Until We Sleep Our Last Sleep

Diary of Emily Ann Millikan Blair

Transcribed and Foreword by
Emily Williams Skinner

Publisher: Emily W. Skinner
Cover design: Labelschmiede, 99Designs.com
Formatting: Book2Bestseller.com
Foreword Editor: Ellen M. Williams
ISBN # 978-0-9994196-7-0

No part of this book may be reproduced or transmitted in any form or by any means, graphic, electronic, digital or mechanical, including photocopying, recording, taping, or by any information storage retrieval system, without the permission in writing from the author.

Books by Emily W. Skinner

Novels by Emily W. Skinner
Marquel
Marquel's Dilemma
Marquel's Redemption

Booktrailer:
Marquel book trailer on YouTube—
featuring actor Eric Roberts & Marquel Skinner
www.youtube.com/watch?v=6e6O7iYqeVQ

Young Adult Novels by E.W. Skinner
St. Blair: Children of the Night
St. Blair: Sybille's Reign
St Blair: The Diary of St. Blair

Memoir:
Master of the Roman Noir

Sign up for email updates at:
www.emilyskinnerbooks.com

Foreword

Dan Brown, author of the *DaVinci Code*, opens his Masterclass on writing thrillers by pointing out that—in a thriller—the clock is ticking. There is time pressure. If a character had his entire life to do something, it wouldn't be exciting.

I write suspense, so transcribing nonfiction—my great, great grandmother's diary—was a practice in extreme patience. The clock was ticking in her mind, but I already knew the end.

As I typed for hours every night after my day job, and some weeks without a single evening off, I realized how sharply the pace of her life contrasted with my multi-tasking lifestyle. I began to see a mystery within the things she hadn't revealed. I also saw within myself our similarities. In keeping our hearts protected and communications informative, how hard we try to distract our self doubt in prayers for others.

I also figured out why I have had this unusual respect and knowledge of death: death conscientiousness is truly in my dna. Henry Louis Gates, Jr., the noted historian and host of Finding Your Roots, might say I have discovered, in my grandmother's words, an intuitive understanding. My genetic memory.

From as young as six years old, I have thought about death and losing family, though I had not lost a single family member until I was about eight years old when my cousin Ben Jr. passed.

My whole life, literally, has been about making sure everyone would be okay if we so part. Being a loving witness.

Foreword

I truly wanted to love my neighbor as my self. However, I was terribly imbalanced in the self-love aspect. That too, seemed to resonate from these pages. My grandmother talks about we humans as "unworthy cretures" roughly 149 times. This is intended as humble speak.

I think of it as "genetic guilt." Because guilt has been at my core and I'm not sure why.

I never really heard the name Millikan growing up. I knew my English great grandmother Esther Hayden married a handsome Quaker named Fred C. Blair. That's about it. Literally.

There were no real stories I could recall from childhood, other than a few mentions of a diary in the family. I heard High Point mentioned on occasion and didn't know why or what High Point was about.

The diary came into my possession after my paternal grandmother Emily Hayden Blair Williams passed. I skimmed the more than 998 handwritten pages to see what the diary contained and was overwhelmed by the multitude of names shared. You'll see in them in the index—I have done my best to organize and avoid duplications where possible.

There is a wealth of ancestral names tucked into these pages. Snippets of family, friends and people one might be looking for when building a family history.

On a second round of skimming, I looked for clues as to her intent and purpose for the diary. Which made me desperate for a photo of her.

We had photos of my 2x great grandfather, John Addision Blair, but at the time I started this project there were none of Emily as a young woman. My cousin Kathleen had one photo of Emily Millikan Blair and John Addison Blair at their 50th Golden Wedding Anniversary. A newsprint photo—better than no photo.

But I wanted to see her as the diarist.

So, I started doing research. I searched my grandmother's name on the internet.

Up popped a woman I had never heard of Hannah Millikan Blair, a Revolutionary War heroine, and her father William Millikan.

Could we be related?

There were no family stories of patriots or war heroes.

I found a dedication my grandmother wrote, a double-sided page, not part of the diary, (which I have now included in date range order) regarding the *Blair-Millikan Union Memorial Exercises at Springfield*, where she mentions Hannah Millikan Blair as a sister to her Grandfather Benjamin Millikan. Enos Blair, Hannah's husband, was the Great Grandfather of John Addison Blair (my 2x great grandfather).

But my grandmother didn't explain what the Blair-Millikan Union event was; she writes that the event was to unveil a Memorial Stone to Hannah and Enos on Springfield Friends grounds.

But why?

As with most things that are current to people of a given time, my grandmother likely assumed everyone knew Enos and Hannah Millikan Blair. Where she lived, they did. She had no way of knowing her future family members would not pass those stories down.

Thanks to Google, I discovered some of them https://www.ncpedia.org/biography/blair-hannah-millikan

Hannah was noted for saving patriots by running food to soldiers in the woods—while she was pregnant; hiding a soldier in the ticking of a mattress as Tories-searched her home, and hiding two soldiers in a corn crib as she shucked corn. This woman stared down Col. David Fanning and his Tory henchmen.

Hannah and Enos Blair raised twelve children they nicknamed the twelve tribes.

Of Hannah's father, William Millikan, I found this brief snippet.

"Being a Quaker, William Millikan was a non-combatant during the American Revolution, but his sympathies were pro-patriot which placed him on a death list. In 1782, William was living on Back Creek in Randolph County, near the Guilford County line. On March 10, a band of Tories came to his farm. Finding William absent, they burned his house to the ground. Still he, himself, was never caught."

Foreword

http://freepages.rootsweb.com/~mygermanfamilies/family/Millikan.html

Like the Revolutionary War, Quakers were considered enemies of the Confederacy during the Civil War. Peace was unpopular with militaries looking for able bodied soldiers.

Many Quakers left the south and headed to northern territories, assisting slaves seeking freedom.

Mary Mendenhall Hobbs writes in her book, *Civil War And Reconstruction Through The Eyes of Mary Mendenhall Hobbs*, "...the New Garden Boarding School was the only school in the South that was not closed during the war or during reconstruction."

In this diary my grandmother writes about New Garden Boarding School with much affection. She also mentions some Mendenhalls as cousins to the Blair family.

However, my grandmother doesn't mention that she and John A. Blair were courting during the Civil War. It is evident this was the case, however, because she mentions being a student at New Garden Boarding School in 1864, and their marriage is recorded in 1864.

Their first daughter Maggie is born seven months after the war ends in 1865.

Soujourners No More – The Quakers in the New South 1865–1920 by Damon D. Hickey provides more details about the school, the period and Quakerism in North Carolina.

It seems New Garden Boarding School/Guilford College could be considered holy ground, as it was not decimated. Nor was the school taken over by soldiers for the war efforts, as other schools and stores and business were throughout the Civil War.

How did this community survive such a bloody, destructive Civil War and still teach and house students—if not, by the grace of God?

My next search took me to Springfield Friends.

I found Brenda G. Haworth, Historian and Editor of the Springfield Memorial Association. She informed me that Emily Millikan Blair, John Addison Blair, Enos Blair, Hannah Millikan Blair and many of the "Twelve tribes" and other family are buried at Springfield Friends Cemetery behind the Springfield Friends Meeting House/Church.

The Springfield Friends annual meeting my grandmother mentions numerous times still happens every August. The Springfield Friends even have a museum of artifacts.

Brenda Haworth, I learned, is my distant cousin on the Millikan side.

She suggested I reach out to Guilford College. It really didn't register at the time, that New Garden Boarding School and Guilford College are the same place. The mecca of my grandmother's entries—well, besides heaven.

Guilford College is still a thriving Quaker establishment.

Through a series of emails to Gwen Erickson, Quaker Librarian & College Archivist at Guilford College, I learned they had a wealth of information on our family.

I booked a research day August 17, 2018 and prayed I'd find my grandmother's photo somewhere in the archives. I was desperate to see her.

As we (my husband Tom and I) drove onto the campus, I started reading the signs. It was déjà vu. I knew this place, though I had never been there.

Gwen graciously had archive records related to the Millikans and Blairs ready when we got there. It also helped that she explained plain Quaker speak and the use of words like thee, thy and humble expressions that reflect reverence for God over self. Erickson also shared how Quakers in the immediate community contributed to the Underground Railroad and assisted slaves in finding safe passage to free territory. Many Quaker churches still exist in the area.

Just as we (my husband Tom and I) were wrapping up, I found in the very last folder, a grainy photocopy of a photograph of Emily Millikan Blair. It was not great.

But I was elated!

Foreword

I took photos of the photocopy and as soon as we left the college, I started emailing artists I knew. Hopeful to get a decent pencil or charcoal rendering.

Saturday August 18, we explored the local historical sites and High Point. I didn't know what I was looking for. I had too much information and not enough context. I was just hoping to find more of my family's past.

I took photos of museum pieces, landmark signs and anything I could eventually match up with diary entries. A backwards way of doing things, but I figured I could always come back.

Sunday August 19th, we attended the Annual Springfield Friends Celebration and potluck, then toured the museum. The museum was once the original meeting house my grandparents attended.

In the museum, which is dusty and rather primitive, are relics of the people I descend from. I saw a wealth of photos hanging in the building and took photos with my phone of as many as I could, knowing many names appear in the diary entries.

Then in the middle of the room, I noticed a desk loaded with photo albums. Could I scoop them up and run away with them? Not a Christian thought…

It was getting late.

Determined to view every photo in every album, I turned pages fast, and moved quickly through each album. And just like the college, almost in slo-mo, there she was in the last pages of the last album in the pile! Eureka! The originals of the grainy photocopy.

Thank you, Jesus!

I took more pictures of the pictures with my phone.

Brenda later had scans emailed to me for the book. The cover photo was greatly enhanced by cover designer, Labelschmiede.

The original scans are in the photo section.

My grandmother looks as she appeared in my mind's eye.

I was overjoyed.

I then went to the cemetery, walked among the many family plots and sat with my grandparents. What a treasure to be where my family rests.

When I got home and began the nightly transcribing task, I reached a point where my grandmother says she is re-transcribing from other tablets. I missed that in all the skimming. I felt I was losing my mind. We were both transcribing her work!

It was hard to be in her head for long stretches. It might be that genetic memory thing. I had to get massages to decompress from the day job to long nights transcribing. I had to break from the routine for a while. I hope you'll appreciate what happens at a pivotal moment in the latter entries of 1890. It's a real a-ha. You begin to realize why she's stressed.

So how will this diary give meaning to its readers?

How does Emily Ann Millikan Blair, a farmer's wife who shares scripture, self-talk, happenings in her community, her family and church life provide value to people in this century?

If you've ever had self-doubt, known depression, want to understand what a faith life is, or have physical limitations, you might find comfort here.

As you read the diary, you'll see how her Quaker life slowly advanced with the times. The typos are her exact words. It was hard to force software to misspell words, which made the transcription a greater challenge. Later the software adapted and didn't pick up typos, so I had to proofread every entry twice. She misspelled peoples names from time to time, so in the index you'll see the variations. I wanted to note this to help others learn the detective work that goes into genealogy searches. Census records often have misspellings, as the census taker writes the data from their own skillset.

Her improvement or changes in grammar, spelling and calendar style are also hers. She uses phrases like, "I have been permitted" or "I have been favored to ...." Which are expressions from the period. Not necessarily someone permitting, favoring or denying her.

Foreword

She wrote in 12 tablets over her lifetime. She was a daughter, wife, mother, sister, cousin, grandmother, neighbor and friend. She was disabled and used a wheelchair or cane for assistance most of her life.

She was intelligent, had beautiful handwriting, and yet believed she and most humans are limited and unworthy. In her 40s, she believed she'd die young. Yet Emily Ann Millikan Blair's physical abilities miraculously improved as she grew older. She outlived many in her immediate family and wrote her final entries 10 days before she died at age 85.

It could be said that gratitude is the prescription to a long life.

At 81, she writes:

Friday April the 30th 1926

As this is the last day of the month, I am reminded that we are another month nearer our journeys end, and the query arises what have I done during this time that will redown to my Makers praise or to the salvation of my own soul, or to the upbuilding of His kingdom in the hearts and minds of others. I plead forgiveness for all my mistakes and shortcomeings for they are many. Oh Father in Heaven accept my heart felt gratitude this morning for all thy mercies to me and mine and help each one of us to serve thee better thruout the remainder of the journey for Jesus sake.

This diary is intended for not only our family (the people who descended from the Millikan and Blair lines), but those who God hopes to speak to through her pen. Which includes her neighbors, their descendants in the historic communities in North Carolina that surround Randolph County including, Guilford, Springfield, High Point, Archdale, Mt. Vernon, Jamestown, Greensboro, Marlboro—and you.

It is with much pleasure and love that I share my grandmother's diary,

Emily Louise Williams Skinner
2x great granddaughter of Emily Ann Millikan Blair

Special thanks to

Gwendolyn Gosney Erickson,
Quaker Librarian & College Archivist at Guilford College

Guilford College
Quaker Library & College Archives
For access to photos & documents

Brenda Gray Haworth
Historian, Curator and Editor of Springfield Memorial Association
(Who I discovered is also a cousin)

Susan Haworth
Springfield Museum
(Also, a cousin)

Paula Kunkle
Interim Transcription Typist

Ellen Williams
Editor of this introduction
(also, a 2x great granddaughter)

Kathleen Sims
(great granddaughter)
For Providing Family Photos

Marian Inabinett
Curator Collections
Highpoint Museum

Blair Dairy Images
Courtesy High Point Historical Society,
High Point, N.C.

Lisa DeSpain
Book Formatter

Barbara A. Lewis

A Reminiscence

In comeing before this large and interesting audience, and for the first time in this beautiful and comfortable new building. I am filled with awe and reverance, for as I think of the great contrast, not only in the appearance of this Church, but the vast difference in the comfortable seating capacity, from the first meeting house I ever entered here at dear old Springfield which was that of the old time frame building which stood just west of the more modern brick building and while thinking of the great evolution that has taken place here, it calls to mind some interesting remarks of our worthy Sunday School Superintendent at Mt. Vernon, on one occasion when he was giving good advice to the classes collectively especially to the young people, that the young generally look forward, while the older people were apt to look backward, back to their childhood or young days, which is very true so I find myself at this time looking back to my childhood, when I had arrived to an age to be sufficiently strong and large enough to hold on to my Father or Mother as I rode behind them to meeting here on horse back often twice a week. how vividly I remember those two white horses, and when mother could leave the baby at home, I rode behind her on Nell, but when she had to cary a baby in her lap which she often did, I rode behind Father on old Dock, and after this tiresome trip of four miles I would sit for an hour or more on a rough slab bench with no back, with my feet bearly touching the floor, and scarcely moving an inch, as I had been taught to sit still in meeting, and thought I must obey. and I did sit still and listened

A Reminiscence

to Uncle **Mahlon Hockette** preach, and it made an impression on me that has followed me, from then until now. and never have I felt the spirit of worship more profoundly than in those days of my childhood, and I seem to see those dear older members sitting in the Galary as we called it in those days, with elevated seats and a hand railing in front of each bench. yes now after more than four score years, in looking back I seem to see Uncle **Sameul** and Aunt **Elizabeth Hunt**, Uncle **Allen** and Aunt **Rachel Tomlinson**, Uncle **Mahlon** and Aunt **Luzena Hockette**, Aunt **Rachel Anderson**, my own dear mother **Mary Millikan** and others, sitting on those seats in profound silence, until Uncle **Mahlon** in his own quaint way would rise and give us words of encouragement to go on in the right way, or warning us to turn from the evil way, and that was to me real worship, and in true reverance we sat still and listened, and some times Aunt **Aseneth Clark** would be here, and I seem to see her take off her neat Colonial silk Bonnett and lay in the lap of one sitting by her and in the deepest reverance fall upon her knees saying "We Bow" in such solemn tones I seem to hear them yet. some may be ready to question the accuracy of these statements, since I was then but a small child, but those who have arrived to old age, I think will agree with me, that we can remember things that took place in our childhood days, more clearly, than many things that have taken place in the past few years. "Train up a child in the way he should go and when he is old he will not depart from it." so I plead with every mother **Unice** and grandmother **Lois** to be diligent in training little **Timothy** the way of truth and righteousness, it will follow him, all thru life even tho he may err from the strait path at times he will come back to it again. for our heavenly Father is watching over his children, and will take care of his own. now as we have observed the contrast in many things, in the way of houseing the flock, and the manner of locomotion in getting to and from service etc in the past and at the present. The query arises have we in this great progress in education, and in all lines of improvement for the comfort of our mortal bodies and the delight of our minds, have we kept pace with those things in spiritual attainment, being as anxious to be fed with that spiritual food which alone can nourish up our souls unto life eternal as we are for the material and temporal comforts of life which perish with the useing? now I hope I may not be understood as criticizeing the present improvement on so many lines, for that would be a sad mistake. for I believe in progress in all things that are necesary for the help and comfort of mankind, and have simply been contrasting the present with the past that we may be the more thankful for, and appreciative of all the blessings we now have to enjoy. and that we may be filled with thanksgiving and praise to the Giver of all good when we enter this beautiful house of God which He has given to man, the material, the wisdom and the strength to build, for without Him we can do nothing, and that we be in earnest to maintain that sincere attitude of worship and faith of our Fathers that they so diligently adhered to when worshiping in their rude buildings, and that we may all strive to enter that house not made with hands eternal in the Heavens, and as the younger generation come in to take the place of those of us who will soon pass over, I trust that they may go forward in building up the waste places in Zion, and if spared to old age, may not have regrets to marr their happiness. now in conclusion I will just mention that I have a birthright membership at dear old Springfield which has ever been a sacred place to me, and now the most sacred spot on the earth to me, since the precious dust of so many of my loved ones lie here. and to see the progress that has been made here and the interest taken to beautify this sacred place, makes me glad indeed. May none grow weary in well doing, is the fervent desire of my heart.

Emily A. Blair
Route # 2. Box 18 Trinity N.C.

July 1889

1889
(Pages 1 to 25 are missing)

Transcribed as originally written

This starts on "Page 26 continued from page 25 in red backed album"

7th *month* 14th 1889

This is a beautiful Sabbath day. And as I am not able to attend the place appointed to worship God. I greatly desire that he will condescend to be with me & enable me to serve him in my own home as I ought. For He who looks at the heart will accept our offering if it is but the breathing of a sigh to him or the falling of a silent tear, if it be in humble contrition and brought forth by a desire to be in entire submission to his will. This afternoon our friends and neighbors are to meet to organize a Sabbath School at Oak Forest our new District School House which I feel thankful for, as I have greatly desired this to be done for the past three months, yes my mind has been deeply impressed since the erection of our new School building with the necessity of a good Sabbath School at this place. Our oldest daughter **Maggie** and our little eight year old son **Freddie** have gone to attend the opening of the same, & oh how thankful I should be to present this poor frail body with them on this occasion. But I desire to be willing to submit to whatever the Lord designs concerning me. Haveing very much regretted that I have not kept a daily account of the most eventful portion of my life thus far.

    I refer to the last twenty five years during which time I have passed through so much suffering. Altho I have penned down some of them as they have been so vividly brought to my mind from time to time. Yet I often feel that if I had taken note daily when I was able to use my pen at all, that it might of kept me more humble & that the many things which has had to be omitted might have been a warning, or a satisfaction to some at least of my own dear friends and family connections. So I will endeavor to me more faithful in the future God being my helper. Altho it is very embarrassing to have to note down so many short comings.

7th month 15th 1889

I feel thankful that I am able to arise from my bed this morning as there is so much of my time that I have not been even able to sit up or to do anything for my family

7th month 16th 1889

Altho I am very feeble this morning my mind is composed &I breathe a silent prayer to God that he will be with me and my dear family & support us in every time of need. I am comforted this morning in believing that whom the Lord loveth he chasteneth and scourgeth every one who he receiveth. Oh that I could always be thus favored but I am sorry to state that such is not the case at all times. For the tempter is always busy. But oh for strength to resist him.

7th month 17th 1889

When I reflect that another whole year of suffering has past, notwithstanding I am still unable to get about only in my wheel chair & have not been able to sit up an half a day at a time, in this length of time. Yet as I have been spared to keep my dear little family together whilst there has been many little ones left Motherless, my soul cries out again and again what shall I render unto my God for all his benefits to me.

7th month 18th 1889

Unto thee oh Lord do I lift up my soul, I thank Thee for even strength sufficient to use my pen. For there has been months at a time since my afflicted days, that I could not do this, no matter how great the desire to do so.

7th month 19th 1889

I desire to be thankful for all my blessings. This day I have enjoyed the company of my own dear aged Mother. For which I rejoice.

7th month 20th 1889

My mind has been deeply inpressed this morning by reading a letter printed in a Tract form, written by Elizabeth Webb to Anthony William Boehm. She sailed from Bristol to America in the 9th month of 1697 with her companion Mary Rogers.

I have been led by this letter, to see that those who have had their robes washed & made clean in the blood of the Lamb have often to pass through great tribulation. But the crown is sure to those who hold out faithful to the Lord.

7th month 21st 1889

The prayer of my heart this morning is help me oh Lord to spend this Sabbath day aright & to be thankful for blessings passed and present. I do feel to rejoice that we have a Sabbath School close at hand, & to know that all my children four in number (two grown and two little ones) are today attending the same, and I trust endeavoring to profit thereby, & help on the cause of Christ, & as my dear husband & I are not permitted to be there on account of my feeble health, yet I rejoice to know that we are happy together & that we have the blessed privilege of serveing the Lord in our home in our own hearts.

7th month 22nd 1889

This has been a day in which my mind has been sorely tried, as I have suffered so much with my lungs, & my nervous system is so racked. Yet I still trust that if it is the Lord's will, he will restore me to health, if not, His will be done.

7th month 23rd 1889

I have realized that as thy day so shall thy strength be sufficient unto the day is the evil thereof go. Yes hitherto the Lord hath helped me, & made way for me where there seemed no way.

7th month 24th 1889

I hope I am truly thankful for even strength to sit up in my chair, oh that I may be kept from murmuring this day.

7th month 25th 1889

Altho I am feeble, yet I have been enabled to do a little work with my hands to day for the help of my dear little family, for which I feel thankful. I desire to be grateful for the smallest favor.

7th month 26th 1889

As we are yet a little unbroken band the desire of my heart is that my husband & I may walk uprightly before our precious children.

7th month 27th 1889

The prayer of my heart is this morning, Teach me thy way oh Lord, lead me in the plain path. For the way so often seems dark, through doubts & fears that unless I am helped to follow my guide closely I so often miss my way.

7th month 28th 1889

Having been spared to see another Sabbath day and my precious children having attend the Sabbath School & returned, & are now singing some good hymns, it fills my heart with gratitude to the giver of every good & perfect gift. And I greatly desire that we may all so live, that when done with time here below we may be permitted to sing the songs of the redeemed in that blissful world beyond the skies.

7th month 29th 1889

The desire of my heart this morning is that the Lord would show me just what to do & what to leave undone, for of myself I can do nothing.

7th month 30th 1889

Being blessed with strength sufficient to arise from my bed, my heart is filled with gratitude, for there has been so many days, yes months that I could not do this. Oh that I may sit humbly at the Masters feet and learn of him.

7th month 31st 1889

Unto thee oh Lord do we give thanks, unto thee do we give thanks, that thou hast preserved our lives & in a degree our health sufficient to enjoy ourselves together as a little family, oh that we may be preserved from sinning against thee.

8th month 1st 1889

Another month with its besetments and blessings has past, & now we enter upon another not knowing what is in store for us. But the desire of my heart is that we may be kept near the Master and do his bidding.

8th month 2nd 1889

Being more feeble this morning I realize how dependent I am upon the care of my dear little family, & the mercy of kind Providence, for when I reflect upon the days, months and years of suffering through which I have past & remember that I have never lacked for food or rainment, nor kind friends to care for me, oh how much I have to return thanks for to the bountiful giver of all good. And as I thus take note of each day as it passes, I am made to realize more fully the flight of time, & the great need of improveing each moment in making our calling and election sure.

8th month 3rd 1889

This day being beset with doubts & fears & struggling for patience to bear with all the trials of this life, it is evident that I am looking too much at my own weakness instead of God's strength. oh that I may not so often look on the dark side, for when I come to examine myself I find it is the enemy who is every ready with his discouragements.

8th month 4th 1889

Another Sabbath day has come & we are nearer our eternal home. Are we better prepared for the final summons should it come to us this day. The language of Holy scripture has arisen in my heart, search me of God and know my heart, try me & know my thoughts, & see if there is any wicked way in me & lead me in the way everlasting.

8th month 5th 1889

I great desire that the remainder of my days may be spent in doing whatever the Master designs for me to do, and that I may no more have to reflect so much on the past, but leaving the things that are behind press forward toward the things that are before.

8th month 6th 1889

As we are fast passing away, it is needful that we should be on our watch & be ready for the summons when ever the Master calls for us. The prayer of my heart at this time is that the Lord would forgive all my sins and heal all my backslidings.

8th month 7th 1889

We have to day been again reminded of the certainty of death. as one **Carras Kerns** who resided near Trinity College, N.C. was today called from works to rewards. Oh how important it is for all of us to be ready.

8th month 8th 1889

The yearly meeting at High Point being now in session and my dear daughter and son (my two eldest children) have left home this morning to attend, my heart breathes a fervent prayer to the bountiful giver of all good that He will be with them and all those who are permitted to be there and bless them abundantly. And as my dear husband, myself, and my precious little children are not permitted to attend on account of my afflictions, I humbly desire that we may be blessed with His presence and yield in submission to His will.

8th month 9th 1889

I have suffered so much to day with my spine and nervousness that it is with difficulty that I can keep in entire submission. Oh for more patience & Christian fortitude to bear whatever the Master sees fit to inflict upon me for his own sake.

8th month 10th 1889

Being more comfortable to day, I hope I am truly thankful for the same. & oh how I still crave to be in entire submission to the Divine will.

8th month 11th 1889

Another Sabbath has come which reminds me that we are all nearer our eternal home. Our two oldest children are still away attending the yearly meeting and as the rest of the family cannot be there, as I am too feeble to go or be left alone, I am thankful that we are happy in our home, for we know that our dear Redeemer is watching over and caring for us.

8th month 12th 1889

I am indeed feeble this morning both in body and in spirit. I do not know why the way so often seems hedged up, unless it is to try our faith & see whether we will trust in the dark hours as well as in the light. If thou whosoever thou art feels at times like thou art hardened as a stone, & that thou canst never even think another good thought, & that thou dost not know how to pray, or what to pray for, & that there has a mountain as it were arisen between thee and thy God, do not think that any strange thing has happened or that thou art more sorely tried than other pilgrims, but only trust in the Lord &wait patiently for him & in his own time which will be the right time, he will remove these mountains of darkness, which may have been our unbelief or some other sin of commission, or omission, but even if this is not the cause, one thing is sure, it is all through love and mercy to make us seek, and trust him more fully.

8th month 13th 1889

The enemy is trying hard to keep me under discouragement in order to gain the victory over me. But thanks be to God who giventh us the victory through our Lord Jesus Christ, I am looking to Him who hath power over sin & satan to help me to trample the old adversary the devil beneath my feet.

8th month 14th 1889

Having been visited to day by a young lady relative from Alamance County N.C. whom we had not seen for several years, our hearts have been gladdened. And especially has my heart been made to rejoice in hearing the testimony of a young man also a relative of ours from Greensboro N.C. who accompanied the young lady here. This dear young man stated to me that he was entirely given up to serve the Lord & that he was not ashamed of it, for said he we are told in the scriptures, That he that is ashamed to confess me before men, of him will I be ashamed before my Father in Heaven. Oh that all the dear young people would thus give themselves to the Lord & let him lead & guide them in the way of all truth.

8th month 15th 1889

Our dear sister-in-law **Elizabeth Starbuck** from Dover N.C. visited us last night & to day, which brought up fresh memories of the past. Her first husband was the brother of my husband, and she being again left a widow we commend her to her maker as her husband and the widows of God.

We have also been visited today by **a Lay** from Indiana, who had visited me twenty three years ago in Gospel service. He was accompanied to day by **Rufus P King** of N.C. we had a most precious meeting one which I hope none of us will ever forget, as the spirit of the Lord was so mercifully showered upon us, we praise his name for his mercies.

8th month 16th 1889

I praise the Lord this morning for his goodness to us. The query arises, why have I been so mercifully spared to my family and my dear ones to me, whilst we are almost daily hearing of some one being consigned to the tomb, but oh that we may ever remember that our time is fast hastening on when we shall be called to give account of the deeds done in the body. So help us oh Lord to be ready is my prayer.

8th month 17th 1889

The prayer of my heart this morning is that the Lord would be pleased to show me plainly what he would have me to do and what to leave undone. Oh Lord let thy light shine upon my path that I may not be groping as it were in midnight darkness at noonday.

8th month 18th 1889

It is the desire of my heart this Sabbath morning, as my dear children have again been permitted to go to Sabbath School & meeting, that the blessing of the Lord may be upon them &all others who may be permitted to be there, and I crave that my husband and myself may be kept nigh the good Shepherd and bishop of souls this day, and that we may be enabled to say from the depths of our hearts, not my will, but thine oh Lord be done. This evening we have been blessed with the company of **Allen Lay** from Indiana. We were wonderfully favored with the presence of the Lord in our midst. **Allen Lay** spoke very encouraging to us all. Oh may we ever remember the message of the Lord for us, through the mouth of his servant.

8th month 19th 1889

Lord teach me to know thy will and to do it, is the fervent desire of my heart this morning. I am thankful that I feel my heart filled with praise to the Father of all our mercies for blessings past and present. Oh that He will be pleased to keep me & my little family as in the hallow of His holy hand that we go not astray.

8th month 20th 1889

It is the earnest desire of my heart this day that I may be fully given up to every requirement of the Lord, and that all my sins and my desires for gratification of self, may be put far from me, and that I can say from the debths of my heart, not as I will but as thou wilt.

8th month 21st 1889

Being sorely tried this morning with some of the cares and vexations of this life. I cry unto Him who is able to succor us in temptation, "Set Thou a watch before my mouth, keep the door of my lips that I sin not with my tongue."

8th month 22nd 1889

The that trust in the Lord shall be as mount Zion which shall not be removed forever. Therefore let us put our trust in Him that we may be steadfast unmmoveable always abounding in the fear of the Lord.

8th month 23rd 1889

What can I write for the encouragement of others; when I feel such poverty of soul myself as is the case this morning. Still I am thankful that I can sing. I am trusting Lord in thee. Blessed lamb of calvery. All my hope on thee is staid, all my help from thee I bring. Cover my defenseless head, with the shadow of thy wing.

8th month 24th 1889

As quarty meeting at Marlboro is in session to day, how thankful I would be to be permited to be in attendance, but as I am not able, I desire to be submissive. And I crave that the blessing of Heaven may rest upon those who may present themselves there this day.

8th month 25th 1889

What shall I render unto the Lord, for all his benefits to me. I am poor and needy, yet the Lord upholdeth me with this own right hand.

8th month 26th 1889

Nothing in my hand I bring, simply to thy cross I cling. I have nothing new in my experience to note at this time, but am endeavoring to trust in the Lord that he will lead me in the way that he designes that I should walk in.

8th month 27th 1889

It is very humiliating indeed to hae to note my failures and short comeings, when the Lord has been so merciful to me. Oh God, forbid that I should be a stumbling block to others in my prayer.

8th month 28th 1889

The Lord is indeed merciful & gracious, for he has prolonged my days, altho so unworthy of his notice, & oh that my life may not be lived in vain, but may I so live that I may answer the end for which I was created which was to glorify God.

8th month 29th 1889

Unto to thee oh Lord do we give thanks for thy bountiful gifts, for we are so plentifully supplied with fruits & vegetables & so many other things necessary for the sustenance of these poor perishable bodies. And we would ask Thee to give us of thy Holy Spirit to sustain life eternal for Jesus sake.

8th month 30th 1889

The day is past & gone the evening shades appear, oh may we all remember well the night of death draws near. As the shades of evening are gathering around us, it brought these lines to my mind. And oh how I do desire that we may all be prepared to meet the night of death with our lamps trimed and burning.

8th month 31st 1889

This being the last day of summer, it reminds me that it may also be the last day of our lives, as we know not what a day or an hour may bring forth. I am suffering to day with my spinal trouble, but am endeavoring to look away from self to Him who suffered such agony on the cross for a poor unworthy creature as I feel myself to be, for help to bear all my sufferings & privations, with patience and entire resignation.

9th month 1st 1889

This beautiful Sabbath morning we desire to return thanks to the giver of all good, that we are enabled to arise from our beds, & I do desire that we may all spend this day in the fear of the Lord. Evening of the same day, I feel again to return thanks that the Father of all our mercies has given me strength sufficient this day to ride out to one of our neighbors, which is the second time I have been permited to do so in over a year, oh it is such a privilege to even get out a little to mingle with friends and acquaintences.

9th month 2nd 1889

Being able to day to do a little work with my hands, I regard it as a great blessing, after the privilege of rideing out yesterday, which caused me to be a little more helpless this morning, but as I am now better again I desire to be truly thankful.

This night **Rachel Baily** from Indiana, and **Amy Trublood** from Florida are to have meeting at our district School House, Oak Forest. Oh that they may be favored to impart the Gospel in its fullness, & that the hearts of the hearers may be opened to receive them, is my earnest prayer.

9th month 3rd 1889

Teach me thy way oh Lord & lead me in a plain path, that I may know just what thou would have me to do & what thou would have me leave undone, to the praise & honor of thy great name. For I do earnestly desire to improve the talent which thou hast given me, instead of being like the slothful servant who buried it in the earth. For altho I feel my great weakness, yet I remember that we all have talents given us, few or many & that we should be willing to improve the little which has been given us. And as He has seen fit to try me in the furnace of affliction, it is my greatest desire that I may thereby be purified from all the dross and reprobate silver and made fit for the Masters use.

9th month 4th 1889

The Lord is my shepherd I shall not want. Yes we are told in the Holy scriptures of truth, that the young Lions do lack & suffer hunger, but they that trust in the Lord shall lack no good thing. Therefore here is great encouragement to trust in Him, for I do believe that if we trust him fully that we shall not lack that which is really necessary for either our natural or our spiritual life.

Many times we think we lack a great many things, which our kind Heavenly Father withholds from us for our good, for God sees not as man seeth, but He who foreknows all things, knows what is best for his dependent children.

9ᵗʰ month 5ᵗʰ 1889

Oh Lord be thou my strong Tower whereunto I may flee to hide me in time of temptation, that I sin not against thee. For there are but few days that pass over our heads but that we are either sorely tried or tempted in some way, by the enemy of our souls peace. Therfore it is necessary to keep close to our guide & watch as well as pray that we enter not into temptation. This day I have suffered more severely with my spinal trouble than for several days previous, & the enemy has been tempting me to repine. But thanks be to Him who giveth us the victory through our Lord Jesus Christ I am hideing underneath thy wings.

9ᵗʰ month 6ᵗʰ 1889

My nerves are so racked to day, that I am scarely able to write, but desireing to do something for some poor suffer in whose hands these lines may sometime accidently or otherwise fall. I am willing to exert what little strength I have, if it may be a comfort to any, or may add an anthem of praise to Him in whose hands our lives are. What I have suffered with my spine, to say nothing of my other infirmities, none can know but Him who knoweth all things. One summer my Physician had running sores made on my back the whole length of my spine, the corruption from these would trickle down my back like water or perspiration, what I suffered for more than three months, all through the hottest of weather, can better be imagined than described when the sores would begin to heal sufficient for the scabs to come off, the medicine was again put on the sores while perfectly raw, which to express it plain was like fire on my back. But my Physician finding that this treatment was too severe & that I was growing worse instead of better he substituted the cold water bath, which was much better in every respect, though not pleasant or very affectual. And altho there has not been a day since that time which has been years ago, nor for a long while before but that I suffered more or less with my spine, yet it has been so light, (with the exception of those severe spells which would prostrate me for several days & sometimes for weeks at a time) in comparison with this torture added to the pain, that I am indeed very thankful for it seems at this moment to add to my pain to look back on these intense sufferings.

9th month 7th 1889

To day our quarterly meeting at Springfield is in session my dear husband and oldest son are in attendance. I am very feeble yet with my spine & nervousness, but have been enabled to do a little work with my hands to day for the help of my family for which I am very thankful, altho still having to use my wheel chair as my means of getting about.

9th month 8th 1889

In noting down a few words each day as they pass, brings to rememberance that there is being a record kept in Heaven, of all idle words and misdeeds which we are speaking & perpetrating whilst on earth. Oh that we may be close on our watch, or many indeed will be the blots on those pages which will be brought up against us in that day when we shall desire to see our names written on a clean fair page in the Lambs book of life. Oh Lord we pray thee to blot out all our sins from thy book & make us pure & clean in the blood of the Lamb, that we may be fit subjects to enter they kingdom to sing thy praise with the blood washed throng who surround thy throne, singing glory to God in the highest, on earth peace, good will toward men.

9th month 9th 1889

This is a day long to be remembered with great pleasure as one of the Lords ministering servants **Wm Wilson** from Providence N.C. who is also a relative of mine altho unknown to me until to day, visited us in gospel love. We had a precious visit indeed, he was favored to speak very edifying oh that we may ever remember the council from the

Lord through the mouth of His servant. He presented me a nice new Testament of larger type, which was accepted very thankfully indeed, as my eyesight is failing. Bless the Lord for his goodness to us all.

9th month 10th 1889

We have great cause to praise the Lord for his goodness to us, for we have never lacked necessary food, neither have we suffered want of raiment, altho many times we feel the lack of a great many things which according to our nature would be gratifying to us all, Yet He who knoewth all things, knows our real needs, & as such supplies them.

9th month 11th 1889

Teach me thy way oh Lord & lead me in a plain path, is again & again my prayer. And now the query arises in my heart this morning, am I being taught the way of the Lord, & am I being led in a plain path, & if not, why am I not? On refection the reason is plain, it is because I am not willing to be taught, & because I am not willing to be shown that plain path for fear it will mark out some duty which I would rather be excused from performing in the service of the Master. Here I am made to cry out Lord help me, & make me willing to abide by the turnings & overturnings of thy righteous hand upon me, make me willing to do all they requireings with an eye single to thy glory. Then I shall not only be willing, but rejoice to learn the full import of the test. Teach me thy way oh Lord, lead me in a plain, path, This is the way, walk thou in it & for we have the promise that, according to thy faith, so be it unto thee.

9th month 12th 1889

More & more each day do I see the great need of living near the Saviour, for only as we are led & guided by him do we walk aright. The scriptures saith draw nigh unto God, & he will draw nigh unto us. Then how needful for us to draw nigh unto Him each day, that we may find grace to help in time of need. And the more we dwell near

Him the greater will be our desire there to abide. Here I remember the lines of a little hymn which is very precious to my heart.

There's a Friend that holds you dearer

Than all other friends besides;

In your gladness or troubles,

Jesus close to you abides.

9th month 13th 1889

The earth is the Lords, & the fullness thereof, the seas & all that dwell therein. Then it remains that we are the works of his hands, & are under his immediate care, altho we see him not and oftentimes are not aware that he is leading us so gentle & so mysterious are his works & ways. For as the wind bloweth where it listeth, & we hear the sound thereof but canst not tell whence it cometh or whither it goeth, so is every one that is born of the spirit. Thus it is evident if we are born of the spirit that Jesus is near us to lead & guide us in the way of all truth as we are willing to obey his gentle voice. But if we stray from the path which he would have us walk in, then we shall know by our conscience condemning us, if not hardened in sin, that we are not following the True Guide, but that he is simply leaving us to our own ways as he did the children of Israel for their disobedience. "When they waited not for His council, he gave them their request; but sent leanness into their souls."

So if we do not follow the Divine guide we shall find ourselves gropeing as it were in midnight darkness at noonday, then we shall be made to cry mightly unto Him to direct us again in the path of rectitude. Therfore we should praise his great name for following us with his convicting spirit, for altho it is wrong in us to cause the Lord to hide his presence as it were from us, yet he is so merciful to his poor weak backsliding children, that as we turn to him again with full purpose of heart he will pardon our iniquities & restore us again to his favor. But oh let us not persist in this way of sinning &

repenting, for the great Shepherd & bishop of souls hath declared my spirit shall not always strive with man.

9th month 14th 1889

It is very humiliating indeed to note the failures which we are prone to more or less every day of our lives, but by so doing we are kept closer on our watch we shall thus be made to cry, If thou shouldst mark iniquities oh Lord who shall stand, but there is abundant mercy with thee that though mayest be feared. Thou oh Lord dost know this day that thy poor unworthy servant, if I may be called thy servant, is fervently desireing that thou will pardon all the iniquities of my past life, that Thou wilt be please to heal all my backslideings & remember them no more forever, & that I may from this time forth throughout the remainder of my stay on earth be found doing that which is well pleasing to the Divine master & I may not be a stumbling block to any. I desire that He whom I am endeavoring to serve will be with me each day & will enable me to serve him in that way & manner which he requires. To Him I look for fitting words each day to note down, that may bring praise & honor unto his great name, for should these lines fall into the hands of any who should feel the need of encouragement, there is nothing which could possibly do my soul more good than to know that I was an instrument in the Lords hands of comforting some poor weary travler in the rugged paths through which we often have to pass in the wilderness journey. And oh God forbid that I should take this work in my own hands & thereby discourage or mislead any from that path which leads to Heaven & eternal happiness. For it is through no merit of my own that I write these things, but for the sake of Him who requires these things at my hands, & for the sake of those for whom Christ died, that I have put forth my feeble effort to note down such things as are brought to my mind from day to day.

The prayer of my heart has been from the beginning of this work, that the Lord would show me just what to do & what to leave undone to his names glory & that he would "hold my right hand." And hereby do I know that the work is owned by the Lord, for when I take my paper each day I am as an empty vessel, I know not what I shall write. But I always ask Him to help me and blessed be his holy name he does help me, for of myself I can do nothing.

When I first began this work, each day as I would finish what was given me, I would say to myself I know I shall not think of any thing to write next time, for so completely was every thing gone from my mind. But I have learned to trust the work to the Lord. On taking up my paper & often feel as though I could never write another word or even thing a good thought. But He to whom I submit this work as well as the ordering of all my life work, is pleased to help me from time to time.

9th month 15th 1889

The Lord be my helper as in days past is my prayer this morning. And as the Lord is willing to help those who help themselves, it is our bounden duty to do whatever our hands find to do to His names glory. As I have this morning been helping to prepare the bodies of my little children to present themselves at Sabbath school I have felt that it was a work for Jesus, & altho done through much feebleness & not able to present myself with them, yet I want to hear those comforting words in the time to come, "she hath done what she could." Therefore it is my earnest desire to do the little I can, in the fear & to the praise of Him to whom I look to clothe these dear little lambs with the robe of righteousness that fadeth not away. And oh Lord help us their parents to walk uprightly before them is my prayer for Jesus sake. Amen.

9th month 16th 1889

I am at this time on a visit to our cousins **B.F.** & **Rachel Blair** who live less than one mile from our home, yet I have not been permited to visit them in considerably over a year on account of my feeble health. My dear husband brought me over last evening, & the weather being warmer than we were really aware of, I became too much fatigued, consequently I spent a very restless night suffering with my spine & nervous debility, & am very feeble this morning, but being sufficiently able to arise from my bed I feel very thankful. For having slept very little during the night I feared that I should not be able help myself any to day, & as it is such a cross to me to be a burden to others, I have feared lest I should be, such on this occasion, but my relatives have such kind consideration for me that I have a great deal to be thankful for. May God in his infinite goodness & mercy be pleased to keep me close to him this day & preserve me from murmuring at my lot, & may I altho feeling much depressed in spirit be permited to look to Him for help & strength in every needful time is my prayer.

9th month 17th 1889

I have been taken from our relatives where I have been visiting, to my dear aged Mother's a distance of about one fourth mile. And as this is the second time I have been to visit her in more than a year I esteem it a great privalige. But these visits have been made through so much bodily suffering that it is very discouraging indeed, for altho the distance is short yet it is very fatigueing. But my physician & others thinking it might benefit my health I have endeavored to bear the suffering for the present in the hope of being better, should it prove beneficial.

9th month 18th 1889

I was barely able to return home from my little aforementioned visits, but as this is our eldest sons twenty first birthday I was very ancious to get home, but after the fatigue of returning home I have not been able to leave my bed to day. But I hope to be patient & willing to suffer whatever the Divine master sees fit to permit to come upon me for his sake. But as the flesh is weak, I confess I have not been more discouraged in quite a while than I have been this week. For after having undergone so much privation & suffering, I had anticipated some relief from suffering by the change, but on finding myself worse for the time, I have been almost ready to give up by the way. But on remembering how fleeting are all joys here, I have been made to look away from all the transient things of earth to Him who alone can comfort us in every needful time. Oh that I may look to no other source for help & comfort for vain is the help of man.

9th month 19th 1889

As I hear the rustle of the leaves this morning in the wind I am reminded that autumn is now here indeed, & soon the trees will shed their beautiful & varied foliage, & the frost will nip bud & flower. Which seems to me to illustrate the cold hand of death which will come sooner or later to all ages. Yes from the tender bud of infancy, the youth, the midle aged & the hoary haired shall all be nipped by the frost of death. And as we are careful to prepare our flowers, our vegetables & to be stored safely before the cold blasts of winter, so should we see to it that we are prepared to be safely gathered into the Heavenly garner when the icy fetters of death is permited to come upon us.

9th month 20th 1889

Jesus gentle gentle shepherd keep me safely guarded from the Lion & the Bear as it were that is daily seeking to devour me, for the enemy of my souls peace would swallow me up. I still being feeble in body, am low in spirit but knowing that satan takes advantage of our weak moments, I desire to be close on my watch lest I should let him come in & rule over me. Oh God be thou my strong Tower whereunto I may flee to hide me, is my fervent prayer for Jesus sake.

9th month 21st 1889

Whom the Lord loveth he chasteneth & scourgeth every one whom he receiveith. These words are comforting to me this morning, for as

I have had to pass through such a scourge of affliction I sometimes become very much discouraged and query why am I thus, or what is my disobedience that I should have to suffer so much. But when I reflect that it is all in mercy for my good & I sincerely hope for the good of others as well, I am made to rejoice that I am counted worthy to suffer for the sake of Him who bled & died for me, & not for me only but for the whole world. Therfore it is comforting to reflect upon the test that has presented itself to my mind this morning causing me to feel that the Lord does indeed love me altho he had laid the hand of affliction upon me, & it is my earnest desire that these light afflictions which are but a season may work out for me a far more exceeding & eternal weight of glory, to the praise and hone of Him who doeth all things well.

9th month 22nd 1889

We are commanded to keep the Sabbath day holy therefore it is my desire this beautiful Sabbath morning to fulfill this command this day, and not being able in body to present myself at the place appointed for worship or Sabbath School, I humbly ask that He who letteth not even a sparrow fall to the ground without His notice, will be pleased to watch over me & mine this day & enable us to serve him in our own home as acceptably as though we were gathered in the Church. But oh if it is the will of my Heavenly Father to raise me up that I may be permited to meet & mingle with those who assemble themselves at the house of God, the praise & honor shall be his.

9th month 23rd 1889

Out of abundance of the heart the mouth speaketh, so also is the pen the silent moniter to convey our thoughts, so may I ever be directed in word, in thought & in deed in that way & manner which is well pleasing to Him who knoweth all things. Oh Lord help me to do my work for thee while it is day, the night cometh where in no one can work. Oh deliver me from presumtuous sins, cleanse thou me from secret faults, so may I be though deciple indeed.

September 1889

9th month 24th 1889

Lord thou hast been our dwelling place in all generations. Therefore we look to thee for refuge in every needful time, and as I am feeling very lowly indeed this morning I feel the need of that everlasting arm of strength to support me. It is comforting to remember the promice, As thy day thy strength shall be.

9th month 25th 1889

When I reflect upon the goodness of God, his long suffering & gentle forbearance toward his backslideing children, I wonder how we shall ever repay him for his mercy toward us. But just here I seem to hear those precious words Jesus paid it all. Thou hast redemption full and free through His own precious blood. And altho we shall never be able to praise him enough to compensate for his mercies, yet he is crying unto us come unto me all ye ends of the earth and be ye saved with an everlasting salvation. All I require of thee is, that thou lay thy burden upon me, and I will bear it for thee. Oh what a precious Savior.

9th month 26th 1889

I am cast down yet not forsaken, yea I feel very unworthy indeed and I know that of myself I can do nothing yet the blessed Master has promiced to hear the cry of the humble, therefore I feel thankful that I have been kept humble under a sense of my own nothingness, and there is but one source where unto we may look for that comfort which is lasting and that which speaks peace to our troubled souls, then let us put our whole trust in Him.

9th month 27th 1889

They that trust in the Lord shall daily renew their strength, & oh how precious it is from day to day to find that altho we are so unworthy, yet we have a kind Father who is touched with a feeling of our infirmities & is pleased to give us strength & grace sufficient for each day, & it is my earnest desire to be found trusting Him more fully & to be willing to do whatever He requires at my hands.

9th month 28th 1889

Another week has past & gone and now the query arises how much better are we prepared for Heaven and eternal happiness. It is the earnest desire of my heart to live more & more in the fear of the Lord, oh that he will blot out all my sins and remove far from me my transgressions so I may be a fit temple for His holy presence to dwell in is my earnest prayer for Christs sake.

9th month 29th 1889

This is indeed a beautiful Sabbath day the sun shines so bright and yet the day is so cool & pleasant. And with my minds eye I look away to that far brighter time and seem to behold those loved ones who have gone before surrounding the throne of God singing hallelujah unto the Lord God and the Lamb. Strange as it may seem to some yet it is nevertheless true, that there has been times during my afflicted days, sometimes when I was alone and at other times when there were loved ones around me, that in my mediation I would seem to hear the innumerable company of angels among whom were loved ones gone before, singing praises so audibly that it seemed to me that surely those around me could hear them singing. These have been some of the sweetest moments of my life. And this bright lovely Sabbath I seem to hear their sweet refrain which brings to my mind the lines of the hymn My Heavenly home is bright & fair, I long to be there. No pain nor death can enter there, I long to be there Angels guide me home, I long to be there.

9th month 30th 1889

I am glad that I can look with an eye of faith to that promiced land of rest, for here we have no continuing City and while passing through the conflicts of this life, if it were not for the grace of God in our hearts and the hope of that promiced rest which remaineth for the people of God, we should feel like giving up by the way, but when we consider His mercies to us poor weak erring cretures, it fills our hearts with love to Him and creates a longing desire to him in the that bright world where we may ever more sing his praise.

10th month 1st 1889

On dating the first of another month it brings afresh to my mind how fast time is passing away, and the importance of being ready when the time comes for the Master to call us home. And it is the earnest desire of my heart to be living a watchful prayerful life so that I may be ready to hear the welcome summons of well done good & faithful servant enter thou into the joy of thy Lord. Oh when I reflect upon the precious promices in the Holy written word, which are laid up for those who love and serve Him on earth, I am awed and ashamed to think of my disobedience to those Divine commands. But it is the earnest prayer of my heart this morning that He will lead and guide me through this wilderness journey in the way which is well pleasing in his sight, that he will cleanse my heart from pride, malice, & deceit, that there may be nothing but love to God and good will toward all my fellow beings abideing in my heart.

10th month 2nd 1889

I have been favored with strength to do a little work with my hands to day for the help of my little family, for which I feel grateful. For altho I cannot walk around to do any work, yet when I have strength sufficient to do a little sewing, knitting, or any thing of the kind it is a great satisfaction; altho it causes me to suffer a great deal worse. But such is my love for my family and the desire to be found doing whatever my hands find to do that my strength will admit of, that I am all the time kept busy makeing, mending & when I am able to sit in my Chair. For which I want to return thanks to the Giver of all good, for the use of my hands & thinking faculties.

10th month 3rd 1889

Glory to God in the highest, on earth peace good will toward men. These words have been rolling over and over in my mind this morning since getting my paper to write, & I was ready to query why should I write them down, then turning with an eye of faith to Him to whom I look each day for fitting words to pen down I am made willing to write whatever He requires of me to his names glory. And by reflection I am made to see that upon this theme hangs the whole sum & substance of true Christianity, for if our hearts are so filled with Heavenly love that we can sing glory to God in the highest, whilst we are still in this vale of tears, & if we are at peace with, & have good will toward all people, it is evident that we are liveing in accordance with the Divine commands. And now it remains for us to examine our hearts and know for ourselves whether this is the happy state of affairs with us or not. And if it is not we should pray God to create in us new and clean hearts & renew a right spirit within us, that we may serve him as we ought on earth, so we may be permited to enter that blessed abode where we may join the innumerable company of those who have come up through much tribulation & have had their robes washed and made white in the blood of the Lamb, in singing glory to God in the highest on earth peace good will toward me.

"Oh for a heart to praise my God,
A heart from sin set free,
A heart that always feels the blood,
So freely shed for me.
A heart resigned, submissions meek,
My great Redeemers throne,
Where only Christ is heard to speak,
And Jesus reigns alone."

10th month 4th 1889

Behold how good & how pleasant it is for brethren to dwell together in unity. Psalm CXXX111. This text has been presented to my mind to day and it seems to me there can be nothing more conduceive of good or more pleasant in this life than for brethren to dwell together in unity. Not only is it pleasant for brethren to be united in the bonds of filial affection, but to be in unity of spirit. For where people are of the same household of faith either in the family circle or in the Church, it will be very pleasant to them indeed to know that they are doing all in their power to make others happy and thereby be doing that which will bring sweet peace to their own souls, and honor and praise to Him who has commanded us to do unto others as we would have them do unto us.

10th month 5th 1889

"By this I know that Thou favorest me, because thou sufferest not mine enemies to triumph over me." Glorious thought, that altho satan is busy raising up enemies against the servants of Christ, yet they are not permited to prevail against them. The Holy scriptures saith blessed are ye when men shall revile you & persecute you & shall say all manner of evil against you falsely for my names sake. It matters not what our enemies say against us if it be falsely. For if our hearts are right in the sight of God nothing that our enemies may do or say can harm us, for if God be for us who can be against us. It is true we are often deeply wounded by the taunts of the enemy. But if we look steadily too, and rely upon Him who was bruised for our iniquities, and by whose stripes we are healed, we shall find that our enemies will be scattered as the mown grass. In the morning it growth up, in the evening it is cut down and withered.

10th month 6th 1889

"Though Thou slay me yet will I trust in thee." Is our faith such that we can adopt this language with true sincereity of heart, feeling that if it were called for to do that which would imperil our natural lives, or that we should be called upon to even lay down our lives for the cause of Christ, would we still trust in him willing to lay down our lives for His sake and the Gospels that we may take them again anew in that Heavenly kingdom where we shall go no more out forever and where the weary are forever at rest. Why I write these things this beautiful Sabbath morning, I leave to Him who foreknows all things and to whom I desire to be faithful even in the little in the discharge of my duty. For our Savior saith what I do thou knowest not now, but thou shalt know hereafter. And moreover these things may be as bread cast upon the waters which may be found after many days. And if it may through Divine help add one crumb to some poor famishing soul who may be ready to perish for want of a word in season to cheer them on their Heavenward journey I shall be richly paid. Then cheer up thou lone one, for in due season thou shalt reap if thou faint not.

10th month 7th 1889

"I am trusting Lord in thee, blessed Lamb of Calvary, humbly at the cross I bow, save me Jesus save me now." These lines of a good old hymn have impressed my mind this evening, & oh that I could always realize as I do at this time that I am trusting in Jesus. For I am sometimes so perplexed with the enemies assaults that I cannot realize for a time that I am truly on the Lords side, but by fully trusting in him in those times of trial & besetments & humbly bowing at his cross, I am made to feel that Jesus does save me, & saves me now. Yes I am made to see with an eye of faith, that it is just as a fond parent watches the unsteady footsteps of a child, altho it may be entirely unconcious of the hand that is streched out to grasp it ere it falls, so our kind Heavenly parent is watching over us & will not suffer us to be tempted or tried above that which we are able, but will with the temptation, also make way for our escape. Then let us trust Him full doubting nothing. For they that trust in the Lord shall daily renew their strength.

10th month 8th 1889

"Though I speak with the tongue of men & of angels & have not charity, I am become as sounding brass, or a tinkling symbol," which is but an annoyance rather than tending to edification. For it matters not with what eloquence words are uttered, if we have not charity which means, love gentleness, kindness and forbearance toward our fellow beings, what doth it profit. But if our hearts are filled with that love which is first peaceable, gentle and easy to be entreated, altho we may be slow of speech and of a stammering tongue, yet a word fitly spoken will be as apples of gold on pictures of silver. Then let us not be discouraged but look to Jesus who is ever ready to help us in every needful time. My heart is filled with thankfulness to His great name for his present help. For altho I am not able to sit up to day and have written this whilst lying upon my bed, yet I feel my dear Savior is very near me, yes helping me in my little endeavor to do something for the upbuilding of His kingdom. Oh how I desire to be faithful even in the little, for by so doing our faith becomes stronger, and we shall realize that He knows all our weaknesses and is ready to come to our assistance as he has to mine this day, for I am so feeble that I have scarcely the faculty of thinking much less the ability to work. But I am leaning upon His everlasting arm of strength for support, for He is not only able, but willing, to help those who will come to him.

10th month 9th 1889

He that waverth is like a wave of the sea driven and tossed, let not that man think he shall receive any thing of the Lord. "Therefore be ye steadfast unmoveable always abounding in the fear of the Lord." When we have so many gentle reproofs in the Scriptures for our folly and so many precious promises for welling doing, why do we so often discard them and go stumbling as it were along the rough untried paths of life without looking to the Guide to help us on in the right way. Let it ever be our prayer to be led and guided by that all seeing eye who is watching over us and is not willing that any should perish, but that all should turn unto Him and live. Here I seem to hear the lines of the hymn, Oh turn ye oh turn ye, for why will ye die, Since God in great mercy, is coming so nigh, Jesus invites you, the Spirit says come, And the angels are waiting to welcome you home.

10th month 10th 1889

The angel of the Lord encampeth around about them that fear him and delivereth them. The Lord is indeed watching over us and his angels encamping as it were around about us when we are not aware of it. Many times has my faith been strengthened by kind friends calling in to see me, which were as Angels of mercy sent to cheer me on my way, when I was least expecting them, showing me that the Lord is putting his spirit into the hearts and minds of his people influenceing them to show kindness to those poor afflicted and lonely ones who are not permitted to meet and mingle with their friends as others do as was shown to me last evening by the visit of two lady friends who had not called to see me for nearly a year, one of them was a lady from the state of Pennsylvania who in stoping in N.C. for a time. she has been very kind indeed to me & has been the cause of my getting to see some of my old friends that I had not seen for years and also of forming new acquaintances, as she always brings someone with her to call on me which has been satisfactory.

10th month 11th 1889

This is a lovely day indeed, the sun shines so brightly and the air is so pure and pleasant, it makes me feel much more comfortable altho I have to be confined to the house, and oh if those who can walk around & see the varied hues of Autumn leaves & the many things which are pleasing to the eye, & gratifying to the mind could only know what blessings they are enjoying they would most certainly give thanks to the Giver of all good for the use of their limbs and the many blessings they are permitted to enjoy, yet strange to state, many of those who are thus so richly blessed seem to carry a load of anxiety and care and a look of bitterness as though life were a burden and had not charm for them. Dear ones let us look well to our condition & endeavor to know the why for all those dark forebodings, when there is so much to be thankful for even in this life, and the promice of everlasting rest & peace in the life that has no end. This morning my mind had be so impressed with the cause for thankfulness that I could not forbear making it my theme. This evening my heart was made to leap with joy at the news that my sister from the state of Missouri who had been gone twenty three years had come to the old home and a visit, I shall expect her to come see us tomorrow, oh that we may praise the Lord for all his blessings.

10th month 12th 1889

Again we are blessed with fine weather, I am thankful that I am able to sit in my chair this morning for I am expecting my dear sister **Ruth Johnson** to visit me to day. Oh that we may all give thanks to Him who has spared our lives and given us the blessed privilege of meeting again with loved ones on earth. My sister came to day, our meeting was mixed with joy and sorrow as it had been so long since we met and both have undergone many trials since that time. Her two little girls **Alta** and **Ermie** aged respectively eight and six years came with her, they and my little children have had a fine time indeed. I desire to be very grateful to my kind Heavenly Father for all his blessings to us poor unworthy cretures.

10th month 13th 1889

This Sabbath morning we have the pleasure of having our dear sister and children to accompany ours to the Sabbath School. Oh that we may all be thankful indeed for our many blessings for notwithstanding I am deprived of the privilege of going around with my friends, but I have the assurance of the company of a Friend that is about all others to whom be praise forever.

This afternoon we were visited by a committee of friends who are visiting the aged and infirm in Gospel service, we had a precious meeting indeed. The presence of the Lord seemed to be in our midst and the ministers **Wm. Richardson,** & **Thomas Anderson** spoke freely of the goodness of God and his many blessings to us all. So did many others who were not recorded ministers. Oh that we may all remember this day with pleasure and profit for surely the Angel of the Lord has encamped around about us this day and blessed us.

10th month 14th 1889

I am desireous to draw very near this Master this morning that he may keep me in the way of the truth, and help me to bear whatever trials I am called upon to meet. This morning we started our dear little eight year old boy **Freddie,** to our district School, there is always anxiety and care in a Mothers heart even to give up her children to go to school, and if we were called upon to give them up entirely in the this world the pang would seem almost unbearable. Our dear little four year old daughter **May** is quite sick indeed this morning we entertain great fear on her account. May the Lord in mercy spare her to us is my prayer, and may we as parents walk uprightly before our precious children, to the praise of Him who hath given us these precious jewels.

10th month 15th 1889

This morning we were favored with the company of **James R Jones,** minister of the Gospel, he gave us an earnest exortation to have full faith in the Lord Jesus Christ, and believe that he hath all power even to heal our bodies knowing that all things are possible to them that believeth. My heart responded to this exortation Lord I believe, help thou my unbelief. I have felt this morning that the Lord was waiting to be gracious to us poor unworthy children of men, and that we are not honoring him as we should, by not believeing that he is willing to do even more for us than we can ask or think, and it is my earnest prayer that thou oh Lord wouldst get thyself honor & praise by

October 1889

restoreing this poor frail body to health and strength, if it be thy holy will, nevertheless not my will by Thine be done. Oh that the words spoken to us this day may take hold upon us with such force that we shall not be able to resist them, and that we may look to the Lord in full faith believeing that he is not only able, but willing to help us.

10th month 16th 1889

My mind is weighed down this morning under a sense of my own weakness and unworthiness that I feel like I could not even lift up my head in hope, but oh that I may be favored as in days past to lean upon that arm of power that alone can support in every needful time. I feel to hunger & thirst for the bread & water of life this morning which alone can nourish up our souls unto life eternal, which cometh down from God out of Heaven. Why I should feel such poverty of spirit at this time I know not, unless it comes from the enemy who is ever ready to discourage us on our way, I pray God that we will give me strength to resist the enemy of our souls peace and trample him beneath my feet, for it is the desire of my heart to be found walking in the commandments of the Lord blameless. And that I may answer the end for which I was created which was to glorify God. For we were all created on purpose of His own glory and I pray that we may all so live, so act, in this life that we may be glorified together in that life that has no end.

10th month 17th 1889

This beautiful autumn day is drawing to a close, & I feel like returning thanks to my kind Heavenly Father for his mercies unto us, I have been able to sit up most of the day & my dear little one who has been sick for a few days is improving for which I do indeed feel grateful. Each day the query arises in my mind am I liveing in accordance with the Divine will, am I leading the life which is required of me to live for my own good & for the good of others. It is my prayer that I may walk in the light & that I may prove a blessing to my family & others by being an example of patience and meekness, & I know that it will only be through Divine assistance that I can be enabled thus to live. Then I pray that the Lord will lead me, so may I walk aright.

10th month 18th 1889

I am suffering great nerveous debility to day. Oh that I may be helped to lean hard on the Arm of power which alone can support in every time of need. Lord teach me so to number my days that I may apply my heart unto wisdom. I feel great need of that wisdom which makes wise unto salvation, and we are told in the Scriptures that if any man (& consequently any woman) lack wisdom let him ask of God who giveth to all men liberally & upbraideth not & it should be given him. Therefore I desire to be enabled to ask in faith for that wisdom which cometh down from Heaven that I may know each day just what is required of me to do, for of myself I can do nothing. And at times I feel such poverty of spirit that it seems that I could never even think a good thought. But God is my helper.

10th month 19th 1889

Praise God from whom all blessings flow, arises from my heart this morning, for his is so merciful unto us. having spared me to my family and they to me, I feel that I cannot be thankful enough for his blessings and on reflecting that we are blessed with a sufficient crop of grain and vegetables & for the sustainance of those poor frail bodies, how grateful we should be, for there are many up and down in the land who have not a sufficiency. And oh that we may daily seek for that supply of spiritual food which alone can nourish up our souls unto life eternal. Then oh God we ask thee in the name of thy dear Son that thou would feed us with this bread of Heaven every day of our lives and that we may give glory to thy great name for all our blessings.

10th month 20th 1889

I feel like praiseing God this beautiful Sabbath morning for his goodness to us poor unworthy children, for altho my dear husband

and myself are still deprived of the privilige of attending Church on account of my feebleness, yet I rejoice to know that we can praise God yet I rejoice to know that we can praise God togeather in our own home, in our own hearts. Our oldest daughter and son are gone to meeting to day, and are also to go on some Missionary work this afternoon, for which I rejoice. And my two dear little children are gone to Sabbath School which does my heart good, and whilst I have helped to prepare their bodies to present themselves there I have prayed Gods blessing upon them & that he would clothe them with the robe of righteousness which fadeth not away oh how I crave that we may all dwell near the Master this day and be willing to learn of him and be obedient to whatever he requires of us to his names glory.

10th month 21st 1889

I desire to thank my kind Heavenly Father for his mercy to me this day as I have been able to sit up most of the day & do a little sewing for my family, altho I am suffering with Neuralgia which makes me very nervous. I hope to be obedient to the Master in whatever he requires of me, and I know that it is only by keeping an eye single unto him that I shall know his will and be enabled to do it. Then I pray thee oh Lord this evening to help me to draw nigh unto thee (for we are told in the Scriptures that if we draw nigh unto God he will draw nigh unto us) and bless me with thy Heavenly love, and that I may be filled with praise to thy great name for thy goodness and thy tender mercies unto a poor unworthy worm of dust.

10th month 22nd 1889

I rejoice this morning in the thought that altho we have so many trials and provacations in this life, that we have a hope of a life beyond the grave where all sorrow and sighing are forever done away. Yes in Heaven where all is love, there'll be no sorrow there. Oh my heart is filled with praise to God this morning for all his love to me, and for the blessed promice of a home beyond the skies where we shall spend one eternal day, in praiseing him who hath washed us in his own precious blood. oh for a thousand tongues to praise him who died to redeem poor sinful fallen man, yea him who is risen and sitteth on the right hand of God to make intercession for the whole world and consequently for a poor unworthy mortal as I, blessed be His holy name.

10th month 23rd 1889

Unto thee oh Lord do we give thanks for thy goodness and thy mercy unto us. Thou hast been pleased to spare us through another day and enabled us to do something we trust for thy glory, but the praise belongeth to Him who hath our lives in his hand and to whom we are to give an account of the deeds done in the body. Then it is my prayer this evening that we may all be closely on our watch that we do not the "abomnable thing which the Lord abhoreth," yea that Thou wilt be pleased to cleanse us from all sin, and make us just what Thou wouldst have us be.

10th month 24th 1889

I have been laboring to day under mental depression, the enemy trying to persuade me that no one had the sympathy for me which my feeble condition needed. But on remembering that we have a merciful Father who is touched with a feeling of our infirmities, who knows all our weaknesses, and is ever ready to stretch forth His omnipotent hand to help those who are desireous to be led and guided by him. I have felt comforted this evening, admidst my trials in believeing that as we look away from our own weakness, to Gods strength he will be pleased to comfort us and give us a hope to press on through this vale of tears to that bright mansion prepared for all those who have taken up their daily cross and followed the Lamb of God who bids us come unto him and love.

10th month 25th 1889

Teach me thy way oh Lord and lead me in a plain path, has been my prayer from time to time, and never did I feel the need of being led in a plain path more than at the present time, for I feel like my way is so hedged up that I know not which way to look. Just here I hear that sweet small voice is ever ready to speak peace to our troubled souls. Yes He is calling us to come unto him, saying this is the way walk thou in it. Oh how precious it is to our souls when we are feeble both in body and spirit as I have been to day, to feel we may flee and find rest and peace.

10th month 26th 1889

We have been blessed last night and this morning with the company of our friends **Allen Moffitt** and wife from Pinewoods, who have started out on a religious visit to Friends in Southern quarter. We were blessed with the presence of our Divine master in our midst during their visit with us, which was refreshing to us all. And altho we feel so unworthy yet we are thankful that we have been so mercifully remembered by Him who is ever watching over us for good & will lead us through the slippery paths of life in safety, as we are willing to be led and guided by him.

10th month 27th 1889

I feel like singing I'm a child of a King, this beautiful Sabbath afternoon. This morning was very dark and rainy, every thing wore a gloomy aspect which naturally makes us feel dull and sometimes sad. But those of us who are blessed with our mental faculties know, that ere long those dark clouds will vanish, and the sun will shine out in all its brightness, so it has been this day and as it will ever be while the world standeth, just so with our joys and sorrows, at times we feel like all hope had fled, that we had as well give up trying any longer, we feel as though we should never be blessed again with the sweet incomes of Heavenly love, all seems so dark, so sad. But how often just as we are about to give up under these conclusions we are suddenly surprised by the light of love, joy, and peace springing up in our hearts, cheering us on our way & causeing us to feel like singing Gods praise.

10th month 28th 1889

This beautiful day we are again blessed with the company of some of our friends. I desire to be very thankful that it is as well with me and my family as what it is altho we have many trials and privations, yet we also have many blessings which no doubt there are many that know not of, for we enjoy the company of each other as a family and the sweet peace and joy in our hearts which none can know but those who are endeavoring to follow the Divine Master in the way of his requireings and I sincerely hope that we may be found walking in the way of all truth, that we be not stumbling blocks to others.

10th month 29th 1889

The grace of God which bringeth salvation hath appeared unto all men teaching us that denying ungodliness & worlds lust we should love soberly righteously & godly in this preasent world, looking for that blessed hope & the glorious appearing of the Son of God. These words have been presented very forceably to my mind this morning & I herewith submit them, knowing that they have been given to me of my Father in Heaven. Now seeing that this grace hath appeared unto us, let us submit ourselves unto its teachings, for if we live up to this text then shall we indeed not only look for, but realize that glorious appearing of the dear son of God, and in the world to come we shall be like him, for we shall see him as he is.

10th month 30th 1889

I am thankful to state that I can rejoice in God my savior, for he is so merciful unto me, for he has blessed me with a kind loving husband, precious children and many kind friends to care for me and I have been provided for with the necessities of life, notwithstanding I am many times deprived of things which would be gratifying to possess, and which many do have that I have not, yet when I reflect how many are worse off in many respects than I am, altho I am so afflicted, I feel that I ought daily to number my blessings. My heart has been made sad to day by the presence of a poor woman & three children, one of them an infant. She is the wife of a drunkard, oh it is as pitiful to see them & to hear their pitiable experience, they call on us often for something, sometimes several times a day. Their case is so trying that I have to plead with my kind Heavenly Father to help me to do what is right toward them, for altho I am willing & do help them as best I can, yet they are not fit associates for my little ones, as their Father teaches them profanity & we know that the Scriptures command that we should have no friendship with an angry man, & with a furious man thou shalt not go, and he is indeed a furious man & abuses his wife & little ones, which is heartrending to think of. I have talked too & plead with him to give up the drink & turn from his evils ways, but it seems to be of no avail thus far, but I am willing God being my helper to try try again & if I do not succeed in reclaiming this poor drunken miserable man I will at least reap the reward of peace for doing my duty.

11th month 1st 1889

The lines of the hymn:
There's a land that is fairer than day,
And by faith we shall see it afar
And our Father waits over the way
To prepare us a dwelling place there.

Impressing my mind this lovely fair day for in that land that is fairer than our beautiful sunshine, what must the splender be, & to remember that our Father has prepared for us a dwelling place there, oh how grand, how glorious, for such a home to be prepared for us poor unworthy cretures. And let us ever bear in mind that if we miss that blessed abode that it is of our own choosing, for we have the commandments given us & the Holy Spirit whereby we are made to know what is right & what is wrong by the dictates of our own conscience. And the great plan of salvation has been laid down in unmistakeable terms so plain that we shall not be justifiable in making shipwreck of our souls peace. Then let us turn to God with full purpose of heart, who is the way the truth & the life, & be saved with an everlasting salvation.

11th month 2nd 1889

I have been favored with the company of my dear sister & her little children last night & this morning & my heart has been deeply tried by having to part with them, I do not know at this time whether I shall see them again before they return home or not, as they have gone to the old homestead & expect to start home in two days. My heart breathes a silent prayer for them that they may be spared to return to their home in safety, & may the blessing of Heaven rest upon them.

11th month 3rd 1889

This has been a dreary Sabbath day it has been very rainy & my heart has been very full, as I had anticipated getting to go to meeting to day a privilege which I have not had for near two years but as our all wise Father saw fit to send us the rain, it is our duty to be content with whatever situation we are placed in & I am thankful that I feel that sweet peace in my soul which is worth every thing else in life. I am thinking of going to the old homestead this evening if the rain ceases, to spend the night with my dear sister who is to start to her home in Missouri tomorrow morning & if the blessed Master gives me strength to go the praise & honor must be His to whom belongeth all praise both now and forever.

11th month 4th 1889

There has been sad hearts to day as my dear sister & her little daughters bid us adieu for their Missouri home & it is very uncertain whether we ever meet again on earth. I had the privilege of spending last night at our old home with them, & our dear aged Mother, Brother, &

Sister & now it is my ancious desire that we may all meet in that land where parting is unknown.

11th month 5th 1889

This is a very beautiful day indeed, everything seems to proclaim the goodness of God. The falling leaves with their verigated hues remind me of the different conditions of people in this life & all hastening to decay, that is these mortal bodies will soon be laid low. But when that part which will live forever has been striped of this earthly tabernacle of clay, if we have lived holy righteous lives, then we shall put on that new robe which is laid up for all who enter the Kingdom. Then we shall not be as the trees of the forest which are striped of their foliage every year by the frost of time. But we shall have put on that new robe which will remain through eternity.

11th month 6th 1889

They that trust in the Lord shall be as mount Zion which shall not be moved. oh that we amy implicitly trust in Jesus, haveing our hearts given to, & in entire subjection to Him who is worthy of all our love. Then we shall be steadfast unmoveable always abounding in the fear of the Lord. My heart is deeply weighed own under a sense of my own nothingness. For I feel that my blessed Master who doeth all things well has been weighing me in the Ballance & I have been found wanting. Oh for more faith, more zeal, more wisdom to understand what thou oh Lord would have me to do & what to leave undone, for it is my earnest prayer that I may not prove a stumbling block to any but that the Lord would make me an instrument in his hands of much good, that he would be pleased to sanctify my affliction not only to my own good, but to the good of others. That I may not of lived in vain, may not of suffered for naught. yea I pray that these light afflictions which are but for a moment compared to eternity, may work out for me a far more exceeding & eternal weight of glory, & that through patience & entire submission I may teach a lesson to others to look and lean upon Jesus alone who can support us through all our trials, temptations and besetments in this life, and He is not only able but willing to save all who will come unto God through the merits of his dear Son.

11th month 7th 1889

I have been engaged to day in writing a lengthy letter to my sister-in-law **Elizabeth Starbuck,** whose first husband was my dear husbands only brother. I am very nervous to day yet & feel thankful for the favor of being able to sit up most of the day & write, oh that I may keep close to the Master that I be not led astray by the enemy who is ever ready to put a stumbling block in our path. The prayer of my heart this evening is that the Lord would keep me as in the hollow of his holy hand that I sin not.

11th month 8th 1889

The Lord has so wonderfully blessed us that I feel like I could not be thankful enough for his kindness. As I sit here in my wheel chair at the window & look up from my work & see my dear husband sowing & plowing in the grain. I remember that altho it is his duty & his part of the work to seed the ground, yet it is God only who can give the increase, therefore my heart is lifted up in prayer to him that He will abundantly bless his labors, that we may be self sustaining while we are permited to stay here upon earth, for it is our bounden duty to provide for the sustanance of our bodies, & it is as much our duty as well as our blessed privilege to ask Gods blessing upon our temperal affairs as that which concerns our welfare in the life to come. And we should ask Him to sanctify these blessings to our good & to the good of others who are in need. For it is only by & through a life thus led & guided by the Master that we shall be prepared to enter into that glorious mansion which is prepared for all those who have improved the talent given them, while time was lengthened out to them, so let us all be up & doing, the night cometh wherein no man can work either temporally or spiritually for then our doom is fixed, we shall then have to appear before the great Judge to give account of the deeds done in the body, whether they be good or whether they be evil.

11th month 9th 1889

Unto thee oh Lord do we give thanks, watch over us this day, preserve us from temptation and keep us from sin. Thou who knows the secret of every heart teach us to apply them unto wisdom, help us to understand thy Holy Scriptures and to apply their teachings to our special benefit, that we may know how to teach our dear children the truths contained therein, for we are poor ignorant cretures, without Thy help we can do nothing. Wilt Thou be pleased to give each of us this day strength sufficient to do that which our hands find to do, and give us that spiritual strength whereby we may be built up in the most holy faith, and have our hearts filled with thanks giving praise and honor onto the Kings of kings.

11th month 10th 1889

This is a most beautiful Sabbath day, our dear children have all attended the Sabbath School this morning, and this afternoon our oldest daughter and son are gone to meet with a committee of Friends at **Thomas Englishes** as he is old and feeble and not able to get out to meeting. This committee has visited a number who like myself are deprived of the blessed privilege of getting out to meeting on account of feeble health. Their labors have been I believe abundantly blessed. In order that some one or ones may be encouraged to be faithful in the discharge of their duty, I will just note the dealings of the kind Shepherd with me this day. This morning I felt it my duty to go to visit a poor family who live nigh to us. I felt that I must go and read a chapter to them, so after getting our children started to Sabbath School altho I was feeling feeble in body, I remarked to my dear husband that we must now make haste and get ready as we had an appointment at eleven o'clock, altho this remark was made in a jovial way yet I did not get shut of the impression so assureing my husband that I felt called to go, he kindly brought out the conveyance and we went, and were kindly received by them, and it seemed that the very Heavens were opened to pour us out a blessing. After reading the twenty fifth Psalm, the spirit of prayer came upon me with such irresistible force that I felt I must bow in humble submission to the Divine will and implore a blessing upon this poor, and we might add degraded family, for the husband had been in the habit of getting intoxicated and spending his earnings in a way that was not profitable either to himself or his family. And we expected that more than likely we should find him under the influence of strong drink but to our surprise and joy he came out met us and cordially invited us in the house. But oh shocking to see, his wife and little children dirty and shabbily clad this beautiful Sabbath day, with appearantly very few of the comforts of life so essential for them. Oh it made my heart sink within me. I do not note these things for my own merit, but the sweet peace which has filled my heart since visiting these poor cretures, to see their appearant conviction and the appreciation of our visit has caused me to feel that such visits are too seldom made, and I desire to encourage all who may feel any work for the Master to be faithful in the discharge of their duty.

11th month 11th 1889

To day I have been reading a tract entitled, Have faith in God. Being an account of the sufferings and wonderful restoration to health by faith of **Carrie Judd** of Buffalo, N.Y. By which I have felt a desire that the Lord would give me such faith and that he would be pleased to heal both my bodily and my spiritual defects. But it has always been my prayer to be submissive to the Divine will and if by keeping me in the furnace of affliction I may be kept pure, I am willing if it is the Lords will still to suffer, yet I know that oh righteous Father hast all power to do whatsoever seemeth good to thee, therefore I ask that Thou in the adorable goodness and mercy when Thou hast kept me in the furnace of affliction long enough to purefy me from all the dross and reprobate silver, that thou would be pleased to say it is enough and bring me out as pure bright silver wherein may be seen the image of the Master, so may I be found glorifying Thee for this great deliverance.

11th month 12th 1889

Greatly to be praised is the name of our God who doeth wonderous works. My heart is filled with thankfulness that I have had strength this day to sit up most of the day and do some work with my hands which is needful for the comfort of my family, oh that I may be faithful to do my duty spiritually as well as temperally for there are souls in our immediate neighborhood I believe that are not in the fold of Christ, and if I may only be instrumental in saveing one soul & feel that it is worth laboring for, and oh that I may be willing to do whatever the Master requires of me, let it be what it may for the upbuilding of the Redeemers kingdom. So it is my prayer this evening that He would be pleased to give me more faith, and help me to act faith by my works.

11th month 13th 1889

I have been suffering with nervous debility to day which is indeed very trying, I have exerted myself to some sewing which was very much needed for the comfort of my family, but by so doing I find myself very much fatigued & the suffering with my spine so great that I can scarely pen down a few lines, but altho I feel sometimes like I should give out by the way, yet I still try to look to that ray of light by which alone we are directed in the right way. Oh Lord let the light of thy countenance shine upon me this day, to cheer me on my way.

11th month 14th 1889

They that dwell in the secret place of the most High, shall abide under the shadow of the Almighty. Oh that I may ever abide so near the Master that his shadow may overhang my path as it were, and that I may be led in the strait and narrow way that leads to life and peace. It is my anxious desire to be found working for the Master in whatever way he sees fit to lead me. And if it is but to wait in humble resignation until He sees fit to call me home, let me by this teach a lesson to others, so that my life be not a blank, for I desire to answer the end for which I was created.

11th month 15th 1889

Being able to sit up this beautiful morning I feel like returning thanks to the Giver of all good for His many blessings. I desire to be kept this day in perfect obedience to the Divine will, for I know except Thou direct me I cannot keep in the right path, for I am so weak I stumble, unless Thou hold me I shall fall. But I thank Thee that thou art holding out thy arm of power for even a poor unworthy creture as I to lean upon.

11th month 16th 1889

I have been able to be up most of this day for which I desire to be grateful, and altho I am suffering with my spine and still have to get around in my wheel chair, yet I have been permitted to day, to do some mending for my family which is a source of comfort to me to know that I can do something for the help and comfort of others.

11th month 17th 1889

This is a very dark rainy Sabbath, so much so that my family are all at home with me. While we are all comfortably situated around our hearth stone I think how much we have to be thankful for, that our little band is yet unbroken and that we are blessed with the necessary comforts of life, Whilst there are many who are surrounded by many luxuries which we have not, yet we enjoy the luxury of a peaceful quiet home, with our hearts united in the bonds of affliction which is worth more than the riches which perisheth not with the using, but by reason of use shineth more and more. Then let us all endeavor to walk in the path, that the light may lead us to everlasting day.

11th month 18th 1889

I have been favored to do some sewing to day altho it is very trying on my spine, yet when it is in my power to do any thing for the help and comfort of my family, altho it be done through suffering, it is a source of satesfaction to me and makes me feel like returning thanks to the Giver of all good for this privilege, for there has been so many months and even years that I could do nothing to help them in the way of household affairs. So may my heart be filled with gratitude to God that it is even as well with me as what it is, and if it be His will I desire that I may receive more physical as well as spiritual strength.

11th month 19th 1889

Another day is passing away, oh that we may all improve each moment as it flies, in order to be prepared to enter that home beyond the skies, my health still remains poor yet I feel that I am rich because I know that Jesus loves, even me.

11th month 20th 1889

As I am able to arise from my bed this morning, I feel like returning thanks to my kind Heavenly Father for his mercies and pray that he will keep me as in the hallow of his holy hand this day, that I sin not.

11th month 21st 1889

To day we have again been reminded of the certainty of death by hearing of the calling home of one of our acquaintances. Oh how important to always be ready for the final summons. Lord teach us so to remember our days that we may apply our hearts unto wisdom.

11th month 22nd 1889

Praise belongeth unto thee oh Father in Zion, therefore I desire to be found doing whatever Thou would have me to do to thy praise and honor. I have been able to sit up to day and do some sewing mending & for which I give thanks. My family are all in good health at this time which is one of our greatest blessings. And altho I do not know what it is to see a well day, yet I am so much better at this time than I have been for months past I feel that there is great cause for thankfulness.

11th month 23rd 1889

This is a beautiful day indeed, the sun shines so nice and warm that it seems almost incredible to think it is near the last days of November, yet when we look about and see the trees laid bare of their foliage by the frost, we are reminded that cold chilly winter is near at hand. This also reminds us that we may soon be cut down by the frost of death. Then let us reverently hope and trust that when this solemn moment comes it may find us disrobed of all unrighteousness that we may put on the new garment which alone is prepared for those who enter the Marriage feast of the Lamb.

11th month 24th 1889

This lovely Sabbath morning whilst I help to prepare the bodies of my dear children for Sabbath School it is is my greatest desire that the Lord would be pleased to clothe them with the garment of righteousness which perisheth nor with the using. And oh that He would help us who are the parents of these dear children to walk in the way of all truth, setting a good example before them to the praise and honor of His worthy name.

11th month 25th 1889

I have been very nervous to day, suffered more with my spine than for some time, yet I hope to be kept from murmuring. I feel like quoting the lines, I have many sore temptations and troubles to my mind, I am so weak I stumble & so am left behind. But thanks be to God who giveth us the victory through our Lord Jesus Christ, that we are permitted to take fresh courage and feel that the Master is holding out his arm of safety to hold up the weak and stumbling ones and place our feet on that sure foundation which cannot be shaken, oh if it were not for these little Oasis in the Desert whereby we are refreshed, we should sink beneath the deep sands and searching suns as it were through which we have to pass in our Haven bound journey. Then oh Father be pleased to supply us with that living water whereof we may drink and live forever for the sake of thy dear Son.

11th month 26th 1889

My mind has been occupied with various reflections this morning and in an especial manner the flight of time, as this is my oldest daughters twenty fourth birth day, and it hardly seems possible, for it seems but as yesterday that she was a little child. Oh that we may all be more concerned to improve each moment as it flies, for our days will soon all be past here on earth and we will go to spend that long long time either in bliss or endless woe, then which is our choice. The prayer of my heart is that we may live so near the Master, walking in his ways and in entire obedience to his will that we may be counted worthy to spend eternity in that blessed abode where the inhabitants never say I am sick.

11th 27th 1889

I have nothing new to note this morning, but glad to record that it is the old story of Jesus and his love, that is most precious to my soul. Oh that I may be made to rejoice more and more in God my Saviour and be permited to know more of his will and do that which is well pleasing his sight. Altho I am feeble this morning, yet I can sit in my chair, and have the use of my hands, and thinking faculties, which is a great deal to be thankful for, and may I realize each day that I am living and working for Jesus, then my life will not have been lived in vain.

11th month 28th 1889

This day being the National thanksgiveing and day of prayer for the prosperity and righteous government of the people, for blessings past and present, my heart has been made to feel as never before the importance of returning thanks for the many blessings that we as a Nation and people have been blessed with, notwithstanding some the States in our Union have been visited by serious calamities in the way of disasterous floods, hericanes & which should tend to humble us as a dependent people, for it plainly shows us that our lives are in the hands of Him who is both able to save and to destroy, and He permits serious calamities to come upon some of his people at times in order that they and others may become more submissive, humble and obedient to Him who holds all the wealth of the world in His hands. For it does seem to me at this time that if there was more charity in dispensing with the good of the land to those who are in real need instead of so much vain show, waste of precious time and money in a manner which is neither beneficial to themselves, nor does it add any thing to the upbuilding of the Redeemers Kingdom by way of benefiting others, that the Master would be better served and would be greater blessed. I have been reading the History of the Johnstown flood in Pa which occurred on sixth day 5th month 31st 1889. As the History expresses it, "Record that awful date Friday May 31st 1889 in characters of funereal hue." Oh that this solemn warning may be universally heeded, for how soon we may be overtaken by some sudden calamity and swept out of time we know not. I have also been reading the life and work of **Eli and Sibyl Jones** whose lives and character we would all do well to follow as they followed Christ. Those dear Friends are universally known and loved, their memories will ever be precious to those who have net them or heard the Gospel declared in plain honest terms from their lips. **Eli Jones** has visited me in my home during my affliction, in the love of the Gospel, which visit was highly appreciated.

    I never met his wife **Sibyl** but I well remember seeing her when I was a girl at yearly meeting at New Garden N.C. and how sweet and diginified her appearance was. Oh if we would only live so near the Master as did those dear friends we should always find a support in every needful time, She and her husband were both so wholly and soully devoted to the work of the Master that they were wonderfully blessed, notwithstanding they had to undergo severe trials. It is true that there are compareatively few that are called to such extensive service as they were, for where much is given much will be required, yet if we have but the one talent let us not bury it in the earth, but improve it to the Masters use and we shall not loose our reward.

11th month 29th 1889

This has been a cold day & windy, which reminds me of the text, the wind bloweth where it listeth & thou canst hear the sound thereof, but canst not tell whence it cometh or whither it goeth, so is every one that is born of the spirit. In our meditation our minds seem to soar away beyond the skies & hearts are made to feel that sweet peace which none can know but those who have given themselves to the Master, & whose souls are hungering and thirsting for that bread & water of life which alone can nurish up our souls unto life eternal. And often the boisterous winds and tempestuous seas seem almost ready to overwhelm us yet as we are willing to trust in the power of the most high He will speak to the angry waves & say peace be still. But I believe that when we have entered the life boat with Jesus for our captain that we should so fully trust him to anchor us safe in the harbor, that when storms arise instead of bewailing our condition & crying out in doubtful anxiety to the Master to save us or we perish, that we should so implicityly confide in the promice lo I am with you always even until the end of the world, that we should lay as it were passive in the Saviours arms believeing that ere long he will anchor us safe in that Haven of rest prepared for the people of God.

11th month 30th 1889

On calling to mind that this is the last day of autumn, I am led to reflect how fast we are approaching our eternal destination. How soon death may lay her icey hands upon us we know not. Therefore it is my desire that each & every one of us may be in earnest to know that we have made our calling and election sure. Oh how fervently my heart desires that those words of the hymn, "oh God & will though condescend, to be my Father and my friend," may be accepted as the prayer of my heart this evening and that I may be kept close on my watch that I go not astray from the path of duty.

12th month 1st 1889

This beautiful Sabbath is the beginning of our winter season, but the sun shines so nice and warm that it does not seem like the approach of winter, yet we are well aware that the chilling blasts can come very suddenly, so we know not what a day may bring forth, so it is with our mortal lives, we know neither the day nor the hour when the Son of man cometh. My mind is deeply impressed with the necessity of being ready when the Bridegroom cometh. I often feel that I am wondering as it were upon the barren mountains & desolate hills where there is neither dew nor rain or fields of offering. But blessed be God he is willing to refresh us at times and seasons, as He knows is best of us.

12th month 2nd 1889

Unto thee oh Lord do I lift up my soul, for Thou alone can supply all my needs. Thou alone can give me that comfort which my soul is hungering and thirsting for at this time. I have felt very much discouraged to day having suffered so much while trying to do some work that was very much needed for the comfort of my little ones. And I have not only suffered in body but have felt such poverty of soul, which no doubt is the assault of the enemy, he takes advantage of our weak moments to discourage us, for when we are weak in body and often times having to pass through trying moments both to our physical and spiritual strength, it is then that he lays his subtile snairs for us. But blessed be the Holy name of Jesus who is ever watching over and careing for his flock, he sees the Wolf comeing

& protects them from the enemy. Since I commenced writing this evening feeling so poor so unworthy and cast down, I have heard the precious words of the Master whispering in my ear, Blessed are the poor in spirit for theirs is the kingdom of Heaven. Blessed are they that hunger and thirst after righteousness for they shall be filled.

12th month 3rd 1889

The lines of the hymn, One sweetly solemn though comes to me oer and oer, I'm near my Fathers house than esr I was before, impressed my mind this morning with deep solemnity, yes each day as it passes brings us near to our never ending home. And whilst it is a solemn thought, yet if we have the blessed assurance that our peace is made with God, that our sins are all bloted out of the Lambs book of life and we are only waiting to be welcomed home when the Master is done with our serveing here below, the thought will indeed be sweet, for then we shall meet with loved ones gone before and no more shall we suffer the pangs of broken ties which we are so often called to experience while passing through this vale of tears. And we shall not be subjected to long years of affliction & pain, sleepless nights & wearisome days of toil, but we shall rest with the people of God there to sing his praise who hath bought and redeemed us with His own precious blood. Oh that we may all be in earnest to prepare for that glorious Haven of rest.

12th month 4th 1889

I am so feeble that it is with difficulty that I can sit up to day, yet I hope I am thankful that the situation is not worse, as I am yet spared to my family & they to me, whilst we are so often hearing of Mothers being taken from their little children, or the children from their parents & of course we know not how soon the summons may come to any of us, for we know not the day nor the hour when the Son of man cometh.

12th month 5th 1889

Today we have been favored with the company of **James R Jones** from Indiana who has been sojourning in N.C. for some time. The day has been spent pleasantly. To night another friend has meeting at our district School House Oak Forest and as Jones is going to spent the night with us he and some of my family are gone out to meeting I hope the power of the most High may overshadow the little gathering & that they may exalt His name together. My grown daughter & my little daughter and myself are left alone, yet not alone for the Master is with us. Blessed by His holy name.

12th month 6th 1889

Our friend **J.R. Jones** left here this morning to attend Deep River quarterly meeting. Our oldest son being appointed as representative started to day to attend the same, oh that the blessings of Heaven may be showered down abundantly upon all those who are permited to attend, and also may all of us who are not permited to be there know of a Heavenly Fathers love abideing in our hearts, purging us from all sin and making us fit temples for His holy presence to dwell in.

12th month 7th 1889

I desire to be kept very humble & not to murmur left my situation be what it may, but I have felt somewhat discourage for a few days past as I have been more feeble & have suffered more with my spine & nervous debility so that I have not been able to do very much with my hands for the help of my family. But the Lord will provide & make a way where there seems to be one as in days past.

12th month 8th 1889

Unto thee oh Lord do I look for fitting words to pen in this book. For unto Thee have I dedicated this work for altho poor and unworthy as I am and knew that my efforts are put forth in a simple unlearned style, yet I feel it to be my duty in obedience to my Heavenly Father, therefore it is my earnest desire that the few simple disconnected sentences which I may write may be sanctified to the good of some poor weary traveler up the rugged paths of time, oh that we may be Gods devoted children, looking unto him for help & direction. That we may be led in the right way, so that when we are called from works to rewards we may enter that rest prepared for the people of God. Oh to know more of Thee to love thee more and serve thee better, is the fervent desire of my heart this Sabbath evening for Jesus sake.

12th month 9th 1889

I will be with thee in thee sixth trouble, & in the seventh I will not forsake thee what a precious promice for troubles & trials come to us in this life until they are many times seven, therefore we feel the need of a kind Father through all these trials and to have his testimonies, some of them which are these, If thy brother trespass against thee, thou shalt not only forgive him till seven times, but seventy times seven. If thine enemy hunger feed him, if he thirst give him drink, for in doing thou shalt heap coals of fire upon his head. Oh here slightly do we heed the precious promises in the Bible. Oh for more faith, & more faithfulness to share forth this faith by works, for faith without works is dead faith.

12th month 10th 1889

True wisdom is the fear of the Lord, therefore let us seek wisdom, that we may serve the Lord in meekness and fear. I have been able to be up the most of this day & use my hands to do some work for which I desire to be very thankful. For altho I am not strong yet it is a great pleasure to do the little I can for the comfort of others, that that I may be more self sacrificing and that the Lord in his mercy would be pleased to give me more bodily as well as spiritual strength so that I may be enabled to do good to those who are in need, either physically, mentally or spiritually, for the sake of Him who died for me.

12th month 11th 1889

This is a most beautiful day for the time of year & how many things we have to be thankful for, as we are spared as a little family together. I have the necessary comforts of life, I say necessary, for altho we lack many things which wealthier people possess, yet we are blessed with many comforts which there are a great many do not have therefore I desire to be content with such things as we have.

12th month 12th 1889

My heart is filled with praise this evening to the King of Kings for his many mercies, oh that I may be always on my guard lest I fall into temptation. For satan is ever ready to discourage us, and when we are the most tried, he watches his chance to take advantage of our weakness. Let us lean upon that strong are of power that is able to support us in every needful time.

12th month 13th 1889

The grace of God hath appeared unto all men, teaching us that denying ungodliness and worlds lust we should lie soberly righteously & godly in this present world, oh how forcibly this text has presented itself to my mind this evening on hearing the vanities and follies of fashion discussed by some young people. Oh Father of all our sure mercies to thee we cry for help both for ourselves and for the dear young people who are exposed to the temptations of this life.

12th month 14th 1889

Twenty five years ago to day my dear husband and I were united in the Holy covenant of marriage, many many have been the changes since that time. Loved ones have passed away. Dear children have been born to us, and some to them grown to womanhood and manhood and oh how thankful I am that they have thus far been preserved from falling into the vile and pernicious customs which are too common amongst youth, and how I crave that they as well as we, their parents, may live nearer the Saviour than we ever have done, and when I look upon two little children who are yet in the untried paths of life, how my heart yearns for them that they may be kept from sin and temptation and that they may live holy righteous lives.

12th month 15th 1889

This is indeed a beautiful Sabbath day and as I am still unable to attend the place appointed for worship, I greatly crave that I may be enabled to worship in my own home in that way & manner which will be owned & blessed of the Lord. As the mountains around about Jerusalem, so is the Lord around about his people, for how precious to have Him around about us watching over and careing for us. He hath said he that cometh unto me I will in no wise cast out. Then let those of us who are weak & heavy laden lift up our heads in hope, for He hath bid all those who are weary & heavy laden to come unto Him & find rest. There remaineth therefore a rest for the people of God. I have been quite feeble for a few days past, but "When I am weak then I am strong, Christ is my strength, and Christ my song."

12th month 16th 1889

This has been another beautiful day and I have been permited to go out a short distance visiting for which I feel very thankful as it has been so long since I have had the privilege of visiting my friends and neighbors.

12th month 17th 1889

The day has been damp and I have been suffering more on that account & also on account of my ride yesterday altho the distance was short, but my spine is so affected that the jostle in rideing often causes me great suffering, yet it is beneficial to my general health, & I desire to return thanks to my Heavenly Father for once more permiting me to get out a little to see my friends & the beauties of nature. Altho I cannot walk around and it is very trying to my natural will to have to be carried in & out as I do, yet it is such a relief from being confined entirely to the house and the bed, that I wish to be very thankful.

12th month 18th 1889

Being permited to be up to day & use my hands to do something for the needs of my family, I feel indeed very thankful, altho it is through suffering that I do what work my strength will admit of. Oh that my Heavenly Father would be pleased to restore me to perfect health & strength, to the glory of his great name & to the comfort and edification of others. I know I am not worthy to be thus favored, yet I know Thou dost condescend to help the lowly, and that thou hast all power in Heaven & on earth to do whatsoever thou wilt, therefore accept this as my prayer oh Lord if it be consistent with thy hold will nevertheless not my will, but thy will be done, to the glory of God the Father & praise of thy dear Son. Amen.

12th month 19th 1889

We continue to have the finest weather & almost ever saw for the time of year, which is very favorable on my afflicted limbs, & also my general health for which I am very thankful. "Oh for a heart from sin set free, a heart that always feels the blood, so freely shed for me." I hope that I may never let any thing hinder me from doing whatever the Lord calls for at my hands, for He doesn't ask more of us than he will give us ability to perform. I have felt greatly humbled for the few weeks past on on hearing of the death of so many of our fellow beings, who have fallen victims to fever and thus passed away. Oh that we may be more in earnest to make our calling and election sure. For there is no bribeing death.

12th month 20th 1889

He that is ashamed of me and my words, of him will I be ashamed before my Father and his holy Angels. I fervently desire that these words of our blessed Saviour may take deep root in my heart and that I may never be ashamed to acknowledge the goodness of God and the tender love & mercy of his dear Son who gave his life a ransom for the sins of the whole world. As the time is drawing nigh which commemorates the birth of the dear Son of God, when the star directed the wise men to Bethlehem where the holy child was, my heart if filled with prayerful desires that we may each one of us be directed by that bright and morning star Jesus our Saviour, to the Holy City whose maker and builder is God. Where we shall ever sing His praise in that world of spirits bright.

12th month 21st 1889

We are again blessed with fine weather for the season. I am able to be up most of my time and do some work altho I still have to roll round in my week Chair. I want to be kept very near the Master that I may learn of him & obey his righteous law.

12th month 22nd 1889

This beautiful Sabbath we have been blessed with the company of some dear friends, & were favored with a precious season of prayer & praise together, for which I thank my kind Heavenly Father for the privilege, & oh that we may look to Him alone to guide & direct us in all our words and deeds.

12th month 23rd 1889

Blessed be the name of the Lord forever for his mercy and goodness to his unworthy children. Amen.

12th month 24th 1889

This lovely day we have been favored with the company of my dear aged Mother, and also my youngest sister and some of her children, which is always a source of joy to myself and family. Blessed be the name of our holy Redeemer.

12th month 25th 1889

Christmas day, a day which we should hold scared in memory of Him who was sent into the world to redeem the people from their sins. This same Saviour who died and rose again, still liveth and will ever live to make intercession for the whole world. Therefore all who will may come unto Him and be saved. My heart is deeply humbled this morning, by looking at my unfaithfulness and remembering the goodness of God to his dependent children, oh that He will be pleased to give me me wisdom and strength to do his holy will is my prayer.

12th month 26th 1889

Trust in the Lord and do good and thou shalt dwell in the land, and verily thou shalt be fed. Here again is some of the precious promises laid down for us. That if we trust in the Lord & do good we had the promice that we shall dwell in the land, & that we shall be fed. Then let us not rebel again the Lord so as top provoke him to anger. But turn to Him & live.

12th month 27th 1889

My husband and I and out little children have been enjoying the holidays quietly in our home, whilst our grown children have been visiting some of their friends. We have so much to be thankful for.

12th month 28th 1889

The weather continues to be very fine, which is a great help to poor afflicted people like myself. Truly the Lord is merciful for he has shown great kindness unto his dependent children. We cannot repay Him for his goodness to us, only by simple obedience to his well. And by so doing we shall mount up like Eagles, we shall run and not be weary, we shall walk and not faint.

12th month 29th 1889

My heart is filled with gratitude to God for his goodness to me & my family, for altho we have had so many trials & afflictions, yet we have been blessed with the overshadowing presence of Him who is able to comfort his children & make a way for them where there seems no way. For often we have felt that our way was entirely hedged up, it seemed that were rocked upon the billows as it were of the temptestuous ocean, where the waves threaten to overwhelm us, but in the midst of these storms which are so common in this life, the Master is please to say peace be still.

12th month 30th 1889

The weather having changed from the very fairest, to dark & rainy makes things have a gloomy outward appearance, & also has affect on the system, yet thanks be to God who giveth us the victory through our Lord Jesus Christ, we can have that within our hearts which bringeth light, life & peace, and which none can take away from us, even the love of God in our hearts which is able to make us wise unto salvation through the merits of our crucified and risen Saviour.

12th month 31st 1889

This will doubtless be the last time I shall write the date of this year, as the last day of the year is fast receding and this even brings to my mind the fact that another year has passed away, with its joys and sorrows, yea and with its many blessings and now the query arise in my heart what have I done to advance my Fathers Kingdom in the way of bringing souls to Christ.

1890

1st month 1st 1890

The beginning of a new year awakens new desires to be more zealous in the work of our Lord and Master, let it be ever so humble, oh that we may all put on the whole armor of God that we may be able to stand in the evil day, for many are the temptations and snares which the evil one endeavors to lead us into. Therefore we ask thee our righteous Father to help us guard again temptation.

1ˢᵗ month 2ⁿᵈ 1890

Being able to rise from my bed this morning, and roll about the house in my chair and help to do some work, I feel that it is indeed a great privilege to even do this, altho I am not able to walk about to see to my daily affairs, but I still hope that if it is the will of the Divine Master, he will give me more strength physically as well as spiritually, to the praise of his worthy name.

1st month 3ʳᵈ 1890

Therefore being justified by faith we have peace with God through our Lord Jesus Christ. Oh for that liveing faith whereby we may be justified and find peace with God, for without this faith and the power to act it out by works, it is impossible to please God. And as faith is the gift of God, we work that Thou would grant it to thy children.

1ˢᵗ month 4ᵗʰ 1890

Haveing this day, been endeavoring to hold up my feeble hands, to mend the clothing for some of my family, and feeling the great need of more strength for even this little performance of duty, how much more do I feel the great need of both physical and spiritual strength to help build up the waste places in Zion. For when I behold the great need of laborers in the fields which are already white unto harvest even as we might say at our own doors, I feel that we should not be willing to sit with our hands folded, altho we shall be ready to cry out who is sufficient for own weakness and nothingness to Him who is able to make wise unto salvation through Jesus Christ our Lord, all those who come unto God by him.

1st month 5ᵗʰ 1890

This has been a dreary Sabbath day, the weather being very dark, & damp & our oldest daughter being sick, my nerves have been over taxed, so that I am scarcely able to be up, yet I am thankful that it is as well with us as what it is, and desire to be kept from murmuring let our situation be what it may.

1ˢᵗ month 6ᵗʰ 1890

My mind is still weighed down under my own weakness, both bodily & spiritually. I feel the great need of a present helper in my trying moments, yet I am well aware that the Master will not try us above that which we are able, but will make a way where there seems to be none, but as our daughter is still sick and myself so helpless about getting around, and we have no one to cook a meal, except my dear husband and he is not very well, the situation seems discouraging. But as we have passed through so many such trying seasons and often times a great deal worse that at the present, we will still hope that the Divine Master who has led us on thus far, will be pleased to again lift the cloud of darkness and that light may shine upon our path & that we may be led on step by step through this wilderness journey, looking unto Jesus who alone can guide and direct our steps in the right way. Then if I know my own heart the very breathing of my soul is unto God this day that he will be near us to lift this burden from us, and restore our family to health and strength, to the praise of His great name.

1ˢᵗ month 7ᵗʰ 1890

The weather remains damp which is very much against my Bronchial trouble. Our daughter, being no better causes anxiety & care. I feel almost like giving up by the way, but I will still trust that He who has promised, not only to be with us in the sixth trouble, but also in the seventh, will still be our stay & helper, for we are in need of both spiritual & temperal help.

1ˢᵗ month 8ᵗʰ 1890

This day is windy, very much like it generally is in the third month, which is very disagreeable indeed, and our daughter is still very sick.

The physician now pronounces the disease Measels, our anxiety is very great, as she is very bad, and the Measels have proved fatal to a great many this winter. My nerves ae overtaxed, but I pray that my strength may be sufficient for each day.

1st month 9th 1890

Our daughter still very sick, our oldest son also taken down with Measels, is very bad to day. My strength is very much exhausted by anxiety and care, as there has been little rest day or night. Oh that we may all feel the Everlasting Arms underneath to bear us up in every needful time is my earnest prayer.

1st month 10th 1890

Truly the Lord is merciful, he does give us help in trouble. Last night my mind was so overtaxed that it disturbed my sleep. I asked the dear Master that he would open the way for us to get someone to help us in our daily affairs, as we are sick and in need. To day help came. And our children are some better also, which is evidence that my unworthy petition has been heard and granted. Blessed be His holy name.

1st month 11th 1890

A beautiful day indeed for the time of year, our children are still suffering, though some better, we as a family have been undergoing hardships, yet if our dear ones may but be spared to us how grateful we shall be, the for the death roll is increasing almost daily in our land, from various causes, there is an alarming epidemic prevalent in our country known as the La-Grippe it is numbering its victims by hundreds.

1st month 12th 1890

We have enjoyed a quiet Sabbath to day as our dear children are much better & visiters fewer so that it seems good indeed to have the peaceful quiet which we so much enjoy, yet we are not unmindful of the great blessings of having kind friends & neighbors to call & see us in our afflictions, & desire that they may be blessed for their kindness. My health is very much the same as for some time past & as I have gone through a great deal of fatigue for the past few weeks I feel almost ready sometimes to give out entirely, but the dear Master has promised that as thy day so shall thy strength be.

1st month 13th 1890

"Oh that men would praise the Lord for his wonderful works to the children of men." He hath indeed been gracious to us poor unworthy children, for he hath spared us as a little family to enjoy the company of each other, and altho we have gone through so many afflictions, yet it has bound us more closely to each other in the bonds of affection and we hope nearer our Divine Master whom we desire to serve.

1st month 14th 1890

True wisdom is the fear of the Lord therefore it is my desire to work in the fear of the Lord daily, that I many learn wisdom of him, for I feel so ignorant and so utterly helpless to do any thing of myself yea without Him we can do nothing.

1st month 15th 1890

Help me oh my God for vain is the help of man. Let me not turn aside after vanity, for my desire is to follow Thee. Help me to walk uprightly before my precious family and thus, that I may by both precept and example adorn the doctrine of God my Saviour is the fervent prayer of my heart this day for Christs sake.

1st month 16th 1890

I desire to return thanks to my kind Heavenly Father for his many mercies, He has spared the lives of my dear children thus far and in a degree their health and as they are improveing for the past few days, I could not be grateful enough and when I reflect that we have been spared as a little family together I feel like we cannot render the praise due unto our dear Redeemers name.

1st month 17th 1890

It is my fervent prayer to be kept very near the Master that I may learn of Him and do his pleasure. Oh for more wisdom to know just what is the Masters will concerning me.

1st month 18th 1890

I sometimes become very much discouraged, as it hardly seems probable that I ever will enjoy good health, yet I desire above every thing else to be kept from murmuring and to be willing to submit to the will of Providence whatever it may be, but if it might please my Heavenly Father to restore me to health and strength, his will be done and his name glorified thereby, for I know that he hath all power in Heaven and on earth to do whatever he sees fit to do, so into thy hands oh Father do I commit myself and my precious family knowing Thou wilt do what is best.

1st month 19th 1890

This day which is the Sabbath has been dark and damp, none of our family have been permited to attend meeting and Sabbath school on account of ill health and inclement weather, yet I feel thankful that we are permitted to enjoy the pleasure of our own dear family in our home for our children have been spared to us, whilst many have fallen victims to the cold hand of death by Measles, fevers, Influenza and as we know that we shall all appear before the judgement seat of Christ to be judged according to the deeds done in the body. Therefore help us oh Lord to live in that way and maner which is well pleasing to thee.

1st month 20th 1890

Teach me thy way oh Lord and lead me in a plain path. These words of Holy Scripture roll over and over in my mind day after day, and if

I know my own heart I desire about every thing else to be led in the way of the Lords requireings.

1st month 21st 1890

Unto thee oh Lord do we give thanks, for thy marvelous loving kindness unto thy dependent children. As I view the setting sun my mind is filled with queries, what have I done for Jesus this day, what have been my most earnest desires, has it been to do thy will oh Lord, if not pardon mine iniquity for it is great and help me to do better in the future for Christs sake.

1st month 22nd 1890

I have been quite feeble to day, not able to sit up all day, yet I hope I am resigned to my lot, oh for patience, meekness, and submission to the Divine will.

1st month 23rd 1890

Sing praise to the Lord most high. I am thankful this evening that I feel the spirit of prayer and praise, altho I cannot even think a good thought without the help of my kind Heavenly Father, yet he is please at times and seasons to let me feel the sweet incomes of his heavenly love which is a balm to my hungry soul.

1st month 24th 1890

I am so glad that Jesus loves me, even me. Yes altho I know that I am not worthy to be called a child of God, yet he showeth mercy to the lowly.

1st month 25th 1890

To day we have been happy to have the company of one of my dear husbands relatives, who had not visited in over eleven years. It was a treat we cannot be grateful enough for all our blessings.

1st month 26th 1890

This Sabbath our family are again deprived of the privilige of attending meeting & Sabbath School on account of poor health, yet I trust we are endeavoring to praise the Lord in our own home & hearts.

1st month 27th 1890

This is the most beautiful morning the birds are singing like spring of the year. oh that our hearts may be filled with songs of praise to our God who has our lives in his hand and who ruleth over all.

1st month 28th 1890

To day I have been blessed with the company of a very dear lady friend, who has visited me several times in the past two years. She is one I regard as an angel of mercy sent to cheer me on my way, for she comes in when I am weak and discourage and speaks a kind word, and always brings me something pleasing & nourishing for the body, and brings some friend with her to introduce to me, in this way I formed new acquaintances that have been very pleasant and profitable, may God bless her earnest efforts to bring joy & gladness to the hearts of lonely ones.

1st month 29th 1890

He that dwelleth in the secret place of the most High shall abide under the shadow of the Almighty, oh to dwell in this secret place, that the shadow of the Almighty may rest upon me and my household is my earnest prayer. For thou knowest oh Father that my desire is that we may all be truly thine, therefore help us to live in thy fear and do thy Holy will, that we may be counted worthy to dwell that long, long time with thee in the blessed mansions above.

1st month 30th 1890

A beautiful day indeed and my family in better health. I am the same feeble one yet somewhat improved, so there is so much to be thankful for, praised be the Lord.

1st month 31st 1890

On taking up my work, the thought came can it be possible that this is the last day of this month, how fast time flies. We are not aware how the moments are gliding by, and how soon time will be to us no more. Therefore how important to prepare for eternity.

2nd month 1st 1890

A nice warm morning with birds singing as it were in the midst of spring. My family all able to go about their daily avocations and myself able to be up, roll about the house in my wheel chair and do something for the help of my family. I feel that we have great cause to thank God for his unspeakable goodness.

2nd month 2nd 1890

Lord thou knowest all things therefore thou knows what is in our hearts & minds this Sabbath day and as we are to give account for the deeds done in the body, we should be constantly on our watch, living day by day yes moment by moment in the fear of the Lord.

2nd month 3rd 1890

Feeling feeble this morning & being tried with the vexations of this life, I have found it hard to be patient and to keep in a meek and quiet spirit. But trust in God to deliver me out of all my troubles, I flee to Him for refuge.

2nd month 4th 1890

Lord thou knowest all my trials & besetments on every hand. Be pleased to help me to bear them with patience for I am weak is my simple earnest prayer this day for Christs sake.

2nd month 5th 1890

To day my mind has been deeply tried as I have many things to contend with that is trying to poor weak flesh, and I have realized that each heart knows its own bitterness. There is none but He that knoweth all things can know what we poor cretures have to contend with in this life. But it is a consoleing thought that He does know all our weaknesses and trials and pitties them as such. Therefore let us cast our burden upon the Lord that he may sustain us in every needful time.

2nd month 6th 1890

The is a very dark dreary day in the outside world, yet I am glad I can state that we as a little family are enjoying the sunshine of a peaceful quiet home. I open thing when I look upon my precious little family, that if we were called upon to be separated it would be more than I could bear. But we will not be called up to undergo more than our Master sees fit to put upon us, for he is our great burden bearer. He has said cast they burden up the Lord and he will sustain thee.

2nd month 7th 1890

My mind is as gloomy to day as the day itself which is dark & rainy, & rain freezing until the timber is bending & breaking with is heavy load of ice, oh that my heart may not grow cold and hardened comparatively to the sleet upon the trees, because my mind is filled with dark forebodings, but may I trust that as the sun will come forth in its proper time and melt the ice away, so will the Son of righteousness cause his light to shine in my poor troubled heart, and purge away all the dross and every thing of a rebellious nature which is causeing me to feel that I am passing through a cloud of smoke and thick darkness, oh Lord pitty my weakness, & forgive all my sins.

2nd month 8th 1890

The day being damp causes me to suffer a great-deal more in body, but as I have my dear little family around me it gives me great pleasure, & I am endeavoring to be patient through all.

2nd month 9th 1890

This is a beautiful Sabbath day my husband and children have attended the Sabbath School for which I feel grateful. I hope those of us who have to remain at home may feel Jesus to be near us, and that he will help us to worship him in spirit and truth.

2ⁿᵈ month 10ᵗʰ 1890

As the sun is setting this beautiful evening my heart is filled with gratitude to God for his mercies to us all this day, and I feel like singing, oh the Lamb the loving lamb, the lamb of calvery.

The lamb that was slain, but lives again to intercede for me. How awfully solemn the thought that He was slain for our sins, yet how glorious to think He lives again to make intercession for us, oh that we may not crucify Him afresh, by sinning against his holy law.

2ⁿᵈ month 11ᵗʰ 1890

It is the earnest craving of my heart this day, that I may be cleansed from all sin, that my heart may be made a pure receptacle for the presence of the Lord to dwell in and that I may triumph victorious over the temptations of the evil one for Christs sake. Amen.

2ⁿᵈ month 12ᵗʰ 1890

Oh Lord thou knowest my sufferings be pleased to give me grace and strength sufficient to bear them and if thou art pleased relieve my bodily suffering. I know thou wilt not put more upon me than thou wilt enable me to bear.

2nd month 13ᵗʰ 1890

Feeling very feeble to day it creates a more earnest desire to be prepared for that better country where the inhabitants never say I am sick, suffering is my position here and it is very trying to the flesh, yet if I may be permited to enter the Celestial City there ever to be with my Saviour and loved ones it will repay for all my sufferings on earth.

2ⁿᵈ month 14ᵗʰ 1890

To day the wind has been very boisterous indeed rocking the timber to & fro which reminds me how we are tossed upon the wings of time, sometimes it seems almost like we would be dashed in pieces so rough seems the way, yet the Captain of our souls salvation is guideing our back, so that if we keep close to him, he will land us safe on Heavens bright shore.

2nd month 15th 1890

Another day has passed with its besetments and its blessings and now we reflect as the sun has gone down, and the shades of night appear, so ere long the curtains of the night of death will be drawn around us, and we shall appear before the Son of righteousness, there to be judged according to our deeds. And my soul doth crave that each one of us may so live that we may hear the welcome language of well done good and faithful servant.

2nd month 16th 1890

This beautiful Sabbath my dear husband and myself have visited a relative who has been feeble for some time. I feel like I cannot be thankful enough for this privilege as we have not been there for several years, and I have not been about to ride even a short distance but a few times for over two years. Thanks to our merciful Father.

2nd month 17th 1890

My mind is deeply weighed down this morning, under a sense of my own weakness and nothingness, and my trying situation both of soul and body, it does seem to me that I never at any time felt a greater need of Divine help than at the present for I feel such poverty of soul, such feebleness of body and mind, that it seems at times that I should sink under its weight, oh that I may be helped to lean hard upon the everlasting Arm of strength for support.

2nd month 18th 1890

I have been blessed to day with the company of my dear aged Mother for which I feel very grateful, she is feeble and I fear she may not be spared to us long. I am suffering to day with my spine, yet I hope I am thankful that I can be up a part of the time.

2nd month 19th 1890

I am thankful I am able to use my hands to day to do a little work for the help of my family altho suffering, and laboring under deep discouragements.

2nd month 20th 1890

The enemy is ever ready with his discouragements so I have been almost ready to faint by the way, but I trust that the everlasting Arm will support me in every time of trial so that I shall be kept from sinning against Him oh for more strength both physical and spiritual for I feel my great weakness, but oh that I may be willing to sit at the Masters feet humbly waiting for and learning of him.

2nd month 21st 1890

Haveing the assurance that I am a child of God it is a source of comfort to reflect up the promises of the Bible, "there remaineth a rest for the people of God, for when we remember how little rest even for these poor frail bodies in this life much less rest for the soul, it is worth everything to have that blessed hope of life eternal.

2nd month 22nd 1890

"And we'll praise Him we'll praise him halla hallelujah we'll praise God for the work he has done glory hallelujah," this song of praise arises with freshness in my mind this evening and I desire that we may ever be ready to sing Gods praise for his glorious works, and his tender mercies to his dependent children.

2nd month 23rd 1890

This is a very dark rainy Sabbath and again I am feeling feeble and discouraged oh that the Son of righteousness will arise with healing in his wings for I am feeling desolate and afflicted yet I hope in His mercy.

2nd month 24th 1890

My suffering has been very severe to day the pain in my spine and head being very great.

2nd month 25th 1890

I have been some better to day but still suffering but am endeavoring to be patient through all, Thou who knowest all things be pleased to help me I pray thee to do thy holy will and not murmur against thee.

2nd month 26th 1890

Another dark rainy day which is very trying on my nerves as it produces more pain and aches yet I feel that a kind Father ruleth over all and we should be willing to accept every dispensation of providence as permited by Him for our good in some way or other, so may we all be kept humble, patient and submissive is my prayer.

2nd month 27th 1890

Truly the Lord is merciful, he hath not dealt with us after our sins, nor rewarded us according to our iniquities, for whereas we have deserved punishment we have received blessing. Blessed be His holy name.

2nd month 28th 1890

Another month has flown oh how fast we are hastening on to eternity, may we improve each moment as it passes, for we wish to spend that long long time with thee our blessed Saviour.

3rd month 1st 1890

This is a very dark rainy day accompanied by snow for the opening of spring. But may our hearts be comparatively pure like the snow so shall we be prepared to meet our God.

3rd month 2nd 1890

It has still been snowing this forenoon so that it was not prudent for our family to go several smiles to meeting, so we are all in our quiet home, except our oldest son who left home yesterday to attend the quarterly meeting at High Point. The sun has shone out this afternoon makeing things look more cheerful though the weather is the coldest we have had for some time. The prayer of my heart is that we may all have our hearts filled with the sunshine of love yet love to God and good will toward men.

3rd month 3rd 1890

My heart panteth for that liveing water which alone can nourish up our souls unto life eternal, for we are fast hastening to our loving home, and it is my greatest desire to be prepared to enter that rest prepared for the people of God.

3rd month 4th 1890

I have been quite feeble to day, yet able to be up part of the time for which I am very thankful. My family are in good health at this time, which is indeed a great blessing, and I desire that we may all return thanks to our Heavenly Father for our many mercies.

3rd month 5th 1890

Lord we feel our dependence upon thee for we are utterly helpless to do anything of ourselves, I am so glad that Jesus loves me even me.

3rd month 6th 1890

Never did I realize the flight of time as I have since takeing down the date of each day as it passes for it hardly seems possible so soon a month is gone, oh how greatly do I crave that we may all be more and more in earnest to do the will of our Heavenly Father here so that we may abide with him forever in the eternity of bliss.

3rd month 7th 1890

This is a cold day and snow falling, when I reflect how many there are who are not well clothed and fed so as to be able to stand the severe weather without suffering it fills my heart with sadness, and a desire to be able to do something for them, for altho I am poor and needy in many respects, yet when I remember how much better I am situated than many others I feel that I have a great deal to thank my Heavenly Father for, so let the praise be his.

3rd month 8th 1890

How much we owe to the giver of every good and perfect gift, for our lives are in His hands and how little we seem to realize the power he has to clip the brittle thread of life at any moment of time.

3rd month 9th 1890

A beautiful Sabbath day though very cold, may this day be dedicated to the service of Him from whom all blessings flow. "Bless the Lord oh my soul and all that is within me bless his holy name."

3rd month 10th 1890

A dark rainy day, and some of my children sick which causes anxiety yet I am thankful that it is the fervent desire of my heart to cling to Him who is the strength and light of my life.

3rd month 11th 1890

I feel that if it were not for the everlasting arms underneath I should faint by the way for I am so feeble and my mind so ocupied with the cares and trials of life, for if it were not for the help of the blessed Master I could not undergo what I daily have to pass through. Our two dear boys are sick with Lagrippe or influenza a disease that is prevailing to a great extent throughout the land, which causes great anxiety at this time. But they are in the Lords hands and I trust he will see fit to restore them.

3rd month 12th 1890

I feel this evening that I have so much to be thankful for, notwithstanding all my afflictions our dear children are better to day for which I am truly grateful and I wish to be more given up to my Heavenly Fathers will, let it be what it may be.

3rd month 13th 1890

This is my forty fifth birthday. "Bless the Lord oh my soul and all that is within me bless his holy name." Oh that this language of holy scripture may be my constant theme, for I greatly desire to be found praising God who has been so merciful to me and mine. May I ever trust in Him.

3rd month 14th 1890

Our dear children being so much improved in health I feel that there is a great cause for returning thanks to our kind Heavenly Father.

3rd month 15th 1890

Oh for grace sufficient to bear the trials and provocations of this life, for I am sorely tried at times but I pray that I may hold out faithful to the end of the journey so that I may be permited to enter that haven of rest where I may forever praise the name of Him who hath bought me with his our precious blood.

3rd month 16th 1890

This Sabbath day has been bitterly cold, so much so that my family have had to stay close indoors, I am indeed thankful that we have the necessaries of life to make us comfortable and altho I am a daily sufferer I wish to be in humble submission.

3rd month 17th 1890

I am laboring under deep discouragements at this time, yet hoping through Divine favor to be kept very humble and submissive to the will of Him who doeth all things well, oh that I may never give up under the trials and besetments which we are daily more or less subjected to, but trust the Lord fully.

3rd month 18th 1890

Truly the Lord is merciful and gracious long suffering toward his dependent children, oh that we may sit humbly at his feet and learn of him.

3rd month 19th 1890

The Lord is my stay and my staff, by his help I will trust in him as long as I live I feel that his arm of power doth bear me up.

3rd month 20th 1890

A dark rainy day, but I am thankful that I can testify that sunshine reigns with in our home oh that we could always realize that we are under the protecting care of our kind Heavenly Father for it is so sweet to bask in the sunshine of his love and as we are only permited the dews of heaven here, what must be the shower of eternal blessedness in the world of bliss.

3rd month 21st 1890

What shall I render unto my God for all his benefits to me. At this moment the following text presents itself to my mind very unexpectedly, "Now when Christ was born in Bethlehem of Judea behold there came wise men to Jerusalem saying where is he that is born king of the Jews for we have seen his star in the east and we come to worship him. Now altho we are poor and unwise yet we have not need to inquire where is He, for we know that he siteth at the right hand of God making intercession for us, so let us worship him in spirt and in truth."

3rd month 22nd 1890

The Lord is my shepherd I shall not want is a great consolation to know that we can claim the lord as our shepherd and if we trust him as we should, we shall not want.

3rd month 23rd 1890

A beautiful Sabbath day and one in which I trust the Lord is being glorified by his dependent children, oh that we may all draw very nigh to him and know of our strength being renewed.

3rd month 24th 1890

I have been undergoing a test of faith and it is my earnest prayer that I may have more of this gift of God for by faith we are enabled to pass through many difficulties that otherwise would seem impossible. Then Lord increase my faith, is my earnest prayer for Jesus sake.

3rd month 25th 1890

This day I have suffered great nervous debility but am trusting in the merits of a crucified and risen redeemer.

3rd month 26th 1890

True wisdom is the fear of the Lord, oh for that wisdom which cometh from above which is first peaceable the gentle and easy to be entreated.

3rd month 27th 1890

"If God be for us who can be against us," this should be a comforting thought for we often feel like we could not press through the cloud of darkness which obscures our path, and we feel like the enemy was ready to devour us, but when new remember that we are on the Lords side and that he will suffer nothing to harm us so long as we put our trust in him, there is great cause to lift up our heads in hope, for we will not suffer our enemies to triumph over us, Blessed by his holy name.

3rd month 28th 1890

The Lord does indeed make a way for his dependent children where there seems to be no way therefore let us put our trust in him for as our day our strength shall be, I am one that has known this promice to be verified for in my extreme weakness God has caused me to feel that underneath were the Everlasting Arms.

3rd month 29th 1890

This day I have passed through great fatigue of body, but the Lord is my helper.

3rd month 30th 1890

This beautiful Sabbath my soul has been deeply stired, I am feeble in body and my mind is almost overwhelmed by trials and discouragements. But I still trust in Jesus to support me through all.

3rd month 31st 1890

This being the last day of the month again reminds us how fast time is passing and the necessity to improve each moment as it flies altho I am deeply tried I trust that I may be kept from murmering for the Lord knows what is best for us.

4th month 1st 1890

The Lord is very precious to my soul.

4th month 2nd 1890

Oh come magnify the Lord with me and let us exalt his name together for his name is above every other name, in Heaven or on earth.

4th month 3rd 1890

They that come unto me I will in no wise cast out saith the Lord, what a consolation to know that whosoever will may come, yea come and find salvation full and free what a joy to know that we have the privilege to come to Jesus and he will not cast us out, will not reject us no matter how poor and unworthy we feel ourselves to be if we come in true believeing and liveing faith. This is our dear little son Freddie's ninth birthday. I humbly commend him to the care of his Heavenly Father and may each succeeding year find him in the service of his Lord and Master is the prayer of my heart for Jesus sake Amen.

4th month 4th 1890

Trusting in Jesus I am endeavoring to press on through trials and temptations and besestments which no doubt are common to many of Gods children oh we may trust him fully to be a present helper.

4th month 5th 1890

Another day of care and anxiety, yet as I am not suffering so much as some days, I am truly thankful and wish to be more humble and submissive to the Divine will.

4th month 6th 1890

A most beautiful Easter Sabbath and as I am still blessed to have my dear little family all with me I feel that I have a great deal to be thankful for and I desire to be found praising God more and more each day as he prolongs my life, that I may be worthy to sing His praise throughout eternity.

4th month 7th 1890

A day in which my heart is filled with longing desires to be more faithful to my calling let it be what it may. The prayer again arises in my heart, "Search me oh God and know my heart, try me and know my thoughts and see if there be any wicked way in me, and lead me in the way everlasting."

4th month 8th 1890

This has been a day of deep trial to me, and I have felt the waves to almost overflow me, yet the blessed Master have been pleased to say thus for shalt thou come and no farther and here shall thy proud waves be stayed. Bless be His holy name.

4th month 9th 1890

Away my doubts be gone my fears, for I have trusted the Lord for years and years, And altho the tempter doth often assail, I have that promise that he shall not prevail, For they that with confidence doth on me rely, The help of salvation I will never deny, These words of comfort are a balm to my soul, For I know He hath power to make perfectly whole, So both soul and body I commit to Thee, Believeing Thou knowest what is best for me, If Thou art willing to show Thy power, I know Thou art able to restore me this hour, From all my afflictions Thou are able canst set me free, That I may be enabled to do more for Thee, But may I be kept humble submissive and meek, And to know Thy will, not mine, may I ever seek, And not only to know, but willingly to do and be, Whatever Thou would have me be, and do for Thee, If it may be only to sit humbly at the Refiners feet, Until in me, Thine image is made complete, So when done with this life's glare and gaze, I may enter Heaven, there to sing Thy praise, Then oh what a recompense for all my pain, Will be this eternal bliss to gain.

4th month 10th 1890

The day of this date will be a day long to be remembered by me and all my family. This being the day of the marriage of our daughter **Maggie** (our oldest child) to her worthy friend **Dougan Clark Moffitt** of Lexington, NC. Whilst we have the consolation that he is a good Christian man and we believe he will be a devoted husband, yet our hearts are filled with sorrow to overflowing at the thought of giving up our precious child, as she has been such a comfort and help to us during my long affliction. May the blessing of Heaven rest richly upon them is my earnest prayer, and may we all look to Jesus for help and strength to bear up under our every trial. At this time also my husband's beloved **Uncle Enos A Blair** is lying a corpse, so that we are all deeply weighed down under our bereavements. But may we all strive so to live that we may meet our loved ones who are gone before, in that blessed mansion above.

4ᵗʰ month 11ᵗʰ 1890

To day the funeral of our dear above mentioned Uncle took place at Springfield, my husband and our oldest son attended, there was a large audience and a truly solemn time. But the bereaved wife and children have such a consoling evidence that he has entered the realms of eternal happiness that it is a balm to their wounded hearts, he was 69 years of age and a beloved Elder in the Society of Friends. This has been a day of deep thought and my mind is impressed with the many changes incident to this life. Our dear daughter having last evening left her parental roof to accompany her dear husband to his home, we feel quite lonely and sad, yet believing that all things work for together for good to them that love the Lord.

4ᵗʰ month 12ᵗʰ 1890

To day I have been permited to ride out a short distance which was quite refreshing and if it is the Lords will I trust my health may be so improved that I may yet be able to do more for my dear little family, and more for the blessed Master who has been so merciful to me a poor unworthy creature.

4ᵗʰ month 13ᵗʰ 1890

The beautiful Sabbath morning I have been blessed with strength sufficient to prepare my little children for Sabbath School, but as I feel too feeble to attend with them my heart goes out in earnest prayer for them and others that the blessings of Heaven may rest up them, and that the work of the Sabbath School may go on prospering more and more as those who have it in charge are faithful in the discharge of their duty, and if it is the will of Divine Providence to restore me to better health I hope I may be faithful to help in this work, as well as all others I feel interested in for the service of the Master.

4ᵗʰ month 14ᵗʰ 1890

I have been blessed with the company of some kind friends last eve and to day for which I feel very thankful oh how kindly I have been remembered blessed be the name of the Lord forever.

4ᵗʰ month 15ᵗʰ 1890

Truly our Father in Heaven is merciful, "He hath not dealt with us after our sins nor rewarded us according to our iniquities," for how often do we see proofs of this, for we see those who have indulged so deeply in sin that those who once regarded them as friends, now shun them as reckless enemies, whilst our kind Heavenly Father still permits them to live and beacons for them to return to their Father's house where there is bread enough and to spare.

4ᵗʰ month 16ᵗʰ 1890

I feel the great need of leaning hard on the arm of my Saviour this day, for I am weak and sorely tried. Be Thou my helper at this moment of time, for I know that Thou alone can know and supply all our needs.

4ᵗʰ month 17ᵗʰ 1890

How truly thankful am I this day that I can adopt the language, my soul doth magnify the Lord and I rejoice in God my Saviour and I feel the great need of dwelling near the blessed Master who has promiced I will never leave thee nor forsake thee.

4ᵗʰ month 18ᵗʰ 1890

"By this I know that Thou favorest me because thou sufferest not mine enemies to triumph over me," Oh that I would ever follow in the footsteps of the divine Master for he has been so merciful to me his poor unworthy handmaiden. At this moment I feel the great need of following close to Him who is able to preserve my feet from falling, for we so often enter the slippery path of temptation that we should have a strong hold on that Arm of power that is able to sustain us in every time of need.

4th month 19th 1890

I am feeble indeed in body to day, yet I am thankful that I am still trusting Jesus to support me.

4th month 20th 1890

This has been a beautiful, and very pleasant day **for our** dear daughter and her husband visited us which was a great comfort to us all and have felt the power of the Most High to overshadow us.

4th month 21st 1890

Another most beautiful day with its joys and sorrows. **To** day our dear daughter and husband went back to their home in Lexington. When I reflect upon the changes that have taken place lately in our neighborhood it hardly seems real, yet this is our common lot in life.

4th month 22nd 1890

I have been favored to help do some work to day with my hands, for which I feel very thankful indeed for there is so much of my time that I am entirely unable to do anything for my family that I feel my heart filled with gratitude for the favor to do something for the comfort of my loved ones altho it is through much suffering at my best days.

4th month 23rd 1890

How much we have to thank our blessed Master for each day of our lives for he so mercifully provides for our real needs. This evening whilst looking around the beautiful flowers, trees, grass, and fields of grain, my heart is filled with wonder, love and praise.

4th month 24th 1890

He that heareth the ravens when they cry, will most surely hear our prayers when we cry unto Him for help for he does not break his promises and he hath promised to be a present help in trouble, then let us go unto Him daily that we may find help for all our needs.

4th month 25th 1890

This has been a day of sore trial and bodily suffering yet the Lord has sustained me, blessed be His holy name.

4th month 26th 1890

To day I have had to keep my bed most of the time as I am very feeble in body and my mind has been deeply tried, having the care of my household in my feebleness it sometimes seems as if I should give out by the way, for since our dear daughters marriage and removal from our home it causes the care to fall so much more heavily upon me as she was always so ready to take all the burden possible off my shoulders and with best wishes to all human kind, I feel quite sure that there is none but those who have had the trial of being afflicted and often having to hire help that does not prove satisfactory, that can truly sympathize with those who are thus situated, and the amount of grace needed to bear up under the trials we so often have to meet when we have those around us that are not congenial. But let us pray, "Father forgive them they know not what they do."

4th month 27th 1890

How great and marvelous are thy works oh God how varied and yet how true. This day has shown the mighty power of the most high, for a little while it will be bright sunshine, then before it hardly seems possible for change, the sky will be overcast with clouds and showing down rain plentifully then again the bright sunshine. I do not recollect to of noticed so many sudden changes in so short a time, this seems to illustrate the many and varied changes in human lives, for often when our prospects look bright and we think now we shall see better days, and not have so many of the cares and perplexities of this to contend with, suddenly as it were a dark cloud comes over us and we find ourselves enveloped in thick darkness and shows of trials, vexations and bestments, both of spiritual and temporal character seem almost ready to wash us down the gulf of dispair. When as suddenly the light breaks forth and we are permited by faith to see the Son of righteousness shining up us with healing in his wings. Oh if it were not for such an oasis as this in the desert of trials we should perish for want of that fountain of life and that rest which is needful for both soul and body, whilst journeying through this life. But our Father knowth all our needs, and will not permit more to come upon us, than He will enable us to bear.

4th month 28th 1890

To day I have not been able to sit up but very little suffering from nervous debility, yet my mind has been composed, trusting that the Master doeth all things well.

4th month 29th 1890

Feeling some stronger to day, yet suffering is my daily portion, but I try with all possible patience to bear whatever the dear Lord permits to come upon me, trusting it may be to His names glory.

4th month 30th 1890

This day closes another month with its varied changes, of joy and sorrows, its besetments and pleasures, and are we better prepared for our eternal home than when the month began? Now my prayer is that the Divine Master will blot our all our past sins from his book and remember them no more forever, and so increase our faith that we may be enabled to press on in the right way.

5th month 1st

This day opens up the pleasant month of May, when the trees are laden with their green foliage and the beautiful flowers blooming, and birds, singing which show forth the mighty power and wonderful works of the Supreme being. Oh that we may all be in entire subjection to His will, and walk in newness of life.

5th month 2nd 1890

Alho I have been quite feeble for the past week, yet I have been enabled to be of some help to my family as regards their clothing which is a great satisfaction to me, and this evening my dear husband took me out into the garden in my wheel chair which gave me great pleasure as it is so seldom that I can get out that much.

5th month 3rd 1890

This is our dear little daughter **Marys** fifth birthday, and I want to dedicate her more fully to the Lord, and it is my earnest prayer that He will keep her, and the rest of us as well, as it were in the hallow of his holy hand that we sin not.

5th month 4th 1890

A very rainy Sabbath so much so that our dear little children could not attend Sabbath School, but we have enjoyed the quiet of our own dear little home, reading, perusing the Sabbath School lesson for which I feel very thankful indeed and humbly desire that this day may be owned and blessed of the Lord to him belongeth all the praise.

5th month 5th 1890

Unto thee oh Lord do we give thanks that thou hast provided us with food and rainment and kind friends to care for us, and especially do I praise thy great name for giving me such a kind husband and loving children to care for me a poor afflicted creture who feels so much need of sympathy and care, and I feel the great need of the loveing arms of my Saviour underneath at all times to support me in my weakness and sore trials. Be Thou my stay and my staff oh my Father in Heaven that I may have a sure support to lean upon for Jesus sake. Amen.

5th month 6th 1890

"Trust in the Lord and do good and thou shalt dwell in the land and verily thou shalt be fed."

5th month 7th 1890

A day of severe suffering with my spine, yet thankful that I am not entirely helpless.

5th month 8th 1890

My suffering has not been so severe to day and I have been able to be taken out in my rolling chair to the yard and garden to see the flowers and vegetables, which has been a great treat to me, oh that those who are permited to go around daily to see and work amongst their vegetables and flowers and enjoy the fresh air and bright sunshine did but know what a blessing they enjoy but alas how little are these blessings appreciated until we are deprived of them.

5th month 9th 1890

As the golden sun is near setting I once more endeavor to write a few words or lines, while my dear little children are playing merily their evening sports, oh Father Divine send down thy blessings upon them touch their young tender hearts with the finger of thy Heavenly love, I pray thee that as they grow in years they may grow in grace and favor with thee. Preserve them from the snares and temptations of sin and satan and make them wholely thine that their lives may not be lived in vain for what greater desire can a mothers heart have for her tender offspring than to so live that they may be prepared to enter Heaven when done with time here below and oh our Father in Heaven I would humbly ask that thou wilt be please to grant unto us their parents wisdom and understanding that we may know how to teach our dear children how to walk in the true path of holiness for we feel the great need of being taught ourselves in order to be able to teach them in the right way. Oh Lord help us now and henceforth throughout our journey here and save us in Heaven we pray the for Christs sake Amen.

5th month 10th 1890

To day I have been blessed with the privilege of visiting my dear aged mother for the first time this year it seems so nice to get out in the fresh air and see different things, the trees the grain and flowers & oh how many beautiful things we are blessed with in this life. Then what will be the joy of the world to come, let us all endeavor to realize it.

5th month 11th 1890

This beautiful Sabbath morning I have returned from my visit to my dear mothers having spent yesterday and last night very pleasantly in my dear old home and I had anticipated the privilege of attending the Sabbath School to day at Oak Forest as it is directly in my way home, but being very feeble this morning it was as much as I was able to do to get home and retire to my bed for the greater part of the day, but such is my lot, and I desire to be very thankful that I have been blessed with strength sufficient to return to my dear little family and enjoy the quiet of my own home. Oh that I may endeavor to be so humble and submissive to the Divine will that I may live in that way and manner which will secure for me an eternal home of rest and peace beyond the skies where I may praise God forever for his goodness to me.

5th month 12th 1890

This has been another day of solemn thought, my husband attended the funeral of **Prof Julius Tomlinson,** son of **Allen Tomlinson** a well known and valued member of the Society of Friends. The funeral was largely attended, his death was sudden which gives us another warning to be prepared for there is but a step between us and death. How often to day my mind wandered back to the time since my afflicted days that I was taken to **Allen Tomlinsons** and **Dr Tomlinsons** (my physician at that time) to visit a few days in the hope of benefiting my health. **Julius Tomlinson** and his brother **Sidney** who also died a sudden death a few years since were then both unmarried and were at their Fathers and were so very kind to me, they would carry me in my chair from one room to another, up and down stairs as I was then as now so that I could not walk around myself. Oh how much I have thought this day of their kindness to me a poor afflicted creature, and of the mysterious works and ways of Providence for I have been made to wonder why I have been spared to live with my dear little family whilst so many have been summond to their long home since I have gone through so much suffering but the final summons will come ere long and it is my greatest desire to be found with my lamp trimed and burning. And my conscience often reproves me which I am tempted to inquire in my mind the why, and wherefore of the mysterious works of kind Providence for he hath said "What I do thou knowest not but thou shalt know hereafter," so we should be in entire submission to the Divine will for he knows what is best for us and permits us to pass through many proveings in order that we may be purefied and made fit for the Masters use on earth. Then when He calls us up higher we shall know the why of the mysterious thing we know not now.

5th month 13th 1890

I am feeling very poor in spirit this evening so much so that I hardly have courage to write but after takeing up my paper the words "Blessed are the poor in spirit for theirs is the kingdom of Heaven" sounded in my ears, so I feel like praiseing God that I am kept humble and that I feel myself to be so poor and weak for "When I am weak then I am strong." Christ is my strength and Christ my song.

5th month 14th 1890

This has been a happy evening to me as my dear daughter came to see us to day very unexpectedly and I had been anxious to see her. Praise the Lord for his goodness.

5th month 15th 1890

Altho I am very feeble and suffer much in body yet this has been a pleasant day with me for my dear daughter is still with me which is such a comfort and satisfaction to me for her cheerful disposition makes sunshine wherever she goes.

5th month 16th 1890

Praise the Lord for his mercies he has been so kind unto us poor unworthy cretures. I feel so thankful for strength sufficient to be in my Chair this morning instead for being entirely confined to my bed as is so often the case. Bless the Lord oh my soul.

5th month 17th 1890

To day the one hundredth anniversary of Springfield Monthly meeting of Friends is being celebrated at Springfield Guilford Co **N.C.** This will be an occasion of deep interest to many people and this has been a most beautiful day which will add greatly to the enjoyment of the occasion. May the name of Jesus be exalted this day is my earnest prayer.

5th month 18th 1890

A beautiful Sabbath day indeed and it has been spent in quiet at home by my husband and myself, our dear little children attended Sabbath School at Oak Forest and our grown son attended meeting to day at High Point. Our daughter **Maggie Moffitt** also attended meeting to day at High Point on her way home to Lexington. After leaving us yesterday and meeting with her husband at the Centennial at Springfield they visited some of their friends and expect to return to their home to night. May the Lord go with them and bless them.

5th month 19th 1890

My soul is cast down this evening under a sense of my infirmities, for I know not what to do as I am not able to do my work and the girl that has been with me for several months wishes to go to her own home. Now as has been my experience in many dark hours in the past, all I can do is look to the Lord Jesus for help, that he will open the way whereby I may get a suitable person to stay with me and my dear little family, for He is a never failing source oh that I may trust him fully in all things.

5th month 20th 1890

I am comforted this evening in believeing that the good shepherd is tenderly watching over his flock and those that are feeble he carefully carries in his bosom. He alone doth know all our trials and our sufferings, therefore I know that at this time there is no human heart that can conceive my travel of soul and the many trying seasons through which I am having to pass both in mind and body, but knowing that we have an High Priest who is touched with a feeling of our infirmities it is a source of comfort to feel that we are watched over by his fatherly care. "Bless the Lord oh my soul and all that is within me bless his holy name."

5th month 21st 1890

This has been a beautiful day and I have been visited by some kind lady friends this evening which has been quite a satisfaction to me as it causes me to feel that I am being tenderly watched over by my kind Heavenly Father who knows all our needs both of body and mind and I have felt for several days past like I should give out by the way so deeply have I been tried in many ways, but the Lord knoweth our frame he rememberth that we are dust and therefore pitties our weaknesses and sends us aid when it is most needed.

5th month 22nd 1890

I am very much discouraged at this time as I still do not know who we can get for our housekeeper but I am endeavoring to trust that the good Master will see fit to provide a way when there seems no way.

5th month 23rd 1890

This is a very warm day which fatigues me very much as I am feeble and the warm weather is very much against me, but I trust that I shall be blessed with strength sufficient for each day.

5th month 24th 1890

This has been another very fatigueing day, yet I have been blessed with strength to be up most of the day and do some work with my feeble hands.

5th month 25th 1890

This is a beautiful Sabbath and I have been blessed with strength enough to accompany my dear husband and children to Sabbath School to day for the first time in many years, which was a great treat to me and I consider it a great blessing, oh that we would praise the Lord more and more his many mercies.

5th month 26th 1890

A day of besetments and discouragements like many others through which I have had to pass, but I have been blessed with strength sufficient for the day.

5th month 27th 1890

I feel the need of the Divine arm to support me at this time for I am passing through great discouragements, but am thankful that I can still trust in Jesus.

5th month 28th 1890

He that cometh unto me I will in no wise cast out, this is a great comfort to know that if we are willing to come to Jesus he will not cast us off, but will welcome us as his children.

5th month 29th 1890

A beautiful day indeed and the flowers are so fragrant and the birds singing so sweetly, all nature seems to be praiseing their Creator which is a gentle reproof to us his so often disobedient children, for we should praise him above every thing else, for he hath created us on purpose of his own glory, and to have dominion over his creation, so let us be found praiseing Him as we ought.

5th month 30th 1890

Praise belongeth to thee oh Father in Zion tune our hearts to sing thy praise.

5th month 31st 1890

This day closes the beautiful spring time. The sun with its scorching heat is withering the lovely flowers that have been so lavishly strewn along our pathway to beautify creation and cheer us on our way, and we want to praise our great Creator for the beauty and sweetness of the flowers, and for the lesson they teach us that we too are but as the fadeing flowers.

6th month 1st 1890

This beautiful Sabbath day being the beginning of another season, we are reminded that we are brought into new fields of labor both spiritually and temporally, for whilst we look upon the fields of grain that are white already to harvest we are made to remember the great field of souls that are not yet gathered into the Heavenly garner and that the harvest is great but the laborers are few. Let us pray therefore that the Lord of the harvest would make instruments of us, even as poor and unworthy as we feel ourselves to be, for the ingathering of souls in this great work for the upbuilding of the Redeemers kingdom.

6th month 2nd 1890

"When thou passest through the waters they shall not overflow thee." This seems to be a great and precious promice especially at the this time when it seems that the waves are darking above my head ready to envelop me in the sea of darkness. Oh God our Father let us know of this precious promice being fulfilled at the moment of time for we know that thou are both able and willing to help us, therefore to Thee will we cling.

6th month 3rd 1890

"Lord who shall abide in thy Tabernacle, who shall dwell in thy holy hill, he that hath clean hands and a pure heart." Oh how close we should examine our hearts to know whether they are pure in the sight of God yea or nay for if our hearts are not pure, our hands will not be clean from covetousness and other evils.

6th month 4th 1890

A day of toil anxiety and care, also of feebleness of body and poverty of soul, yet these are times of deep proveing, let us be close on our watch.

6th month 5th 1890

I have been quite feeble to day indeed having spent a very restless night, and the weather being quite warm, but I crave to be kept from murmering and to be patient through all my sufferings altho it is my daily lot to suffer more or less. But my only hope is in looking away to that promiced land of rest where I hope to enter when done with the pain and toil of this life, God being my helper to do his will on earth that I may praise him forever in Heaven.

6th month 6th 1890

This has been a day of trial to me as I am so feeble in body that I am not able to labor for my family and our good house girl that has been with us this year up the present time had to go home on account of poor health, is it has been a trial of faith to know how we are to get along, but we are promised in the holy scriptures that the Lord will provide, so it is our duty to trust him fully that he will provide for all our needs.

6th month 7th 1890

We have been favored to day beyond our expectations to get along with our little household affairs, my dear husband has done the cooking for our little family, and I have been favored to have strength to go around on my rolling chair and give some assistance, and our little ones are very helpful and can do a great many little turns to help on with our work, so altho we are passing through difficulties, yet we are happy in the enjoyment of the company of each other, and the love God is filling our hearts with thanksgiving that it is as well as what it is.

6th month 8th 1890

A quiet Sabbath day spent at home as usual with my dear husband as I am not able to get out to meeting, our dear children have attended Sabbath School to day which is a great comfort to us. It would be such a pleasure to attend with them, but I want to learn to be content with whatever situation I am placed in.

6th month 9th 1890

I have nothing to note except the continued mercies of kind Providence for He makes a way for us each day where there seems to be no way.

6th month 10th 1890

Deal bountifully with thy servants oh Lord for we are in great need of thy help, let us not give out by the way, forsake not the works of thine own hands.

6th month 11th 1890

Oh Thou who knoweth all things, thou knowest how poor and how cast down I feel this evening, help thou me according to my need, for I feel myself desolate and afflicted.

6th month 12th 1890

Our dear daughter and her husband attended the Commencement at Trinity College to day and paid us a short visit this evening. We enjoyed their company very much that at times it seems almost out of the question to give her up, but we must be in subjection to the will of Providence.

6th month 13th 1890

This beautiful day I have been quite feeble but have endeavored to be composed and not let the enemy overcome my weakness, for he is ever working our weak moments to come in and destroy our peace.

6th month 14th 1890

Another day of toil and pain, yet I desire to be kept humble and not murmer at my lot, for a few more fleeting days or years at most and we shall all have done with time here then if we are prepared to meet our God what a glorious change from the toil anxiety and pain through which some of us have to pass in this life, will be changed for one bright eternal day where we shall be forever at rest.

6th month 15th 1890

This has been a bright Sabbath but very warm indeed which has added greatly to my suffering as I am feeble and warm weather does not agree with me as well, as moderately cold. Our dear little ones were not well enough to attend Sabbath School to day so we have all except our oldest son who went to meeting, spent a quiet Sabbath at home. I am thankful that we are so happy together, for we have to pass through so many trying seasons and are deprived of so many privileges which we would so much enjoy.

6th month 16th 1890

My suffering increases daily as the weather gets hotter, but I hope to bear it with true Christian fortitude and as the Master has promised strength sufficient for each day, I want to trust Him fully for help and strength to bear me up through all my trials and sufferings.

6th month 17th 1890

Now faith is the substance of things hoped for the evidence of things not seen, therefore if we have that living, believing faith, we shall wait with patience for the coming of Christ knowing that when he shall call for us, all will be well, for he has a manner of rest prepared for all those who through faith in his name have walked uprightly before him and are now prepared to enter His eternal rest.

6th month 18th 1890

My heart is filled with gratitude to God for his mercies.

6th month 19th 1890

My soul doth magnify the Lord and I will trust in God my Saviour who had spared me through so many trials and besetments and days, months and years of suffering. Oh that my life may be forever at an end when called from works to rewards, to the praise of His name.

6th month 20th 1890

My heart is filled with gratitude to God for his remembrance of us poor unworthy children. Today I have been visited by some kind friends who are so considerate of our situation and who came on errands of mercy. May the Lord bless them for their kindness and may we ever be grateful for favors and praise God for his goodness is my prayer.

6th month 21st 1890

The Lord has blessed me with strength sufficient to help my dear family some to day and altho it has been done through sufferings, yet I am glad that I can possibly do something to help them as it has been so seldom that I could do this and I praise God for his goodness and trust him for strength sufficient for each day, according to his will.

6th month 22nd 1890

To day we have been visited by my youngest sister and her husband had quite a good time, our children attended Sabbath School. Bless the Lord for his mercies which are extended to us every day.

6th month 23rd 1890

A very hot day which causes great fatigue and suffering, but I have been favored to be up most of the day.

6th month 24th 1890

To day we have been favored with the company of my dear aged Mother for which we are very thankful.

6th month 25th 1890

Another very hot day my suffering has been greater than for some time past, but my desire is to be kept humble and not murmur altho it is trying to poor weak flesh, Lord be thou my refuge in every needful time.

6th month 26th 1890

A broken and contrite spirit oh God thou wilt not despise, this is a great consolation to me to day for I am indeed broken down in spirit feeling the very least of the Shepherds flock for I am in deep poverty of soul and so feeble in body, that if it were not for assurance that we have a merciful Father who is touched with a feeling of our infirmities and who is not willing that any should perish, I sometimes would be ready to give up in dispair. But I feel this evening like crying unto God my rock to hold me on this sure foundation against which nothing can prevail.

6th month 27th 1890

And now oh Lord what wait I for my hope is in thee.

6th month 28th 1890

I have been favored to roll round in my wheel chair to day and see after some of the household affairs, but am feeble and the weather is very warm.

6th month 29th 1890

This Sabbath day has been intensely hot and I am still unable to attend Sabbath school or meeting yet I believe the Lord is careing for his dependent ones therefore my heart is in Him.

6th month 30th 1890

Oh how fast time is fleeting and there is scarcely a day but what we hear of some one in the surrounding country being called from works to reward, how essential to be ready for the call.

7th month 1st 1890

In thus keeping dates I am made to wonder at the flight of time, it hardly seems possible that so many months have elapsed since I have been writing down a few words each day. But it brings fresh to my mind each day that we should make haste to be wise and sin not, for the day of the Lord cometh as a thief in the night and there is no bribeing death.

7th month 2nd 1890

My heart is filled with thankfulness this evening in remembering my blessings notwithstanding my afflictions.

7th month 3rd 1890

Unto thee oh Lord do we give thanks, for thy mercy unto us, we are cast down but not forsaken, help us to put our whole trust in Thee.

7th month 4th 1890

A very hot day which increases my suffering but I am trusting Jesus to give me strength sufficient for each day, for the Bible tells us "As thy day thy strength shall be."

7th month 5th 1890

How fast the weeks pass by, and we have been reminded again to day of the uncertainty of life and the certainty of death on hearing **of Rev Stamey** the presiding elder of the Methodist Church at the time for this district, passing away.

7th month 6th 1890

Today **Rona** the only daughter of **Prof Lemuel Johnson** of Trinity College was consigned to the Tomb she being just grown into young womanhood reminds us that all ages are called from works to rewards, then how important to be ready for the summons let it come when it may and to whom it may for all shall give account.

7th month 7th 1890

Oh Lord make haste to help me is the cry of my soul this evening for thou knowest I have great need of thee, forsake not the works of thine own hands.

7th month 8th 1890

Truth is my shield and buckler lead me into the light of thy truth every day of my life oh righteous Father, for it is only as we are led by thee that we can walk aright, and I feel the great need of thy everlasting arms to support me.

7th month 9th 1890

Lord thou alone doth know my trials and thou alone can bear me up under them, so I ask thee oh righteous Father to be very near me

July 1890

at this time and help me in a wonderful manner for I am passing through deep waters as it were, where the billows threaten to overflow me.

7th month 10th 1890

My sufferings seems almost unbearable at times but the Lord helps me to bear my infirmities, praise to His name.

7th month 11th 1890

"Trust in the Lord and wait patiently for him and he will bring it to pass, yes believe in His word and whatsoever is best for us he will fulfil, for he hath testified whatsoever ye ask when ye pray believe that ye receive them and ye shall have them."

7th month 12th 1890

Another day of toil and pain as I have often stated as I have still been spared to my little family and they to me I have a great deal to be thankful for. To day the second wife of **Wm Plummer** was buried at Springfield she leaves two little children one of them an infant she is the daughter of **Wm Jones.** When I think how many poor little motherless children are left in this world, I feel very grateful that I have been permited to keep my dear little family together.

7th month 13th 1890

A very hot sultry Sabbath and it has been through great fatigue that I have prepared my little ones again for Sabbath School but the Lord does still graciously condescend to help me, blessed be his holy name.

7th month 14th 1890

I am trusting Lord in thee, blessed Lamb of Calvary, all my hope on thee is stayed, all my help from thee I bring, cover my defenceless head with the shadow of thy wing.

7ᵗʰ month 15ᵗʰ 1890

I feel very grateful that I have even strength to write some to day but it has been through suffering for that is my daily lot, yet I hope to be patient in suffering in the assurance of a final release from it when done with time here below, if obedient.

7ᵗʰ month 16ᵗʰ 1890

I am very feeble indeed this morning if is with great fatigue that I can sit in my chair, but trusting that the Lord will watch over and care for me I submit my all to him.

7th month 17ᵗʰ 1890

This has been a day of severe suffering but I have been favored to be kept in quiet submission to whatever the Divine Master sees fit to permit to come upon me.

7ᵗʰ month 18ᵗʰ 1890

"Thy mercy oh Lord is from everlasting to everlasting upon them that fear thee." This has been another trying day to the flesh, as the weather is very warm and I have been bedfast the most of the time for the past three days and my suffering great, yet the Lord has been merciful to me and kept me in a composed state of mind for which I am very thankful.

7ᵗʰ month 19ᵗʰ 1890

"Oh sing unto the Lord a new song for he hath triumphed victoriously, his right hand and his holy arm hath gotten him the victory." Oh that each one of us may have a new song as it were in our mouths ever praises to our God, for he hath so mercifully spared our lives thus far and hath been pleased to watch over and care for us even when we were not conscious of his care. Oh that the remainder of our days let be few or many may be spent in Thy service and in thy praise.

7th month 20th 1890

I am very feeble indeed this morning cannot sit up but a little while at a time, yet with great effort I have prepared my little ones for Sabbath School a duty which I feel that I owe the blessed Master so long as I can hold up my hands to help and I pray that the Lord will abundantly bless them and all others who are permitted to attend and I greatly desire that He will condescend to be with us who are not permitted to attend either Sabbath School or Church and bless us in our home, for He alone doth know the desire of our hearts and how rejoiced we would be to meet and mingle with His people at the house of God. Oh Father help us to say not as I will but as thou wilt.

7th month 21st 1890

"To day if you will hear His voice harden not your hearts." This text presented itself to my mind whilst meditating upon the many calls from works to rewards of all ages in the part of the Lords vineyard. To day the little motherless infant of **Wm Plummer** that I took note of a week ago has followed its mother to the better land. It seems very necessary that we should heed that still small voice which is speaking unto us as unto children be ye also ready for in such an hour as ye think not the Son of man cometh. Then let us not harden our hearts against those gentle warnings which in mercy has been so often sent to us.

7th month 22nd 1890

"Foxes have holes and birds of the air have nests, but the Son of man hath no where to lay His head." Oh when I meditate on those things, how the dear son of God was so shamefully treated on earth after leaving his blissful home on high and condescending to mans low estate and even laying down his life for poor fallen man, how my heart burns with shame, that we so often murmur at our lot, when perhaps we are lying upon downy beds or feasting upon the good things of the land.

7th month 23rd 1890

I am still feeble not being able to sit up but a little while at a time, but am endeavoring to bear all with us much patience as I can, looking to Jesus for help and strength sufficient for each day.

7th month 24th 1890

A dark rainy day and I feel very low in spirit as I am so feeble in body, but trusting that the Lord will yet give me more strength I submit my all to Him.

7th month 25th 1890

I will be glad in the Lord for he doth so mercifully provide for me each day notwithstanding I am a daily suffer yet He bears me up through all my trials. Blessed be His name.

7th month 26th 1890

My heart is filled with gratitude to God this evening in remembrance of his mercies for he makes a way for us each day where there seems no way for he puts it into the hearts of kind friends to come and lend a helping hand when it is most needed. Today my dear single sister came in and did some work for us which was very much needed, for which I feel very grateful and pray that the Lord will blessher abundantly and all those who have been so kind as to show mercy to us. I am so feeble that I cannot even sit up near all day and I see so many needs that it is only by clinging to Jesus for support that I am enabled to withstand the trials that I daily meet.

7th month 27th 1890

Our dear children have attended Sabbath School to day for which I am glad and oh how gladly I would have presented myself with them if I had strength, but as I cannot I am thankful for the peace and quiet I enjoy in our little home, for my kind husband is so patient in careing for me and watching over our home affairs in general that I have a great deal to be thankful for.

7th month 28th 1890

A very rainy dark day which makes me feel low in spirit as I had anticipated a visit from my dear daughter to day but such petty disappointments we meet with in every day life and are comparatively nothing to the grievances which we often have to meet but as I am so feeble in body I have to keep close on my watch or I become discouraged for the enemy tries to persuade me that my lot is hard indeed and that the Lord has forgotten to be gracious, but He does not forget his weak dependent children so I will still lift up my head in hope.

7th month 29th 1890

As I have been favored to sit up and write some to day I feel very thankful for the privilege and hope I shall be kept in a patient humble state of mind whereby I may be made to rejoice in time to come that I have submitted myself to the discipline of the great head of the Church who is able to make us wise unto salvation.

7th month 30th 1890

Altho we are not permitted to know what we are to have to pass through in this life and it is a wise plan that we do not, yet if we are simply trusting in Jesus we shall leave the future all to him believing that he knows and will plan that which is better for us than we can know for ourselves. Yes then we can adapt the language of the hymn, "I feel the sweet assurance and thats enough for me."

7th month 31st 1890

How fast the months pass away its only by keeping the day of each day as it passes that we realize how quickly the months and even years pass away. But we are all fast hastening to the Tomb, are we prepared to meet its gloom, and be carried air, on Heavens bright share.

8th month 1st 1890

"Bless the Lord oh my soul and all that is within me bless his holy name" for he hath been so merciful and kind to us this day poor and unworthy as we are, and as this is the beginning of another month may we begin with new courage and diligence to do whatever the Master requires.

8th month 2nd 1890

Trust implicitly in Jesus is the language that presents itself to my mind this morning on taking up my paper to write, and I greatly desire to do this myself and that others may be constrained to put their whole trust in the Savior who alone can help us through all our difficulties. Lord give us help from trouble, for vain is the help of man.

8th month 3rd 1890

"Is my name written there." This line of the hymn impressed my mind after takeing up my paper to write, and the query has arisen in my mind, have we been diligent to know for ourselves that our names are written in the Lambs book of life. I rejoice in believeing that my name has been written there altho so unworthy, and I have so often made blots on its fair page by my many shortcomings, yet I believe that my kind Heavenly Father in his pity for my weaknesses is pleased to erase these blots from his book according as I have been willing to humble myself and ask this favor, as so will He do for all others who come to him in true penitence and faith.

8th month 4th 1890

This has been a day of severe bodily suffering sometimes I am made to wonder why I have been so afflicted and almost ready to give up in despair, but when I reflect how much sorer afflictions that of the mind, has fallen upon many that has yet been permited to come upon me, and I pray may never come, that of having a reckless dissipated husband or child. I feel that I should be willing to bear my bodily suffering with Christian fortitude without a murmur, for I have such tender care and sympathy from my dear family. Praised be the name of the Lord.

8th month 5th 1890

I feel thankful that I have been some freer from pain to day altho no means exempt, but have been able to be up most of the day and do some work therefore I feel like praising God for all his goodness to me.

8th month 6th 1890

Bless the Lord oh my soul and all that is within me bless his holy name.

8th month 7th 1890

Thou who knowest the thoughts and intent of the heart, and who art watching over thy dependent children, knoweth that I am poor unworthy worn of the dust so to speak, am desirous to do Thy will in all things notwithstanding I so often err but oh Father forgive all my sins blot out all my transgressions from thy Book for the sake of Him who died that all might have eternal life, is the prayer of my heart this evening.

8th month 8th 1890

I have felt the great loss of not being able to attend the yearly meeting at High Point which is now in session, but am desirous to be content with my lot and that the Lord will greatly bless all who may be permited to attend.

8th month 9th 1890

I am cast down yet not forsaken for the Master hath testified I will never leave thee nor forsake thee. Oh that I may be enabled to draw nigh unto God at this time for I feel the need of his Fatherly care.

8th month 10th 1890

Whilst our neighbors and friends in general have gone to attend the yearly meeting at High Point this Sabbath day, my dear husband and little children and my poor frail unworthy self are spending the day as usual in our humble home. Oh that we may realize that the hand of the Lord is upon us for good and altho we are so deprived of the blessed privileges which others enjoy, yet we know that He who heareth the ravens when they cry will be pleased to listen to the yearnings of our souls for help and strength to obey Him even in adversity.

8th month 11th 1890

Be still and know that I am God. This text of scripture has arisen in my mind this evening and I desire to realize its full import, to enter into solemn silence before Him who is the judge of all the earth and know of having my strength renewed, for I feel so weak both spiritually and physically that I have great need of Divine help, and it is only by entering into this solemn stillness having our minds turned away from all outward hurry and bustle of this life that we shall know of our strength being renewed.

8th month 12th 1890

To day I have had the pleasant surprise of my dear daughter **Maggie Moffitt** comeing in to spend a few days with me, oh it is such a sweet treat as I am often so lonely. Bless the Lord oh my soul.

8th month 13th 1890

This is a lovely day and as my daughter is with me I feel very grateful indeed my bodily suffering is still great, but I am still relying on Gods mercy for strength sufficient for each day.

8th month 14th 1890

This is my dear husbands forty seventh birthday we have been favored to still have our dear married daughter, and my dear aged mother with us to day. We have enjoyed this occasion very much for which I feel like giving God the praise, for from him all blessings flow.

8th month 15th 1890

To day our daughter left us for her own home in Lexington and took with her our dear little daughter to spend a few days with her. I am very lonely indeed as she is so much company to me when she is at home prattleing around me. May He who hath all our lives in his hands be with them and take care of them soul and body is my prayer and may each of us look to Him to be kept in the way of His requirings.

8th month 16th 1890

Praise God from whom all blessings flow. I feel glad that I can pen down these words from sincerity of heart, for I feel like ascribing praise and honor unto Him who is watching over and careing for us at all times.

8th month 17th 1890

This is a beautiful Sabbath day but as usual I cannot get out to Church on account of my feeble health, but I trust that it is the hand of the Lord that has been thus laid upon me therefore I submit myself to Him.

8th month 18th 1890

I desire to be very grateful that I have been so I could be up most of this day and help some in our household work.

8th month 19th 1890

Lord what wilt thou that I should do for thee is the query of my heart this evening.

8th month 20th 1890

Blessed are they that consider the poor the Lord will deliver him in time of trouble. These words were brought to my mind this evening by a poor little boy comeing in to get something for their supper, and I do desire to do that which is pleasing in the sight of God at all times.

8th month 21st 1890

To day my dear little daughter and her oldest brother returned from a visit with their sister in Lexington. I am very thankful for their safe return, and desire to be grateful for every favor and to be close on my watch that I be not led astray from the path of rectitude.

8th month 22nd 1890

Oh Lord have mercy upon me for I am weak, yea not only weak but suffering and thou alone can heal all mine infirmities, therefore I pray thee that if it is thy holy will to heal me both soul and body for thou hast all power to do whatsoever seemeth good to thee.

8th month 23rd 1890

True wisdom is the fear of the Lord, oh that I may be found living in the fear of the Lord that I may be made wise unto salvation, is the prayer of my heart for Christs sake.

8th month 24th 1890

This is a beautiful Sabbath, quarterly meeting at Marlboro is in session but none of our family except our oldest son were permited to attend on account of my feeble health, but we have been favored to spend a quiet happy day in our own little home for which I feel very grateful.

8th month 25th 1890

"Rock of ages cleft for me let me hide myself in thee." Yea under thy wings would I seek my refuge for there is none other name given whereby we may be saved but Jesus Christ the righteous.

8th month 26th 1890

"Oh give thanks unto the Lord for he is good for his mercy endureth forever." When we remember that his mercy endureth forever we know that it is still extended to us for which we should give thanks.

8th month 27th 1890

"They that trust in the Lord shall daily renew their strength."

8th month 28th 1890

Nothing new to note only the goodness of the Lord is still extended to us poor unworthy cretures, which is precious indeed, and is new every manifestation.

8th month 29th 1890

Surely the Lord has been with me a poor weak creture for he has enabled me to help do some work for my dear ones to day. Bless the Lord oh my soul.

8th month 30th 1890

"To day if ye will hear His voice harden not your hearts." This language comes to me oer and oer, and I feel like exhorting others also to hearken to the voice of him who willeth not the death of a sinner but is anxious that all should come to Him and live.

8th month 31st 1890

This beautiful Sabbath being the last day of summer brings many serious reflections to my mind. As we know not but it may be the last summer of our existence on earth, but if we are prepared for that glorious immortality all will be well, but if not it is time we were up and doing, for at midnight the cry may be heard "behold the Bridegroom cometh go ye out to meet Him." We should have our lamps trimed and burning.

9th month 1st 1890

As autumn begins to day, it again reminds us of the flight of time, for it hardly seems possible that a whole year has passed since noting down the beginning of Autumn of last year. But oh how much suffering and privation I have had to endure during this length of time, but the Lord has graciously supported me through it all.

12th month 1st 1890

Note.

Three months have elapsed since I have written anything in my diary this has been on account of not being able to do so.

I will endeavor once more to write, but oh how can I write, how can I record the trials through which I have past in the last three months, yes the last time I took up my pen to write a few words for my diary was the first of ninth month last, on that very date 9th month 1st 1890 the Lord in his condescending goodness and mercy was pleased to give me a precious little daughter, and as we had not had a babe in our home for over five years we regarded it as a great treasure. No doubt our hearts were set too much upon it for I never saw a brighter babe. It had beautiful features, dark brown hair and the most lovely bright eyes for a little babe I almost ever saw. But alas, alas how transient are all our hopes in this world, the pale faced messenger death came and nipped this lovely little bud when only two months old. Oh how our hearts have been saddened by the loss of our dear little treasure for altho we know our loss is her gain, yet she was such a comfort to us and in an especial manner to myself who has had to bear so much affliction and privation. She was so much company to me in my lonely hours for she was so bright to notice for one of her age, having begun to laugh and coo like a little dove, no one but a parent and He who made a parents heart can know the pang of parting with the dear little daughter who was but lent to us for so short a time, surely it was sent as a dove to our window to warn us to enter the ark of safety whereby we can and all our household may be saved. Therefore it is my earnest prayer that this dispensation of Providence may be heeded by us all and that we may make a full surrender of both soul and body to Him who holds the brittle thread of life in his hands, that we may all one day meet our little cherub beyond this vale of tears.

5th month 7th 1891

As I last wrote concerning the birth and decease of our dear little babe, I will now write some things concerning my visit some months later to our son-in-law **D.C. Moffitts** who as I have before stated married our oldest daughter and at the time lived in Lexington **N.C.** and altho I was very feeble and not able to walk at all and had not been outside of our home in more than a year and but few times in more than three years, yet through the kindness of my dear husband and other loved ones I was prevailed upon to make this visit.

Further notes as recalled in 1909

Consequently on the morning of 5th month 7th 1891 my dear husband and our oldest son **Jesse C. Blair** and my youngest brother **Thomas C Millikan** took me to the train at Fraziers sideing and our son Jesse and brother Thomas accompanied me to Lexington and as my wheel Chair was taken with me, when we arrived at High Point those dear boys (grown young men they were) took me in my Chair from one train to another as we had to make a change at High Point and oh how fresh the memory of this day comes up in my mind as I note these things, and what a pleasure it seemed to be to those dear ones to have the care of me that day and they both expressed themselves as its being one of the happiest days of their lives, and said they were so proud of the privilege of takeing care of me, and in turn I was so fond of them and so thankful to them for their kindness to me, and thankful to my kind and loving Heavenly Father both then and now that he gave sufficient strength for the trip and so thankful for such tender care from our dear son and my dear brother, and it brings a solemnity over me as I reflect on those things for whilst I am now transcribing this in the year 1909. They are both mouldering away beneath the sod our dear son is laid to rest in the Cemetery at

Until We Sleep Our Last Sleep

Thomasville Davidson Co N.C. and my dear brother at Springfield Guilford Co N.C. around the throne of God. But oh the many things which present themselves to my mind as I thus note these things, for at the time of this visit our dear son and brother both seeming healthy and so full of life and fun. While they were on this trip after they had seen me safely in the home of my daughter they went on a fishing trip to the big Yadkin river and spent near a week camping out and fishing and having a good time together, then they returned to Lexington and spent a little time with us there and then returned to their homes in Randolph, leaving me to spend some time in the family of our son-in-law **D.C. Moffitt** and as I was in such a feeble state of health it was deemed necessary to call a Physician in a few days after my arrival to see me and after a thorough examination he said it was necessary to perform an opperation for internal trouble, and I was also suffering with Catarrh of the stomach could not digest any solid food, had to subsist mainly on soups, raw eggs & for a long time, and my suffering was so intense and being in such debilitated state I had to remain there under the care of the **Dr Paynes** for four months, as I had to go through an opperation during this time and suffer many other things I was the greater part of my time helpless not even able to turn myself in bed a part of this time which brought a great deal of care of our dear daughter and her husband but their kindness will ever be remembered with the deepest gratitude and I feel sure that great will be their reward in Heaven for their kindness and true hospitality to one who was so afflicted and helpless as I was in their hands, and as I write this I pray Gods blessing upon them in this life for what they have done for me and many others, and a crown of blessedness upon them beyond the vale of tears for they have been so faithful to me I can never repay them myself for what they have done, but a kind word or act never loses its reward, even in this life, and we have the promice that after the judgement we shall receive the reward according to the deeds done in the body therefore I commend them to our loving Heavenly Fathers care knowing that the Judge of all the earth will do right, and that they will receive a crown of righteousness that fadeth not away if they hold out faithful to the end.

Bush Hill, N.C.

Rules to be observed in keeping the Sabbath

I will pen a few brief resolutions on the observance of the first day of the week which I wish to be observed as far as circumstances will admit, in my own family and others. I will propose that on the evening preceeding the Sabbath there should be such necessary preparation made as will lend to abandon all worldly persuits on the Sabbath day. If physically able rise early Sabbath morning resolve to bear in mind the commandment of our Saviour "remember the Sabbath day to keep it holy." Adopt the plan of having breakfast and all ordinary morning persuits done as soon as possible. Then proceed to clothing ourselves in clean apparel so that all may be ready to enter jointly upon the services of the day. Thus giving opportunity for those that can to assemble themselves at public worship while those that remain at home have the hour between ten and eleven for reading Scriptures and other good books and conversing upon their contents.

Then I propose that the hours from eleven until two o clock be a time of rest and for nourishment and necessary recreation for the body, refraining from all light worthless conversation, preferring such conversation as may be a lasting benefit to all who are under its influences. Then after the usual time for returning from public service all may assemble themselves and read portions of scriptures as will be most interesting and profitable. Also read some Tracts or sketches from other good books, asking questions, conversing freely about such things as will interest the little company and be most suited to occasion. Inward to recognize such faults as may have been committed during the past week and resolve to forsake them and do better in the future. Make a true acknowledgement of all wrong doings and unkind words or evil thoughts towards each other, asking pardon, granting it and remembering that we much forgive if we would be forgiven. Thus we will become united in the bonds of love and affection towards each other which we are sure will be well pleasing in the right of Jesus for he hath testified by this ye shall know that ye are my disciples if ye have love one to another.

I propose that there be no limited time for this afternoon service but that we be governed by our own feelings and circumstances and be careful not to prolong the time until all become wearied and disinterested. Now after this service is over we may if time and opportunity be offered us, spend some time in beholding the scenes of nature not merely for our pleasure alone but for the sake of improvement and instructing our children about that great Being who created all things.

After this we may speedily go about our evening turns such as are essentially necessary to be done that all thing may be done decently in order. This being done we may gather our little family around us, read a chapter and after a solemn pause and committing ourselves and children and others to the care of our Heavenly Father quietly retire to our beds, resolving as did Joshua of old, "let others do as they may as for me and my house we will serve the Lord."

Also bear in mind the lines of the poet. "A Sabbath well spent, brings a week of content, And health for the cards of the morrow But a Sabbath profaned whatever is gained, Is a sure forerunner of sorrow."

These rules were written by my own feeble hand in the early stage of raising our family, and were observed as far as practicable considering our afflictions and the observance of them has proved a blessing to us and our children, and I hope they may inspire others to train up their children in the way they should go.

Emily A. Blair
Progress

Rules to Be Observed–Compilation of Thoughts

Compilation of thoughts 1895 to 1914

If I mistake not it was the year 1895 that our dear son-in-law with this young family moved from Lexington to the dear old Moffitt homestead about two miles west of Thomasville. After they had been living there about two years I went on a visit to them at a time when I had lost my voice from a severe attack of Laryngitis. I had not been able to speak a word above a whisper for nine weeks before I went to visit them and suffered greatly from irritation in my pulmonary organs and as I had tried so many remedies to so little affect and feeling that I could not long survive in this manner I wished to pay them this visit thinking at the time that it no doubt would be my last visit to them as it was a distance of nine miles from my home and my suffering was so intense that there was little hope of recovery at that time, but while there my dear ones plead with me to have **Dr. Julian** of Thomasville called to see me. Consequently he came and finding me in such a critical condition he under took my case and I had to remain there two months under his care, and what I suffered none can know but Him who knoweth all things, nor none imagine but those who were my constant daily attendants who were my dear daughter and her estimable husband and his dear aged Mother who were always ready to do everything in their power to relieve my suffering, so I was a constant care on them again day and night for two months for my suffering was so great and it was with difficulty that I could speak even in a whisper so as to be understood, and was suffocating for breath so much of my time, and a great deal of the time could not lie down at all to rest but had to be propped up in bed to get what little sleep I got, and as there had to be a Nebulizar used to spray oil into my pipes, or bronchial tubes to heal the mucus membrane this had often to be done five or six times a day, but my dear ones never slacked their diligence toward me but performed every duty without a murmur altho some of it was very irksome and even loathsome as my expectoration was something terable, and the Dr. sometimes used a Camel hair brush three or four inches long with long crooked handle inserting this in my throat and down into my chest until it touches as far down as the lower edge of my breast bone in order to remove the corruption that had gathered there which I could not get relief from in any other way. This was suffering indeed, it seemed at such times like it would take my life, and I suffered so much from having the Electric Battery used on my throat and back so often that is seemed at times that it was more than I could endure, besides the many other remedies which were used to remove the cause and restore my voice, but through the mercy of kind Providence and the tender care of those He used as instruments in his hands my voice was restored sufficient to speak out again, my first impulse was to speak praises to the name of the Lord. The first audible sound was the word yes in reply to some of my Physicians questions this was made with a great effort, and the first sentence that I could frame to speak audibly was Jesus blessed Jesus, and on hearing my own voice again my dear daughter and her dear husband joined in the praises to God, my dear son-in-law exclaiming "blessed God blessed God," while my dear daughter sang "Jesus blessed Jesus". These were moments never to be forgotten while life lasts. In a short time after this, as soon as I had gained sufficient strength I returned to my home to join my dear husband who had so faithfully assumed the care of our home affairs to improve for a time, but for many years afterward I would be deprived of my voice for sometimes two and sometime three months at a time especially during the winter and spring seasons, suffering greatly from the same cause Laryngitis.

During the four years which our son-in-law lived on the farm at the old Moffitt homestead of which I have mentioned, his dear aged Mother passed from works to rewards an account of which I have written in a plain simple way and which was printed at the request of her children and other and which will be found lying within the leaves of this diary, so I will omit to write more there concerning it and after her decease her son D.C. Moffitt with his family moved to Thomasville, N.C. where they have since resided, but alas, in the year 1911 our hearts were again saddened by having to give up another dear earthly tie, for our dear son-in-law **D.C. Moffitt** after a lingering illness of almost a year with a serious stomach trouble and other complications was called away from his family by the cold hand of death on Easter Sabbath the 16th of 4th month 1911 and was laid to rest on Easter Monday in their family burying place at dear old Pinewoods by the side of his parents and other relatives, he leaves a wife and six children and a host of close friends and relatives to mourn their loss, which is his gain, for he fell asleep so sweetly as it were in the very arms of Jesus. His children are one son **David Blair Moffitt (the third child)** and five daughters namely **Marguerite Elizabeth (the eldest child) Emily Anita, Lula Maie, Ethel Tomlinson, and Wilma Almina Moffitt.** The second daughter **(Emily)** is now wife of **Joseph Franklin Bodenheimer** of Elkin N.C. There was many true and beautiful tributes paid to the life and death of D.C. Moffitt by his friends which were printed in the Papers some of those will be found lying within the leaves of this memorandum. It will be remembered that I have previously stated that my dear youngest brother **Thomas C. Millikan** and our dear oldest son **Jesse Carter Blair** had both departed this life. Brother **Thomas** passed way on the **23rd of 12th month 1895** and was laid to rest in the dear old Springfield Cemetery on Christmas day. He was born 10th month 16th 1859. Therefore a little more than 36 years of age, he had remained single all his life, he had been in feeble health for some time and finally succumbed to exhaustion.

 About two weeks after this dear brother was laid to rest, our dear son **Jesse C. Blair** was married to **Miss Emma Clodfelter** of Davidson Co on January the 8th 1896. Of this union three children were born one son and two daughters names **Jesse Lelen, Emily Corene, and Sadie Clodfelter Blair.** When Sadie was less than one year old our dear son their father passed away Sept 22, 1901, after a lingering illness of seven weeks of Typhoid fever, at the age of 33 years and 4 days. He had been living in Statesville N.C. for some time and his death occurred at that place, his remains were brought to Thomasville by rail and kept over night at our son-in-law D.C. Moffitts then taken to Bethany Church out in the country among his wifes people for interment, then after he had lain in the Cemetery there for four years his remains were taken up and interred in the Cemetery at Thomasville to which Town his wife with their three little fatherless children had moved, and after they had lived there for some time her dear little son was killed by a freight train while returning home from school, this was another severe trial to us all. A brief account in print is lying within these leaves. The widow is now married to **Luther Conrad** of Davidson Co and still lives in Thomasville. It seems that as a family have had large share of afflictions and sorrows in this life, but are trying with Divine help to fulfill the following lines.

"Build a little fence of trust around to day, Fill the space with loving work and therein stay, Look not through the bars upon tomorrow, God will send what comes of joy and sorrow." 1914 **Miss Lou Johnson** second daughter of **J. Alvin and Ruth Johnson** died of Inflamitary Rheumatism soon after her parents moved from Indiana to Missouri, she was born in Randolph County North Carolina, her parents went to Ind. soon after the Civil War and lived in that State a few years then moved to Mo. She was a dear little neice of mine and grew up to be a lovely young woman.

1908

10th month 10th 1908

Written for the Blair-Millikan Union Memorial exercises at Springfield

To those who have met for the purpose of honoring the name of our worthy ancestors **Enos** and **Hannah Millikan Blair** by erecting a stone to perpetuate their memory, I will state that **Enos Blair** was the Great grandfather of my husband **John Addison Blair**, and his wife **Hannah** was a sister to my Grandfather **Benjamin Millikan** therefore my great Aunt and altho I was quite a little girl at the time and am now past three score and three years, I remember almost vividly as though it was but yesterday of being in the old ancestral home, and in the family of their son **John Blair** and being taken into a room to see dear aged **Aunt Hannah** who was lying in bed which made a solemn impression on my young mind. and how well I remember the pleasure of runing up and down the high rock steps that led into an old house which then stood south of their dwelling and of being taken into it by some of the family to crack the nice dry walnuts that had been hulled and stored there to please children and others. [This same old homestead is now owned by **Capton Parkins** of Trinity] and since those things have recently been brought fresh to my mind I have reviewed them with a degree of awe that had never moved me so deeply before, for as I have meditated upon the changes that have taken place since those days, the joys and sorrows and afflictions in various ways which we have all passed through to a greater or lesser degree, and how our merciful Heavenly Father has watched over us all and kept us through all, I am almost lost in wonder, love, and praise. And now I come to the most vital questions that has to do with a meeting together for this memorial service. have we lived up to the standard of moral excellence and true righteousness which we believe our worthy ancestors desired we should?

are we living in that way and manner that will show to generations following a more lasting monument than granite or marble. lives that show forth an example of truth and uprightness worthy of imitation by our own posterity and others and as we have met on this both solemn and festive occasion it is my earnest prayer that it may be a union of kindred minds and hearts, discarding everything contrary to the Divine will, and that we may all be united in the bonds of true christian fellowship as children of one Father even God and joint his heirs with his dear son. having nothing but love to God and good will to men abideing in our hearts, and let this show forth in our lives and conversations so that our decendants may behold how good and how pleasent it is for brethren to dwell together in unity.

Emily A. Blair
Progress N.C.

1909

9th month 1909

In meditating upon the many mercies of my kind and loving Heavenly Father in spareing my life thru so many sore trials and afflictions one thing comes before my mind with vividness at this time, that of the severe operation which I had to undergo at the Junior Order Hospital at High Point this was performed by **Dr Burrus** assisted by **Drs Duncan and Reitzel** which was counted a grand success at the time for one of my age I then being past my sixty fourth year, but what I suffered I cannot express in words, altho I was cared for by kind nurses and many kind friends and relations visited me during the four weeks I remained in the Hospital and brought me many beautiful flowers and spoke words of comfort and good cheer, then after I have been nursed in the Hospital four weeks **Dr Burrus** took me in his arms and carried me down a long flight of stairs and out to his nice closed Cab and took me to our son **Fred C. Blair** there in Town and carried me and placed me on a bed there to be nursed by our sons wife who is also a trained nurse, two weeks longer before recovering sufficient to return home. There many kind friends visited me and brought in flowers and delicious luncheons which by this time I began to relish and for which I was most grateful for their kindness, and to all my nurses from first to last. I am grateful and above all to Him who had seen fit to prolong my days through the efficiency of kind Drs and nurses. Therefore the praise belongeth to "Him in whom I live and move and have my being."

1914

6th month 18th 1914

Many interesting things have taken place since I wrote last in my Diary which I cannot now recall sufficiently to pen satisfactory, but so far as my own career is concerned it has been much the same of several years past, and I am still endeavoring to press forward altho it is with faultering steps and often times makeing sad mistakes as I am but a poor weak worm of the dust so to speak and realize that of myself I can do nothing which will redown to the glory of God or to the upbuilding of his kingdom in the hearts of the children of men, yet in casting a backward glance over the many years that have elapsed since my childhood days and realize the many mercies which my kind Heavenly Father has bestowed up me his poor unworthy child as I feel myself to be and especially during those many years of affliction I feel that I cannot praise Him enough. If my dear husband and I should be spared to see the 14th day of the 12th mo of this year 1914 we will have spent a half century of married life togeather and happy indeed has been this union notwithstanding all our suffering, bereavement, and afflictions in many ways yet we realize that the loveing hand of our precious Saviour has held us up. and my dear husband has already passed his three score and ten and I am now in my seventyeth year we are now going down the western horison of life and are anxious that every step of the remainder of the journey may be heavenward to the praise and honor of our blessed Saviour for we desire to serve and glorify him on earth that thou would guide our faltering steps and overlook all our short comeings, for we acknowledge that they are many, and "as far as the east is from the west so far remove our transgressions from us" for we desire to live the life of the righteous that our last end may be like his, so that we may praise God forever in the home of the blessed. Amen.

1917

7th month 26th 1917

There has sometimes been long intervals that I did not pen down anything in my Diary therefore many interesting things have been omited, but as what I have written has been mainly for my own family and well known friends who have known of and often been eyewitness of the suffering through which I have had to pass from time to time, it is not important that I should take note of the many things that have taken place for the last few years, many of them know how I have been deprived of going to Church and Sabbath School etc this has been one of my heaviest burdens for I so love to go to the places appointed for worship there to praise God with those who assemble for this great and noble purpose and are thus obeying the injunction to "not neglect the assembling of your selves together as the maner of some is." but there has been many years in succession that I could not present myself with those thus assembled on account of my afflictions, and since being able to get out at all have not gotten to the place of worship more than one or twice during a year. and it will be one year in the next month since I was able to join others in a meeting capacity, and that was at our anual roll call and memorial session at our dear old

Springfield, it had been two years since I had been there, and the roll call made a profound impression on my mind for I thought how very uncertain it was that I and many others as well, would be permitted to thus meet together in this life (and some that were present have gone from works to rewards since) and was my earnest desire that we might all so live that "when the roll is called up yonder we would be there." haveing been washed in the blood fo the Lamb so that we might have an abundant entrance into the kingdom there to sing Gods praise togeather thruout the endless ages of eternity and if I should never again be permitted to present my body at the place appointed for worship my prayer is that all who can thus assemble may be faithful to attend as long as life and health sufficient is given, and may I be faithful to render unto my blessed Saviour his due of praise in my own heart and home if not permitted to attend Church here on earth that I may meet all my faithful and loved ones in the Church Triumphant is my prayer for Jesus sake. Amen

It was only four days after I had attended the a foresaid roll call at Springfield that I was more than two months, and have still continued to suffer with a complication of diseases up to the present writing 7th month 26th 1917. but am leaving myself in the hands of the Lord to do with me as he see best for he knows what is best, and if he should see fit to restore me to a better condition physically the praise be his and if not His will be done. for I feel sure that if he give me sufficient strength each day to perform it, and if my days are fulfilled here on earth he will take me to His home in Heaven. "Then adue to earth for all is well, all is well with me forever." Amen.

1918

5th month 1st 1918

As my life has been mercifully spared through much suffering to the present date, I will again attempt to take down a few notes in regard to what has transpired since I last wrote in my memoranda which was 7th 26 1917 and in which I noted the fact that I was suffering greatly with complications of diseases which continued to be my lot through the following months with no relief except at shore intervals, so it was decided by my dear husband and children the I should be taken to a Hospital for treatment accordingly I went to the Tranquil Park Sanitorium at Charlotte, N.C. the last week in October 1917 and on the 29th underwent an operation and remained at the Hospital for three weeks under the care of **Dr. John Myres** and his nurses in which time my suffering was very severe. Then **Dr Myres** took me in his easy limozene to our son **Fred C. Blairs** as he and family had moved to Charlotte a short time previous to my going to the Hospital and as his wife is a Trained nurse she cared for me until I gained strength enough to be taken to our daughter who is the wife of **Arthur Lee Stilwell** they have lived in Charlotte ever since their marriage. I remained with them the past winter. My dear husband joined me soon after I left the hospital and remained with me at our son-in-law Stilwells also during the winter. We left for our dear old home on the 8th of March, spent a few days with relatives in High Point but reached our home in time to spend my 73rd birthday (the 13th) in our dear old home where we have lived so happily for 53 years.

1919

2nd month 28th 1919

This being the last day of winter my mind has been deeply impressed with the flight of time and the many changes that have taken place within the past year which seems to have flown so quickly not withstanding we have had sickness and also bereavement during that time. I wrote in my memoranda concerning what had transpired the few months previous to that date was 5th month 1st 1918. The following summer in the 8th month I was taken down with fever,

February 1919

suffering greatly for several weeks but by medical aid and tender care I was again mercifully restored sufficiently to be up and attend to our household affairs, although still a daily sufferer from chronic disease. And now it is with sadness of heart that I take note of our sore bereavement in the death of our beloved soninlaw **Arther Lee Stilwell** which occured the 23rd of October 1918 after a short but severe attack of Influenza followed by Pneumonia, he only lived one week after taken sick. Words will fail to express our sorrow at this loss for he was such a kind and faithful husband to our daughter who had been very much afflicted at times during their married life, and was sick with Influenza at the time of his death and could not attend the funeral. And he was so kind and generous to my husband and I when we spent the winter of 1917-18 with them as I have before stated and he being a Christian man was greatly missed in Church affairs as Stuard and in many other ways as he was constantly in the work of the Sunday School and loyal in all the activities of Church work and also a conciencious business man of much ability and trust. A copy of resolutions of respect will be found in print lying with the leaves of this Tablet. We greatly mourn our loss but have a blessed assurance that our loss is his gain. He passed peacefully away without a struggle to be forever with the Lord. But while we rejoice in the belief that he is forever happy. We sorrow so much for our daughter who feels her loss so greatly. And as we only had two daughters to live to enter married life and they are now both widows it is a great trial to us their parents, but we commend them and theirs to the tender loving care of Him who has promised to be "a father to the fatherless and a husband to the widow."

"For God is faithful ever faithful.
He will surely keep his word
To the uttermost fulfilling
Every promice I have heard."

Until We Sleep Our Last Sleep

1920
Sabbath Day

May the 9th 1920 Progress N.C.

This is indeed a lonely Sabbath day as I sit alone reflecting on the many changes that have taken place in the last few months. When I last wrote in my Diary it was concerning the loss by Death of our dear soninlaw **Arthur Lee Stilwell** which occured on the 23rd of October 1918. And now I have come to the point where I must state that I am left a poor bereaved widow myself. My precious husband **John Addison Blair** having deceased the 21st of March 1920. No one only that who have experienced the loss of a dearly loved companion can know the deep sorrow of heart and the lonelyness thru which I am passing for no one ever had a kinder or more sympathetic husband in every way than he was to me, during all of our journey of life togeather and we had the happy lot of living togeather a little more than fifty five years, and during all those years I was so very much afflicted, and he was so faithful and tender to me all the while as a mother over her tender babe. So I miss his loveing sympathy and care so much that at times it overcomes me so much that I feel like I should faint by the way, and it is only as I lean on the strong arm of my merciful Heavenly Father that I can bear up under this <u>sorest of all</u> my trials, bereavements and afflictions in various ways all along my line which I have now reached a little over my seventy fifth year there has never fallen to my lot as sore a trial as as the loss of my dear husband who was more precious to me than all else in this world, and now my earnest prayer is that I may so live that I may meet him in that world where all sorrow and suffering atone away, where I trust my precious one is now basking in the sunshine of Gods love, while I his poor lonely widow am left to mourn the loss of one so very near and dear to my heart, but I am thankful that I do not sorrow as those who have no hope, for I believe my loss is his gain and if it is my Heavenly Fathers will I hope that it may not be long until I can join him in that better land, but am willing to bide His time and do whatever duty calls me to do in His name. dear Lord help me to be faithful to the end.

The prayer of his bereaved wife
Emily A Blair

1923

Sabbath day Sept the 9th 1923
Rout #2. Box 18. Trinity N.C.

This beautiful Sabbath morning as I have been reflecting on the past, and have been refering to what I wrote last in my Diary concerning the trial of having to give up my dear earthly companion, I feel so very lonely. And as I have noticed that it was the 9th of May 1920 when that was written, and as this is the 9th of Sept 1923 it hardly seems possible that more than three years have passed away since I had to give up the one that was the most precious one on earth to me, and while I am blessed with dear children and grandchildren and many kind friends, there is still a vacant chair and an acheing void that none other can fill, people have said to me that "it looks like you could not get lonely when you have so plenty of company," yet I often feel the most lonely when in company for I see others with their friends and companions and I miss mine so much. But I am so thankful to know that I have a Friend above all others that is always ready to look down from His holy habitation and brings comfort in someway to one as I look to Him for help and consolation. And just now the children in this home (the home of **J.W. Peace**) are singing togeather and playing on the Organ and as they sing "yes He included me" when they refer to the words "whosoever will may come", it is such a consolation that we can all come to this bless Saviour and find that he has included us in his great plan of salvation, and that "we can lean on The Everlasting Arms," and I have never known it to fail when I have felt the most lonely and the need of comforting word from some one, that some kind friend would come in to cheer me on my way, or my eyes would fall on some comforting lines written by some one to cheer others, so I just now came across the following lines which were selected and sent to me by my husband's cousin **F.S. Blair** which seem to of been written expressly for me at this time.

"Sigh not o'er the days departed,
Nor old times wish back again,
In the present live brave hearted
Tears for vanished joys are vain,
Steer they back serenely securely,
All the world before thee lies,
Striveing suffering hopeing surely,
Thou shalt gain the prize.

As I have previously stated the last I wrote in my Diary was concerning the Decease of my dear husband and now I will try to take note of some experiences since that time, I have also stated in the past that my youngest daughter **Mary Eliza Stilwell** was left a widow while living in Charlotte, N.C. She since married **Jerome W. Peace** of Randolph Co., N.C. and it is in her home that I am now writing. I staid in the home during the summer of 1920 after my dear husbands death, then in the fall of the same year, I went to my widowed daughter **Margaret E. Moffitt** who lives in Kansas City, Mo. arriveing there the day before Thanksgiving and on the following day her children and grandchildren all assembled in her home to celebrate Thanksgiving and give a welcome reception to me as Mother Grandmother and Greatgrandmother who had been mercifully spared to come to them; and it was indeed a day of rejoiceing and Thanksgiving at that time I had six greatgrandchildren there, and since that time there has been more born, so I now have six greatgrandaughters and three grandgrandsons, my daughter **Maggie** as we always called her from infancy, had written an urgent request for me to go out there and spend the rest of my days with her. I staid one year and a half with her and her children and grandchildren and had a fine visit indeed, but my health failed so much while there that their family Physician advised me to return to N.C. which I did in May 1922 but before returning to N.C. I visited my oldest sister **Ruth Johnson** widow of **J. Alvin Johnson,** she at that time lived in the Town of Deepwater Mo. had a very interesting visit with her and her children and grandchildren, she was so peart and joval and could get about like a young person and was then eighty one years of age. She since passed away on March the 20th 1923. Lacking only one month of eighty three years. For several months she had been having slight strokes of paralysis then came a severe one that proved fatal. She was spared to an advanced age and all her life she had been a very enerjitic and useful woman in all her avocations in life. I am so thankful that I had the privilege of visiting her in her home while out West as it was my last opportunity.

After returning to N.C. I spent the following months in the home of my soninlaw **J.W. Peace** until November of the same year, then I went to my son **Fred C. Blairs** home in Charlotte, N.C. and spent the following winter with him and family, his wife who was **Miss Esther Hayden** before marriage is a native of England, she is a Trained Nurse and was often called from home to care for the sick and suffering and I am so thankful that for the most of my time while there I kept able to be of some help and I hope of some comfort to my dear son and children while the wife and mother had to be away from them ministering to the sick.

I met many interesting people while there and was treated most kindly by all, so I had a pleasant sojourn. Then in the spring of 1923 I returned again to the home of my daughter **Mrs JW Peace** and have spent the spring and summer very pleasantly in this home the pure country air giving me more vitality and have enjoyed the fresh vegetables, melons, fresh egges poultry & have had the precious privilige of attending Sabbath School and Church at Mt. Vernon with this family a good part of the time, for which I am very grateful. And I was also blessed with strength and the oppertunity of attending our yearly meeting of Friends this year which is now held at Guilford College N.C. it convened on Tuesday Aug the 7th 1923. I have previously written to **Miss Gainey** who is the Secretary, for the use of a room on the first floor of Founders Hall during what time I should stay at the meeting, as I did not have strength sufficient to hold out to climb the steps to the uppers stories, and received a reply that I should have my request, and there had also been arrangements made for me to go in a Car with the Blair sisters. Therefore on Wednesday am Aug the 8th **J.W. Peace** and wife took me to the **Blair Dairy** and **Elva Blair** drove her Car and took two of her sisters **Emma** and **Martha,** and **Nerius Barker** and wife **Mary Barker,** and **Dora Richerdson** and myself over to Guilford College had a fine drive arrived on time enjoyed the good service at eleven o'clock, then drove out to Founders Hall where there was a nice little room already prepared for me. Met **Miss Gainey** who received me most kindly, also **Miss Sarah Benbow** the Matron who met me in like manner, and also met **Miss Rayle** a helper in the work who was very kind and nice to me. After eating dinner in the large dineing room in Founders Hall I went to my room undressed and lie down and took a good rest, as I felt too much fatigued to go out to Church that pm. But dressed again in time for supper, then when meeting time came, as those that had been takeing me out to Church were gone home for the night, Cousin **F.S. Blair** got a conveyance for me and I attended the meeting that night had good service largely attended. Then next morning cousin **Elva Blair** was back again in time to take me to Church, and also brought me back to the Hall. Then after dinner I sat on the front porch and met many old acquaintances and formed many new ones, and not feeling able to attend all the regular services I staid at Founders this pm also and rested, and mused on the many

September 1923

changes that had taken place at this dear old institution since I was here last which has been more than forty years ago, so the many new College buildings that are here now have been erected since that time. I attended yearly meeting at this place and some of our dear good neighbors who use to live near us in Randolph Co now reside at Guilford College. I will mention **Gurney Frazier** and family in whos home I had the pleasure of dineing with them one evening at supper, and their nephew **Lee White** who is one of the Fackulty at Guilford at this time was with us to help us enjoy the bountiful repast that had been prepared for us, he also drove the Car for his Aunt and myself and took us to Church that night, then took me back to the Hall this was a visit I shall ever remember with pleasure. And we had a most wonder meeting that night so interesting and instructive in every way. Truly all the sessions of the meeting were interesting and helpful and I greatly enjoyed all I was favored to attend. I very much regreted that by a misunderstanding in the way of a conveyance from Founders Hall to the Church as I could not walk that distance I missed the special memorial service which was held on Friday pm the 10th for our late beloved **President Warren G. Harding** which was held at the same time in Marion Ohio. I dressed in black just as tho I was going to the funeral of a near relative for I felt that it was fitting that we should pay due respect to his memory as our nations beloved Cheif, and although I did not get to attend the services I mourned our loss as a nation and as a people just the same, and that same pm there was memorials read for **Priscila Benbow Hackney** and **Laura Balinger Winston,** I especially regretted not getting to hear the Memorial of **Laura Balinger** who was my school mate in 1864 when this dear old place was called New Garden Boarding School at that time Founders Hall was the only building of note at this place and it has since been remodeled so that not very much of it looks as it did in those days, nevertheless it was a dear old spot then as now. But it is interesting to see the improvements and the progress along many lines that have been made since those farmer days for the advancement of education. And it is sincerely hoped that with all those improvements that the fundimental principals of this dear old institution which were incorporated in the very foundation may not be last sight of, but strictly adheared to and regarded as steping stones to present day progress. It has filled my heart with gratitude to God and good will to my fellow beings that I was permited to hear and to enjoy the Gospel sermons and the many interesting things that was said and done, not only in the services at the Church, but also at Founders Hall for there I met with so many kind friends who by giving me the right hand of fellowship and kindly greeting helped to cheer me on in my lonely walk of life. Many of those I have known for years but on account of my affliction have seldom had the oppertunity of meeting them. I will insert the names of some those who I met and had pleasent converse with at this yearly meeting, especially I wish to mention **Wm Worth** who was one of the kind Friends who helped to carry me in and out of Church at this place more than forty years ago as I have previously stated was the last time until this year that I had been able to attend yearly meeting at that time I did not have the use of my lower limbs to walk and as I did not them have my Wheel Chair which I was blessed with a short time after and in this way had to get about for many years in succession but thankful to state that at this time I can get about the house and yard with the aid of a staff, but then I had to be carried in a chair by two men and **Wm Worth** was one of those on that occasion and at that time was a strong man and had the use of all his limbs, whereas at this yearly meeting his way of walking was on two crutches but by the aid of these he would walk to and from Founders Hall to the Church and was the same cheerful even joval person that he was in those past years which was an inspiration to me to not give out by the way on account of bodily affliction, but to press on not looking back on the past, but "Leaving those things which are behind, press forward toward the mark for the prize of the high calling in Christ Jesus." I met with dear **Miriam Mendenhall** who is the sister of my soninlaw

September 1923

D.C. Moffitt and had such a pleasant time with her, and also daughter **Erma** who is the wife of **Rev Joseph Peele** of Guilford College.

I cannot at present recall the names of near all those that I met with so pleasantly at Guilford at this time but will insert some of them. **Margaret B. Hackney** Greensboro N.C. **Ada E Lee Stanley. Rettie S. Harding** and husband. **Mary M. Petty. Laura Petty Hadgin, Roe Petty Smith.** Their Mother **M Victoria Petty** Archdale N.C.

J. Winston Blair and wife of Archdale. **Hattie R. Tomlinson** Archdale N.C., **Annie M Couch** Guilford College, NC, **Leanna Wibborn,** Deep River, **Martha E Marshall,** Mt. Airy NC, **Alice Dunman** and her Father **W.C. Welch,** Mt. Airy. **Catherine Paff** Winston Salem, N.C., **Emily R. Newlin Smith** Wilmington NC., **Elvira Lowe Smith** Burlington. **Nereus M Hodgin** A Minister and wife **Melissa F Hodgin** of Bangar Iowa. **Elwood C. Perisho** and **Inez Beele Perisho** Guilford College. **Lewis W McFarland** and wife **Pearl McFarland. Lewis Linden Hobbs, G.C. Samuel Haris** Guilford College. **Anna Perisho White. Fernando Cartland White** Guilford College. **Mrs H.E. Shore** Kernersville NC. **Mrs Myrtle W Nelson** Kernersville N.C. **Annie Pegram Simpson** St Burlington N.C. **Louella Night** S.C. **Alta Winslow Night. Elizabeth Levering. Lee White** S.C. **John J Blair** Raleigh. **F.S. Blair** Guilford College. **Gurney Frazier** and wife **Lou,** their son **Ruffin,** their youngest daughter **Louise,** also their daughter **Addie Smith** and her oldest son and daughter. S.C. **Lydia C. Anderson. Daniels H.P.** wife **Alice Paige White. Mrs. H.A. White** High Point N.C. **Ada Blair. Emma Blair. Martha Blair. Elva Blair.** H.P. **Nellie Thompson** of Philadelphia. **Artie Barker** High Point. **Addie Spencer** and her daughter **Pattie Spencer Davis,** Deep River. **Artilica Hill** and her daughter **Edith Hill,** High Point. **Eliza Barker** and her daughter **Jennie Reynolds. Arrilla Balinger** Osborne, Greensboro N.C. **Miss Sarah Benbow. Miss – Gainey.** Guilford College.

I staid at Guilford from Wednesday morning until Saturday evening, then came with **John J. Blair** and Sisters to High Point, they left me at cousin **Jesse Millikans** I staid over night there, and the following day which was the Sabbath we were invited to the home of their nephew **Willie Johnson** which is a very pleasent home he being a splendid fellow himself and has a good smart wife and nice family of children fared sumptuously at their Table. Then after dinner **Willie** took us in his nice Car over to dear old Springfield to the Cemetary to visit the graves of our dear ones who lie there, we were grateful to him for this favor. Then after a nice little drive in the fresh air we returned to **Johnsons** and had some excellent Music his wife playing the Piano and **Willie** and their daughters singing with her some beautiful Hymns. After this **Willie** took us back to his uncle **Jesse's** in High Point, where I again staid with them overnight. And Monday pm cousin **Maggie Millikan** and myself went across the St to **Wm Andersons,** his **Mother Nannie Anderson** who is my first cousin was with them. I staid there and took supper with them, then cousin **Nannie** went back with me to cousin **Jesse's** and staid until bed time we all had a very interesting time togeather. Then Tuesday am cousin **Maggie** and I went over to their son **Roger Millikans** which is next door had a nice little visit there, then **Roger** took me to **Junius Barkers** whos wife is cousin **Tommie** and **Nannie Andersens** daughter spend the day pleasently with them, then in the evening **Junius** and his **wife Artie** took me to **Henry Winslows,** they were for several years our good neighbors in the Country, I staid with them until Thursday evening then their son **Robert** took me over to see his nice new home he was married some time this year, from there **Robert** took me to **Nerius Wilborns** familiarly called **Dock** his wife **Pearl** is **Lenard Marshes** daughter and her mother is a first cousin of mine, staid with them until Friday evening then cousin **Pearl** took me in the Car over to **Fridella Barker** whose wife **Mattie** was cousin **Benjamen Millikans** daughter, staid over night with them then Saturday morning cousin **Pearl Wilborn** came for me and brought me to Springfield to the Memorial Association this was a very interesting occasion, in the forenoon **Joseph Peele** preached a most wonderful sermon, and had excellent music, both vocal and instrumental, prayer, good talks &. A Memorial was read for **B. Franklin Blair** written by his son **Augustine W. Blair** and read by his son **Walter E Blair** which was very interesting and true to his picknick on the grounds which long Table was loaded with good things to eat and plenty of ice water and ice tea to drink. The services were very good from the beginning to close, remanisences were read of the rise and progress of the Church, good talks on various subjects good prayers, good music, and met with many kind friends and kindred, all these thing contributed to making it an interesting instructive, and enjoyable occasion; which I shall cherish while memory and life lasts.

1924

In August 1924 I again had the precious privilige of attending yearly meeting at Guilford College as it is still held there in Aug from year to year. My daughter **Mrs JW Peace** and husband took me up to the Blair Dairy and from there I was favored as I was the year before for **Elva Blair** took me in her nice closed Car and two of her sisters and **Dora Richardson** were with us and we had a very pleasent drive over to Guilford, and there I found a nice little room prepared for me as was the case the year before as I had previously spoken for it. I enjoyed this yearly meeting very much as I was able to attend most of the sessions which were very interesting and instructive as we had many good sermons and much good advise and met so many kind friends with whom it was a pleasure to converse, many of them I had not met the year before during the yearly meeting week in 1923 and formed many new acquaintance which was also very pleasent. And now to the Great Giver of all our blessings I iscribe all praise and honor now and forever for He watches over me daily poor and unworthy as I am and puts sympathy and kindness into the hearts of those with whom I meet and mingle to do favors for me, and I pray His richest blessings upon those who have shown me kind favors and words of comfort which I daily feel so much in need of as I am now aged and lonely. But I am still striveing to do my Heavenly Fathers will as He makes it known to me by His holy spirit and by reading of His sacred written Word. And am praying for ability to hold out faithful to the end. Amen

August the 5th 1924

Our yearly meeting of Friends convened at Guilford College on Tuesday morning Aug the 5th 1924. I was favored to attend from the opening until the close. There was quite a number of Preachers present from different States and brought excellent mesages, and the meeting was largely attended. I shall always feel indebted to dear **Clara I. Cox** for her kindness to me in being instrumental in the Lords hands in getting me over to Guilford College for indeed the good Lord sent her to answer my poor simple prayers in regard to my attending this meeting, for I had felt that it was right that I should go, but felt my weakness so much that I became discouraged, and finally desided that I would not go, but still I did not feel satisfied, so I took the dear Lord in prayer and plead with Him to show me wheather or not I should go, that if it was right and best for me to go, that He would open a way for me to go, and if it was not right and best that He would keep the way closed so that I could not go, so after thus pleading for several days and nights, one afternoon very unexpectedly dear **Clara I. Cox** our Pastor at both Springfield and Archdale at that time, drove up to where I was staying to visit me, and in her conversation she asked me if I was going to yearly meeting. I told her I had desided not to go, and she said if I would say I would go she would come and take me over there and bring me back, or see that some one else did all right. So I saw at once that my prayer was heard and that the good Lord had sent her to open up the way. So I could no longer doubt that it was all right for me to go. So I went and was favored to attend most of the sessions which I enjoyed, and also met with so many kind friends that I had not seen for years, and formed many new acquaintances, which I enjoyed. I had the pleasure of meeting with a school mate that was at New Garden boarding school with me sixty years ago. That was before it was called Guilford College. After the meeting was over I visited my kindred in and around High Point for a week and had a good time. So I have much to thank the Lord for his goodness to me in giving me strength each day to perform this visit, and in blessing me with so many kind friends to minister to me.

This sketch rightly belongs with that on page 219 (in the handwritten diary) for it took place the same year and the same yearly meeting, but by some oversight I missed transcribing these notes where they should of been, connected with what was written on page 219 (in the handwritten diary). So they were left out of my Tablet in their proper place.

1925

August 4th to the 9th 1925

I was again taken to the Blair Dairy as seems to be the starting point each year for yearly meeting, but this time instead of it being Dear **Elva Blair** as in the two previous years it was Dear **Clara I Cox** our beloved Minister who took **Rev Louis McFarland** and myself with her in her nice Closed Car, and we sure had a pleasant drive over to Guilford their conversation on the way was an inspiration to me. I had the pleasure of attending the meeting from Wednesday morning until Sat evening. Had a splendid meeting largely attended, and I met so many friends who were so congenial that it was refreshing to be there. Then on the 15th of Aug I attended the Memorial Association of Friends held at dear old Springfield where my precious companion lies just north of the meeting house, and so near that I can see his grave from the door while sitting in Church. And is the most sacred spot on earth to me now, for in his this hallowed Cemetary there lies not only the precious dust of my husband, but also my dear parents, brothers, and sisters, and our own precious little babe, and many other loved relatives and friends. And dear old Springfield where I have a birthright membership in the Friends Church has been a place dearly beloved since childhood, for there I attended Sabbath School when Uncle **Allen Tomlinson** was Superintendent. These are hallowed memories and fill my heart with awe as I meditate on what I have endured since those days, and in my loneliness I feel the greatest desire to so live that I may meet my loved ones in the better land when done with this vale of tears.

As this Tablet is now filled up I will have to resort to my new bluebacked Tablet in which I shall insert many different things which I have taken note of from time to time. I will first begin by giving a faint outline of my interesting visit which I was blessed to make in Oct 1925. I feel that I cannot be thankful enough to my merciful Heaven Father for permitting me to enjoy this good visit, meeting with and enjoying the company of so many loved ones, it was a treat I greatly appreciated for the many favors bestowed upon me by so many kind friends, for which I ask Gods richest blessings, upon all.

Continued in Tablet 4

Monday a.m. Oct 26th 1925

This a.m. came to **Blair's Dairy** spent the remainder of the day and the following night in that hospitable home. then Tuesday a.m. **Elva Blair** took me and some others with her to the **Evangelist Rev George Stephen's** meeting at the Tabernacle in High Point heard a grand sermon. Then in the afternoon visited **Mrs. Ellen Jerald,** and also visited **Mrs. Mary Barker.** Then Wednesday a.m. went to the Tabernacle again, and in the p.m. went to **Winston Blairs,** there I met with two of **Zebidee Crokers** granddaughters **Miss Aldred** and her sister **Mrs. Davis,** I had a good visit there in general. Then on Thursday A.M. went to the Tabernacle and came back to **Mary**

Barkers and took dinner and spent the afternoon very pleasently with her, she is the Widow of **Nericus Barker** who is a Minister in the Friends Church. Then Friday we went to the Tabernacle in the morning and from there went to cousin **Roger Millikans** took dinner with them and spent the afternoon. **Florence Meredith** and her daughter **Mabel,** and **Anna Cranford** also went there and we had quite a pleasent visit together. **Rogers** Mother was also in his home and is spending the winter with them. It hardly seems necessary to mention that we all enjoyed the meeting at the Tabernacle, for words would fail to express our appreciation for we were so well pleased with every session that we had the chance to attend that we wanted each time to go back worse than the last. It was indeed a great meeting and I hope will do much lasting good. Saturday the 31st I staid with the **Blair sisters** all that day had a good visit with them all togeather as **Ada and Emma** are Teaching and not at home other days in the week.

Sunday morning Nov the 1st 1925

I went with the Blairs to Sunday School and meeting at Springfield and heard an inspireing talk by **Mrs George Stephens** the Evangelists wife. That morning a **Mrs Coval** of Indianapolis Ind., who was formerly **Miss Laura Nixon** of N.C. had Phoned down to Blair's from the Sheraton Hotel at High Point for some one to bring her down there so **Elva Blair** went up and brought her and took her with us to meeting, she made some very appropriate remarks in the meeting. We had splendid Music by the Choir, and also a lovely Hymn by several young men who had been attending the Tabernacle meeting.

She **(Mrs. Coval)** and myself both returned to Blairs after meeting, and in the afternoon **Walter Blair** of Greensboro came and brought his Mother **Rachel Blair** there, she had been visiting him and family for five weeks and wished to stop over a few days or perhaps a week with her Neices, so we all had a very interesting visit together. I was very thankful for the opportunity of visiting my dear husbands grave at Springfield after meeting for it is so seldom I get to visit it, and as I have often remarked it is now the dearest spot on Earth to me, oh how I pray to meet him in the Glory land.

Monday Nov the 2nd 1925

This afternoon I visited at **Wm Churches** had a good visit with his **"Grandma Church"** and daughter, and felt constrained to read a chapter and offer prayer which I did in my poor simple way as I had done in other of the homes I visited and am trying hard to be more faithful to do my duty, as I have been made to realise the dear Lord would have me do. Tuesday a.m.

Nov the 3rd 1925

Cousin **Rachel Blair** and myself are still at the Blair Dairy, this day we were both invited to spend the day with **Miss Emma King** which we did most pleasantly, **Annabella** was Teaching so was only home for Lunch and their Mother was visiting friends in Beaufort, N.C. so we of course did not get to see her, but **Emma** was equal to the occasion, so we had a great time. **Elva** went in the p.m. and brought **Mrs. Coval** there from the Hotel again, and at three oclock we all took Tea togeather, then **Elva** took us all out for a drive over Town and out by the Country club etc. Then that same night **Clara Cox, Dara Richardson** and others met at the Blair Dairy and organised a Bible Class which is to be kept up once each week at that place, this was very much enjoyed by all.

Wednesday Nov the 4th 1925

this morning **Elva** brought me to cousin **Fannie Englishes** at Archdale had a good time with her, then evening **Elva** came and took me over to her son **Murly Englishes,** they had just buried their little four months old son about two weeks before, I staid with them until Thursday afternoon, then **Rettie English** took me to **Ginnie May Englishes** and I remained with them very unexpectedly for two nights but had a good time at Professers with **Venie** and **Ginnie May,** then her son **Tom** took me Saturday morning back over to cousin **Fannie Englishes** as she was not satisfied that I had not staid a night with her, so I spent the time pleasently there again, she now lives in the home of her youngest daughter **Amos Kerseys** widow who has a neat and comfortable home in Archdale. Then Sunday morning **Tom English** came for me and took me to meeting at Archdale, a very interesting occasion and from there cousin **Ed** and **Anna Blair** took me home with them for dinner and in the evening took me back to **Jerome Peaces** from whence I had started out and enjoyed such a very pleasent visit among relatives and friends, and I feel like ascribeing all honor and praise to Him from whom all blessings flow, that He put it into the hearts and minds of so many to treat me so kindly, especially dear **Elva Blairs** kind favors will ever be remembered with a grateful heart, for she conveyed me so much from place to place in her comfortable Car.

1926

March the 13th 1926

This being my 81st birthday I feel like giving thanks to my kind and merciful Heavenly Father for his goodness to me all the days of my pilgramige so far and I know he will ever be my stay and my staff as I look to Him for comfort and strength, for he is ever ready to comfort those who are cast down, and I feel humbled today under a sense of my unworthyness of the many favors bestowed upon me, not only by my blessed Redeemer who is ever ready to speak peace to my soul, but also to those in whos hearts He puts the law of kindness to do for me that which I can not do for myself, and my hearts desire is that he will abundantly bless all those who are my helpers. I am now in the home of my dear daughter **May (Mrs. J.W. Peace)** and she is kindly remembering me by making my favorite birthday cake, and other nice things. She had planed to have **Grandma Peace,** cousin **Rachel Blair,** and cousin **Roxie Hill** brought over to spend the day with me, but it was so cold and windy and snowing as we have not seen it snow so fast for several years, so her plans could not be caried out. I sure would been glad to of had company of those dear aged ones but I could not on account of the weather. I gave it up cheerfully and spent the day contentedly by a good fire and was thankful for the privilege for I had suffered so much when down with the Gripp that it was a treat to me to be able to be up and sit by the fire and read. I have not been able to get out at all since the new year came in, so I greatly miss getting out to Sunday School, Church, prayer meeting etc. but feel that I have a great deal to be thankful for, as we can enjoy the presence of our gracious Redeemer in our own hearts and homes, when it is so we can not present ourselves at the place appointed for worship. And I was kindly remembered by my dear children and grandchildren and others by lovely birthday cards of greeting and also by a nice box of confectionery from my dear **Maggie Moffitt** of Kansas City Mo. all these things I appreciate with my whole heart, and ask Gods richest blessing may rest upon all my dear children and upon every member of their households from the oldest to the youngest inclusive. And may we all so live in love to God and good will to all our fellow beings thruout the remainder of the journey here, that we may all be reunited in the better land is my prayer for Jesus sake.

March the 23rd 1926

This being the sixth anniversary of the last time I looked upon the form of my precious husband I am feeling sad indeed, as this day six years ago he was laid to rest in the cemetary at dear old Springfield he passed away March 21st 1920. And was consigned to the grave on the 23rd which this day brings the memory of trying days and the loneliness that I have endured all these years, so fresh to my mind that I can not refrain from pening down a few lines. For it seems almost

March 1926

like a rehersal of those sad days to me, for I seem to see so plain the precious remains of the one that was so dear to me, and that being the last chance for me to see even his lifeless form. And although it is six years ago to day since he was laid away, it seems in one sense as tho it was but yesterday and in another as if a half century had passed, for I have missed him so much all those years. It seems so natural to mourn the loss of loved ones that in the weakness of the flesh we can not overcome these things at all times. But I often think we do an injustice to our loveing Heavenly Father by leting these things grieve us overmuch, for he is the all wise being who sees the end from the beginning, and makes no mistakes as we poor weak mortals do, but does that which is best both for those he calls away, and those of us who are left to fight earths battles a while longer until our work is finished. So I greatly crave to be kept from murmering or repining at my loneliness on account of loved ones gone from us, but to be kept in perfect submishion to the will of Him who seeth not as man seeth and who is watching over and careing for those that are left behind and as we are faithful to perform whatever duty he assigns to us he will be with us to strengthen and help us to endure whatever comes to our lot. And the greatest desire of my heart is to be so conformed to the will of our divine Lord and Master that he may have full possession of my heart and make it a fit recepticle for his holy presence that I may be purified and made a fit subject for the Masters use, and not only for myself do I crave this but for all my loved ones, that we may all be permited to enter those mantions prepared for all those who love and serve Him on earth.

As I have just been writing in my Diary concerning my 81st birthday spent here in Randolph Co N.C. at my daughter **Mrs. J.W. Peaces** it calls to mind my 80th anniversary which was spent in the home of my son **Fred C. Blair** in Charlotte N.C. which I will give a little version of after stateing a few other facts as they occured previous to this time. That I had taken note of. I had spent the winter and spring of 1923 and 4 in Charlotte with my son and his family during my sojourn, there was a Bible Class organised in my name, and I was blessed to attend it the greater part of the time, as **Mrs Clyde Neely** a very kind and generous lady would come in her nice Closed Car and take me to the different homes where the Class was held, so I shall ever remember her with the greatest affection while memory last for she was so kind and nice to me every way. In order that I may be better understood I will insert that during these past few years of which I am now writing I was staying at my sons in Charlotte in winter and spending my summers in the country with my daughter changeing places in the spring and fall.

So on Nov the 16th 1924 I returned to Charlotte again and Thursday Jan the 29th 1925 I wrote thus.

This has been a very dull rainey winter so much so that I have been deprived of going to Church or attending Bible Class, this is the day of the week on which it is held (Thursday) and to day it is held not far from where I reside, but as I am not able to walk but a short distance and the ground is covered with ice and a sprinkle of snow it is out of the question for me to be there, as I have no conveyance as my kind lady was not able to be out, but my prayer is that our blessed Lord may be with those who are permitted to attend and open up to them the Scriptures so that they may behold wonderous things out of Gods law, I have been meditateing upon the goodness and mercy of our lives and to whom belongeth all praise now and forever. And as the month of Jan is nearly out I am reminded fo the flight of time. And how necessary it is that we should be prepared for eternity.

March the 24th of 1925 Charlotte N.C. on account of an attac of "Flu"e and other hinderences I have not written anything for my Diary since January I was quite sick for several weeks and then the weather became so inclement that I have been deprived of getting out to Church or prayer meeting and Bible Class all the past winter. I have stated that there was a Bible Class organised here in my name in 1923. Called the Emily A. Blair Bible Class it was first organised with me in the home of my son **Fred C. Blair.** (it was a neighborhood

March 1926

Cottage prayer meeting as well). And **Mrs. U.C. Hollingsworth** and **Mrs Clyde Neely** were the efficient Teachers, but **Mrs Hollingsworth** continued faithfully to cary on the Class. It was held weekly on Thursday afternoon at three oclock but Friday March 13th 1925 being my 80th anniversary **Mrs. Hollingsworth** proposed to hold it with me on Friday that week. Accordingly the Emily A. Blair Bible Class was held Friday afternoon March 13th with its name sake, in the home of my son **Fred C. Blair** in Carolina Heights Charlotte N.C. in honor of my 80th birthday. The class responded loyally, there being many present, and was conducted by our faithful Teacher **Mr. U.C. Hollingsworth** who read and commented on the 11th chap of St. John, prayer being offered then they sang a portion of that lovely Hymn How Firm A Foundation. They also sang Blest be The Tie That Binds. Then just before closeing the meeting with prayer, **Mrs W.D. Rogers** rendered a beautiful Solo. The End of A Perfect day, playing the accompaniment on the Guitar. Then immediately after the services were closed my sons wife **Esther Hayden Blair** who had prepared Cake etc for the occasion served refreshments, one of the Cakes was ornimented with violets and hyacinths showing the outlines of the 80 years and also the date of birth 1845 in the iceing. All enjoyed the day immensely. On this occasion I wore my lovely grey all wool crape dress that I wore on the celebration of my Golden wedding. I received many nice and valuable presents.

    The dress I wore was a present to me from my oldest daughter **Margaret Ellen Moffitt** sent me from New Orleans LA for my Golden wedding, when she and her children resided there for a time after the death of her husband **Dougan C. Moffitt,** as one of her daughters and husband had previously gone to New Orleans, but later they all moved to Kansas City, MO. My 80th birthday was for me a day of both gladness and sadness for it brought the past so vividly to my mind for it seemed almost like rehearseing Golden wedding as I wore the same costume that I wore then and receiving presents, etc, but alas my precious companion was not with me as then, only in mind and heart, but I am so thankful that I have the blessed hope of meeting him in the Better Land. I feel that as I have now rounded our my four score years that the journey will not be many years longer at most. But if my dear Heavenly Father sees fit to lengthen our my days awhile longer my prayer is that he will use me in whatever way that will redown most to his honor and praise, for I want to glorify him on earth that I may glorify him forever in Heaven. But am waiting his own good time, when he sees fit to call me to His blessed abode.

March the 31st 1926

I am still in the home of my daughter **Mrs. J.W. Peace** haveing been here since the first of the year. This is the first time I have spent the winter here since I left my dear old home, for as I have before stated that I had been spending my winters in Charlotte and my summers here, but I did not return to my sons last fall as I had been doing, but after spending a month before Christmas with my cousins **John** and **Roxie Hill** at Progress N.C. I returned to my daughters. I was quite sick with Gripp for a few weeks but thru the mercy of kind Providence and the kind and efficient nurseing of my dear daughters I was again able to be up and about the house as usual and now as I meditate on the past the flight of time in forceibly brought to my mind for as this is the last day of March it hardly seems possible that three months have fled, for it seems but as yesterday that the year 1926 was ushered in and as the days go by, I am more and more concerned to be prepared for that better land, when done with time here. And in order to be prepared I am earnestly praying that I may be kept patient and submissive to the will of Him in whom we live and move and have our being. For although I have many trials and provocations which many times are hard to bear, as we are not all spirit and the flesh is weak, and unless we are constantly on our guard, we will become discouraged and feel like giving up trying to press on any farther but as we look to Him from whence cometh our help we are strengthened to preserve and thus overcome the many discouragements that come to us on our journey here below, so let us be close on our watch, for there is nothing that pleases the enemy of our souls peace more than to get us thoroughly despondent for that gives him the victory over us. I am so thankful that my kind and merciful Heavenly Father who knows all things knows that it is the fervent desire of my heart to be kept from the allurements of satan, for I do not want to listen to his cunning devices, for he would try to deceive if possible all those that put their trust in Jesus by making us believe that many things which he would dictate to us are no harm to indulge in. but if we listen attentively to the voice of concience that which our blessed Redeemer has put in our hearts to teach us, the way that leads to truth and happiness we shall be able by His divine help to overcome the temptations of the evil one.

April the 1st 1926

As this is the beginning of another month I realise that the month just past has brought us that much nearer our journeys end here on earth, and now my pleading is, Hear my prayer oh Lord and let my cry come unto thee for "I will lift up mine eyes unto the hills from whence cometh my help, my help cometh from the Lord that made Heaven and Earth." and my cry is unto thee oh Lord, for vain is the help of man. For when I look for a comforting word I find none only as thou speaks to me thru thy divine presence, or as thou puts it into the heart of some one or ones to speak a word of encouragement and good cheer to help me to keep pressing on, and thou knowest that I cry unto thee daily for help to serve thee in the way of thy requireings and to day whilst I am sorely tried with some of the problems that often confront us as we are passing thru this wilderness journey. And my pleading is unto thee my Heavenly Father that thou wilt help me to draw so nigh to thee, that thou wilt draw nigh to me, to keep me from getting despondent that the enemy may not have the victory over me. But that I may take fresh courage to press on by remembering my many blessings which the Lord has bestowed upon me thru all my pilgrimage journey up to this time, and who will fulfill His promice to be a present help in trouble, and will not suffer us to be tempted about that which we are able, but with the temptation also make way for our escape that we may be able to bear it.

April the 2nd 1926

I am very thankful to of had a quiest nights rest and to be able to arise from my bed this morning and go about the house and yard, and my prayer is that my merciful Heavenly Father will lead me this day and all succeeding days, as it were by his divine hand so that I may be kept in the path which he has cast up for those who have been redeemed by the precious blood of His dear son to walk in and that I may not err therefrom but follow him faithfully and this being Friday before Easter the day on which our Lord was crusified fills my heart with sadness as I reflect up the agony that our dear Saviour suffered for us poor sinful creatures, that we might be redeemed by his precious blood. Oh that I may not crusify him afresh by my disobedience to his divine commands.

April the 3rd 1926

As I meditate up the Word as laid down in the Gospel of St John 20 that I have just been reading it fills my heart with solemity, as I seem to see with the eye of my mind the agony of soul of the Mother of our blessed Saviour and others who had witnessed his suffering on "the Old Ruged Cross," and now greif of his Mother and followers as they were in suspense as he lies in the silent Tomb, not knowing that He would shortly come forth and be seen of them alive again. And I seem to see the consternation of Mary Magdalene when she went to the Tomb and found that her Lord had been taken away and she knew not where they had laid him. And as I reflect that all this suffering and death was for the redemption of all mankind, therefore it was for each one of us individually, and He rose again that all might have life thru his name for we learn from His holy written Word that whosoever will may come and partake of eternal life which was perchest for all, thru sheding His precious blood.

April the 4th Easter Sabbath

This is a day in which we should rejoice in realiseing as we read the Word, that God in his infinite goodness and mercy saw fit to send his dear Son into the world to die for the sins of the whole world, and rose again for our justification and redemption. And not only should we rejoice on this the day of the resarection of our dear Saviour but we should rejoice every day thruout all comeing days to us, that we have such a merciful Saviour and bless his holy name and do the things that are well pleasing in his sight. As I am not physically strong I did not feel able to present this poor mortal body at the place appointed for worship, but kind Father thou knowest I have endeavored to come to thee according to the ability which thou hast given me to worship thee in my own heart and I trust thou wilt hear and answer my poor simple prayers as it seemeth good to Thee for oh God thou knowest all things so I can say like Peter thou knowest that I love thee, help me to do thy will I ask for Jesus sake.

Amen

April the 5th 1926

Haveing been spared to see another day and having had a quiet nights rest in sleep also, I feel that I have much to thank my precious risen Lord for, and desireing to be kept entirely in obedience to His will, and in the language of the Hymn I am saying in my heart, "wash me cleanse me in the blood that flowed on Calvery." And as it is now evening as I write and have had the company of a kind friend in whom I confide I feel that it has been an inspiration to me to keep on praying and trust God for help each day.

April the 6th

This is a lovely spring day beautiful sunshine and so calm no blustering winds as we have been experiencing the past month. And my prayer is that I too may be kept calm and patient thru all the changeing scenes of life, and filled with love to God and good will to all my fellow cretures, obeying all the commandments laid down in his holy Word that I may be prepared to meet my loved ones where parting is unknown, there to sing everlasting praises to Him from whom all blessings flow.

April the 7th 1926

I have nothing of interest to take note of to day except the goodness and mercy of our blessed Lord who has watched over us all thru another night and given us rest in sleep, and strength to rise from our beds and go about our daily avocations and as I have been able to do a little work with my own hands to help some in the things which were necessary to be done. I feel very thankful to my kind Heavenly Father and praise his name for his many blessings to his dependent children.

April the 8th

I have been meditateing upon the wonders of Creation, as I have been reading in Gods word of creation of all things and especially of man in his own imige, and the things He has prepared for him, and for all things which he has created, and have said over and over in my mind how wonderful, wonderful, wonderful, are the works of Him who created and made all things. And my cry is unto thee oh God that thou would direct my steps so that I may walk aright and praise thy holy name for all thy benefits.

April the 9th 1926

This is a nice morning rather cool but pure fresh air which is congenial to health and as I do meditate upon the goodness, mercy and power of God who ruleth all things, my desire is unto him that he will cleanse my heart and make it pure as the fresh air which we breathe this morning, that it may be a pure recepticle for His holy presence to dwell in and help me to be so close on my watch that I do not say or do anything contrary to thy will. "Set thou a watch before my mouth keep the door of my lips that I sin not with my tongue." For thou who didn't give me life knows that I like Peter of old who loved thee, am naturally impulsive and quick spoken so as I pen my prayer thou knowest that I also love thee, and my desire is to be kept from the natural tendency to yeild to temptation when meeting with the many things that naturally try our patience beyond endurance, but for the help of Him "who was tempted in all points as we are yet without sin." Help me to follow in thy footsteps that I go not astray from thee, is my prayer for Jesus sake.

Sat. April the 10th 1926

This is a very cloudy damp morning which causes my aged frame to ache, but so thankful to be able to arise from my bed, and do a little something to help my dear daughter if it is only to do some mending which at times I could not do as my eyesight is failing so badly, and it is with much dificulty that I write from the same cause, which makes it so poorly done as to hardly be readable but feeling it required of me to do this, I am trusting in the Lord who is careing for his dependent children at all times, and I praise his name to day that I can claim to be one of his children unworthy as I feel myself to be, for thou knowest that I have given myself to thee many many years gone by and has made thyself so manifest to me that in my great affliction which I endured for so many years it seemed many times as if thy loveing arms were underneath to be bear me up. And "now when I am old and grey headed oh God forsake me not," and let my mouth be filled with the praise and with thy honor all the day, for I feel like repeating Davids prayer, "Cast me not off in the time of old age, forsake me not when my strength faileth."

Sunday April the 11th 1926

For the first time this year I was able to get out to Sunday School at Mt Vernon, and having been shut in all winter it seems good to go to the house of God which is dedicated to his service, and I praise his name for his goodness and mercy to me in granting me this privilige and that I may follow him closer each day is my earnest prayer for Jesus sake.

Monday April the 12th

I certainly thank my Heavenly Father that I am able to arise from my bed this damp morning for although the dampness causes more suffering in body I am so glad that I can wait on myself instead of being a burden in that way to others, and that I am still blessed with my thinking faculties so that my greatest desire is that I may not grieve the Holy Spirit by any disobedience to his commands for I acknowledge all my transgressions both of omission and commission and I know that Thou art ready and willing to forgive, for it is written in thy Word "they that come unto me I will in no wise cast out" and I come to thee day by day pleading that thou wilt help me to do thy will and praise thy Holy name.

Tuesday April the 13th 1926

As the mind sympathises with the infirmities of the body I am feeling very much depressed in spirit as I should faint by the way, as I am weak in body, but thankful to be up and able to read some this morning, and since reading of the bravery of **Dr** and **Mrs Gofarth** who are mishionaries to China I feel like takeing fresh courage to press on and not give up under physical weakness when it is possible to overcome it. **Mrs. Gofarth** was so physically weak that she was advised by her Physician to go to the Hospital for several weeks for rest, for since her return from China in July 1923 there had been almost continuous illness of so serious a nature that the previous week the Dr had said that an Operation had seemed imperative but she refused to allow it, but finally agreed to the Hospital treatment as a necessary alternative so feeling very frail and weak she was waiting to go and while siting waiting the telephone and the door bell both rang at the same time. **Mrs Gofarth** went to the telephone, **Dr Gofarth** to the door the phone call was from **Mrs Gofarth's** physician teling her that he could not get the room he desired for her just then and she would have to wait two or three days before coming. The door bell was rung by a messenger delivering to **Dr Gofarth** a cablegram from China. It had been sent by the Secretary of the Netherlands Legation upon the order of **General Liu Chin Ling** requesting that **Dr Gofarth** come immediately to China to assume the office of Chaplain in Peking in **General Feng's** army. As **Mrs Gofarth** was hanging up the receiver **Mr Gofarth** handed her the cablegram, what shall I say to this he asked her? You should say Praise God from whom all blessings flow but he argued that he could go and leave her when she was ill. You do not have to leave me she quietly replied I am going with you, and the next time her physician visited her she said Doctor I am not going to the Hospital I am going to China he told her he could not give her permission for her to go, but her faith was firmly fixed, and she said I am going with my husband to China and she did go. And I have felt that if that woman in her febleness could go thru the hardships there I should not give up because I am aged and feble but keep on trusting in the Lord for strength to do whatever he calls for my hands, for his promice is "as thy day thy strength shall be."

Wednesday April the 14th 1926

Being permited to see the light of another day I am praying that I may be kept so close to the Divine law giver, that I may not disobey any of his riteous laws in word or deed and that I may do something for the up-building of His kingdom in the hearts of those with whom I meet and mingle, for I do not want my life to of been spent in vain, but that I may so live that I may answer the end for which I was created which was to glorify God even if it is but little that I can do, I want to do that little to His honor and to his praise and thou knowest oh Heavenly Father that it is not for any merit of my own, that I have strained my weak nerves and eyesight as I have done from time to time thru those many years but for the sake of my dear children and grandchildren and other relatives and friends, should there be any interested enough to read what I have made an effort to write, whatever the dear Lord puts into my mind and heart for it is unto Him I look and ask each time what he would have me pen down so it is both for a warning to all to be close on their watch to resist evil, and for encouragement to press on in the right way, looking unto Him who has watched over and cared for me from my infancy until now, and as I have passed my four score years, I know I can trust him the remainder of the journey to help me to do his will here on earth tho I may praise him forever in Heaven.

Thursday April the 15th

I have much to be thankful for this morning that I have had a quiet nights rest in sleep and able to be about the house to day, for when I reflect on the many days, months, and even years when I was much younger than now. I could not even help myself from the bed or do anything in the way of helping do any kind of work, and now although feeling the weight of my more than four score years and failing eyesight, I can do some things to help others, and can still read and write, altho I make a very poor out at it, but still keep trying. To day I received a good letter from my dear relatives which gave me fresh courage to not give out by the way, and having been shown a kind favor to day by one who is very dear to my heart by the presentation of a little bouquet of flowers so much like thou my dear husband would bring me every spring it went home to my heart, for I miss his tender thoughtfulness more than I can express, and when anyone shows by any little act of kindness that coresponds to his many ways of makeing me happy, I appreciate it more than gold, and pray Gods blessing upon them. I have just been reading the 37th Psalm, Davids exortation to have patience and confidence in God, and the different estate of the Godly and the ungodly, and the 25th verse he says, "I have been young and now am old; yet have I not seen the righteous forsaken nor his seed begging bread." And as I think of the loved ones that are gone before who were righteous in their generation and have known by experience that their children have never begged for bread, I feel that there is no place for doubt of Gods goodness and mercy and faithfulness to His promises to those who obey him.

And in the same chapter 27th verse is the Text that is engraved on my dear companions Tomb Stone. "Mark the perfect man and behold the upright for the end of that man is peace." Oh that we may all follow on to know the Lord that we may all lay down our lives in peace is the fervent desire of my heart for Jesus sake.

Friday April the 16th 1926

Having heard this morning of the Death of **Mrs Nathan Robins**, whose sweet smile and kind hand shake I have appreciated so much when meeting her at Church at Mt Vernon and in her home I feel like I had lost a personal friend that will be greatly missed, and she being only a few years my seniour I realise that the time is not far distant at most when I shall be called to lay this earthly Armor down, and go to receive a Heavenly Crown if I have kept the faith unto the end, which I pray I may do, God being my helper.

"Oh for a heart to praise my God, a heart from sin set free, A heart that always feels the blood so freely shed for me."

Saturday April the 17th

I am so thankful that I have been blessed with strength this day to attend the Funeral of **Mrs. Robins** at Mt. Vernon which was largely attended and was presided over by the **Pastor Rev Reed Haris** and **Rev JEWoosley.** This was a most solemn day impressive occasion and the mention of her great devotion to her children, to the Church, and her Saviour was most beautiful, and which I greatly desire to emulate.

Sunday April the 18th 1926

This day calls for much thankfulness on my part, as I was able to attend Sunday School and Church **Prof Bivens** of Trinity conducted the class of the older people which was greatly enjoyed and the Presiding Elder **Rev Craven** of Greensboro preached a most wonderful and practical and inspireing sermon from the 4th Chapter of 1st Peter takeing his Text from the 5th chap and 8th verse Be sober etc, which was greatly appreciated. After Church **J.W. Peace** and wife **May** and **Mary Lee Stilwell** and myself visited **Mrs Joseph Sikes** who has taken into her home the little one week old motherless babe of **Mrs Walter Farlow.** We had a very interesting visit with **Mrs Sikes** who for the time at least has the little girl baby of **Mrs Edna Farlow** who passed away in a short time after its birth they have named it **Edna Clarice.** I feel that **Mrs Sikes** is doing a great work for the Lord in helping and careing for those in great need.

Monday April the 19th

Quite cool this morning but pretty sunshine and I am so thankful to be able to be up and pen down some of the incidents of the past two days.

Tuesday April the 20th

This morning it is quite cold for the time of year, but I am thankful to have a comfortable room, and to be able to use my hands and my thinking faculties and my greatest desire at this time is to fulfil the mishion for which my life has been spared, for we are put here on earth for a purpose, and if we are to expect a home with the blest when done with time here, we should strive with all our might God being our helper to do his holy will here that we may be counted worthy of an entrance in His Kingdom, where there is no more sorrow nor parting with loved ones, but we shall be happy togeather to sing our Saviours praise thruout eternity. This pm I was visited by Cousin **Anna Blair,** cousin **Elva Blair** and **Mrs Holman.** Had a very interesting visit with them, it does my heart good to meet with Christian friends who are interested in Church work, and I pray that we may all dedicate our lives to the work of the Lord in whatever capacity he calls us to fill. That we may by both example and precept, show to others that we are endeavoring to follow where the Master leadeth.

Wednesday April the 21st 1926

Still quite cool but a bright morning, and all nature seems to be putting forth into new life, so my hearts desire is that I may put forth a greater effort to grown in grace, and do the will of Him who created all things for his own glory.

Thursday April the 22nd

Today it is much warmer and the leaves on the trees and shrubs are growing fast, and my heart is still yearning for more grace to fulfil the divine command to love God with all my heart and mind and my neighbor as myself, I often wonder who of us does this. I freely acknowledge that I do not come up to it as I should, but pray daily that I may be kept closer on my watch to do what the Lord would have me to do his honor and praise, and that my heart may be kept clean so there may be no room for malice or any root of bitterness against any one.

Friday April the 23rd

A beautiful spring morning, all nature seems to be obeying the word of the Creator, oh that we who are accountable beings would be as faithful to do our Masters will in thing pertaining to our happiness and Gods glory.

Until We Sleep Our Last Sleep

Saturday April the 24th

As we look out upon nature and see the development of bud and flower, it creates in us a desire to follower closer to the Divine plan, examining ourselves lest we fall short of doing the things which we have been commanded to do in Gods holy word and by pening down from day to day o from time to time His tender watchful care over us we are kept closer on our watch lest we go astray, so my prayer this day is, dear Lord lead, guide and direct my steps so that I may follow thee aright.

Sunday April the 25th

A beautiful Sabbath morning, all the family here with one exception are gone to the Baptiseing by emersion at Glenold, and I am in my room alone meditating upon the goodness and mercy of God who has spared our lives unto this day, may we all keep this day holy as unto the Lord, for we shall have to give account of how we spend our time here. Oh that my heart may be filled so full of love to God and good will to my fellow beings, that there may be no room for anything that is contrary to the Divine will, is the desire of my heart. This afternoon I was able to go with the family to Sunday School at Mt Vernon. I love to go to the house of God to learn more of his word, and to do the little I am called upon to do, but to day I was so unexpectedly called upon by the Teacher **Mrs Ledwell** to offer prayer in the Class, before entering into the work of the class. If felt my unworthyness so much that it was rather embarising to me, but I endeavored to do my duty, but no sooner than I had finished the tempter came telling me that I made a very poor effort, for he is ever ready to discourage us when he sees that we are doing what the Lord calls us to do. Therefore knowing his devices I am trusting that my poor feeble effort will be accepted of Him who has bid us come to him in faith and he will answer, and knowing as He does that my simple petitions come from the heart, he does not require florishing words. So I feel like I can thank God and take courage.

Monday April the 26th

So much to be thankful for this morning that it is as well with as it is, may we all be kept on our watch that we do nothing which would grieve the Holy Spirit but endeavor in all earnestness to draw nigh to God that he may draw nigh to us, and thereby be enabled to overcome all the temptations of the enemy of our souls peace.

Tuesday April the 27th 1926

My hearts cry this morning is, Teach me thy way oh Lord lead me in a plain path that I go not astray from thee, for my greatest desire is to be found doing the things that are well pleasing in thy sight. Oh give me aboundtiful supply of thy grace to enable me to overcome all the temptations of evil one, for we are told in thy Word that "By grace ye are saved through faith in Christ Jesus." So in order to be saved we must have believeing faith, and ask him to fill us so full of His grace that we will not permit any root of bitterness to spring up in our hearts against anyone, not even those who have spoken very unadvisably against us.

Wednesday April the 28th

We are again reminded that we have no lease of our lives, as we know not the day nor the hour when we shall be called from works to rewards. We learn this morning of the funeral to day of my soninlaws uncle **Wiliam Peace,** familliar by know as (**Uncle Bill**) who is 83 years of age. It is said the aged must die, and the young do die so we realise that all ages are called from the infant to old age, so although we may be spared to a long life our time will come, so at whatever age we are called for, the important thing is to be ready for the change, therefore I pray with my whole heart that we may all make ready for the summons that our calling and election may be sure, so that we may enter into that rest prepared for the people of God.

Thursday April the 29th

Inasmuch as we of this household are all able to be up this morning to go about our daily avocations I feel that we have much to be thankful for, and my prayer is dear Lord keep us as it were in the hallow of thy divine hand, that we may be so close to thee, that we can feel thy presence and keep us from wandering off and disobeying thee in word and deed. I ask in Jesus name, Amen.

Friday April the 30th

As this is the last day of the month, I am reminded that we are another month nearer our journeys end, and the query arises what have I done during this time that will redown to my Makers praise or to the salvation of my own soul, or to the upbuilding of His kingdom in the hearts and minds of others. I plead forgiveness for all my mistakes and shortcomeings for they are many. Oh Father in Heaven accept my heart felt gratitude this morning for all thy mercies to me and mine and help each one of us to serve thee better thruout the remainder of the journey for Jesus sake.

May the 1st 1926

This is a beautiful May morning, all things in the vegetable kingdom seem to be obeying the injunction of Him who created all things and saw that they were good, and it behooves us who were created on purpose of His own glory, to be close on our watch lest we fall short of doing his holy will, and forfeit our right to a home in that beautiful land of the blest. Where we are so desireous to meet our loved ones gone before and those who will follow after, there to sing, praises togeather to Him who died for us that we might have eternal life with him.

"With my whole heart have I sought thee: O let me not wander from thy commandments. Thy word have I hid in mine heart that I might not sin against thee."

Sunday A.M. May the 2nd 1926

This beautiful Sabbath morning the birds are singing among the new green foliage on the trees, the sunshine is warming the earth to make the plants grow, everything seems to be takeing on new life. And the cry of my very soul is that He who rules the universe, would help me to grow in grace, and in favor with God and my fellow beings, for I want to be faithful to do my duty in all things to his honor and praise. This p.m. there was preaching at Mt Vernon at three oclock, I was favored to be able to attend which I greatly appreciated. The Pastor **Rev Reed Haris** was favored to give us a message from the fountain of all good, he gave us a splendid lesson from the second chapter of Exodus, which I hope will sink deep in all our hearts and cause us to reflect seriously on our condition and see if there is anything in our hearts that is contrary to the Divine will for I know that it is only as I look to Him for help and strength that I can endure the many trials and privations that I have to bear while travling thru this trancient life, for I miss my dearest earthly friend so much that it is only as I trust in Him who is a friend above all others that I can find rest and peace. So my prayer is come Lord Jesus and help me to overcome all temptations and obey thy holy will.

Monday May the 3rd 1926

This being my daughter **Mary Eliza Blair Stilwell Peace's** forty first Birthday I am again reminded of the flight of time, for it seems in a sense as but yesterday that she was a little child, and to think that she has since been twice married, and now has a little son about two and one half years old playing around her door, as my little **("May")** did in our dear old home hardly seems possible. But such are the changes in this life. But there is much to be thankful for to our merciful Heavenly Father for his many blessings to us.

Tuesday May the 4th

This is quite a cool morning for May, but all things are ordered by the all wise being, and as I listen to the gentle wind blowing I am reminded of the Text, "The wind bloweth where it listeth and thou canst hear the sound thereof, but cannot tell from whence it cometh or whither it goeth, so is every one that is born of the spirit." So we realise that we can not understand the misteries of Him in whom we live and move and have our being but we believe that He <u>is</u> and that he is a rewarder of all those who diligently seek him. So I am thankful that I am takeing him at his word and trying to obey his holy will by his help, and leaveing the results to Him.

Wednesday May the 5th

As we are spared from day to day we realise that God is so good and merciful to us all, blessed be his holy name. and oh may we not crucify his dear Son afresh by disobedience to his commands, but be ever ready to follow it his call. altho we are often led in misterious ways, like "Abraham going out not knowing whither he went, but we find that he received a blessing by obedience, so will we if we are faithful.

Thursday May the 6th

I feel very grateful for having had a quiet nights rest in sleep, and protection from all harm, for how often do we hear or read of people having to hasten from their beds into the chilly night air in their night clothes with no protection from wind or storm of rain or snow, to save themselves from the raviges of fire, and besides the exposure of themselves, to have to witness the destruction of their property which they have labored hard and long to procure, so we have much to be thankful for that it is as well with us as it is.

Friday A.M. May the 7th 1926

This morning I have enjoyed a ride in the fresh air, with my daughter and her little son, out to Progress to cousin **Ed Blair's** Store. It seems so refreshing to get out a little after being housed up so much. I feel like giving thanks to our merciful Heavenly Father for his goodness to me and to mine. and having had the privilege of attending the Prayer meeting last night at Mt Vernon for the first time this year, I feel very grateful indeed that I was able to attend, we had a very interesting and helpful meeting, there being many prayers offered, and testimonies from all down to the little children, which was very touching and encourageing to see so many of the young people and children takeing their stand for Christ, was an inspiration to us older people who have journeyed this for, at least I can say for myself that it caused a great desire in my heart to be faithful and be a living example of truth and righteousness, and thus be a steping stone toward Heaven for the younger people instead of being a stumbling block. Lord help me to do my whole duty is my prayer for Jesus sake.

Saturday AM May the 8th 1926

This beautiful morning my heart is lifted up in addoration to Him from whom all blessings flow. and as I hear the sound of music in the Parlor as one of the daughters in this home is playing the Organ, it makes it seem to me like I can hear those dear ones that are gone before playing on their golden Harps singing praises to Him who prepared that glorious home for them, that gave them an abundant entrance into it, there to praise him thruout all eternity. oh that I may be prepared to join them in that beautiful land is my earnest prayer, for Jesus sake.

Sunday AM May the 9th

Thankful that all are able to arise from our beds after having a refreshing sleep, and prepare for the events of the day. This pm I was able to go with the family to Sunday School at Mt Vernon, and after school we went to hear the anual commencement sermon at Trinity by the **Rev J.W. More** from Winston Salem. he gave us a very interesting and practical sermon which seemed to be very much appreciated by the large audience. I feel that I cannot be thankful enough for this days blessings, for I so love to go to hear the Gospel preached and as I have been deprived so much from attendance at Church on account of my afflictions for many years, it is a treat to be so I can get out altho I am not strong, yet I am so thankful to have strength sufficient to attend worship, some of my time.

Monday A.M. May the 10th

This pretty morning I feel like giving thanks to the great Giver of all good that it is as well with us all as it is, for while we so often hear of sad accidents, we have so far escaped and have gone to and from Church yesterday safely, and then had a quiet nights rest in sleep, and able to day to go about our daily avocations praised be the name of the Lord.

Tues May the 11th

This is a cloudy damp morning, which causes me to have more bodily pains and aches, but, my heart aches as is sorely burdened as I reflect upon the sin and folly that is going on in the world to day, which is worse than bodily aches and pains. It does seem that the time is nearing when Gods judgements will be sent to destroy the wickedness on earth, unless a sincere repentance and a turning therefrom, for He bore long with the people before the flood, but as they would not repent, and turn from their sinful ways, he sent the flood and destroyed them, and as we have the promice that it shall not be so done by water any more, we are standing on His promice, but it is also stated in his word that fire shall consume the wicked, and that God is not only a God of mercy but also of vengeance, for the saith "vengeance is mine I will repay saith the Lord." so I pray thee our gracious Redeemer that thou wouldst touch the hearts of the people of our nation that they turn from their wicknedness and folly before it is forever too late. and that we may all individually cease to do evil and learn to do good, that we may be accepted of Him who what bought us with his precious blood.

Wednesday May the 12th 1926

Still cloudy but only a sprinkle of rain. the farmers are troubled over not having a suffiency of rain, and fear there will be a drought like last year. I cannot help feeling that if farmers would leave off raising Tobacco and turn their attention to raising grain we would have rain when needed. for we are promiced in Gods word, seed time and harvest. and I believe if the same interest and care was taken to fertalise and prepare the soil for <u>grain</u> that there is to raise that which is not fit for food for man or beast, we would be blessed with good seasons for if man does his part God will give the increase. I state this from my own convictions, for I am standing on the promices to "Trust in the Lord and do good, and thou shalt dwell in the land and verily thou shalt be fed."

Thursday May the 13th

As I hear the little cheerful birds singing in the branches of the trees, I feel like praiseing the Creator of all things, that he has given us the birds to cheer us on our way. for we are so often filled with sadness on account of the many trying things we have to contend with in this life that it is hard to be cheerful at all times. but as we meditate upon the goodness of God for beautifying this world with the various kinds of flowers and nice things to enjoy, we are more able to bear our trials, and our hearts are filled more and more with praise to Him who created all things, on purpose of his own glory. so may we praise him with all our heart and mind. and to our fellow beings be true, just, and kind. is the desire of my heart.

Friday May the 14th

A pleasant morning as we had a refreshing show last night, for which I hope we are all thankful, for it was needed, likewise we need showers of grace to fill our hearts with love to God and good will to our fellow beings. "Behold how good and pleasent it is for brethren to dwell togeather in unity." then let us all shun discord that we may feel pleasent at all times is my prayer.

Saturday evening May the 15th 1926

This day the quarterly meeting of the Methodist Church was held at Mt Vernon, it was not largely attended but reasonable number of attentive listeners to one of the best sermons I think I ever listened to by **Rev -Kirk** of Greensboro, N.C. The sermon was greatly enjoyed by all interested persons, and the weather was very pleasent thru the day, and soon after we reached home there came a good shower of rain which was much appreciated for the vegetables were needing rain, and planters needed rain to moisten the soil, so we have much to be thankful for that it is as well with us all as it is. and I am rejoiceing in God my Saviour who gives us the sunshine and the rain and all that we have to enjoy. Blessed be His holy name.

Sunday a.m. May the 16th

A lovely Sabbath morning and my prayer is Lord help us to keep this day holy unto thee. we expect to attend the S.S. as usual and the further services of the quarterly meeting, this p.m. Later we attended S.S. and a meeting of the Epworth League, and also the Laymens meeting, all was very interesting and large attendance. It was my first oppertunity to attend either of those meetings, and I enjoyed them to the full.

Monday a.m. May the 17th

As we have been spared to see another day with its sunshine and flowers, I am again reminded of our blessed Saviours goodness and mercy to his dependent children yes we are entirely dependent upon him for every pulse we beat, and we know he has the power to clip the brittle thread of life at any moment of time, so it behooves us to be close on our watch least we loiter on our way and neglect the preperation necessary to receive a welcome into that home that is prepared for the children of God. and oh what a privilige to be one of Gods children and as unworthy as we are of his mercy to us we know it is our own fault if we do not claim to be his children for he has made it possible for us to do so, and if his children then heirs and joint heairs with His blessed Son. oh that we may all by entire obedience to his holy will be able to inherit that glorious promice given us in this Word.

Tuesday a.m. May the 18th

As I am able to arise from my bed this pretty morning I feel like saying with the Psalmist, "oh give thanks unto the Lord for he is good because his mercy endureth forever." The Lord is on my side, I will not fear: what can man do unto me?

Wednesday May the 19th 1926

I am so glad that I again this morning feel like lifting up my heart in thanksgiving and praise to Him who has watched over us another night and given us quiet rest in sleep, and suffered no harm to come to us, blessed be His holy name.

Thursday May the 20th

The weather is quite cool this morning and cloudy, but I am praying in my heart not to conform to the gloom of the weather, but to be transformed into a bright and cheerful spirit, so that I may be able to overcome all the trials that come to me wherever my lot is cast, in a meek and quiet spirit, to the praise and honor of Him who hath said "blessed are the meek for they shall inherit the earth."

Friday May the 21st

A nice cool but sunshiney morning, and I am comforted with the thought that All seeing eye has watched over us thru the night and kept us safe from all harm, and I feel like saying with David, "The Lord is my light and my salvation who shall I fear, the Lord is the strength of my life of whom shall I be afraid." Psalm 27 this Psalm has been a great consolation to me, as well as many others which help me to have full confidence in Gods word, for when I have cried unto the Lord, in his mercy and goodness he has answered me, for in time of trouble he has hiden me as it were from those that would harm me by putting all the discouragements possible in my way, and if it was not for my crying daily unto my gracious helper, "Teach me thy way oh Lord and lead me in a plain path because of mine enemies," I should faint by the way. but I know that He hears my poor simple prayers and answers them as he sees best, for he is no respector of persons and will hear the most lowly as they come to him in true believing faith, and he knows I have endeavored to do this by his help, for of ourselves we can do nothing.

Saturday May the 22nd

In reading and studying the Sunday School leson in regard to the characters of Abraham, Isaac, and Jacob we follow Gods dealings with the faithful, and how he makes good his promices, bearing with them thru all the sad mistakes that they made in not exerciseing their faith at all times as they should. which shows that they were human just as we are and when tempted they did not stand firm and trust God to take care of the situation, and we see what trouble they brought upon themselves, and but for Gods faithfulness in his promices they would have been undone, just so with us he overlooks our mistakes as we go to Him for forgiveness, and mend our ways.

Sunday May the 23rd 1926

As we are spared to see another Sabbath day we have much to be thankful for, and my hearts desire is that we may keep this day holy, as we have been enjoined in the holy scriptures to do, and we should also remember that it is not only our duty and also our blessed privilige to keep the Sabbath day sacred, but we should keep every day in the week in a manner that will redown to the praise and honor of His holy name, is my prayer.

Monday a.m. May the 24th

While some of the family here are busily engaged planting and tending flowers etc. I am reminded that it is their part to put the seeds and plants into the ground, but that they will have to look to thee our Heavenly Father for the germination and growth for thou alone hath the power of life, and as we look to thee for our beautiful flowers and for our crops of grain, vegetables, fruits etc, so we look to Thee for our spiritual food to nourish and strengthen us to grow in grace and in favor with God and man. and as we behold the beauty and loveliness of the flowers etc, we are made to realise that it is only as we have the sunshine of Gods love in our hearts that our fellow beings can see that we are growing in grace and endevoring to do according to his commandments and that we are looked upon as being plants of Gods own tending, keeping out the nocious weeds of contempt, hatred and strife, so may we fulfil his word, and thus be made plants fit for the Masters use.

Tuesday May the 25th

A very busy day, overhauling and looking after things which need attention in the way of makeing them more sanitary by sunshine and fresh air ready to be stored away for future use when the cold season rolls around again. and oh how necessary that we should examine ourselves and see that we are cleansed and purified not only by the sunshine of Gods love and mercy, but by his touching our lips as it were with a live coal from off his holy alter that we may be of clean lips and pure hearts ready for the gathering into His kingdom of those who have been faithful to do his biding on earth, so that we may be forever with him, in that home where neither moth nor rust doth corrupt nor theives break through nor steal, and where they that have had their robes washed and made white in the blood of the

Lamb are forever praiseing him who has bought them with His own precious blood.

Wednesday May the 26th 1926

Being sorely tried with some of the problems which often confront us in this life, I am earnestly praying to be kept calm, and not say or do anything which I should regret on delibertly meditateing on these things, and I drop this caution to my children or any one whose eyes may chance to fall on these lines, to always be close on the watch lest the enemy of our souls peace take advantage of our weakness in our tried moments, and thus cause us to transgress the Divine law of forbearance and loveing kindness toward those to whom we should "turn the other cheek" instead of avenging ourselves, dear Lord help me to practice what I am preaching in my prayer for Jesus sake.

Thursday May the 27th

A lovely cool morning, but we are needing rain badly and I am earnestly praying, and I trust many others are, that if it is the will of Him who has power over the clouds and all things that he will give us rain in due season, but in order that our prayers may be heard and answered we must fulfil the conditions laid down in Gods holy word, for we are told that "If we regard iniquity in our hearts God will not hear us." so let us refrain from evil that we may receive his blessings, oh for more obedience on our part, and more faith in Him who fulfils all his promices, and more faith in prayer, for in the evening the same day we were blessed with a good refreshing shower to moisten the dry earth and revive the vegetation etc for which I feel very grateful indeed to Him from whom all our help cometh, and I am saying in the very depths of my soul the words of scripture "not unto us oh Lord, not unto us but unto thy name give glory for thy mercy and thy truths sake." for it is not of any merit of our own that our prayers are heard, but only of the goodness and mercy of our blessed Saviour who hears the ravens when they cry and he satesfies

May 1926

them from his bountiful hand, and that not a sparow falls to the ground without his notice, and that we are of more value than many sparows. so it certainly behooves us to be filled with thanksgiving and praise for his wonderful manifestation of his divine goodness and power in sending the much needed refreshing showers to us who are so unworthy of his gracious love and care. Oh for more and more of His holy spirit each day. That I may be kept in the strait and narow way. Is my prayer.

Friday May the 28th 1926

In looking out this morning upon the thing of nature and seeing them revived after the refreshing showers of the previous evening, and the air so pleasent, and after having a good nights rest in sleep, I feel that I have much to be thankful for, and feel like takeing fresh courage to press on the remainder of the journey, looking to the blessed Master to be my guide and leader.

Saturday May the 29th

This morning as I prepare to write a few notes, the words of the Hymn, "Father I strech my hands to thee no other help I know, If thou withdraw thyself from me ah whither shall I go" comes to me with such force and earnestness that I cannot refrain from pening them down. yes indeed I feel that if the hand if my Heavenly Father was not extended to help me in all my helplessness where should I look for help and comfort, for none other will have the compasion for me that thou hast, for vain is the help of man. therefore I am looking to thee our Father for saveing grace here on earth and for an everlasting home with thee in Heaven, when done with this fleeting life, Thou being my Redeemer.

Sunday a.m. May the 30th

This lovely Sabbath morning as I hear the little birds singing among the branches of the trees which seem to say cheer up, cheer up I am trying to be cheerful too and praise the great giver of all things for His goodness to us his unworthy children, but to realise that I am one of his children although so unworthy and insignificant as I feel myself to be is worth all else beside to me, and in my spirit I cry "oh for a heart to praise my God, a heart from sin set free, a heart that always feels the blood so freely shed for me." This is the greatest desire of my heart, that I may be obedient to his will, and daily be filled with His love and praise for this means much more to me, than any earthly treasure.

Monday a.m. May the 31st

This being the last day of the month it reminds me again how fast time is passing away, for it seems but as yesterday that I dated May the 1st instead of the 31st and I am desireing to make the very best use of time as it flies, for we know not the day nor the hour when we shall be called to give account of the deeds done in the body, and I am sure we all want to enter the home of the blessed. so dear Lord help us to do thy will in all things to thy names honor and praise, that we may be permited to enter into rest, is my prayer for Jesus sake.

Tuesday June the 1st 1926

My heart is filled with thankfulness this morning for the good rain sent us last evening and night for it is such a blessing to moisten the dry ground to make the crops flourish, for they soon would of withered and we should been deprived of those things which we need for the sustanance of these perishable bodies. so our hearts should be filled with thanksgiving and praise to His holy name for these blessings and for all that we receive from his bountiful hand both temporal and spiritual, for he is faithful to come to our help in every time of need. I had been feeling very much discouraged for several days passed and felt the need of some kind friend to give me a word of good cheer, so last evening to my great delight I was blessed with company of our Pastor dear **Clara I Cox** of High Point. she is Pastor for both Archdale and Springfield meetings, my membership is at Springfield Friends Church and she visits me in Christian love whenever she can, and I feel shure that the dear Lord sent her to me, for I was feeling very much depressed, and almost ready to faint by the way, but the promices of our blessed Saviour never fails and he comes to those who trust him, with help in time of need.

Wednesday June the 2nd

To day I have a very bad headache so that I am not able to insert anything in my Diary as usual, but am trusting the dear Lord to me to bear all my pain.

Thursday June the 3rd

As I have still continued to suffer with my head, and am so weak and nervous, that I have had to keep to my bed the most of the day, but thankful to be with my daughter who cares for me, when I am not able to care for myself, and I pray that she may be blessed an hundred fold for all she does for me, for "blessed are the merciful, for they shall obtain mercy."

Friday June the 4th

Still weak and scarely able to arise from my bed, but can be up most of the day, for which I am very grateful to the Great giver of all good; for His watchful care over us all.

Saturday June the 5th 1926

My heart is sad indeed as I just received a message that my dear cousin **Joshua Anderson** is to be buried to day at Springfield, I regret so much not to be there, but as the foregoing will show I have been very much indisposed this week, so it was thought best for me not to undertake to go. There is now but one member of that large family left, his sister dear cousin **Rachel Blair** and she is getting quite feeble. May the Lord help her to bear her bereavement is my prayer.

Sunday June the 6th 1926

I am very thankful to have been able to attend, Sunday School and Church to day, heard a splendid sermon by **Rev Reed Haris** the Pastor; on the Ten Commandments, which I greatly enjoyed, then after services I went to see my dear cousin **Rachel Blair** whose brother as I have stated was buried Saturday. I felt it my duty to go to see her, and try to comfort her in her bereavement. I also met her soninlaw **Rev Olin P Ader** and his two youngest daughters, and others who were visiting in this home. I remained with them over night, had a very interesting visit every way, at night in the family devotions **Rev O.P. Ader** offered a most excelent prayer, after he had sang a lovely Hymn, which was quite an inspiration to us all.

Monday a.m. June the 7th

Still in the home of cousin **R.L.M.Blair** and his mother, spent a pleasent day, and very unexpectedly staid over night with them again and had a good time.

Tuesday June the 8th

This a.m. I left this pleasent home and went and spent the day with cousin **John** and **Roxie Hill**, had a fine visit with them, then in the evening returned to the home of my daughter **Mrs. J.W. Peace.**

Wednesday June the 9th

To day we are again reminded of the uncertainty of life and the certainty of death, I was favored to have strength to attend the funeral of the eleven year old son of **Benjamin Hill** who was buried at Springfield this afternoon, he is another one of my kindred passed away, he was taken with Meningitis and only lived about forty eight hours, he was a grandson of **Sidney T Hill** who is a first cousin of mine. How often we are reminded that there is but a step between us and death, let us "therefore be ready, for in such an hour as ye think not the son of man cometh."

Thursday June the 10th

I feel very thankful to be so I can do a little work to day for there has been so much of my time for many years that I could not even wait on myself, but I have been so wonderfully favored for the past few years, that I could do quite a bit to help on in the domestic affairs of life, and able to get out to Sunday School and Church, so although I am aged and not strong, I am very grateful that it is as well with me as it is. to God be the praise.

Friday June the 11th 1926

This morning I feel like ascribing all praise and honor to Him from whom all blessings flow, for his goodness to us all, I was favored to accompany my daughter and others to the weekly prayer meeting at Mt Vernon Church last night, which was an inspiration to me to see so many both old and middle aged and so many dear young people and children, stand up for the Lord and testify to his goodness to them and ask for the prayers of the people that they may live for Jesus.

Saturday June the 12th

This beautiful morning I feel very thankful to be so I can be up and go about my daily associations and have my eyesight sufficient to read my Bible and study the Sunday School lesson, the praise belongeth to Him in whom we live and have our being, now and forever.

Sunday June the 13th

As we are favored to see another Sabbath I realise that we are that much nearer our journeys end than we were a week ago, and may we realise that we are accountable beings, and will have to answer for the deeds done in the body, therefore let us be close on our watch that we sin not in word or deed.

Monday June the 14th 1926

Another beautiful morning, and as I was favored yesterday to attend Sabbath School, I feel that I have much to be thankful for that it is as well with us all as it is. and to realise that we are watched over by that all seeing eye that sees even the sparrows and not one of them falls to the ground with His notice. yes, "His eye is on the sparrow, and I know he watches me."

Tuesday June the 15th

To the great Giver of all good do I lift up my heart in grateful praise that I am able again this morning to arise from my bed, and that I have the use of my hands and my thinking faculties sufficient to do that which my hands find to do. Praise the Lord for his goodness and mercy to his unworthy child, oh what a privilige to realise that we are a child of God, for if we are not it is our own fault for He has said in his word, "They that will come unto me I will in no wise cast out," so we dishonor God by not takeing him at his word, and claim him as our Father although we are unworthy, yet we are his children by faith and obedience, to His divine commands.

Wednesday June the 16th 1926

This nice cool morning the fervent desire of my heart is that I may be so close on my watch this day that I may not say or do anything which would not be well pleasing in my makers sight, I am so thankful to day that my heart is filled with love to God and good will to my fellow beings, for we are commanded to "love even our enemies, those who despitefully use us, and say all manner of evil against us falsely for his names sake."so while it is trying to the flesh to have to bear these things, it is a consolation to know that if we bear them patiently, and pray the Father to forgive them as I have endeavored to do, I know that I shall reap a reward in the end, for we are told in His word, "Blessed are they that are persecuted for righteousness sake for theirs is the kingdom of Heaven." oh God help me to be faithful to end for Jesus sake.

Thursday June the 17th

The language of Scripture that comes to my mind this morning is, "Trust in the Lord and do good and thou shalt dwell in the land, and verily thou shalt be fed." What a gracious promice to us if we only will fulfil the conditions, to trust in the Lord and do good, I know that I sadly fail to fulfil the conditions as I should, but it is the greatest desire of my heart to be found trusting in the Lord implicitly and doing that which is well pleasing in his right, and my prayer is that I may daily observe the Golden Rule, to do unto others as we would have them do unto us, for in doing I should never be guilty of wounding the feelings of others, as I have been made to suffer, by the thoughtlessness of others to me. but I am thankful I can say Father forgive them, for Jesus sake.

Friday June the 18th

A very warm day and we are needing rain in order that the crops do not fail, but we should have faith to believe that the good Lord has not forgotten his dependent children, and that he will be ready to help in time of need, and even now while I write there is a little shower of rain beginning to fall, oh we are so unworthy of the many blessings that we receive from day to day, but our Heavenly Father is so merciful and kind to use as unworthy as we are, that he will condecend to listen to our cry as we come to him with our burdens for he had promiced to be our burden bearer, and He is true.

Saturday June the 19th 1926

This morning we again realise how merciful our great Redeemer is to us his unworthy children, for during the past night we have had lovely showers which have so refreshed all vegetation that everything seems to lift themselves up in hope. and I feel like adopting the language of scripture, "let the people praise thee, oh Lord let all the people praise thee." for the wonderful blessing which has been showered down upon us. I feel that we cannot praise thee enough for the nice gentle rain which came in due season, for thou sees and knows our needs, and knows what is best for us, for while many were murmuring because of the delay of rain, the good Lord was withholding it until the people could reap the grain that was already made, and then sent these refreshing showers to save our other grain and vegetables, "oh that men would praise the Lord for his wonderful works to the children of men." for He is worthy to be praised now and forever. "Blessed is every one that feareth the Lord that walketh in his ways, for thou shalt eat the labor of thine hands: happy shalt thou be, and it shall be well with thee."

Sunday June the 20th

We are still having a nice rain for which I feel very thankful. I shall not be able to get to Sunday School and preaching to day, but am very willing to stay in on account of the needed rain, I hope to keep the day holy left my lot be cast where it may, for we are commanded to keep the Sabbath day holy, and my desire is to be kept on my watch each day of the week that I do not transgress Gods holy law in word or deed, for the flesh is so weak that if we do not watch unto prayer and seek Gods guidance, we are so apt to be thrown off our guard and say or do something which we exceedingly regret on deliberate reflection, at least this has been my sad experience many times, as I am praying with all the fervency of my soul to be more faithful in the future that I may not transgress in word or deed.

Monday June the 21st

We are told in Gods word that "In the world ye shall have tribulation, but be of good cheer for I have overcome the world." oh how true I have found it, for I have gone thru such trials that it would be impossible to bear them if it was not for the help of the Great burden bearer, for I have been made to suffer both in mind and body by the unmerciful onslants of those who delight in trying my faith by thoughtless words and acts, for if we suffer in mind the body also suffers, likewise if our bodies is made to suffer our minds sympathise with them, so in this way I have been made to suffer beyond endurance until in my weakness of the flesh I have been angered like Moses at the rock so that I have spoken unadvisedly with my lips, which has caused me much sorrow of heart on reflecting on the vanity of so doing, but I am so glad that I have a great Mediator to whom I can confess my errors and find pardon, for if we are willing to confess our sins he is ready and willing to forgive our sins blessed be his holy name now and forever. I write these things acknowledging my weakness, that others may take warning to be close on their watch that they may not give way to the tempter who is ever ready to entrap us in our weakest moments, whom he seeks we are thrown off our guard.

Tuesday June the 22nd

A very bright day, and we have the bright prospect of having my little granddaughter **Mary A Blair** from Charlotte N.C. to visit us tomorrow, and as they have not visited us in over two years we are expecting a happy reunion, I hope we shall not be disappointed.

Wednesday June the 23rd 1926

I am very thankful that it is as well with us all this morning as what it is. and as is my daily plea, I come to thee my gracious Redeemer asking that thou will be my guide and direct my steps so that I walk aright, This evening I can now state that our company which were expecting came this p.m. and we have been enjoying ourselves to the full. "Behold how good and how pleasent it is for brethren to dwell togeather in unity."

Thursday June the 24th

Our company still with us, and we are having a good time. Praise God from whom all blessings flow, praise him all creatures here below.

Friday June the 25th 1926

A nice cool morning. Crops are growing fine since the blessing of a good rain. so we have much to be thankful for. The prayer meeting was held last night as usual at Mt Vernon Church, several of this family attended, and also my daughterinlaw went with them, they repart a good meeting. Praised be the name of the Lord.

Saturday June the 26th

We have still been blessed with the company of my little granddaughter and her mother, but the mother is now going to leave us for a few day to visit relatives and friendsi n High Point then return for a night before leaveing for her home in Charlotte.

Sunday June the 27th 1926

Again we are being favored with a nice gentel rain, which is such a blessing at this time that I can not refrain from pening it down, for it is one of Gods greatest blessings to man, for if it was not for the rain, and the sunshine, we could not have the increase of our fields for the sustanance of man and beast, so we cannot be thankful enough to our merciful Heavenly Father for all his benefits to his unworthy children.

Monday June the 28th 1926

I feel like saying what I shall I render unto thee my Heavenly caretaker who watches over us all from day to day, for I know that thou in thy goodness and mercy art careing for thy dependent ones at all times even when we are not aware of it.

Tuesday June the 29th

I am thankful this morning to realise that we have all been watched over again during the past night and given us rest in sleep, so we have much to praise our merciful Heavenly Father for, oh may we be obedient to his divine commands that we may inherit that blissful home above, where all is joy and peace and love, and where we can sing His praise togeather throut eternity, is my prayer.

Wednesday June the 30th 1926

As this is the last day of the month, I realise afresh the flight of time, and oh how necessary that we should be prepared for eternity, for we know not the day nor hour nor the moment when we may be called from works to rewards, our company took leave of us to day for their home in Charlotte. we shall miss them, but will hope to meet them, if not here again, in the better land where parting is unknown. is my prayer.

Thursday July the 1st 1926

This is a pleasent morning for the begining of July, and although feeling weak, I am thankful to be able to arise from my bed, but am being most sorely tried in spirit, but am praying for strength to bear all the trials that come to me from the assaults of those who are listening to the voice of satan who is well pleased when he can get people to serve him by saying and doing things that will discourage those who are trying to serve the Lord, and although I know that I do not obey him at all times as I should, yet I am so glad that He who knows all things knows, that I am trying with all my heart, soul, and strength to do His will, and that I may not render evil for evil, altho tried as it were passing thru fire and deep water, but I believe in Gods written word as true, and he says "when thou passest thru the waters they shall not overflow thee, and thru the fire it shall not kindle upon thee." so I am thankful to believe that He is watching over me and will make a way for me where I see no way as in the past, for I know he has taken care of me all those years, and will take care of me the rest of the journey, for He is no respector of persons.

Friday July 2nd 1926

In order that I may have my mind staid on the rock Christ Jesus more closely, I find it profitable to write down each day some thought of his goodness, and some of his marvelous deliverances from the many temptations and snares, which the enemy of our souls peace lays for to entrap me therein, so I feel that I cannot praise God enough that he watches over me daily, and helps me to bear up under my many sore trials thru which I have to pass, and causes me to rely more and more each day on Him who is ever ready to listen to the cry of his needy dependent children who put their trust in Him. oh that I may obey him more perfectly.

Saturday July 3rd

Unto thee oh Lord do I lift up my soul, for in thee alone do I find refuge and strength to bear the assaults of the enemy, who is going about daily as a roaring lion seeking whom he may devour. I am so glad that I have such a strong refuge whereunto I may flee from the storms and tempest which would overcome me if it were not for my hope and trust in the Lord. for vain is the help of man. so I come to Thee blessed Lamb of Calvery to hide me from the impending storms.

Sunday July the 4th 1926

I cannot call to mind when Independence day the fourth of July came on Sunday before to day, but I think I shall remember while memory last the solemn occasion I attended this fourth of July, that of the funeral at Mt Vernon of **Martha Elder** wife of **Haley Elder** one of the the largest funerals I ever attended at that place. and was conducted by the Pastor **Rev Reed Haris** and the **Rev JE Woosley,** and it so happened that **Haleys** brother **Neice Elder** was here on a visit from Virginia and attended the funeral. he leaves tomorrow the 5th for his home in Virginia.

Monday July the 5th

Yesterday July the fourth comeing on Sunday, people could not celebrate Independence day in the usual way, so to day many are enjoying a holliday being exempt from their work in the various occupations. oh that we all would be more thankful to the Giver of all good for the many priviliges we enjoy, bless His holy name, for his goodness and mercy to us all. **Miss Jewell Baker** is spending the day here with the young people, and they are having a nice time.

Tuesday July the 6th 1926

I feel so thankful this morning to my gracious Heavenly Father that it is as well with me as it is, for although I am not strong, I am glad to be so I can wait on myself for the most part, for there has been so many years in the past when I was much younger, that I could not do this.

Wednesday July 7th

"Teach me thy way oh Lord and lead me in a plain path," is the cry of my soul this morning, that I may know what is they will concerning me, for I delight to do thy will oh Lord. I know that thou seest me at all times, and knows that I often make mistakes as the flesh is weak, and I am so glad that thou knowest also that I do not transgress they law willingly, but it is by not being close enough on my guard at all times, that the tempter takes the advantage of my weakness, but I am so thankful that the One that knows all things, knows that my greatest desire is to be faithful to serve Him and not give way to the temptations of the enemy, so my prayer is that he will help me to be close on my watch, for the Scripture saith, "What I say unto you I say unto all." Watch so let us watch and pray.

Thursday July the 8th 1926

This is a very warm day, so much so as to be very oppresive, but thankful than none of use have been overcome by it. To night is the regular time for the prayer meeting at Mt Vernon, and my fervent desire is that there may be many gathered into the fold of Christ at those meetings, for they seem to have been owned and blessed of the Lord from the time they were first organised up to the present time, and have gained in numbers and interest, and I trust will continue to do. for there are yet many precious souls to either be saved or lost, and we know that our blessed Lord wills that none shall be lost but that all may come to him and be saved. Dear Heavenly Father keep us all so close on our watch that we may not sin against thee.

Friday July the 9th

"I will lift up mine eyes unto the hills from whence cometh my help, my help cometh from the Lord which made heaven and earth." I am so glad that I have such a helper, that I can look to in every needful time, for He has promiced to be with us not only in the sixth trouble but also in the seventh, and his promices are always fulfiled in his own good time.

Saturday July the 10th 1926

Another very warm day, but we have much to be thankful for that it is as well with us all as it is, so my heart is lifted up to Giver of all our blessings in praise and honor to His holy name.

Sunday July the 11th

Like as a father pittieth his children, so the Lord pittieth them that fear him, these lines came to me to day with almost the force of words and I have written them down, knowing that the dear Lord does pitty those that fear him, and is ever ready to help those that call upon his name, for there is no such thing as failure to keep what

He has promised, therefore I am trusting in His word, and am in constant fear of offending him, which causes me to be closer on my watch than I otherwise would be, for I do not want to offend Him in word or deed, neither do I want to offend any of my fellow beings, but I desire to be thoughtful of the feelings of others and not to wound them as I have been wounded by thoughtless and unkind words of those from whom I expected better things. so again my cry is, "Set thou a watch before my mouth, keep the door of my lips that I sin not with my tongue."

Monday July the 12th 1926

A nice cool morning. I am not feeling at all well, but thankful to be able to be up and have the use of my limbs so I can get about and wait on my self, praise the Lord for all his benefits to me and to mine, for He has brought us thru many trying seasons, and still blessing us more than we are worthy of, blessed be His holy name.

Tuesday July the 13th

We have been blessed with a wonderful good rain to day, which was beginning to be much needed so we have much to praise the Giver of all good for his mercy to his unworthy dependent children.

Wednesday July the 14th

Praise belongeth to thee oh God, therefore I will life up my heart in thanksgiving and praise to they most holy name this morning for thy goodness and mercy to us, in giving us quiet rest in sleep, and protection from all harm, oh keep us this day as in the hallow of they divine hand, that we go not astray from Thee.

Thursday July the 15th

We have again been blessed with a good rain which is so refreshing to the growing crops, vegetables, and flowers. so we have much to thank our merciful Heavenly Father for each day, for he knows we stand in need of at all times, and supplies all our real, let them be what they may. oh that we may be more obedient and thankful for all our blessings, is my fervent desire.

Friday July the 16th

"Trust in the Lord and do good, and thou shalt dwell in the land and verily thou shalt be fed." This is a promice which so often presents itself to my mind and my wish is to be found doing good in whatever way the Lord requires, then I shall realise that this promice is fulfiled from day to day, and I shall not lack food.

Saturday July the 17th

"Oh Lord our lord how excelent is thy name in all the earth." These words come to me as I look our upon the trees, the flowers, and everything lovely, and see how wonderful is the Creator of all things, for there is no one that can make even a blade of grass to grow, or tree to yeild fruit, but Him who in the begining created all things by the word of his mouth, for we are told that darkness covered the earth, and he spoke and said let there be light and there was light, and there was light. so we see that it is incumbent upon all things to obey His word. so help me dear Father to be more obedient to thy divine commands, I feel so unworthy of the care which thou hast had over me all these years, that I want to do whatever Thou calls for at my hands.

Sunday July the 18th 1926

Remember the Sabbath day to keep it holy. This injunction is upermost in my mind this morning and I trust we shall do our utmost to obey it. Now it is evening and I am thankful to state that I have had the privilige of attending Sunday School at Mt Vernon and also heard a most excelent talk by **Mr Woosley** son the **Rev Woosley** which I greatly enjoyed, and I think the congregation in general enjoyed it very much.

July 1926

Monday July 19th

My heart is filled with praise to the Giver of all good for his mercy to us all, for he has watched over us thru another night and given us rest in sleep, and suffered no harm to come to us, and now my prayer is that we may be so close on our watch thru this day, and thru all succedeing days, that we go not astray from the path of duty, and that we may be careful to obey The Golden Rule more implicitly.

Tuesday July 20th

We almost daily in contact with things of the world that are so allureing, that if we were not close on our watch we would conform to them, for the tempter takes advantage of our weakness, so it keeps me calling daily for strength to overcome the evil one, for the Lord hath said call upon me and I will answer thee, and so He does.

Wednesday July 21st

Bless the Lord oh my soul, who stoops to listen to my poor simple prayers.

Thursday July the 22nd

Praise the Lord for his goodness and mercy to us all.

Friday July the 23rd

I am meeting with disappointment, but oh Father keep me so close to thee, that I can lean on thee the great burden bearer.

Saturday July the 24th

For several days I have been deprived of my near glasses, so that I could only make out to jot down the day of the days as they have passed, and a brief word of prayer or praise. to Him from whom all blessings flow.

Sunday July the 25th 1926

This morning my prayer is Lord help me to keep this day holy according to thy commandments. And now in the evening of same day I feel like ascribeing all praise to Him from whom all our help cometh, for I have had the privilige and pleasure of attending the Township Sunday School convention at Mt Vernon, which was greatly appreciated. The Music and general exercises were fine, and I listened to two of as grand lectures as I ever heard, one by **S. L. Davis** of High Point on Palestine and his travels and observations in that land, and the other by **Rev Milo Hincle** of Friends Church of Greensboro on the importance of Bible Schools, both were fine. truly to me least, the most inspireing lectures I ever heard, and I am sure were enjoyed by the majority and altho it was a warm day, I was favored to have physical strength to hold out thru all the exercises of the day, which I regard as almost a mericle now in my eighty second year of age, after being a helpless invalid for many yearsk and I must not fail to mention the excelent Picnic dinner that was served at the noon hour and greatly enjoyed by all. And now as is so often the case in the one way or another in this life, this evening after a day of religious and social enjoyment, our hearts are sadened on learning of the death of one of my first cousins **Nancy Almina Hill Anderson**, widow of **Thomas E Anderson** who was a minister in Friends Church and he was also my first cousin. **Cousin "Nannie"** passed away this morning at six oclock in the home of one of her daughters at Rural Hall and was brought to High Point to the home of one of her children there and will be buried Tuesday the 27th at ten oclock at Springfield Guilford Co N.C.

Monday July the 26th 1926

We are again blessed with a refreshing rain to day, for which I hope we are grateful to Him who supplies all our real needs, and we were needing this good rain to revive the grain. blessed be His holy name.

July 1926

Tuesday July the 27th

To day my soninlaw **J.W. Peace** and wife and myself are favored to attend the funeral of cousin **Nannie Anderson**, which was largely attended and the appreciation of the departed was shown in the most immense profusion of lovely flowers I ever say on such an occasion. services were conducted by **Rev Louis McFarland** of Greensboro and **Rev Tom Sikes** of High Point, ministers of Friends Church. we were given mesages which sink deep into our hearts and be acted upon accordingly. for we know not the day, the hour, nor the moment, when we shall be called from works to rewards. therefore let us be ready, and our calling and election sure.

Wednesday July the 28th

I am thankful to state, that after a good nights rest and sleep, I am able to be up and use my pen to put down the uppermost thought in my mind, that of praise to Him who has seen fit to lengthen my days to this time. And I trust that my life may have not been spent in vain, for the One that knows all things, does know that I have looked to Him for help and strength to serve him. and although I have often made mistakes, for I am but poor weak flesh not all spirit, for the spirit is willing but the flesh is weak. so I know that thru all my mistakes and short comeings God has been faithful to his promice and has forgiven me for Christs sake, and I am leaning on His strong arm for strength and protection for the remainder of the journey.

Thursday July the 29th

A very damp morning, which causes more pains and aches, but I am thankful to still be able to wait on myself, and this I owe to the goodness and mercy of Him who gave his beloved son to die for me, and in him we live and move and have our being, and to Him belongeth all praise. now and forever. I now hear one of the daughters in this home playing a beautiful hymn on the Organ which fills my heart with awe and reverence. Well just as I had gotten this far in scribling down my thoughts I have a very pleasent surprise, as dear cousin **Terelias Hill** call in to see me. he had on getting the news of his sister **Nannie Andersons** death, left his home in Tenisee to come to attend her funeral, but had to lay by for several hours at different places so did not arrive in time to be at the funeral, but is now visiting his two brothers **John** and **Sidney Hill** and other relatives for a few days, so called to see me this morning I was more than glad to see him, as he seems very near to me as his mother was a sister to my Father **Sameul C Millikan** and I know him from a little child, he left N Carolina forty years ago. came back on a visit twenty three years ago and I had not seen him since, but knew him at first sight, and he seemed so glad to see me that it was indeed a happy meeting, and it brought up so many recolections of former days that we wished to converse about, that our time was much too short, but thankful to even meet again in this life, and hope to meet again in the better land.

Friday July the 30th 1926

I am thankful to be able to do some work with my hands to day, for my dear daughter, which does my heart good, for I want to be doing something every day for the help of some one either in word or deed, or both, something that will not only be beneficial to those with whom I meet and mingle but also that which will redown to the glory of Him who gives us strength to do that which our hands find to do, and ability of mind and heart to know his will, and to do that which He calls for each day as time goes by, to do that which is well pleasing in His sight, to the honor and praise of his holy name, is my fervent desire for Jesus sake.

Saturday July the 31st

As this is the last day of the month, it brings again afresh the thought of how fast time is passing away, and that we should make the best use of our time, for it will not be long at most until we will have to give an account of the deeds done in the body. oh Father in Heaven keep me pure in thy divine sight, so cleanse my heart and make it a fit recepticle for thy holy presence to dwell in, is my prayer for Jesus sake Amen.

Sunday August the 1st 1926

As this Sabbath day ushers in a new month, oh may we all renew our covenent with thee our Heavenly Father and may we keep this day holy and in true reverence to thy name, may we gain something from the study of thy Word that will help us on, in our heavenward journey and that will honor and praise His name who has prepared a home of rest for us when done with earth if we have fulfiled the conditions laid down in his holy word The Bible. I was blessed to attend the Sunday School and Church at Mt Vernon to day and enjoyed a good sermon by the pastor **Rev Reed Haris** from the text Grow in grace and in the knowledge of our Lord Jesus Christ.

Monday Aug the 2nd

While reflecting this morning on the excelent sermon I heard yesterday, I have a very great desire to grow in grace, not merely to have grace in my heart which I trust I have, but to grow in grace, having more and more grace each day, and more knowledge to understand what the will of the Lord is concerning me, that I may obey him more perfectly as the days go by, and that there may be a growth in grace which may be perceived not only in the strengthening of my own spiritual welfare, but which will be manifest in the sight and hearing of those with whom I come in contact, for I want to be a stepping stone toward Heaven to those with whom I meet and mingle instead of a stumbling block by being unfaithful and disobedient to the live commands. God grant that I may be so filled with thy grace, that there may be no room for envy or malice or anything contrary to thy will that I may answer the end for which I was created which was to glorify thee, Lord help me to glorify thee on earth, that I may glorify thee forever in Heaven, is my prayer for Christs sake.

Tuesday Aug the 3rd 1926

To day our anual meeting of Friend Church convenes at Guilford College. my heart is lifted up in praise for the many blessings of the past, and I pray that our gracious Heavenly Father will meet with those who may be favored to meet in this capasity and help them to worship him in spirit and truth, and enable them to transact the business of the Church in harmony and love. and that he will also be with those of us who cannot assemble with them to day, and help us to praise him in our hearts and homes.

Wednesday Aug the 4th 1926

This morning my daughter **May** and her husband **JW Peace** took me up the Blair Dairy. from there **Elva Blair** took her sisters **Ada** and **Martha,** and **Winston Blair, Chester Haworth**, and myself over to Guilford College. Elva left the others at the Church, took me on out to Founders Hall where I registered paid my fee for my room and meal tickets for the rest of the week, then back to Church attended the forenoon session, then came back to Founders ate dinner, talked with many friends who I was glad to meet again at this place as I had done last year. I was very much worn down after my ride over there, and sitting for a lengthy session at Church, so I did not go out to the afternoon service, but went to my room and lie down and took a rest, feeling very thankful for the privilige of being there and give the praise to the Giver of all good and the kindness of my dear friends. Then I went to the night sesion heard a grand lecture by **Edgar T Hole** on his mishionary work in Africa. and also a good talke by **Rev Milo Hincle** Pastor of Friend Church, Elm St Greensboro, NC.

Thursday Aug the 5th 1926

Had a good nights rest, and after a good breakfast, went to Church, heard the business of the Church transacted in harmony and love.

August 1926

Then listened to the Memorial of **James R. Jones, Gertrude Mendenhall, Sara E Wilson Winslow** and others all of whom were prominent in the activities of the year meeting in past years, which caused a hush to fall over the crowed assembly as in a quiet and distinct voice read these Memorials. I enjoyed all of them very much, and especially those of whom I had had acquaintance. This was a solemn good meeting. after which I returned to Founders and visited with kind friends, many who I met last year, others many years ago.

Friday Aug the 6th

Thankful to be feeling rested after a good nights sleep. Last night I was favored to get out to Church and enjoyed the services to the full. Rev Tom Sikes gave us a view of some of the scenes in China by the pictures of the various places and people of China by the Lantern slides the most in number and the largest and most interesting pictures I ever saw, and to cap the climas he showed life sise pictures of **Eli** and **Sibyl Jones** first mishionaries to China, and as I had seen them years ago at New Garden yearly meeting they looked so natural it seemed like I might walk up and shake hands with them. It is wonderful indeed what man can do by the wisdom and power given them by the great Giver of all things, and I praise the Lord for his goodness and mercy to us his unworthy children as we too often prove ourselves to be, at ten oclock we had a very favored meeting. **Rev Louis McFarland** gave us one of his best sermons which was very much appreciated.

Saturday Aug the 7th

Thankful to be able this morning to arise from my bed and prepare for Church. I was favored to get out last night to the young peoples Christian Endeavor meeting which was very much enjoyed. and this forenoon we had a splendid meeting. then I got out again at night, heard a good lecture by a young Friend from Baltimore on education. then three of the graduating students of Guilford College received their Diplomas at this time, two young men rec the degree of Batchelor of Arts and a young lady the degree of Batchelor of Science. **Dr Perisho** remarked that this was something unusual to take place in the yearly meeting. But it seemed to have a unique place in the meeting.

Saturday Aug the 8th 1926

Thankful to be able to be up this morning and prepare for breakfast, and trusting in the Lord that He will be with me and lead me in the way I should go this day, and leaning on His arm as it were for help and strength, I was favored to have the opportunity to visit an invalid friend **Miss Dora Balenger** this morning, which was much appreciated by her, and was an inspiration to me to see her bright cheerful countainance as she lay there upon her bed where she was lain for the past two years, not being able to walk, or do anything in the way of domestic help, but her patience and resignation to her Masters will, is a benediction to those who visit her. she has in her home two of her sister **Mary Yates'** daughters who are Orphans, and a nephew son of her brother **Cyrus Balenger**, and another little child who if I mistake not is fatherless, it seems like a real Orphans home, and a good home it is. Neither **Dora** nor her sister **Julia** have either one married so far, both been missionaries to Mextco for many years. **Julia** left her field of work, for the present at least, to minister to her invalid sister. for which I am sure she will be abundantly blessed, as it is also doing a great work for the Master in this dear home. After this precious little visit, **Julia** accompanied me back to the meeting for worship at the Church, there were many other meeting held at the various other buildings on the grounds. After church went back to Founders Hall, ate dinner. I did not stay for the afternoon service, but gathered up my baggage and came with cousin **Ed** and **Anna Blair** over to High Point and stoped at cousin **Roger Millikans** where I staid over night.

August 1926

Monday Aug the 9th 1926

I am in cousin **Rogers** nice hospitable home takeing a rest and having a nice time. This evening his wife and I went over to cousin **Will Andersons** and had a nice interesting visit with them, then back to Rogers at supper, then gathered around the family Alter and endeavored to return thanks upon the bended knee for the many priviliges our merciful Heavenly Father has permited us to enjoy. Then retired for the second night in this home where I have met such a kind of reception that the memory of this visit will be sweet while memory lasts, and I am not likely to ever have such an opportunity again. Cousin **Will Anderson** promiced me this evening that he would take me over to cousin **Fridella Barkers** in the morning to pay them a visit.

Tuesday Aug the 10th 1926

This morning cousin **Will Anderson** true to his offer took me to **Fridela Barkers,** there I met again with **John S. More** and wife, whose maiden name was **Tuelma Barker**. This is a lovely home, and I am enjoying the company and hospitality of cousin **Mattie** the wife and mother in the home I staid at **Fridela's** thru the day and until after supper, then **Fridela** took me to **Henry Winslows** where I spent the night, with those kind generous people.

Wednesday Aug the 11th

Having had a lovely welcome into this home and a good nights rest. I am now enjoying the hospitality of this home, feeling that I have so much to be thankful for to my Heavenly Father for takeing care of me, spareing my life and in a degree health. oh how I crave that I may be faithful to do his holy will to his honor and praise. I feel so grateful for the opportunity of being in his home, time past having been our kind neighbors in Randolph Co and the husband having lost his life companion, I have deep sympathy for him, knowing what it means to be thus deprived as I am, and for those dear children my heart goes out in deep sympathy for them who had to give up such a loveing and kind Mother who was such a help and guide for them in many ways, and they have so nobely born then loss and are so energeticaly takeing care of themselves and their aged Father, may the Lord bless and keep them all from the oldest to the youngest, and unite them all in the better land, when done with the conflicts of this life is my prayer. Wednesday Aug the eleventh I am still in this hospitable home. I am so thankful for the kindness I have received by all the inmates of this home. This afternoon their son **Robert Winslow** who lives not far from them came and took me over to his nice new home, I spent part of the p.m. there with his splendid wife and little son Robert jr then she and I went a little way to cousin **Joseph Worths jr** had a fine short visit at both these places, then **Robert** brought me back to his fathers, and after supper he took over to **Wright Jones** spent a short time with cousin **Leora** and her mother **Maggie Millikan** very pleasently, then returned again to **Henry Winslows**.

Thursday a.m. Aug the 12th

As had been planed by my friends the **Winslows**. I spent the second night with them, very comfortably and this morning I feel that I can not be thankful enough to my merciful Heavenly Father for his divine favors for putting into the hearts of these people to treat me so kindly. May the Lord bless them abundantly. I staid in this home until the afternoon of the same day when cousin **Joseph Worth** and wife **Minnie** came for me and brought me to **R.B. Stricklands** who now live at Montlieu Ave H.P. right on the National Highway from H.P. to Greensboro where I am enjoying the kind hospitality of this home to the full, as cousin Bettie and I conversed togeather it brought up so many things of farmer days that I had long since forgotten, that it seemed like rehearseing things of the past. **Cousin Bettie** is daughter of **Abner** and **Hannah Blair Grey**, her sister **Emma Grey** who has spent many years teaching in several different capacities in the Oxford

August 1926

Orphans Home, Oxford N.C. and who is now Matron in the home, was spending her vacation with her sister **Bettie** and family, so I had the pleasure of her company also, she has been faithful in performing her duty in this Orphan home may the Lord bless her abundantly in this work and when done with time here have an abundant entrance into the home of the forever blessed. I feel this morning that I cannot praise my merciful Heavenly Father enough for the kind hospitality I have received in this home. I have enjoyed the company of cousin **Bettie** so much, and her interesting youngest son **Sameul** who was in the home, their daughter **Elizabeth** was at this time visiting one of her sisters in Goldsboro, she is going to Teach in High Point again this year as she has been doing. I also met one of the married sons and his sweet little wife and lovely little daughter. may the dear Lord bless and keep all who represent this home as in the hallow of His holy hand is my fervent desire for Christs sake.

Friday Aug the 13th

As I have stated cousin **Joe Worth** and his wife brought me Thursday p.m. to **R.B. Stricklands,** where I spent the night and until this p.m. (Friday) when cousin **Joe** came by for me to take me to visit in his home, he had been to Greensboro to meet his sister **Lorena**, who is now **Mrs. John** of Fayetsville N.C. to visit them a days, so I had the pleasure of seeing and conversing with her, as well as cousin **Joe,** his wife **Minnie** and daughter **Phoebe** and others. Then after a sumpeous supper, went for a drive of several miles, and had a fine view of the most picturesque places in High Point by the Electric lights, then after returning had a pleasent chat togeather before retireing. Cousin **Joe Worth** has a most beautiful home, furnished up to date in every way, and nice green year and shade trees his oldest daughter **Clara** who is now **Mrs Bryan** lives rite by him and also has a lovely home we all had a pleasent time togeather sitting in a lovely breese; Blessed be the name of the Lord for his favors.

Saturday Aug the 14th 1926

I shall ever remember with pleasure the kindness I have received in this home. This morning we have been sitting on their lovely porch in a fine breeze chatting togeather most pleasently. And now according to cousin **Josephs** arrangement he is going to send me over to dear old Springfield to attend The Annual Memorial Association his daughter **Pheobe** who is an expert driver drove the Car for her **Aunt Lorena John** also accompanied me. This was a very interesting occasion, plenty of both vocal and instrumental music, good prayer, etc. **Rev Louis McFarland** gave us a splendid talk and **Milo Hincle** Pastor of Friends Church Elm St Greensboro gave us an excellent sermon. Then an intermition and fine Picnic dinner, where I met with many friends and relatives that I had not seen for quite a while. Then in the afternoon after a season of worship my own dear mother **Mary Carter Millikans** Memorial was read, and also a Memorial of **Yardley Warner**, I met his widow and daughterinlaw who I had met and had pleasent converse with over at Guilford College during year meeting. This Memorial day, was a day of both gladness and sadness, as on hearing my dear Mothers Memorial read, and it also being the eighty third anniversary of my dear departed husbands Birth, it brought so many things fresh to my mind.

Sunday Aug the 15th 1926

Yesterday my daughter **May** and husband **JW Peace** met me at the Memorial at Springfield and brought me home with them, where preperations were in order for a wedding to take place that night it was also the twenty second aniversary of their daughter **Ollie's** birth. The ceremony was performed at eight oclock by **Rev Reed Haris** by a beautiful Ring Ceremony makeing their daughter **Ollie Bulah Peace**, become the wife of **Gideon Bowman** of Glenola N.C. The Parlor and dineing room were both beautifully decorated for the occasion, and after the ceremony was over, congratulations, and greetings of friends etc were in order, then Bride and Groom and Guests repaired the Dineing room where after **Bro Haris** had asked the blessing all pertook of a bountiful supply of Ice cream and Cake, everything passed off nicely and it was a very interesting occasion. And now this lovely Sabbath I feel that we all have much to return thanks for our Heavenly Father for his goodness and mercy to us all. This afternoon we of this household went to S.S. and preaching at Mt Vernon **Bro Haris** gave us one of his best sermons, his theme being "ye are the salt of the earth and the light of the world." I hope this message may be as seed sown in of the world. Good ground to the glory of God the Father.

Monday Aug the 16th 1926

This is a lovely day and all are gone about their daily work, and as we now have one less in the home it seems rather odd not seeing her helping in the household work. but as she has given herself to another to share the joys and burdens of life, we not longer have **Ollie Peace** with us, but shall look for her to visit us, but when she comes it will not be **Ollie Peace** as usual, but **Mrs. Gideon Bowman** I am wishing for her a long and happy life with the man of her choice, ad that they may be blessed both spiritually and temporally.

Tuesday Aug the 17th

A beautiful morning, all able to be up and go about our daily avocations. Caning Peaches is in full blast for to day, fine ones from the Sand Hill Orchard, we have much to be thankful for that we are blessed with fruit, and vegetables, and so many other things, all of which come from the Great Giver of all things, and to whom belongeth all praise forever.

Wednesday Aug the 18th

A lovely morning, all able to be up and go about our daily work. so much to praise our blessed Saviour for that it is as well with us as it is to day.

Thursday Aug the 19th 1926

A very warm day, all have been busy, cooking, ironing etc. I am so thankful that all are as well in this home as we are. I was favored to be of some help in the work for which I am very grateful to the Giver of my strength. Blessed by His holy name.

Friday Aug the 20th

A nice cool morning after a little shower of rain, peeling and caning fruit is the order of the day, I am so thankful to the Giver of all good, who is so merciful to His unworthy children.

Saturday Aug the 21st

Another nice cool morning, all able to go about our daily avocations. The Bride and Groom spent last night with us, and are now leaveing for **Mr Bowmans** Fathers. May happy be their lot.

Sunday Aug the 22nd 1926

The most of the family here are going to a family reunion over at D. Browns, but as I cannot go to Sunday School to day I chose to go and spend part of the day with **Nannie** and **Earl Peace**, had a nice quiet visit with them, then returned home in the evening. There were several young people here; I love young people but there are times when I love to withdraw from all human companionship and commune with my blessed Saviour, who is friend above all others, and who has promiced to be a husband to the widow, and a Father to the Fatherless.

Monday Aug the 23rd

A nice cool morning all nature seems revived, I praise the Lord for his goodness and mercy to us all, his dependent children, oh what a blessing that we can claim to be His children, let us worship Him in spirit and in truth.

August 1926

Tuesday Aug the 24th

This is a lovely morning, all nature the flowers and the birds etc, all seem to be praiseing the great Creator of all things but oh how my heart has been pained at witnessing the exceeding sinfulness of the human heart, as it is made manifest by the words and acts of those who transgress the law of our gracious Redeemer, who has given us the Golden Rule that we should do unto others as we would have them do unto us, and that love is the fulfiling of the law, and Christ says in his Word, "by this ye shall know that ye are my deciples if ye have love for one another." and we know that we cannot be Christs deciples if we have envy, hatred and malice in our hearts toward any of our fellow beings for these things are the opposite of love, and shut out everything that is gentle and kind and loveing toward our fellow cretures. Therefore I am praying that my heart, and the hearts of others may be filled with that love that knows no ill to his neighbor.

Wednesday Aug the 25th 1926

We have been blessed with a nice shower of rain last night, for which I am grateful. as it was needed to help the crops to mature. and my great desire this morning is, that my gracious Heavenly Father will send me a refreshing shower of his grace and love, that I may feel revived and strengthened to overcome all the trials and discouragements that daily more or less come my way. and that I may take fresh courage to press on toward the mark of the high calling, as it is in Christ Jesus.

Thursday Aug the 26th 1926

A nice cool morning after rain in the night. This is **Clemons Peace's** fourteenth birth day. And I am praying that the dear Lord will so touch his heart, that he may make a full surrender to Him now in the days of his youth; that he may become a good and useful man in this world being in favor with both God and man, and that he may so glorify God on earth that he may glorify Him forever in Heaven when done with this world. and may we who have long borne the burden and heat of the day, set a good example for those who are younger, that we may be a stepping stones toward Heaven, and not stumbling blocks, is my earnest prayer. for Christs sake.

Friday Aug the 27th 1926

A nice cool morning, all able to be up and go about our daily avocations. My daughter is busy making preparations to entertain some of her first husbands people from Sailsbury, hope we shall not be disappointed, for they are worthy people, and good company.

Saturday Aug the 28th

Another lovely cool morning, our company who came last evening according to arrangement spent the night with us, and have just started back on their journey home. They were **Mr and Mrs Homer Fesperman** and **Mrs Fespermans** sister **Miss Eva Stilwell**, they are daughters of **Mr George Stilwell** of Sailsbury N.C. who is a brother to Mr **Arthur Lee Stilwell** of Charlotte N.C. my daughters first husband. it always brings a touch of tenderness to my heart when I am privaliged to see any of those people for "**Lee Stilwell**" thru all the fifteen years that he lived after he married my daughter was as kind and affectionate to me as if I had been his own Mother and I feel the loss in his death as tho he were my own son. so his people feel near and dear to me, and I am always delighted to meet with them and may they and all of us follow his feet steps as he followed Christ is my great desire.

Sunday Aug the 29th 1926

Another week has passed, and another Sabbath ushered in, oh may we keep it holy according to the commandments, that we are to study in our S.S. lesson to day. We have just heard of the death of an elderly day a **Mrs Brewer** of Glenola N.C. who is to be buried this pm at Mt Vernon, the funeral was preached by her Pastor the **Rev Burr** a Baptist Minister, Assisted by **Rev Reed Haris** the Pastor at Mt Vernon. This was another occasion to cause us to realise the uncertainty of life and the certainty of death. oh may we all be ready for the summons, that we may enter into rest where we can praise Him, who gave his life for us, more perfectly than we can here on this earth His footstool, oh may we live to thus praise Him thruout all eternity is the fervent wish of my heart.

Monday Aug the 30th

I feel very thankful that we have all had a good nights rest and sleep, and able to go about our daily avocations praise God from whom all blessing flow.

Tuesday Aug the 31st

This date reminds me that another month has passed with its joys and sorrows, and still we are pressing on, and I trust trying to fulfil the purpose for which we were created which was to glorify God, oh that we may be more faithful as the days and months go by. Last evening we were blessed with company of **Miss Jinnie Redding** and her sisterinlaw **Mrs Daisy Redding**, we were so very glad to have them as they are ladies that we dearly love and have full confidence in and the time was spent so pleasently, that it passed off too quickly. Praise the Lord for His favors.

Wednesday September the 1st 1926

Now that we are entering upon another month and another season of the year, we realise that as we are spared to see the days as they pass, that we shall meet with different people and different things, some of which will be pleasing and some things which will try our patience as in the past, so it behooves us to be close on our watch, lest we transgress the commandments which we have been studying the past month, and thus fall short of doing that which is well pleasing in the sight of our blessed Redeemer who is willing to favor us with his divine presence if we will only open our heart and let him in to rule and reign there as we should.

Thursday Sept 2nd 1926

A lovely morning after a refreshing rain, which was being needed. We have so much to thank our great Giver for all His benefits to us his unworthy dependent children, but oh the blessed privilige of being a child of God. we can not praise Him enough for bearing with us in all our weakness as he does. but He is so merciful and kind, and so faithful to His promices that He remembers that we are but poor weak flesh, and that the spirit is willing, but the flesh is weak and liable to err. oh may we all be more thoughtful and close on our watch to do His holy will is the fervent desire of my heart this morning. for Jesus sake.

Friday Sept the 3rd

A cool cloudy morning, part of the family here are going to Town to day. I was favored last night to go with them to the prayer meeting at Mt Vernon. had a very interesting meeting, many prayers offered in behalf of themselves and others, that they be more faithful to duty. oh that we would all cary out each day of our lives, the resolutions that are set at these prayer meetings, and not have merely a religion for the prayer meeting and Sunday, but practice what we preach, every day at all times and every where, is the great desire of my heart.

Saturday Sept the 4th 1926

This is a dark cloudy morning, which coresponds very much to my feelings, as I reflect upon my many short comeings, for I feel that I fall short of obeying the commandments of the Great law giver as I should, but am thankful to know that the Lord is my shepherd and that He is watching over me as one of his flock least I wander too far from the fold and be lost in the wilderness of temptation and sin. Blessed be His holy name for his care over me.

September 1926

Sunday Sept the 5th

I am reminded that this is the day of the week which our Great head of the Church has commanded that we should keep it holy. Oh that we may be more diligent to obey His word, not only should we keep the Sabbath day holy, but should be on our watch each day of the week that we may not break any of his commandments which are laid down as a law for us to go by, and if we disobey them, we may expect to incur the penalty of our own misgivings. To day the protracted meeting commences at Mt Vernon. This afternoon I was able to go with the family here to the services at 3 oclock had a good sermon by the **Rev Hiker** who is visiting the **Pastor Reed Haris** in the meeting. May the presence of the Lord be in our midst and much good accomplished is my prayer.

Monday Sept the 6th

A damp morning but nice and cool, I feel very thankful that are in pretty good health at this time, we all attend the protracted meeting last night at Mt Vernon heard a good sermon, my prayer is that the Lord in his mercy will stir up the minds of the people, that there may be a great revival in the neighborhood and community, and that many who are out of the fold may be brought to Christ. for although He bears long with us, he will not suffer his people to go on in sining against him without reproof in some way or other, for He loves us too much to let us go without correction, therefore we should count it a blessing when He convicts us and shows us our wrong doings and causes us to turn to Him for the salvation of our never dying souls, for He wileth not that any should perish but that all should come to Him and be saved.

Tuesday Sept the 7th

Last night my daughter and I went out to see a neighbor woman who was suffering severely with a gathering in one hand; knowing that she could not do for her family what was necesary, we felt it our duty to go there instead of going to Church as we had aimed to, believeing to assist them in any way we could would be owed and blessed of the Lord as done unto Him.

Wednesday Sept the 8th 1926

I have just been reading the story of the little girl that had been going to Sunday School only a short time when she began to want to do something for Jesus, she said if I was as big as Miss Seaver I could go to China and be a mishionary. but as she was just a little girl she could not think of anything that she could do. but said "dear me I wish there was something that I could do for Jesus." she sat very quiet with her elbows on her knees and her chin cupped in her hands, Suddenly Aunt Kate appeared in the doorway of the play room and exclaimed I've left my ball of yarn downstairs, Pattie dear please run down and get it for Auntie. For an instant Pattie felt cross, and stretched her arms and legs lazily, then she thought if I jump right quick and get the ball I will have more time to sit and think afterwards, so she hurried downstairs and in a few minutes put the ball in Aunties lap. Then mother called her to go feed the chickens, she hesitated at first, but remembered she should obey her mother, and went and did as she was bidden. Afterward she asked her mother, "if there was anything a little girl could do for Jesus"? then her mother reminded her of what she had done for mother and Auntie and was told that what she had done for them was doing something for Jesus, then she remembered that she had not done those things as willingly a first as she should "as she didn't want to be disturbed while she was trying to study our some plan to do something for Jesus. Here is a great lesson for us to learn, that whatever our hands find to do for the help and comfort of others we should do it with cheerfulness and as quickly as it is in our power to do so. for it is written "inasmuch as ye did it unto the least of these ye did it unto me." and knowing that we shall reap our reward for doing small things in the name of the Lord as well as great things. I was favored to attend the meeting again yesterday afternoon and again last night, had a good meeting no demonstration, but a most excelent sermon by **Rev Hiker**, and good songs and prayers, which I trust was owned and blessed by the Lord. to Him be all the praise.

Thursday Sept the 9th

I feel very thankful that I had strength to get out to Church again yesterday afternoon, and again last night. had a good meeting both sessions, last night two persons went to the Alter, one a young girl who professed conversion, the other a man past middle age. I have not learned whether he became satisfied or not. if not I hope he may yet be saved. May the Lord send a double portion of His spirit down upon us all, both friend and foe, and give us a great revival is my prayer for Jesus sake.

Friday Sept the 10th 1926

A lovely morning. I feel that I cannot thank our Heavenly Father enough for his care of us his unworthy children. we often meet with difficulties in this life, but as we put our trust in Him in whom we live and move and have our being. and to whom we look for help in every needful time, he will make a way for us where we see no way. Last night we went to Church trusting in the good Lord to take care of us, The Car proved not to be in good runing order, and as my daughter was driving and no one in the Car except women folks, we got dear **Lee White** to drive home for us after Church, and we came to a hill that the Car could not pull up, so **Lee** went and got help and **Emery Peace** came with his Car and pulled us up and the rest of the way home, so we see that as we were asking for help and trusting, that we would get it the dear Lord sent us the assistance we needed may a rich blessing rest upon those for their kind helpfulness in time of need. and I know He will accept this kind favor as done unto Him. I am so thankful that the man that went to the Alter the night before, came out conquer last night, and gave evidence of a true conversion. Praised be the name of the Lord.

Saturday Sept the 11th 1926

This morning it is quite cool, and reminds me that the fall season of the year has come. oh that we may remember that we have to give account of the deeds done in the body when done with time here, no matter what season of the year it is, and we should be close on our watch that we do not transgress Gods law, by our disobedience either in word or deed. oh Father in Heaven keep me this day, as in the hallow of Thy divine hand, that I go not astray from Thee, is my fervent desire, for the sake of Him who died for me. The protracted meeting at Mt Vernon closed last night, I trust that there may have been good seed sown, and that it may have fallen in good ground, and will bring forth fruit, to the honor and praise of the Great Husbandman. And that there may be many stars in the Crown of Gods mesengers for their faithful service in His name.

Sunday Sept the 12th

A lovely Sabbath day, but as I have no conveyance cannot get out to Sunday School, but trust I shall get some one to take me over to Fairview to the protracted meeting to day or tomorrow. My prayer is dear Lord keep me so close to do thy holy will.

Sept the 13th 1926

I went to **W.W. Merediths** last evening to be ready to attend the protracted meeting, but found that we had been misinformed, for the meeting in Fairview does not commence for two weeks yet. but we went to the prayer meeting there last night which was conducted by **Clarence Meredith** who gave a good talk and we had a very interesting meeting, many prayers being offered, and many testifying to the goodness of the Lord to them and their families. and to day I have had a good visit with cousin **Florence Meredith** and others, and this evening we stoped for a short while at **Sidney Blairs** and had a good short visit with him and **Della** then **Julius Meredith** and his mother brought me back to **J.W. Peaces** where we enjoyed melons etc togeather **Julius** who was home on vacation, will return to Chapel Hill this week for another term in School there. I feel that I have much to be thankful for that I have been able to make this visit. All praise belongs to Him who raises up friends to be kind and helpful to me.

Tuesday Sept the 14th

A nice cool morning and looks like the fall season was surenough here. and we know that each day as it passes brings us that much nearer our journeys end here on this earth and my fervent desire is that I may improve the moments as they fly, and be found doing things that are well pleasing in my makers sight. oh to be found faithfully performing my duty, is my prayer for Jesus sake.

Wednesday Sept the 15th

They that trust in the Lord shall be at Mt Zion which cannot be removed, why this scripture comes so forceably to my mind this morning I do not know, but I believe it is to remind me that I should be so firmly settled on the rock Christ Jesus that sure foundation, that none of the trials and troubles that I have to pass thru will move me from my purpose of serving Him who has been my stay and my staff thru all the years of my pilgramage here so far, and I know He will never leave nor forsake me if I trust in Him as I have in the past, for I know that he has watched over and cared for me all the days of my life up to the present time, and now that I am old and grey headed, He will not forsake me if I still put my trust in him for He has said I will never leave thee nor forsake thee. and I am more determined by Gods help to press on toward the mark of the high calling, that I may gain the prise Christ has laid up for me.

Until We Sleep Our Last Sleep

Thursday Sept the 16th 1926

As I go to write this morning, my heart is raised in thanksgiving and praise to the Giver of all our blessings, for His mercy to me his unworthy child, for he has taken care of me thru the night and kept me from all harm and given me quiet rest in sleep, and strength to arise from my bed and go about my daily avocations doing whatever my hands find to do, that I am able to do in helping my dear daughter in her work and entertaining my dear little grandson in his play. Blessed be the name of the Lord for His goodness and tender loveing kindness to us all.

Friday Sept the 17th

I feel like giving thanks to my Heavenly Father this afternoon that he has given me strength to day to do some work that was necessary to be done for myself to prepare for a visit next week to spend with my grandaughter **Miss Sadie Blair** and her mother who is now the wideo of **Mr Luther Conrad** and whose first husband was my son **Jesse C. Blair.** As I have a special invitation, and who I have not visited this year, I hope I shall be able to go, and weather favorable, May the Lord bless and keep us all in His holy hand.

Saturday Sept the 18th

"As the Hart panteth after the water brook as panteth my soul after thee of God." this is the cry of my soul this morning, for I am passing as it were thru deep waters, that threaten to overwhelm me. and I seem to be confronted by a great bearier that I cannot penetrate. and to look back or from side to side, there are obsticles that I cannot overcome. so my only hope is in the Lord who created all things on purpose of His own glory, so my cry is unto Him again and again as in the past, Lord help me to know what is thy will concerning me in all things, that I may see so clearly what Thou wouldst have me do that I may not err therein, for I desire to conform to thy will even in thy choice of an earthly home while I am permitted to abide on earth, for I desire about all else to have a place where I can feel the welcome of the inmates and where that peace and quiet and love rules in the hearts of all who obey the golden rule, and the law of love, for Christ has said that love is the fulfilling of the law, and by this ye shall know that ye are deciples if ye have love for one another.

Sunday Sept the 19th 1926

This is a lovely Sabbath morning. I am expecting to go to Thomasville to day, so will not get to Sunday School and Church, but hope that by his divine guidance I may be able to worship Him acceptably is the desire of my heart. we are told in Gods word that not even a sparrow falls to the ground without his notice, and that we are of more value than many sparrows, so I am trusting that He will keep me from falling into temptation, or at least make way for my escape, for it is written that we shall not be tempted above that we are able, but with the temptation thou will also make way for our escape that we may be able to bear it. and Thou who knows all things knows that my soul is hungering and thirsting for that living bread and water of life which alone can nourish my soul unto life eternal, so that I may not only be permitted an entrance in the home of the blest when done with time here below, but where I can see my blessed Redeemer face to face, and where I can praise him thruout eternity much better than I can on this earth His foot stool, is the desire of my heart, for Jesus sake.

Monday Sept the 20th 1926

A nice cool morning, I came to my daughterinlaws last evening according to arrangement, my grandaughter **Sadie Blair** and a young man **Mr Hobert Lee Fouts** came and brought me. I have been enjoying this visit fine, and feel that I have so much to be thankful for that I have sufficient health and strength to enjoy the company of loved ones. may the dear Lord help me this day and every day as they pass to do His holy will. for He knows that I crave to be found doing the things that are pleasing in His sight. "Trust in the Lord and do good, and thou shalt dwell in the land and verily thou shalt be fed," is the Text that comes to me this morning. oh may I obey it.

Tuesday Sept the 21st

A lovely morning. I feel thankful that I have had a quiet nights rest, and on looking out upon the hurry and bustle of the Town of Thomasville. I am glad that I can have an inner Sanctuary where I have sweet communion with Him who has watched over and cared for me all the days of my life up to this time, and I know if I do not forsake Him he will still be my helper, for he hath said "I will never leave thee nor forsake thee" blessed be the name of the Lord who has taught me to look to him for comfort, for vain is the help of man, and if God be for us who can be against us, bless the Lord.

Wednesday Sept the 22nd 1926

A cloudy day but no rain. We had quite an interesting visit last night from our friends **Mr.** and **Mrs Murphy** and their daughterinlaw and two sweet children. I am so thankful for a good nights rest, after our good time with friends, and that we are all feeling better today after being indisposed for the past few days. All praise and honor is due to our Great giver of all good for His benefits to us his unworthy dependent children. I hope to be able to attend the prayer meeting to night with my grandaughter and her mother to the praise to our gracious Heavenly Father, who watches over us.

Thursday Sept the 23rd

A lovely morning, I am still suffering from cold but thankful for rest in sleep after attending a good prayer meeting at the Church which I enjoyed very much. Then after Church **Sadie** and her mother and myself went and paid a short, but sweet visit to **Mrs. Lee Rice,** her daughter **Mrs. Martine Barker** was with her, having recently gone thru an opperation at the Hospital. Then leaving here we went to **Clarance**

Tomlinsons new store, had a happy little time with him and **Corene**, eating Ice cream etc then back to our starting point where we found rest and sleep, feeling grateful to our great Benefactor for all His favors.

Friday Sept the 24th

I am so thankful to be able to arise from my bed this morning for altho I am far from feeling well I am very much better than yesterday. Last night we were favored with the company of some of our friends, **Mrs Myres** for one who I am always glad to meet, and **Mrs Periman** who is such a sweet little lady, and others, **Miss Daisy Leach** has also been to see me this week I am always glad to her, for I knew her people years ago.

Sat Sept the 25th

A lovely morning, I am thankful that it is as well as it is. **Miss Daisy Leach** came to see me again last night I enjoyed her company very much, I praise the Lord for his goodness and mercy to me His dependent child, although unworthy of His many favors.

Sunday Sept the 26th

A beautiful Sabbath morning, I hope to attend Church to day at Thomasville, then I aim to return this evening to my daughter **Mrs J.W. Peace.** Yesterday p.m. my grandaughter **Sadie Blair** took me over to visit **Mrs. Ben White** who is a cousin to my dear deceased husband, and her husband is a cousin to myself, I had a splendid visit there, then back to my daughterinlaws where I had a good nights rest, for which I praise the Giver of all good, oh may I look to Him at all times for help and strength to do His holy will for he alone knows my heart, and my desire to be found walking in the footsteps of my dear Redeemer.

Monday Sept the 27th 1926

This morning it is quite cool, seems nice to set by a good little fire. I returned last evening from Thomasville to my daughter **Mrs J.W.**

Peace where I have resided for the past year, but as I am wanted elsewhere I do not think I shall spend the comeing winter here, but I have given myself into the hands of the Lord to lead and guide my steps so I may keep in the right path.

Tuesday Sept the 28th

A cloudy morning but no rain yet which is beginning to be needed badly, I am still suffering from cold and my eyes are so dim I make a poor out at writing but thankful to be able to state Gods goodness to me.

Wednesday Sept the 29th

Still cloudy but no rain as yet. I am thankful to be feeling stronger, and I realize that my help comes from Him who is the strength of my life and to whom belongeth all praise now and forever. Amen.

Thursday Sept the 30th 1926

This morning finds me in the home of cousin **Clarance Meredith** having come her last night after Church at Fairview had a good meeting splendid sermon by the **Rev Byram** of High Point. my daughter **Mrs J.W. Peace** brought me over to **Charlie Crokers** and they brought me to Church and from there I went home with **Merediths** where I have had a good nights rest and a good time with them. I have enjoyed this visit so much for I have know **Clarance** from his childhood. he spoke of the inspiration that he had received for his life work when he went to Oak Forest Sunday School when I was the Superintendent there for two years, This was while I was yet so afflicted that I had to be lifted in and out of the Buggy and the same way in and out of the doors; but all praise to Him who helped me, ang gave me strength sufficient to cary on this work.

Friday Oct the 1st 1926

From the 3 oclock meeting last evening at Fairview I went home with cousin **Ann Cranford,** took supper with them, then **Mr. Hobert**

Mills and **wife** took **Mrs Cranford** and myself back to the Church at night. had a splendid meeting. the Gospel Team from Mt Vernon, Archdale etc were there and we had many prayers testimonies from them and others in the congregation in general. **Mr. Archie Spencer** read the 12th chapter of Romans which was commented on, and **Mr Cisero Peace** led the meeting. the **Pastor Rev Reed Haris,** and his helper in the revival **Rev Byram** of High Point gave us much good advice. I praise the Lord for giving me strength and opportunity to attend this meeting. Blessed be His holy name.

Saturday Oct the 2nd 1926

After the meeting last evening at Fairview, **Walter Meredith** and wife **Florence** took me home with them, then we went back to Church at night, had a splendid meeting which closed last night, I went back with **Merediths** where we had a season of prayer before lying down for rest thru the night and I feel this morning that I cannot be thankful enough to my merciful Heavenly Father for His care over us during the night, and for strength to arise from our beds and go about the rotine of the day, oh may I be faithful to discharge my every duty. Thou our Father has spared me for a purpose, help me to fulfil that purpose to Thy names honor and glory. is my prayer for Jesus sake.

Sunday Oct the 3rd 1926

Last night **Walter** and **Florence** took me to **Mr Charles Burtons** where I spent the night with them, had a pleasant visit and now this holy Sabbath morning my prayer is that I may keep this day not only holy, but wholely unto the Lord. I shall return to may daughter to day, and it is was not convenient for me to go to Church and Sunday School to do. I desided to go and spend the p.m. with **Grandma Peace** as she was not able to go to Church, and thus be company for each other while the members of each family were away at different places. Bless the Lord oh my soul.

Monday Oct the 4th 1926

After spending the afternoon with **"Grandma Peace"** I returned to my daughter **Mrs J.W. Peace** in the evening and found that some of my specials friends had been to see me while I was away. I regreted very much to miss seeing them, but as I did not know they were comeing and feeling it my duty to go and stay with one that was lonely like myself, I feel that it will not be set down against me for the great judgement day. so this morning I am trying to take fresh courage to press on bearing my losses and crosses which are many, and strive for the crown which is ready for me if I run with patience the race that is set before me, endeavoring to do the Masters will as He makes it known to me, to His honor and praise so my prayer is dear Lord keep me as in Thy divine hand that I go not astray from Thee.

Tuesday Oct the 5th 1926

A cloudy dark morning, which has a tendency to make one feel rather gloomy, but as I reflect upon the goodness and mercy of our blessed Saviour, I feel that I can not thank Him enough for his long suffering and forbearance with those of us who are so prone to neglect our whole duty to God a heart from sin set free, a heart that always feels the blood so freely she for me. oh that my heart maybe a fit temple for His holy presence to dwell in his prayer for Jesus sake.

Morning
Wednesday Oct the 6th 1926

We were blessed with a good rain last night, and I hope we are all thankful for it, as it was being needed. and grateful for a degree of health to go about our daily avocations. Last night we received a message that **David Gurney Davis** passed away at 8:30 oclock last night, he was paralyzed suddenly last Sunday night at 8 oclock and was entirely unconcious the two days that he merely breathed before his life went out, we learn that he will be buried at Marlboro to day but have not yet learned the hour. In his death we are again reminded of the uncertainty of life and the certainty of death. It seems that there was but one step between him and death, it was so very sudden. Later in the day we learn that the funeral is to be at 2:30 oclock, so **Jerome, May** and myself made ready and went to the home, then to the funeral at Marlboro which I feel sure was the largest I ever attended, and was conducted by **Rev Tom Sikes** of Friends Church High Point and **Rev Reed Haris** Pastor of Mt Vernon Methodist Church and others, it was a very solemn occasion, and much exortation and warning given to all to be ready for the final summons. Dear Savior help us all to be ready, is my prayer.

Thursday Oct the 7th 1926

It is quite cool this morning, which seems such a contrast to the hot weather we have had for some months past. We have much to be thankful for that we have health and strength sufficient to attend our affairs, and do that which is necessary to be done for the comfort and sustainance of our perishable bodies. Praise the Lord for His goodness to us.

Friday Oct the 8th

Still cooler this morning than yesterday, it seems nice to sit by a good fire, and makes one feel that winter is on the way, and time flies so fast it wont be long until it will be here. This is a very busy day here and altho I am not strong I am very thankful that I can help some in the work. Praise the Lord.

Saturday Oct the 9th

A nice fall morning, much to thank the Giver of all good for, that it is as well with us all as it is. This is my prayer again and again. Teach me thy way oh Lord and lead me in a plain path that I go not astray from thee. and that I may see clearly what Thou would have me do, to Thy names honor and praise.

Sunday Oct the 10th 1926

This morning my heart is lifted up in supplication to the Creator of all things, in the language of the Psalmist, "Create in me a clean heart oh God and renew a right spirit within me." for I am overcome with grief and almost ready to faint by the way, so Thou art the only one that can help me to overcome the firey trials that fall to my lot, for vain is the help of man. Help me oh my Father in Heaven to trust thee fully for I am standing on thy promices which are written in thy Word that when thou passest thru the fire it shall not kindle upon thee and thru the waters they shall not overflow thee.

Monday Oct the 11th

A dark rainy morning, which according to nature does not have a tendency to make one feel as cheerful as a bright clear day. but I remember that it is both the dark and the light that we have to contend with in this life, for the power of darkness which is the devil himself is going about like a roaring Lion seeking whom he may devour, by putting all manner of coruption into the hearts and minds of those who he knows will listen to him, to say all maner of evil against those who have given themselves to the Lord to be his children, and are trying by his help to obey Him, but the enemy of our souls peace does all in his power to turn us away from our blessed Saviour who died for us that we might live forever with Him in Heaven. so my prayer is this morning dear Heavenly Father that thou would preserve me from the snares of the devil that he daily lays for me to try to foil me in the battle that I am fighting against him, and help me to overcome all evil and obey thee in the way of thy requireings so that I may have an entrance into that blessed abode which Thou hast prepared for all who love and serve thee on earth, Lord help me to fulfil the conditions to thy honor and praise.

Tuesday Oct the 12th 1926

A nice cool morning. My heart is filled with thanksgiving and praise to Him who has seen fit to spare my life and a degree of health and strength, to bear up under the sore trials thru which I am having to pass, for He alone has enabled me to bear them, by looking as it were upon the form of my blessed Savior who while on earth was falsely accused, not only threatened by actually struck with the palm of the hand by his enemies, spat upon, and crowed with thorns, crucified, and died for me, as well as for the sins of the whole world, that I can bear the false accusations and trials in various ways that fall to my lot, to bear up under the many provocations and trials that are so often my portion. but blessed be the name of the Lord who is my great burden bearer.

Wednesday Oct the 13th 1926

A cloudy damp morning, which causes more acheing limbs, but thankful that I can now use them as well as I can, for when I look upon the years that I spent in helplessness, not being able to walk at all, and passing thru so much suffering and privation, I feel like I can not grateful enough to my merciful Heavenly Father for his goodness to me. for Thou knowest that in days and years gone by my suffering has been almost beyond human endurance, and only as I leaned hard upon Thy strong arm, was I able to endure it, for many times in the past has my life been dispaired of by my physicians and my family and friends called in to see me pass away from them. And as He who has seen fit to spare me to the age of more than four score years, and has been with me all those years, careing for and preserveing me from all harm, and even given me more physical strength than I ever hoped to gain. I want to tell the generation following what a precious Savior I found many years ago, and how by leaning on His everlasting Arms of mercy and love, I have been enabled to bear all my crosses and losses even to having to give up my precious companion, who was ever ready to speak a word of comfort to cheer me on my way, and now to have to contend with the thing of the world as they come, and often hedged in as it were with briars and thorns in the flesh. I cry to my great Helper to go with me the rest of the journey and help me to hold our faithful to the end, that I may receive the crown of life, and praise Him forever and forever. Amen.

Thursday Oct the 14th 1926

Another cloudy dark morning, but I am so glad that I can look on the bright side and see that every dark cloud has a silver lineing. for altho we are encompassed about with many infirmities and dark surroundings, yet we can look away to that bright future where all is joy and peace and love. and as we look to Him who is the source of light, we are made to take fresh courage and press on thru the darkness to Him in whom we are told in his Word that He is light, and in Him there is no darkness at all, and it is to Him that I am looking to keep me from sining against him, and direct my steps. and the morning, as has so often been the case the words of the Hymn sound again in my ears. "oh for a heart to praise in my God, a heart from sin set free, a heart that always feel the blood so freely shed for me." Yes it is the fervent desire of my heart that it may be kept free from all sin, and kept a clean receptacle for His holy presence to dwell in. that I may continually praise Him who died for me, yes even me, unworthy as I am.

Friday Oct the 15th 1926

A nice cool morning but I as I have spent a restless nigh, not getting the sleep I needed, I feel exhausted and weary. but I praise the Lord for strength enough to arise from my bed, for I crave to do this as long as possible, that I may not be a burden to others.

Saturday Oct the 16th

This morning I am so sorely tried with some of the problems of this earth, that I have to cry nightely to Him who is my helper in every time of need, for strength to withstand the assaults of the enemy, for he takes advantage of our discouraged moments to keep us if possible from pressing on to serve our dear Saviour who died that we might live forever with Him in that happy home that is prepared for all who love and serve him on earth. Blessed by His holy name forever and ever.

Sunday Oct the 17th

A lovely Sabbath morning, which makes one feel refreshed by the pure air, and is something to remind us of that pure and holy atmosphere of Heaven, which I desire so much that we all may bask in when done with time here below. and am praying that I may live so obedient to my Heavenly Fathers will that I may gain an entrance into that blessed abode where I hope to meet all my loved ones. There to sing Gods praise togeather thruout all eternity.

Monday Oct the 18th 1926

This is a nice clear cool fall morning, I feel very grateful that it is as well with us all as it is, for we learn daily of sickness, and death by fatal accidents etc in various ways and places, while we as a family have thus far escaped any serious injury, for which I feel that we should render thanksgiving and praise to Him who watches over us His unworthy children by day and by night, and I am thinking what a sad thing it would be for any of us, to so disobey our Heavenly Father that he is in justice to His holy divine law would have to withdraw himself from us, which brings the Hymn to mind. "Father I strech my hands to thee, no other help I know, if thou withdraw thyself from me oh whither shall I go." There is none other to whom we can go for refuge but to Him who created and made us on purpose of his own glory. oh that we may all glorify Him on earth that we may glorify him forever in Heaven. is my prayer for Jesus sake.

Tuesday Oct the 19th 1926

Another nice cool morning, and a earnest desire arises in my heart, that I may be more faithful to do my Masters will every day that my life is spared, that I may be doing something worth while for the upbuilding of the Master Kingdom, in the hearts of the children of men, to His names honor and praise.

Wednesday Oct the 20th 1926

Nice weather, and I feel thankful this morning for a degree of health to be able to arise from my bed, and in my heart and with my pen, take note of the goodness and mercy of our blessed Saviour to us his unworthy dependent children, for we are so prone to neglect our whole duty, that is laid down in His holy Word for us to follow. but I am so thankful that He knows that "I will to do his will." and that it is thru weakness and forgetfulness that I often fall short of doing the things that I should do, instead of wilfully disobeying Him. but I do plead that I am justified accordind to the Word laid down in the Book of Books in comeing to Him and pleding forgivness for those things which I do, or leave undone thru weakness and thoughtlesness, and I am praying with my whole heart for forgiveness for all my sins borth of omishion and commission. that they may be bloted out of The Book of Thy remembrance and that my name may be written on a clean fair page in the Lambs Book of life so that I may have an entrance into that blessed abode where I can praise Him more perfectly than I can here on earth. Dear Father accept this as the sincere prayer of thy unworthy child, for Thy dear sons sake. Amen.

Thursday Oct the 21st 1926

Another nice cool morning. I am thankful that we are all in compareatively good health, nothing of interest to note only the continued goodness and mercy of our blessed Lord and Saviour who is still watching over us and shielding us from all harm. oh may we be closer on our watch this day and every day that is lengthened out to us, to do His holy will is the fervent desire of my heart for Jesus sake.

Friday Oct the 22nd

This nice morning, I am so glad that I can say the Lord is my shepherd I shall not want, for I feel so poor and lonely that if I did not look to the great shepherd of our souls for help and strength to press on I should utterly fail. but by looking to Him I can say "Yes tho I walk thru the valley of the shadow of death I will fear no evil for Thou art with me." "Thy rod and thy staff they comfort me." oh that I might feel the presence of the Lord at all times as I do this morning, but He see fit to hide his face as it were from us at times to try our faith, and see whether we will trust him in our dark moments as well as when we feel his divine presence. Oh merciful Father help me to love thee more and serve thee better, for Christs sake.

Saturday Oct the 23rd 1926

This morning while thinking of the many changes that have taken place in the years gone by it came into my mind that eight years ago to day our dear soninlaw **Arthur Lee Stilwell** passed away, as he died Oct the 23rd 1918. this was a great loss us all. and he was so very nice and kind to me, I miss him so much. and when I reflect on the still greater loss to me of the death of my own dear husband who meant so much to me, I can hardly realise how I have gotten thru the past six years and more without him as he passed away on the 21st of March 1920. but it has only been by looking too, and depending upon, the strong arm of my gracious Heavenly Father for strength and courage to press on to meet him in the better land, that I have been able to endure the trials thru which I have had to pass since being bereaved of my dearest earthly friend, and I pray that I may draw closer to the Lord each day and not wander from His love and care. "Prone to wander Lord I feel it, prone to leave the God I love, here my heart oh take and seal it, seal it for Thy courts above." For Jesus sake I ask it.

Sunday Oct the 24th 1926

A very cloudy day, but by faith we will look to the Great Head of the Church for an opening to go to His house for worship. which we were permited to do in the afternoon, and enjoyed an interesting Sunday School class taught by our Teacher **Mrs Wm Ledwell**.

Monday Oct the 25th

A cool windy morning. I feel very thankful to of had a good nights rest in sleep, and to be able with others to resume our general rotine for the day. and my heart is lifted up in praise to the great givers of all good for His mercy to us all.

Tuesday Oct the 26th

The language comes to me this morning "Why art thou cast down oh my soul and why art thou disquieted within me, hope thou in God for I shall yet praise him who is the health of my containance and my God." In my great poverty of spirit this verse of Scripture comes to me as though it were whispered in my ear by my merciful Heavenly Father to cheer me on my way, for everything seemed so dark before me that I could not see my way, nor know what to do that would be well pleasing in His sight, but by listening to that still small voice which speaks as never man spake, I am persuaded to still hope on and hope ever, for I shall yet praise God in that home he has prepared for me and for all who hope in His mercy if we will only be faithful to trust Him fully and not listen to the discouragements of the tempter who is ever ready to try to put us out of the right path but blessed be God who giveth us the victory thru our Lord Jesus Christ, he has power to help us to overcome the enemy of our souls peace as we look to him with an eye single to His glory. "I waited patiently for the Lord and he inclined his ear unto me." and now my prayer is, oh Father in Heaven never let me doubt thy mercy to me thy poor unworthy child, but still hope in thy mercy for it has been shown to me that Thou art ever ready to hold up the hands of those who are ready to hang down and give out by the way. for we are told that "mans extremity is Gods opportunity" Therefore He is ever ready to hold out a helping hand ere we fall.

Wednesday Oct the 27th 1926

A cold cloudy morning. I am thankful for having passed a quiet nights rest, and this morning I feel like praising God from whom all blessings flow. I am so glad that I can say truly that I am resigned to the Lords will, and that I can say in the language of one who has now passed over the river of death. "I am ready to live or ready to die." I am in the hands of the Lord and am waiting his own time to take me from works to rewards, and if He sees fit to lengthen our my days, I am willing to remain on earth until He is ready to call me home let the time be longer or shorter, and my earnest prayer is dear Lord help me to follow thee so closely that I may not go astray from thee, but that I may abide under the shadow of thy wings as it were at all times, doing thy holy will, so that I may be a fit subject to enter Thy kingdom to praise thee forever.

Thursday Oct the 28th 1926

A clear cold morning there was ice this morning for the first I had seen this fall (but perhaps I had been getting up too late the past week) the air feels like winter weather was near. oh that we all may prepare for that time where the cold blasts of winter never come, and where we can praise the Great Giver face to face for preparing such a haven of rest for his dependent children is my sincere prayer for Jesus sake.

Friday Oct the 29th 1926

A nice morning, all able to be up, for which I feel very grateful to our merciful Heavenly Father for his gracious love and care over us. oh that I may never grieve his holy spirit by my disobedience to his divine commands, for I desire to do thy will oh my Father in Jesus name.

Saturday Oct the 30th 1926

Thankful for strength to arise from my bed this lovely morning, and can truly say in the language of Scripture "As the Hart panteth after the water brook so panteth my soul after thee oh God." when shall I see thee and behold thy glory, oh help me to do thy holy will this day and every day whilst I am spared here on earth, that I may be prepared to meet thee in the glory land to praise thee with the dear Son of thy love thruout eternity, is my prayer for Jesus sake.

Sunday Oct the 31st

As this is the last day of October it again reminds me of the flight of time, and that we are all one month nearer our journeys end, oh that we may all be nearer ready to enter that blest abode which is prepared for all who do the will of the Lord while travling thru this vale of tears, I passed hours last night in agoniseing prayer that I might have strength and courage to resist the assaults of those who should be my helpers and comforters, and pleading earnestly that my heart may be so cleansed from all evil, and filled so full of love that there would be no room for envy or malice against my most bitter enemies, that I may be more like my blessed Savior who "when reviled reviled not again" but prayed for those who despitefully used Him. and I am so thankful that by the grace of God I can love even those who treat me unkindly and can pray for them that they turn from all evil and be saved with an everlasting salvation, for we are told that love is the fulfiling of the law, and if we do not love one another we can not expect to enter into that rest, which has been perchased by the precious blood of Him who loved even siners so much as to die upon the Cross that we might all be saved.

November the 1st 1926

A nice cool November morning, and as is the case from day to day, we all have much to be thankful for, and I trust as the days go by that we may be closer on our watch to do the things that are well pleasing in our Heavenly Fathers sight, for he sees us at all times, for as His eye is on the sparrow, we know that his all seeing eye is watching us, and knows all we do and say therefore my prayer is, "Set thou a watch before my mouth keep the door of my lips that I sin not with my tonque." for I find that the tongue is indeed an "unruly member" and has to be closely guarded least in a moment of weakness and excitement it causes us to transgress.

Tuesday Nov the 2nd 1926

A cool cloudy morning. Just as I was preparing to pen a few lines the message comes to me "**Mamie White** died this morning" **Mamie Steed White** wife of **Earl White** who passed away this morning Tuesday November the 2nd 1926 will be greatly missed she was a sweet loveable woman. my heart has been made sad by this message for I was always met by a sweet smile an friendly handshake when we were at Church at Mt Vernon, and my desire is that I may so live that I may be prepared to meet her in the better land where I feel sure she has gone. Oh Thou who knows the minds and hearts of all people thou knows that my poor sad heart is desireous about everything else to be found doing the things that are well pleasing in Thy sight, and that I look to Thee from day to day for help and strength and ability to know what Thou requires of me to do, and in answer to my simple petitions Thou hast made it plain to me that it was required of me to keep a Diary as I have been doing, not merely to just be doing something to be seen or heard by those who may chance to see or hear what I have written, but in obedience to Him who has held my right hand as it were, and directed my thoughts to pen down such things as would be an inspiration to others to press on through all the hardships thru which we have to pass in this life, looking to Him who is able to keep us from falling as we follow in His footsteps along lifes pathway. And in whos name and for whos sake I have used my pen from time to time, as He has bid me do this simple work.

Wednesday Nov the 3rd

A clear cool morning, and as I am expecting to attend the funeral of Mamie White at Mt Vernon to day at two oclock if I keep able, my thoughts are centered on the uncertainty of life and the certainty of death, and I am striveing with all my mental faculties and physical strength to do that which is just and right in the sight of Him to whom I shall have to give account in the judgement, and I want not only to be ready to enter into that rest which He has prepared for those whos robes have been washed and made white in the blood of the Lamb, but I want to feel His divine presence while travling thru this wilderness journey, and that I may love, honor and praise Him here on this earth his footstool as well as around His throne in Heaven. "That Thy will may be done on earth as it is in Heaven," is my prayer for Jesus sake.

Thursday Nov the 4th 1926

A clear cold morning. I have just been reading the 10th chapter of Romans, and in it I find so much instruction who to call upon for help and in whom to believe in order that we may be saved, that we cannot plead ignorance for not knowing the way, for in the ninth verse we are told, "That if thou shalt confess with thy mouth the Lord Jesus and shalt believe in thine heart that God hath raised him from the dead thou shalt be saved" and the 13th verse it is stated. "For whosoever shall call upon the name of the Lord shall be saved" and as Paul has made it plain to all believers that God is not only a God of the Jews, but also of the Gentiles we can all have hope in Him and Paul further says there is no difference between the Jew and the Greek for the same Lord over all is rich unto all that call upon him. and we who from childhood have know the holy Scriptures cannot plead ignorance for not obeying them, for we have read for ourselves and our Preachers have told us that we must call upon God with true sincereity of heart and purpose, for it is written that, "not every one who saith Lord Lord shall enter into the kingdom of Heaven, but they who do the will of our Father in heaven, so we see that altho we are told that "Whosoever shall call upon the name of the Lord shall be saved we are not to expect the mere calling to save us, unless it is done in spirit and in truth, believeing and taking God at his word, For with the heart man believeth unto righteousness and with the mouth confession is made unto salvation.

November 1926

Friday Nov the 5th 1926

As I have been spared to see another day I feel like giving thanks to the great Giver of all our blessings and ask that He will go with me thru this day and thru all comeing days, that I may be prepared to meet Him in the glory land, where we can praise Him more perfectly than we can upon this earth, and it is the fervent desire of my heart to do his holy will, and I know that I may walk uprightly before Him.

Saturday Nov the 6th

A nice cold morning, and I am very thankful to be able to arise from my bed to enjoy the braceing fresh air, which gives vigor to our bodies and buoys up our spirits in, Thanks to Him from whom all blessings flow.

Sunday Nov the 7th 1926

A lovely Sabbath morning, and all able to get out and enjoy it. **Miss Carrie Cranford** and her brotherinlaw **Mr Jeter Montgomery** called to see us a little while this morning so glad to see them. I am aiming to attend Church and Sunday School at Mt Vernon to day if I keep able, and go home with **Mrs George Robins** for a little visit, I feel very grateful for this kind invitation, and also for a degree of health which I trust will enable me to do these things. The praise belongeth to Him from whom we receive all blessings.

Monday Nov the 8th

A damp foggy morning, I am now takeing down a few notes in the home of **Mrs George Robins** as I came home with her from Church yesterday as I had planed to do, had a good friendly visit, and at night we had Bible reading and prayer before retireing. This home is on the same farm where I was born and raised, and it brings many things of the past fresh to my mind. The Cedars in the yard that were there from my childhood in my dear old homestead, which is just a few hundred years north of where **Mr Robin's** new house now stands, look so natural, and where I played as a child with my brothers and sisters and other playmates on the pretty green grass in the year, it hardly seems possible that more than a half Century has passed since those days, yet if I am spared until the 13th of March 1927. I will be 82 years of age. and my heart has been made glad by reading this morning the 71st Psalm which shows that our blessed Saviour does not forsake us when we are old and grey headed if we put our trust in Him. Blessed be His holy name now and forever saith my soul.

Tuesday Nov the 9th 1926

A rainy morning. I am still in the home of the **Mr Robins** his wife and I have been having quite an interesting visit togeather, their two boys are in school at Trinity and their Father has gone on a trip to Winston Salem I feel that I have much to be thankful for that I am able at this time, before real winter sets in to visit some of my friends and kindred for a fews days, and I praise the Lord for his goodness and mercy to me in enabling me to do this. Evening of the same day **Mr Robins** conveyed me me to cousin **Robert Blairs** where I found cousin **Ocid** his wife quite busy prepareing for the Ladies Club of Archdale to meeting in their home the following day, I also met with cousin **Anna Blair** wife of **E.C. Blair** who was helping to get ready for their guests had a jolly good time with them.

Wednesday Nov the 10th 1926

A nice cool morning. I spent a very comfortable night here at cousin **Roberts** and feel so grateful that I am able to be up and enjoy the nice cool breeze "Praise the Lord oh my soul, and all that is within me bless His holy name.

Thursday morning Nov the 11th

A lovely morning but quite cold. I spent last night also at cousin **Roberts**, and I am thankful that we are all in usual health. I must not omit stateing that yesterday in the afternoon The Ladies Club of Archdale met in this home, about thirty in attendance among them dear **Clara I Cox** who is our Pastor at Springfield at this time, and I met with many that I had not seen for quite awhile, so it was a very interesting occasion. I feel that I have much to be thankful for, to my merciful Heavenly Father for directing my feet this way. for I had comited my self to His divine care and keeping. Praise His name.

Friday Nov the 12th 1926

The coldest morning we have had this month, but I am thankful that it is as well with us all as it is. I returned to my daughters last evening from cousin **Robert Blairs**, and found my little grandson **J.A. Peace** suffering from Rupture which necesitated their takeing him at once to High Point to a Dr which did and soon had him relieved of his suffering for the present, but we still have great anxiety about him as the Dr thinks it will be necessary to perform an Opperation later. I am praying that the dear Lord will heal him sound and well if it is His holy will. I am also praying that we may all be in perfect subjection to His will in whatever He permits us to pass thru in this life, for He has promiced to not leave or forsake us.

Saturday Nov the 13th 1926

A clear cold morning. and since having some rain the leaves from the trees are falling fast, the ground is already covered with foalage of various colors, and the trees begin to look bare which reminds us that cold bleak winter is near us, and it also reminds us that we sooner or later will be disrobed of our mortal bodies and have to appear before the Great Judge of all the earth and oh how necessary that we be prepared to have a good account to give, that we may receive the welcome of well done good and faithful servant enter into the joy of thy Lord. for oh the dreadful thought of being cast into outer darkness, oh God forbid that we should disobey thee, thus be lost.

Sunday Nov the 14ᵗʰ

A lovely morning, not so cold as for the past few days. I lift up my heart in praise and thanksgiving to the Great Giver of all good, that we are all able to arise from our beds and prepare for the services of the day, we hope to get out to Church as usual this afternoon, if it is the will of our loveing Heavenly Father, but later as I do not feel quite strong enough to go to Church and Sunday School I am in submishion to His will in this also. Blessed be the name of the Lord.

Monday Nov the 15ᵗʰ

A cloudy damp morning, which causes more aches and pains in my aged limbs, but so thankful that I now have the use of them sufficient to get about and wait on myself, a privilige that I did not have for so many years, having then to go on my Wheel Chair when I had strength enough to be put in it and get around in that way. If feel that I cannot be thankful enough to my merciful Heavenly Father that he has seen fit to restore me even as well as I am, for in the past I had little hope of ever walking again, and now instead of being a helpless invalid, altho not strong as I would wish to be but to be so I can do for myself the things that I could not do for so many years when I was helpless, I feel that I cannot be grateful enough, to Him who has promiced, "That as they day they strength shall be." and as I have realised this to be true and sufficient for each day, I have day by day taken fresh courage to press on to the end looking unto Him who is able to keep me from falling as I put my trust in Him, and now the lines of the Hymn comes to me. "Trust and obey for there is not other way, to be happy in Jesus but to trust and obey." So I am praying for the help of the Lord that I may obey him in all things to his honor and praise.

Tuesday Nov the 16ᵗʰ

A very cloudy morning. I am so thankful that I have strength sufficient to arise from my bed, and be of some help to my daughter, which some light work she is doing to day, for I love to be doing something helpful whenever there is anything I have strength to do. I now feel like pening the lines, "I am trusting Lord in thee blessed Lamb of Calvary; all my hope on thee is staid, all my help from thee I bring, cover my defenceless head with the shadow of thy wing."

Wednesday Nov the 17th 1926

The weather is very changeable one day quite warm for the time of year, the next cold or rainy, which makes one feel the effects of the change quite perceptably. The changes reminds me of the fickleness of human nature tone time we may meet with a person who seems kind and generous, and at another time the same person will be cold and distant. These are like those described in Scripture "He that wavereth is like a wave of the sea driven and tossed, let not that man think that he shall receive anything of the Lord." and as we poor human beings are all subjects of this penelty, my earnest prayer is that I may be steadfast, unmoveable, always abounding in the fear of the Lord, so that my prayer may be heard and answered to His honor and praise.

Thursday Nov the 18th 1926

A rainy morning, the dampness causes me to suffer more with pains and aches, and I have suffered more with acutely for the past forty eight hours than for several months, but I feel that I have much to be thankful for that I am with my daughter at this time who is very kind and helpful to me. which I appreciate so much. Praise the Lord from whom all blessings cometh.

Friday Nov the 19th 1926

This is quite a cool day. I am not at all well at this time, and as I feel so weak and nervous, it causes me to also feel sad and lonely, but so thankful that I can still wait on myself, for I do not want to be a burden to others, and I am looking unto Him from whom all help cometh for strength and courage to press on thru the dark hours as well as in the light, and as we poor weak mortals often feel the need of a sympathiseing friend, it is a great consolation to know that we have a friend about all others who never fails us, but is ready at all times to help us as we come to Him in true confidence and faith. So my earnest prayer at this time is, oh God help me to put my whole trust in thee, for vain is the help of man. and Thou who knows the hearts and minds of all people, knows that I have given my heart to thee, and desire above all things to be found walking in the way that is well pleasing in they sight. and now oh my Father be my guide and leader thruout the remaind of this life, keep me so close to thee that I go not astray. bless all my loved ones, and even my enemies, for I want to follow in Thy footsteps loveing those that do not love me, and thus follow the example of our blessed Redeemer who loved his enemies and even died for them.

Saturday Nov the 20th 1926

A very cold morning. I am still suffering in body, but thankful that my mind is staid on that firm foundation Christ Jesus, who is able to comfort and help us in our most trying moments. and it is much to be thankful for to the Giver of all our blessings, and to those with whom we reside, to have food and shelter, and fuel to keep us warm these cold chilly days, and it makes me want to prepare for that land where, "no chilling winds nor poisness breath can reach that healthful shore, where sickness and sorrow pain, and death are felt and feared no more." "When shall I reach that happy place and be forever blessed, when shall I see my Fathers face and in his bosom rest."

Sunday Nov the 21st

This is a cold Sabbath, but we are blessed with company to dine with us to day. The **Pastor Rev Reed Haris** and his wife and two little boys. Mrs **Archie Spencer** of Trinity and wife and their little son. **Mr** and **Mrs. Bowman,** of Glenola, also their son **Gideon Bowman** and wife **Ollie Peace Bowman.** They will all attend Church this after at Mt Vernon, but I shall not be able to go, as I have not been at all well for several days, I am sorry to have to miss Church and Sunday School, as I am one that is always glad when it is staid "Let us go up to the house of the Lord," or words of that effect, but I am thankful to be in submishion to my lot, and am trying not to murmer at whatever changes comes to me whilst travling thru this lif's journey, and wish that at all times I may be able to truthfully say like Paul, "I have learned in whatsoever state I am therewith to be content. but as the flesh is weak we are often sorely tried and have to plead hard for help to overcome all obsticles and not give out by the way, and as I cannot go to Church to day my prayer is, Heavenly Father help me to keep this day holy for altho I cannot go up to thy house, help me to worship thee in my heart and in the house in which I reside or wherever I be, I ask for Jesus sake.

Monday Nov the 22nd 1926

A cold morning. I am still feeling weak and regret not being able to attend the funeral of **Mr. J.R. Wall** at Mt Vernon to day at eleven oclock, we are almost daily called upon to witness the uncertainty of life and the certainty of death, by either some friend or some one we have known being called from works to rewards. oh that we may all make diligent search of our hearts, the we may be ready to meet the messenger death, with our lamps trimed and burning.

Tuesday Nov the 23th 1926

Another cold morning, but I am thankful to be feeling some better, and feel that I cannot praise my merciful Heavenly Father enough, that he watches over us by day and by night, and protects us from all harm. oh that I may not grieve the holy spirit least He depart from me. for I desire to do thy will, oh gracious Lord for thou knowest our every thought. Blessed be the name of the Lord.

Wednesday Nov the 24th

A cool cloudy morning. I am truly thankful to be feeling some stronger to day. for I have suffered so much the past two weeks. Tomorrow is Thanksgiving day and I feel like it would be impossible to enumerate the things that we all have to be thankful for. one of these great blessing is health sufficient to be so we can care for ourselves, and not be a burden to others. and above all to realise that we have a great burden bearer, our blessed Saviour who is watching over, and careing for us at all times.

Thursday Nov the 25th 1926

Thanksgiving day. This day is set apart to remind us of our obligations to the Creator and maker of all things, that we are indebted to Him for even the breath we draw, and the food to sustain life, and the clothing that we wear, and for everything that we have to enjoy both spiritually and temporally. It is impossible to enumerate the blessings which are showered upon us unworthy cretures by our gracious Heavenly Father, for which we should give thanks, and who sent us the greatest of all blessings the gift of his dear Son Jesus Christ to die upon the Cross for our sins, that we might have eternal life with Him if we obey and serve him with the whole heart as we should, oh let us be more thankful for all our blessings, and praise Him more and obey him better here on earth, that we may be prepared to enter into that rest which He has promiced for all those who love and serve him here on earth, that we may praise Him forever in Heaven.

Friday Nov the 26th 1926

A cloudy damp morning. In my meditation upon the past I call to mind that to day is my oldest childs Birthday **Mrs D.C. Moffitt** who has been a widow for nearly twenty years and is now living in Kansas City Mo. it hardly seems possible but to day November the 26th 1926 is her sixty first birthday. oh the trials and beseting seasons that she

November 1926

and I have both gone thru during those years, both having to give up kind and loveing husbands by the cold hand of death. but I am thankful that we have known where to look for help and strength to bear us up thru all the hardships that have come to us during those years, and my prayer this day is, dear Lord help us both to be faithful and true to follow Thee wheresoever thou leads, and that we may be instrumental in thy hand in helping others to serve and praise thy most holy name. Just now while pening these lines our mail was brought in, and a Thanksgiving Card was handed me from my dear daughter that I was just writing about, and again reminds me of her faithfulness to her aged Mother. for from childhood she has been one of the most obedient children I ever knew, always faithful to care for her Invalid Mother while she remained in the home, and after Mariage she always did what she could when in reach to help, and when far away always rememered me with kind mesages.

Saturday Nov the 27th 1926

A clear morning after a nice rain last night. Again the words of scripture comes to my mind "Teach me thy way oh Lord and lead me in a plain path, how often my mind and heart cries out as it were in these words, for I want to be found walking in the footsteps of Jesus, so that I go not astray from him. That I may answer the end for which I was created which was to glorify God. and He says, "Come unto me all ye that labor and are heavy laden and I will give you rest, take my yoke upon and learn of me, for I am meek and lowly in heart, and ye shall find rest to your souls, for my yoke is easy and my burden is light. oh that we might always look to this great burden bearer, who is ready at all times to help us.

Sunday Nov the 28th

This is quite a cool Sabbath, and as I have not felt able to go to Church, I was taken down to **Grandma Peaces** while the rest of the family were away, I had a very interesting visit with her and her daughterinlaw **Mrs Earl Peace**. and I wish to return thanksgiving and praise to our merciful Heavenly Father for His tender care over us all this day.

Monday Nov the 29th 1926

Cool and cloudy this morning. The language comes to me at this time. I know that my Redeemer livith and because he lives I shall live also. These words are such a consolation to me, to think of a blessed Saviour where unto we can look for life eternal if we will follow him in the way of his requireings. dear Lord help me to do thy holy will to thy names honor and praise is the prayer of my heart for Jesus sake.

Tuesday Nov the 30th

A cloudy damp morning. As this is the last day of the month. I am again reminded how fast time flies, for it seems but as yesterday that I noted the last day of October. and I am also reminded that tomorrow will begin the winter season, and not doubt we shall have to face chilling winds and perhaps storms of rain and snow. oh that we may all bear patiently and obediently with all the storms and trials thru which we have to pass in this life, that we may be prepared to enter on this blissful shore. "Where chilling winds nor poisonous breath can reach that healthful shore where sickness and sorrow pain and death are felt and feared not more." oh God help us all to be ready to enter into that haven of rest, there to sing thy praise forevermore.

Wednesday December the 1st 1926

A nice cold morning for the first day of winter. The neighbors are met togeather for regular hog killing to day, their place of dressing them is near **Grandma Peaces** spring. How nice it is for people to help each other in their domestic affairs, and "Behold how good and how pleasent it is for brethren to dwell together in unity." oh that all would do this.

Thursday Dec the 2nd

Another nice cold morning. which is favorable on their fresh killed pork. oh how much we have to be thankful for as we are spared from day to day, for our merciful Heavenly Father seems to take notice of all our needs both physically and spiritually. Blessed by His holy name for he is worthy of all praise now and forever.

Friday Dec the 3rd

A nice winter morning. I am very thankful that we are all able to be up and go about our daily duties. "Oh for a heart to praise my God, a heart from sin set free, a heart that always feels the blood so freely shed for me. A heart resigned submisive meek my great Redeemers throne, where only Christ is heard to speak and Jesus reigns alone." These words of the Hymn which came to me as I was takeing up my paper to write a few lines this morning, express the fervent desire of my heart that Jesus will rule and reign supreme in my heart and thoughts this day, and all succeeding days.

Saturday Dec the 4th 1926

A nice morning. We have much to be thankful for that we are all able to be up, and go about our daily ocupations. may the dear Lord direct our every step so that we walk aright, is the desire of my heart this day, for unto Him belongth all praise new and forever, for "He hath not dealt with us after our sins nor rewarded according to our inquities." but has watched over us from day to day and blessed us beyond what we deserve, and set us the example of paitience and forbearance one with another that we should do well to emulate, God help us so to do for Christ our Redeemers sake.

Sunday Dec the 5th 1926

A cold cloudy morning. oh that I may make a Sabbath days journey toward Heaven this day, is the fervent desire of my heart, to the praise of Him who has told us in his Word to remember the Sabbath day to keep it holy, for I desire to do thy holy will thou knowest. and it is only by keeping my mind staid on thee, and trusting in thee for help that I can keep in the right path.

Monday Dec the 6th 1926

This is one of the coldest, and most disagreeable mornings we have experienced this season so far, the wind is so piercing. oh that we may all be in earnest to prepare for that land where chilling winds, nor cold can ever enter, but where peace and happiness reigns supreme. but we have so much to be thankful for that while we are sojourning here, we have shelter from the stormy blast, and food and clotheing and fuel to keep us warm. so I want to praise thee our Heavenly Father for what thou hast provided for us they dependent children. and that I may love thee more and serve thee better. yes "Let thy tender love to me, bind me closer closer Lord to thee." is my prayer for Jesus sake.

Tuesday Dec the 7th 1926

A very cold morning. But I am thankful that we of this household are all in usual health, and trying to do whatever duty calls us to do. Heavenly Father I plead that thou will lead and guide us this day so that we walk uprightly before thee, for we want to have a good account to give of this days work, and my earnest desire is that I may each day as they are lengthened out to me, be found doing the thing that are well pleasing in thy sight that I may be a living epistle of love and good will, owned and read of all with whom I meet and mingle, to Thy names honor and praise.

Wednesday Dec the 8th 1926

A rainy morning. I am thankful to my merciful Heavenly Father for having passed a quiet night in rest and sleep and for strength to arise from my bed, and to use my pen to note down His goodness to all of us his unworthy creatures, and I want to praise his name for his watchful care over us by night and by day. "I love the Lord because he hath heard my voice and my supplication. Because he hath inclind his ear unto me, therefore I will call upon him as long as I live."

Thursday Dec the 9th 1926

Another rainy morning. We are told in the Book of Books that all things work togeather for good to them that love the Lord. and I am thankful that I believe all the words of that Book are true, and we learn from it that Gods ways are not as mans ways, and that he sees the end from the beginning, so we should be entirely in subjection to his divine ordering, for He makes no mistakes. altho we poor short sighted mortals can not see the why of many things that take place. For instance the case of the sweet little babe of **Charles White** and wife that was found dead in bed yesterday morning without any appeared cause, and which has almost broken the hearts of its parents to have to give it up, may be in the all Wise plan the means of saveing some soul or souls that are out of the Ark of safety. and also the great Burden Bearer can heal their wounded hearts if they will only lean on the Everlasting Arms and be able to say the Lord gave and the Lord hath taken away. Blessed be the name of the Lord.

Friday Dec the 10th 1926

Still cloudy, but I think the sun is going to shine to day. The changeable weather coresponds very much to our habits and feelings, as we are passing thru this wilderness journey of life, for sometimes our way seems so dark and hedged in that we can not see any way to go any farther. but if we will only be patient and trust in the Lord he the Sun of righteousness will cause his light to shine as it were in our hearts and minds and cheer us on our way. just as the morning sun breaks forth from behind the clouds and dispels the gloom and everything becomes bright and cheery. oh that I may fully trust Him to lead and guide me all the way is my greatest desire, for the sake of Him who died for me and all others.

Saturday Dec the 11th 1926

A lovely morning The sun is shineing so brightly, after having several days of dark rainey weather. It makes me long for that beautiful land where dark dreary days never come, where there is no night, but all is light, and sorrow never comes "oh for a closer walk with God a calm and Heavenly frame a light to shine upon the road that leads me to the Lamb." yes that is the greatest desire of my heart to be found daily walking in the light which leads to life evermore; where I can sing Gods praise, thru all my days, with loved ones gone before.

Sunday Dec the 12th 1926

Another cloudy morning. To day is my little grandson Jerome Addison Peace's third birthday. my prayer is that his parent wholely dedicate him to the Lord. and that they may teach him to love the Lord and obey his Commandments, and that he as he grows in years may grow in grace, and in favor with God and man. and become a good and useful man and be a blessing to his parents, and to the Church and to the world. for Christs sake. And that may early take heed to the Scriptures injunction to "Remember now thy Creator in the days of thy youth while the evils days come not, nor the years draw nigh when thou shalt say I have no pleasure in them."

Monday Dec the 13th 1926

A very cloudy morning, which coresponds very much with my feelings, for I am sorely tried this morning, which makes me feel dull and gloomy. but I am praying to the source of light and life for help to overcome all my trials, and not give by the way. remembering that He who came to earth to live for a time, and die for us poor unworthy mortals, was insulted and badly treated even being spat upon, and crowned with thorns so I am trying with the help of my gracious Redeemer to bear all the briars and thorns as it were in the flesh, that I may when done with this wilderness journey, be prepared to enter where all trials are done away. and where I can praise His holy name forever. where the enemy can never enter.

Tuesday Dec the 14th 1926

Still cloudy, but more prospect of sunshine to day. My heart is sore this morning because of the trials I have to meet with in this life, but am trying by faith to trust and believe that there is a better day comeing. for Jesus hath said; In the world ye shall have tribulation, but be of good cheer I have overcome the world. so by His help I am trying to be of good cheer, and overcome my trials that I may find a home of rest at last.

Wednesday Dec the 15th 1926

Cloudy again this morning. But I know that the clouds will scattered, and the sun will shine fourth at the word of the Creator of all things for He holdeth the world in his hands and knoweth all things. so I feel like saying with David the psalmist, "oh Lord thou hast searched me and know me. Thou knowest my downsitting and mine upriseing thou understandest my thoughts afar off. Thou compasest my path and my lying down and art acquainted with all my ways. For there is not a word in my tongue but lo oh Lord thou knowest it altogeather." Therefore I am praying fervently that Thou who sees me just as I am and knows my thoughts and desires will keep me as in the hallow of Thy holy hand that I sin not against thee in word or deed. And thus I pray for all my loved ones and for all for whom it is my duty to pray that they may follow Thee in the way of thy requireings here on earth, and that we may be an unbroken band in the better land. To be with Him forever of whom some one has written. "Without begining or decline Object of faith, and not of sense: Eternal ages saw Him shine. He shines eternal ages hence."

Thursday Dec the 16th 1926

A very cold morning, but I am thankful that we of this household, are all to be up and go about our daily duties, and my great desire is that we may all be of the household of faith, that we may be found doing the things that are well pleasing in the sight of Him who is the Auther and finisher of our faith, and in whom we live and move and have our being, and to whom belongeth all praise now and forever. For I believe indeed that God is true, That he sees and knows all I do. So help me Lord day by day, To walk the strait and narow way. That I may have a good account to give, And with thee in heaven forever live. This is my prayer in simple rhyme, That with Angels I may praise Thee all the time.

Friday Dec the 17th 1926

Another cold morning, some of the family not very well. but I am thankful that it is so well with us all as it is. for we have so many things to be thankful for, altho we have many things to contend with in this life that are not pleasent to our human nature. but I feel like giving praise to God this morning, for all his benefits to us, his poor erring children, for He bears with us according to our iniquites. but bears with our many short comeings. Blessed be His holy name.

Saturday Dec the 18th 1926

Still cold but bright sunshine, and I am thankful that we are all feeling better to day, and going about our daily avocations. "Bless the Lord oh my soul, and all that is within me bless His holy name."

Sunday Dec the 19th

A very cold morning, so much so that the flowers that had withstood the cold so far are now frozen in the rooms this morning. To day we are to have the Christmas lesson in the Sunday School, oh that we may all bear in mind the true significance of Christs coming into the world. That God in his infinite goodness and mercy toward poor fallen mankind. sent his beloved Son into the world, to suffer and die upon the Cross to save us from our sins. and as we think of His suffering on the "old ruged cross," let us be careful that we do not crusify Him afresh by our disobedience, but let us be close on our watch to do the things which are well pleasing in His sight to his names honor and praise. "Glory to God on high, let Heaven and earth reply praise ye His name. His love and grace adore, who all our sorrows bore, worthy the Lamb."

Monday Dec the 20th 1926

A very cold morning. I trust we are all thankful to our merciful Heavenly Father for all our benefits for he provides us with food and clotheing and fuel to keep us comfortable this bitter cold weather, for if we did not have a sufficiency of these things we should suffer greatly. and I also feel very grateful to those who are kind and thoughtful enough to see that those thing which are provided for our use by our great Benefactor are put within the reach of those that are not able to wait on themselves, to make them comfortable for by so doing they obey the Masters words when he said "In as much as ye did it unto the least of these ye did it unto me. And let us ever remember the Golden Rule to do unto others as we would have them do unto us, for by so doing we shall be happy ourselves and make others happy.

Tuesday Dec the 21st

Much warmer to day. I am thankful that we of this household are all able to be up, to do what is necessary to be done for the comfort and sustanance of life. The people in general are in a hurry and bustle prepareing for the hollidays. oh that we would all be as eager to do everything to please Him every day in the year, who came to earth and suffered so much for us poor unworthy mortals as we are to do something to please our friends and loved ones at Christmas time, how loyal we would be. and my prayer is that we may all have our feet planted on higher ground, so that we will not stoop to do the lowe debaseing things, such as harboring evil thoughts and hatred in our hearts toward any of our fellow beings, but that our hearts may be filled so full of the love of God that there will be no room for envy or malice or evil speaking against any one, but that we may be gentle loveing and kind toward each other, and with all with whom we meet and mingle. for love is the fulfiling of the law. The following lines is the most fervent desire of my heart. Loveing Jesus, gentle Lamb, In thy gracious hands, I am; Make me, Saviour what thou art; Live thyself within my heart. I shall then show forth thy praise, Serve thee all my happy days; Then the world shall always see Christ, the holy Child in me.

Wednesday Dec the 22nd 1926

A cloudy morning, and altho the dampness causes more pains and aches, I am thankful to be able to arise from my bed. and write to some of my friends, sending them letters of sympathy, and to some Cards of Greetings for the comeing holidays and my very best wishes for the comeing New Year. oh that we all would be more obedient to Him whose birth we profess to commemorate at Christmas time.

Thursday Dec the 23rd 1926

Another cloudy morning. I feel at a loss to know how to express my feelings to day. For as the Christmas time draws nearer. It brings to mind those that are dearer, Than any earthly store of perishable things. But altho for our loss of them here, we sigh, We rejoice to think of their home on high, Which is the Palace of the king of kings. And in order that we all may meet them there. We should be obedient and watch unto prayer. As these thoughts come to me at this time, I write them down in this simple rhyme Trusting that my children dear, in the far hence or near, May meet me in that happy home above. To dwell with loved ones in eternal peace and love.

Friday Dec the 24th 1926

Cloudy again this morning. As Christmas day is nigh my heart is filled with both gladness and sadness, for it makes me sad to think of what our dear Saviour suffered for us poor unworthy cretures. and it also makes my heart rejoice to think of what a precious Redeemer we have, and now as the time is near when we commemorate the birth of this wonderful babe which God the Father sent into the world to save the people from their sins. I am greatly desireing that we may keep the day in a way, that will glorify God the Father, God the Son and Holy Spirit three in one.

Christmas day. Saturday Dec the 25th 1926

A very cloudy day. But there seems to be plenty of sunshine indoors, in the hearts and minds of us all, rejoiceing over Christmas presents received from loved ones far and near, and while we greatly appreciate these things. I am so glad and thankful that we have a gift above all others, the precious Babe of Bethlehem that was given to us by God the Father, Creator of all things, to be our loving and merciful Redeemer. who reveals himself to His children by and thru the Holy Spirit the Comforter. oh that we would all serve Him with all our heart and mind, is the fervent desire of my heart, for Christs sake.

Sunday Dec the 26th 1926

Still cloudy this morning. But I am thankful to state that we were all able to arise from our beds and make haste to get to the Parlor to see the Christmas Tree, which was loaded on, and beneath the boughs, with presents for every member of the family, for each other, and to and from other loved ones. It is nice to be remembered so kindly at Christmas time. and how nice it would be if we would all maintain the Christmas spirit all the year round, not merely in giving presents, but in treating each other with due respect, and loving kindness in every way. oh that we would have the spirit of our blessed Saviour, who is so gentle and kind, and bears with our many mistakes and shortcomeings so should we bear with one another for "Behold how good and how pleasent it is for brethren to dwell togeather in unity." To day those of us who compose the class of most aged attendents of the Sunday School at Mt Vernon, has the pleasure of presenting to our Teacher **Mrs Nora Ledwell**. A Teachers Bible. which she appreciated very much. and I for one, and I believe all the others did the same, felt "that it was more blest to give than to receive." And as Christ has given himself to us, let us give ourselves to Him.

Monday Dec the 27th 1926

Much colder this morning. Now as I meditate on the pleasures of the past two days, that of Christmas day Saturday and the next day being Sunday, of the many things given, and received both temporally and spiritually by ourselves and loved ones. I have thought how important it is that we examine our selves and assertain the the facts, whether with all the things we receive from our Heavenly Father the bountiful giver of all things. we are giving Him anything in return for us poor erring cretures He sent into the world to redeem us from sin and woe. we know that we can never compensate Him for all he has done for us, but let us do our utmost by His help to obey his divine commands which we should hold sacred about everything else. Blessed be His name.

Tuesday Dec the 28th 1926

A very rainey day. But we have all been spending the holidays very pleasantly, as those of the children of this family. (The family of **Jerome W. Peace**) who have recently married have visited us, and other friends have called in to cheer us. **Grady Peace** and **Clara Ward** were married Christmas eve Dec the 24th 1926. There has been quite a resorting to the Hymeneal Alter in the **Peace families**, in the past two years. **Gradys** sister **Ollie Peace** was married to **Gideon Bowman** August the 14th 1926. Her brother **Fred Peace** and **Jenette Kerns** were married Oct the 14th 1925. And **Fred's** cousin **Emery Peace** and **Nannie Crotts** were married in November 1925. and **Emerys** brother **Everette Peace** and **Jewel Baker** were married Dec the 19th 1926. The fervent desired of my heart is that all the coupels may live long and happy and useful lives, being on honor to themselves, to their people and to the Church and serve God according to all His commandments. so that when death separates them here on earth they may be reunited in that better land where parting is unknown.

Wednesday Dec the 29th 1926

A nice clear morning. All up and going about our daily duties. much to be thankful for that we have a degree of health and strength for these things The Mother in this home and the two girls are busy to day tacking comforts for the home of some of those who have recently emigrated to the state of Matrimony. These things we know will perish with the useing. The fervent desire of my heart is that we may all be as diligent to prepare for that home where neither moth nor rust doth corrupt nor theives break thru nor steal.

Thursday Dec the 30th 1926

A clear cold morning. I am so thankful that we are all able to go about our daily avocations. I was blessed last evening with a visit from our dear Pastor **Clara I Cox** of Friends Church. Springfield N.C. I always enjoy a visit from her, she is so very congeniel, and gives me such encouragement to press on in the way of our blessed masters requireings. May the dear Lord bless her abundantly in her work for Him is my prayer.

Friday Dec the 31st 1926

Another cold morning. And as I reflect that this is the last morning in the year 1926. I am filled with awe at the flight of time, and the wonderful works of the great Creator of all things. And my heart and mind are also filled with wonder love and praise, as I meditate upon the goodness and mercy of a loving Saviour, who has watched over us and spared our lives, whilst many loved ones have been taken away either by natural death or by some sad accident during the past year. and that we have a degree of health and strength, so that we can go about our daily avocations. and have food and rainment and all the really necessary conveniences of life. so I feel that we cannot praise our Heavenly Father enough for his goodness and mercy to us, His dependent ones.

1927

Saturday January the 1st 1927

A cold morning for the beginning of the New Year. There is so much to be thankful for that we have been carried safely over into the new year, that I am at a loss to know how to express myself. I know that I feel very grateful to our merciful Heavenly Father for the degree of health which I have at this time for altho I feel the infirmities of age, yet I can still wait on myself, and can also do some things to help in the work of the family, which is a great pleasure to me. and my great desire is that I may not become a burden to the family. It has been said that earnest desires are prayers, so I am earnestly praying my blessed Saviour to help me to begin this new year in a way that is well pleasing in His sight, that I may love, fear and worship him all the days, not only of this year but all the days of my life, should He see fit to lengthen my days a few years longer, that I may be prepared to enter that blissful abode which is prepared for all those who love and serve Him here on this earth his footstool. I want to sing this morning. oh for a heart to praise my God a heart from sin set free, a heart that always feel the blood so freely shed for me.

Sunday Jan the 2nd 1927

A clear cold day. Now that we have launched upon a New Year, my great desire is that we may all get into the life Boat and press forward, leaveing the things of the Old year behind, not carying over into the New Year anything that should be entirely forsaken and in the future have nothing but love to God and good will to all mankind abideing in our hearts for it is only by obeying these admonitions of our Great lay giver, that we can have the peace and comfort which is so desireable in this life, and we can not expect to have an entrance into the haven of rest which is prepared for those who do the will of Him who suffered death on the cross that we poor sinners night be saved from the penelty of our deeds while in the flesh, so help us dear Lord to forsake all evil, and learn to do good, is the sincere prayer of my heart this holy Sabbath day, to the praise and honor of His sacred name.

Monday Jan the 3rd 1927

A cloudy day. All in usual health. We were favored yesterday afternoon to get our to S.S. and Church at Mt Vernon heard a good sermon by the Pastor **Rev Reed Haris**. which was very much appreciated. Then last night we were visited by kind friends and kindred, which we enjoyed.

Tuesday Jan the 4th 1927

Another cloudy morning. But all are up for which I am very thankful. I have nothing specil to take note of at this time only the continued goodness and mercy of our dear Lord and Saviour, to His unworthy dependent children, for while our lives have been spared, and a good degree of healthe. we almost daily hear of some friend or some person that we have known of, being consigned to the grave, and we know not how soon it may be our lot, so dear Heavenly Father help us all to be ready, is my prayer. To day we learn that **Mrs. Wall**, widow of **Henry Wall**, and mother of **Mrs. Kinsey Myres** is to be burried this p.m. at Marlboro. I sympathise with all and especially with **Mr Myres'** motherless children who loved their Grandmother so fondly. May the Lord comfort all the bereaved ones, and help them to love so as to meet their loved ones in the Glory land. is my prayer

Wednesday Jan the 5th 1927

Clear and colder this morning. I am looking to Jesus who has taken care of us all during the past night, as He has all our past lives, to watch over us all this day. and I am desireous to do the things that are well pleasing in His sight. Our blessed Saviour has said in His Word I am the door, by me if any man (consequently any woman) enter in, he shall be saved and shall go in and out and find pasture, St. John 10-9. And my hearts desire is that I may so walk each day and my that may enter that door which is Christ the living way, and go in and out as it were in His very presence, realiseing him so near that I am being fed from His bountiful table of divine love and mercy which he shares with those who obey his holy will here on earth. Then what shall be the glory of His presence in his Palace above, where all is joy, peace and love.

Thursday Jan the 6th 1927

A nice clear morning. I am very thankful that it is as well with us as it is to day, and trust that we may be careful not to disobey any of the commands which are laid down in Gods holy word for us to follow, for we all want to meet Him in that glory land where we shall praise him forever, for here we have no continuing City and are subject to pain and sorrow, but there these things are done away. "And God shall wipe away all tears from their eyes, and there shall be not more death neither sorrow nor crying, neither shall there be any more pain: for the former things are passed away." Rev 21-4

Friday Jan the 7th 1927

Nice clear morning. All up and going about daily avocations. for which I feel very grateful, for it is such a blessing to be able to do that which is necessary for our comfort while passing thru this journey here below, and we often feel that we are almost ready to give up under the discouragements that come to us, and we feel cast down. But we are told in the Book of James 4-10 to Humble yourselves in the sight of the Lord and He shall lift you up. so I desire to live humbly and walk uprightly in the way the Lord directs, for often we are cast down and become so discouraged it is thru weakness and lack of faith rather than true humility. so help us dear Lord to lift up our heads in hope. is my prayer

January 1927

Saturday Jan the 8th 1927

Motto for the day Matt 5-48
Clear and cold this morning. I am solemnly impressed with the flight of time, for when I think that one week has alredy gone, of the New Year 1927. it hardly seems possible. and I am more and more impressed each day as they pass, with the necessity of being prepared for our final destiny, and oh that we may be so in earnest to do the will of Him who is perfect and who has said Matt 5-48.

Sunday Jan the 9th 1927

Sunday School lesson for to day Luke 6-27 to 38
We have a light skiff of snow this morning, for the first here this season. but it is soon gone. In thinking of the whiteness of snow. I am reminded of the Hymn Whiter Than Snow. and it seems to us poor mortals that nothing could be whiter than snow. but how often we see its pure white surface darkened and soiled by coming in contack with unclean things. But when we think of the pureity of Him who shed his precious blood to wash away our sins, and that not one joy of tittle of sin shall enter the kingdom of Heaven we realize that if we are prepared to enter into that blest abode, we shall there be whiter even purer than the snow; for there will be nothing to marr the beauty and purity of the situation. so let us endeavor to fulfil the words of our lesson to day, so that we may hae an inheritance in the Palace of God. where we shall have no enemies, none to hates us, or speak evil of us, but all will awell in perfect harmony in peace and love. praiseing Him who gave his life for us.

Monday Jan the 10th 1927

2nd Timothy 3-14 to 17
This morning we have six inches of snow on a level. The pretty white snow make me more and more desireous to obey all of Gods commandments, that I may praise Him in that beautiful land. where all is <u>joy</u> and <u>peace</u> and <u>love</u>.

Tuesday Jan the 11th 1927

Isa 40-31

Cold morning the ground still covered with snow. I am thankful that we are all able to be up and enjoy the fireside. And have strength of mind and eye sight to read Gods holy word. and we are told in Isaiah that They that wait upon the Lord shall renew their strength. so I am desireous that we may all daily be found waiting upon Him, and doing his will that we may grow stronger and stronger each day in the Lord, and doing the things that are well pleasing in His sight.

Wednesday Jan the 12th 1927

Col 4-2

A very cold morning. and the ground still covered with snow. but we have much to be thankful for, that we have shelter food and clothes, and fuel to keep us warm; for we should suffer greatly if we were not well provid for with these things, and we know that they all come from our merciful Heavenly Father, therefore I desire to "Continue in prayer and watch in the same with thanksgiving." for I know He will hear my humble petition for he is no respector of persons, but will hear the cry of the most lowly as they come to Him in true humility and faith and love. Love it the fulfiling of the law. Dear Father fill my heart with thy love, so there will be no room for any evil.

Thursday Jan the 13th 1927

John 7-37

Cold morning and the snow still stays with us. But I am very thankful that so far, we have all kept able to be up. and stand the weather fine. I am so glad that a child I have been taught the Holy Scriptures, for beside going to our blessed Saviour in prayer in my own simple way. I cam turn to my Bible and there find help for may thirsty soul. for in the words of my Text we are told that "If any man thirst let him come unto me and drink." so we see than any one who will, may

January 1927

come to this precious fountain and partake of this living water, which is Jesus Christ our gracious Redeemer.

Friday Jan the 14 1927

Joshua 23-14

Much warmer, thawing some this morning. In meditateing on the goodness and mercy of the Lord I feel that we should all remember that He has not failed to do for us, all that we have really needed, just as Joshua told the children of Isriel a short time before he passed away that they knew that the Lord had not failed them of all that He promiced to do for them. And now He warns them that as they failed to obey Him, after he had given them all things which He had promiced them. That He will now permit evil things to come upon them. so it behooves us to be close on our watch that we do not turn aside from the strait and narow way and do evil things which we are commanded not to do, least we be cut off in our sins, after having been so wonderfully provided for, and blessed far beyond what we deserve, in our disobedience. We know that He has told us in his word that He will not always chide, neither will He keep his anger forever. so we see that He bears long with us and does not chide us for our many short comeings for He has not dealt with us after our sins nor rewarded us according to our iniquities. for He is so merciful He remembers that we are but dust and in our weakness we are liable to err from the path of rectitude, but God is a just God and if we sin wilfully after all our blessings from Him, we may expect to be justly punished, for he hath said vengeance is mine I will repay saith the Lord. So we see we shall reap the reward of our deeds. oh God help us that our deeds be not evil, is my prayer for Jesus sake.

Saturday Jan the 15th 1927

Psa 119-105

The warm sunshine on yesterday melted all the snow away. And if we are so filled with the sunshine of Gods love in our hearts, it will do away with all evil.

Sunday Jan the 16th 1927

2nd Timothy 3-14-17

Much colder again this morning. so much so that I do not think it prudent to go to Sunday School, for at my age, I have to be very careful of my health to keep up. I am very thankful that it is as well with me as it is. for altho my eyesight is failing I can still read my Bible which is a great comfort, for when I cannot go to Church to hear the Gospel preached I can turn to His holy word and find soul food. Blessed be the name of the Lord who has sustained me all my life up the present time, and I am trusting Him to care for me the remainder of the journey. oh that I may truly reverence Him this day and keep it holy according to His word, is my prayer for Christs sake.

Monday Jan the 17th 1927

1st Peter 5-10

Another cold morning. and I feel the weakness of the flesh. But I trust we shall all still press on being strengthened and settled in the faith which leads us to follow our blessed Lord and Saviour Jesus Christ in the way of his requireings. that we may answer the end for which we were created which is to glorify Him. and my hearts desire is to glorify Him on earth that I may forever glorify him in Heaven. Blessed by His holy name.

Tuesday Jan the 18th 1927

Luke 11-5-13

A cloudy morning. In reading the 11th chapter of Luke we find that when Jesus was praying in a certain place when ceased one of His deciples said unto him Lord teach us how to pray as John also taught his deciples and all who read the Scriptures know that he taught him the familliar Lords prayer or at least a portion of it at that time and Jesus asked them as we find in verse five to thirteen. "if a son should ask a Father for bread would he give him a stone."etc and said if ye being evil know how to give good gifts to your children how much more shall your heavenly Father give the Holy Spirit to them that ask Him. and as we who are parents know so well how we love to give good things to our children what great encouragement it should be to us, to ask our blessed Lord to fill us day by day with the Holy Spirit that there may be no room for anything that is evil in thought, word or deed. so this is my fervent prayer this morning. dear Lord keep me this day and every day from sining against Thee for thou art more ready to help us than we are to help our own dear children much as we love them for Thou art infinite in goodness and mercy and will not deny us anything that is for our own good and Thy own glory.

Wednesday Jan the 19th 1927

St John 15-8

A cloudy chilly morning. As I have just read the 15th chap of St John. my heart has been filled with gratitude to our gracious Redeemer for the precious promices vouched to us, if we who are the branches will abide in the true vine. Dear Lord help us to abide in Thee that we may bear fruit to thy names honor and praise. for without Thee we can do nothing.

Thursday Jan the 20th

1st John 3-5

A foggy morning. I am feeling the infirmities of the flesh. But I am so thankful that my blessed Saviour knows that the spirit is willing even if the flesh is weak. and I am praying for strength to overcome the temptations and trials which so often come to be my lot, for I do not want to give way to discouragement for that gives the enemy advantage over us, for nothing pleases the enemy of our souls peace better than to get those who are trying to serve the Lord thoroughly discouraged, so help me dear Lord to put my whole trust in Thee that I may day by day follow in the way that thou hast pointed out for thy children not walk in that they sin not against Thee. and I feel that it would be dishonoring Thee not to claim to be Thy child when Thou hast so wonderful blessed me. and given me this privilige.

Friday Jan the 21ˢᵗ 1927

Luke 18-1-8

A cloudy damp morning. In reading my Scripture lesson this morning. I see how important it is to humble ourselves before God in the very dust of humility that He may lift us up. for we do not want to be like the Pherisee who boasted of what great things he had done, and also exalted himself over his fellows, and yet had not done that which was essential to the salvation of his own soul, for he had set his heart on the perishable thing of this world. please read for yourselves and see the result. The Publican merely cried God be merciful to me a sinner, and was justified rather than the other. And if we see ourselves as poor undone sinners without the grace of God in our hearts we will cry mightily to Him in whom we live and have our being, to create in us a new heart and renew a right spirit within us, and He will hear and answer us, see how the Widow was heard when she asked to be avenged of her enemies, and I know that the dear Lord does hear and answer the prayers of those who humble themselves and ask in true believing faith for a "broken and contrite heart of God thou wilt not despise." but will listen to the cry of the humble.

Saturday Jan the 22ⁿᵈ 1927

Matt 7-7

Another cloudy morning. and the dampness cause more aches and painse in my aged limbs but thankful to still be able to wait on myself and I find so much comfort in the Text that I have chosen for to day, and in reading the whole chapter for I believe if we ask in the right spirit in faith believing that we will be heard, we will receive an answer in the Lords own good time which will be the best time for us, for He knows what is best for us, better than we know for ourselves. My heart has been saddened this morning on just now

January 1927

learning of the death of **Rev J.C. Woosley** a Methodist minister who is well and favorably known in this community and thruout this land far and wide his funder is to take place to day but I have not yet learned the place of burial, he was a Preacher I had great confidence in, for altho I did not belong to his denomination he was eer ready to give me the right hand of fellowship and welcome me in his Church. his was a good example in this that we would all do well to follow for I believe in true Christian fellowship. And altho my membership is in the Friends Church which is my choice I am no sectarian, and can worship with any of Gods people.

Sunday Jan the 23rd 1927

Matt 6-9-13

Nice and warm this morning. As I have been spared to see another Sabbath day. my great desire is to show my gratitude to my Heavenly Father by doing whatever he calls for at my hands, and to be very grateful for all past blessings, and keep this day holy unto the Lord, and that I may present my body a living sacrifice wholely acceptable unto Him, doing his will from my heart. and as I now look out on the beautiful sunshine this day, which makes everything look so cheerful and bright after days of dark cloudy weather. I think what a glorious sabbath day this must be to **Rev J.E. Woosley** in that bright and happy land where no clouds ever dim the sky; and I am shure he has entered that land, for he passed away with songs of praise on his lips, we now learn that his burial took place yesterday at three oclock at Mt Olive in Davidosn Co some distance from Lexington N.C. and was very largely attended. We also learn that **Miss Emma White** daughter of the Late **Thomas** and **Susana Wall White** was laid to rest this evening at three oclock at Trinity N.C. we are daily reminded of the uncertainty of life and the certainty of death. Let us be ready.

Monday Jan the 24th 1927

Col 3-2

A very damp morning. In reading the chapter out of which I have chosen my Text I find so much that is so essential for us to observe and do in order that we may reap a rich reward when done with the things of this world. we must be kind, humble, long suffering forbearing one another and forgiving one another, and above all have charity one for another which is the bond of perfectness, for charity means love and if we are made perfect in the love of God we will love our fellow beings. Altho we may often times see things very differently one from another. But God sees the heart and will reward us according to our deeds done in the body, so whatsoever we do, "let us do it heartily as to the Lord not unto men."

Tuesday Jan the 25th 1927

Psa 62-6

Another damp morning. I am very thankful to be able to wait on myself, and do some work and am trusting the good Lord to take care of me, for in His goodness and mercy He daily watches over his dependent children, and my prayer is Lord help me to do thy holy will. thruout the remainder of lifes journey.

Wednesday Jan the 26th 1927

James 5-8

A very damp morning. I desire to "let patience have its perfect work" and that the Lord will teach me his way and lead me in a plain path, that I may know His will in all things that he would have me do. for thou knowest dear Lord that it is my fervent desire to serve thee here on earth that I may have a home with thee forever in heaven where I can praise thee more perfectly than I can here on earth and I know not how soon I may be called to give account of deeds done in the body. and I desire to be patient and have my heart and affections set on things above, not on the things of earth. For as we are told in the Book of James "the comeing of the Lord draweth nigh" and we know not how nigh it may be to any of us when we shall be called therefore I want to be ready. And let us all be ready.

Thursday Jan the 27th

Matt 9-38

A clear cold morning altho I feel that it is little that I can do in the vineyard of the Lord toward gathering in the vintage of precious souls, yet I do not want to bury the one talent in the earth, nor hide it in a napkin, but use it to the glory of God the Father and our Lord Jesus Christ. and to the upbuilding of His kingdom.

Friday Jan the 28th 1927

Prov 15-3

A cold morning. "The eyes of the Lord are in every place beholding the evil and the good." Therefore He sees us just as we are, whether we are doing the things that are well pleasing in his sight, or whether we are doing evil. and it behoves us to be close on our watch to resist evil. for we want to be found walking in the way of his precepts, for we know not the day nor the hour, when we shall be called to give account of the deeds done in the body whether they be good or whether they be evil. and some one is being daily called. Yesterday **Sidney Davis** was buried at Marlboro. He is a brother to **Jesse Davis** that married my youngest sister **Rachel Almina Millikan** who bother deceased several years ago.

Saturday Jan the 29th 1927

Heb 2-18

A cloudy damp morning. I am suffering from deep cold but have much to be thankful for. I am so glad that we have such a merciful Saviour who bears with all our trials and temptations. For in that he himself hath suffered being tempted, he is able to succor them that are tempted. but we should be careful not to yeild to temptation and thereby grieve his holy spirit. for yeilding is sin.

Sunday Jan the 30th 1927

Col 3-2

Another damp morning. In this Scripture Text we are admonished to "Set our affections on the things above not on things of the earth." and I am trying more and more each day to wean myself from the perishable things of this world, and center them on things above. Yet it is my earnest desire not only for myself but for all my loved ones, that we set our affections on things which pertain to our eternal happiness and to Gods glory, so that we may be permited to dwell in that happy land, to praise Him forever. Help us dear Lord to keep this Sabbath day holy and live closer and closer to thee the remainder of lifes journey let it be longer or shorter, for Jesus sake.

Monday Jan the 31st 1927

Deut 33-25

Cooler this morning. I am feeling rather feeble this morning, but thankful to be able to arise from my bed, and as we are promiced thus "as thy day thy strength shall be," I am standing on the promices and trust I shall have strength sufficient for the day to do what is required of me to do, both spiritually and temporally to the praise and honor of Him, who gave me my being, and who died that I might live.

Tuesday February the 1st 1927

Heb 10-24

Colder to day. In reading the tenth chapter of Hebrews we are admonished to consider one another to provoke unto love and to good works. And we know that if we do not love our fellow beings with that true Christian love which we are commanded to do we can not have fellowship with the Father who gave his dear Son to die for us all that we might be redeemed from all sin, and live with him forever.

January–February 1927

Wednesday Feb the 2nd 1927

Malachi 3-7-12

Clear and cold to day. In reading the 3rd chapter of Mal I see plainly laid down the difference between those that serve the Lord and those that serve Him not. and altho I so often make mistakes, it is my earnest desire to do the will of the Lord, and I am craving more and more to be able desern each just what He would have me do, and when he would have me leave off doing, to the praise and honor of his holy name, for I want to be as an obedient child should be to a kind and loveing parent. While first commenced this series of writing I mentioned my regrets that I had not been as obedient to my parents and as kind to my brothers and sisters as I should have been, and this was done in true penitence for the same. And I am glad that I could see my mistakes so that I could warn others to be more obedient and kind, but I have been made to wonder what will the feeling be of those who now go so far beyond what I ever did in disobedience, if they ever come to see their folly. for as I have advanced in years and witnessed the disobedience of children towards their parents in these days. and in looking back to my childhood and young days, and seeing the contrast, I am so thankful to my Heavenly Father that I was as obedient to my earthly parents and as kind to my brothers and sisters as a general thing as I was. for I loved them dearly and did not transgress thru any malice or any ill will but just thru the thoughtlessness of youth, when not being on guard against the advances of the enemy of our souls peace, and as I sought forgivness for my mistakes I rejoice to know that my merciful and loveing Saviour has forgiven for his own sake and I not longer have these things to hinder me on my heavenward journey, for he watches over me all the time and sends His mesengers to cheer me on my way. This evening dear **Clara I Cox**, and a dear Friend **David White**, came to visit me and gave words of comfort.

Thursday Feb the 3rd 1927

Gal 6-14

Cold this morning. I am very thankful that it is as well with me as it is this morning. and am glad that I can say with Paul, "God forbid that I should glory save in the cross of our Lord Jesus Christ by whom the world is crucified unto me, and I unto the world." I want to note the continued goodness and mercy of the Lord to his dependent children, for having been visited last evening by two of His mesengers as I mentioned has strengthened my faith and given me fresh courage to press on the remainder of the journey, trying with all the strength of mind and body to do that which He calls for at my hands, for I know he will not require more of any of us than he will enable us to perform, and when He sees that we have grown feeble and discouraged and almost ready to faint by the way, he sends us help thru the mouths of his obedient servants to speak words of encouragement to cheer us on our way. and I am so thankful for the privilige of being in the home of my dear daughter who is kind and loveing to me, and I pray Gods richest blessing both spiritually and temporaly to the praise and honor of Him who shed his blood for us <u>all.</u>

Friday Feb the 4th 1927

Mark 8-34

Warmer this morning. The more I read the Bible the more anxious I become to take up my daily cross and follow Him who has borne so much for me, for we are told that in the world we shall have tribulation so it does not come to us unawares, but if we will only be patient and bear all trials for the sake of Him who bore so much for us even the death on the Cross, we shall reap a rich reward when done with the things of the earth. oh heavenly Father help me to do thy will this day, and every day thruout the remainder of my journey here below, for Christs sake.

February 1927

Saturday Feb the 5th 1927

Matt 25-21

A foggy morning. The Hymn. "Father I strech my hands to thee no other help I know" sounds in my ears this morning, andI feel that there is no real help only in looking to the Father of all our sure mercies, who is ever ready to help in time of need, and I feel the need of Him at all timnes, and I want to fufil the words of the Golden Text, and be faithful even if it is but little that I can do; that I may gain strength both spiritually and physically to do more for the upbuilding of the Masters kingdom in the hearts of those with whom I meet and mingle.

Sunday Feb the 6th 1927

Matt 25-21

Clear and warm this morning. In reading the 25th chapter of Matthew, it brings to my mind the great need to be ready to meet the Bridegroom at any moment of time, for we know not the day nor the moment of time when we may be called for to give account of our stewardship – so I am desireing about everything else to be found faithful in doing whatever the blessed Lord requires of me. for He purchast a home for all with His own precious blood, who will be faithful to observe the rules that are laid down in His holy written word. so let us keep our lamps trimed and burning, so that we may hear that welcome of well done good and faithful enter into the joy of thy Lord, for on the other hand if we have been slothful and negligent and not make the proper use of what the Master has entrusted to us, and the door shut upon us and have to hear that awful sentence depart from me I know you not. oh God forbid that I should spend this life in such a way that would cause such a doom to be my portion, and help me dear Lord to do thy holy will in all things to thy names honor and praise. Bless the Lord oh my soul.

Until We Sleep Our Last Sleep

Monday Feb the 7th 1927

Matt 10-38

Cooler this morning. We are told that, "He that taketh not his cross and followeth after me is not worthy of me." So it is my hearts desire to be faithful to take up my daily cross and follow where the dear Lord leadeth so that I may be worthy to be called a child of God. for I daily meet with crosses that are hard for poor weak humans to bear, and it is only by putting my whole trust in the Lord that I am able to bear them, for He makes a way where there seems no way, as I cry to my heavenly Father for spiritual strength to withstand the trials, temptations and crosses that I am daily more or less subjected to. Blessed be the name of the Lord who is my stay and my staff.

Tuesday Feb the 8th 1927

Pro 103-13

Raining this morning. I am glad the Psalmist has told us that, Like as a father pittieth his children, so the Lord pittieth them that fear him. for my heart is filled with thankfulness that I do fear the Lord in the way of offending Him in word or deed, altho I too often fail to come up to this standard of obedience, but I think this is what He means when he admonishes us to fear Him it means that we may fear to do things against His holy will for He so often tells "to be not afraid, fear not to come to me" etc and bids us come boldly to the throne of grace that we may find help in time of need. so I do not think He means us to be afraid in the way of horror and dread in comeing to him for fear of punishment altho we deserve punishment if we transgress his laws and will receive it if we persist in disobedience just as we deserve chastisement when we disobey our earthly parents. but when they give us correction it does not prevent us from loveing them, and we know they love us and only chastise us for our own good, and pitty us even when we are naughty enough to need correction. And we know that our merciful heavenly Father sees us when we have done wrong and bids us come to him for forgiveness and not to be afraid to come, and He is ready and willing to forgive all our transgressions if we come to Him in sincerity.

Wednesday Feb the 9th 1927

Psa 25-14

Cloudy and cool. I feel like saying with David, "oh my God I trust in thee, let me not be ashamed, let not mine enemies triumph over me. "The troubles of my heart are enlarged oh bring thou me out of my distresses." These words express my confession that I do trust in the Lord, and a plea that he would help me at all times to not be ashamed to confess Him before my fellow beings and that He will not let my enemies triumph over me. for I love their souls and altho they cause my heart to ache, I want them saved for Christs sake.

Thursday Feb the 10th 1927

Isa 65-24

A dark damp morning. But there is no time so dark and dreary that our blessed Lord does not see us and listens to our cry to Him for help and is ready to answer if we are his obedient children and there is nothing that I so much desire as to be a child of God doing his holy will. so my heart is filled with praise to his name this morning in believeing that he will harken to my simple plea for strength and ability to do this day what is well pleasing in his sight, and to refrain from doing anything that would offend Him or my fellow beings and that my heart and mind may be filled with love to God and good will to all mankind, for Jesus sake.

Friday Feb the 11th 1927

Hebrews 4.12

Cooler this morning. In the chapter which contains this Text, we are told to come boldly to the throne of grace that we may obtain mercy and find grace to help in time of need. and I feel very needy this morning, so I am comeing to thee our heavenly Father that thou wilt give me strength for this day both spiritually and physically. that I may be able to withstand all the assaults of the enemy and press on to serve Thee. for I delight to do thy will.

Saturday Feb the 12th 1927

1st John 4-7

Still cool this morning. This Text says, "Beloved, let us love one another: for love is God's. my great desire is that I may have nothing but love to God and love to all with whom I meet and mingle and for all the human race. and that I may have such perfect love abideing in my heart, that it will cast out all fear of man. for perfect love casts out fear. Let us all read and study the Scriptures more and abide by its teachings, for Christs sake.

Sunday Feb the 13th 1927

Eph 6-4

A rainy morning. The subject for Sunday School lesson to day is how to make our homes Christian. We know that if we do not have Christ dwelling in our hearts we can not have a Christian home. for the word Christian means Christ like, so if we do not love each other in the home, and try to make each other happy, we are not Christ like, and have not a Christian home. which is one of the greatest institutions on earth. There is no place like home has been said and sung for many years gone by, and there is nothing truer, for I know what it has meant to me in the past to have a happy Christian home, for the inmates dwelt in love. and where love is supreme there is happiness in the home. and one knows the sorrow of having a good home broken up by the cold hand of death only those who have it to bear. But our gracious Redeemer will give us strenth to bear all our trials and we can not be thankful enough for a happy home, and that when they are broken up that is was not on account of disagreement, ill will and strife as is the case in many instances, that we hear of. So help us dear

Father to say. "The Lord gave and the Lord hath taken away blessed be the name of the Lord." and help us to meet them in Heaven.

Monday Feb the 14th 1927

Col 3-1

St Valentines day. I am feeling feeble and very nervous this morning, but trusting that the Lord will give me strength for the day, for He hath said as thy day thy strength shall be. and I am seting my affections on things above; for vain is the help of man.

Tuesday Feb the 15th

1st John 1-9

A nice bright day. I am so glad that our blessed Saviour has told us that, If we confess our sins he is faithful and just to forgive us our sins, and to cleanse us from all unrighteousness. And we are told in His word that all unrighteousness is sin, and we know that none of us are so pure but that we transgress, in one way or another altho we may not sin wilfully but are thrown off our guard by not watching close enough for the snares that the enemy lais for our feet. So we can not be thankful enough that we have such a mericiful Father that watches over us and convicts us our sins, and brings us back to him when we have wandered in forbiden path, oh righteous Father keep us from all sin, and help us to do Thy holy will for Christs sake. We were blessed with the company of dear **Grandma Peace** to day I always enjoy being with her so much. for I know that she is one that loves the Lord and serves him, and tries to influence other to walk in the strait and narow way. This p.m. we had the company of her grandaughter **Lena White**. We are always glad to have her.

Wednesday Feb the 16th 1927

Psa 62-8

Another nice morning. I am not feeling at all well but thankful to be up and wait on myself and am endeavoring to do as the Psalmist says to trust in the Lord at all times, for He is a refuge for us. and I feel the great need of a refuge whereunto I can flee for help and comfort, and I know our blessed Lord will fufil all his promices to be with us in every needful time, and I feel that I need Him all the time for comfort, help and strength.

Thursday Feb the 17th 1927

Acts 1-1-11

A beautiful sunshiney day. We have again been reminded of the uncertainty of this life, by the mesenger of death entering the home and calling away one of our dear neighbors **Mary Davis,** wife of **Wm Davis** from works to rewards, and indeed she was taken from works, for she worked faithfully until taken with violent pain, and having such a weak heart she only survived about twelve hours. She passed away Feb the 16th 1927 at the age of 35 years leaving seven little children four boys and three girls.

Friday Feb the 18th 1927

Prov 2-6

Lord give me wisdom to know just what thou wouldst have me to do this day. "Let thy tender love to me bind me closer Lord to thee." I am now prepareing to attend the funeral to day of our beloved neighbor **Mary White Davis**, at Mt Vernon May the Lord sustain her bereaved husband and dear little children in this great trial is my prayer. Afternoon of the same day, I am thankful that I had sufficient strength to attend the funeral at eleven oclock to day, a large concourse of relatives and friends in attendance. A good sermon by the Pastor **Rev Reed Haris**, and a profusion of flowers.

Saturday Feb the 19th 1927

1st Cor 3-9

Much cooler this morning and rainy quite a contrast from yesterday "We are laborers together with God." This Text causes me to realize

February 1927

what a great privilige we have in being permited to be laborers with God our heavenly Father, for when he bids us do something for Him no matter what the task may be, he will be with us to help us to perform it, and thus we are made coworkers with him. oh what a blessed thought to be found working with and for our blessed Master who has done and suffer so much for us poor unworthy cretures.

Sunday Feb the 20th 1927

Matt 5-13-16

Some snow on the ground this morning. We learn of another funeral thqta is to take place today, that of one of my friends **Mrs. Nannie Lowe Jones** which of **Thomas Jones**, The funeral and burial at dear old Springfield. I regret very much not having the opportunity to attend, for she was one that I thought a great deal and her Mother **Mattie Marsh Lowe** and I were great friends from our childhood have gone to school togeather from our first schooling until we were grown up to young womanhood. she passed away several years ago. while I still linger here. but feel that it wont be much longer at most until the journey will be ended.

Monday Feb the 21st 1927

Galatians 5-22

Clear and cold this morning. I am feeling feeble but thankful to be so I can still wait on myself, I am trying with the help of Him who has my life in His hands to do whatever is called for at my hands, not looking for the praise of men, but to Him who knows every thought and intent of the heart. Bless me oh Lord as thou seest I need, and help me to glorify Thee on earth, that I may glorify He in Heaven.

Tuesday Feb the 22nd

Rev 22-12

Cool this morning. This is the birthday of the Father of our Country George Washington. I am not feeling at all well as I spent a sleepless night which causes me to feel weak and nervous. but "Thanks be to God who leaning on the strong arm that has borne the burden from me all those years, and He will never fail me, so long as I cling to Him which I ever shall do, He being my helper Blessed be His holy name, now and forever.

Wednesday Feb the 23rd 1927

Isa 2-22

A very rainy day. If it was not for the consolation I get by reading the Bible and believeing that it is the word of God I should become so discouraged that I should faint by the way. for I am so sorely tried in the flesh, having hard things to bear because of the oppression of the enemy. for the more I strive to do right the harder the enemy of our souls peace tries to keep me from doing the things that God would have me to do, by putting into the heart of those who will listen to his devices, something to discourage me and the weaken my influence for good, in the sight of others, but I am so thankful that God knows my heart and knows that I ask Him daily to bless my enemies and help me to love and forgive them, according to His word.

Thursday Feb the 24th 1927

James 4-7

A nice bright day. I am suffering to day but thankful that I am not helpless, for I tried walking a distance of several yards, which was farther than I had walked in over fifty years. It is true any one that is able to walk would think that little distance ought not to hurt me, but it sure did, and I shall never overdo myself again by trying to see what I could hold out to do for I am certainly paying dear for it with suffering caused by doing too much. but I never could of done it, if I had not prayed for strength all the way there and back. Blessed be the name of the Lord he is so good to me. Tonight is the prayer meeting at **Grandma Levina Peaces**.

February 1927

Friday Feb the 25th 1927

Colo 3-15

Cooler to day. I am still suffering with soreness and lameness because of overstrain on my nerves but thankful that it is as well with me as it is, and am trusting the dear Lord to take care of me, and provide a way for me where I see no way for the flesh is weak but I am so glad that He knows that the spirit is willing and that my greatest desire is to do the things that is well pleaseing in His sight. so dear Father in heaven come into my heart and rule and reign there, to thy names honor and praise.

Saturday Feb the 26th

Eph 5-11

Another cool day. In my lonelyness and sadness, my heart cries out to thee dear Heavenly Father for help to bear my sore trials, for I cannot bear them alone. Thou who knows all things, know my heart and that I want to have nothing but love mine enemies, even those who "despitefully use me and say all manner of evil against me falsely, for thy names sake oh Lord." help me oh God for vain is the help of man, I want to have no "Fellowship with the unfruitful works of darkness, but rather reprove them." for I can truly say that I have sin but do not hate the sinner. for I would that all mankind might be saved.

Sunday Feb the 27th 1927

Eph 5-11

Colder this morning. We are again reminded to be ready for the call to leave this stage of ixistance and give account of the deed done in the body. To day the funeral of **Mr J. Wesley Wilborn** is to take place at Mt Gilliad at 3 oclock which I hope to be able to attend. oh Father in Heaven help me to so live here on earth, that I may be ready when Thou calls for me. for I want to dwell with thee, there to praise Thee forever, for Jesus sake.

Until We Sleep Our Last Sleep

Monday Feb the 28th 1927

Phil 4-19

A cold morning. And as I reflect on this being the last day of the month and the last month of the winter season, I see how fast time is flying, and that every day brings me nearer the time when I shall be called to give an account of the deed done in the body, and I am striveing more and more each day to be ready. I know that I have made many mistakes, for who is there that has not? and have many short comeings for which I sincerely repent, and for which my gracious Redeemer has forgiven me for His own names sake and for my never dying souls sake. for He knows my hearts desire is to serve him in the way of his requireings and that it is only the weakness of the flesh, that I ever give way to be tempted to say or do anything contrary to His divine commands, and He knows the spirit is willing, and his is so merciful to his poor unworthy child which I claim to be, that he forgives me and strengthens me to overcome the temptations of the evil one, and press on amidst all the trials, and crosses which I have to contend with which are many altho I am feeling weak yesterday, the dear Lord give me strength sufficient to attend the funeral of **Mr. J. Wesley Wilborn** for which I am thankful, for to hear such an excelent obituary of him was an inspiration to me, to try harder and harder live, ao as to "die the death of righteous and my last end to be like his." his Mother **Mattie Johnson Wilborn**. a woman that I loved dearly, was a sister to **J. Alvin Johnson** who married my oldest sister **Ruth Millikan Johnson**, which makes **J.W. Wilborn** seem like one of my kindred. He has now gone to rest.

Tuesday March the 1st 1927

Psa 32-8

A cold morning, and some snow on the ground which fell last night. I am not feeling well at all which causes me to feel sad and lonely, but I am so thankful that is can still wait on myself so that others do not have it to do, for I do not want to become a burden to any one. and altho I have in contending with the things of the flesh, great cause for discouragement, as I have no real earthly companionship to speak a comforting word as in the past, but I know that I still have a Friend above all others that cares for me. and the content of my Text to day give me fresh courage to press on, for He says, "I will instruct thee and teach thee in the way which thou shalt go: I will guide thee with mine eye." oh to be led and guided by that all seeing Eye is the greatest desire of my heart. for Christs sake.

Wednesday March the 2nd 1927

1st Cor 18-25

Another cold morning. and we have the deepest snow which fell during the night that we have had in many years. which makes me think of the days of my childhood for then, big snows were common almost every winter. And sometimes the ground would be covered with snow the whole winter long. But there has been quite a change since those days, here in North Carolina, for we have had very few snows in the this part of the State and those very light, so when the Sun shone out it soon melted away. so this is the largest snow many of the young people ever looked upon. I am thankful that we have food and shelter, and fuel to keep us from suffering. but I fear there are some who may not have. and the snow is from eighteen to twenty inches on a level and badly drifted in places so that it very dificult to get about even on feet and the roads impasable for vehicles.

Thursday March the 3rd 1927

Eph 4-40

A bright clear morning and the sun shining on the snow almost blinds my eyes. It will take quite a while for all this snow to melt away unless it soon turns much warmer, the roads are so that the boys who work at Town cannot go to their work, and it is so cold that the women folk cannot do much house work, but we have much to be thankful for, that we are not any of us down sick, and that we have shelter and food and clothing and fuel to keep us warm. "Bless the Lord oh my soul and forget not all its benefits."

Friday March the 4th 1927

Psa 1-6

A cold day and still plenty of snow. My Text prompts me to be closer on my watch least I transgress the law of the Lord, for I want to live a righteous life that I may die the death of the righteous and my last end be like his. For we are plainly told that the way of the ungodly shall perish.

Saturday March the 5th 1927

Act 1-8

Still cold but bright and clear. I am thankful that we are all able to go about our daily duties. We learn this morning of the death of **Irey Kennedy's** little son Cameron about five years old, which was caused by getting badly burned yesterday morning. he was standing before the fire in his night gown, and in some way it caught afire and burned him in such a way that he only lived about twenty four hours. So we are again reminded that any of us are liable to be called at any time in some way to give up our existence here below, for the realities of another world. It has often been said that the old must die and that the young do die. which we see verified almost daily. so it behooves all ages to be ready for the summons.

Sunday March the 6th 1927

Acts 8-4-8

A nice bright morning overhead, but very bad underfoot, which makes it bad for the burial of little **Cameron Kennedy** which is to take place this afternoon at Mt Vernon. Later I was favored to attend the funeral this p.m. which was largely attend. heard a splendid sermon by the Pastor **Rev Reed Haris**, his subject was well chosen for the occasion. and there were many lovely flowers from kindred an friends. I praise the Lord for his goodness to me in giving me strength to attend. Blessed by His holy name, who watches over me day by day.

Monday March the 7th 1927

Matt 4-18

Cooler this morning. I am suffering from deep cold but thankful to be up. In reading the 4th chapter of Mathew we see what great power Jesus has to do whatsoever he finds to do when He sees the peoples needs. He went about healing the sick, and those who had lost their minds, had those that were possessed with evil spirits. and he called those fisherman to be his disciples, so they meant that they were to call men for their sinful ways to repentance, and salvation in Jesus Christ.

Tuesday March the 8th 1927

1st Cor 16-13

Cloudy this morning. I am feeling the effects of the dampness, but thankful to be able to arise from my bed. and to note the continued goodness and mercy of my gracious Heavenly Father to me his unworthy child, as the days go by. for we are told in His word that "As thy day thy strength shall be "and I find it verified for even in my weakest moments He bears me up. for so much of my time since being broken up from my dear old home I feel so weak and discouraged that if it was not for leaning on the arm of Him who is a friend above all others I should give out by the way. But blessed be His holy name. He is my strength and my song and has become my salvation. Glory be to the Lamb.

Wednesday March the 9th 1927

Psalm 34-15

A very rainey morning. I am thankful that it is as well with all the members of this household as it is, for there is much sickness in places, and almost daily we learn of the death of some person that we have known, either kindred or friend. The time is set for the funeral to day at 3 oclock of **Mrs Robert McGee**, who is a sister to **Mr Walter Johnson** who married my first cousin **Rhoda J. Millikan Johnson** now deceased. so it seems that nearly all those who have passed away in the last few years that I have known of, have in some way been connected with my people. and it keeps me constantly reminded that my time is surely comeing and may be nigh at hand, so I want to be on my watch at all times, so that I may be ready when the Bridegroom comes, and what I desire for myself, I desire for all my loved ones, and all others that we may all be found with our lamps trimed and burning so that we may be permited to enter into the joy our Lord to praise him thruout all eternity.

Thursday March the 10th 1927

Luke 10-1-9

Sun shineing to day. Yesterday was such a very rainey bad the funeral of **Mrs Robert McGee** had to be postponed until to day at eleven oclock. I was thankful to be able to go with those of this family who attended, heard a good sermon by **Pastor Rev Reed Haris**. **Mrs McGees** Grandsons were the Pall bearers, and six of her Grandaughters caried lovely flowers. it was a touching scene. We were again reminded of the uncertainty of life and the certainty of death. My prayer is oh God help us all to be ready when thou send the summons. for Jesus sake. Amen.

Friday March the 11th 1927

John 15-7

A nice clear day, and I am so thankful that we of this household are all as well as we are at this time, for there are many suffering in one way or another. I was favored to attend the prayer meeting last night at **Mr Monroe Spencers**. there was good attendence and good interest in the meeting. I praise the Lord that he made himself manifest to us poor unworthy children. Glory be to His holy name.

March 1927

Saturday March the 12th 1927

Matt 28-19

A nice warm morning. I am feeling very nervous and weak, and feel the need fo a strong arm to lean upon. and knowing who has been my stay and my staff thru so many years of affliction. I cray unto thee oh Lord for strength sufficient for this day, for without thy help I should utterly pail both physically and spiritually. but I am so thankful for such a Friend who is ever ready to respond to the cry of those who put their trust in Him, altho I feel so unworthy of His kind favors. I know that He is no respector of persons and condescends to hear the prayer of the lowly.

Sunday March the 13th 1927

John 15-14

A nice warm day. And this being my eighty second Birthday brings many things of the past fresh to my mind. I am thankful that my health at this age, and at this time is sufficient to be able to wait on myself and do some things for others. Praise the Lord for all His benefits to me, and to mine.

Monday March the 14th 1927

Rom-5

Rainey this morning I am feeling the effects of the dampness, but thankful to be so I can be up and help what I can with the things necessary to be done for which I feel like noteing down praise each day as I am given strength to use my pen and thinking faculties, for the Great Giver of all good belongeth praise hone and glory now and forever.

Tuesday March the 15th 1927

1st John 2-17

A nice morning. and I am thankful that all the inmates of this household are in usual health. and I am so anxious that we all abide by the words of this Text, for "he that doeth the will of God abideth forever" and I know that I want to do His will, and praise him forever for what He has done for me and mine, that that we may all ponder well this whole chapter and not walk in darkness for "he that hateth his brother in in darkness," but the that loveth his brother is in the light which includes all human beings. So I pray that we may all walk in the light.

March the 16th 1927

Matt Chap 25

A damp morning, and I am not feeling well but thankful to be so I can still pen down the continued goodness and mercy of my dear Saviour to me a poor unworthy creture as I feel myself to be. and I am going to try my best with the help of the Master to improve the one talent given me instead of burying it in the earth, and altho it has been done in a simple way I have endeavored to make use of the one Talent given me, as it has been made known to me by Him who is my strength my wisdom and my all. that I should note down from time to time such things as would be an inspiration to others to press on in the right path which they had entered, or a warning to turn from walking in the broad road that leads to destruction and I have tried to be faithful in doing that has been made plain was required of me. and I am so thankful God knows my heart and knows that I love Him and that I love all my fellow beings with that true Christian love that knows no ill to my fellow beings, and that I hate sin, but do not hate the siner. for altho I have had to suffer many reverses from my enemies, I do not want any root of bitterness to spring up in my heart against them. but I pray that they may be forgiven and turn to God with the whole heart and be saved, with an everlasting salvation.

Thursday March 17th 1927

2nd Sam 22-7

A nice morning. I am so thankful to be able to again use my pen to note down the goodness and mercy of the Lord to me. I have been in great trouble, passing as it were thru deep waters that threaten to overflow me. but like David, "In my distress I called up the Lord and cried to my God and he did hear my voice out of his temple and my cry did enter into his ears". oh to know that the great God of heaven and earth will stoop to listen to the cry of one so unworthy as I feel myself to be, humbles me in the very dust. but we are told that "not a sparrow falls to the ground without His notice." and in St. John 10-9. our blessed Saviour says, "I am the door by me if any man enter in, he shall be saved and shall go in and out and find pasture." what a gracious promice this is to us all. and my great desire is, that not only myself but all others may enter in thru that door, that we may be saved there to praise our Blessed Redeemer forever. for "He wileth not that any should perish, but that all should come to him and be saved.

According to the appointment the weekly prayer meeting will be held in this home to night. May the Lord meet with us and bless us to His names honor and praise, is the sincere pray of my heart.

Friday March the 18th 1927

Matt 10-32-33

A nice spring moring the flowers comeing forth into bud and flower. Which seems to acknowledge the great power and goodness of the Creator of all things, and so should we acknowledge Him in all our ways, for as in the verse 32 if we confess Him before men, he will confess us before his Father in heaven, but as in verse 33 if we dney Him he will also deny us before his Father in Heaven. This chapter is full of admonition to His deciples, and shows us plainly that if we would be His deciples we must follow the precepts that He has given us, in order that we may enter into that Heavenly abode which he has prepared for all who love and serve Him here on earth.

The program for the prayer meeting in this home last night was carried out to good satisfaction a good attendance and much interest taken in the meeting for which I praise the Lord for the manifestation of His divine promice.

Saturday March the 19th 1927

John 14-2

Nice warm morning. All nature seems to be responding to the call of the great Giver of all things. oh that we who are responsible beings may be as prompt to obey His will, for we know that ere long we shall have to give account of the deeds done in the body. Father in heaven I pray that thou wilt keep me this day and every day as in the hallow of thy divine hand that I go not astray from Thee. "Let thy tender love to me bind me close closer Lord to thee." for I want to walk as it were by they side, and do thy bidding, to Thy names honor and praise.

Sunday March the 20th 1927

John 14-1-13

A lovely Sabbath morning. I am anxious that we may all keep this day holy, looking to Jesus who is the author and finisher of our faith. oh for more faith for without faith it is impossible to please God, and if I know anything of my own heart it is that I want to do the things that are well pleasing in His sight. oh God be my strength, my wisdom and my all.

Monday March the 21st 1927

John 8-31

A cloudy morning. I am feeling feble and lonely, yet I realize that altho the family are away, and I have no one to speak a word of comfort to me, that I have a Friend above all others who speaks peace to my soul, and as is be not afraid, "Lo I am with you always."yes altho I am alone so far as human company is concerned, yet I know that the all seeing Eye is watching over me, and helping me to put my whole trust in Him. and I am by his help going to continue in His word, that I may be His deciple indeed. For thou Lord who knows all things knows that I believe on Thee.

March 1927

Tuesday March the 22nd 1927

Eph 5-11

Cooler to day. I am feeling the need of the strong arm of my blessed Saviour to bear me up thru all my trials for I am weak in body and in spirit, and I want to be strong in the light of the Lord, and walk in the light. and as in my Text I want to have no fellowship with the unfruitful works of darkness but rather reprove them. Afternoon of same day. I have been favored with the company of our dear Pastor Clara I Cox this evening which I greatly enjoyed and feel that this visit will be owned and blessed of the Lord for I know He sent this mesenger to me at this time to strengthen my faith, for I was wadeing as it were thru deep waters that threaten to overflow me, and by her kind words and earnest prayer for me has helped me to realize that my gracious Heavenly Father is still watching over and careing for me for many times in the past when I would feel so weak and discouraged and almost ready to faint by the way some of the Lords mesengers would come to see me and give me fresh courage to press on. And I do not look upon these visits as mere hapenings, but that they were sent by Him who is ever watching over His dependent children, to comfort and to bless in real needs.

Wednesday March the 23rd 1927

Heb 10-23

Much cooler to day. I am not feeling strong in body but thankful to be as well as I am. and I am more determined by Divine help to press on doing whatever the Lord shows me in his will concerning me, leaveing those things which are behind, and pressing forward to the things that are before, for I want to hold fast to my profession of faith, for "He is faithful that promices," for I have had experience enough to know that He is faithful to do for us whatever he has promiced, if we put our trust in Him.

Thursday March the 24th 1927

1st Tim 6-11

Still quite cool to day. All of this family are able to be up and go about their daily avocations, for which I feel very thankful, for health is one of the greatest blessings in this life, and there are some in this neighborhood at this time suffering with diseases; I hope and trust that we may all so live that when done with the things of this transient world. may God help us to live humbly before him at all times, for we are told in this 6th chap that "godliness with contentment is great gain, for brought nothing into this world and it is certain we can carry nothing out. having food and rainment let us be therewith content. this is the desire of my heart, for Christs sake.

Friday March the 25th 1927

Col 3-16

A nice cool morning, I am suffering with my spine so that I am scarcely able to be up, so do not feel like writing much at this time, but will just state, that I am still leaning on he strong Arm that alone is able to support me thru all my suffering both temporally and spiritually. Blessed be His holy name.

Saturday March the 26th

Pslm 24-3-4

Cool again to day. I am still suffering with the pain and soreness in my spine, a trouble that I have suffered with for many years, added to my other afflictions, but I am thankful that I still have strength to walk about instead of being down helpless as I was for many years in the past. and my greatest desire is to conform to the words of my Text to have clean hands and a pure heart, that I may "ascend into the hill of the Lord and stand in his holy place," that I may receive the blessing of the Lord and praise him face to face forever around the throne in Heaven. oh God I plead that thou would help me to me so close on my watch at all times that I go not astray from thee, for the enemy of my souls peace is seeking to devour me by puting stumbling blocks in my path which if not carefully avoided would cause me to fall into the hands of the enemy, for he watches our weakest moments in order to overcome us and draw us into his net. so my prayer is unto thee oh God in a needful time, for vain is the help of man.

Sunday March the 27th 1927

Luke 10-27

A nice bright day. I am still suffering with pain in my spine, and fear that I shall not be able to attend Sunday School, but if not I hope to be submisive to my lot and endeavor to worship my Maker in my heart and in this home or wherever I may be, for I want to keep this day holy, according to the commandments. Evening of the same day. By the goodness and mercy of the Lord I was given strength sufficient to attend S.S. this afternoon which I very much enjoyed, and praise Him to whom I look for all my blessings, and soon after returning from Church I was blessed with the company of my daughterinlaw and grandaughter **Sadie Blair** and two other acquaintances from Thomasville N.C. which helped to cheer me on my way.

Monday March the 28th

Isiah 4-29

A clear cool morning. I am thankful to have the use of myself so as to be able to be up and wait on myself, altho still suffering with my spinal trouble and weakness, but I am so glad that we are told in Gods word that "he giveth power to the faint and to them that hath no might He giveth strength. Blessed be His holy name, for it is only as I look to Him for strength that I can keep pressing forward, toward the promiced land.

Until We Sleep Our Last Sleep

Tuesday March the 29th 1927

Heb 7-25

A cold morning. I am feeling weak and nervous this morning but thankful to be able to be up and use my pen to note down the goodness and mercy of the Lord, knowing that He is a friend that has pitty on those that are weak and infirm, I am going to try my utmost to hold out faithful unto the end. for we are told that "Jesus is able to save to the uttermost those that come unto God by him, seeing he ever liveth to make intercession for them." So my prayer is unto thee oh God in a needful time. I failed to take note of the pleasant call I received a few days ago from a relative from Bloominton Indiana **Mrs Mary McCauley** who like myself has been a widow for several years, so we have great sympathy for each other. her father and mother **Mahlon** and **Nancy Millikan** had twin daughters **Mary** and **Martha,** they moved to Ind when the children were small. their Father is a cousin to my Father **Sameul C. Millikan** who deceased many years ago. **Mrs McCauley** has a son **Lee Charles McCauley** who is a Teacher and has charge of Public Schools in Asheville, N.C. and she comes to visit him and spends some time in Asheville, and also visits her relatives and friends in Randolph and Guilford Counties. which is very pleasent to all concerned.

Wednesday March the 30th 1927

1st Peter 3-4

A cloudy damp day. which adds to my aches and pains, but thankful to still be able to wait on myself instead of being a helpless burden to others, and I am anxious to maintain a meek and quiet spirit which is the sight of God of great price, this whole chapter of 1st Peter should be carefully read and adhered to, in order to be happy in this life, and in the world to come receive a crown that fadeth not away.

Thursday March the 31st 1927

Psa 62-5

A cloudy day. As this is the last day of the month it again reminds me of the flight of time, and the necessity of preparing for eternity. and my soul cries out wait thou only upon God for my expectation is from Him. yes my only hope, my only plea is that Christ has died and died for me, poor and unworthy as I feel myself to be for He died for the sins of the whole world therefore my sins, and rose again that those who believe on him and trust in him might have life eternal. Blessed by His holy name. "Let all who look for hasten, The coming joyful day, By earnest consecration, To walk the narow way, By gathering in the lost ones For whom our Lord did die, For the crowing day that's comeing by and by."

April the 1st 1927

Matt 6-33

A warm damp morning. I am still suffering with my spine, but thankful that I can still wait on myself, and I rejoice to think there is a place prepared for the children of God when done with this life, where we will not suffer pain or sorrow, but where we shall be forever in the presence of Him who is ever ready even now to listen to the cry of those on earth who seek His help. and I know that I am His child unworthy as I am, so I will call upon Him as long as I live and expect him to heed my cry. For "my expectation is from Him." for as we are told in the Text to "seek first the kingdom of God and his righteousness and all these things shall be added unto you." I am so thankful that I have the privilige to be a child of God as well as all others who will come to Him and obey his holy will, and I am striving by His help to be ready to receive a welcome into His kingdom.

Until We Sleep Our Last Sleep

Saturday April the 2ⁿᵈ 1927

Mark 1-17

A damp morning. I am still feeling the effects of the dampness. but thankful to still be so I can wait on myself and I feel that the good Lord is watching over and takeing care of me. Blessed be His holy name now and forever.

Sunday April the 3ʳᵈ 1927

Mark 1-7 Golden Text

A clear cold morning. I am thankful to be up this bright Sabbath morning, and altho not feeling strong I hope I shall be able to attend Sunday School and Church for I am always glad when I can go to the place for worship. for the time will soon come when I can no more go to the church Militant, but I hope to then enter the Church Triumphant in Heaven. In calling to mind that his is my son **Fred C Blairs** forty sixth Birthday it hardly seems possible that he has arrived to that age, but time flies so fast we can hardly realize what had taken place from one year to another.

Monday April the 4ᵗʰ 1927

1ˢᵗ Cor 10-13

A cold cloudy day. As has been my condition for the past week and more, I am still suffering with lameness in my spine, but I am thankful to still be so I can help myself, for I don't want to be a burden to any one, and I am also so thankful for the blessed promice of our merciful heavenly Father that we shall not be tempted about that we are able, but will make way for our escape, for I have been sorely tempted and tried lately, and the fervent desire of my heart is that I may not yeild to anything that is not well pleasing to the sight of Him in whom I live and move and have my being.

April 1927

Tuesday April the 5th 1927

Psalm 121

This is a very damp morning. I am suffering more severely this morning than for several days, I think the dampness has something to do with my pains being more severe, but I am hoping that I may not become helpless again, for I am looking unto the hills from whence cometh my help. for my help cometh from the Lord which made heaven and earth. for I know he has power to heal me if it be his holy will, so I am trying to bear my pain with all the patience possible for the sake of Him who has borne so much for me, hoping that I may find a place of rest and peace when done with this life, where pain and sorrow are forever unknown. Blessed be the name of the Lord forever.

Wednesday April the 6th

A warm day. I am suffering still more with my spine to day and am less able to help myself, so that I ahe had to have some help in getting up and down from bed and chair, but thankful to be with my daughter who is ready and willing to help me. I am hoping to soon be better, for I received a fresh invitation to day on a standing one for the past six months or more, to visit my dear friends **Mr** and **Mrs George Stilwell** and family in Salisbury, N.C. If it is the Lords will. I hope to make this visit.

Thursday April the 7th 1927

Romans 5-6

A nice morning. I am still suffering with the excruciating pain in my back, but thankful that I can sit in my chair part of the time, for altho I can not be at ease while sitting in it, I am glad that I do not have to be entirely confined to the bed as I have been in years gone by. and I have hoping and praying that I may yet recover this suffering which takes all the patience I can conceive to endure it. May the dear Lord help me to endure it for His sake.

Friday April the 8th 1927

Psalm 27-14

A warm cloudy morning. I am very thankful to of had a quiet nights rest in sleep, and some better of the lameness in my back, but not free from pain and soreness, but I am so glad to be so I can help myself more this morning. and I feel like asorbeing all praise to Him in whom I put my trust for help and for restoration if it be his holy will, for I do not want to again become a helpless creture as I was for many years as in the past for it grieves me to think of becomeing a burden to others. and since having to give up my dear companion. I know there is no one that would have the patience and sympathy for me that he had, and always a word of comfort, instead of reproof.

Saturday April the 9th 1927

Matt 14-27

A cloudy day. I am still suffering with my infirmity, but so thankful to be so I can arise from my bed, altho it is with much pain that I do so, and I am feeling very sad and lonely. but in listening to that still small voice which speaks as never yet man spake, I seem to hear Jesus speak to me as he spake to his deciples when He went to them walking on the water saying, "Be of good cheer it is I be not afraid." So in my fear and trembling I come to thee blessed Lord to plead that thou wilt keep me from sinking into the sea of despond, and give me faith that will hold me above the waves and storms of this, tempestuous life, and at last land me in Thy haven of rest where I shall see thy face, and praise thee forever.

Sunday April the 10th 1927

Matt 14-27

Another cloudy morning. I am still suffering with the tortureing pain in my spine, so that get little rest, but I am still trusting that rest will come when I am done with the things of this life, for we have the assurance in Gods, holy written word, that they that come unto him shall find rest unto their souls, and that will compensate for all the suffering we have to endure in this trancient world. Blessed be the name of the Lord.

Monday April 11th 1927

Heb 2-18

A clear cold day. I am so thankful for to of had a good nights rest, and that my pains have not been quite so severe to day, for altho I am not free from suffering I am so thankful to be some better to day and thank the good Lord for answering my dear daughters prayer on my behalf, for she pled for me a good nights rest, and that I might not have to suffer so severely as I had been doing. And I praise Him for hearing and answering my own simple prayer. Blessed be His name.

Tuesday April the 12th 1927

Psalm 141-8

A nice clear morning. I am so thankful for another quiet nights rest, and altho still suffering, I am not so helpess as I have been for a week past. for which I praise the Lord for His goodness to me, for I am so anxious to get able to wait on myself again, so that I may not be a burden to my dear daughter or anyone. And in the language of David "mine eyes are unto thee oh God the Lord in thee is my trust: leave not my soul destitute." and dear heavenly Father thou knowest that I call upon thee daily for help to serve thee in the way of thy requireings, give me faith to believe thou wilt not leave me destitute for thou knowest that I do trust in thee. oh my Father.

Wednesday April the 13th 1927

Psm 25-10

A nice bright day. I am thankful that it is as well with me as it is altho I am still suffering, and did not get as good a nights rest, as I had for the two previous nights, but as I can now help myself enough to get from my bed to my chair alone it is a source of comfort to me, for as I have repeated over and over that I do not want others to be burdened on my account, but there is no one but what needs a friend especially when afflicted in any way. and affliction has been my portion the greater part of my life, so I am desirous to keep the covenant of the Lord. that I may obtain mercy, by walking in His paths and obeying His holy will to His honor and praise. We are to day reminded of the uncertainty of this life. and the certainty of death. To day the sweet little seven year old daughter of **Mr George Fraizer** is to be laid away at Mt Vernon. little **Ociania** it is said was a most remarkable inteligent child. Our blessed Saviour hath said in his word. "Suffer the little children to come unto me and forbid them not for of such is the kingdom of Heaven." oh that we may all become innocent as little children, that we may have an inheritance with them, in that blessed abode.

Thursday April the 14th 1927

Prov 29-25

Cloudy to day. I feel very grateful to my merciful heavenly Father to be so I can sit in my chair and take note of His kindness to me in granting me more rest the past night, and altho not free from pain that they are not so severe. And I am fervently praying this day that by the help of the Lord I put my whole trust in Him. for I have too often let the fear of man hinder me from doing what the Lord required of me. Yes for fear man would make light, or speak reproachfully of me I have at times yeilded to the fear of man rather than the fear of Him who holds my life in his hands and can fix my destiny at any moment of time, so I am determined to put my whole trust in the Lord, remembering the words of my Text that "The fear of man bringeth a snare, but who so putteth his trust in the Lord shall be safe." so herein I have backsliden at times to great sorrow, and have had to repent of it most bitterly, and just here I will caution any one who may chance to know that I have written this, to not let the tempter have right of way in this matter for it will bring sorrow. so Let us not care what man can say or do unto us for if the Lord be for us who can be against us. Blessed by the name of the Lord. now and evermore.

Friday April the 15th 1927

John 14-26

Another damp morning. I am thankful to be so I can arise from my bed, altho feeling feeble, for I have suffered so much during the past two weeks that it has reduced my strength so that I am weak and nervous but I find so many precious promices in this the 14th chapter of St John that I gives me courage to press on knowing that if I do the will of my heavenly Father I shall be free from suffering when done with the trails of this life.

Saturday April the 16th

1st Peter 2-1-10

Cloudy again this morning, and I feel the effects of the dampness, but thankful to be up and testify from my heart and with my pen the goodness of the Lord to me one of His unworthy children, for altho unworthy I am so glad that I can claim to be one of His according to his precious promice, for He watches over and takes care of me by day and by night, and I am strieving to obey His holy will, and altho weak in body, I am trusting "His spirit to help mine infirmities."

Sunday April the 17th 1927

Cloudy again this morning. I am suffering more to day, but thankful that I am able to sit in my Chair and read my Bible, and I remember the injunction to keep the Sabbath day holy and by the help of the Lord I will do my best to obey, for altho I am not able to attend Sunday School and Church, I know we can worship God in our own homes and hearts. Heavenly Father keep me this day as in the hallow of thy holy hand that I go not astray from thee, is my prayer for Christ sake.

Monday April the 18th 1927

1st John 3-1

A nice clear morning. I am thankful to be feeling some better this morning. and hope thru the goodness and mercy of Him who has all power to heal to soon be much stronger, and that I may press on in the strength and wisdom which He is pleased to give me, to do whatever He may require at my hands, to the praise and honor of His holy name.

Tuesday April the 19th 1927

Romans 8-17

A nice morning. I am very thankful to be so I can be up to day. All nature seems to be obeying the great Creator of all things, who gives life to bring forth the bud and bloom, and the trees are being covered with their green foliage which the warm breath of spring time brings forth, and we know that it is all from the power and goodness of God, for the pleasure and benefit of mankind, for whom Christ died. oh that we poor erring children would be as ready, to put forth our efforts to obey Him in word and deed.

Wednesday April the 20th 1927

1st Peter 1-4

A nice warm morning. I feel like praising praiseing God from whom all blessings flow, that I am so I can again wait on myself and walk about a little for it is from Him that all our help cometh, and it is to Him that I look for an inheritance incorruptible that fadeth not away when done with time here, dear Lord help me to be diligent to make ready, for we know not the day nor the hour when we shall be called upon to give account of the deeds done in the body.

April 1927

Thursday April the 21st 1927

Mark 5-19

A warm morning. I am thankful to be so I can be up and use my pen, for every day and at all times we have cause to give praise to the Great Giver of all our blessings, for we are bound to confess that they all come from Him and to him belongeth all the praise with his dear Son our blessed Saviour.

Friday April the 22nd 1927

Gal 2.20

A rainy morning. I feel very grateful to our merciful heavenly Father that it is well with us all as it is, and to realize that altho so unworthy as I feel myself to be, that The Son of God loves me and gave Himself for me, as we are told in Gods holy word, so I want to be found doing that which is well pleasing in His sight to His names honor and praise. The weekly prayer meeting was last night held at the home of Mr June Peace. I was not able to attend, but learn is was well attended and had a good meeting. "Blest be the tie that binds."

Saturday April the 23rd 1927

Mark 9-7

A bright cold morning. And again I would return thanks to our merciful Father for having taken care of us all during another night, and for rest in sleep, and I wish to give heed to the voice that comes out of the cloud as it were telling us "this is my beloved son hear him." oh that we may listen and obey. yes that we may obey to the salvation of our never dieing souls, and to the praise of Him who died our souls to save. Bless His holy name.

Sunday April the 24th 1927

Golden Text for today Mark 8-7

A lovely morning as we of this household have all been spared to see another Sabbath day, I feel that we have much to be thankful for, as we are all able to arise from our beds, and the most if not all of us will go to Church. I have not felt strong enough to go to Church for a few weeks, but as I am gaining I hope to be able to attend Church next Sunday. The first Sabbath in May will be the dedication of the Friends, new Church at Springfield. I hope we may all listen to Him who speaks to us through the Golden Text.

Monday April 25th 1927

Heb 9.28

Cloudy this morning. I am very thankful to be able to be up to day, as I desided to risk my strength yesterday to attend Sunday School, but I do not think I am any worse for my trip and I always enjoy going to S.S. and I was blessed with a good nights rest which was largely the result of rideing out in the fresh air, which is always so helpful to me when I am at all able to do so. and I trust that I shall be more and more concerned at all times to press on, and to do the will of him who shed his prepious blood for the salvation of us poor unworthy cretures. Bless the Lord oh my soul.

Tuesday April the 26th

John 15-16

A nice clear morning. All able to be up for which I am very thankful. And my great desire is that we all abide in the True and living Vine that we may bring forth fruit to the honor and praise of Him who created us on purpose of His own glory. for if we abide not in the Vine we shall be cast forth as a branch and wither oh that none of us may so transgress Gods holy law, as to be cast forth from His presence into outer darkness for it makes me shudder at the thought and what would the reality be. oh Father in Heaven. help us all to abide in Thee the true and living Vine that we may be nourished up unto life eternal to praise Thee forever is my prayer for Jesus sake who died that we might live.

April 1927

Wednesday April the 27th 1927

1st Cor 3-16

Warmer this morning. I feel very grateful to my merciful heavenly Father for a good nights rest in sleep and for strength to wait on myself to day. and as we are told in the "3rd chapter of 1st Corinthians that we are the temples of God and that the Sprit of God dwells in us, so I greatly desire that I nor any one may not defile these temples by disobeying His holy commandments in any way, but that we may worship in spirt and in truth, and not defile these mortal bodies by saying and doing things which are not well pleasing in His sight, for we know we shall be called upon to give account of the deeds done in the body when these temples shall crumble into dust. God help us all to do thy holy will in all things, is my prayer for Jesus sake.

Thursday April the 28th 1927

1st Peter 1-18-19

A nice clear morning, all able to arise from our beds and go about our daily avocations, for which I trust we are all very thankful. nothing special to Chronicle to day, but the continued goodness and mercy of our kind Heavenly Father. Praise his name.

Friday April the 29th 1927

Gal. 6-9

A nice clear morning. We have much to be thankful for that it is as well with us all as it is, and I desire that we all may be more careful to do the Masters will in all things to His names honor and praise. so Let us not be weary in well doing for in due season we shall reap if we faint not.

Saturday April the 30th 1927

1st Cor 10-12

A lovely morning as this is the last day of the month it again reminds me of the flight of time. I am thankful to my gracious Redeemer for his loveing kindness to me, as He puts into the hearts of loved ones to do me favors. Last night my dear daughter invited me to go with her to see and hear the exercises at Trinity High School Commencement, it was conducted by a clas of young students of the seventh grade and was very entertaining. In years gone by before Old Trinity College was moved to Durham N.C. I have enjoyed commencements there. But I have gone thru much sorrow since those days, so I appreciate the kindness of any one who tries to divert my mind from my troubles as much as possible and I want to be close on my watch that I do not give way to temptation and discouragement thru being sorely tried in many ways, so I am trying to remember the words of my Text and to take heed lest I fall. oh God help me to stand firm in the faith which I have in Thee is my prayer for Christ sake, who died for all.

Sunday May the 1st 1927

Psa 51-1-19

Bright morning, after a nice rain last night as this is the day set apart for the Dedication of the new Church at Springfield I am glad we have such a fine day as some of use wish to attend. Evening of same day. Glad to note that my daughter and husband and their little son and myself had the pleasure of attending the Dedication of the new meeting house at dear old Springfield, quite a large gathering and a very interesting ocasion, many good speakers. This was the one hundred thirty seventh anniversary of the Founding of Springfield meeting.

Monday May the 2nd 1927

Isa 12-2

Nice clear day. I am very thankful to be as well as I am to day, after quite a lengthy stay at the Church yesterday, which was rather fatigueing to the body but was so interesting that it seemed to buoy me up I enjoyed the services so much, that I seemed to forget that I had been afraid I could not hold out for all the services. so I wish this time forth to not be afraid to lean on the Everlasting Arms for strength in every needful time. and abide by my Text. "Behold God is my salvation I will trust and not be afraid." As I was very tired last evening I only pened a few lines, so I will not enter a few more lines concerning this interesting meeting. The opening service was Bible School at 9:45 a.m. but we did not get there for that, but at 11:00 am Meeting for worship **Sameul Haworth** brought the message, and it was grand. Hymn O Worship The King was nicely rendered, and then Scripture Reading and prayer by **Reuben Payne.** Then Selected Music by **Violet Millikan, Chester C.** and **Byron A. Haworth.** I will not attempt to note all that was said and done, but this sesion was closed by singing the Hymn, O For A Thousand Tongues To Sing. And Benediction. The Memorial Service at 2:30 p.m. **William A Blair** Presideing. There was to of been Scripture Reading and Prayer by **Tom Alderman Sikes** but for some cause he was not present. Then we had Greetings from Baltimore yearly meeting by **John C. Thomas**. Then Music Selected by **Norman Fidler**. Then the Address by **Dr. Elbert Russell** of Duke Univesity. Then some Reminescenses and Remarks. Then the Hymn Faith of Our Fathers and Benediction.

Tuesday May the 3rd 1927

Luke 5-32

A nice clear day. As this is my daughter **Mary Eliza Blair Stilwell Peaces** forty second Birthday it brings many things of the past fresh to my mind. remembering her childhood her youth and her young womanhood days, and her marriage to **Arthur Lee Stilwell** of Charlotte N.C. on her twentieth birthday with whom she lived happily for fifteen years. Then she was deprived of him by the cold hand of death, which was indeed a sad shock to her, and her people and his people. but as he was such a good Christian man we could the more cheerfully give him up knowing that our loss was his gain. After endureing widowhood for a time, she united in marriage with **Mr Jerome W. Peace** of Progress, N.C. Their present address being Route #2. Box 18. Trinity, N.C. and I am sojourning with them at this time, as I have now been a widow for seven years, and during those years have lived with my children. I feel that I have much to be thankful for, that I still have children living to have a place of refuge under their roof. May the dear Lord help us to live in harmony and love and at last reunited in His home above, to praise Him togeather.

Wednesday May the 4th 1927

Eph 5-17

Nice warm morning. Al nature seems to be obeying the voice of Him who created all things on purpose of His own glory. Therefore we who are accountable beings, should not be "unwise but understand what the will of the Lord is, "that we may obey as readily as the trees bring forth their foliage and the plants their bud and bloom "Proveing what is acceptable unto the Lord," for we know that we shall receive our reward if we are faithful to follow His leading, and have no fellowship with the unfruitful works of darkness as is enjoined upon us in the holy Scriptures but rather reprove them. and we are also told that blessed are the pure in heart for they shall see God, and again that not a jot nor tittle of sin shall enter Heaven, I pray thee oh God to cleanse my heart and make it pure that I may see Thee face to face and praise thee forever with thy dear Son whom thou didst give as a sacrafise for the sins of the whole world therefore for my sins, so from the depth of my heart I pen these words. Blessed be the name of the Father and the Son and Holy Spirit now and ever more.

Thursday May the 5th 1927

Psa 73-24

A beautiful clear day. All able to be on the stage of action, which is much to be thankful for, and I am looking to the source of our strength to be led and guided in the way that I should go, and it is such a source of comfort that we have One that we can look to for help and council and the promice of reward if we fulfil the conditions. As in the following Text. "Thou shalt guide me with Thy council and afterward receive me to glory." oh that we may all be so diligent in doing the Lords will here on earth that we may be received into glory. is my prayer for Jesus sake.

Friday May the 6th 1927

Isa 43-25

A nice warm day. All the members of this household are in usual health, for which I feel very grateful to the Giver of all blessings. I was favored to have strength to accompany them to Trinity last night to hear the Graduating exercises of the Seniour Class, twenty four in number, six boys and eighteen girls, all did fine. it was very entertaining. One of the daughters in this home **Miss Minnie J Peace** was one of the number. And to day at eleven oclock **Dr. Perisho** of Guilford College is to deliver the Address and present the Diplomas.

Saturday May the 7th 1927

1st Peter 1-5

Cloudy this morning. All able to be up and going about daily avocations. I feel like giving thanks to our merciful heavenly Father for his kind favors to me a poor unworthy worm of the dust as I feel myself to be. I was favored yesterday to attend the exercises of the Graduating Class at eleven oclock at Trinity that all did fine and looked pretty. **Dr Perisho** gave a splendid Address. and the Diplomas were presented by **Congressman W.C. Hammer** instead of **Dr Perisho** as I stated yesterday.

Sunday May the 8th 1927

Golden Text 1st Peter 1-3

Nice morning. Thankful that we are all able to be up and prepare for Sunday School and Church, and as this day is set apart universally as Mothers Day it brings many things fresh to my mind from my childhood to the present time. and having had such a good Christian Mother, I have so much to be thankful for that she taught me the way of truth and righteousness. and altho I have not at all times kept to the straight and narrow path as strictly as I should, her good advice and Christian council and example in life has been an inspiration to follow on in her footsteps and to day as I wear the white flower in memory of my dear Mother who passed over the River of death more than a score of years ago, and has put on the White Robe that Angels wear. I feel so thankful to my Heavenly Father that he gave me such a precious Mother. may I so finish my course on earth that I may meet her in the better land, is my prayer for Christs sake.

Monday May the 9th 1927

2nd Timothy 1-7

Nice warm morning. All able to go about daily duties, which is much to be thankful for. and I am so glad that we are told in the holy Scriptures to come boldly to the Throne of grace that we may obtain help in time of need, this I interpret to mean that we should come with meekness and in the right spirit of fear; but of power and of love and of sound mind. and as we have full confidence that God is as good as his word, and has given us a sound mind to know good from evil. let us hold fast our faith in Him and come to him day by day for help to do His holy will. that we may inherit a home with the redeemed, there to sing His praise forever with loved ones gone before. For Christ sake.

Tuesday May the 10th 1927

Rom 12-2

Cloudy this morning. I am feeling weak and nervous, but trusting in the promise that as thy day thy strength shall be. I am endeavoring to press on looking unto Him who has been my stay and my staff thru many years of weakness and trials in various way, and to whom I shall look for help unto the end. Bless His holy name.

May 1927

Wednesday May the 11th 1927

Isa 30:-15-18

A bright morning. I am still feeling feble but thankful that it is as well with me as it is, and trust in in the Divine helper to keep me passive in His hands, for we are told in my Text that "in quietness and confidence shall be your strength. and Blessed are they that wait for Him." so I desire not only for myself, but for all for whom it is my duty to pray, that we may live quietly and obediently and wait patiently for His comeing that we may receive His blessing. And praise Him forevermore.

Thursday May the 12th 1927

Psa 84:11-85-12

Much cooler this morning. I am thankful that we of this home have sufficient strength to go about the daily rotine of work. for in the language of Scripture the night cometh where in no man can work and conciquently no woman, so I wish to do whatever is required of me to do while it is called to day, for we know not how soon we may be called from works to rewards to give account of the deeds done in the body. It was with sadness that I learned last evening of the sudden death of **Mrs Elizabeth Hendrix** widow of **Millard Hendrix** she was burried a few days ago at Springfield and we very much regret that we did not learn of her funeral at the time. she was a very useful Christian woman. and a friend in whom I put great confidence and thought a great deal of. She was a daughter of the late **Martin Taylor**. I believe she is reaping the reward of well done good and faithful servent enter into thy rest. For she was so faithful to care for the sick and suffering. oh that I may fulfil my mishon on earth, and be ready to meet her in the better land.

Friday May the 13th 1927

James 5-16

Cool enough for fire to mak one feel comfortable. to day. and oh how Thankful I am to the Great Giver of all good, that we can look to Him for comfort in our weak and tried moments thru which we often have to pass in various ways, and I desire to be faithful to fervently pray not only for myself but for all others that we may so live the life of the righteous that the words of my Text may become effectual and avail much. For Jesus sake.

Saturday May the 14th

Acts 2-12-38

Cloudy this morning. All well as usual for while I hope we are truly thankful to our Heavenly Father who watches over us by day and by night and we know that He hears every word that we speak, and beholds every act whether kind or unkind, so it behooves us to be careful what we do and say, for we are told that we shall have to give account of every idle word. Therefore if we have transgressed in anywise we should do as Peter says in the Text, repent and be baptized with the Holy Ghost.

Sunday May the 15th 1927

Golden Text for to day Acts 2-38

A clear cool Sabbath morning. and the words Remember the Sabbath day to keep it holy; sounds in my ears, and I am anxious to obey this injunction of holy Scriptures. and not only to keep the Sabbath day holy, but each and every day should be regarded as belonging to the Lord and to Him we shall have to give account of how we make use of them.

Monday May the 16th 1927

Jer 29-13

A cool morning. I feel very thankful that all in this home are as well as we are. and hope that we are endeavoring to do our whole duty and seeking the Lord while He may be found for He tells us thru His Prophet Jeremiah, "ye shall seek me and find me when ye shall search for me with all your heart." so I am anxious that we seek Him with all our heart, that we may be found of Him and bless us with His presence while here on earth, and thus prepare us for an entrance into His happy home above. where we shall praise Him forever.

Tuesday May the 17th 1927

Luke 14-23

This quite a cool morning. I am thankful to be up this morning and able to ride out, as I wish to visit my dear cousin **Roxie Hill** to day. she has to sit in her Wheel Chair day after day and knowing as I do what that means, as I have had that experience for years in the past I have great sympathy for her.

Wednesday May the 18th 1927

Luke 15-10

Warmer to day. I am grateful that was favored with strength to visit **Roxie** and **John Hill** yesterday and staid over night with them and had a very pleasant visit with them then this morning I came to cousin **R.L. Blairs** he was not at home, but I spent the forenoon and took dinner with **Ocid** and as always had a good visit with her.

Thursday May the 19th 1927

Rom 8-

Nice morning. I am thankful that we of this home are all able to be up and go about our daily avocations and atho we meet with many things while passing thur this vale of tears that is trying to our natural inclinations. we should be in entire submishion to the Divine will. for "We know that all things work togeather for good to them that love the Lord." and I am so glad that He who knows all things. knows that I love him and desire to obey Him in all things.

Friday May the 20th 1927

James 5-13-20

Cloudy this morning. I am thankful for having a quiet nights rest, and to again be able to be up and doing. and my daughter and I are makeing preperations to go on our visit to Salisbury on the morrow, the Lord willing and she is also aiming to go on to visit friends in Charlotte besides my dear son and family which I would love to visit but as I am not strong think best not to go that distance at present. Bless the Lord oh my soul.

Saturday May the 21st 1927

Acts 4-12

Cloudy and cooler this morning. I am thankful that it is as well with us all as it is this morning. my daughter and I are aiming to go to Sailsbury to day, and I am trusting our blessed Lord to preserve us from all danger and give us a safe journey Blessed be His holy name now and forever.

Sunday May the 22nd 1927

A nice warm morning. According to our expectation my daughter **Mrs Peace** and myself arrived at **Mr George Stilwell**, last evening, spent the night with them very pleasantly, and to day aim to go with the family to Church. I praise the Lord for His goodness and mercy to us in granting us a safe journey to this place. Later in the day, I will state that we were blessed to attend Church and Sunday School at Sailsbury and heard a very interesting and inspireing sermon by the **Rev R G Tuttle** and certainly did enjoy the splendid remarks of the Teacher of the ladies class which I was invited to attend, the Teacher **Mr Taylor** expounded the Scripture equal to any Preacher I ever heard and it is as greatly enjoyed. Then in the afternoon the family of **Mr Stilwells** was visited by kind friends and relatives to visit them which was a pleasure for us all. Praise the Lord.

Monday May the 23rd 1927

Acts 15-17-26

Nice morning. I am thankful to of had a quiet nights rest, and am enjoying the hospitality of this kind and interesting family. Praise the Lord oh my soul.

May 1927

Tuesday May the 24th 1927

Rom 8-26

A warm morning. I am so thankful to of had a good rest in sleep the past night, for often when away from my usual sleeping place do not rest well. so I feel that I can not thank my merciful Heavenly Father enough for His goodness to me and that He puts it into the hearts of those whom I visit to be so kind and nice to me. may the dear Lord bless them abundantly for their thoughtful kindness to me, is my prayer.

Wednesday May the 25th 1927

Much cooler this morning and very dry and dusty. I am still enjoying the hospitality of this home. Thankful to be able to take note of the goodness and mercy of the One in whom we live and have our being. Blessed be the name of the Lord now and forever. Evening of same day, This afternoon **Mrs. Stilwell**, her **daughter Margaret**, and myself paid a visit to their daughter **Mrs. Shoe** in Sailsbury and met with one of their other daughters **Mrs. Fesperman**, also met with **Mrs Fred Lauglin** one of their neighbors, and met with the Minister **Rev Tuttle** and his daughter, we had a very enjoyable evening for which I feel very grateful and for a safe journey to and from Town. Blessed be the name of the Lord. now and evermore.

Thursday May the 26th 1927

Cloudy this morning, had a little rain during the night which has cooled the air and laid the dust which has made it much more pleasant. Thankful all are well here as usual. To day my daughter **Mrs Peace** will return home from Charlotte, but I will remain in Sailsbury for some time longer. with **Mr George Stilwells** family who are so very kind to me.

Friday May the 27th 1927

Beautiful morning. Last evening **Mr Stilwells** daughter **Mrs B.D. Shoe** brought me to visit her sister **Mrs Homer Fesperman**, and I remained over night with them, and we went out for a drive last night over the main streets of Sailsbury and had a very fine drive as the Electric lights in the buildings showed up beautiful. and now this morning I am still enjoying the hospitality of these fine people whom I love so much. May the blessing of the Lord rest upon these dear young people who are starting on this journey of life here below, with a sweet little lamb **Rachel** commited to their care, may they train her in the path of truth and virtue, so that when all are done with the things of earth we may all meet in the better land is my prayer for Jesus sake.

Saturday May the 28th 1927

Rainey this morning. Last evening **Mr** and **Mrs Fesperman** brought me back to **Mrs Fespermans** Fathers staid over night and had a good nights rest, and this morning I am enjoying the hospitality of this home. I had a very interesting visit at **Mr Fespersmans**. They took me up to Town to do a little trading before coming back here.

Sunday May the 29th 1927

Raining this morning. I am still in the hospitable home all able to be up and prepare for the services this holy Sabbath day. but the weather being so very damp and rainey I thought it prudent to stay in as I am very easy to take cold, so **Mr Stilwell**, their daughter **Mary**, and myself remaining in the home and spent the time most happily togeather. Blessed by the name of the Lord.

Monday May the 30th 1927

Rainey again this morning Still in the home of this kind family. I had a good nights rest after rideing out yesterday afternoon to see some friends, as I have stated it was too rainey for some of us to go to Church this forenoon we spent the evening very pleasently with those friends and after returning to **Mr Stilwells** found two of their daughters and their husbands had called in the parental home so we had a nice time with them. Then before retireing as is their practice every night we had Bible reading and prayer togeather. oh that this precious practice might be observed in every home what a blessing it would be. and now to day **Mrs Stilwell** is makeing my Crepedechine dress, she is such a nice dress maker, and I love her so much for she is so kind and nice to me, and so are all the family.

Tuesday May the 31st 1927

A nice morning after a good rain last night. I am still in the home of these hospitable people. I had a good nights rest, and feel refreshed as the rain has cooled the air, all are well in this home at present and are busy caning cherries for future use. my great desire this morning is to be found walking in the path of tore righteousness and peace. oh that I may live the life of the righteous, that I may die the death of the righteous and my last end be like this. "Teach me they way oh Lord and lead me in a plain path that I go not astray from thee" is my prayer for Jesus sake.

Wednesday June the 1st 1927

Cooler this morning. all able to be up and go about daily avocations. This morning their daughter **Virgie (Mrs Smith)** and her three sweet little girls and their **Auntie Mrs Jinnie Garver** gave them a call. **Virgie** had to return home, their Auntie is going to visit in this home, and her people in Sailsbury. Praise the Lord for His goodness and mercy to us all.

Thursday June the 2nd 1927

Cloudy this morning. Again we have so to be thankful for that we are all able to be on this stage of action. I have been enjoying the hospitality of this home to the full for all are so very nice to me. May the Lord bless them abundantly both spiritually and temporally for their kindness to me.

Friday June the 3rd 1927

Thankful to of had a good nights rest in the home of **Mr and Mrs B.D. Shoe** with whom I spent the night. I am so glad that they are true Christians and have Bible reading and prayer in their home. oh that all young people starting out in life would observe this rule in their homes it would prove such a blessing. I praise the Lord for His goodness and mercy to me for He raised up kind friends to minister to my need of sympathy for all have been so very kind to me in all the homes I have visited, this afternoon **Mrs Shoe** took me to see her sister **Mrs Fesperman** to spend the afternoon, as she did when I was in this home before I am spending the time very pleasently and expect to return to their Fathers **Mr George Stilwells** this evening. I feel that I can not praise my loveing and merciful Heavenly Father enoug for His goodness to me. Blessed be His holy name now and forever.

Saturday June the 4th 1927

Romans 10-12

Cloudy and cool this morning. I returned to **Mr Stilwells** last evening, spent a quiet night in rest and sleep and am so thankful to be able to arise from my bed this morning. I greatly desire to be kept close on my watch least I transgress God commandments by not watching close unto prayer and meditating on His holy word.

Sunday June the 5th 1927

A nice Sabbath day. I still being in the home of my friends the **Stilwells.** I had the opportunity to go to Church again at Sailsbury and hear another good sermon by the **Rev RG Tuttle** and also went into the Sunday School class which was very interesting. I feel that I cannot praise the Lord enough for His kindness to me in raiseing up kind friends to care for and sympathise with me. May the Lord bless them abundantly both spiritually and temporaly for Christs sake. We just now heard that **Mr Callier Cranford** is to be burried this afternoon at Trinity N.C. his daughter **Carrie** was called home from her teaching here in Sailsbury on account of his demise. He was burried at Trinity June the 5th 1927.

Monday June the 6th 1927

2nd Cor 12-9

Much cooler this morning. I am thankful to of had a good nights rest after a drive last evening out to a neighbors by the name of **Mr and Mrs Webb**, spend a pleasent evening with them, and returned to **Mr Stilwells**, and this morning all are busy with their work, the women folk with their sewing and other house work, and the men folk to their work in the cotton field. oh how much we all have to be thankful for that the good Lord gives us health and strength to perform the work that is necessary for the sustanance and comfort of our bodies, and a mind to know what He would have us do if we will only listen to His divine commands. oh Heavenly Father in Heaven help me to know, and to do thy holy will I ask for Jesus sake.

Tuesday June the 7th 1927

Cloudy and cool to day. I am still in the home of **Mr George Stilwell**, had a quiet nights rest and am so thankful to be able to be up and note the goodness and mercy of the dear Lord to me a poor unworthy worm of the dust as I feel myself to me. Later in the I received a letter from my daughter **Mrs J.W. Peace** telling me of the funeral of **Mr Callier Cranford** which was held at Fairview Church which was the first funeral held in that Church and was very largely attended. I very much regreted not being up there to attend the services, as he was a near neighbor of ours when we were in our dear old home in Randalph. And his wife a first cousin to my husband. May the Lord bless and comfort the bereaved ones, and be ready to meet him in the better land, where parting is unknown.

Wednesday June the 8th 1927

A cloudy morning. Still in **Mr George Stilwells** home as usual. in the afternoon of same day. "**Aunt Carrie**," **Margaret**, and myself visited **Mrs Fred Laughlin** over in Sailsbury, had a very interesting visit and returned home for the night and slept well. Praise the Lord for His goodness and mercy to us all.

Thursday June the 9th 1927

Rom 5-8

A nice morning. Thankful all are able to be up and going about daily avocations. Just now **Mrs Jessie Shoe**, and **Mrs Kathleen Fesperman** came to visit at their Fathers. I enjoy all their company so much. Praise the Lord for His goodness to us all.

Friday June the 10th 1927

A clear morning. I am very thankful to be able to be up this morning, for I was feeling quite feeble last night, and had a headache so I was not able to read or write. I praise the Lord for His goodness to me, for later in the day **Mr and Mrs Stilwell**, their two little boys and myself took a drive over to China Grove, this trip seemed to do me good as my headache got better after pertaking of some ice cream. and having a general good time.

Saturday June 11th 1927

A pretty morning after a big rain. I am thankful to be feeling some better this morning than I did yesterday. Praise the Lord for His goodness to me and to mine. oh may we all praise His holy name.

Sunday June the 12th 1927

Cloudy this morning, but rain held up so that the whole family of **Mr Stilwells** and myself got out to church and Sunday School at Sailsbury. this was also childrens day and they had some very good exercises and songs by the children which I enjoyed very much. There came a very hard rain and thunder during the exercises, which somewhat mared the exercises being enjoyed as they would have been, as we could not hear all that was said, but the rain stoped so that all had a chance to get home without getting wet, but before we reached home we had a punctured tire which hindered us quite a while and the roads were very muddy, and it was quite a task to get patched up so we could get home.

Monday June the 13th 1927

A nice clear morning. All in this home able to be up and go about daily avocations. I feel like giving thanks to the great giver of all good for His mercy to me, His poor unworthy child.

Tuesday June the 14th 1927

1st Peter 3-18

A nice clear morning. after a heavy rain last evening and heavy thunder. I am thankful that all in this home are able to be on the stage of action. **Miss Mary Stilwell** went to Tannapolis last night to begin her work of inspecting cloth in the cotton mill. she works at night and sleeps in the day she is now takeing her morning nap.

Wednesday June the 15th 1927

Raining this morning. I am not feeling at all well but thankful to be able to be up and take note of the goodness and mercy of the Lord to us all. Tomorrow morning is the time set for us to go to Randolph this is the fourth week I have been with **Mr Stilwells** family, and have enjoyed it so much that I am loathe to leave them, but feel that the time has come for me to return to my daughters home in Randolph and **Mr** and **Mrs Stilwell** and their daughter **Mrs Fesperman** and baby **Rachel** are aiming to accompany me home. I trust we may have a good day for the drive as we are aiming to go by private conveyance

May the Lord bless this family abundantly in every way need for this kindness to me. I ask in Jesus name.

Thursday June the 16th 1927

Isa 43-2

A nice clear morning. all able to be up, and those of us who are bound for Randolph Cc to day are making ready for the trip. I praise the Lord for the beautiful sunshine after the rain. and trust the good Lord will give us a safe journey to our destination. Praise the Lord for His goodness and mercy to us all. We feel that we should give God all the praise for our safe journey to my daughters in Randolph as we arrived here in good time and found all well and ready to give us a hearty welcome I hope we may all watch unto prayer and be thankful for all our mercies. Bless the Lord oh my soul.

Friday June the 17th 1927

Luke 12-37

Cloudy this morning. We arrived here at my daughters **Mr J.W. Peace** yesterday about eleven oclock, then after eating a sumpteous dinner, in the evening we all took a drive over the home of **Mr Bowman** at Glenola to see their daughter **Ollie Bowman** and others. and now **Mr** and **Mrs Stilwell** are going back to Sailsbury this morning, and their daughter **Mrs Fesperman** will remain with us until tomorrow then visit in High Point. May the Lord bless them all abundently is my prayer for Jesus sake.

Saturday June the 18th 1927

Cloudy this morning. all able to be up, and my daughter and husband are going to take **Mrs Fesperman** over the High Point to day to visit her friends there. And now as our Sailsbury friends have all taken their leave of us we feel to miss them greatly for the time was spent so pleasently during my stay with them in their homes and so glad to have them visit us here. May the Lord bless them all in His name. Yes we are sorry indeed to have to give up **Mrs Fesperman** up to day for she is such good company and so are all her Fathers family I enjoyed my visit with them so much that it will always be a source of pleasure to think of my visit in Sailsbury N.C.

Sunday June the 19th 1927

Rom 13-10

Clear and cool this morning. I have deep cold and am hoarse so that I cannot speak plainly. as I would like, but so glad I able to read my Bible and pen down the continued goodness and mercy of the dear Lord to His dependent children, for I am so thankful that it is as well with us all as it is this holy Sabbath day. To day the Township Sunday School convention is to be held at Trinity N.C.

Monday June the 20th 1927

James 1-22

A nice clear morning. All able to be up in this home and go about daily avocations. I am not feeling at all strong, but thankful to be so I can wait on myself, and pen down the goodness and mercy of the Lord to me and mine. blessed be His holy name now and forever more.

Tuesday June the 21st 1927

Cool and cloudy this morning. I am still feeling feeble, but thankful to be so I can be up and have the use of my right hand and thinking faculties so I can take note of the goodness and mercy of the dear Lord who has suffered so much for me. Blessed be His holy name.

Wednesday June the 22nd 1927

Rev 3-11

Cloudy this morning. all able to be up in this home. I am still feeling weak but thankful to be up and again take note of the goodness and mercy of the Lord to his unworthy dependent children.

Thursday June the 23th 1927

A nice warm morning. all able to be up in this home I am still feeling weak, but thankful that it is as well with me as it is. To night is the time appointed for the weekly prayer meeting to be held at **Grandma Peaces**. May the dear Lord meet with those who are permitted to attend and cause His presence to be felt in their midst.

Friday June the 24th 1927

Nice morning. I am still suffering from deep cold so is my daughter, the rest of the family are well. Last night the cottage prayer meeting was held at **Grandma Peaces**. I was sorry none of us were there. **May** and I were ready to go but were prevented by the storm. we learn this morning they had a good prayer meeting for which I am glad.

Saturday June the 25th 1927

Cloudy this morning. All able to be on the stage of action for takeing care of us all thru another night. some one will perhaps be ready to say there is nothing worthy of notice in these lines, that it is the same thing over, day after day. yet and it is the same good Father watching over us all day and by night and His goodness is worthy of note from day to day. so let us not be weary of proclaiming God's goodness in whatever way we may. either in writing or in the sound of our voices, either in the congregation or in the whispered prayer when alone with God in the quiettude of our rooms at night or in the early morning. let our hearts ever be filled with praise to His holy name.

Sunday June the 26th 1927

A nice warm morning. My daughter brought me over to cousin **John Hills** last evening staid over night with them, they seemed so very glad to see me, I was glad I made the effort to go, for altho I was not feeling well. when I saw **Cousin Roxie's** condition since getting her fall and getting so badly hurt I felt that I had so much to be thankful for that I am as well as I am, and so glad I could do a little something for her comfort and help which they appreciated so much I felt doubly paid for what assistance I could give. Praise the Lord for His goodness to us all.

Monday the June the 27th 1927

Clear and cool this morning. It was late last evening when I returned from cousin **John Hills**, but I had a good nights rest, and am so thankful that I am able to be up this nice morning to note the goodness and mercy of the Lord to His unworthy children. Blessed be the name of the Lord now and ever.

Tuesday June the 28th 1927

2nd Thess 3-5

Nice clear morning. I am thankful to of had a good quiet rest the past night, and for strength to be up and wait on myself. I count this a great blessing, and praise the dear Lord for it. and I desire to be faithful to obey His holy will in all things and what I desire for myself I desire for all my loved ones. and as in the Text, "and the Lord direct your hearts into the love of God and into the patient waiting for Christ." The same day Tuesday the 28th just after I had written the foregoing lines, we were surprised by a large Car rolling up with some of our friends from Charlotte and **Miss Margaret Stilwell** from Sailsbury This was indeed a pleasent surprise and we enjoyed it to the full, they took dinner with us and then we enjoyed a feast of Ice cream togeather. Then in the afternoon we had another glad surprise, **Sidney Blair** and wife **Della** and their daughter **Mrs Charlie Lee** of High Point and also their grandaughter **Mrs Barnes** of Greensboro gave us a pleasent call. we were very glad to see all of them.

Wednesday June the 29th 1927

2nd Cor 1-20

A nice clear morning. All able to go about daily duties, but I am feeling very much depressed under a sense of weakness and my situation

I greatly desire to be instrumental in the Lords hands in doing whatever He requires of me, and am earnestly praying that He will show me just what His will is concerning me in all things to His honor and praise. for I want to glorify Him on earth that I may glorify Him in Heaven. Blessed be his holy name now and forever.

Thursday June the 30th 1927
Rom 15-13

A nice warm morning. As this is the last day of the month, it again brings to mind the flight of time, and as I believe on the Lord Jesus Christ, I am now filled with joy and peace in believeing, and pray the I may ever be faithful in dischargeing my duty let the consequences be what they may, for altho I have many things to bear that are trying to the flesh, yet I am determined by the help of God to bear no malice or ill will in any way toward any living soul. for we are told that love is the fulfiling of the law, therefore we should obey Gods law even to the loveing our enemies, for Jesus sake.

Friday July the 1st 1927
Rom 1-16

Cloudy this morning. All well as usual I am thankful to state, and thankful also that I am not ashamed of the Gospel of Christ for it is the power of God unto salvation to every one that believeth as stated in our Text. and I am so glad that I can say truly that I do believe and am not ashamed of the Gospel of Christ but confess it full and freely. Blessed be the name of the Lord now and forever.

Saturday July the 2nd 1927
Micah 6-8

Cloudy and warm this morning. All are busy as usual. I am not feeling well but thankful to be able to arise from my bed. and am trying to obey the requirements of my Text. Lord help me so to do this day and every day thruout lifes journey. I pray for Jesus sake.

Sunday July the 3rd 1927

1st Sameul 9-11

A nice Sabbath morning. All able to be up and prepare for Sunday School and Church. May the dear Lord help us to understand more of His holy word and keep this day holy.

Monday July the 4th 1927

Psa 46-1

A nice clear morning. All able to be busy this morning with things pertaining to household duties and farm life here in this home. while hundreds are going to different places making a great ado over the 4th as Declaration Day of Independence. oh that we may all remember the deeds done in the body. and that we may prepare for the time when we shall have to give account of how we have spent our time here on earth for we all want to spend eternity in Heaven, so I pray that we may listen to Him who bids us obey His voice.

Tuesday July the 5th 1927

Eph 2-8

A nice day. all able to be up, and are very busy caning fruit, beans, and crout, and also prepareing for the wheat threshers here for supper. so all are useing the strength they have for the work that is necessary to be done. and herein is the words of Scripture verified "That as thy day thy strength shall be." Praise the Lord for His goodness.

Wednesday July the 6th 1927

Eph 4-32

A nice clear morning. All in this home are able to be on the stage of action. The house wife busy makeing preserves etc and the men folk threshing the wheat and other grain to day. There is so much to be thankful for, that we are blessed with grain for bread and that we have strength to take care of what is made for our benefit. oh may we all be more diligent to partake of the bread of life, by doing the things that are required of us for the preservation of our bodies and the salvation of our immortal souls. and may we all live according to the words of our Text. being kind and forgiving one another. for love is fulfiling of the law. "For behold how good and how pleasent it is for brethren to dwell togeather in unity."

Thursday July the 7th 1927

Heb 9-27

A niece cool morning. I am thankful that it is as well with us all here as it is to day. and in the language of the Scripture Text that, "It is appointed unto men once to die, and after this the judgement." So we know that sooner or later, we all shall be called to day down these mortal lives, and then to give account of the deeds done in the body. so it behooves us to be close on our watch that we do not transgress Gods holy law. For we want an entrance into the better land when done with time here below. So we should obey Him with our whole heart in order to receive the welcome language of good and faithful servant, enter thou into the joy of thy Lord.

Friday July the 8th 1927

1st John 2-25

Cloudy and warmer to day. All well as usual and I am thankful that I still have the use of my hands and the use of my thinking faculties so that I can note the goodness and mercy of the Lord to us His dependent children. and I am very anxious to obey His word. for "This is the promice that He hath promiced us even eternal life." And we all want to inherit eternal life.

Saturday July the 9th 1927

Psa 26-3

We have had a very rainy night, and it is still cloudy this morning, all able to be up and some of the family are aiming to go to High Point to day if rain holds up, as **Mary Lee** has been visiting in Charlotte and will expect some one to meet her in H.P. on return to day. "The loveing kindness of the Lord is before mine eyes." in beholding the effects of the refreshing showers that was so much needed to save the crops. oh that we may all obey Him and "walk in His truth." is my prayer.

Sunday July the 10th 1927

1st Sameul 12

A nice Sabbath morning. All nature seems to be praiseing the Great Giver of all things. oh that we who are responsible beings, may be close on our watch that we do not disobey Him this holy Sabbath day, but be diligent to do His holy will in all things to His honor and praise.

Monday July the 11th 1927

Matt 7-12

Cloudy this morning. I am thankful to still be able to use my pen, for by takeing note each day if it is only a few lines, it keeps me closer on my watch to do the Masters will. Heavenly Father help me to obey thee this day and every day. thruout lifes journey.

Tuesday July the 12th 1927

Acts 3-10

A nice day all able to be busy with household duties and other work. I am so thankful that I have long ago confirmed to the words of my Text and repented of my sins and that they are all boted out in that blood that was shed on Calvery for the sins of the whole world therefore for my sins. and altho I have often made mistakes when I have been thrown off my guard, and not followed my Guide as closely as I should, yet I know that He who watches over us at all times knows my heart and knows that I do not willfully transgress His law, and my earnest prayer is that I may never so backslide into sin as to forfeit my claim of a home in Heaven when done with the trials of earth. and what I desire for myself I wish for all others, for Jesus sake.

Wednesday July the 13th 1927

Isa 55-6

A nice warm day. and I am very thankful that we are all in usual health going about our daily avocations, and I am so glad that I have found the dear Lord to be very gracious to my soul and I desire that all may conform to the words of my Text to seek the Lord while He may be found call upon Him while He is near.

Thursday July the 14th 1927

Psa 37-23

A nice bright day. all able to be up and doing this morning, for which I am very grateful for I was feeling very much indisposed last night. I am also glad of this beautiful day for the sake of the couple that are to be joined in Wedlock We understand that **Mr Walter Farlow** and **Miss Muriel Lowe** are to accomplish their marriage to day at ten oclock in Friends Church at Marlboro N.C. I trust that the steps of the Groom may be in accordance with the words of my Text. "The steps of a good man are ordered by the Lord and He delighteth in his way." and may he and his Bride go hand in hand as it were thruout this lifes journey in promoting the way of truth, and righteousness, and be a blessing to the home, to the Church and to the world, is prayer for Jesus sake.

Friday July the 15th 1927

Psa 107-9

Nice warm morning. All able to be attending to the necessary duties, for which I am thankful, and hope that we may all be anxious and diligent in doing the things that are well pleasing in the sight of Him in whom we live and have our being, and that we hunger and thirst after righteousness that we may be filled, for "He satisfieth the longing soul, and filleth the hungry soul with goodness."

July 1927

Saturday July the 16th 1927

1st Tim 4-12

A nice morning. All well as usual I am thankful to state. but many hearts are made sad on account of another death in the community To day **Mrs Nelle Robins** an aged widow is to be consigned to the grave at Mt Vernon which reminds us that the aged must die, and the young do die.

Sunday July the 17th 1927

1st Tim 4-12

A warm morning, with some clouds to obscure the rays of the sun. oh that we may all obey the words of our Text, that we may be examples of the believers in word, in conversation, in charity, in spirit in faith in purity. that we may not do anything to cloud our spiritual sky, and thus shut out from us the Sun of righteousness who designs that we should obey Him in the beauty of holiness. oh for more grace to serve Him as I ought.

Monday July the 18th 1927

Gal 6-2

Cloudy again this morning. All able to be up and go about daily avocations, for which I feel very grateful to the Giver of all good. and we are again reminded of the uncertainty of life and the certainty of death. as to day the remains of **Mr Scales Eldrige** are to be laid away in the Cemetary at Mt Vernon. The words "be ye also ready for in such an hour as ye think not the Son of man cometh," sounds in my ears. yes we are all liable to be called at any moment of time to give account of the deeds done in the body, therefore let us be ready to meet the Bridegroom with our lamps trimmed and burning, so as to hear the welcome mesage of "well done good and faithful servent enter thou into the joy of thy Lord." oh to receive this message is worth more than all this worlds goods. So let us all be ready for Jesus sake.

Tuesday July the 19th 1927

1st Cor 6-20

Nice warm morning. All able to be on the stage of action for which I am thankful. Our Text tells us that we are bought with a price. Yes that price was paid with the blood of our blessed Saviour. therefore we should do all to glorify God in our bodies, and in our spirits which all belong to God. my prayer this morning is Lord help me to glorify thee in all I do or say. And that I may obey Thee in all things now and always. And as almost daily some one we know, or know of are being laid in the grave, we are kept in mind that we also may be called at any time to face the enemy death. I stated yesterday the funeral of **Mr Eldrige** at Mt Vernon. The same evening the funeral of **Mr Isaac Marsh** was held at Ebeneezar.

Wednesday July the 20th 1927

Rom 10-10

Fine morning. All nature seems to be rejoiceing after a refreshing rain last evening. oh for a fresh baptism of the holy spirit this morning to strengthen our faith and help us to press on in the way of everlasting peace, to the praise of Him who hath said. "With the heart man believeth unto righteousness, and with the mouth confession is made unto salvation." Praise the Lord oh my soul.

Thursday July the 21st 1927

James 4-17

Nice morning. all able to be about daily avocations for which I am thankful, and trust that as we are blessed with the use of our mind, that we will obey the words of our Text. for them that knoweth to do good, and doeth it not, to them it is sin. Lord help us to do good, and resist evil at all times to the praise of Him who died to save us from sin.

July 1927

Friday July the 22nd 1927

Matt 11-23

Another nice morning. Thankful to note that all are able to be busy with the burdens of the day. and some of us are laboring under the trials that beset us more or less every day our lives. but we have the words of our blessed Saviour come unto me and I will give you rest.

Saturday July the 23rd 1927

A nice warm morning. All able to be up and prepareing for a great social event of the day. oh that we may all remember to be accountable to God for all our words and actions, and be on our guard lest we transgress the commandments of the Lord in word or in deed. Help us oh Father to obey Thee in all things, for Christ the Redeemers sake.

Sunday Jul the 24th 1927

Psa 27-1

A lovely Sabbath morning. I am so thankful that we are all able to arise from our bed, and prepare for Sunday School and Church. May we keep this day holy unto the Lord and may observe each succeeding day in the way of His requireings is the desire of my heart for Jesus sake, "The Lord is the strength of my life of whom shall I be afraid." Keep me close to Thee.

Monday July the 25th 1927

2nd Peter 3-18

A nice day. All able to be up for which I am thankful altho I am feeling quite feeble to day. but am trying to conform to the words of the Text which I have chosen which is to "Grow in grace and in the knowledge of our Lord and Saviour Jesus Christ." Father in Heaven help me to do Thy names honor and praise. is my prayer.

Tuesday July the 26th 1927

Psa 34-9

A nice clear day. I am thankful that we are all able to be about our daily avocations, alth I for one do not feel strong, but praise the Lord for what strength I have to be so I can do somethings necessary to be done. and am praying for grace to enable me to do that which the dear Lord would have me to do this day in His name and we are promiced "That as thy day thy strength shall be, and I am standing on the promices of God my Saviour."

Wednesday July the 27th 1927

Heb 12.6

Another fine day. All able to be on the stage of action for which I feel very grateful. and altho I am laboring under discouragements which are very trying to bear, I am comforted in the thought of my Text that. "Whom the Lord loveth He chasteneth and scourgeth every son whom He receiveth."for I as a child of His, which I claim to be by promice have been chastened very sore many times by the trials I have had to meet, and to think that my blessed Saviour permits these things thru love for my spiritual good, is a great comfort to my mind, for they are often hard to bear in the weakness of the flesh.

Thursday July the 28th 1927

Isa 26-3

Still another fine day. and I am thankful this morning and doing that which is necessary for the comfort and sustainance of these mortal bodies. and I trust that we may be kept in perfect peace having our minds staid on Him in whom we live and move and have our being. and that we may be in earnest to do that which will redown to His honor and praise, that we may have a home with Him in Heaven, there to praise Him forever.

July 1927

Friday July the 29th 1927

John 13-35

A nice clear day. All able to be busy with the work of the day, which is something to be very thankful for, as there are those in other places who cannot even rise from their beds. and oh for a full supply of grace to fufil the words of my Text to love one another for by this saith our blessed Saviour ye shall know that ye are my deciples if ye have love for one another. oh to be a true deciple of Jesus is my most fervent desire for His sake. "Jesus lover of my soul let me to thy bosum fly While the nearer waters roll while the tempest still is high Hide me oh my Saviour hide till the storm of life is past ets."

Saturday July the 30th 1927

Prov 18-24

A nice morning. All as well as usual I am thankful to state and the Parents in this home are now on their way to High Point to do their shopping etc. I am so glad to realise the truthfulness of my Text that, "there is a friend that sticketh closer than a brother. oh to obey this friend is the fervent desire of my heart, that I may have an inheritance with Him when done with earth, for Jesus sake

Sunday July the 31st 1927

Psalm 27.1-5

A lovely Sabbath day. All able to be up and prepare for Church and Sunday School, and as this is the last day of the month I am again reminded of the flight of time, but am comforted by the words of my Text, and desire that my loved ones may read the whole Chapter and be profited by its contents. the words of the fifth verse has especially impressed my mind, for in times of trouble I have hidden as it wherein the secret of His tabernacle and found strength to bear my troubles. Praise His name.

Monday August the 1st 1927

Gal 6-10

Raining this morning. All able to be up and go about household duties for which I am thankful. And I am desireous to conform to the words of my Text. for I want to do good in every way I can to those who are in need of help either spiritually or temporally, as far as the dear Lord gives me ability and opportunity, to the honor and praise of His ever worthy name.

Tuesday Aug the 2nd 1927

A very nice day for the opening of yearly meeting and this morning my daughter **Mrs J.W. Peace** and her husband took me up to the Blair Dairy to meet with **Miss Clara I. Cox** who took me over to Guilford College, and I was favored to go to both services that day and attended services again that night and heard some very inspireing sermons which I enjoyed very much. I praise the Lord that I had strength and was permited to attend the opening session of this yearly meeting and most of the sessions thruout the entire week to the close, for which I praise the Lord for his goodness to me.

Wednesday Aug the 3rd 1927

A lovely morning. I am thankful to of had a good nights rest after going out to Church and hearing a good sermon. and meeting with many kind friends both at the Church and here at Founders Hall where I have a neat room for the whole week. I praise the Lord for His mercy to me, and all His dependent children.

Thursday morning Aug the 4th 1927

Cloudy this morning. I did not feel able to go to Church last night, but after a good nights rest I hope I shall be able to go to part of the sessions to day but think I shall rest until the afternoon session. I praise the Lord for giving me strength to be up and mingle with friends.

August 1927

Friday Aug the 5th 1927

Nice morning. I was not feeling well so I did not go out to meeting last night, but was able to sit on the porch and convers with some friends which I enjoyed very much. I hope to get out to some of the sessions to day. Praise the Lord for his goodness to me.

Saturday Aug the 6th 1927

Fine day. I was able to attend the morning session which was presided over by **Mrs Milener Angel Cox** also by **Miss Huff** of Indiana. I also went to the afternoon session which was mostly concerning the report of Guilford College which was satisfactory.

Sunday Aug the 7th 1927

Nice morning but quite warm. I am thankful that after having a good nights rest, I feel able to arise from my bed, and prepare for meeting and I shall leave Guilford College to day, and go over to High Point to visit some of my relative and friends.

Monday Aug the 8th 1927

A nice clear morning. Last evening **Miss Clara Cox** brought me from Guilford College over to **Henry Winslows** whos Address at this time is 1205 E Green St High Point N.C. where I spent the night most pleasantly and remained with them until Tuesday afternoon, then in the evening of same day **Miss Clara Cox** came for me and took me to Cousin **Winston Blairs** where I expect to spend the night with them. I praise the Lord that He raises up friends to minister to my needs. oh that I may be faithful to do His holy will, is my prayer for Jesus sake.

Tuesday Aug the 9th 1927

A nice morning. I spent last night at cousin **Winston Blairs** as I had anticipated had a good nights rest for which I feel very thankful to the Father of all our sure mercies. Blessed be His holy name now and forever. This forenoon cousin **Roger Millikan** came to cousin-**Winstons** for me and took me to his home where I spent the day very pleasantly with them and in the evening **Roger** took me over to cousin **John Branson Blairs** where I spent the night.

Wednesday Aug the 10th 1927

Cloudy this morning, had some rain last night. I am takeing a good rest here to day after going from place to place it seems good to get to such a quiet place and I am enjoying it fine. **John B Blair** is the son of **Enos T and Prisila Branson Blair** of Randolph County N.C. he is their only child, he married **Miss Carrie Louise Welch** and they now live in High Point Guilford Co N.C. he runs quite a good Dairy business there I went out to the Barn and was shown the fine cows they have had milked that morning they have all the modern equipment for carrying on the work, he also owns a large Farm over on Deep River known as the **Elihu** and **Samuel Mendenhall** farms in the past, at this Farm they were milking twelve fine cows at the time I was visiting them and they had a number of other fine cattle. **John B Blair** has brought up seven fine sons the youngest now twelve years of age. they never had any daughters, The sons have all stuck to them in the Dairy business and on the farm. There is no other as fine a record in my knowledge any where. The first born **Enos Cyrus Blair** married **Miss Muriel Cook** of High Point. the second son **Garland Augustine Blair** marries **Miss Gladys Edmons** of the State of Georgia. **Donnel Jesse Blair** married **Miss Pansy Meadows** of N.C. The other four sons are single at the time. namely **John Robert Blair, Albert Welsh Blair, Wiliam Ivey Blair, and Joseph Branson Blair.** All of High Point N.C. **John B. Blair** built a neat cottage in his yard and moved **Mrs Samila Branson** into it where she remained until her death, she was burried the day after her ninety first Birthday. she was **John B Blairs** Step Grandmother being the widow of **William Branson.**

August 1927

Thursday Aug the 11th 1927

Cloudy this morning. I was prevailed upon to stay at cousin **John B Blairs** another night, which I did very unexpectedly, but also very pleasently, had a good nights rest, for which I am very grateful to the Giver of all good, and am looking to Him to direct my steps this day. Later in the day one of the **Johns** son **Garland Blair** brought me to **Mr June Barkers**, where I am writing this note. Barkers wife, **Arta Barker** is the daughter of my first cousin the late **Thomas Anderson** a Minister in Friends Church. I am visiting my relatives here in High Point and expect to attend the Memorial Association at Springfield next Saturday if I keep able. I will here insert cousin **Arta Barkers** Address, as I find I am getting more forgetful than when I was younger. **Mrs Arta Barker** 230 Otteray Drive High Point N.C.

Friday Aug the 12th 1927

Cloudy again this morning. I spent last night with cousin **June** and **Arta Barker,** After supper **Arta** and myself called at the home of **Jerome Barker** who is an Uncle of her husband, and whos wife is a neice of my soninlaw the late **Dougan Clark Moffitt.** his widow **Maggie E. Moffitt** lives in Kansas City Missouri. I had not seen **Emma Moffitt Barker** for quite a while so it was pleasant to meet with her again if only for a little while. returning to cousin **Artas** I had a good nights rest and am enjoying the hospitality of loved ones and this beautiful home. The same evening **Mrs. Stella Hiatt** a neice of **Arta Barkers** took **Arta** and myself over to the Cemetary at Springfield to place flowers on the Graves of our loved ones. Then she brought me to **Mrs Mary Barkers** who is the widow of the late **Nerias Barker** a Minister in the Friends Church. he two grandchildren who live with her, being on vacation she and I spent the night togeather alone, yet not alone, for the dear Lord watched over us as He does at all times and takes care of His dependent children. Praised be His holy name.

Until We Sleep Our Last Sleep

Saturday morning Aug the 13th 1927

A lovely morning. I had a good nights rest here in the quietude of **Mary Barkers** Christian home, and we are expecting to attend the services of the Memorial Association at dear old Springfield Later in the day, just at the right time **Elva Blair** came and took **Mrs Barker** and myself over to Springfield. There was a good attendance and many good interesting things said, and read, a Memorial for **J. Winston Frazier** was read by his Nephew **Cyrus P. Frazier** which was very interesting and satisfactory. After the meeting closed dear **Clara I. Cox** brought me to where I now reside, the home of my daughter **Mrs J.W. Peace**. I feel under great obligations to dear **Clara Cox** for her never failing kindness to me in provideing a way for me to get too and from Church. May the Lord bless her abundantly.

Sunday Aug the 14th 1927

Psa 67

A bright warm morning. I am very grateful for a good nights rest, after going thru the week of our yearly meeting, then visiting relatives and friends in High Point the past week and lastly the Memorial Association at Springfield yesterday. I am so thankful for the kindness of dear **Clara Cox** for takeing me to Guilford College and for bringing me home herself last evening that I can not refrain from repeating her kindness and for the kind hospitality I received from so many friends all the time I was away from home I praise the Lord for His goodness to me and may His blessing rest abundantly upon all who were so kind to me and showed me many favors in various ways. This afternoon I attended Sunday School at Mt Vernon with my daughter and family as I always do when in this home and able to go. For altho my membership is in Friends Church at Springfield, I am no sectarian and as it is more convenient for me to go with the family to their Methodist Church I go and worship with them, altho it would seem more natural to attend my own Church if I was situated so I could. After we

August 1927

returned home for S.S. we were visited by **Mr** and **Mrs Lee Roils** and family had a very interesting time eating Watermelons and conversing freely togeather. This day Aug the 14th being the 84th anniversary of my dear deceased husbands birth it brings many things fresh to mind, and having to be deprived of his precious companionship for the past seven years, I feel my loss so much I can't hardly content myself at times for he was so kind and loveing to me I miss hm so much oh God help me to so live that I may meet him in the better land.

Monday Aug the 15th 1927

Psalm 103

Cloudy this morning. I am thankful to be able to be up and walk about some, altho I am still suffering with my right limb from my knee down, which was sprained by a fall I got at the Church steps while at Guilford College, it was after night meeting and I could not see very well so I made a misstep at the top of the long flight of front steps, and but for the presence and timely aid of **Rev Reuben Payne**, Pastor of Friends Church at Archdale I should of gotten a very dangerous fall and perhaps been seriously hurt, as I praise the Lord that I came off as well as I did, for altho a bad sprain is very painful I am so thankful that I escaped having any broken bones, so I praise the Lord for His care over me.

Tuesday Aug the 16th 1927

1st Peter 5-6

A nice warm morning. I am not feeling well but I am thankful to be so I can wait on myself and attend to what is necessary to be done. and I hope to be able to attend the County Sunday School Convention to day, which is to Convene this afternoon at Mt Vernon, and will continue thru tomorrow. many Delegates are expected from all over the County. Later in the day. I feel like praiseing the Lord that he has permited me to attend the Convention this afternoon, and I certainly did enjoy all the exercise, there was a large attendance.

Until We Sleep Our Last Sleep

Wednesday Aug the 17th 1927

Nice morning. All Able to arise from our beds this morning and prepare to go to the Convention again to day, for which I am very thankful, and also for the opportunity of attending the session last night which was interesting. The devotional session was presided over by **Rev Reuben Payne** of Archdale Friends Church and was very much enjoyed and I hope we shall be much benefited by his discourse. The same night (Tuesday night) **Miss Daisy Magee** of Hickory N.C. gave a splendid lecture on the principals and methods of Work with Older Children in the Sunday School. **Mr D.W. Sims** gave a lecture on the Methods of Teaching. This the Wednesday morning session, the Devotional service was opened by **Rev S.M. Penn** followed by Miss Daisy Magee and **Mr D.W. Sims** of Raleigh on their Sunday School work. **Mr Sims** is General Superintendent of North Carolina Sunday School Association at this time. The Afternoon Devotional service was presided over by **Rev J.H. Haynes**, followed by **Rev J.E. Pritchard** on Daily Vacation Bible School work and another good lecture by **Miss Daisy Magee**. It seems that in my absent mindedness I have made the mistake of partly putting "The last first and the first last." As I should of stated at first that this Randolph County Sunday School Convention was held at Mt Vernon Methodist Church near Trinity, on Tuesday and Wednesday Aug the 16th and 17th 1927. and was for all Sunday School workers of all Denominations, and the first session was opened with Devotional service by their Pastor **Rev W.R. Haris** Trinity N.C. followed by an Address on Cooperation by **Rev Ramond Smith,** Director of Religious Education. Wesley Memorial Church, High Point. also an Address on Principals and Methods of Work with young children of Sunday Schools, by **Miss Daisy Magee** Director of Religious Education, First Methodist Church Hickory N.C. The Delegates to this Convention were entertained in the different homes of the neighborhood. For our Guest in this home we had **Mrs H. Lee Fearns** of Farmers Randolph Co. she is a very interesting and congenial Lady and we were highly pleased to have her with us, I had never met her before, but she seemed like an old time friend, and she being a widow as well as myself we know how to sympathise with each other. I think The Convention was very much apprecited in general.

Thursday Aug the 18th 1927

A nice warm morning. All able to again resume the rotine work of the day after takeing a good nights rest which was very much needed after the fatigue of yesterday, for altho we enjoyed the exercises of the day so much, yet the day being very warm, and such a vast throng of people it was tiresome to the flesh, for it was the largest crowd I have ever witnessed at Mr Vernon.

Friday Aug the 19th 1927

A nice breeze this morning, which is very refreshing after being so warm. I am thankful to be as well as I am after going thru several days of attending Church, and Convetions etc. I praise the Lord for His goodness and mercy to us all.

Saturday Aug the 20th 1927

Cloudy this morning. All in this home able to be up and stiring, for which I am thankful. The Parents are going to High Point shopping. The other members busy in the home.

Sunday Aug the 21st 1927

Heb 1-8

Cloudy this morning. I am so thankful for a quiet nights rest, and my prayer this morning is dear Lord keep me so close to Thee this day that I may not transgress they commandments in anything I do or say, and that my heart be made pure and clean in Thy sight. It rained so hard at the time to go to Sunday School and Church service that some of us did not get out to day. but trust that our desire to "assemble our selves togeather as the manner of some is" will be accepted of Him who knows that we will do His will, altho we can not always accomplish our desires.

Monday Aug the 22nd 1927

Heb 13-8

Cloudy again. to day. The dampness causes more pain and aching limbs, but I am so thankful to not be confined to my bed as for many years in the past, that I try to bear all with Christian courage. knowing I have so much to thank the Lord for.

Tuesday Aug the 23rd 1927

Psalm 142

A nice clear morning. I am so thankful that I am still able to be up and doing what my hands find to do, that is in my power and ability to do for I am not strong physically, but so glad that I can do many little things for myself, so as to not burden others. Praise the Lord oh my soul.

Wednesday Aug the 24th 1927

Psalm 119-105

A nice clear morning. All able to be on the stage of action, for which I feel very grateful to our merciful Heavenly Father, for he cares for us by night and by day, oh may we obey Him always is the prayer of my heart for Jesus sake.

Thursday Aug the 25th 1927

Heb 10-37

Cloudy this morning, had quite a rain last night. All able to go about our daily avocations for which I am thankful. Dear Heavenly Father pardon all our transgressions, over look all weakness and help us to grow stronger and stronger as the days go by in faith and true righteousness; help us to glorify Thee on earth, that we may glorify thee in heaven is the fervent desire of my heart for Jesus sake.

Friday Aug the 26th 1927

Lam 3-22-23

Cool this morning. All able to go about daily avocations which is much to be thankful for, I realise the truth of the Text, "His compassions fail not they are new every morning, yes great is the faithfulness of our Lord to his dependent children. oh that we may be more faithful to do the will of Him who shed His precious blood, that we might have life eternal.

Saturday Aug the 27th 1927

Psa 51-17

Cloudy and cool again this morning. I am glad that it is as well with us all at this time as it is, for altho I often feel broken hearted over many things that I have to bear while passing thru this journey here below, yet it is sweet to reflect upon the words of my Text which assures us that "a broken and a contrite heart oh God thou wilt not despise." So whatever may be my lot I want to be humble and submisive to the divine Master who has watched over and cared for me thru so many years of affliction, privation and bereavement, and made a way for me where I could see no way. so I want to be more diligent each day to obey Him while here on earth that I may have a home with Him in that land that he has prepared for all who love Him and serve him on earth, there to praise Him with the son of his love and the loved ones gone before thruout all eternity. Oh for a heart to praise my God, a heart from sin set free. A heart that always feels the blood so freely shed for me. yes and not only for me but for all who will come to Him and be saved by that all attoneing blood.

Sun Aug the 28th 1927

Psa 51-17

Cloudy and cool this morning. Thankful to state that all are up and prepareing to go to quarterly meeting at Marlboro to day. I hope we shall receive a message from the Lord thru the mouth of some of His servants that we shall take to heart and profit by it to the salvation of our souls, and to the glory of God our heavenly Father who has spared our lives to see another Sabbath day while many others have been consigned to the grave, during the past week. Later in the day. We were favored to attend quarterly meeting at Marlboro as we had hoped to do and heard a very inspireing sermon by a Friend from the State of Mishign. I did not not learn his name, but he certainly gave us warning to be prepared for the final judgement where we shall all have to give account of the deed done in the body. This was at the eleven oclock service, we did not stay for the afternoon service, but came back to Sunday School at Mt Vernon, heard a very interesting lesson. And I hope that all who have sined in any way. May like Dave repent of their transgressions, and be restored to Gods favor "A broken and contrite hear, oh God thou wilt not despise."

Monday Aug the 29th 1927

Heb 12-28

Cool this morning, so that it is pleasant to sit by a nice little fire which I am thankful to have the privilige of doing. and I desire to conform to the words of my Test. That I may have grace in my heart, so that I may serve God acceptably with reverence and fear. Yes with reverence to His holy name, and fear offending him in word or deed, so help me dear Father to obey thy will.

Tuesday Aug the 30th 1927

Phil 1-6

Nice morning. All in usual health and going about daily tasks, and my great desire is that we may all strive to do that which is well pleasing in the sight of Him who has our destiny in His hands, and have power to clip the brittle thread of life at any moment of time. oh God help me to be ready.

Wednesday Aug the 31st 1927

Psalm 108

Nice bright morning. All in usual health. And part of the family have gone to High Point shopping. the rest busy with home duties, my feelings this morning conform to the words of my chosen Psalm for in my heart I bless the Lord for His goodness and mercy to us all His dependent unworthy children. oh that we may all love Him more and serve Him better. for Jesus sake.

Thursday Sept the 1st 1927

Heb 13-9

A nice morning. I am again, reminded of the flight of time as this day ushers in the beginning of another month. And I am desirous that I may conform to the words of my Text, for it is a good thing for the heart to be established with grace. oh that I may grow in grace from day to day is my prayer, for the time is fast approaching when I shall be called to give account of the deed done in the body, "By grace ye are saved." nd "grace has led me safe thus far, and grace will lead me home" yes by looking unto and trusting and obeying Him who died to redeem all mankind we shall be saved. This morning in thinking of many friends an acquittances that I met with again this year at Guilford College at yearly meeting, which was held the first week in Aug – I find the name of **David Ensley** who was born in Ohio March the 14th 1837. But for many years he has lived near Winston-Salem N.C. he is now ninety years of age. And for one of his past times, he whittles out little paddles about a foot long with his knife out of well seasoned hickory wood, and gives them away to his friends as Souvenirs. I prise mine much as I feel highly honored to be presented with one of them, as he has given them out to the first ladies of the land, to the Presidents wife, the Governors wife and other Dignitaries, and to his acquaintance, so I humbly accept it as a mark of kindness and good friendship. He married **Miss Hannah Delphina Thomas** of Guilford Co N.C. a friend of mine in our young days. and I have met with them for the last four years at yearly meeting at Guilford College and found much pleasure in conversing with them.

Friday Sept the 2nd 1927

Psa 66-18

Cloudy this morning. I am thankful that we of household are all in usual health. and the desire of my heart is that we may all conform to the words of my Text, for if we regard inquity in our hearts, the Lord will not hear us. Lord help us to resist evil and learn to do good, is my prayer.

Saturday Sept the 3rd 1927

Psalm 133

A lovely morning. and I am so thankful that we are all as well as we are to day, and I hope we shall be close on our watch that we do not disobey the commandments of our Lord and Master who has suffered so much for us poor unworthy cretures that we might have a home with Him in Heaven if we do his holy will here upon Earth as we are commanded.

Sunday Sept the 4th 1927

Prov 3-13

A lovely Sabbath morning. I desire that we may keep this day holy to the praise and honor of Him who gave his precious blood that we poor sinful cretures might have life, and joy and peace with him when done with this earth, so I pray that we may get more wisdom and understand from the holy Scriptures as we study it every Sabbath day and thru the days during the week that we may profit thereby to the saveing of our souls and to the glory of God the Father and Son Jesus Christ.

Monday Sept the 5th 1927

Psa 55.22

Nice morning. All able to be up and go about daily avocations, for which I feel very grateful to the Giver of all good, and am endeavoring to obey my Text and cast my burden upon the Lord that he may sustain me thru all my trials, for I cannot bear my burdens alone, but cast them on the Great burden bearer, our blessed Saviour Jesus Christ.

Tuesday Sept the 6th 1927

James 2-5

A nice clear morning. All in usual health I am glad to state, and it is a consolation to reflect on the words of my Text. and I am so glad that God knows I love him. Lord help me to be rich in faith is my prayer.

Wednesday Sept the 7th 1927

Rom 13-11

Nice morning. All able to be busy at the work most necessary to be done for the comfort and sustanance of these mortal bodies and I am disireous that we may all remember that "The night cometh where in no man can work" so let us be up and doing for my Text tells us that it is high time to awake out of sleep for now is our salvation nearer than when we believed yes every day that passes brings us nearer our journey end here on earth. Heavenly Father help us to prepare to meet Thee in the better land.

Thursday Sept the 8th 1927

James 1-4

A lovely morning. Thankful to be able to pen down the goodness and mercy of the Lord to his unworthy children. and I am trying to "Let patience have its perfect work, that I may be made perfect and entire wanting nothing." For we are told that they that love the Lord shall not want any good thing. I am thankful that He who knows all things knows that I love Him, and I want to love him more and more, and serve him better every day of my life here on earth, that I may have an inheritance with Him where I can praise him more perfectly than I can here.

Until We Sleep Our Last Sleep

Friday Sept the 9th 1927

Matt 25-13

Cloudy and raining a little this morning. I am feeling the effects of the dampness but thankful to be up and wait on myself. And am bearing in mind that "We know neither the day nor the hour when the Son of man cometh, so I am endeavoring to be close on my watch to be ready when He calls for me to give account of the deeds done in the body. help me dear Heavenly Father to do thy holy will in all things, for Jesus sake.

Saturday Sept the 10th 1927

Psalm 103

Cloudy this morning. we had quite a down pour of rain last night, and the nearest an Electrical storm we have had this season, the lightning came nearest to us with loud claps of thunder. I feel that we have a great deal to thank the one who has all power in His hand over all things that we were all graciously preserved from all harm, for we often hear of some one or ones being killed or stuned by lightning. "But the mercy of the Lord is from everlasting to everlasting upon them that fear him and his righteousness unto childrens children." oh let us leave this blessed heritage to our children.

Sunday Sept the 11th 1927

Psa 122-1

It was raining this morning when I awoke but has now cleared off and bids fair to give us a nice day to attend Sabbath School. And in the language of the Golden Text, I am always glad when it is said, "let us go up to the house of the Lord" or words to that effect, for I do love to go to Church to learn more of Gods holy word, so let us not "neglect the assembling ourselves togeather as the manner of some is." and go in the true spirit of worship, for "God seeketh such to worship Him."

September 1927

Monday Sept the 12th 1927

James 2-5

A nice clear morning. Thankful we are all able to be up and go about daily affairs. my daughter **Mrs J.W. Peace** has gone to High Point for a slight opperation for a small growth on her neck I hope it will be successful. I am feeling weak and very much discouraged this morning as I so often do since having to leave my dear old home. for the mind will revert back to the days when I was so happy and contented with my dear companion in our dear old home, for no matter where you are or how situated, "There is no place like home." but I am trying to make my sojourn here on earth a pleasent as possible and endeavoring to so live that I may meet my loved ones in that Home above, where all sorrow is forever done away. for altho we may be poor in the worlds goods and feel very unworthy yet if we are rich in faith we shall be heirs of the kingdom, surely this is worth loveing and strieving for, to be heirs of the kingdom.

Tuesday Sept the 13th 1927

John 4-35

Cloudy this morning. Thankful for a good nights rest. and that all are able to be about daily duties, and we should look unto the fields that are already ripe unto harvest, and endeavor to gather in the souls that may be lost by neglecting to gather them into the fold, while there is hope and salvation offered to all. so come let us be up and doing, "for the night cometh wherein no man can work." and let us know for ourselves that our own "calling and election is sure" that "both he that soweth and he that reapeth may rejoice together." I have felt constrained to quote these portions of scripture to incite those who may chance to read this, may search the scriptures more thoroughly and prayerfully and know for themselves whether they are prepared for the ingathering of souls which will be joy and peace thruout all ages, and praise to Him who shed his precious blood for all. I will just state here that the oppertation for my daughter which I mentioned yesterday, was postponed indefinitely.

Wednesday Sept the 14th 1927

Rom 8-37

Nice morning. All in usual health for which I feel very grateful, and desire that we may all endeavor to obey the commandments that we may have a right to the Tree of life, for on obedience hangs our destiny, and by obeying them. We may be "more than conquerors through Him that loved us, and gave himself for us." oh help me dear Father to obey thee, for Jesus sake.

Thursday Sept the 15th 1927

1st Peter 5-6

Nice warm morning. All in usual health I am thankful to state **J.W. Peace** went out this morning and killed three squirrels, some of us are very fond of them, so we are glad to get them. we are blessed with food each day for the sustanance of these mortal bodies, for which we are indebted to the Great Giver of all good. and I trust that we may "Humble ourselves under the mighty hand of God that He may exalt us in due season. and by His help lead clean and pure Christian lives to his honor and praise, so that when we are done with time here below, we may go to be with him in the better land, where we can see Him face to face. and praise Him forever.

Friday Sept the 16th 1927

Psa 31-24

Warm morning. all able to be up and go about daily avocations, for which I give thanks to our merciful Heavenly Father, for his goodness to us unworthy as we are of his divine favors, but I trust we shall take fresh courage to press on endeavoring to do that which is well pleasing in strength and wisdom that we can do these things as we should, so my prayer is dear Lord help me to do thy holy will this day and thruout lifes journey to thy names honor and praise.

Saturday Sept the 17th 1927

Psa 116-1-2

Nice warm morning. I am feeling quite feeble this morning but thankful to be so I can arise for my bed. the rest of the family in usual health glad to state. "oh for a closer walk with God a calm and heavenly frame. A light to shine upon the road that leads me to the Lamb." yes this is the fervent desire of my heart, that I may walk closer, and do His holy will.

Sunday Sept the 18th 1927

Golden Text Prov 16-18

Lovely Sabbath day. All able to prepare for Sunday School and preaching this afternoon at Mt Vernon, this is the day for the Protracted meeting to begin there. The **Rev-Davis**, Pastor of South Main St ME. Church of High Point, is the help **Rev Reed Haris** in the meeting. Glad that I can now add that we were favored to attend this meeting at three oclock and hear a splendid sermon by the **Rev -Davis**.

Monday Sept the 19th 1927

Revelations 3-19

A very warm day and somewhat cloudy. we are all favored to be so we can go about the work necessary to be done for the comfort and sustanance of these mortal bodies, I hope we shall attend services again this afternoon, as there is to be services every afternoon this week at three oclock and at seven thirty at night. I am so glad that we are told in Gods holy Word that, "As many as I love, I rebuke and chasten; be zealous therefore and repent." For knowing as I do what it means to be rebuked and chastened for not being as obedient as I should be, it is such a comfort to know that it is through love that I am made to feel the chastening hand, to bring me back to Him.

Until We Sleep Our Last Sleep

Tuesday Sept the 20th 1927

Psa 94-18

Much cooler this morning, since the rain yesterday and last night. We were deprived of getting to the afternoon session on account of heavy rain, but it held up so we got out to Church last night. had a most splendid service. **Bro Davis'** theme for this service was on prayer, and handled it well, and brought forth results. We are such poor weak mortals, that we are so open thrown off our guard, and it is such a blessing that our Heavenly Father sends his mesengers to us to warn and to encourage us to be close on our watch least we slip away as it were from Him thus loose our hold on things which concerns out eternal welfare, so I am thankful for the words of my Text. "When I said my foot slipeth Thy mercy O Lord held me up." yes I feel that through all those years of affliction and privation, and the many changes that have taken place in my life, I can truly say that the dear Lord has held me up, and watched over me and kept me many times from giving way to the temptations and snares that have been laid for my feet as it were to cause me to stumble and thus be a cast away. so I can not praise the blessed Lord enough that He has held me up thru all the trying sessions of my life. Blessed be His holy name.

Wednesday Sept the 21st 1927

1st Cor 13-5

Nice cool morning. We were favored to attend the three oclock service yesterday and also the seven thirty last night, we have heard good mesages each time. in the afternoon we have a grand lesson from the parable of the Prodigal Son, and altho **Rev Davis** did not preach last night from the Text which I have chosen this morning his theme was largely on examining ourselves, whether we have faith and how we stand in the sight of Him to who we have to give account.

September 1927

Thursday Sept the 22nd 1927

Gal 5-14

The weather is quite cool to day, so much so that it is pleasent to sit by a fire, and I am so glad that I am able to do so. At the first of the week it was so very warm for the season of the year, that so many of us expressed the wish that it would turn cooler I am wondering how many of us are thanking the great Giver of all good, for granting our wish. I must state that I was permited to go to Church yesterday and again last night, and from Church in the afternoon I was invited to go and take supper in the home of **Mr Allen Robins**, where the Preachers dined that evening. and also dear **Grandma Peace** was invited and accompanied us, and we spent a very happy evening togeather socially and then returned to the Church and had quite a feast spiritually last night, and afterward a good nights rest in sleep for which I praise the Lord for all the blessings which He confered upon us, for our neighbors and friends entertained us so kindly and so bountifully with many good things at their Table. I have chosen my Text to day because it speaks so much in One word, namely "all the law is fulfilled in one word, even in this Thou shalt love thy neighbor as thyself," for it is an obligation that we should all fulfil in order to obtain eternal life. for we are told in Gods word "By this ye shall know that ye are my deciples if ye have love for one another." Help us our Father to do this.

Friday Sept the 23rd 1927

Col 1-10

Still quite cool this morning. I am thankful that it is as well with us all as it is. we were unavoidably detained from attending church yesterday which we regreted very much. but for our disappointment in not getting to Church we were blessed with some of our kind friends from Salisbury to visit us they came very unexpectedly to see us, but we enjoyed having them so much that it made up largely for not getting to Church. And we got out to the services last night and had a wonderful good meeting presided over again by the **Rev William Baxter Davis** (I have learned his full name) he preached a very inspireing sermon which was much appreciated by the people in general, and I hope will bear much fruit to the glory of God, whose mesenger he is, and who has labord so earnestly to reclaim lost sinners, beging, pleading, with them so kindly to come to Jesus and be saved, and altho he did not get as much response as he desired, yet I believe it will be like "Bread cast upon the waters it will be found after many days," for God will not suffer his word to return to Him void, "but will accomplish that whereunto He hast sent it." so I praise the Lord for his goodness to us all, his poor unworthy children. We were favored to get out to the services again this afternoon and also at night, which was greatly enjoyed. As the meeting is to close to night we regret that it could not continue at least a few days longer. but we have had a spiritual feast with **Rev Davis** and **Rev Haris** and also enjoyed their company socially, my daughter and myself were invited to dine with them this evening for supper which we did at **Dr Bulla's** and was entertained most kindly and hospitably in every way. Then returned to Church for another spiritual feast, and a happy Goodbye.

Saturday Sept the 24th 1927

Psa 9-10

Nice cool day. I am thankful to state that all are in usual health. We were favored to attend the services at three oclock yesterday and again last night. and as I have before stated my daughter and I were invited to dine with the Minsters at **Dr Bullas** we had a very nice time socially, then returned to the church for another spiritual feast. And as this was the last session of the meeting we enjoyed it so much we regreted that it could not of gone on at least a few days longer, there is time for all things, and the time had now come to close.

September 1927

Sunday Sept the 25th 1927

Psa 103-19

A lovely Sabbath day. My daughter **Mrs Peace** and her daughter **Mary Lee Stilwell** and myself went to Springfield to day for the eleven oclock service heard a most splendid sermon by the **Evangilist Rev -Hobson** from California and also the great singer **Evangilist** which was very inspireing I enjoyed it to the full. And would love to of heard them more, but could not stay for the night services owing to circumstance, I returned home then went to Sunday School at Mt Vernon this afternoon we had a very interesting lesson and was much enjoyed by the School in general.

Monday Sept the 26th 1927

Psa 71-16

A nice cool morning. I am so thankful to be able to be up, and testify with my heart and hand pen and ink on paper to the goodness and mercy of the Lord to me His unworthy child, as I feel myself to be, but I am going to strive to live each day according to my Text. "I will go in the strength of the Lord and Thine only." For there is none other that can see and know my heart, and that can and will speak peace to my troubled soul. oh Father in Heaven help me to bear all my trials and disappointments cheerfully for Jesus sake. and "Let my mouth be filled with thy praise, and with thy honour all the day. Cast me not off in the time of old age: forsake me not when my strength faileth." And "now also when I am old and grey headed, O god forsake me not." I ask in Christ name.

Tuesday Sept the 27th 1927

Psa 119-11

A very pleasant day. and I am so thankful that all of this household are able to go about our daily avocations. And I am so glad that I am trying in all sincerely to confirm to the words of my Text. "Thy word have I hid in mine heart, that I might not sin against Thee." Help me oh holy One to ever abide in Thee, is my prayer.

Wednesday Sept the 28th 1927

James 1-4

A damp morning. and I am feeling very much indisposed, hardly able to arise from my bed, but with my usual determination to "try try again," I am doing my best to not give up to lie in bed as long as it is possible to do otherwise. but when I have to submit to the chastening rod of laying by for a time I am going to try to abide by my Text and let "Patience have her perfect work, that ye may be perfect and entire wanting nothing." For I know by experience what it means to have to be deprived for years of not getting out to Church, and of not being able to meet and mingle sociably with kindred and friends, so I feel that I cannot praise the Lord enough that I have been blessed to get out to services this year as much as I have and I greatly desire that it may be of lasting benefit.

Thursday Sept the 29th 1927

1st John 5-4

Nice clear morning. I am still feeling feeble but thankful to be able to be up and testify to the goodness and mercy of the Lord which is new every morning to His dependent children. and I am going to try to abide by my Text, to have that faith which overcome the world, so that I may inherit the Kingdom when done with the things of this world.

Friday Sept the 30th 1927

Psa 139-17

As this is the last day of September It reminds how fast time is getting away and that we should live each day prepared for eternity for we may be called at any moment of time. I am still feeble, yet I realise that I have much to be thankful for that it is as well with me as it is, and the words of my Text is comforting to me. "How precious are thy thoughts unto me, O god how great is the sum of them." If I should count them, they are more in number than the sand: when I awake, I am still with thee." verse 18. oh what a blessing to know that the dear Lord is with me, and careing for me from day to day, unworthy as I am. Bless His holy name.

Saturday Oct the 1st 1927

Psalm 121

A nice clear morning, for the begining of Oct. I am feeling quite feeble, but in the language of my Text, "I will lift up mine eyes unto the hills, from whence cometh my help. My help cometh from the Lord which made heaven and earth." "As for God his way is perfect" Psa 18:30. God always has His own Right Way, When our way seemeth blocked; Just for some small "back-door" we pray, Then find His Hand unlocked: The "royel gates" that open where We never dreamed of in our prayer.

Sunday Oct the 2nd 1927

Golden Text Joshua 24-15

Beautiful Sabbath day. All able to be on the stage of action, part of the family are going to Church and part cannot to day. As my daughter had the opperation performed on her neck yesterday that had been postponed for several weeks, and she has to go again to day, to High Point to the Dr to have the place dressed. So some of us can not go to Church and Sunday School to day. So I am thinking of going as far as Archdale with them to see cousin **Fannie English** and her daughter **Mrs Amos Kersey** with whom she makes her home they are both widows as well as myself so I have great sympathy for them, and cousin **Fannie** has been quite sick lately, Sunday evening I can now state that I went to Archdale and had quite an interesting visit, it was all too short but very mph enjoyed and the drive did me good.

Monday Oct the 3rd 1927

Matt 5-5

A very rainey morning. The family here in usual health I am feeling the effects of the dampness, and suffering in body, causes more depression of the mind, I am trying to abide by my Text, which says, "Blessed are the meek for they shall inherit the earth." Lord help me thus to live for Jesus sake.

Tuesday Oct the 4th 1927

Neh 1-7

Cooler this morning. The family are well. I am weak but thankful to be so I can be up and note the goodness of the Lord in giveing his children sleep and rest and protection thru the night, and watches over them by day. and He knoweth them that put their trust in Him. Blessed be His holy name.

Wednesday Oct the 5th 1927

Mark 9-23

Much cooler this morning. All able to go about daily avocations but I am still feeling weak and nervous but thankful that it is possible for me to do what my hands find to do. and the words of my Text "If thou canst believe all things are possible to him that believeth," the reply from my heart is "Lord I believe, help thou mine unbelief," and help me each day to live according to Thy commandments and let not the adversary have dominion over me.

Thursday Oct the 6th 1927

John 5-24

A nice clear morning. All up and doing, I am thankful that I can still be able to use my pen to give silent testimony to the goodness and mercy of our dear Saviour to His dependent children. and oh to think of the precious promice in my Text. He that heareth my word and believeth on Him etc.

October 1927

Friday Oct the 7th 1927

Psa 143-8

A nice clear morning and all are able to arise from our bed, for which I thank God who has taken care of us three another night, and now in the language of my Text, my prayer is, "Cause me to know the way wherein I should walk; for I lift up my soul unto Thee.

Saturday Oct the 8th 1927

Rom 10-10

Cloudy this morning. I am feeling weak, but am glad that it is as well with us all as it is, and I am so thankful that I can say truly that I conform to the words of my Text. "For with the heart man believeth unto righteousness, and with the mouth confession is made unto salvation." For He that knoweth all things knows that I believe on Him with all my heart and that with my mouth I confess the Lord Jesus.

Sunday Oct the 9th 1927

Psalm 27-14

Cloudy again this morning. I feel thankful that we are all as well as we are, and hope we shall be favored to get out to Sunday School. For I do not want to give way to despondency, but rather take fresh courage to press on, for we are told in Gods holy word to "wait on the Lord be of good courage and he shall strengthen thine heart. Wait I say on the Lord" oh that I may obey this injunction for His sake.

Monday Oct the 10th 1927

Psa 71-9

Clear and cool this morning. Thankful that we are all in our usual health, and altho I am aged and worn I will still look up in faith to Him who has all power to help and say with David, "Cast me not off in the time of old age; forsake me not when my strength faileth."

Until We Sleep Our Last Sleep

Tuesday Oct the 11th 1927

2nd Timothy 4-18

A clear cool morning. All able to be performing the duties of the day. and I desire to be obedient to the divine Master in all things, then I will realise the words of my Text. "And the Lord shall deliver me from every evil work, and will preserve me unto his heavenly kingdom to whom be glory forever and ever Amen.

Wednesday Oct the 12th 1927

Matt 6-8

Rainey this morning. The dampness causes more pain and aches, but I am so thankful that I can still wait on myself and do some work that is not beyond my strength. and I am so glad that our "Father knows what we stand in need of before we ask Him." and we have the promice that is we ask in faith we shall receive." So I am standing on the promices of God my Saviour, standing standing on the promices of God." oh never let me fall.

Thursday Oct 13th 1927

James 1-5

Clear and cool this morning. All able to be up and doing and I hope that we are all trying to know and to do the things required of us, by Him who knoweth all things, and that if we go to Him in faith believing his word, he will hear our humble petitions and give us wisdom to know his will for we are told in His Word that. "If any of you lack wisdom, let him ask of God and it shall be given him" What great encouragement to ask.

Friday Oct the 14th 1927

Jude 3

Clear and quite cool this morning. All in usual health, for which I feel very grateful to the Giver of all good. and Jude tells us to "Earnestly

October 1927

contend for the faith which was once delivered unto the saints." oh for more faith to serve my Maker as I ought is the fervent desire of my heart for Jesus sake.

Saturday Oct the 15th 1927

Psa 9-9-13

A cold morning plenty of frost last night. We are all so we can go about our daily avocations I am thankful to state, and also thankful to know that the Lord is a refuge for the oppressed a refuge in times of trouble." for thou hast "considered my trouble, which I suffer of them that hate me, thou that liftest me up from the gates of death."

Sunday Oct the 16th 1927

Num 32-23 Golden Text

Clear and cold this morning. All preparing to attend the Birthday dinner given to **James Isom** a neighbor, and from there to Sunday School and Church at Mt Vernon. oh may we all spend this day in the way of Gods requiring's, is my fervent desire for Jesus sake.

Monday Oct the 17th 1927

Psa 63-7

Cold this morning. All up I am thankful to note. But I am suffering from deep cold. If I had been well as usual, I would have been in Sailsbury this morning instead of here, as my kind friends **Mr** and **Mrs Shoe** of Salisbury came to visit us last evening and one purpose to take me home with them to spend some time for a change, which I appreciate with all my heart, and regret very much that I was feeling too much indisposed to take the trip at present. But hope to be able to visit them before this year is out. They are so very kind and obligeing to me, and so are all their people in every way. May the Lords richest blessing rest upon them all, in this life when we are done with the things of earth may we all meet around that great white Throne there to sing Gods praise togeather thruout and all ages is the pray of my heart. for Christs sake.

Tuesday Oct the 18th 1927

James 2-26

Cloudy and cold to day, I am still suffering with deep cold, but thankful that I am so I keep up and try each day to do something, if its only to pen a few lines in remembrance of the goodness and mercy of our blessed Saviour who watches over and cares for us every day of our lives, and my greatest desire is to be doing something for the upbuilding of His kingdom in the hearts of the children of men. oh Father give me more faith to work for thee, for we are told that "as the body without the spirit is dead, so faith without works is dead also."

Wednesday Oct the 19th 1927

Psa 18-3-6

Another cold day. I am still suffering with deep cold, but still keep so I can be up, for which I am very grateful to Him in whom I live and have my being, and "I will call upon the Lord who is worthy to be praised; so shall I be saved from mine enemies," for thou wilt save the afflicted people; but wilt bring down high looks. And I know that thou dear Lord hast raised up friends for me time and again when I was in trouble and in need of sympathy, so I know that thou has heard my poor sympathy, so I know that thou hast heard my simple prayers according to Thy promice. Blessed be the name of the Lord now and forever.

Thursday Oct the 20th 1927

Psalm 103

Clear and windy to day, it seems more like March than October. We are all up and doing, but I am still suffering from cold in my chest, but thankful that it is as well with me as it is, for I am so glad not to be confirmed to my bed, as I was for so many years in the past. and I know that those of us whose lives have been spared are spared for a purpose, either that we may be better prepared for the future, or that there is yet some work for us to do, that has not been accomplished so let us be up and doing whatever the Lord commands, for "He hath not dealt with us after our sins; nor rewarded us according to our iniquities." For he knoweth our frame he remembereth that we are dust."

Friday Oct the 21st 1927

Romans 12th chap

Clear and warmer this morning. All up and going about daily work. I am not yet relieved of my cold. I have suffered more from deep cold in the past two weeks, than I have in the same length of time in two years. but I am so thankful not to be confined to my bed, that I feel like I cannot praise God enough for his watchful care over a poor unworthy child as I feel myself to be. oh that I may be more faithful and obedient to His will, is my prayer.

Saturday Oct the 22nd 1927

1st John 14th chap

Nice clear morning. I am still suffering, but thankful that I keep so I can be up and take note of the goodness of the Lord to his dependent children, and I find such comfort in reading the fourteenth chapter of St John for our blessed Saviour tells us that he wail not leave his deciples comfortless, and as He is no respector of persons we can all claim to be his deciples by obeying His holy will. and I am standing on the promices for when he said whosever will may come be included me, "yes he included me." dear Lord help me to so live that I may be worthy to be included is my prayer.

Sunday Oct the 23rd 1927

A beautiful Sabbath day. I am still suffering with deep cold in my chest, but keep trying to press on. My mind has been deeply impressed to day in reflecting that nine years ago to day my dear soninlaw **Arthur**

Lee Stilwell of Charlotte N.C. passed from works to reward. I miss him so much all those years for he was so kind and obligeing to me, never did an unknind word to me ever pass his lips but always words of sympathy and I miss him all the more since having to give up my dear husband who was so good and kind to me in every way.

Monday Oct the 24th 1927

Psa 90-10

A nice bright day. All up and busy. I am not at all well, but thankful to still keep up. I had to miss Sunday School yesterday as I cough so badly. I always regret missing S.S. and Church, but remember that we can worship in our own homes and in our own hearts, when we cannot attend Church. yes no matter where we be we can lift up our hearts in thanksgiving in praise to Him who watches over us and cares for us at all times. Praise His name.

Tuesday Oct the 25th 1927

Psalm 37

Nice morning. All up and attending to daily duties. my cough troubles me quote a goodeal yet, but I a thankful to still be so I can wait on myself, for I am xo anxious not to become a burden to others, and it is such a relief to my mind when I can be so I can do for myself that which is necessary to be done for the comfort of the body, instead of having to depend entirely upon others as I did for many years in the past. and I know that I had righteous parents, so "I have been you and now am old; yet have I not seen the righteous forsaken nor his seed begging bread." Therefore I am trying to "Trust in the Lord, and do good: so shalt thou dwell in the land, and verily thou shalt be fed." His Glorious Promice. Lord help me to fulfil it.

Wednesday Oct the 26th 1927

Matt 5-6

Cloudy and warm this morning. All busy at the morning Chores. I am still suffering from cold, but so thankful to be able to be up

October 1927

and I am so glad that I can say truly that I hunger and thirst after righteousness and the promice in my Text is "that they all be filled." And I know that our merciful Heavenly Father never fails to be good as his word, and sends help to us in every time of real need. I must not fail to take note of the splendid visit I receive last evening from some relatives and friends I had been feeling quite lonely all day and rather discouraged, when cousin **Elva Blair** drove up brings her sister **Martha** and her **Aunt Rachel Blair** who is my first cousin, and the Evangilest the **Rev Hobson** and wife of California who had been holding meetings at Springfield and Archdale etc. This visit was a source of comfort to me.

Thursday Oct the 27th 1927

Clear ad cooler this morning. Altho I am still suffering from cold in my chest. I am thankful to have strength sufficient to arise from my bed. and the words of the 23rd Psalm keeps sounding in my ears, and oh how good it is to feel that the Lord is my shepherd and that I shall not want for things readily needful in my life. for I know that the dear Lord has watched over and cared for me from my youth until now. Unworthy as I am of His favors, but He knows my heart and knows that I love Him and desire about everything else to obey his commandments, for He tells us in this 21st verse that "he that loveth me shall be loved of my Father, and I will love him, and will manifest myself to him." and I know that He has manifest himself to me time and again, when I have been the most discouraged and almost ready to faint by the way from assaults of the enemy who is ever ready to put a stumbling block in our pathway, so I feel that I cannot praise the Lord enough for his watchful care over me, and I pray that I may be more faithful to obey His holy will in all things, that I may have a right to the Tree of life when done with the earthly journey and be permitted to join loved ones in singing praises to the Lord God and the Lamb that was slain for the sins of the whole world, therefore for my sins, oh the glorious thought of having our robes washed white in the blood of the Lamb, and to be forever in that happy land where all sickness and sorrow pain and earth are felt and feared no more," oh it will be worth all our toil, suffering and trials here to gain that happy home of rest. Bless the Lord oh my soul.

Friday Oct the 28th 1927

Psalm 91-2

Cloudy this morning. In my weakness this morning my heart cries out. "Teach me thy way oh Lord lead me in plain path." that I may know what is Thy will concerning me, for I want to do thy will in all things to Thy names honor and praise, "I will say of the Lord He is my refuge and my fortess: my God; in him will I trust. Yes help me to trust in Thee at all times so that I may be able to resist all the temptation and snares which the enemy of my souls peace lays for my feet, as it were by putting enmity in the hearts of those who should be my true friends instead of my enemies. oh Father forgive them, and help them to turn to Thee with full purpose of heart, that they may have nothing but love to God and good will to all human kind, and that all who are out of Thy fold may come to Thee and be saved before it is too late. and oh Heavenly Father cleanse me from all sin, making my heart a clean recepticle for thy holy presence to dwell in, that I may be a living example to others of thy tender love and care, by my upright Christian walk in life, for I desire to be a steping stone toward Heaven for the riseing generation instead of a stumbling block. Father help me to do thy will for Jesus sake.

Saturday Oct the 29th 1927

Rom 13-8

Clear morning. All able to arise from our beds but some of us are not at all well. but I am very desireous that we obey in the injunction laid down in my Text, for we are told to "Owe no man any thing, but to love one another: for he that loveth another hath fulfilled the law." and again that Love worketh no ill to his neighbor therefore love is the fulfilling of the law." Heavenly Father help us to obey thy righteous laws and commandants that we may have an inheritance with thee when done with things of this life, that we may praise thee forever in that home that thou hast prepared for those that love Thee.

Sunday Oct the 30th 1927

Psalm 116-1-2

A nice warm morning. I am feeling feble but I am so thankful to be so I can be up, and I trust that I shall have strength to attend Sunday School, for we are told in Gods Word "That as thy day thy strength shall be," and I have learned to lean on the Everlasting Arms for support for many times in the past years of my affliction when I was not able to even lift a hand to pen a line of recognition of His goodness, I have felt His arms as it were underneath to bear me up.

Monday Oct the 31st 1927

Eph 4-1-2-3

Cooler this morning. All are up doing that which their hands find to do, and altho I have not strength to do much, I am so glad that I can still wait on myself and do that which is most necessary for the comfort of the body. and I am more and more concerned as the days go by, to do the things that make for our everlasting good when done with the things of this trantient world. and today being the last day of the month, again reminds me of the flight of time. and that it wont be long, at the longest until we will be called to gave account of the deeds done in the body.

Tuesday Nov the 1st 1927

Prov 3-5

Cloudy and cool this morning. I am still suffering from deep cold. But thankful to be so I can wait on myself, and am trying to obey the injunction of my Text to Trust in the Lord with all my heart and lean not to my own understanding, for I know that my understanding is limited and I cannot know just what is required of me to do only as I look to the source of all good for help.

Wednesday Nov 2nd 1927

Luke 6-22-23

A nice day. All busy as usual. I am thankful to be able to use my pen to note the continued goodness and mercy of our bless Saviour to his unworthy dependent children. we are blessed to day to have he company of dear **Grandma Peace** we are always so glad to have her with us, she was seventy four years of age yesterday. May the Lord bless her abundantly both spiritually and temporally. And may we all obey His holy will.

Thursday Nov the 3rd 1927

Psalm 141-3

Cloudy and raining some this morning. the dampness causes more pains and aches, but thankful that it is as well with me as it is. and I ask the dear Lord to accept the words of my Text as the prayer of my heart, for I desire to be faithful in word and deed, to the praise and honor of His holy name.

Friday Nov the 4th 1927

Josh 1-5-6

Much colder this morning as we predicted after the rain. but if it will stay cold long enough for us to get use to it, I think we would all much better, for it has been too warm all fall to be healthy. I haven't much strength, but in thinking of the promice to Joshua in the words of my Text I feel encouraged to try still harder to be strong in faith and take fresh courage, remembering that God is no respector of persons and that He will not fail nor forsake me, if I put my whole trust in Him. oh God help me to be strong and of good courage, I ask for Jesus sake.

November 1927

Saturday Nov the 5th 1927

Psalm 121

Much colder to day. All able to be up I am glad to note. But I am still suffering from the effect of deep cold, but trying to bear it with patience, and Christian courage.

Sunday Nov the 6th 1927

St John 15-7

A cold morning, but clear and bright. And I am thankful that we are all able to be up, and I trust that we shall get out to Sunday School. I am so thankful for the precious promice of my Text, and I pray that it may be fulfilled in me by abideing in the blessed Saviour and his word abideing in me to His honor and praise. Blessed be His holy name.

Monday a.m. Nov the 7th 1927

Psalm 94-18-22

Cold enough for plenty of Ice this morning which is quite a contrast to the weather we have had all fall. I am thankful that it is as well with us all as it is, but we have some anxiety in this home at this time, as the eighteen year old daughter **Miss Minnie Peace** is being taken to High Point Hospital for an opperation for something growing on the left side of her neck. The opperation may be post poned for a time, so I will have to wait until later to state the results of the opperation. We were all favored to attend Sunday School yesterday at Mt Vernon Methodist Church as usual and after school we were entertained by the County Sunday School Institute, which was largely attended and was very interesting. It was essentially for the Methodist, but for all Denominations in the County to take part, so the **Rev Reuben Payne** Pastor of Friends Church at Archdale at this time was called upon to preside over the Devotional service. He read a portion of the seventh chapter of Mathew and commented on it beautifully admonishing us to first pull the beam out of our own eye that we might see clearly to cast the not out of our brothers eye. **Miss Carrie Cranford** of Trinity had the general oversight of the different groups which were represented by their different offices and Teachers etc from their respective Churches over the County. I repeat the exercises were very interesting from first to last. And I hope I will do much lasting good.

Tuesday Nov the 8th 1927

Raining this morning. I am in the home of cousin **Robert Blair** at this time, as their son **Robert jr** came for me last evening to pay them a visit. so I spent last night with them very pleasently. and this forenoon cousin **Ewd Blair** came for me and took me to his home to visit his wife and Mother cousin **Rachel Blair** who is staying with them at this time. I had not had the opportunity to spend a day with cousin **Rachel** for quite a while so I am enjoying the day fine. In takeing notes Monday I mentioned about **Miss Minnie Peace** being taken to the Hospital and I stated that the opparation might be postponed for a time, but it was not, for the Cyst on a gland of the neck, and also had her Tonsils taken out and she is now getting along fine I am glad to state.

Wednesday Nov the 9th 1927

Still very cloudy and damp. I was prevailed upon last evening to stay over night at cousin **Ed Blairs** so spent the time very pleasently with them, and this morning cousin **Ed** took me over to cousin **John Hills** to spend the day with him and cousin **Roxie**, who is getting quite feeble, and she gets so lonely having to sit there in her Wheel Chair day after day so she enjoys having kindred and friends visit her. Then this evening cousin **Ocid Blair** and son **Robert jr** came over there for me and brought me back to **J.W. Peaces** to my daughters where I call it home. and found them all well, and they had been to High Point to day and found their daughter improveing

Thursday Nov the 10th 1927

Rom Chap 1

Cloudy and damp yet this morning. all able to be up and go about daily avocation for which I am thankful I feel that I cannot thank the Father of all our sure mercies enough for His goodness and mercy to us his unworthy children. I desire that all may ponder well this first chapter of Romans and see for themselves the fate of those who disobey God by giving way to their own lust and carnal minds and disobeying His divine commands and we should also take to the instruction given in the second chapter of Romans for we are too apt to judge others, when we should be examining ourselves, so I pray thee dear Heavenly Father to help me to be close on my watch at all times that I do not disobey thee but that I may be faithful to do my duty in all things to thy names glory.

Friday Nov the 11th 1927

1st Timothy 4-12

The sun is shineing to day which makes things look more cheerful, and I am glad that it is as well as it is with us all as it is yesterday **Lena White** and myself went with **J.W.** and **May Peace** to the High Point Hospital to see their daughter **Minnie** and found her doing fine. I greatly desire to conform to the words of my Text, for I want to be an example of the believers in word in conversation in charity in faith in purity. dear Lord help me so to be. for Jesus sake is my prayer.

Saturday Nov the 12th 1927

A clear nice morning. and I am so thankful that it is as well with us all this morning as it is all able to go about daily duties, and they brought **Minnie** home from the Hospital yesterday and she is doing fine so far, as we have much to praise the Lord for, that she has gotten along so well.

Sunday Nov the 13th 1927

Much colder this morning. All able to prepare for the services of the day Sunday School etc except the daughter **Minnie** who has to go back to the Hospital again to have the incision on the neck dressed she is going along fine I am thankful to state. Praised by the name of the Lord now and forever.

Monday Nov the 14th 1927

2nd Tim 3-15

Cold morning. All able to be busy doing that which is most necessary for the comfort our bodies. my eye sight is failing but am so thankful to still be able to read the Scriptures, for we are told in my Text that the holy scriptures are able to us make wise unto salvation, so we should peruse them daily and thoroughly in faith asking Christ to help us to understand them for our own salvation, and to His honor and praise.

Tuesday Nov the 15th 1927

Cloudy and some rain all able to be up and busy. **Minnie** is going to the Hospital again to day to have the incision in her neck dressed. She is getting on fine. In meditating on the words of my Text. I feel that it is necessary that we should all remember that we are bought with a price, therefore we should glorify God in our bodies and in our spirits for we belong to God. so we should keep ourselves pure in body and soul. that we many merit an inheritance with Him in glory.

Wednesday Nov the 16th 1927

A very damp morning, which is rather depressing to my feelings, but thankful to be able to arise from my bed, and wait on myself and note the goodness and mercy of the Lord to us all.

Thursday Nov the 17th 1927

Psalm 17-5

Still cloudy with some rain, all able to be up and doing. The parents are going to take **Minnie** to the Hospital again to day to have her neck dressed. We have so much to be thankful for that it is as well with us all as it is. My prayer is dear Lord "Hold up my goings in thy paths that my footsteps slip not." "Keep me as the apple of the eye, hide me under the shadow of thy wings." for thy names sake oh Lord.

Friday Nov the 18th 1927

Psalm No 8

Clear and much cooler this morning. All in this home able to be up and busy, so I feel like saying with David, "I will praise the Lord with my whole heart," for thou hast maintained my right, and thou will also be a refuge for the oppressed a refuge in times of trouble. Praise His holy name.

Saturday Nov the 19th 1927

Cold morning. All able to be on the stage of action. Some of them going with **Minnie** to the Hospital again to day to have her neck dressed she is getting along find and I hope will soon be healed. I am trying hard to obey the precepts taught in this Psalm. Oh Lord help me to be wholey thine is my prayer for I want to see Thee face to face. when done with the things of time here below.

Sunday Nov the 20th 1927

Micah 6-8

Clear and cold this morning. I am very thankful that we are all as well physically as awe are. and we are told in our Golden Text for to day that the Lord requires of us to do justly and love mercy and to walk humbly with God. oh Heavenly Father who art God over all. help us to do this for the sake of thy dear Son Jesus Christ who died for us.

Monday Nov the 21st 1927

John 14th chap

A very cold but beautiful morning. I am certainly thankful to be as well as I am, after my long ride of forty six miles last evening from the home of my soninlaw **J.W. Peace** in Randolph Co to the home of **Mr BD Shue** in Salisbury; **Mr Shue** and wife **Jessie Stilwell Shue** are such fine people, so very kind and obligeing to me, I appreciate them so much and my prayer is that the dear Lord will bless them abundantly both spiritually and temporally I have been comforted this morning in reading the fourteenth chapter of St. John which has such very precious promices, oh that we may all live such lives that we may be permitted an entrance into those Mansions which our Heavenly Father has prepared for those who love and serve Him on earth.

Tuesday Nov the 22nd 1927

Clear and cold this morning I feel that I have so much to be thankful for, that I have had a quiet nights rest and am able to be up, and am enjoying the hospitality of those kind people in the home of **Mr** and **Mrs B.D. Shoe.** May the Lord bless them abudently in every way needful is my prayer for Jesus sake who shed His precious blood for us all.

Wednesday Nov the 23rd 1927

A lovey morning for the time of year, I am still in the home of **Mr** and **Mrs Shoe**, had a good nights rest and am so very thankful to be keeping as well as I am. I feel that I cannot praise the dear Lord enough for His goodness and mercy to his dependent children.

Thursday Nov the 24th 1927

Warmer this morning. All in the home able to be up and are prepareing to spend this Anual Thanksgiving day with kindred and friends. I feel that we should give thanks with our whole heart to the bountiful Giver of all our blessing, not only this day but every day of our lives, for His goodness and mercy to His dependent children.

Friday Nov the 25th 1927

A beautiful morning. I am back again in the home of **Mr** and **Mrs Shoe** after spending yesterday Thanksgiving at the home of **Mrs Shoes** Father, **Mr George Stilwell** a few miles out in the country.

There was most of their children and several of the relatives and friends there to spend the day with them, the men folk takeing their guns and haveing a big Rabbit hunt in the forenoon, then comeing in and prepareing to sit down at a Table of bountifully loaded with all the good things necessary for the sustanance of the body, and luxuries in abundance, and before all had gotten seated at the table there was the report of a gun and the scream of a child. All rushed to the back porch to find little **Harley Stilwell** the youngest child in the home, with the blood running down from his head and neck which was caused by scattering shot striking him, and we also found that **Mr Stilwells** soninlaw **Mr Homer Fesperman** had received quite a quantity of shot in his body and some in his head. The gun being inside the room and the load going thru the wall and tearing a large hole in the weatherbording broke part of the force of the shot before it reached them, otherwise as they were so near to it they would both undoubtedly been instantly killed, so we have much to be thankful for that is was not more serious, they were both painfully but not seriously hurt. They got the Drs attention at once and had their wounds dressed and are going to take the Antitoxine treatment to prevent lockjaw and also to prevent danger of blood poisoning. The trouble was cause by one gun being left loaded, after the men came in from hunting and was laid in a room on a bed, the others guns had all been unloaded and stacked by a tree in the yard, but there was one young son that was not by when the Father cautioned the two little boys not to bother the gun as <u>it</u> was loaded and they did not but this other son did not know that it was loaded so went in and thinking he was old enough to learn something about a gun got to fooling with it and finally pulled the triger, with the results mentioned.

Saturday Nov the 26th 1927

Clear and cooler this morning. I am still in this hospitable home had rest thru the night and thankful that all are able to be on the stage of action this morning for which we are indebted to the Giver of all our sure mercies oh that we would praise the Lord more and obey Him better for in Him we live and move and have our being. I have an invitation to visit at **Mr Fespermans** to day so I shall perhaps spend the day with them.

Sunday Nov the 27th 1927

A beautiful Sabbath morning. I am so thankful to once again be able to arise from my bed and prepare for Church. I made my anticipated visit yesterday to my kind friends and returned to **Mr Shoes** again for the night. and to day I am to go to Church with them in Salisbury this forenoon, and this afternoon go out to **Mrs Shoes** Fathers **Mr George F. Stilwell's**. oh that we may all praise the Lord for His goodness toward us His dependent children is my prayer for Jesus sake.

Monday Nov the 28th 1927

A nice warm morning. All in this home able to be on the stage of action. I was permited to attend Church yesterday in Salisbury, heard a splendid sermon by the **Rev H. H. Jordon**, then came out to **Mr G.F. Stilwells** and spent the evening pleasantly with **Mr Stilwells** family and some of their married daughters and their families, and I remained overnight and this morning I am enjoying the hospitality of these kind people. I praise the Lord for his goodness to us.

Tuesday Nov the 29th 1927

Cloudy and damp this morning. I am still in the home of **Mr G.F. Stilwell** being entertained most kindly Two of the daughters. Two of the daughters **Mary and Eva** are in High School in Salisbury, the three small boys **Everette, Ottis, and Harley**, go the District School, one daughter **Margaret** is now helping in the home, she is also a nurse and goes out when called to nurse the sick in the homes of their neighbors or others wherever the case may be one grown son **Murry Stilwell** is now working in Salisbury as a delivery salesman. The parents **Mr** and **Mrs George** and **Carrie Stilwell**, are actively engaged in the work of the field and in the home and are exemplary people. The gather their family around them at night to hear the Scriptures read and prayer offered in thanksgiving and praise to the Great Giver of all our blessings, and asking forgiveness for all short comeings, etc. In the name of Father, Son and Holy Spirit.

Wednesday Nov the 30th 1927

Cloudy again this morning. I am still in the home of **Mr Stilwell** all able to arise from our beds and go about daily avocations some to household duties, some to school, others to the fields, etc. and in meditateing upon this day being the last day of the month and how fast time flies my heart and mind cries out as it were. oh that we all may be ready to enter into the work of the Lord in whatever field He calls us to labor that we may answer the end for which we were created which is to glorify Him on earth that we may glorify Him forever in Heaven.

Thursday Dec the 1st 1927

Still cloudy and much cooler this morning. for the beginning of the month of December. I am still in this hospitable home. all in usual health for which I feel very grateful. for it is a blessing to be able to go about our daily avocations doing those things that are necessary for the comfort of our bodies. oh that we might be as anxious to be faithful to do the things that pertain to our everlasting welfare that we may be prepared to enter into that home which has been made ready for those who do Gods holy will on earth and that may enter into glory there to sing Gods praise with loved ones gone before thruout all eternity.

Friday Dec the 2nd 1927

A very rainy day. I am still in the home of **Mr Stilwell** and all are in usual health. and we are again reminded of the uncertainty of life and the certainty of death as **Mr Stilwells** soninlaw **Mr Home**

Fespermans Father is to be consigned to the grave he passed away yesterday morning about four oclock Dec the 1st 1927.

Saturday Dec the 3rd 1927

It is still very rainey to day. I am yet in the good home of my kind friends, and altho the dampness affects me quite a goodeal, I am thankful that it is as well with me as it is, I am thinking of going to my son **Fred C. Blairs** in Charlotte, N.C. tomorrow if the weather gets fit and I am able.

Sunday Dec the 4th 1927

The ground is covered with sleet this morning, so I think I shall be defeated in getting to my sons to day, I had expected to leave my kind friends to day after spending a week in this hospitable family, but on account of the bad weather it hardly seems probable neither can we get out to Church to day, but I hope we shall endeavor to keep this day holy in this home.

Monday Dec the 5th 1927

After several days of cloudy and rainey weather and quite a sleet last night; the sun has come out so bright this morning that it makes things look so much more cheerful. That I feel like we all should take fresh courage to press on in the way we should go, so that when we are done with the dark days of trial and privation here on earth, we may go to enjoy that bright clime where all is joy and peace and love. I felt some what defeated in not getting to go to Charlotte yesterday as I had hoped to do, but as it was on account of the inclemency of the weather, I gave it up cheerfully, knowing that He who ruleth over all will do all things for the best, and we should be in subjection to His will at all times to His honor and praise. Blessed be His holy name.

Tuesday Dec the 6th 1927

Cool and damp this morning. All able to be on the stage of action for which I am very grateful. Some the family are gone to Town, the children to school etc. I feel like I cannot praise the Lord enough for His goodness to me in raiseing me up kind friends to comfort and help me in time of need.

Wednesday Dec the 7th 1927

This has been a very dreary looking morning but now the sun has shown out and bids fair to be a nice day. I am still the home of **Mr Stilwell** and having a good time, and they are going to kill a nice hog to day, so we will be blessed with fresh meat. And last night we had a real social feast for fun exchanging presents for Christmas, as I do not expect to be with them for Christmas, as I aim to go on to my sons in Charlotte to spend the hollidays. oh that we would all be as much concerned to honor and praise Christ our Redeemer for what He does for us, which is so much more than we can do for each other as we are to try to make our friends happy by presenting them with temporal things which perish with the using. For in Him we live and move and have our being, and without Him we can do nothing.

Thursday the 8th Dec 1927

Cloudy this morning. I am still in the home of **Mr Stilwell**. All in usual health. If feel that I have so much to be thankful for, for the kindness I receive in this home of their dear children, may the Lord bless them all abundently for Jesus sake I ask it.

Friday Dec the 9th 1927

The coldest day we have had for several week. I am very thankful that this family and myself are all able to be up and go about daily duties. This is the day for the Roan County Farmers Union to meet at the Yost School house, and the Farmers wives prepare large quantities of food to supply the long Table for the big Public Dinner, and there is always a large Deligation attend. Yesterday we were favored with the company of two of **Mr Stiwells** daughters **Mrs B.D. Shoe** and **Mrs Homer Fesperman** we had a very good social time, and I feel like saying praise the Lord for His goodness to us all.

Until We Sleep Our Last Sleep

Saturday Dec the 10th 1927

Heb 10-24

A very cold morning. I am thankful that all are able to be up this cold day and attend to the things necessary to be done for the comfort of our mortal bodies. oh that we may all be as ready to do the things which pertain to the salvation of our immortal souls. so "Let us consider one another to provoke unto love and to good works." "For we have need of patience that after ye have done the will of God ye might receive the promice."

Sunday Dec the 11th 1927

A bright cold Sabbath day. All in this home in usual health. **Mr Stilwell**, his daughter **Mary** and two of his sons **Everette** and **Ottis** are gone to Sunday School and Church. I am aiming to leave this hospitable home to day and go to visit my son **Fred C. Blair** and family in Charlotte N.C. I hope I shall have health and strength sufficient to enjoy a stay of a few weeks with them as I have not been there for three years. May we all be filled with thanksgiving and praise to the Giver of all good for His mercy to us His dependent children is my prayer for Jesus sake.

Monday Dec the 12th 1927

A cloudy damp day. After two weeks in the hospitable home of **Mr G.F. Stilwell**, most pleasently, **Mr. Floyd Wolf** and wife brought me last evening to my sons here in Charlotte, found them all in comparatively good health for which I feel glad indeed as my son has suffered so much during this year. I stood my trip from Salisbury, to Charlotte by private conveyance very well for one of my age as I am in my 83rd year. Praise the Lord for His tender care of me. His unworthy child.

Tuesday Dec the 13th 1927

A bright morning and much warmer. My eyes are so weak to day I can scarcely see how to write, but feel grateful to my merciful Heavenly

Father that I am able to be up and wait on my self instead of being helpless as I was for so many years in the past, at this time as I write I am in my sons home alone for a few hours as part of the family are gone to Town, some to work some to school etc. so in the quiet I am meditateing on the goodness of God to us all his dependent children. Bless His name.

Wednesday Dec the 14th 1927

A warm day for the time of year, I am still in the home of my son **Fred C. Blair,** had a quiet nights rest for which I thankful to the great Giver of all good for all His benefits, for He watches over me by night and by day and I feel that I cannot praise Him enough.

Thursday Dec the 15th 1927

A very cloudy day. This damp weather is very hard on those who are in anyway afflicted with Rumatism but I am so thankful to still be able to wait on myself, and that our dear Lord has seen fit to spare my life, and a degree of strenth sufficient to do this, for we are at this time again reminded of the uncertainty of life and the certainty of death, and that the young as well as the aged do die. A young boy in this neighborhood was taken ill very suddenly and only lived one hour after being taken, he is to be buried to day, so we see we should always be ready for we know not the day nor the hour when the mesenger of death will summons us to give account of the deeds done in the body. Later in the day, since comeing here I have met **Mrs M.L. Smith** who lives next door to my sons and she has been in this evening and I have enjoyed her company so much she is such a lovely woman. I have not yet had the opportunity to see my friends that I appreciated so much when I staid in Charlotte three years ago. but I hope to see them soon.

Friday Dec the 16th 1927

Still very cloudy, and we have had the most rain for the past week that has fallen in one weeks time for several years, the ground is so thoroughly soaked that travel is almost impossible where there is no hard serfice roads. which is very trying to those who are compeled by circumstances to go to their work thru mud and water, for in places they can not run their cars. but we should all be in entire submishion to the will of kind providence. who not only knows the present but foreknows all things and doeth all things well, and He has a wise purpose in sending all this rain, then when it turns off dry there is complaint about the drought. Instead of saying "Have Thine own way Lord have Thine own way." "Thy will be done not mine," it seems that we poor mortals ae never satisfied, so I say Father forgive us, for Christ our Redeemers sake.

Saturday Dec the 17th 1927

Clear and much colder this morning. I am still in the home of my son and expect to be until after Christmas. I have not been feeling well this dark damp weather for the past week. so it looks good to see the Sun shining again, so it is when we feel discouraged and almost ready to faint by the way that if we look to the Son of righteousness for help He will let His light shine into our hearts and help us to press on thru the darks days of adversity and help us to glorify Him at all times so no matter what our situation in this life. so I pray dear Heavenly Father to take full possession of my heart.

Sunday Dec the 18th 1927

A lovely Sabbath morning. oh that we may all keep this day holy as we are commanded in Gods written Word. I am so thankful that it is as well with us all as it is. The family here were able to go to Church, this morning and expect to go to a Sacred Concert this afternoon. Praise the Lord for His goodness to us all. I can now state that I was favored to be able to go with the family this afternoon to the Sacred Concert which was held in the Auditorium of the Cathlic College, it was very entertaining as the Bible caracters were so well personated. The Title of the Play was No Room in the Inn it was a Christmas

Play, the caracters were The Blessed Virgin, St Joseph, the Guardian Angel, Misael the Blind Artisan, Sara his wife, their children Rachel, Martha and Mirriam, and the Angel and the Shepherds. All this was carried out to perfection and their costumes was most beautiful and of gorgeous colors, and a most perfect imitation of costumes worn in the old Bible times when our Blessed Saviour was here on earth, oh that we may all take home the lesson that was pictured out to us that we may be more obedient.

Monday Dec the 19th 1927

A very cold day. It seems more like Christmas weather than any we have experienced lately, but it is much to be thankful for that we have shelter, a good warm fire to sit by and food and rainment, so we should be content and praise the Lord for His loveing kindness to us His poor unworthy children. oh Father in Heaven help me to be thy obedient child for the sake of Thy dear Son who was born and died not only to save us from our sins but for the sins of the people world over. Praise His name.

Tuesday Dec the 20th 1927

This is one of the coldest days of the season, but I am so thankful that we are all able to be up and do that which is most necessary for the comfort of the body, oh that we may be diligent to do those things which are well pleasing in the sight of our gracious Redeemer is my most earnest desire for Christs sake. and I feel that we have so much to thank Him for that my grandaughter **Emily Hayden Blair** was not hurt to day, when another Car ran into the one she was driving, and did damage to both Cars, and she came out without any hurt to herself more than a bad scare which weakened her for the time. so I repeat we have so much to be thankful for that she came off as well as she did. Altho of course the repairing of the Car cost money that they needed for other things, but as her life and limbs were spared, we feel like turning our regrets, unto Thanksgiving and praise.

Wednesday Dec the 21st 1927

A bright morning all able to be on the stage of action, for which I am grateful to the Giver of all good, and desire to be obedient unto Him.

Thursday Dec the 22nd 1927

Another nice morning. All are busy here prepareing for Christmas, oh that we should all be as anxious to celebrate our dear Saviours birth in the most appropriate way to give honor and praise to His most holy name. oh that we all may prepare to meet our God, when we are called from works to rewards that we may hear that welcome sound, of well done good and faithful servent enter thou into the joy of the Lord. To day the weekly Cottage prayer meeting is held in the home of **Mrs Rogers** and I regret so much not having a conveyance too and from the place so that I might of met with them, but my prayer is dear Lord be with them and bless them.

Friday Dec the 23rd 1927

A clear cold morning but not quite so severe as for the past few days, I am so thankful that we are all as well as we are to day, for there are many who are suffering in this and other States, I received word a few days ago that my only living brother **E.B. Millikan** was in a serious condition and has to be taken to the Hospital in Indianapolis Indiana so I am very anxious about him, and pray that if it is the dear Lords will that he may be restored to health again.

Saturday Dec the 24th 1927

Cold to day, and altho I do not feel strong I hope I shall have strength enough to enjoy the hollidays with my sons family and other kind friends I praise the Lord for His goodness to me and to mine.

Sunday Dec the 25th 1927

Christmas day. A clear cold but beautiful day. I am so thankful that we have been spared an in comparatively good health this lovely

December 1927

Xmas morning. oh how I praise the name of our blessed Lord who was born and died to save us from our sins, all of us here in my sons home have been so kindly remembered with the many good things which has been sent in by our loved ones. and we know that it all comes from the great Giver of all good. Blessed be his holy name.

Monday Dec the 26th 1927

Another cold cay. All in this home are able to be up and on the move, after spending a pleasent Christmas day with kindred and friends. I feel that I have so much to be thankful for that I have kept able to enjoy the Xmas exercises and the childrens joys over their many nice things that "Santa" brought them. I hope they may be taught to know where all their good things come from to the praise of Him from whom all blessings flow and so live as to be with Him in the better land.

Tuesday Dec the 27th 1927

A pretty day but quite cold, I am thankful to be able to enjoy the Hollidays with my relatives and friends, and I have been so kindly and generously remember by, not only those whom I am visiting but also by my daughter and her children in Kansas City Mo, and many loves ones in Thomasville and other places by Boxes of good things and Cards of greeting. Praise the Lord for His goodness to me and mine. Later in the day. I had the pleasure of visiting **Mrs A.C. Hollingsworth** this afternoon, who was one of the Teachers in my Bible Class when I staid in Charlotte some years ago. and **Mrs Clyde Neely** who was my other Teacher, came over there to visit me, so I certainly did enjoy the evening with those kind friends. Praise the Lord.

Wednesday Dec the 28th 1927

A nice morning. I am so very thankful that I am keeping up as well as I am. I think I shall probably go to Salisbury tomorrow on my way home in Randolph.

Thursday Dec the 29th 1927

A very cloudy day, so much so that it is uncertain about my getting to Salisbury to day, but I am leaving myself in the hands of my blessed Lord to do with me as He sees best, so if He opens the way for me to go His will be done and His name glorified.

Friday Dec the 30th 1927

A very dark damp day, which causes more pains and aches in my limbs, but I am thankful to still be able to wait on myself, and trust that I shall be favored to keep able to return home before many days, altho my friends did not come for me yesterday to go to Salisbury on my way home as I had expected them to do.

Saturday Dec the 31st 1927

Still cloudy and damp. This being not only the last day of the month, but the last day of the year 1927. It brings to mind the flight of time for it hardly seems possible a year has passed since 1927 came in. oh that we may all be ready to hear the final welcome summons of well done good and faithful servent enter thou into the joy of the Lord. Help me Father to do Thy holy will.

1928

Sunday January 1st 1928

A cold windy morning for the first of the year. I am thankful that all the inmates of this household are in comparatively good health and I hope we all shall begin the new year with a firm resilution to do better in the future than we have ever done in the past, and that these resolutions may be kept to the honor and praise of Him who has spared our lives to see this holy Sabbath day of Jan the 1st 1928. This is the prayer of my heart for Jesus sake.

December 1927–January 1928

Monday Jan the 2nd 1928

A very cold morning. I came from my sons **F.C. Blairs** in Charlotte last evening, and spent last night at **Mr B.D. Shoes** they are so very kind to me I shall ever remember them with the greatest appreciation and this morning **Mrs Shoe** brought me over to her sisters **Mrs Homer Fesperman** to spend the day, which I have enjoyed very much.

Tuesday Jan the 3rd 1928

Still very cold, the past few days it is said has been the coldest weather we have had for the past ten years, water pipes frozen and general freze. But thankful that we have been kept warm and comfortable. Praise the Lord for His gooness to us.

Wednesday Jan the 4th 1928

I am still at **Mr Shoes**, have had a good nights rest, and am so thankful to be as well as I am this cold day. for this afternoon I am aiming to go back to my daughter in Randolph where I make my home at this time. Yesterday I went with **Mrs Shoe** to the funeral of **Mrs Mary Elizabeth Loflin** which was held at Coburn Memorial Methodist Church in Salisbury at two oclock, which was conducted by the **Rev H.H. Jorden** Pastor of that Church at this time, assisted by **Rev W.A. Rollins** of Greensboro former Pastor of this Church, also **Rev R.G. Tuttle**, and **Rev C.U. Ryne**. The Interment was in Chestnut Hill Cemetary. **Mrs Loflin** before her marriage was **Miss Mary E. Penington.**

Thursday Jan the 5th 1928

Another cold day. I am so very thankful to be able to be up to day, after my long ride last evening from Salisbury here to my daughters home the home of **J.W. Peace**. **Mrs B.D. Shoe** brought me back home her Mother **Mrs George Stilwell** accompanied us. I was loathe to seperate with those kind friends but glad to get back to the place

I call home. But when I arrive found a letter awaiting me bring me the sad message of the Death of my dear brother **E.B. Millikan**. For several years he has been my only liveing brother and now that he is gone, there is only two of us left of the family of twelve children, my sister **Mattie C. Millikan** and myself. Brother passed away on Dec the 28th 1927 at five twenty oclock in the morning without a struggle. He had known for sometime that he could not live, and had chosen his Pall bearers and some songs. The funeral was held in the Church and he was placed in the West Union Cemetary which is a Friends burying ground, he had been for many years in Monrovia Indiana. and for the past year or more he had been a great sufferer with a complication of diseases. And as he grew worse they removed him from home to a Hospital in the hope that he might be helped and return to his sons home in Indianapolis, but was there only a short while and passed away in the Hospital, we are sad at the loss of our dear brother but are so thankful to believe that our loss is his gain, so we do not sorrow as those who have no hope, for he had lived a concerted Christian life and had ample time to prepare for the final change. Which I am sure he did. And now my greatest desire is to be ready to meet him in the better land where parting is unknown.

Friday Jan the 6th 1928

Still quite cold, but the weather has moderated some. I am thankful we are all able to be up and go about our daily duties of course I am feeling the loss of my dear brother who so recently passed away. for altho I could not see him, it was a pleasure to hear from him and see his own handwriting. But he has only paid the debt that we all will have to pay sooner or later. Father help us to be ready.

Saturday Jan the 7th 1928

The weather is some milder to day, after being so severe cold for some time. and I am thankful to still be able to be up and note down the goodness of our blessed Saviour to me and mine. Praise His holy name.

Sunday Jan the 8th 1928

Cloudy this morning. oh that we may none of us let the clouds of unbelief or doubts possess our hearts and minds this day, but that we may look unto Jesus with full faith, and the sunshine of joy fill us with thanksgiving and praise to the great Giver of all good. Is my wish for Jesus sake.

Monday Jan the 9th 1928

A very cloudy dark morning, had rain during the night. I am very glad to be as well as I am at this time, I am very grateful to the Giver of all good, that I was able to go to Mt Vernon Sunday School yesterday, and take part in the exercises of the day. Praise God from whom all blessing flow.

Tuesday Jan the 10th 1928

Cooler again this morning and clear and bright I feel greateful to our merciful heavenly Father for a quiet nights rest in sleep, and for strength to arise from my bed and go about my daily duties, and this family are all in good health.

Wednesday Jan the 11th 1928

Another nice morning. All able to be up and go about daily avocations, for which I feel very grateful to the Giver of all our blessings. Praise His holy name.

Thursday Jan the 12th 1928

A nice clear morning, all able to be up and go about household duties. and I desire that we all may ever be mindful of our obligations to our heavenly Father for all His mercies to us His unworthy dependent children. and that we will adore Him and His dear Son who gave His precious blood as ransom for our souls. that we might find pardon for our sins and live with Him forever in heaven when done with time here below. Blessed be His name forever.

Friday Jan the 13th 1928

Damp this morning which causes my limbs to ache more, but I am glad to be able to use them, and that the family here are in good health. I have just been answering the letter from my sisterinlaw **Mrs E.B. Millikan** of Monrovia Ind. which brought the message of my dear brothers death. And as I reflect upon the past, the days of our childhood and youth that we spent togeather in our dear Fathers home here in Randolph Co. N.C. comes vividly to my mind. for altho he had been gone to the State of Indiana for many years, and I had not seen him for about thirty years yet I miss him, for it is always such as pleasure to receive letters from him written by his own hand which I always know at first sight, oh how I crave to meet him in that happy land where parting is forever unknown.

Saturday Jan the 14th 1928

A nice warm day. All as well as usual in this family for which I am thankful, and I desire to be kept close on my watch, that I may not transgress Gods righteous law, by doing things that are not well pleasing in His sight, but that I may be concerned for the upbuilding of His kingdom in the hearts and minds of those with whom I meet and mingle from day to day. oh heavenly Father help me to do thy will every day of my life. I ask for Jesus sake.

Sunday Jan the 15th 1928

Another nice warm day. I am thankful that I can state that the family here and myself are in reasonable good health, and I trust we shall all get out to Sunday School and preaching to day. and worship in spirit and in truth, for God seeketh such to worship Him.

January 1928

Monday Jan the 16th 1928

All up again this warm morning, and busy with daily duties, the women folk of this household are making a quilt to day to ready for the time when cold weather returns again. We were all favored to get out to Sunday School and preaching yesterday heard a good sermon by **Rev Reed Haris** the Pastor at Mt Vernon Church at this time he read the first fifteen verses of the eighth chapter of Romans takeing his Text from the third verse. "God sending his own Son in the likeness of sinful flesh and for sin condemned sin in the flesh." he made it plain that we are to condemn sin in the flesh and forsake it if we would see Jesus and dwell with Him in those mansions above that he told his deciples that he was going away to prepare for them. oh that we may all so live that we may be numbered with His deciples and go to see Him face to face, and live with Him forever.

Tuesday Jan the 17th 1928

Cloudy this morning. All able to be up and busy at things necessary to be done for the comfort and sustainance of these mortal bodies, and I greatly desire that we may all be kept close on our watch that we do not disobey the Divine Commands, that we may have a right to the tree of life when done with time here below, and where we can praise God face to face forever, who gave his dear Son to die for us poor unworthy cretures that we might live forever with Him in that land where sickness and death never comes.

Wednesday Jan the 18th 1928

Cloudy and warm to day. All in usual health for which I feel grateful to the Giver of all good, There is nothing special to take note of to day only the continued goodness and mercy of the Lord to his dependent children in spareing our lives and keeping us in a good degree of health. Blessed be His holy name.

Thursday Jan the 19th 1928

Still very cloudy and damp, which makes my aged limbs ache more, but I am so thankful to still be so I can be up and wait on myself that I try to bear all pain or whatever comes, with patience trusting in the Lord to help me, for of myself I can do nothing. So dear Lord lead and guide my steps.

Friday Jan the 20th 1928

Much cooler this morning which is more conducive to health, and makes me take on fresh courage to press on until called from works to rewards. oh that I may be faithful in discharging my every duty while on this stage of action, that I may be prepared a good account to given when done with the things of earth and praise God forever and ever in that happy land.

Saturday Jan the 21st 1928

A very cold morning, all in usual health except my little grandson **J.A. Peace** who is suffering from deep cold, the Parents had the Dr called this morning to see him, but thankful that as yet he does not seem to have any serious symptoms. My head and mind goes up the Giver of all our sure mercies, for His goodness to us, in that He has seen fit to spare our lives and in a good degree our health. Praise Father Son and Holy Spirit.

Sunday Jan the 22nd 1928

Another severe cold morning, but I am thankful that we are comfortably situated, having food and rainment and fuel to keep us warm, while there are many no doubt who are not blessed with a sufficiency of these things to make them comfortable. so I feel like praiseing God for His goodness to us His dependent children.

January 1928

Monday Jan the 23rd 1928

Still quite cold to day, but all are able to be up and go about daily avocations, for which I feel very thankful. And desire to be kept close on my watch least I deviate from the strait and narrow way which leads to everlasting life and peace when done with this life here below. Heavenly Father lead, guide, and direct my steps so that I walk aright is my prayer for Jesus sake.

Tuesday Jan the 24th 1928

Cloudy to day. All up and busy at work doing the various things necessary to be done for the comfort of the perishable bodies. oh that our chief concern may be to prepare for the time when we shall be called upon to give an account of the deeds done in the body. The lines of the good old Hymn seem to sound in my ears this morning. "come thou fount of every blessing tune my heart to sing thy Praise. Streams of mercy never ceaseing call for songs of loudest praise. Oh to grace how great a debtor daily Im constrained to be, Let thy goodness like a fetter bind my wandering heart to Thee. Prone to wander Lord I feel it prone to leave the God I love. Here's my heart oh take and seal it, seal it for thy courts above. These lines express the desire of my heart more acurately than I could express them.

Wednesday Jan the 25th 1928

Still cloudy to day. We had quite a wind and rain storm last night, the strongest wind we have had for several years. I feel thankful that we were preserved from all harm. for we know that our kind and merciful Heavenly Father has all power in His hands to do whatever he wills so we have much to thank Him for that he suffered no harm to come to us.

Thursday Jan the 26th 1928

Still cloudy and cool All in usual health for which I feel very grateful to Giver of all benefits. Praise His name.

Friday Jan the 27th 1928

A clear cold morning. All able to be up and attend to the daily rotine of work, for which I am thankful. oh how little we realise how much we are indebeted to our Great Benefactor for all we have to enjoy. A quiet nights rest in sleep in a good warm bed, food and clotheing, and fuel to keep us warm this cold weather, whilst no doubt there are many who are suffering so that they can not sleep, and perhaps do not have the other necesitities of life, and as I have suffered so much in the past, my heart is full of sympathy.

Saturday Jan the 28th 1928

Cold this morning, with a skiff of snow on the ground. We have had very little snow this winter so far. I am thankful that with a few exceptions, we have all kept reasonably well. for which the Giver of all our blessings. Praise His holy name now and ever.

Sunday Jan the 29th 1928

One of the coldest mornings we have had this winter. I am so thankful that we are all able to be up and sit by a good warm fire, instead of being confined to the bed, which was my experience for so may years, I feel that I can not thank my heavenly Father enough for His goodness and mercy to me and mine. I hope we shall be able to get out to Sunday School this afternoon and that we keep this day holy unto the Lord.

Monday Jan the 30th 1928

Still quite cold. All able to be up and keep busy. I was favored to get out to Sunday School at Mt Vernon yesterday, had a very interesting session, and well attended for such a cold day. Praise the Lord for all His benefits to his dependent children. "Ask the Saviour to help you, comfort, strengthen and keep you. He is ready to save you. He will cary you through."

Tuesday Jan the 31st 1928

A very cloudy morning, and the ground covered with sleet. I am thankful that it is as well with us all physically as it is, and this being the last day of the month again reminds me of the flight of time, and every mounth that passes brings us that much nearer our journeys end. and that we should be diligent to make our calling and election sure, that we may have a home with the blessed.

Wednesday February the 1st 1928

The ground and trees are covered with ice this morning, there having come a heavy sleet during the night, which is beautiful to look out upon and will be more beautiful when the sun shines out, which will make things look like they are covered with silver. Oh how wonderful are the works of Him who has rule over all things, it fills my heart with wonder, love and praise. I am truly thankful that we as a family here have been preserved in a good degree of health this damp weather for which we are indbted to the Giver of all our blessings. Praised and honored be His holy name. "O Praise the Lord all ye nations: praise him, all ye people, For his merciful kindness is great toward us: and the truth of the Lord endureth for ever. Praise ye the Lord.

Thursday Feb the 2nd 1928

Clear and cold this morning. All able to go about daily work, which is a great blessing, for it is such a pleasure to be able to attend to household affairs. Praise the Lord for His goodness and mercy to his dependent children.

Friday Feb the 3rd 1928

A nice clear morning, all in usual health and going about daily work, for which I feel thankful to our heavenly Father, for all our blessings come from Him. And if I only pen a line or two each day it is in grateful remembrance of his continued mercy and goodness to us his dependent children, and to cause me to be closer on my watch at all times least I transgress His divine commandments

Saturday Feb the 4th 1928

A nice clear morning. All in this home are able to be up and go about daily avocations for which I am truly thankful. oh that we may not neglect the most in important thing, that of directing our lives aright, so that we may have a good account to give when done with time here below is the vervent desire of my heart. Father keep me as in the hallow of thy divine hand had I go not astray from Thee is my prayer for Jesus sake.

Sunday Feb the 5th 1928

Raining this morning, which causes my limbs to ache more as the dampness seems to affect them, but I am thankful to be able to again note down the continued goodness and mercy of the Lord. and I hope we shall all endeavor to keep this Sabbath day holy for Jesus sake.

Monday Feb the 6th 1928

Cloudy and much cooler this morning. I have nothing special to take note of at this time, but the Old Old Story of Jesus and his love to ys, His unworthy dependent children. for we are all able to be up and go about our daily avoications which is much ineeded to thank Him for. Blessed be His name.

Tuesday Feb the 7th 1928

A very dark cloudy day, and quite cool, but we are favored to be in usual health, and to day we have again been reminded of the uncertainty of life and the certainty of death. as we have just returned from the funeral of cousin **Maggie Millikan** which was held at Springfield to day at eleven oclock conducted by **Rev T. A. Sykes** Pastor of Friends Church High Point and **Clara I. Cox** Pastor of Springfield Church and **Rev-Moore** Pastor of Wesley Memorial Methodist

Church High Point. The deceased was the widow of **J.H. Millikan** he preceded her to the grave three years ago. she was in her seventy fourth year of age. she will be greatly missed as she was so endeared to her immediate family and was much loved by kindred and friends. There was a most beautiful tribute paid to her memory and the floral offerings were beautiful. The weather being to inclement there was not as large attendance as there otherwise would of been, but a very good attendance for such an unfavorable day and was a most interesting and beautiful occasion on account of the good advice we received from God mesengers and the assurance that the dear departed now rests from her labors in the Home prepared for the blessed. She was stricken with Paralysis on Friday Feb the 3rd and passed away on Sunday night Feb the 5th and was burried Tuesday Feb the 7th 1928. She never regained conciousness at all after she was taken, but just simply breathed to the last.

Wednesday Feb the 8th 1928

A rainey morning but some warmer, all able to be up and go about daily duties, for which I am thankful to the Giver of all good, for we are entirely dependent on Him for the breath which we draw, for in Him we live and move and have our being. Praise His name.

Thursday Feb the 9th 1928

Cloudy and cool this morning. All in usual health I am thankful to state, and I hope that we may all make proper use of the talents given us let them be few or many, if we have but one let us not bury it in the earth or wrap it in a napkin, but let us improve it to the glory of God the Father and his dear Son who died for us. to redeem us from our sins, and give us eternal life.

Friday Feb the 10th 1928

Clear and cold this morning. All up and busy with household affairs. **J.W. Peace's** married daughter **Mrs Gideon Bowman** has come to visit them to day bringing her infant son **Gideon jr** which seems to be a great treasure to all concerned.

Saturday Feb the 11ᵗʰ 1928

A pretty bright morning but still quite cool. All able to be up and go about daily work for which I am thainkful to the Giver of all mercies and blessings.

Sunday Feb the 12ᵗʰ 1928

Clear and cool this Sabbath morning. All able to arise from our beds, and I trust will be able to get out to Sunday School, oh that we may all keep this day holy according to the commandments. For our Redeemers sake.

Monday Feb the 13ᵗʰ 1928

Cloudy this morning and still quite cool. The members of this family are I usual health. I am feeling more feebl to day than for some days past, but thankful to be able to be up and note down a word of praise to Him in whom our lives are, I desire more and more each day to live closer to the Lord and do his holy will in all things that I may be worthy of an inheritance with Him when done with the things of this transient world, here below. I was favored to get our to Sunday School yesterday for which I praise the Lord for his goodness to us all.

Tuesday Feb the 14ᵗʰ 1928

A rainey morning. all able to be up and go about daily avocations. The weather being so damp causes more pain and acheing in my spine and limbs, but I am so thankful that I am not confined to the bed as had been my lot for may years in the past, that I try to bear all my infirmities with patience and Christian courage, looking unto Him who is able and willing to help. Yesterday I came across a piece that had been printed in a High Point Paper concerning the death

February 1928

and funeral of cousin **Maggie Millikan** and I desided to insert it in my Diary as it stated some things I had not.

Mrs Millikan Is Paid Last Rites.

Services conducted at Springfield Friends Church, Burial in Church Cemetery. Funeral services for **Mrs Maggie Millikan** who died at her home 710 Morris Street last Sunday night, were conducted Tuesday morning at 11 oclock at the Springfield Friends Church. **Rev Tom Alderman Sykes** Minister of Central Friends Church, **Rev John W Moore** pastor of Wesley Memorial Church, **Clara I. Cox** of Springfield officiated. During the service the Choir sang favorite hymns of the deceased. They were, Abide With Me. Jesus Saviour Pilot Me and Nearer My God To Thee. As a special number **Leon Millikan** sang Where We'll Never Grow Old. Pall bears were **Jerome A. Barker, Eugene H. Jarett, Banner Davis, L.L. Farlow, Ruben C. Davis**, and **William Farlow**. Flowers were carried by **Miss Mamie Farlow, Mrs Ralph Parker, Mrs W.M. Farlow, Mrs. Tom Sykes, Miss Anna Mendenhall, and Mr Ruben Davis**. Burial followed in the Church Cemetery.

Wednesday Feb the 15th 1928

The sun is shineing brightly this morning which makes everything look more cheerful, and causes one to more on the bright side of life, oh that we all like the dark clouds that pass away, and the brightness of the sun shines out to give us light and warmth, may we so let all dark forebodings pass from our minds and the light of the Son of righteousness shine in our hearts and take fresh courage to press on toward the mark of the high calling in Christ Jesus to honor and praise Him who died that we might have eternal life.

Thursday Feb the 16th 1928

Cloudy and damp this morning, which is rather hard on those of us who have acheing limbs, but I am thankful to be able to use my pen to take note of the continued goodness and mercy of God to his dependent children, for we know that we are dependent upon Him for every breath we draw, and that He has power to clip the brittle thread of life at any time, so we should be close on our watch at all times, least the mesenger of death come unawares and find us unprepared for the summons. "I will lift up mine eyes unto the hills, from whence cometh my help. My help cometh from the Lord which made heave and earth." Psalm 121. Praise His name.

Friday Feb the 17th 1928

Cloudy this morning, all able to be at work. and I greatly desire that we all may be faithful this day to do whatever the Lord requires at our hands, for we are told that "the night cometh wherein no man can work." and we know according to the Scriptures which we believe are true, that we shall be called upon to give account of the deeds done in the body while here on earth, so we should be very careful what we do and say, that we may "Live the life of the righteous, and that our last end may be .like his." And thus be prepared a good account to give. Lord help us to live aright, to Thy names honor and praise.

Saturday Feb the 18th 1928

Cloudy again this morning, and has raind most all night. We are all able to be up and go about daily affairs as usual, for which I am very thankful, and hope we shall endeavor to be on our watch that we yeild not to temptation, for yeilding is sin, we are told in Gods holy word that our blessed Saviour was tempted in all points like as we are, yet without sin. so we see He has set us an example that altho we may be tempted to do things which we aught not. it is no sin if we like him do not yeild to do them. Lord keep us from all evil.

Sunday Feb the 19th 1928

Clear and cold this morning. I am thankful that we are all in usual health this bright Sabbath morning. and I hope we will all take fresh courage to press on in the way we should go. I trust we shall all be able to get out to Sunday School and Church to day, and that the dear Lord may give us a message thru the mouth of His servant the **Pastor Reed Haris** that we may all profit by the praise of our Redeemer.

Monday Feb the 20th 1928

Cold this morning. We are all able to arise from our beds and go about daily affairs, for which I feel very grateful to our merciful heavenly Father and desire to draw nigh unto Him. that he may draw nigh unto me. "Oh for a closer walk with God, a calm and heavenly frame, A light to shine upon the road, that leads me to the Lamb."

Tuesday Feb the 21st 1928

A nice clear morning, but still quite cold. I am thankful that we of this household are in usual health. The Parents of this home, are gone to Winston Salem to day. My prayer is that they may have a safe journey to and from that City, for there are at times evil disposed persons who are watching their chance to interupt travelers on their way, as they go from place to place.

Wednesday Feb the 22nd 1928

It is cloudy this morning and cold enough for plenty of ice. All up and busy. And in writing the date Feb the 22nd called to mind that this, is our first President George Washingtons Birthday, and with what pomp and grand display it is generally celebrated every year. and it is by many people in recognition of the true worth of the man, while others just make a big hurrah for their own gratification. just a Christmas is celebrated, some spend it in true adoration of our blessed Saviour who was sent into the world to redeem people from their sins. while others spend it in light and frivolous conversation and sports, sometimes even in those things which are of a questionable character. oh that we may all be closer on our watch, that we do not disobey Him who was born and died for us all to save us from eternal punishment, and live with Him forever. And as we honor our earthly Heroes may it not be in merely exalting the flesh, but in recognition of the character and true worth of the man who served God and his country according to the dictates of his own concience, and his example in worthy emulation, according to his trust in God.

Thursday Feb the 23rd 1928

Cloudy and damp this morning. All well as usual except the Father of the family **J.W. Peace** who has a bad headache. We all have our times of Physical suffering while sojourning here below, but let us prepare for that haven of rest, where we will be free from all pain and where the inhabitants never say I am sick. And where we can dwell with the Lord forever, to praise Him for what he has done for us.

Friday Feb the 24th 1928

Clear this morning and much warmer. All able to be up and going, either to work, or to school or on buisness, oh that we would be faithful to do the work that the Lord has spared us for, and be taught in the school of Christ, and attend to the Kings business which He requires of us, that we may reap the reward of well done good and faithful servent enter into the joy of thy Lord, where we can praise Him more perfectly than we can here upon earth His footstool, for then we shall see Him face to face and behold His glory. To be permited to enter such a home of rest and peace is worth all else to gain Lord help us to gain it, is my prayer for Thy sake who suffered for us.

Saturday Feb the 25th 1928

Cloudy and the air feel like we might have snow. All are able to be on the stage of action. **Mr** and **Mrs J.W. Peace** have gone to High Point to day the children careing for the home. I hope we will all be careful to be on our guard, least we yeild to temptation while we have to endure many things that are trying to human nature. and that we may trust God to take care of us, each and every day, and preserve us from all evil, for Christ the redeemers sake.

Sunday Feb the 26th 1928

Clear and cool this morning. All able to be up, and I hope we may all be favored to attend Sunday School to day as usual, and that we may keep this day holy according to the commandments, for in the language of the Poet, "A Sabbath well spent brings a week of content. And health for the cares of the morrow. But a Sabbath profaned whatever is gained is a sure forerunner of sorrow." Attended Sunday School, and on my way home stoped at the home of **Mr Wm Fry** and spent part of the evening with them, called on Cousin **Rachel Blair** the rest of the evening, then returned to **Mr Frys** and staid over night with them.

Monday Feb the 27th 1928

A nice clear morning, but still quite cool. This morning I am writeing this in the home of cousin **E.C. Blair**. Yesterday I went to Sunday School as usual at Mt Vernon and came back by Progress and stoped with **Mr Wm Fry's** family and staid with them awhile, then came out and spent the rest of the evening here at cousin **Ed Blairs** with his Mother cousin **Rachel Blair** and others. here I met up with her son **Walter Blair** and wife **Mary**, from Greensboro, and two of her Grandaughters **Ruth** and **Anna Ader** who had come to visit her. they are daughter of **Rev O P Ader** who married her only daughter **Ruth Blair Ader** who deceased several years ago, and her husband since maried again. **Ruth Ader jr** is teaching in High Point, her sister **Anna** is a Seniour in College at Greensboro and will graduate this year. I had not seen those girls for several years, and was pleased to see them such nice little ladies, so well accomplished in every way, **Ruth** is almost the image of her dear Mother. They had other company here also besides those I mentioned. The **Rev Ruben Payne** Pastor of Archdale Friends Church. and cousin **Robt Blair** and wife **Ocia** and their sons **Robt jr** and **Edward Charles**, I spent the evening pleasantly with this interesting company of kindred and friends, Then went back to **Mr Fry's** and staid over night, and came back to day to visit with cousin **Rachel** who is quite feeble at this time.

Tuesday Feb the 28th 1928

A nice clear morning, all able to be up and go about daily affairs. I came back to my daughters last evening, after spending most of the day yesterday with cousin **Rachel Blair** very pleasantly she is quite feeble and cheerful and contented which makes it a pleasure to visit her. and in the evening my daughter and I went to cousin **Roxie Hill** and was agreeably surprised to find her so cheerful as she has to sit there in her rolling Chair day after day. but altho she often sits there alone at times, yet she is not alone, for the dear Lord watches over her and comforts her. It is no mistry to me that she can be cheerful and contented in her isolation for I know by experience what it means to be a shut in and have to go on my Wheel Chair for many years when strong enough to be put in it, and many months at a time not able to even be put in it, but my dear Saviour was so near and dear to me that it seemed that His arms were underneath to bear me up thru my afflictions. so I know He sustains cousin **Roxie** in her afflictions. I enjoyed my visit at all the places very much **Mrs Fry** was so very kind to me and did so much to make me comfortable, which I appreciate with all my heart. Her daughter **Jessie** came home with us she is a sweet Christian girl and is so nice and kind to me.

Wednesday Feb the 29th 1928

Cloudy and some cooler this morning. All in usual health I am thankful to state. and as this is the last day of this month, it brings fresh to my mind the flight of time, and how fast we are hastening on to eternity oh let us be ready.

Thursday March the 1st 1928

A bright morning for the beginning of the month All able to be up and at work as usual, for which I feel like returning thanks to the Giver of all our blessings, and desire that we may take fresh courage to press on doing whatever the dear Lord calls for at our hands, to His names honor and praise.

Friday March the 2nd 1928

Clear and cool this morning. All in usual Health I am thankful to state. and that I was favored to attend the prayer meeting last night at **Mrs Gurney Davis's** which was well attended and good interest taken. There were many earnest prayers offered and many testimonies given which added to our faith in prayer and trust in God, for many of us have gone through deep proveings and experiences which tested our faith and as we have taken our trials and afflictions to God in prayer we have found relief. so we may strengthen each other by converseing togeather on those things.

Saturday March the 3rd 1928

A nice bright morning, but quite cool. All in this home are able to be up and go about daily affairs for which I am very thankful. The Parents are going to their Methodist quartly meeting at Trinity to day. Later They have returned from quarterly meeting and report a good attendance and a splendid sermon by **Rev W.B. Davis** of High Point. And business meeting.

Sunday March the 4th 1928

Cloudy this morning. all well as usual and hope to attend Sunday School again to day as custom is. and as this is Preaching day trust we shall have a grand message. Evening of the same day. Yes we were favored to attend Sunday School and Preaching, had a very interesting lesson explained to us by a member of our Class. And hear a good sermon by the **Pastor Rev W.R. Haris**. his Scripture reading was the 18th chapt of Ezekiel and his Text was taken from Galations the 5th chapter and 7th verse. "who did hinder you."

Monday March the 5th 1928

Rather a gloomy looking morning, which corespons to my feelings, as I am feeling feeble and discouraged as the flesh is weak, but I am praying for strength to overcome all my trials and temptations. And I know the dear Lord will help me now, as He has been my stay and staff for many years.

Tuesday March the 6th 1928

The sun is shineing, and it is much cooler this morning but I am thankful this morning to be able to be up, and sit by a nice warm fire. and I am desireous to have my heart so warmed with the love of God that I may be instrumental in His hands in saying or doing something that may be an inspiration to some one or ones, to press on in the way the dear Lord would have them go. And as it was plainly made know to me year ago by the spirit of the Lord that I should take note of His dealings with me, in order that I might leave a record that would be an inspiration to others after I have laid down this mortal body, to have more faith in prayer, and press on in the Lord would have them go. For I certainly know that the dear Lord has heard my poor simple prayers time after time and has answered them in a way that was so plain that I could not doubt His loveing kindness to me in answering them. and knowing as I do that it is my duty to daily acknowledge His goodness and mercy to me, by inserting a few lines to be left on record for my children and grandchildren and others if they are so disposed, to read what I have written. I have tried to be more faithful in the discharge of this duty, for when thru great weakness I neglected it for some years in the past, and altho I was so greatly afflicted and at times felt that perhaps this work was useless, I became condemned for not attending to it, and promiced the dear

Lord that I would do my best to be more faithful in the future while I have physical strenth and eyesight to attend to it, for I now miss many interesting things that I should of recorded in the past that would be a great spiritual help to me, and perhaps others. To the honor and praise of Him who has done so much.

Wednesday March the 7th 1928

Clear and cool this morning. All able to be up and on the stage of action, for which I feel grateful to the Giver of all good, and my greatest desire is to be found walking in the footsteps of Jesus doing his holy will in all things. but altho the spirit is willing, the flesh is week and we are so prone to neglect our whole duty, by not being close enough on our watch, that we often do things that are not well pleasing in His sight. Father keep me this day and throughout all the comeing days of my sojourn here on earth, as in the hallow of Thy divine hand, that I go not astray from thee is my prayer for Jesus sake, who died for me.

Thursday March the 8th 1928

Still quite cool but a nice clear morning. I am thankful to of had a quiet nights rest in sleep and strength to arise from my bed, and again testify with my pen the goodness and mercy of the Lord to me his dependent child. I am so glad that I am His child, and that "he loves even me"and glad that I am dependent on him, for he knows what is best for me, so much better than I know for myself. And he has promiced to never leave nor forsake those that put their trust in Him, and he knows I am standing on his promices, and am trusting in the sure mercies of God my Saviour, yes "Standing on the promices of God." oh that I may ever follow in the way that has been pointed out for me to follow, and be faithful in the discharge of my duty, let it be what it may. for as the flesh is weak, I often find the cross very heavy when I am called upon by His spirit to do or say something in the presence of those who do not understand my calling. so I have to plead with the dear Lord to take away the fear of man, and remember we are told in His word That if "God be for us who can be against us." and thus take fresh courage to press on to do His holy will.

Friday March the 9th 1928

Rainey this morning, and the dampness causes more aches and paines, but I am thankful to be able to be up and again use my pen in noteing down praise from all harm through another night. and my prayer is dear Lord keep us all this day, from sining against thee in word or deed, and help us to do something for the upbuilding of they kingdom, in the hearts of those with whom we meet and mingle. for Jesus sake.

Saturday March the 10th 1928

A beautiful bright morning, the sun is shineing so nice and warm, that it makes me feel glad, for it reminds me of the sunshine of Gods love toward us poor needy children. I am thankful that we are not needy at this time for the comforts of our physical bodies for the dear Lord has provided us with things necessary for our bodily needs. but we are so often neglectful of the things pertaining to the salvation of our immortal souls that we should daily have not only for ourselves, but for these with whom we daily come in contact, and we know that it is only by looking unto Jesus and abideing in His love that our hearts are kept pure from the many vain things that the enemy of our souls peace would have us indulge in, as he is ever ready to take advantage of our weakest moments to ensare us in the traps that he so cuningly sets for us. so my prayer is, heavenly Father help us to avoid all evil for Jesus sake.

Sunday March the 11th 1928

Very cloudy and damp this morning, and as I am suffering with my spine, this dampness seems to add to my pain, but I am trying to be brave and look to the source of all help for strenth to keep up, and I trust the dear Lord will enable me to get out to the Sunday School to day if it is his will, for I do not want to miss a day, but if I can not go, I want to be in entire subjection to His will for I praise his name for his goodness and mercy to me, in giveing me the use of myself sufficient to get about even as well as I now do, for altho I suffer greatly at times with my spine and other afflictions yet it is so much to be thankful for that I am not at this confined to my bed in a helpless condition with my spinal trouble, as I have been for many months at a time in the past. so my heart cries out. Bless the Lord oh my soul and forget me not His benefits.

Monday March the 12th 1928

Still cloudy this morning and I feel sad and lonely, as I am suffering so much with my spine to day, but thankful not to be confined to my bed, but able to be up and use my hands and thinking faculties to do that which I feel required to do, in obedience to the Master and as I have just been reading the fourth chapter of the Ephesians, I have felt constrained to call the attention of my readers to the great need for us all to take heed to the exortations given us in this whole chapter and especially the three last verses which tells us whereby we are sealed unto the day of redemption. "And grieve not the holy Spirit of God, whereby ye are sealed unto the day of redemption." "Let all bitterness and wrath, and anger, and clamour, and evil speaking, be put away from you, with all malice: "And be ye kind one to another, tender hearted, forgiveing one another, even as God for Christ's sake hath forgiven you. I am sure if we would take heed to the instructions given in the chapter we would be much hapier ourselves and make others happy. for we will be held responsible not only for own sins, but for causeing others to sin, by exciteing them to anger. I do not want to be a party to such evil, so I pray Father give me a kind, loveing, and forgiveing heart for Christs sake.

Until We Sleep Our Last Sleep

Tuesday March the 13th 1928

A bright sunshiney day, and as this my 83rd Birthday it brings many thing of the past, both of joy an sorrow fresh to my mind, as there has so many changes taken place from time to time during all those years. and when the month of March comes round, it not only brings to mind the date of my birth, and the many changes in many ways, but also the date of my bereavement as my dear companion passed away the 21st of March 1920. And during those eight years of widowhood I have spent many sad and lonely days. and it is only by looking away from my own weakness, to Him who has promiced. "That as the day thy strength shall be." that I am kept from giving out by the way. Blessed be His holy name now and forever.

Wednesday March the 14th 1928

Cloudy this morning. I am thankful to be so I can arise from my bed, but am still suffering with my spinal trouble so that I am not able to do much. the rest of the members of this household are busy with Spring cleaning, in order to have everything sanitary for the comeing of warm weather, oh that we may examine ourselves and see whether our hearts are pure and clean in the sight of the Lord and whether we are doing the work the Lord calls for at our hands.

Thursday March the 15th 1928

Cloudy again this morning, but I am thankful to have the sunshine of Gods love in my heart, and altho I am suffering more severe pain in my spine to day, I am thankful that I can still get about enough to wait on myself, even if it is thru much suffering for I have been so anxious not to become a burden. For it is is such a consolation to know that during all my helpless years in the past I was not considered a burden, by my loved ones. at one time when I was so very helpless I said to my dear companion that I was so sorry to be such a burden to him, and he replied that he never considered me any

March 1928

burden to him, but said if "he was to consider me a burden at all, he would consider me a precious burden." No one can know how much these kind words so gently spoken helped me to bear my suffering and to exercise all the patience possible, in order to make the burden lighter on my loved ones who were so untireing in their ministrations to me, not only for days, but for months and for years in succession. And my dear Saviour was so precious to me, and seemed to abide with me to comfort and cheer, for at times when I would be alone, He permitted me to hear the songs of the Angels so audibly that it seemed that my room was filled with the sweet refrain. I very well know that it would be like "casting Pearls before swine" to tell some people this experience they would not believe it but would say I was either dreaming or out of my right mind, but there are others of Gods children who have had similar experiences and know that they are true. At one time more than a half of a Century ago, after I have given myself to the Lord, I was lying on my bed in my weak helpless condition, and meditateing on the goodness and mercy of the Lord, when all at once there appeared descending into my room two large and most lovely Waiters suspended by Chords at the corners and in one of them was filled with the largest and most beautiful Apples that ever I saw, and the other was filled with glasses of the purest Wine, and close beside them there was a large strong single Rope just near enough for me to reach the end of it, and the Spirit said lay hold of that rope which is the hope set before thee and thou shalt receive of those precious gifts. The Apples and the Wine in their beauty and purity were to represent the good Spiritual things in the kingdom of Heaven that I should receive if I would be faithful and lay hold of the offer of redeeming love, and obey what the dear Lord has for me to do in this life to His honor and praise. then a happy home above where all is peace and love. In all the years which I have spent since that wonderful vision, for it was nothing less, I have tried to hold on to that strong Rope which was sent for me to cling to, and which I seem to see as plainly at this time, as I did the day it came. And altho

I have at times seemed to let it get to far out of my reach, but being overcome with weakness and the assaults of the enemy, yet as I turn again with full purpose of heart to Him who has sustained me all those that blessed hope is again and again suspended low enough for me to reach and I lay hold with more determination to never let it escape my grasp. For He who is the rope to which I am clinging has ever been ready to comfort and sustain me thru all my comflicts in various ways, for the tempter was ever ready to try to take advantage of my weakness. but blessed be the name of the Lord, he has always made a way for my escape according to His promice, and so will he ever do if we will follow him and obey His will. Faith help us to do this for Jesus sake.

Friday March the 16th 1928

Rainey this morning. I am still suffering with the pain and acheing in my spine, but feel so grateful to of had rest in sleep, the past night, and to be so I can arise from my bed, and take up my pen to note the goodness and mercy of the Lord to his dependent children in watching over and careing for them. oh that we may all endeavor to do the things that are well pleasing in His sight. To day is the nineteenth Birthday of **Miss Minnie Peace** daughter of **J.W. Peace** by his first wife **Sallie Ingram Peace**. I am wishing her many happy birthdays, and that she may live a true and concecrated life, bringing happiness to others with whom she comes in contact. In calling to mind that last Tuesday the the thirteenth was my eighty third Birthday. I am thinking how much she has before her, of both joy and sorrow, if she should be spared to live to see that age. So I commend her to the God and Father of our Lord Jesus Christ who has cared for me thru all those years of varied experiences. To watch over and keep her as in the hallow of His holy hand, that she go not astray from the path of truth and virtue. but putting on the whole Armor of God may she adorn the doctrine of God our Saviour to His honor and praise.

Saturday March the 17th 1928

Very cloudy and deamp this morning. I am still suffering with Lumbago in my back. but thankful to even be so I can be up, and use my thinking faculties and my hand to take note of the loveing kindness of our blessed Saviour to us his unworthy dependent children. for He watches over and cares for us, and often makes a way for us where we see no way. Blessed by His holy name.

Sunday March the 18th 1928

Still cloudy and damp, which seems to add to my pains and aches, but thankful to still be up and wait on myself. And if way opens, I hope to have strength to ride out to Mt Vernon Sunday School and preaching to day, as I hae been favored to attend every Sabbath so far this year, altho many times I have not felt realy able for the trip but feeling it my duty for examples sake to go as long as I have physical strength, I have kept up the resolution to still "try try again" looking unto the Source of all my help for both physical and spiritual strength to help me thru each day, and I have seen the precious promice verified which says "As thy day thy strength shall be." oh heavenly Father help me to lean harder each day, on the everlasting Arms.

Monday March the 19th 1928

A real cold morning, plenty of ice and the ground frozen in places. I am thankful to still be so I can get up and use my pen in praise to the Great Giver of all good that it is as well with us all as it is, altho I am not strong I am so glad to be able to wait on myself that I may not be a burden to others, The little grandson in this home is not at all well at this time but I hope nothing serious. The rest of the family well. Praise the Lord.

Tuesday March the 20th 1928

Nice clear and cool morning. I am thankful that my little grandson is better, and that I am also feeling some stronger and the rest of the family well as usual. so I feel that we have much to be grateful for to the Giver of all good, and I praise His holy name for His mercy to us all. "Blessed be the name, blessed the name, blessed be the name of the Lord." oh that I had a voice to sing His praises.

Wednesday March the 21st 1928

Clear this morning and still quite cool. All able to be up and go about daily duties, and as usual in looking to the source from whence cometh my help, the words again sound in my ears. "Trust in the Lord and do good and thou shalt dwell in the land and verily thou shalt be fed." So I have the assurance that I shall not lack for food either physically or spiritually if I obey His holy will.

Thursday March the 22nd 1928

Clear and still quite cool. I am thankful that I can state that we are all feeling some better to day as to health, but it is so hard to keep the many depressing thoughts out of my mind, that this month naturally brings fresh to my mind, as yesterday the 21st rounded out eight years since my precious companion was taken from me by the cold hand of death. oh how I miss him, and as I sit here, with his picture hanging over the little table on which I am writing, it looks so natural that it seems like I ought to hear him speak to me in gentle tones as in the past, but alas his voice is stilled on earth, but I trust he is singing praises to the King of Kings in that land where I hope to meet him, in the better land where parting is unknown, and praise Him togeather.

Friday March the 23rd 1928

A lovely bright morning. All feeling better and are prepareing to go to the Protracted meeting at Glenola to day, for which I give thanks to the Giver of all our blessings. Evening of same day, my daughter and myself and some others, were favored to attend the eleven oclock meeting to day and heard a most excelent sermon, and many good testimonies, which were very encouraging to us all.

Saturday March the 24th 1928

Another nice clear morning. I am thankful to be so I can arise from my bed, altho suffering severely again this morning with pain in my back and hip, but I do not think going to Church yesterday made me any worse, for I have suffered to a greater or lesser degree every day for more than a month. and was such a lovely sunshiney day the fresh air seemed to do me good, and it is seldom that I have such an oppertunity, and had never been to Church at Glenola. and I listened to such a splendid sermon by **Rev – Drauhn** (or some such name) from Yaadkin County, it inspired me to try hard to press on the remainder of the journey, which won't be much longer at the longest, as I have now past my four score and three years. The only regret I have in not staying at home yesterday is that dear **Clara I. Cox** our pastor of Friends Church at Springfield came to see me while I was away, but such is this life, we meet with disappointments in many ways. and as I did not know that she was comeing, neither did she know that I was away, so I look upon it as one of the comon incidents of life. And thank God that we were both able to ride out in His warm sunshine. and trust that our hearts have been filled with the sunshine of His love, and that we will daily praise Him, and his dear Son Jesus Christ our Saviour is my prayer.

Sunday March the 25th 1928

Rainey this morning. The dampness adds to my aches and pains, but glad I can still get out of my bed and wait on myself, for I count this one of my greatest temporal blessings. And I am so thankful that I have a Friend above all others, that I can look to for all my blessings both physical and spiritual, for He knows our frame and remembers that we are but dust. and He knows the fervent desire of my heart is to love and obey Him according to His commandments. oh heavenly Father keep me so close to thee, that I may know thy will, and do the thing that are well pleasing in thy sight. preserve me from the temptations and snares of the enemy, that I may not be overcome with evil. "Oh come magnify the Lord with me, and let us exhalt His name together." saith my soul.

Monday March the 26th 1928

Nearly clear this morning, and warmer. All up to day except Miss Minnie Peace who is suffering from a deep cold. I am thankful to keep up as I do, altho I suffer more or less all the time, but I was blessed with better rest and sleep last night than for some time, for which I thank and praise the dear Lord with all my heart, for from him cometh all our blessing.

Tuesday March the 27th 1928

Clear, windy and cool this morning. All up but the sick girl and she is better, so we have much to be thankful for. And over and over these same words of Scripture come to me, as I am spared from one day to another. "Trust in the Lord and do good and thou shalt dwell in the land, and verily thou shalt be fed". and it seems it is a perfect garentee, that I shall not lack for a place to dwell in, nor lack for food, if I will abide by and fulfil the conditions, to "trust in the Lord and do good."so my prayer this morning is that I may fully trust the Lord to guide and direct my steps in every way, and that I may know to do good, in whatever way He calls for at my hands. and by thus obeying Him on earth I may merit a home with Him in heaven where I can praise him forever, with loved ones gone before. Lord help me to do so.

Wednesday March the 28th 1928

A nice bright morning and quite cool. all stiring except the sick girl and she is improveing, and I trust will soon be out again. I am feeling rather feeble, but thankful to be able to read God's holy word, which is my daily practice, and while some of it is readily understood, there are other portions that are so misterious that I can not comprehend the meaning as I would wish, yet I just say dear Lord altho I can not understand all I read, but I believe thee and know thy word is true, and can understand enough of it to know that if I obey thee, according to thy word all will be well with me, and thus leave myself in His hands to lead, guide, and direct my steps unto the end, for of myself I can do nothing, so abandon myself to His care and keeping that I may walk uprightly and obey him to His honor and praise.

Thursday March the 29th 1928

Cloudy this morning. but all are feeling some better and I am very thankful to our merciful heavenly Father for all our blessings, and that it is as well with us as it is. Yes this morning I can say with Ralph Waldo Emerson.

"Far flowers that bloom about our feet,
For tender grass so fresh and sweet,
For song of bird and hum of bee,
For all things fair we hear and see,
Father in heaven, we thank thee.
For blue of stream and blue of sky,
For pleasant shade and branches high,
For frragrant air and cooling breeze,
For beauty of the blooming trees,
Father in heaven, we thank thee." Amen.

Friday March the 30th 1928

Raining this morning. The dampness adds to my aches and pains, but glad that I can still arise from my bed and pen a line in the name of Jesus, and for his sake, for I want to be found walking in his footsteps, and obeying his holy will. that I may answer the end for which I was created, which was to glorify Him, on earth that I may glorify him forever in heaven.

Saturday March the 31st 1928

Clear and cool this morning. and as this is the last day of the month, I am again reminded afresh of the flight of time, and that we are fast hastening to eternity. oh that we may be ready when the time comes for us to give account of the deeds done in the body. "oh for a closer walk with God. A light to shine upon the road that leads me to the Lamb." Yes dear heavenly Father let thy light so shine into my heart that I may see clearly what thou would have me do and that I may do, all to thy names honor and praise yes "Come as the light; to us reveal our eptiness and woe; And lead us in those paths of life, Where all the righteous go." "Come as the fire and purge our hearts. Like sacrificial flame; Let our whole souls an offering be. To our Redeemers name."

Sunday April the 1st 1928

Still cold this morning. All able to be up, and as this is preaching day at Mt Vernon I trust the most of the family will be favored to attend. We were blessed to have **Grandma Peace, Jeromes** Mother to dine with us to day. also his brother **Ferney Peace** and family, and his son **Grady Peace** and wife and baby. and after takeing a sumptuous dinner togeather all with the exception of one person, went to Sunday School and preaching, heard a splendid sermon by the **Pastor Rev J.R. Haris** which was very much enjoyed, at least it was by myself, for his theme was helpfulness and I desire that we may all be loveing and helpful to each other in every way, as the dear Lord would have us do, For we told in the holy Scriptures, "By this ye shall know that ye are my deciples if ye have love one for another" "Therefore love is the fulfiling of the law."

Only, O Lord in thy dear love,
Fit us for perfect rest above,
And teach us this and every day,
To live more nearly as we pray,

Monday April the 2nd 1928

A nice clear morning, and some warmer, All able to be on the stage of action, for which I am thankful, but I am feeling quite lonely and sad, as I so oftend do since having to give up my dear earthly companion, and am praying that if it is my heavenly Fathers will, that he will this very day send a mesenger to me to comfort and strengthen me, so that I may not faint as it were by the way, but take fresh courage to press on and not give up until the journey is ended. and wonderful to relate. In the evening of same day, who should drive up but our Pastor of Friends Church at Springfield where I have my right of membership, but dear **Clara I. Cox**, the very one that I had asked my blessed Saviour this morning that He would be pleased to send to me this day. and oh how it has strengthened my faith in prayer. to realise that just this morning I plead in my simple but sincere way that if it was consistent with His will, that he would send my dear true friend, who is one of His faithful handmaidens to me, and in the evening of same day she came and ministered to my spiritual needs. I shall ever remember her earnest prayer on my behalf and may the Lord bless her abundantly in her helpfulness to others. and Blessed be the name of the Lord now and forever.

Tuesday April the 3rd 1928

Cloudy this morning, all able to be on the stage of action, for which I feel grateful to our merciful heavenly Father, and as I stated yesterday that our Pastor dear **Clara I. Cox** came to see me last evening. I feel that she is indeed one of my helpers, and that that I am still being watched over by the All seeing Eye who never slumbers nor sleeps. and has watched over us during the night. and I am looking to Him to day for strength, for He hath said, "As thy day thy strength shall be." and I want to obey Him faithfully, who will be with us unto the end if we will only trust and obey Him as we should. Lord help us to obey.

Wednesday April the 4th 1928

Still cloudy this morning, and much warmer. All again able to be up and go about daily avocations some to one thing and some to another. **J.W. Peace** and his daughter **Minnie** are gone to Asheboro to day, his son **W. C. Peace** to work on the farm, his stepdaughter **Mary Lee Stilwell** to high school at Trinity, which leaves my daughter **Mrs. J. W. Peace** and her little son **J. A. Peace** and myself in the home to day to care for the things of the household. oh that we may all be as careful to prepare to enter, That House not made with hands, eternal in the Heavens.

Thursday April the 5th 1928

Nice clear, warm morning. All up and attending to what is necessary to be done for the comfort of these perishable bodies. Oh that we may be even more diligent to do that which pertains to the salvation of our immortal souls, to the honor and praise of Him who created us on purpose of His own glory.

Friday April the 6th 1928

Cloudy and warm to day. All in usual health, some of the family were going to High Point to day, so I decided to go with them and have my eyes tested and my glasses changed. I feel very thankful for this opportunity for I have been so bothered about seeing for some time, and have been going to **Dr J. Fred Tesh** of High Point for the past eight years and he does all he can to keep my eye sight, for which I feel very grateful to him, and above all to Him from whom all blessing flow.

Blessed be His holy name.

Saturday April the 7th 1928

Cloudy and misting rain this morning, all able to be up and go about daily duties, for which I am very thankful to the Giver of all good, for to have health and strength sufficiend to arise from our beds and go about our work, which is necessary to be done for the comfort of our bodies is one of our greatest blessings. Praise the Lord.

April 1928

Sunday April the 8th 1928

A beautiful Easter Sabath morning. All able to be up and preparing for the services of the day, and altho I am feeling rather weak physically, I have a strong spiritual desire to attend Church on this memorable day of the Resurrection. and I very much wished to attend at dear old Springfield where I have a birthright membership in Friends Church and also wished to place flowers on my dear husbands grave. It is always a source of comfort to me to go to Springfield where I went to Sabath School and meeting in the days of my childhood and young womanhood and it is now still more sacred to me since the precious dust of so many of my loved ones lie there, but as I did not have the opportunity of attending service there today I went with the family to Mt Vernon Methodist Church to Sunday School as usual, for I am no Sectarian and when I am situated so I can not attend my own church I am glad of the opportunity to worship with others. and as **Mrs. Tedwell** the Teacher of our Class called upon me to offer prayer before taking up the work of the class I of course responded, and in my poor simple but sincere manner from my heart invoked a Divine blessing upon all for whom it is my duty to pray. which I trust will be owned and blessed of the Lord. Praised be His holy name.

Monday April the 9th 1928

A nice morning, all able to be up to day, but as this is Easter monday and a Legal holliday people are not going to their daily tasks as usual, some going on pleasure trips, some to service in various Churches and some to funerals. Many are gone to day to the funeral of a dear young girl of this community. A **Miss Mary Burge** who only lacked a few days of twenty years of age, who commited suicide by shooting herself in the head there seems to be no clue to the cause of this rash act. oh how sorrowful to think of her untimely death, but it is to be hoped that she was not in a state of mind to be accountable for the deed. but it should be a warning to all people to be close on our watch least we be overcome by temptation, for the enemy of our souls peace is ever ready and watching our weakest moments to try to draw us into his subtile snare which he has ready at all times for our feet. and we know that we are told in Gods written word that we shall give account of the deeds done in the body whether they be good or whether they be evil. and we know whether in youth or in age we shall all be called sooner or later to give account. And I have so often since thought of an Epitaph which I read on a Tombstone in the Cemetery at Guilford College when I was in my twentieth year of age in school at that place which was then called New Garden Boarding School. It made a deep impression my mind. and I wish that many on others It as follows

Stop blooming youth as you pass by.
As you are now so once was I.
As am now so you must be.
Prepare for death and follow me.

Tuesday April the 10th 1928

Rainey and quite cool this morning. All in usual health I am thankful to state. And I trust that we may all be trying to obey our Masters will in all things, and by His help we shall secced, to His honor and praise.

Wednesday April the 11th 1928

A very rainey day, and colder than yesterday. I am thankful that all are able to be up, even if we can not do much but sit by the fire, we can meditate upon the goodness and mercy of Him who gives us the rain and the sunshine at the appointed time, and we can read his holy word, wherein He gives us instruction how to follow Him. oh Father give us wisdom that we may more fully understand thy Word, and obey its teaching is my prayer.

Thursday April the 12th 1928

The sun is shineing this morning, which makes things look more cheerful. And I greatly desire that we all may have the sunshine of

Gods love in our hearts and praise Him for his care over us during the past night, and for strength to go about the duties of this day, and that all our days thruout the remainder of this journey here below may be spent in doing His will to his honor and praise, so that when done with the things of earth we may go where we can see Him face to face, and with the loved ones gone befor, sing His praises forever.

Friday April the 13th 1928

A nice clear morning. All able to arise from our beds and go about daily avocations, after having a quiet nights rest in sleep, for which I thank the Giver of all our blessings, for I often spend many sleepless hours, but the words, "He giveth His beloved sleep", came to me while pening these lines, and are a comfort to me. For altho I feel so unworthy, it proves to me that my merciful heavenly Father is watching over and caring for me at all times. Blessed be His holy name.

Saturday April the 14th 1928

Cloudy this morning. All able to arise from our beds and go about the duties of the day. oh that we may all rememer the duty and praise that we owe to him in whom we live and move and have our being, for His mercy and goodness to us his dependent unworthy children.

Sunday April the 15th 1928

Still quite cloudy, and has been raining during the night, but I am thankful for a good nights rest and for strength to be up, and use my pen to mutely testify to the goodness and mercy of my blessed Saviour to me and to mine, for He has watched over us all of our lives up to this time, and will take care of us unto the end. And will give us a home with Him when done with earth, if we love and obey Him as we should. Dear Lord help us to be faithful to the end is my prayer. Sunday evening, the weather turned out to be so very inclement, that none of us got out to Sunday School and Preaching this afternoon, which I very much regret as I have been favored to be there every sunday so far since this year came in, but we have no controll over the elements, so are in entire submishion to the will of Him who doeth all things well. Blessed be His holy name.

Monday April the 16th 1928

Clear and cold this morning, quite a goodeal of ice on tubs of water ets and we greatly fear that the fruit is injured in the bud, but leave it all in the hands of Him who hath the life of all things at His command. And I pray that we may all live in that way and manner of obedience unto him which will give us life eternal with Him forever and forever. Monday afternoon my daughter and I went over to Progress to cousin **Robert Blairs,** and in the evening **Robert jr** took his mother and myself over to cousin **Ed Blairs** to see his mothers cousin **Rachel Blair** who is quite sick in his home. Then came back to cousin **Roberts** and spent the night with them.

Tuesday April the 17th 1928

A most beautiful morning. All able to be up in this home the parents at work and the children gone to Trinity High School. I had a quiet nights rest in sleep last night and am feeling some stronger than when I left home as my ride in the fresh air yesterday seemed to do me good. I must take note of the pleasant visit I had last evening over to see cousin **Rachel Blair** she was so cheerful and seemed so glad to see me she was too weak to talk much but greeted us all with her sweet smile and seemed so perfectly resined to her lot. And Pastor dear **Clara I Cox** was there at the same time to see her and read an appropriate Psalm and offered a most excellent prayer which we all enjoyed so much. Praise the Lord for His mercy and tender care over us all. Well this afternoon I had the chance to go back to see cousin **Rachel** again and spent the time very pleasantly with her. cousin **Roxie Hill** also came over there on her wheel chair, or rather was brought on her chair for she is not strong enough to get about in it without help. she came to see her **Aunt Rachel**, who is in weak condition, **Mrs Wm Fry** who who lives near by, also came in and we all had a very interesting time together. Then I went back to cousin **Robert Blairs** and spent the night with them again. I had not been over to see them for several months I had a very pleasent and interesting visit both nights I was with them. And praise the Lord for this opportunity.

Wednesday April the 18th 1928

A very nice morning. Thankful to to be able to be up. And after spending the night again with my cousins as I have stated. This morning cousin **Robert Blair Sr** brought me over to cousin **John Hills** to spend the day with him and cousin **Roxie** who has to sit in her Wheel Chair all day and some times gets very lonely, and knowing as I do by experience, what it means not to be able to get about only on wheels for so many years, I have great sympathy for her and desire to be all the comfort to her that I possibly can. I feel that I have so much to be thankful for that I have been restored sufficient to get around with the aid of a staff without having to go on my Wheel Chair. Praise the Lord for His goodness and mercy to us all. Then this same evening cousin **Robert Blair jr** came with the car for me and brought me from cousin **John Hills** over to **Mr Wm Frys** and spent the night most pleasently with them.

Thursday April the 19th 1928

A lovely bright morning. After having a good nights rest in sleep at **Mr Frys** and feeling refreshed, **Mr. Frys** son **Paul Fry** brought me over to **Mr George Robins** to visit **Mrs Robins** as I had not been to see her for two years past. Their home is located on the same tract of land where I was born and raised, It brings many things of the past fresh to my mind as I look out at those dear old Cedars and the dear old home place which was so very dear to my childhood. I spent the day very pleasently with **Mrs Robins** and also staid over night with them.

Friday April the 20th 1928

Cloudy this morning. I am thankful to state that all are in usual health in this home, and I am feeling some stronger after a good nights rest. **Mrs Robins** has been so very kind to me, I feel that I can not be grateful enough. I think of going to see cousin **Sidney T Hill** to day if way opens to do so, as he is aged and lonely since his companion passed away. (Later in the day) I will now state that this morning after I had made my wish known, **Mr Robins** volenteered at once and took me to see cousin **Sidney Hills** as I had not been there since before his wife died more than two years ago. I had a very interesting visit with him and his son **Thomas** and family who live with him. before parting with them it was impressed upon my mind to read a chapter, and was led to read the encouraging chapter of the 14th of st John and also in my simple but sincere way invoked a divine blessing upon them. Then in the evening **Mr** and **Mrs George Robins** drove over there and brought me back home with them and was prevaild upon to stay over night again with them, they also drove out to the old buildings of my dear old home where I gathered Lilacks and other flowers and put them in a vace wher I could sit and look at them and meditate on the past, part of the buildings that were there in my young days were gone and things changed in many ways but still many things looked natural the main living room with the chimney built of stone up to the hips and brick the rest of the way looked so much like home that I had to stand and gaze at it and a large fig bush in one corner of it just like there was over half a Century ago, and those pretty old tall Cedars looked so very natural, and I drank water from the same well that my dear Father had dug almost as long ago as I can remember. I feel like I can not praise the Lord enough for the privilige of visiting that dear old place once more.

Saturday April the 21st 1928

I am thankful to state that all are well as usual here at **Mr Robins**. I had a very good nights rest and am spending the time very pleasently here having now spent two nights with them. And think of going to see cousin **Della Blair** to day if it is convenient for some one to take me over there, as she is in a rather critical state of health, having had a light stroke of paralyisis a few weeks ago. So **Mr Robins** kindly offered to take me over to **Sidney Blairs** to see him and **Della** they both gave me a pleasent smile and a hearty greeting. Altho **Della** was too weak to converse much, yet she seemed so glad to see me that she just would talk some, I took her a boquet of flowers that I gathered at my dear old home Lilack, and other things which she said she appreciated as much as I did, having visited that place in past and loved my dear Mother "**Aunt Polly Millikan**" as she called her, and she was familliarly called by that name by her many friends and acquintances far and near, and was much beloved. **Sidney** is getting quite feeble, hardly able to wait on himself but keeps up and seems very cheerful Their daughter **Anna Lee** who lives in High Point was there waiting on her Mother, the children all have been so good to come to see and care for their Mother and Father. Their son **Roland** was there, and before he returned to his home in High Point he took me over to **Walter Merediths** to visit them as I had not been to see them in near two years. **Roland** took his Father along with him for the ride in the fresh air, he is so kind to his parents, that I feel like he will reap the promised reward and I feel sure that all their children will be blessed for their faithfulness to their parents.

Sunday morning April the 22nd 1928

Cloudy this morning I did not rest very well last night as I was not feeling well, so feel rather dull this morning but thankful to be able to arise from my bed, am so glad to of had the privilige of visiting in this home for I have loved cousin **Florance** so much ever since she was a little girl and her dear Mother before her. I trust that I may be able to go with the family from here to Sunday School at Fairview to day.

Sunday afternoon. **Merediths** took me with them to S.S. at Fairview, which I regard as a great favor, as my dear husband and

I attended there often when we lived in our dear home which was but a short distance away. And we enjoyed it so much together as long as he lived. And to day brought memorys of the past so fresh I could not refrain from tears. They had a very interesting school session to day **Mrs Anna Cranford** who has been the Superintendent for years was present, and also her assistant **Clarence Meredith**, who taught the adult class, and gave a splendid lecture on the lesson. At the beginning of the service in opening the school **Mrs Cranford** called on this poor unworthy creature as I feel myself to be, to lead in prayer, of course I responded in my simple but earnest way from my heart looking to Him who has promised to be unto us "Mouth and wisdom tongue and utterunce" for of myself I can do nothing. And I praise his name that he is ever ready to help those who put their trust in Him, Then after school **Charlie Croker** took me home with him, his sister **Fannie** was also with him, I took dinner with them, and spent part of the afternoon with them, **Charlies wife** has a little babe three weeks old it is a very small and weak little creture and they have little hope of getting to raise it, but it is in the hands of the Lord who gave it to do what he sees best and he never makes any mistakes. Then in the evening **Charlie** brought me back to my daughters **Mrs J.W. Peaces** where I make my home, he had his sister also with us as he was taking her back to her place of work in High Point. but he came out of his way to bring me home and also called by cousin **Ed Blairs** for us to see **Eds Mother** dear cousin **Rachel Blair** who at this time is very critically ill. **Charlie** took his two little girls and his only little son with him in all his rounds, as he is so kind to care for them while their Mother is not able.

Monday April the 23rd 1928

Cloudy this morning. I am so thankful to be able to be up and do some little work for myself that was neccessary to be done, for it is a pleasure to do anything that I possibly can for myself so as to be that much help to some one else. And as I was blessed to have strength to visit the sick and afflicted the past week. I feel that I can not praise my blessed Saviour enough for His goodness to me in giving me strength and the opportunity to make those visits.

Tuesday April the 24th 1928

A beautiful morning. After having so much rain it seems nice to have such bright sunshine, and I am so thankful that we of this household are all able to arise from our beds to enjoy it. My daughter **May** and her little son **J.A**, and her husband **J.W. Peace** have just started to spend the day with **Mr** and **Mrs Charlie Fulp** who use to be close neighbors to them but now live at Trinity. Praise the Lord for all His blessings to us His dependent children. This evening we learn of the death of the little two year old daughter of **Mr** and **Mrs Walter Burr** who live in High Point, **Mrs Burr** is a sister to **Mr Gideon Bowman** who married **Mr J.W. Peaces daughter Ollie**.

Wednesday April the 25th 1928

Nice morning. All able to be up and go about daily vocations. I feel it to be a great blessing to be so I can wait on myself at the age of eighty three and ride out to see my friends occasionally and attend Church when the weather will permit, and my heat is filled with thankfulness to Him from whom all blessings flow from his goodness and mercy to me, for He has watched over me from my infancy until now, and will be with me until the end.

Wednesday evening. Well last evening I mentioned that we had learned of the death of the **little daughter** of **Mr** and **Mrs Burr**. This evening we have just returned from the funeral of **little Lois** at Glenola it was a touching scene. their first and only child and she looks like the picture of an angel which of course she now is, she was laid to rest in the new Cemetery at Glenola and her graves covered with flowers.

Thursday April the 26th 1928

A lovely bright morning. The birds are singing among the beautiful green foliage on the trees so cheerfully, and all nature seems to respond to the Creator of all things, and my hearts filled with praise to our blessed Saviour for all His blessings.

Friday April the 27th 1928

Raining this morning. The dampness causes me to have more aches and pains, but I am so thankfuk to still be so I can be up and care for myself and pen a few lines each day, to the praise of my merciful Heavenly Father who holds my life in his hands. I have a little Poem which was sent to me recently by my very dear friend **Fannie Croker** which I praise so much that I wish to insert it in my Diary for future reference, as it is so tiny it might otherwise get misplaced and no one reap to benefit of its words which we should all take heed to, I feel that I need to refer to its contents daily to keep me closer on my watch. "To be still and know" of God.

Be Still and Know

"Have faith in God; His love infolds;
No sparrow falls but He beholds;
No task too hard, no need too small
For Him whose love embraces all.
Have faith in God; Give Him your hand,
His heart of love will understand;
No lack too great for Him to fill;
O soul of man, be still, be still;
Have faith in God; He may not show
The how and why he will bestow
The strength to meet all winds that blow;
O child of God, be still and know;"

Henry Victor Merzan The Master Christian

Saturday April the 28th 1928

Another cloudy day and quite cool. I am very thankful to be able to arise from my bed, and that the others in this home are able to do the same. I wish to mention that my dear friend that sent me the nice piece of poetry, also referred me to some Texts of Scripture which I will insert here, in the hope it may help some one or ones as it has me. Second Corinthians 4-8 to 18. Matthew 5th chap. 10 to 12. For altho we may be greatly troubled and cast down and persecuted, yet if we cling to our dear Saviour he will enable us to bear all our trials and besetments in various ways, and help us to press on to follow Him, to the end of the journey. "For our light affliction which is but for a moment (compared with eternity) worketh for us a far more inceeding and eternal weight of glory.

Blessed be His holy name saith my soul.

Sunday April the 29th 1928

A beautiful sunshiney morning. All nature seems to be responding to the will of the great Creator bringing forth leaf and flower. Oh that we who are accountable beings may be as obedient to do His holy will in all things is my prayer for His dear names sake. I am so thankful that it is as well with us all as it is, and hope we may all do whatever is required of us to day, and each day as they go by, thru out the remainder of life journey to the praise and honor of Him who gave his dear Son to die for us all.

Monday April the 30th 1928

Clear this morning and much warmer. And this being the last day of the month it again brings afresh the flight of time. And that we are fast hastening eternity. I am so thankful that we are all able to arise from our beds and attend to our neccessary duties, for while life is lengthened out we have many things to attend to for the comfort and sustenance of these mortal bodies and we should be much more concerned for the preservation of our immortal souls which never die. "Lord who shall abide in thy tabernacle? who shall dwell in thy holy hill?" Psalm 18 will tell.

Tuesday May the 1st 1928

Cloudy this morning, had rain during the night. I am thankful to state that all are able to be up and go about daily avocations. This being the begining of another month, makes me feel desirous to renew my efforts to serve the Lord more faithfully than in the past. I am thankful that from my heart I can say with David. "I love the Lord because he hath heard my voice, and my supplication. Because he hath inclined his ear unto me, therefore will I call upon Him as long as I live." God being my helper

Psalm 116 1-2

Wednesday May the 2nd 1928

A lovely bright morning. After so much rain the sunshine seems all the more cheering. I am so thankful to be so I can still wait on myself, for I have such a dread of being a burden to others. And I also know what it means to be helpless and in a suffering condition for many years, so I feel very grateful to my merciful heavenly Father for raising me up to be even as well as I am. The praise belongeth to Him now and forever.

Thursday May the 3rd 1928

A nice warm morning. All in usual health. And this is my daughters **Mary Eliza Blair Stilwell Peace's** forty third Birthday it hardly seems possible that she has arrived to that age, for I seem to see her as a little plump baby, sitting on a pallet when she was but little more than four months old. Oh the changes that have taken place since then, she has since been married then left a widow, and now married the second time, and myself now a widow and making my home with her at this time, and in looking back with my minds eye, I see her a little girl going to the district school, near our home, then later going to high school in Thomasville N.C, and boarding with her brothers family there, And also at that place she met her first husband **Mr Arthur Lee Stilwell** of Charlotte N.C. who was A Merchant. with whom she lived with happily for fifteen years until he was taken down with that dreaded disease Influanza and also took on pneumonia and only survived about one week. And oh how we all missed him, he was a fine Christian gentleman and treated me as though I had been his own Mother. And as time passed my daughter married again, this time a farmer Mr **Jerome W. Peace** of Randolph County who lived but a short distance from where she was raised also on a farm, he always provides well for his family etc.

Last night I went with some of the family to the childrens exercises which was the beginning of the Trinity High School Commencement. the children gave a delightful entertainment, which I think was very much enjoyed by all. I am thankful I could attend.

Yesterday afternoon **Prof Pegram** was buried here at old Trinity. **Dr William Howard Pegras** eighty two years of age, died at his home in Durham N.C. Monday April the 30th 1928. And his remains were brought to old Trinity in Randolph county for burial he was laid beside his wife who died some years ago, she was the daughter of **Dr Braxton Craven** who was the founder of old Trinity College.

Friday May the 4th 1928

A lovely morning, all able to be up and enjoy the bright sunshine everything seem to be responding to the voice of Him who gave them life. I feel that we have so much to thank our great Benefactor for, for He fulfils all his promices to us, unworthy as we are.

Saturday May the 5th 1928

All able to be up and attend to the duties of the day. **Mr and Mrs J.W. Peace** are going to quarterly meeting to day at Mt Giliad hope they will have a good meeting. Later in the day. Their daughter **Minnie** and myself both desided to accompany them to Giliad, heard a good sermon by the presiding elder **J.D. Craven** and enjoyed a bountiful noon day lunch. Praise the Lord for His goodness to his dependent ones.

Sunday May the 6th 1928

Quite cool this morning. All in usual health in this home, and are preparing to go to Sunday School at Mt Vernon, as it is to be held this morning instead of afternoon as usual, in order to attend thr Annual Comencement sermon this afternoon at Trinity which will be preached by the presiding elder the **Rev J,D. Craven**, My heart is filled with thanks to the great Giver of all our blessings for strength sufficient to attend the "assembling togeather as the manner of some is." (A Correction.) My mind was so occupied with the thought of Rev J.D. Cravens good sermon on Saturday that I made the mistake of writing his name instead of **D Rondthaler**.

Monday May the 7th 1928

Still cool and also cloudy this morning. All well as as usual for which I am thankful. I will state that we were favored to attend Sunday School yesterday at Mt Vernon at nine thirty. Then in the afternoon at three oclock attended the services at Trinity The Baccalereate Sermon was preached by **Dr. Howard E. Rondthaler** President of Salem College, which was very interesting and instructive. The twenty three Graduates eleven girls, and twelve boys, made a lovely background for the Rostrum, my prayer for them is, that they may all live good, useful and successful lives, and obtain a crown of righteousness in the end.

Tuesday May the 8th 1928

Cloudy and cold this morning. All able to be up and attend to daily affaira, for which I am thankful.

May 1928

Wednesday May the 9th 1928

Still cloudy this morning. All able to arise from our beds and go about daily avocations for which I am grateful, and hope that we will all remember the debt we owe our blessed Redeemer for giving his precious life for us, and day by day obey his devine commands

Thursday May the 10th 1928

A nice bright day, which seems delightful after having so much rain, but we should never murmer of these contrasts, for the great Creator who holds the elements in his hands knows what is best. And both the rain and sunshine are necessary to life and growth. We have just returned from attending the Annual Literary Address to the Graduates at Trinity by **Dr Charles E. Brever** President of Meredith College, he gave a fine Address so practical and instructive it seemed to be greatly appreciated in general. The attendance at Trinity Commencement brings many things of the past fresh to my mind for I attended them there in my young days.

Friday May the 11th 1928.

Another nice clear morning. I am thankful that I can state that we of this household are all able to be up, and attend to the neccessities of life. We were favored to attend the final class of the Commencement exercises last night at Trinity and see the Graduates receive their Diplomas it was a pretty sight and was very entertaining from start to finish. and I wish for them all great success in life.

Saturday May the 12th 1928.

Clear and some cooler this morning. All able to go about daily avocations. I feel very grateful indeed that I still have the use of my hands and thinking faculties to express with my pen the goodness and mercy of our gracious heavenly Father who takes care of us from day to day. Oh that we may all be close on our watch that we do not disobey His divine commands, for we want to have a right to the tree of life that never decays, when done with the things of earth that perish with the useing.

Oh God help us to do thy will in all things for Christs sake.

"I will lift up mine eyes unto the hills, from whence cometh my help. My help cometh from the Lord which made heaven and earth," Psalm 12 –1-2.

Sunday May the 13th 1928.

A lovely Sabbath morning. All are able to be and prepare to attend Sunday School this afternoon at Mt Vernon as usual. And as this day the second Sunday in May is set apart Anually Mothers day, I hope we shall have a good attendnce and much interest manifested in praiseing the Lord for our good Mothers.

Monday May the 14th 1928

Another nice morning. All in usual health, I am thankful to state. We were all favored to attend the Sunday School, and Mothers day exercises yesterday. There was a large attendance, and a very interesting program, appropriate songs recitations etc. I feel that we have much to thank our heavenly Father for that He has confered so many blessings upon us all.

Tuesday May the 15th 1928.

Nice clear morning. All this family able to be on the stage of action. I am feeling rather weak and nervous, but thankful that it is as well with me as it is and desire to be faithful in dischargeing my duty whatever it may be. "O Lord, thou hast serched me, and known me. Thou knowest my downsitting and my uprising, thou understandest my thought a far off." Hold me by thy rite hand that I go not astray.

Wednesday May the 16th 1928.

A nice clear morning, and also warmer. All able to arise from our beds and attend to household affairs which is much to be thankful for, as there are several at this time lying upon sick beds, with no prospect of recovery. Yesterday my daughter **Mrs J.W. Peace** took **Grandma Peace** and myself to visit the sick. We first went to see **Della Blair (Sidneys wife)** she is Parylised and is very lowe. next we visited Cousin **Rachel Blair** widow of **B.F. Blair** she is in a very critical condition having some kind of an internal growth. and not expected to recover. Then we went to see **Ellen Gray** widow of **Oscar Gray** she is suffering from Cancer and near deaths door. I surely know how to sympathise with the sick and afflicted, having suffered for so many years. And as my blessed Saviour has seen fit to raise me up for a time, my greatest desire is to be forward doing whatever He calls for at my hands, for I know that I have been spared for a purpose and my prayer is that I may fulfil that purpose to the honor and praixe of Him who shed His precious blood for me and for all his dependent ones.

Thursday May the 17th 1928

A nice warm morning. All in usual health. This night is the appointed time for the neighborhood prayer meeting to be held in this home, my greatest desire is that our hearts may be prepared to receive any message which the dear Lord may send us thru the mouth of His servants or handmaidens, and this His presence may be graciously felt in our midst, to his honor and praise.

Saturday evening May the 19th 1928

This has been a nice warm day. But I have had to keep my bed to day, for the first time in several months, I have suffered severely last night and to day with pain in my left side, and with a nervous breakdown, but thankful that I am now feeling some better. Praise the Lord for His tender care over me.

Sunday May the 20th 1928

A nice Sabbath morning. The family here are all well except myself, and I am feeling some better to day, than I did yesterday. I am sorry to have to miss Sunday School and Preaching to day, for I have not missed but one time this year, and that day it rained so hard we could not go. I am so very thankful that I have strength to use my pen to again take note of the goodness and mercy of the Lord to me who feels so unworthy of His protecting care.

Monday May the 21ˢᵗ 1928

Clear this morning. All able to be up and going except myself. And I am thankful to be feeling some better, and hope I shall be able to sit up more to day. I praise the Lord that He gave me more rest in sleep last night. Later in the day. I have been blessed this afternoon, with the company of our Springfield Pastor **Clara I Cox** of High Point, her visits are always so welcome, for her presence and her excelent prayers seem to reach the throne of grace and do me so much good, for often when I feel almost ready to faint by the way her message cheers me up and helps me to take courage to press on. Blessed be the name of the Lord now and forever.

Tuesday May the 22ⁿᵈ 1928

Another nice morning. The family here are all up and attending to daily affairs. I am trying to sit up this morning and take note of the blessings we enjoy. I was blessed to spend most of the latter half of the night in sleep, which I so much needed, and for which I thank my merciful heavenly Father, for it is He who watches over and cares for us at all times, and last evening dear **Clara Cox** plead so earnestly that the Lord would give me relief from suffering and grant me quiet rest in sleep, so I feel that He heard and answered her prayer on my behalf. And I prayer that the Lord will bless her abundantly with His holy spirit and give her great success in her work for Him. Praise be His name.

Wednesday May the 23ᵗʰ 1928

A nice warm morning. The family here are not all as well as usual, the little son **J.A. Peace** is not at all well spent a restless night with high fever, but seems better this morning. I also spent a restless night, but finally got some rest in sleep in the latter part of the night, so I am trying to be up and take note of the goodness and mercy of the Lord to us his dependent children, for He watches over us by day and by night. Last night our hearts were made sad by news of the death of dear cousin **Rachel Blair,** sad at the thought of how we shall miss her from our social circle here below, but we have such a blessed assurance that she is now forever at rest, that we can the more cheerfully give her up, for her suffering had become great. And while it is is so natural that we can not help but weep at the loss of our dear friends, yet when we realise that our loss is their gain, we should be in entire subjection to the Masters will, and prepare to meet them in the better land. Cousin **Rachels Mother** and my Mother were sisters, and we have been intimately associated from our youth and loved each other dearly. And her husband and my husband were second cousins. So we were intimately associated in many ways, her husband was the late **Benjamin Franklin Blair** who passed away several years ago, my husband the late **John Addison Blair** passed away eight years ago so cousin **Rachel** and myself have know how to sympathise with eah other in our widowhood. Cousin **Rachel Blair** passed away on Tuesday evening May the 22nd 1928.

Thursday May the 24th 1928

Nice clear morning, and cool enough to be pleasent. The family here in general are well as usual, the little son is much better to day I am glad to note, and in regard to my own health, I am far from feeling strong, but after a quiet nights rest, I am so very thankful that I had sufficient strength to ride over to cousin **Ed Blairs** to see the remains of dear cousin **Rachel** before she was taken to Springfield for burial, The profusion of flowers was a beautiful sight to see. I regreted very much not being able to attend the funeral for I know there would be an interesting service.

Friday May the 25th 1928

Cloudly this morning and warmer, all better here to day, I was able to ride out a short distance to day for which I feel very thankful to my heavenly Father for it semes to strengthen my nerves to ride out in the fresh air, and as I have felt quite feeble for a week past I am so grateful for strength sufficient to ride out.

Saturday May the 26th 1928

Nice morning, all so we can arise from our beds but I am still feeling feeble this moring but I am so glad that I am not bedfast as was my lot for so many years in the past, that I feel like I can not thank my merciful heavenly Father enough that he gives me strength to arise and use my pen in honor to His ever worthy name.

Sunday May the 27th 1928

Cloudy and misting rain this morning. we are all able to be up I am thankful to state, but I do not get to feeling strong. Yesterday we learned of the death of **Ellen Gray**, widow of later **Oscar Gray**, her funeral is to be held at three oclock to day at Marlboro and she will be laid in the Cemetary there by the side of her husband. **Ellen** passed away, May the 26th 1928. I wish very much to attend the funeral but have not sufficient strength to do so, but hope I may be able to go to her home, to pay my last respects. Later. I went to the home and saw her and the many beautiful flowers in rememberance of her, but could not attend the funeral.

Monday May the 28th 1928

Clear this morning, after rain during the night. I am still feeling weak, but thankful to be so I can be out of bed. Another of this family is sick this moring. Mr Peaces step daughter **Mary Lee Stilwell**, but I trust it will not prove serious, we have much to be thankful for, with all the trials and besetments in this life. for our merciful heavenly Father does not permit more to come upon us, than He will enable us to bear.

Tuesday May the 29th 1928

A lovely bright morning. All are feeling some better for which I feel very thankful, and praise the Lord for His goodness and mercy to us all.

Wednesday May the 30th 1928

Another nice morning all improving the stepdaughter is able to be up this morning. I am still feeling weak but thankful that we are all so we can be out of bed. I praise the Lord that is as well with us as it is, for it has been our lot for some time for some one of the family to be indisposed. So we have much to thank God for.

Thursday May the 31st 1928

A nice clear morning. All able to arise from our beds. I am very thankful for this favor, and as it is the last day of the month, I am again reminded of the flight of time and that we should be prepared for eternity. When I look at the lovely flowers that God has made to beautify this Earth. I think what must be the beauty and splendor of that Home that we are told of in His word, That it has never entered into the heart of man to conceive the things which He has prepared for those that love Him. Praise the Lord.

Friday June the 1st 1928

A lovely bright morning. All able to be up, and altho I still feel weak in body, yet my mind is strong in the faith that God is love, and He will take care of those who put their trust in Him. and now at the beginning of another month I want to be more and more faithful to obey the commandments of Him who has done so much for me.

Saturday June the 2nd 1928

Cloudy this morning and much warmer. All up and going about daily avocations, I had a good nights rest in sleep, for which I feel very grateful to the giver of all good for His tender mercies over us all. "I will lift up mine eyes unto the hills, from whence cometh my help. My help cometh from the Lord which made heaven and earth." Help me dear Lord to put my whole trust in Thee.

Sunday June the 3rd 1928

Cloudy and raining some this morning. All able to arise from our beds, for which I am thankful, but the dampness causes more aches and pains in my limbs. but I hope if the rain holds up I shall be able to get out to Sunday School, as I have had to miss the last two Sabbaths, and I regret to have to miss. Later in the day. Thankful to state I was favored to attend Sunday School and preaching. Praise the Lord.

Monday June the 4th 1928

Still cloudy this morning. All able to be up and go about daily duties, for which I am very thankful.

Tuesday June the 5th 1928

Cloudy again this morning. Nothing of interest to note only the continued goodness and mercy of the Lord to us unworthy cretures, for He has given us rest the past night, and strength to arise from our beds and go about daily avocations, for which I give Him thanks. "Though I walk in the midst of trouble, thou wilt revive me; thou shalt stretch fort thine hand against the wrath of mine enemies, and thy right hand shall save me." "The Lord will perfect that which concerneth me; thy mercy O Lord, endureth for ever forsake not the works of thine own hands." Psalm 138-7-8

Wednesday June the 6th 1928

Clear and warm this morning. All able to be up and go about daily avocations. Altho I feel weak and very much discouraged by the onslaughts of the enemy, yet my prayer is unto Him who has promiced that we shall not be tempted beyond that which He will enable us to bear, so I am standing on the promices and trusting that I shall be made to conquer over the enemy of our souls peace, through Him that loved us and gave himself for us. Blessed by His name.

Thursday June the 7th 1928

Cloudy and cool this morning. The weather is so very changeable that it gives people colds. I am weak and nervous, but thankful that I can keep up as well as I do. but it is only by trusting in the Lord and leaning on His strong arm to give me strength to arise from my bed, and wait on myself, which I am so anxious to do, that I may not be a burden to others, and so thankful to have sufficient eyesight to read His holy word, and to have the use of my hand to pen a line in honor of His goodness and mercy to me and all His dependent ones. Blessed be the name of the Lord in whom we live and move. For of ourselves we can do nothing.

Friday June the 8th 1928

Nice clear morning. All in usual health I am thankful to state. and I am looking to the Great giver of all good for strength sufficient for the day. for He has promiced "That as thy day thy strength shall be." and I am standing on the promices. So I say with one of old. "Hear my prayer O Lord and let my cry come unto thee" "Hide not thy face from me in the day when I am in trouble incline thine ear unto me; in the day when I call answer me speedily." "Bless the Lord O my soul; and all that is within me, bless his holy name. Bless the Lord O my soul and forget me not all his benefits, who forgiveth all thine inquities; who healeth all thy diseases." Psalm 103-1-2-3

Saturday June the 9th 1928

Clear and warm this morning. All able to be up and go about daily avocations. I was blessed to spend last night in quiet sleep, for which I am thankful for. I have spent so many nights in wakefulness and suffering. We are expecting my son **Fred C. Blair** and family from

Charlotte to spend this Saturday night with us if the weather keeps favorable. Praise the Lord.

Sunday June the 10th 1928

Clear and warm this morning. All in usual health. We were favored to have our company arive safely last night, they were late coming and we were anxious for fear they had met with an oxident, but all was well with them for which I am very thankful. My son and wife and their two daughters **Emily** and **May** went to Church in High Point this morning and came back and took dinner with us, then returned to their home in Charlotte in the evening, it made me sad to give them up. Their only son **Fred jr** was out on a camping trip with a crowd of the Young Mens Christian Temperance Union, so we did not have the pleasure of his company.

Monday June the 11th 1928

Cloudy this morning had rain during the night. I have a headache and am weak and nervous this morning but thankful to be so I can be up and use my pen and thinking faculties. I must note the glad surprise we had yesterday afternoon by the arrival of **Mr** and **Mrs Homer Fesperman** and little daughter **Rachel** from Salisbury. It was entirely unexpected, but we certainly did enjoy this company. **Mrs Cathleen Fesperman** is the daughter of **Mr** and **Mrs George Stilwell**. I spent some time in their homes last year in Salibury and was so very kindly entertained. I shall ever appreciate them.

Tuesday June the 12th 1928

Still cloudy this morning. All in usual health I am thankful to state. and altho I am so unworthy of all my blessings, I know that the dear Lord has watched over me during another night, and has given me rest in sleep, and strength to arise from my bed this morning, and also all the members of this household, for which we owe Him reverence and obedience, now and forever. Blessed by the name of the

Lord for his goodness and mercy to us his poor unworthy cretures. They that trust in the Lord shall be as mount Zion, which cannot be removed, but abideth for ever. Psalm 125-1

Wednesday June the 13th 1928

Clear this morning and much warmer. All able to arise from our beds and go about daily work for which I am thankful to the Giver of all good, and my prayer is, Teach me thy way oh Lord and lead me in a plain path, that I may know what thou would have me to do, and what thou would have me leave undone to Thy names honor and praise.

Thursday June the 14th 1928

Clear and warmer this morning. I have a bad headache this morning, and sick at my stomach and nervous, but thankful to be so I can be up. The rest of the family are well as usual. Praise the Lord for his goodness to us.

Friday June the 15th 1928

Nice clear morning, All up and busy at daily avocations, I am weak and nervous but thankful to be so I can be up and wait on myself. Nothing of interest to note this morning only the continued goodness and mercy of the Lord to his dependent children. Blessed by His name. "I love the Lord, because he hath heard my voice and my supplication. Because he hath inclined his ear unto me, therefore will I call upon him as long as I live." Psalm 166-1-2

Saturday June the 16th 1928

A nice clear morning. All in usual health for which I feel very thankful and desire that we all may be kept close on our watch that we do not disobey the Divine commandments for we want to have a home with the blessed when done with the things of earth. and we know that if we do not fulfil the conditions laid down in Gods holy word, we cannot hope to have an entrance into that City which is prepared for those who love and serve Him on earth. Father help us to obey.

Sunday June the 17th 1928

Cloudy this morning. All able to be up, and I trust will be able to get out to Sunday School and Church. Later. We were all favored to be at Sunday School, had a splendid lesson. The Teacher **Mrs Ledwell** called on me to offer prayer before beginning the lesson, this I felt very unworthy to do, but responded in my simple but sincere way, as the dear Lord gave me utterance I have often been called upon the invoke a divine blessing before the class, and I always say in my heart dear Lord speak through me, for of myself I can do nothing, and trust that no matter how simple the words, that they will be owed and blessed of the Lord to his names honor and praise.

Monday June the 18th 1928

Cloudy and warm this morning. All able to arise from our beds, and go about our various duties. Praise the Lord for this goodness and mercy to us all.

Tuesday June the 19th 1928

Clear and quite warm this morning. All in usual health and busy at work, for which we have much to thank the great Giver of all good for sufficient health and strength to do that which our hands find to do. Praise His holy name.

Wednesday June the 20th 1928

A nice clear morning, all up and busy as usual, The prayer of heart this morning is, Teach me thy way oh Lord and lead me in a plain path, that I may know just what is well pleasing in thy sight, for I want to do thy will oh Lord thou knowest, for thou knows my heart.

Thursday June the 21st 1928

Cloudy this morning. The dampness causes my limbs to ace, but thankful to be up and use my pen to mutely testify to the goodness and mercy of my blessed Saviour who watches over me by day and by night, and suffers no harm to come to me and mine. Blessed by His holy name.

Friday June the 22ⁿᵈ 1928

Still cloudy this morning. All in usual health, for which I am thankful. and in my meditation this morning the words of this Hymn comes to my mind. "Oh for a closer walk with God a calm and heavenly frame, A light to shine upon the road that leads me to the Lamb." yes my desire is to walk closer and closer each day, that I may know His will concerning me, and walk in obedience there to, and that the light of His holy spirit may shine in my heart to enlighten my understanding, that I may not miss my way, and be led into the darkness of doubts and fears and unbelief, for thou who knows my heart, knows that I believe on Thee and on thy dear Son who died for me, yes for me, for it was for the sins of the whole world therefore my sins, and when He said whosoever will, may come unto me, He included me. "Have mercy upon me, O God according to thy loveing kindness; according unto the multitude of thy tender mercies blot out my transgressions. Wash me thoroughly from mine iniquity and cleanse me from my sin." Psalm 51-1-2

Saturday June the 23ʳᵈ 1928

Still some cloudy, and quite warm this morning. All able to be up and doing. The Parents gone to High Point shoping, the children attending to the various chores to be done, and I am trying to pen a few lines to leave on record to show that I am endeavoring to live close to the Master, and do whatever He requires, at my hands if its but to pen a line in honor to His holy name, that I may be a liveing example to those with whom I meet and mingle, for although I often make mistakes and come short of doing and being what is my chief desire to do and be, yet I rejoice that the One who knows all things knows that I am striveing day by day to do His holy will, and by

His help I am found for the promiced land, where I can praise Him throughout eternity, with loved ones gone before.

Sunday June the 24th 1928

Cloudy again this morning. All well as usual and most of the family are preparing for Sunday Schoool at Mt Vernon which is to be held this morning in order to attend the Sunday School Convention at Archdale this afternoon. I shall not go to Mt Vernon, as I wish to attend the Convention. and do not feel strong enough for both.

Monday June the 25th 1928

Cloudy again this morning. All able to be up and go about daily affairs. for which I am very thankful. I was favored to attend the Methodist Sunday School Conferance yesterday at Archdale, with others of the family, and enjoyed it very much. We arrived in time for the seven oclock service which was presided over by their Pastor the **Rev – Jones**. he gave us a splendid message. The Choir did fine. The Superintendent of this Township Convention **Miss Carrie Cranford** had a splendid Program for the day, good Addresses by good speakers, were attentively listened to by a large congregation, and the childrens demonstration of how their splendid Teacher had taught their class etc all was fine, and very instructive, especially to other Sunday School classes of children. There was a long Table in the grove laden with the good things to strengthen and refresh our bodies which had been prepared by the ladies in general of the community and made welcome for one and all. The afternoon service was led by the **Rev Ruben Payne** Pastor of Friends Church Archdale which was very much enjoyed and the rotine of the business of the conference carried out, more good speaking etc ets and close by singing. Blest Be The Tie That Binds.

Tuesday June the 26th 1928

Still some cloudy this morning. All so we can be up and attend to things necessary to be done I am thankful to state. and after pertaking of food for the nourishment of the perishable bodies, I am desireous to be fed with that spiritual food from the Masters table which alone can nourish up our souls unto life eternal, thru Jesus Christ our Lord.

Wednesday June the 27th 1928

Nice and cool this morning. All able to be on the stage of action, for which I am thankful, for I know what it means to be helpless for many years, in the past, and as the dear Lord has been pleased to give me sufficient strength to wait on myself, and to walk once more, instead of having to go on my Wheel Chair altogeather as in the past, I feel that I cannot thank Him enough for His goodness to me. We are favored to day to have the company of **Mr Peaces** daughter **Mrs Gideon Bowman** and sweet babe **Gideon jr** and **Miss Dora Peace** daughter of **Mr June Peace**. with us to spend the day which we are enjoying very much. and I wish to return thanks to our merciful heavenly Father for all His benefits to his unworthy, dependent children.

Thursday June the 28th 1928

Another nice cool morning. All in usual health I am thankful to note. And my prayer is heavenly Father help me to know thy will, and to obey it this day and every day thruout the remainder of this lifes journey to Thy names honor and praise, that I may merit a home with thee, where I can sing Thy praise forever with the loved ones gone before.

Friday June the 29th 1928

Cloudy this morning, had a refreshing shower during the night. All are able to be up and go about the necessary work for the day. We have much to thank our Great Benefactor for. Praise His holy name.

Saturday June the 30th 1928

A nice clear morning, after a refreshing rain in the night. All are in usual health thank the Great Giver of all our blessings, for in Him we live and move and have our being. Praised be the name of the Lord, saith my soul. I am glad that I can truly say with the Psalmist, "I love the Lord because he hath heard my voice and my supplication. Because he hath included his ear unto me, therefore will I call upon Him as long as I live." Psalm 116-1-2

Sunday July the 1st 1928

A nice Sabbath morning. I am very thankful that I can again state that all are in usual health. and this being the beginning of another month again reminds me of the flight of time, and that we should all be prepared for eternity, for we know not the day nor the hour nor the moment when she shall be called to give account of the deeds done in the body. Father in Heaven help us to so live at all times, that we may be ready for thy sumons, to thy names honor and praise. We were favored last evening with the company of the Mt Vernon Pastor **Rev Reed Haris** and wife and three fine little boys, which we all enjoyed I told his wife they were bound to keep up the name of **Haris**, I wish that those boys may all be as fine men as their Father. Praise the Lord oh my soul.

Monday July the 2nd 1928

A nice warm morning. All able to be up and go about daily duties, for which I praise the Lord, and desire to be close on my watch, that I do not transgress His commandments in word or deed. We were favored last evening with the company of some of our kindred and children, **Mr** and **Mrs Bayles** and their two little girls. Which we enjoyed.

Tuesday July the 3rd 1928

Nice clear morning. All in usual health and busy at daily avocations. Father in heaven keep me close to thee this day, and every succeding day thruout the remainder of my journey on earth, that I may know thy will and obey it, that I may be a living example to others, that I am endeavoring to walk in the footsteps of Jesus. for vain is the help of man. Praise the Lord. "Praise ye the Lord. Praise O ye servants of the Lord, praise the name of Lord. Blessed by the name of the Lord from this time forth and for evermore." Psalm 173-1-2

Wednesday July the 4th 1928

A beautiful bright morning. All in usual health, for which I thank Him in whom we have our being. This the fourth of July being set apart to Celebrate the Declaration of Independence. I feel that we should not only Celebrate our liberty as a nation but that we should give God the praise for all our blessings, and remember that we are all Dependent upon Him for even the breath we draw. and endeavor to honor His name above every name and obey His holy will in all things, for Jesus sake.

Thursday June the 5th 1928

A bright warm morning. All in usual health, for which I feel very grateful, for when we have a degree of health sufficient to wait on our selves and go about out daily duties I consider it one of our greatest blessings. Praise the Lord for it. "Bless the Lord oh my soul; and all that is with in me, bless his holy name. Bless the Lord, O my soul, and forget not all his benefits; Who forgiveth all thine iniquities; who healeth all thy diseases." "Like as a father pitieth his children, so the Lord pitieth them that fear him." Psalm 103

Friday July the 6th 1928

A nice clear morning. All able to be up and doing whatever is necessary to be done, that the hands find to do, and I am so thankful that I still have the use of my hands, and mental faculties so I can pen down a reminder of the goodness and mercy of God to his dependent children, in that He has given us rest in sleep, and given us strength to arise from our beds, and go about our daily work. Blessed be His holy name. "From the riseing fo the sun, to the going down of the same Gods name is to be praised."

Saturday July the 7th 1928

A fine morning. All in usual health, and busy at work, some of them are planting their fall potatoes to day. the good housewife busy in the kitchen. I am thankful to of had a good nights rest, and strength sufficient to wait on myself this morning. I must take note of the glad surprise we had yesterday. My daughterinlaw **Mrs Fred C. Blair** from Charlotte and their son **Fred jr** and little sister **May**, came driveing in about twelve oclock. They came to attend a funeral at High Point, the Aunt of **Mrs – Sayers** who my daughterinlaw has known favorably for many years and wished to pay her respect by attending her funeral, I do not remember the aged ladies name. After they received the Telegrahm they decided to come to High Point and while this near to run out here to see us all a little while, which we all enjoyed very much indeed, for it is so seldom we see them. Praise the Lord for all His benefits.

Sunday July the 8th 1928

Some cloudy this morning, rain during the night. All able to be up and prepare for the services of the day. Praise the Lord.

Monday July the 9th 1928

Cloudy again this morning, and very warm. All in usual health I am thankful to state. I had strength to attend Sunday School yesterday at Mt Vernon, and after returning home we were favored with the company of our friends and relatives. Cousin **R.L.M. Blair** and wife **Ocid Redding Blair** came they had not called on us for some time, as the sickness and death of their Mother, cousin **Rachel Blair**, had kept them close at home for several months, we enjoyed having them with us very much. Praise the Lord, for it is from Him we receive all our pleasures and benefits.

Tuesday July the 10th 1928

Raining this morning. The dampness causes my limbs to ache more, but I am thankful to be so I can be up and wait on myself, and that the rest of this family are in usual health. Praise the Lord for His goodness and mercy to us His dependent cretures. for He takes care of us by day and by night, and suffers no harm to come to us. "O give thanks unto the Lord for he is good; for his mercy endreth forever." Psalm 107-1

Wednesday July the 11th 1928

Cloudy and very warm this morning. All able to be up, for which I thank the good Lord for all His benefits to us. I have nothing of importance to take note of at this time, but by pening down a line or two each day it keeps me closer on my watch least I let the tempter come into my heart and mind and cause me to disobey the golden rule when I am so sorely tried as I am, more or less every day in various ways, for my greatest desire is to live in obedience to Gods holy will, and obey His commandments and altho I fall short of doing this at all time, yet I know that God knows my heart, and that He has forgiven my transgressions, and pitties my weakness for He knows the spirit is willing, but the flesh is weak. We were favored last evening with a call from **Mr** and **Mrs Gideon Bowman** and their sweet babe **jr.** Also by short visit by **Mr** and **Mrs Ferney Peace** and their two children, all of which we enjoyed very much.

Thursday July the 12th 1928

Cloudy again this morning. I am thankful to of had a good nights rest in sleep, and to be able to be up and use my pen, and that the rest of the family are well as usual. Praise the Lord for His goodness and mercy to us all.

Friday July the 13th 1928

Still cloudy and damp. I am feeling rather feeble this morning, but thankful to be able to be up and wait on myself, the rest of the family are all up and at work. Praise the Lord for His goodness to His dependent children.

Saturday July the 14th 1928

I am thankful to state that all are about in our usual health at this time. The sun comes out this morning, then suddenly closes again, which reminds me of the voyage of life, for sometimes our lives seem to be filled with the sunshine of love and happiness, then some unforeseen calamity comes upon us to cloud our minds with dark forebodings and discouragement, and we have to look steadfastly to the Source of all our help and comfort, trusting that the clouds of doubt and fear will be dispelled from our hearts and minds, and the Son of righteousness shine forth in our hearts to give us courage to press on our way rejoiceing that we have such a kind and loveing Saviour who cares for us. Last evening something over thirty young people boys and girls and their chapherones went on a Sunday School Class Picknick from Mt Vernon to Wilomore Springs. They report to of had a very enjoyable time, but got well drenched with rain and mud before they got home, but as they were favored to not have any accident, the pleasure of the trip attoned for their baptism with rain and red mud. Thanks be to Him in whom their lives were, for their safe return to their many different homes.

Sunday July the 15th 1928

A pretty bright Sabbath morning. All in usual health I am thankful to state. But this morning we are again reminded of the uncertainty of life and the certainty of death sooner or later to us all, as we hear of the death of **Esq. Nease Elder** who passed away last Friday July the 12th 1928. At Hopewell Virginia. where he and his family have lived for several years, since leaveing North Carolina he was a man I always thought a greatdeal of and he and my dear husband who has gone before him were special friends, they were play mates and school mates in their childhood and youth, and close friends as long as life was spared to them.

Monday July the 16th 1928

Another nice morning. All able to be up and go about daily avocations, which is much to thank our merciful heavenly Father for. Blessed be His holy name, for all His benefits to us. Last evening we were favored with the company of cousin **Edd** and **Anna Blair** which was quite a treat as they had not been here for quite awhile.

Tuesday July the 17th 1928

A nice clear morning. All able to be up and attend to the affairs of the day. I am thankful to state. Yesterday **J.W. Peaces** son, **Grady Peace** who lives at Archdale, and works at Wilsons Garage in High Point had the misfortune to get painfully but we trust not seriously burned when the Gas caught fire at the Garage and blistered his face and arms, so thankful its no worse.

Wednesday July the 18th 1928

Some cloudy and quite warm this morning. All able to go about daily avocations I am thankful to note. May the dear Lord help us to be close on our watch this day that we go not astray fom Him is my prayer. Blessed the Lord o my soul. Psalm 104

Thursday July the 19th 1928

A nice clear morning, and quite warm, Glad that I can still state that all are up and able to go about the affairs of the day. The Lord be praised for His goodness and mercy to His dependent children. not unto us O Lord, not unto us, but unto thy name give glory, for thy mercy, and for thy truth's sake. Psalm 115-1

Friday July the 20th 1928

Another nice morning, All still in our usual state of health, I am thankful to note. And the Wheat Thrashers are expected here to day, to thrash out the grain, oh how thankful we should be for the grain God gives us for our bread. All our blessings come from Him, in whom is all life and power. "Praise God from whom all blessings flow. Praise Him all cretures here below, Praise Him all ye heavenly host, Praise Father Son and holy ghost."

Saturday July the 21st 1928

Clear and very warm this morning. All able to be up and at work, for which I am thankful. "I will lift up mine eyes unto the hills, from whence cometh my help, my help cometh from the Lord, which made heaven and earth." for vain is the help of man.

Sunday July the 22nd 1928

A clear morning, and very warm again to day. I am thankful we are all able to be up and prepare for Sunday School its this afternoon. "Blessed the Lord o my soul; and all that is within me, bless his holy name. Bless the Lord O my soul, and forget not all his benefits."

Monday July the 23rd 1928

Still clear and very warm. Nothing special interest to note this morning, only the continued goodness and mercy of the dear Lord to us dependent cretures, in giveing us a degree of health and strength sufficient to go about our daily avocations. Blessed be His holy name.

Tuesday July the 24th 1928

Nice warm morning. I am feeling rather feeble this morning, but thankful to be up and so I can wait on myself, and that the rest of the family are well as usual. for which I praise the Lord for all His benefits to us all, His dependent children. He watches over us by night and by day.

July 1928

Wednesday July the 25th 1928

A bright morning and still very warm. I am not feeling at all well, but so thankful not to be bedfast, but to have strength to wait on myself. And so glad the rest of the family are keeping well. Praise the Lord for His goodness to us dependent ones. Afternoon of the same day. I have been favored by a precious visit from our dear Pastor of Springfield meeting **Clara I Cox** who gave me encouragement to press on in the way the dear Lord would have me go. I had become very much discouraged as I had been thinking of trying to go to yearly meeting again this year, but did not see any opening for a way to get there, and dear **Clara** just volenteered to take me if I would go, so I feel that I can not thank the good Lord enough for his watchful care over me his unworthy child, but altho I am so unworthy of His love and care I am so thankful that I can claim to be His child thru His precious promices, for He has said they that come unto me I will in no wise cast out, Blessed be His holy name.

Thursday July the 26th 1928

Another hot morning. but I am thankful that none of us have been overcome by the heat as many have been in the Cities. I love the country where we can get more pure air and see the many different trees, and the fields of grain and the many beautiful and useful things, which our merciful heavenly Father gives us to enjoy I feel that I can not praise Him enough for his goodness and watchful care over us His dependent cretures. "Oh that men would praise the Lord for His wonderful works to the children of men."

Friday July the 27th 1928

Bright sunshine and still very warm this morning. All in usual health and actively on the job whatever is necessary to be done for the needs of these mortal bodies. and my heart is filled with a fervent desire, that we may be as much and even more, in earnest to do that which pertains to the salvation of our immortal souls, that we may be permited an entrance into that blessed abode which is prepared for all who love and serve God here on earth.

Saturday July the 28th 1928

Another clear and very warm morning. All in usual health, and busy with the work of the day, for which I feel very grateful to our merciful heavenly Father, for He has taken care of us thru the night and given us rest in sleep, and given us strength to arise from our beds, otherwise we should be helpless cretures. for of ourselves we can do nothing. Blessed be the name of the Father, the Son, and the Holy Spirit.

Sunday July the 29th 1928

A lovely Sabbath morning. All in usual health, and some of us have just returned home from **Sidney Blairs**, where we went to view the remains of his dear wife **Della Blair** who passed away Friday night the 27th about ten olock after lingering for several months. The funeral is to be this evening at Springfield which I hope I may be able to attend. Later in the day, I was favored to get to **Della Blairs** funeral which was largely attended and presided over by the Pastor **Clara I Cox** and and also **Dougan Cox** who gave a very interesting talk and fervent prayer. and **Louis McFarland** also gave a good talk and offered a wonderful prayer everything was carried out in a beautiful way, there was quite a profusion of lovely flowers, and a quartet sang some appropriate songs.

Monday July the 30th 1928

Cloudy this morning. I am feeling quite feeble this morning, having become rather much fatigued yesterday on account of the heat, which causes me to feel weak to day. but I am so thankful to be able to be up and, and so I can wait on myself, and that the family here are all well as usual. Praise the Lord for His goodness to us all.

July–August 1928

Tuesday July the 31st 1928

A nice pleasant morning, after a week or more of extreme heat. All able to be up and go about daily avocations, for which I feel very thankful to the Giver of all our blessings. "Bless the Lord O my soul; and all that is within me, bless his holy name, Bless the Lord O my soul, and forget not all his benefits: Who forgiveth all thine iniquities; who healeth all thy diseases. oh how applicable are these words of Scriptures to my individual case, for I have realised the forgiveness of all mine iniquities which I acknowledge to be many. And has so wonderfully healed my many diseases sufficiently to enable me to get about with the aid of a staff after being helpless for so many years, and to get out to Church and Sabbath School etc after being deprived of those privileges for so many years, and suffering great bodily pain for a complication of diseases from which I did not have any hope of relief. and altho I am not strong and feel the infirmities of age, and at times feel almost like giving out by the way, on account of feebleness, yet I feel that I can not be thankful enough that it is as well with me as it is, for indeed I am a Miricle to those who knew of my great affliction in the past that I am living much less be so I can be up and get about. But I know the journey can not be very much longer at the longest, and am looking to Jesus to keep me close to Him, for I am so prone to wander, and I want to keep so near, that I may be ready for the summons, at any moment of His call. "Yes I am waiting by the river where the evening shadows fall. Only waiting for the Boatman listening for His gentle call. I will wait in calm submission, meekly kneeling on the shore Till my Saviour please to call me, then He will gently lead me oer."

Wednesday August the 1st 1928

A beautiful morning for the beginning of another month. and oh how fast time flies it seems almost as if it was but yesterday that I dated the 1st of July. and we have been reminded the past month of the uncertainty of life and the certainty of death by the removal of some of our loved ones from works to reward. Oh that we may be in earnest to be ready to meet them in the better land, for we know that altho we are all in comparatively good health at this time, that we can be taken at any moment of time if the Master calls, let us all be ready is my prayer for Christs sake. Later in the day. This evening I had the glad surprise of the appearance in this home of the fine form and pleasent countenance of cousin **Roland Blair** of High Point, he was certainly a welcome caller. My heart was filled with sympathy for him and his sisters and brother and grandchildren in the loss of their dear Mother and Grandmother, but we have such a blessed assurance that their loss is her gain, that we should rejoice, rather than mourn for she is relieved from suffering. Praise the Lord.

Thursday August the 2nd 1928

Beautiful day. All up and on the move, The parents gone to High Point shoping. others attending to the affairs in the home. I am feeling rather weak in body to day, but feel strengthened in spirit since cousin **Roland Blairs** visit last evening as he gave me such good advice in kind words of sympathy and encouragement to press on doing whatever the Lord calls for at my hands. oh that all people would be ready to give a kind word of sympathy to those who feel cast down and lonely, instead of words of scorn and derision, for they would not only make the sad and lonely ones happy by so doing but would be much happier themselves. oh how often I think of the words of Scripture, "Words fitly spoken are as Apples of gold in pictures of silver. For I know that there is no liveing that prises a kind word or deed more than I do, and no one feels the sting of unkind words more keenly than I do, for I have a sensitive nature that responds easily to kindness, and easily wounded at the thoughtlessness of those who are ready to offend. Father help me to lean hard on Thy Everlasting Arms that I may find help in every time of need. Is my prayer.

August 1928

Friday Aug the 3rd 1928

A clear and very warm moring. All well as usual and busy at work which is a great blessing. oh that we would all appreciate our blessings as we should, and be obedient to the call of our blessed Redeemer, and do His biding in all things, that we may inherit a home with Him when done with the things of earth, where we can praise Him forever with our loved ones gone before.

Saturday Aug the 4th 1928

Clear and still very warm this morning and we are very much in need of a good refreshing rain, and our merciful heavenly Father will send it to us when the proper time comes, for He is so kind to his unworthy dependent ones. oh that we may learn to be more obedient to do His holy will. I feel very thankful that He has given us a degree of health sufficient to go about our daily affairs, but we know not how soon we may be called from works to rewards. for we learn to day of another death in the community.

Sunday Aug the 5th 1928

Cloudy this morning. All able to be up this morning I am thankful to state, and prepare for Church services. and we learn there is to be a funeral at Mt Vernon to day at two oclock, that of a middle aged maiden Lady. A **Miss Crissie June Mcgee**, altho she never married and had no children of her own, yet she was a great caretaker, as two of her married sisters died and left three children to be cared for, and this kind woman took them and raised them and some of them are now married. It seems to me, that there will be many bright stars in her crown. Sunday evening. I was favored to go with the family here, to the funeral of **Miss Mcgee** at Mt Vernon this afternoon which was very largely attended, and **Rev Reed Haris** gave a splendid sermon, the Theme being The Good Samaritan which was so fiting to the occasion, for the Lady whose funeral he was preaching has certainly done the part of a good Sameritan. Praise the Lord for His goodness to His dependent children.

Monday Aug the 6th 1928

A clear hot morning, we are needing rain. but all things are in the hands of Him who has all things in His power and we should be in subjection to the holy will. we are all in usual health for which I feel very thankful. I am very busy to day prepareing to go to yearly meeting at Guilford College tomorrow if able.

Tuesday Aug the 7th 1928

A beautiful morning, but very warm indeed. I left home this morning to go to yearly meeting at Guilford College, and am now on my way as far as the Blair Dairy, where I am sitting on their porch and takeing a few notes while waiting for **Miss Clara I Cox** who was to meet me here and take me over to Guilford, she is the Pastor at Springfield at this time. I am so thankful to be able for this trip, for altho I do not feel strong, the dear Lord holds me up so I praise His name for His goodness to me and to mine. I am so glad that the family at home are all well. as usual. **J.W. Peace** and **May** his wife, who is my daughter, brought me this far on my way. May the Lord bless all who have been so kind to me is my prayer in His name. Lather in the day **Miss Clara Cox** brought me over here to Guilford and I enjoyed the opening session of the yearly meeting forenoon, but desided to rest this afternoon in my room as I am tired after my ride over here, and then sitting in a lengthy session of the opening meeting. we are now having a good shower of rain which was very much needed. Praise the Lord.

Wednesday Aug the 8th 1928

Another hot morning. I am feeling rather feeble but thankful to be so I can arise from my bed and prepare to attend services this forenoon. Afternoon of same day, I was favored to attend the forenoon session of the meeting for worship and enjoyed it very much. and I also listened to a fine Address by a Colored Lady by the name of **Crystal Bird**, who was born and educated in the North. I think in New York, and is said to be one of the most brilliant speakers of her race to be found in the United States, she is young and comely dresses well and becomingly, is of light color, but with no trace of the Mulatto, she speaks distinctly, has a fine delivery, and is pleding in behalf of her race for the betterment and the education of them, and as she expresses it, to bring about "The new Negro," to get them to bestir themselves come out of such a thriftless immoral and unchristian way of living as many of them are persisting in, and to get them elevated to a true, honest, and Christian citizenship, and she did not seem to have any tendency whatever to want the colored race to usurp authority over white people, and only plead that there might be a better understanding between them, that each one in their proper sphere might do their part to live in peace and harmony with each other, not only for the betterment of each race, but for the whole nation. I have not attempted to quote her, for that would be out of the question to reach one so schollarly in my limited capasity of education, but merely have tried to express the sentiment which ran thru her Address, I had never thought of hearing anything equal to it by a colored person, as our negrous in the South had mostly grown up in ignorance and not until recent years had they turned their attention to Schools, and become interested in educating themselves for useful citizens, but there is quite a change in many places for the betterment of the colored race and I hope they will be benefited by this intelligent and well educated woman comeing among them. It was the first time I ever knew of A colored person making, or rather giving an Address in a Friends Church, but all enjoyed it fine, and took it as it was meant, which was to bring about a true Christian relationship of peace and good will between the races to avert war. and to be helpful to each other in every way needful for the betterment of mankind, Not in the least was it meant to uphold the mingling of blood relation, nay verily. but for the Christianisation and salvation of immortal souls of both the white, and negro race. I did not feel able to go out to the afternoon session so went to my room and took a rest which was very much needed, as I had a headache and the weather was very warm. I praise the dear Lord for His tender care over me.

Thursday Aug the 9th 1928

A lovely morning. I was quite sick last evening, but got some rest in sleep last night, so feel much better this morning. and cannot praise the dear Lord enough for relieveing me of my suffering, and for favoring me with kind friends to minister to my needs while at this place. I hope I shall be able to get out to Church to day, at least to part of the sessions. Praise the Lord for His goodness to me. Thursday afternoon, I was favored to get out to the forenoon session, and enjoyed it very much, especially the Address by **Dr Garrett** of Philadelphia and **Dr Pateats** Address on Peace.

I remained at the Founders Hall this afternoon for rest as the sessions are quite lengthy, and I am not very strong, and the day very warm, so as to be able to get out some tomorrow, but I had the pleasure of conversing with many kind friends who joined me at the Hall. As the days go by I have enjoyed the opportunity of seeing once a year as we meet at this place for our Annual gathering for Worship and to transact the buisness of the Church. Praise the Lord for this favor.

Friday Aug the 10th 1928

Some cloudy this morning. I am so thankful to be able to arise from my bed, and prepare for the services of the day. I hope I shall be able to get out to Church to day. As I did not in the afternoon yesterday nor last night, but I feel like praising the Lord for blessing me with kind friends to assist me in every needful time, for they have been so good and obligeing to me.

Friday night, well I was favored to get out to the forenoon session. And heard the interesting report of the Evangelistic and Church

August 1928

Extension Committee and of the Superintendent **Lewis W. McFarland** which was highly entertaining and very satisfactory. also listened to another excelent Address by **Dr Alfred C Garrett** of Philadelphia. but as I did not get out to the afternoon session, I missed hearing the report of the Woman's Mishionary Union and the Address on the same by **B. Willis Beede** of the five years meeting. but my not getting out this p m and to night, was largely made up for, by an Address in one of the rooms in Founders Hall by **Marie Carrell** on the plans for carying on the Sabbath School many plans and interesting sugjestions were made to many interested listeners. Praise the Lord for His benefits.

Saturday Aug the 11th 1928

We were blessed with a bountiful rain last night, which was very much needed, and it is still raining, so I did not get out to Church to day, but this lack was bountifully supplied by a wonderful session held in one of the rooms in Founders Hall, lead by **Ivey Clark** and his wife who are both Ministers from California and also Mishionaries, and have traveled extensively in Foreign Fields. they each one gave us a splendid sermon, which I hope everyone present will cary home with us, and that we may keep our Lamps trimed and burning, and replenished with the oil of Gods holy spirit to His names honor and praise. There was another Minister and his wife in this particular meeting **Benjamin Millikan,** who is one of my kindred his is the Minister in this couple he is the son of **Sheriff Benjamin Milliken**, and his wife **Pearl** is the daughter of **Thomas Andrews** who is also a Minister in Friends Church. **Pearl** is one of the sweetest women I ever met her very presence is a benediction they are all native Carolinaians. **Cousin Ben** as I learned to call him gave us a splendid message in this meeting also, and nearly all in the room either gave testimony, or offered prayer during this service. This was one of the most spiritual meetings of all the sessions, and was greatly enjoyed by all. The praise belongeth to our Heavenly Father. The yearly meeting proper Closed with the buisness sesions etc to day. But as the rain ceased this evening I went our with some kind friends to the Church to night and enjoyed listening to the grand Address on education by **Dr Elbert Russell** of Duke University, and the presentation of Deplomas to nine graduates, eight girls and one young man. out of the twenty three graduates in all this year at Guilford those nine had not quite finished, so as to receive their Deplomas at Commencement time, so be it said to their honor, they would not give up but persevered thru Summer School and came out victorious, and all clad in their Caps and Gowns of the Graduate, received their Degrees and Deploman on the platform in the Friends Church, something which had never been witnessed before. **Dr Perisho** of Guilford College delivered the Deplomas. I did not get out to Church on Friday afternoon so missed hearing the report of Christian Endeavor Union, and of Young Friends Activities, and also the Address on the same by **Stokes S. Rawlins**, President of North Carolina Christian Endeavor Union, Greensboro.

Sunday August the 12th 1928

Cloudy this morning. I am very thankful to of had a good nights rest, as I am aiming to leave this place to day. I am very grateful for the many kind favors I have received since attending this meeting. The thoughtful care of the Matron and Nurse at Founders Hall **Miss Laura Worth** who ministered to my needs, when I was indisposed. And the kindness of the Secretary **Miss Maud Gainey.** and also the Matron of the Dining room and Kitchen. **Miss Alma Rayl** who has the care and oversight of the cooking and prepareing everything ready for the Table, which is an immense job not withstanding all of the Modern Equipment for the business. And the nice girls that waited on the Tables were very corteous to me, especially will I remember **Elizabeth Levering** who was also a Table waiter last year at the Table where I ate. she has been so sweet to me ever since I first met her, and so was her Mother **Mrs Levering,** who was the Matron in New

August 1928

Garden Hall. And of the nice young men I will mention one **Paul Reynolds,** son of **Paron Reynolds,** he has been so very kind and helpful to me, during the yearly meeting week for the past three years when I first met him. It shows such a noble mark of him and of all the nice young people both boys and girls to show so much respect to the aged and infirm like myself, that it fills my heart with true Christian desires for their best welfare in every way both in this life and in the world to come. And while I met and conversed with so many kind and interesting friends, that I had the same pleasure of doing last year, I also was made sad at the loss of some dear friends to us, who have gone to their reward since we conversed with them here during yearly meeting of 1927. One was **Aunt Jemima White** aged ninety three. And **Hannah Ensley** who was older than myself, and I am past eighty three, I have forgotten her exact age. she was a special friend of mine, her brother **Eli Thomas** was in School here with me (when it was New Garden Boarding School) in the year 1864. And his sister visited him and we became fast friends and we have had much pleasure togeather here in Guilford College during yearly meeting week and I did not know of her death until I got over here, and was expecting to meet her again this year. her husband **David Ensley** attended this yearly meeting and he is in his ninety third year of age. They lived together sixty five years, they lived near Winston Salem. Well as I have stated I aim to leave this place to day, so after being favored to get out to Church at eleven oclock and hearing a splendid sermon, then returning to Founders Hall and partakeing of a sumptuous dinner, and chating with many friend who were leaveing for their various homes I too prepared for the return trip to my place of abode. And the prayer of my heart is, that as we leave this place that the dear Lord will go with us to our homes and bless and keep us close to Him that we may obey Him in all things to His honor and praise. Now that a conveyance has come for me, I am ready to say goodbye to this dear place.

Until We Sleep Our Last Sleep

Monday Aug the 13th 1928

Some cloudy this morning. I am very grateful to be feeling some stronger to day. **Elva Blair** and his sister **Martha** were very my kind friends who came over to Guilford College last evening to take me home, but on the way I desided to stop over at cousin **Jesse Davis's** and spend the night with them as I had so often been invited there and had not every had the opportunity since they have been liveing in Old Trinity. **Jesse Davis** and his wife **Mary Coltrane Davis** are at this time staying with their soninlaw **Archie Spencer** who lives in what was called the Wilbor Boarding House, in the time of **Dr Braxton Craven** when he was President of Trinity College at this place, and his grave is quite near this home, and as **Prof John Blair** had joined his sisters as we came by the Blair Dairy on our way from Guilford, he and his sisters and some others went out to view the grave of **Dr Craven.** I am so happy to of had the opportunity of being here, and am enjoying the hospitality of this home. The daughter **Miss Laura Davis** who has taught School both in the North and in the South for several year was with her Parents and others at this time and I enjoyed her company also so much, she was such a friend to me while over at Guilford during the yearly meeting. This afternoon **Jesse Davis** and **wife Mary** took me over to the home of the late **Prof Nerious English** where I spent the night with his widow **Jinnie May English** and his sister **Venie English.**

Tuesday Aug the 14th 1928

Clear this morning. I am very thankful to be able to arise from my bed this morning, as I had a quiet nights rest in sleep and feel refreshed. I have had a most pleasent conversation with the widow of **Prof English,** and his sister **Venie** who is eighty five years of age and very much afflicted I pray Gods blessing upon the inmates of this home, and upon all for whom it is my duty to pray, and that He will lead guide and direct my steps this day and every day thruout the remainder of lifes journey in the way that I should go. for I am in His hands to will and to do of His own good pleasure. "Praise God from whom all blessings flow. Praise Him all cretures here below." This is my prayer for Jesus sake.

Wednesday Aug the 15th 1928

Cloudy this morning. I was prevailed upon to remain over night again with **Jinnie May English** and family, as **Venie** wanted me to stay longer to talk with her, so I have been enjoying the hospitality of this home, and I trust that I have been in my proper place with them, for the past two days and nights. but feel that the time has now come, to part with them for the present, and go to visit some others who are sick and afflicted in this community, and I shall endeavor to follow where the Lord leadeth. So **Jinne Mays son Tom** took me over to Archdale to see cousin **Fannie English** who has been very sick, but some better, but still not strong enough to have company in her room but a little while at a time. but she was so glad to see me I felt that I had done the right thing to call to see her, she lives with her widowed daughter **Mrs Amos Kersey.** From there I was taken to the home of cousin **Fannies** son **Merley Englishes,** who lives in Archdale, a short distance from his Mother, so he makes it his practice to go to see her twice every day, since she has been sick.

Thursday Aug the 16th 1928

A rainey morning. I spent the night very pleasantly at cousin **Merleys** and at their request shall spend another day or two with them as I had not visited with them for the past three years, and his wife **Rettie Blair English** was one of my neighbors, before she was married. Later in the morning. **Merley** was going to High Point and offered to take me with him as far as the **Amos Ragan** place to see **Amos's** daughter **Anna Armfield** who is a widow, and has been partially paralysed so that she can not use one hand very well and is lame in one leg, and not at all strong. They keep a Nurse with her all the time to wait on her and care for all her needs, but she can be taken out for a short ride occasionally, and was able to be taken the following Saturday over to Springfield to the Memorial Association. She seemed so glad to see me and gave me such a hearty welcome, that I was thankful I went to see her, and so did her Nurse **Miss Rodema Harney** a fine Maiden Lady that was raised over at Jamestown N.C.

On **Merleys** way back from High Point he stoped for me and took me back home with him again. We had aimed after lunch to go again a little while to see his Mother but it kept raining at intervals all afternoon so I did not get there that day with him, but I spent the afternoon very pleasently with **Merleys** family, and expect to stay over to see **cousin Fannie** a few minutes again tomorrow.

Friday Aug the 17th 1928

Still cloudy this morning, but not raining. and according to my expectations I spent last night in this home and shared their kind hospitality and am so thankful for a good nights rest in sleep, and for strenth to arise from my bed this morning. and so I can wait on myself. Later in the day. **Murley** took me over again to see his Mother again a little while, and I am glad to state we found her some better than on my previous visit, and was so glad to see me and wanted to talk with me, but she was still so weak. I did not permit this but a little while.

Saturday Aug the 18th 1928

Still some cloudy this morning. I am still in the home of cousin **Merley English**, but he and family are going to take me over to Springfield to day to the Memorial Association. and I expect from there to return to my daughters **Mrs J.W. Peace.** I have been so hospitality entertained in the homes of my kindred and friends since visiting in this community, that it will be a pleasure to look back to while life lasts. May the blessing of Heaven rest upon them all. May they be abundantly blessed spiritually and temporaly according to their needs, and that we may all live in that way and maner which will give us assurance of meeting in the better land where parting is unknown, and where we can sing Gods praise togeather with our loved ones gone before thruout eternity. Praise the Lord for His goodness and mercy to us all, for He has watched over us from the Cradle until the present time, and will still care for us throut the remainder of this lifes journey if we put our trust in Him, as we should.

Sunday Aug the 19th 1928

Clear this morning. I am thankful to of had a quiet nights rest in sleep the past night in the place I call home, and to be able to arise from my bed and wait on myself this morning. and I count it a great blessing that I was favored to attend the Memorial Association at Springfield yesterday as I had hoped to do. I greatly enjoyed the Memorial exercises, and the excelent sermon by **Ruben Payne** Pastor of Friends Church at Archdale at this time. and also heard the interesting Memorials read for **Harison Frazier** and wife **Gracett Frazier**. The Memorial of **Harison** was read by his Grandson **Robert Frazier** son of **Cyrus P Frazier** and **Cyrus** himself read the Memorial of his Mother **Gracett Frazier** it was all very touching to me, as I personally knew those dear friends, when I lived in my Fathers home in my young days. They were our good neighbors, and we loved them dearly, and continue to reverence their memory, and dearly love their children and grandchildren some of whom I met most pleasently at this Memorial. and I also met with so many friends that I do not get to see oftener than once a year as I meet them here at the Memorial service. and also many others that I do not even get to see that often, as many live at a distance and are not here every year. According to my expectations my daughter **May** and her husband **J.W. Peace** met me at Springfield and took me home with them where I am sojourning at this time. and if I keep able I expect to go with the family to Sunday School at Mt Vernon this afternoon as I make a practice of doing when I am in this home. for altho I do not belong to the Denomination that carries on that School. I am no Sectarian and enjoy the privilige of attending there as way opens as I am not situated so as to attend my own Church at Springfield. and I do not know what a day nor an hour or moment may bring forth, but am trusting the dear Lord to take care of me throut the remainder of lifes journey as He has in the past. for I know that he has watched over and cared for me during all the years of my afflictions, and will be with me to the end, and may the Lord be with us all and help us to serve Him forevermore is my prayer.

Monday Aug the 20th 1928

Nice and clear this morning after so much rain. I am very thankful to be as well as I am after my two weeks of Church going and visiting. for while I keep so I can wait on myself, I feel that I have much to be grateful for to the Giver of all good. Praise His holy name.

Tuesday Aug the 21st 1928

Cloudy again this morning. I am not feeling well, but thankful to be so I can be up and wait on myself. The family here are all in usual health, for which I am grateful, for it is one of the greatest blessings. Praise the Lord.

Wednesday Aug the 22nd 1928

A clear warm morning. I am very thankful that we of this household are all up and go about daily duties. The praise belongeth to Him in whom we live and move and have our being. So let us all praise Him with all our heart.

Thursday Aug the 23rd 1928

Cloudy to day. All in usual health I am thankful to state. and hope that we shall all be obedient to our merciful Heaven Father whos all seeing eye is watching over us at all times and He upholds us by His mighty hand. Praise God from whom all blessings flow.

Friday Aug the 24th 1928

Clear and warm to day. All up and busy doing whatever our hands to find to do, and may we do all to the glory of God the Father and Son and Holy Spirit Three in One. Is my prayer.

Saturday Aug the 25th 1928

A clear warm morning, All up and busy with the affairs of the day, I am so thankful for a good nights rest in sleep, and I can once again take up my pen to note down the goodness and mercy of the dear Lord to me and to mine, poor and unworthy as I feel myself to be, but His eye is on the sparrow so I know He watches over and cares for me. For He hath said in His holy word. "Mine eyes shall be upon the faithful of the land, that they may dwell with me; he that walketh in a perfect way, he shall serve me." But, He that worketh deceit shall not dwell within my house; he that telleth lies shall not tarry in my sight." God help us to be the faithful of the land is my prayer.

Sunday Aug the 26th 1928

Some cloudy this morning. I am thankful that we are all able to be up, and I trust we shall get out to Sunday School to day. **J.W. Peaces** soninlaw **Gideon Bowman** and wife **Ollie** and **jr** spent last night with us, we are always glad to have them. My prayer this morning is the words of the Psalm 67-1-2-3 "God be merciful unto us, and bless us; and cause his face to shine upon us; That thy way may be known upon the earth, thy saveing health among all nations; Let the people praise thee, O God; let all the people praise thee."

Monday Aug the 27th 1928

A nice clear morning, and quite warm, all in usual health. **J.W. Peace** and wife **May,** and **Mary Lee Stilwell** are gone to High Point on business others at work. I hope we shall be faithful in the work of the Master, whatever He has for us to do, at all times and in all places, to His honor and praise.

Tuesday Aug the 28th 1928

Another clear warm morning. All able to be on the stage of action, and attend to various duties, I am thankful to state, and I hope we shall all be mindful of our duty to God, and to our fellow beings, for we should love God supremely and our neighbor as ourselves, for love is the fulfiling of the law. Therefore we should love even our enemies and those who despitefully use us, and say all manner of evil against us, for so hath the Lord commanded us to do. and I desire to obey his word for His names sake, so, "I will lift up mine eyes unto the hills, from whence cometh my help, my help cometh from the Lord which made heaven and earth. "The Lord shall preserve thy going out and thy coming in from this time forth, and even for evermore." Psalm 121-1-8

Wednesday Aug the 29th 1928

A clear bright morning. Some of the family are not very well. **J.W. Peace** spent a restless night, suffering with a hurting in his left side, but is up and going to day. I am thankful to be able to be up and wait on myself as usual. The mercy of the Lord is from everlasting to everlasting upon those that fear Him, and for all who hope in His mercy. Praise His holy name.

Thursday Aug the 30th 1928

A nice clear day. All able to be up and go about daily avocations, for which I praise the Lord.

Friday Aug the 31st 1928

Another nice day. All feeling better to day. I am very grateful to the Giver of all good for a quiet nights rest and for strength sufficient to wait on myself and do what my hands find to do and this being the last day of the month, reminds me how fast time is passing away, as tomorrow will usher in the beginning of the fall season of the year. Then it will not be long until the time when the frosts will begin to bite the leaves on the trees, and they begin to fall to the ground. And thus will come the cold frost of death. To summons some of us to fall, at its beck and call, To give up our mortal breath. So help us dear Lord, To obey thy holy word. So that when we are laid beneath the sod. Our spirits will beat home with God.

Saturday September the 1st 1928

Cloudy this morning. All able to be up and on the move. My daughter and I are aiming to go to quarterly meeting at Archdale to day if it does not rain so as to prevent us. I praise the Lord that He gave me a good nights rest, so as to have strength for the day, and I pray that He will be with us wherever we be and go with us wherever we go, to lead, guide and direct our steps, to His names honor and praise.

Sunday Sept the 2nd 1928

A very rainey morning. I am thankful to of had a good nights rest, and to be able to be up and wait on myself. I am in the home of cousin **Robert Blair,** having come here yesterday afternoon. I stated yesterday that my daughter **Mrs J.W. Peace** and myself aimed to go to quarterly meeting at Archdale, but we failed to get there as we desided it was not safe for us to undertake it without some man person with us, as it had been raining and the roads slippery. so she brought me over here thinking I could go with cousin **Roberts** to quarterly meeting but they had already gone. so I went over to **Mrs Frys** and visited with them until after dinner, then their son **Paul Fry** brought me over here, and I spent the evening very pleasently with cousin **Ocid Blairs** sister **Miss Jinnie Redding** who chanced to be in their home at this time, and I staid over night as I have already stated. and to day it has been so very rainey that none but cousin **Robert** and his boys could go to Archdale to Sunday School and Church. To day the Protracted meeting begins at Mt Vernon, but if it keeps raining I dont know whether any of us will get there or not. but we are in the hands of the good Lord to take care of us wherever we may be. Praise His name.

Monday Sept the 3rd 1928

A cloudy morning. All in usual health. Well it did keep raining so hard that none of us at cousin **R.L.M. Blairs** got out to meeting at Mt Vernon, so in the evening when the rain held up some, cousin **Stanley Blair** brought me back to my place of abode that of **J.W. Peaces** and family. **Stanleys** brother **Charles Edward Blair** also came with us, and when we got here there was a glad surprise in store for us, especially for me, as my son **Fred C. Blair** and family had just arrived from Charlotte, N.C. so we spent the rest of the evening and until bed time very pleasantly with them, and this morning **Fred** and wife **Esther** and their son **Fred jr** and my daughter **Mrs J.W. Peace** have gone to visit some of their friends in High Point and their two daughters **Emily** and **May** are with us, until they return for them this evening, then we will have to give them all up for the time as they expect to go to their home in Charlotte this evening. May the dear Lord go with them and bless them spiritually and temporally is my prayer.

Tuesday Sept the 4th 1928

Still cloudy this morning. All able to be up and go about daily avocations. My son **Fred C. Blair** and family left us last evening for their home in Charlotte. I miss them so much that it makes me feel lonely. Lord help me to be resigned to my lot, let it be what it may, is my prayer. Evening of the same say. I was favored to get out to this afternoons session of the Protracted meeting at Mt Vernon, and heard a splendid sermon by **Rev – Jones** Pastor of the Methodist Church at Archdale at this time. His theme was the Barren Fig Tree.

Wednesday Sept the 5th 1928

Raining this morning. All in usual health. The weather was so unfavorable I did not go to Church last night, The young folks went, and report a good attendance and good interest. Praise the Lord.

September 1928

Thursday Sept the 6th 1928

Still rainey this morning. All able to be up I am thankful to state. It was so rainey none of us got out to Church yesterday nor last night, and it looks very unfavorable about getting out to day. But the rain may cease in time for the three oclock sesion, I am always glad when it is said "Let us go up to the house of the Lord," or words to that effect, but when it is not so I can go I endeavor to be in either submision to "The turnings and overturnings of the hand of the Lord upon me. And bless His holy name.

Friday Sept the 7th 1928

Cloudy this morning, All in usual health, I am not strong, but thankful to be so I can get about and wait on myself. And as the rain ceased in time I was favored to get out to the three oclock service yesterday and also to the service last night at seven thirty, which was well attended, and we have heard an excelent sermon by the **Rev – Jones** of High Point and fervent prayer by him and the **Rev Reed Haris** the present Pastor at Mt Vernon, also by some of the members. I praise the Lord for strenth to attend these services.

Saturday Sept the 8th 1928

Some cloudy this morning, but I think the Sun will shine some for us to day. All in usual health for which I feel very thankful. I was favored to get out to Church yesterday at Mt Vernon to the to three oclock service, but did not get out last night, which I very much regreted as it was the closing service of the meeting. But I praise the Lord that I had the opportunity to get out as much as I did.

Sunday Sept the 9th 1928

Nice clear morning. All able to be up, for which I feel thankful, and hope we shall all get out to Sunday School this afternoon as usual. To the praise of the dear Lord who is so good to us His unworthy children.

Monday Sept the 10th 1928

Another nice clear morning. All in usual health. The young people in this home got out to Sunday School yesterday, but I did not, as I have aimed to, as some of our friends from a distance came in very unexpectedly and we do not generally get to see them more than once a or twice a year, it was **Mr** and **Mrs Shoe** and baby son, and **Mr** and **Mrs Fesperman** and little daughter, and **Mrs George Stilwell** the Mother of **Mrs Shoe** and **Mrs Fesperman** all of Salisbury N.C. **Mr George Stilwell** is a brother to my soninlaw **Mr Arthur Lee Stilwell,** who was the first husband of my daughter which is now **Mrs J.W. Peace.** I have visited in the home of **Mr George Stilwell** and those of his soninlaw and they are such a fine people and treat me so very kindly that it makes me dearly love them all. And I pray Gods richest blessings may rest upon them.

Tuesday Sept the 11th 1928

Clear and warm this morning. All in usual health. My heart cries out this morning in the words of the Hymn. Oh for a Closer Walk with God, a calm and heavenly frame. A light to shine upon the road that leads me to the Lamb. For I am so sorely tried, that I want to walk so close to the Master that I may be kept from saying or doing anything that is contrary to His holy will. And I am so glad that He knows my heart and knows that I do not want to do anything that is not well pleasing in His sight. and I pray for the strength from him to help me to walk in the way that leads me to the Lamb, for vain is the help of man.

Wednesday Sept the 12th 1928

Cloudy this morning. All in usual health I am leaning on the strong Arm of my blessed Saviour for suport thru all my trials which are many, for it is only as I look to Him and trust in His mercy that I can keep able to press on toward the better land, Praise His name.

September 1928

Thursday Sept the 13th 1928

Clear this morning. All up and busy with the duties of the day. The parents gone to High Point on buisness. the rest of us doing what our hands find to do. And my desire is, that we may do all to the honor and praise of Him, who holds our lives in His hands.

Friday Sept the 14th 1928

A nice clear morning. All up and busy doing the things our hands find to do. oh that we may be more concerned to do the things that pertain to the salvation of our immortal souls that will return to the dust, "For the soul that sineth it shall die." but will wake up in everlasting punishment if we do not repent of our sins and forsake them while time on earth is lengthend out to us. oh God for the sake of thy dear Son who died for the sins of the whole world therefore for my sins help me this day, and every day the remainder of lifes journey to do thy bidding in all things to Thy names honor and praise. Is my prayer.

Saturday Sept the 15th 1928

Another nice clear morning. All able to be up and go about daily avocations, To day is quarterly meeting at Fairview. My daughter and husband and little son are gone to attend. I should been so glad to have had the opportunity of being there also, as it is a place my dear husband I attended togeather the last few years before his death.

Sunday Sept the 16th 1928

Clear and warm this morning. All in usual health. I am invited to go with **J.W. Peace** and wife **May** to dine at the home of **M. Kerney Peace. J.W. Peaces** brother. I appreciated the invitation very much but do not think it right to make a practice of visiting on the Sabbath. Praise God from whom we have life and strength for all our efforts. Sunday evening. We were favored to get to **Mr Kerney Peaces** and were received most kindly and faired sumpteuously at their Table. Then in the afternoon we and our Hosts all went to Sunday School and Preaching at Mt Vernon heard an excelent sermon by the Pastor the **Rev Reed Haris,** his Text being from the 23rd Chapter of Mathew 25 and 26th verse, I hope all of us that heard him will take a good lesson from it, and endeavor to keep the inside of the cup and platter clean, which represents having our hearts clean and pure in the sight of God. for we are told in His word, "Blessed are the pure in heart for they shall see God."

Monday September the 17th 1928

A nice warm morning. All able to be up and go about daily avocations, for which I feel very grateful to the Giver of all our blessings. Dear Lord help us all to be more obedient to Thee in all things to Thy names honor and praise is my prayer.

Tuesday Sept the 18th 1928

A very rainey morning. All able to be up, but I am feeling the effects of this damp weather, which causes aches and pains. This is a very unfavorable day for the opening of the High School at Trinity. **Mary Lee Stilwell** the stepdaughter in this home started this morning. This is her Seniour year, I hope she will succeed well in her studies, in every way. for I greatly desire that she may become a noble virteous woman, and be a blessing to the Church and to the world. For Jesus sake.

Wednesday Sept the 19th 1928

Still rainey, and was quite stormy during last night. I feel that we have much to be thankful for that that we have so far, been spared from such dreadful storms as has visited some places. and that we have a degree of health sufficient to go about our daily avocations. Praise the Lord for His goodness and mercy to us, His unworthy dependent children.

September 1928

Thursday Sept the 20th 1928

Clear this morning. All in our usual health. And as the Law against hunting Squirrels was out the 15th of this month, people are availing themselves of this opportunity, so **Rev Reed Haris** has come this morning to take a hunt with **J.W. Peace,** both seem to enjoy this kind of sport very much. **Mary Lee Stilwell** has gone to school this morning, and the rest of the family about daily duties. I praise the Lord that it is as well with us as it is, for in many places people are suffering from the effects of the recent storms.

Friday Sept the 21st 1928

Clear again this morning. All able to be up and are trying to do whatever our hands find to do. oh that we may do all to the glory of God and to His dear Son who He gave to die for us poor unworthy cretures. Praise His holy name.

Saturday Sept the 22nd 1928

A nice clear day. All in usual health I am glad to state, for health is one of our greatest earthly blessings, for having been deprived of it for so many years. I know whereof I speak. Praise the Lord for His care over us all.

Sunday Sept the 23rd 1928

Some cloudy this morning. All able to be up and prepare for Sunday School to day. My daughter **Mrs J.W. Peace** is going to Marlboro to Church with some of **Grandma Peaces** family to hear the Missionaries **Ivey Clark** and wife of California. Oh may the dear Lord be in their midst, and also with those of us who are not permitted to be there.

Monday Sept the 24th 1928

Clear and cooler this morning. All able to be up and go about daily avocations, for which I am grateful to the Giver of all good. Bless

His name. "Be thou exalted O God above the heavens: and thy glory above all the earth;" This is my prayer for Jesus sake.

Tuesday Sept the 25th 1928

Clear and quite cool to day. All in usual health I am glad to state for it is one of our great blessings to be able to be up and attend to whatever is necessary to be done. I have nothing else of importance to note at this time except the continued goodness and mercy of the Lord to His unworthy dependent children. Bless His name.

Wednesday Sept the 26th 1928

Still nice and clear and cool this morning. All able to be up, and go about the duties of the day. oh God keep me so close to thee this day that I may not sin against thee in word or deed, is prayer this morning for Christs sake.

Thursday Sept the 27th 1928

A clear lovely morning. I feel feeble this morning but thankful to be so I can be up and wait on myself and thankful for the health of the family. Bless the Lord O my soul; and all that is within me, bless his holy name. Bless the Lord O my soul, and forget not all his benefits; Who forgiveth all thine iniquities; who healeth all thy diseases. Psalm 103-1-2-3

Friday Sept the 28th 1928

Nice morning. All in usual health. I am feeling sad and lonely as I so often do since my bereavement. But in the language of the Psalmist. "I will life up mine eyes unto the hills, from whence cometh my help. My help cometh from the Lord which made heaven and earth. He will not suffer thy foot to be moved; he that keepeth thee will not slumber." "The Lord shall preserve thy going out and thy comeing in from this time forth and even for evermore." Blessed be His holy name.

September–October 1928

Saturday Sept the 29th 1928

Clear and some warmer this morning. All about as usual in this home I am glad to state, and hope we shall be very thankful for all our blessings. And that we may be close on our watch to guard against all even. for Jesus sake.

Sunday Sept the 30th 1928

Cloudy this morning. We had quite an Electric storm last night. and hard rain. but after the storm was over, I spent the rest of the night in quiet sleep, for which I feel very grateful to our Great care taker. and thankful that this family and myself are all able to be up, and I trust shall be able to attend Sunday School and perhaps Preaching somewhere, as there is preaching at several places not far away, but none to day at Mt Vernon. Father keep us close to Thee.

Monday October the 1st 1928

Cloudy this morning. All able to be up and attend to the duties of the day, I am thankful to state. and as to day ushers in the begining of another month it reminds me of the flight of time, and as this week the Protracted meeting at Fairview is in session, it also reminds me of the many Sabbaths that my dear husband and I went there togeather to attend Sunday School and preaching. and it hardly seems possible that he Deceased more than eight years ago, for I miss him so much, and if I should get to Fairview during this meeting I shall in imagination seem to see his dear form sitting on one of those benches. My great desire is to live in that way and manner which will assure me an entrance into that blessed abode, where I believe he has entered. Evening of the same day. My daughter **Mrs J.W. Peace** and myself were favored to get to the three oclock service at Fairview and I thought of those things which I stated this morning. but the Pastor **Rev Reed Haris** gave us such a splendid sermon on the 121st Psalm "The Lord shall preserve thy going out and thy comeing in from this time forth, and even for evermore." This sermon made such a deep impression on my mind, as he spoke of the tender care over His children, that I was made to feel that he was indeed watching over and careing for me at all times even when I was not aware of it, and altho so unworthy of His care, that I having an eye single to His glory and thru all my loneliness and privations in this life to look away from this things and prepare for that glorious meeting where there is no more separation, but where we shall join our loved ones in singing praises to Him who gave His precious life for us.

Tuesday Oct the 2nd 1928

Some cloudy this morning. All in usual health for which I feel very grateful, and also feel very thankful for a quiet nights rest in sleep for I often have spent many wakeful hours during the night. and it is so refreshing to spend several hours in sweet quiet sleep. I feel like I can not praise our blessed Redeemer enough for His mercy and watchful care over us poor unworthy cretures. Bless be His holy name. Evening of the same day. I have mentioned that my daughter and I went to Fairview Monday to the 3 oclock service. I came back home with her and staid over night. Then Tuesday afternoon she took her stepdaughter **Miss Minnie Peace** and myself, also **Grandma Peace** and **Mrs Earl Peace** in the Car with her to the three oclock service, and left me over there, as I was invited to the home of **Mrs Anna Cranford** to spend the night. So after Church **Rev Reed Haris** the Pastor took **Mrs Cranford** and myself to her home where we partook of a bountiful supper, then all went to Church had a good meeting, then I returned to **Mrs Cranfords** where I spent the night in quiet rest.

Wednesday October the 3rd 1928

Cloudy this morning. I am very thankful to be able to arise from my bed and wait on myself as I had good nights sleep here in the home of **Mrs Cranford,** and expect to attend Church again this afternoon if the dear Lord so wills. Blessed by His holy name, for He takes care of us all his poor unworthy dependent children.

Thursday Oct the 4th 1928

A lovely sunshiney morning. I am now in the home of **Clarence Meredith** where I spent last night. I was favored to get out to Fairview yesterday at the three oclock service. The Pastor **Rev Reed Haris** came by **Mrs Cranfords** and took her and myself out to Church. Then after service he took us back to **Mrs Cranfords**, where we partook of a sumptuous supper then all of us went back to Church last night and **Rev Earnest Harberson** of High Point came and gave a message which was a most excelent one indeed. Then both **Rev Haris** and **Rev Harberson** and **Mrs Walter Meredith** and myself were invited to take supper at **Clarance Merediths** so we went and were treated with the very kindest of hospitality. and after partaking of an excelent supper, we all went back to Church. **Rev Harbison** preached a wonderful sermon on the exceeding sinfulness of Sin. Then after Church I went back home with **Clarance** and his wife **Effie** and staid over night, and then the remainder of the time until time to go to Church was spent most pleasantly in this home. Then we all went to the 3 oclock service and listened to an excelent sermon by the **Rev Reed Haris** on the Parable of the Ten Virgins. we had a good meeting. and I praise the Lord for the opportunity of being there for I feel that the name of the Lord was highly exalted on this occasion. Blessed be His name.

Friday Oct the 5th 1928

Cloudy this morning. I am now in the home of **Walter Meredith, Clarances** Father. All able to be up in this home, for which I feel very grateful having had a good nights rest in sleep, This is the second night I have spent in this home very unexpectedly. as no one from home came to Church last night I have no conveyance. I have been takeing down notes from my Diary at every home where I have been invited and went. and I find that in this one instance in transcribing my notes that I should of mentioned early on these pages. That after the 3 oclock meeting Thursday, I was invited to take supper at **Mr Kinsey Myres** and I went and several others were invited beside both Preachers **Rev Reed Haris** and **Rev E. Harberson, Mrs Anna Cranford** and daughter **Miss Carrie**, also **Mrs Carina Kenedy** and **Mrs Walter Meredith** and a **Mr Lamberth** and some others. There was a bountiful supper prepared which we all enjoyed very much. Then all went back to Church and listened to a splendid sermon by **Rev Harberson.** Then after Church instead of going back to **Mr Myreses,** I was invited to **Walter Merediths** to spend the night which I accepted and spent the time very pleasently in this home, until time to attend Church Friday afternoon when we all went to the three oclock service and heard a good sermon by the **Pastor Rev Reed Haris.** Then as I have stated had no conveyance to get back home with then again I had other invitation but desided to go back with them, I enjoyed still more if possible for **Rev** and **Mrs Harberson** were both there to partake of the good supper with us also **Rev Reed Haris** and **Miss Bernice Myres.** Then as usual we all went back to Fairview for the closing service of the meeting had a most excelent sermon by **Rev Harberson.** All parted in great unity of spirits. And as there has been much good seed sown I hope it may mature into an abundant harvest. Then after service I went back with **Merediths** and had a good nights rest.

Saturday Oct the 6th 1928

Still cloudy this morning. I am so thankful to be able to arise from my bed, and prepare to go back to my daughters this morning, so after partakeing of a good breakfast, **Miss Mabel Meredith** took me back home. but before we started, I felt it my duty for to have us all assemble in the Parlor and have a little service togeather, so I read the 121st Psalm and in my simple but earnest way offered prayer, that we might all be faithful and profit by the good mesages that we had heard and live in love and unity with each other and with all our fellow beings, all enjoyed the service and we parted with love and unity. "Behold how good, and how plesent it is for brethren to dwell togeather in unity."

Sunday Oct the 7th 1928

A beautiful Sabbath morning. All in usual health for which I feel very grateful to our merciful Caretaker for His watchful care over us, at all times, I feel that I can not praise Him enough for blessing me with kind friends to help me in time of need I am so grateful to **Miss Mabel Meredith** for her kindness to me in bringing me back to my place of residence. And for the kind hospitality I received in their home. I was so glad to find all well in this home when I got back yesterday, and I also found some good letters awaiting me one from our dear Pastor of Springfield Church **Miss Clara I. Cox**. And one from my dear son **Fred C. Blair** of Charlotte. so glad they were all well, so I feel that I have so much to thank my kind heavenly Father for, for all His benefits to me.

Monday Oct the 8th 1928

Clear and some cooler this morning. All able to be up and trying to do what our hands find to do. but I feel rather feeble to do much to day, and my eye sight has become so dim that it is dificult to write a creditable hand, which I regret very much for I wish to keep my Diary as long as possible to note down the goodness and mercy of the dear Lord to me His unworthy child. And I am so thankful to know that I am His child for I have given myself to Him many years ago, and altho I have made many mistakes and come short of doing His will at all times, but I know that God has forgiven me for all my short comings for Christ sake who died that I might live, for He died for the sins of the whole world therefore for my sins, and I know that He has bloted out all my transgressions. Blessed be His holy name. saith my soul now and forever.

Tuesday Oct the 9th 1928.

A nice bright morning. I am feeling rather feeble this morning, and very much discouraged as the enemy of our souls peace watches us still more closely when he sees that we are trying the hardest to serve the Lord in the way of all His requirings. And He knows that at this moment of time my greatest desire is to be found doing His holy will, and that I do not harbor my hate or ill will toward any of Gods creation but desire the souls salvation of all for Christ the Redeemer sake.

Wednesday Oct the 10th 1928.

A clear warm morning. All able to be up and go about daily avocations for which I am thankful. My prayer this morning is. Dear Lord keep us all as in the hallow of thy holy hand, that we go not astray and sin against thee, for it is my fervent desire to do thy will on earth, that I may inherit a mansion in heaven where I can praise thee, thruout all eternity.

Thursday Oct the 11th 1928.

Clear and cooler this morning. All in usual health for which I am thankful to the great Giver of all good. And like the Psalmist I want to ever put my whole trust in the Lord. And I can say from the debths of my heart this morning like David in the 31st Psalm 1st verse "In thee O Lord do I put my trust; let me never be ashamed; deliver me in thy righteousness." Yes I hope I shall never be ashamed to confess God before my fellow beings, for "Into thine hand I commit my spirit; thou had redeemed me O Lord God of truth." Blessed be His holy name now and ever more.

Friday Oct the 12th 1928

Nice clear morning. All well as usual except myself. I am feeling quite feeble this morning, but thankful to be able to note down the continued goodness and mercy of my Heavenly Father and I am so glad that

I can call him Father for I know that I am His child for I gave myself to Him many years ago, and I am still His child, altho unworthy of his many blessings, for I often make mistakes and fall short of being as obedient as I should be and wish to be, but He knows the spirit is willing but the flesh is weak, and I know that in pity as a loving Father he has overlooked all my shortcomings and pardoned all my sins both of omishion and commission, and I feel that I can not praise Him enough for His tender, watchful care over His unworthy dependent child. He has often favored me with the company of kind friends and relatives, which I count a blessing as it helps to cheer me on my way. Last evening we were visited by cousin **Merley English** and his wife **Rettie Blair English**, and their daughter **Mildred** and her little sister, we were highly pleased to have them with us. May the Lord bless and keep them in my prayer. "I love the Lord, because he hath heard my voice and my supplication. Because he hath inclined his ear unto me, therefore will I call upon him as long as I live." Psalm 116-1-2.

Saturday Oct the 13th 1928

Fine morning. All in usual health. The Parents are gone to High Point shoping, the rest of the family attending to the various duties of the day I am thankful to still be able to pen down a few lines each day, to note the goodness and mercy of the dear Lord to His dependent children.

Sunday Oct the 14th 1928

A lovely Sabbath morning. All in usual health for which I am very grateful to my heavenly Father and for a good nights rest, and for strength to arise from my bed this morning, and I trust I shall be given strength to attend Sunday School this afternoon at Mt Vernon with the family as I have for some time past. **J.W. Peaces** son **Grady Peace** and wife **Clara** and little son **Joseph** spent last night with us. we are always pleased to have their company my little grandson **J.A. Peace** went home with them this morning to stay until Sunday

School time. "Not unto us O Lord not unto us, but unto thy name give glory, for thy mercy and for thy truths sake." Psalm 115-9

Tuesday Oct the 16th 1928

Still some cloudy to day. I am still in the bed but feeling some better than yesterday. I got some sleep during the night, but still feel quite feeble and nervous, but I praise the Lord for watching over me, and that He has blessed me with a kind daughter to care for me while in bed, and not able to wait on myself.

Wednesday Oct the 17th 1928

Not quite clear yet. The family all except myself are in usual health. I am feeling badly and not able to sit up but very little, but still hope I shall sonn be better if the dear Lord so wills. The praise belongs to Him.

Thursday Oct the 18th 1928

The elements are much the same as yesterday, and so is the condition of the family much the same also, I am weak and swimming headed but some better than yesterday as I can get off and on the bed myself to day with my daughters help to get into my chair to rest a while from my bed. I am so thankful to be so I can help myself that much, for my daughter as had to help me in and out of bed all this week so far, and she has so much work to do that I am sorry for her to have to wait on me, but she does it kindly and willingly, and I know she will get her reward tor this, both in this world and the next. I have been favored with some kind and interesting letters from loved ones this week since being confined to the bed. which has been a great comfort to me. One from my dear young friend **Miss Fannie Croker** from High Point she is such a lovely girl to me. And one from my dear sisterinlaw **Mrs Sadie Millikan** of Monrovia Indiana, who is now left a lonely widow like myself, her husband, my dear brother **E.B. Millikan** having passed away Dec the 28th 1927. I have such deep sympathy for her in her bereavement for I know what it means to give up a dear companion. This moring **Mrs Earl Peace** came to see me and brought some lovely Crysanthemums I appreciated the kindness so much. Last night **Mr.** and **Mrs Gideon Bowman** were here and came in to see me. they have such a sweet babe little jr he is a pleasure to us all. and the joy of his Parents and Grandparents. Praise the name of the Lord.

Friday Oct the 19th 1928

Nearly clear this morning. I am still in bed but glad and thankful to be some better. The rest well as usual.

Saturday Oct the 20th 1928

Clear and cooler to day. I still have to keep my bed, as I suffer so much with my head and spine and amy loud noises seem to almost take my life as my nervous system is so broken down, and it is only as I lean on the Arm of the dear Lord that I am able at all to bear these things. Praise His holy name.

Sunday Oct the 21st 1928

Clear and cool this morning. I am still not able to be up but a little while at a time, and suffer so much with my head and spine and in fact a general acheing of my whole body, but I praise the Lord that He helps me to bear it each day.

Monday Oct the 22nd 1928

Clear and cool. The family here are in usual health, all except I am not able to sit up but very little yet as I suffer so much with pain and acheing in my head. but so thankful that I have better use of myself today. Praise the Lord for His goodness and mercy to me and to mine.

Tuesday Oct the 23rd 1928

Cloudy and cool this morning. I am still in my bed. **Dr Bulla** came to see me yesterday he said I was suffering with Virtigo and from high blood pressure kidney trouble etc. I am too weak to be up but very little yet, and I have many things on my mind that does not help to strengthen me. This day ten years ago my soninlaw **Arthur Lee Stilwell** passed away. I miss him so much, for he was so very kind to me, and I loved him and honored him as my own son. I praise the Lord that my daughter has been spared to care for me in my feeble and declining years. and I know He will abundantly reward her both in this life and in the world to come for "in asmuchas ye did it unto the least etc, ye did it unto me."

Wednesday Oct the 24th 1928

Cloudy and cooler to day. I rested pretty well the latter part of last night, and have been able to sit up about one hour this morning, for which I am very thankful, to the dear Lord for strength to do that much. and I am so thankful for the kind friends that visit me. **Mrs Allen Robins** has been to see me, and this week. **Grandma Peace. Aunt Nannie,** and **Jewel Peace.** All came.

Thursday Oct the 25th 1928

Clear and much cooler to day. I had a better rest last night than for two weeks past, for which I feel very grateful to the Giver for all good. as it has given me strength to sit in my chair awhile which is relief from having to lie in bed all the time. I am always so glad for some one to come to see me to help while away my loneliness. Yesterday **Mrs Earl Peace** came and conversed with me a while to relive the monotiny. the night before **Mr** and **Mrs Fred Peace** came and staid awhile. always glad to see them. Today Oct the 25th 1928 is my little grandaughter **Mary Ann Blairs** tenth Birthday. I expect she will have some her little Charlotte friends invited to help to enjoy it.

Friday Oct the 26th 1928

Clear and cold to day. I had rather a restless night not being so I could get any sleep until after midnight. but thankful for some rest this morning and to be so I can sit in my chair awhile to rest from the bed. The family here are in general good health I am glad to note. Praise the Lord for His tender care over His unworthy dependent children.

Saturday Oct the 27th 1928

Clear and cold again this morning. I had a better nights rest in sleep, than for several nights past, and can sit in my chair awhile to rest from the bed. this morning, for which I am very thankful. I will note that just now we learn that **John Hill** of Hillsboro passed away this morning at five oclock. he is Father of **Mrs Merriman Cranford** of Trinity. he was in the Guilford General Hospital at High Point for several months but nothing could do him any good so he went home, he had Cancer, he died at his home in Hillsboro but was brought to Mt Vernon for burial. The funeral largely attended.

Sunday Oct the 28th 1928

Clear and cold. I am still so I have to keep my bed the most of the time, but can sit up a little while to rest from the bed. I praise the Lord for His care over me. The family here have gone to Sunday School and to attend the funeral of **John Hill** at Mt Vernon this afternoon at three oclock. After they return home they report the funeral was very largely attended, and was conducted by **Dougan C. Cox** of Thomasville and a Baptist Minister of High Point I did not learn his name.

Monday Oct the 29th 1928

Clear and cold again this morning. I am so thankful to of had a better nights rest than usual and can sit in my chair awhile to rest from the bed Praise the Lord for all His benefits to me and to mine.

Tuesday Oct the 30th 1928

Still clear and cold. The family here are well as usual. I had several hours rest in sleep the past night. so thankful that I can sit up awhile in my chair to rest. I cannot write but a few lines at a time just merely keep the date, and express my thanks to my blessed Redeemer for His goodness to me.

Wednesday Oct the 31st 1928

Clear and cold this morning. And as this is the last day of the month, it brings to mind how fast time to us all is passing away. I have now been confined to my room and mostly to my bed, for two weeks and a half today. and I am not yet strong enough to sit up half of the day and have not been able to more than pencil a few lines each day, which I hope I can yet be able to Transcribe with pen and ink in my Dairy. I am so very nervous that I have had to leave off many things that I would loved to of taken note of, but praise the Lord that He has given me strength sufficient to do the little that I have done.

Thursday November the 1st 1928

Still clear and cold. The family here are in usual health, and I am gaining some from day to day. I slept better last night, and arose from my bed about nine oclock, and put a dress on for the first time since I was taken sick, hope I can sit up more to day.

Friday November the 2nd 1928

Cloudy this morning. I am very thankful to be so I can sit awhile in my chair and pencil a few lines for my Diary for I have had suffered so much with Virtigo and weak eye sight that I have had to leave off many things that I would loved to touch upon, but praise the Lord for His goodness, in careing for me each day.

Saturday Nov the 3rd 1928

Cloudy and some warmer this morning. I am still feeling weak and nervous, as I suffer so much with pain and acheing in my head and spine. The rest of the family are well, I am glad to note. Praise the Lord for all His benefits. "O Lord thou hast searched me, and known me, Thou knowest my downsitting and mine uprising, thou understandest my thoughts afar off. Thou compassest my path and my lying down, and art acquainted with all my ways." Psalm 139-1-2-3

Sunday November the 4th 1928

Nice morning. I am so thankful that I have strength enough to arise from my bed this morning, and take my bath, and I desire that I may not only be clean in the flesh, but clean and pure in heart, for we are told that. "Blessed are the pure in heart for they shall see God." I was favored last evening with the company of some of my friends and relatives. **Sidney J. Blair** from Fairview and his two daughters, **Mrs Charlie Lee** of High Point and **Mrs Murley English** of Archdale also his grandaughter **Mrs Clara Barnes** of Greensboro she is **Roland Blairs** daughter. I was so glad to have them visit me, for they seem so much the same as in earlier days, and seem to have so much sympathy for me now in my loneliness which I appreciate so much. I praise the Lord for sending them to visit me.

Monday Nov the 5th 1928

Clear and cooler this morning. My head and eyes are still in bad condition, but so thankful to be feeling some better and hope I shall be able to be up more to day than yesterday. Well yesterday dear **Clara Barns** came again, this time bringing her Father **Roland Blair** to see me which I appreciated so much. and that same day (Sunday) **Allen Blair** and his wife **Mary Mendenhall Blair** came to see me. I appreciated their visit very much as I did all the others that came to see me that day among others were cousin **Emma Blair** and her sister **Elva Blair** and **Mrs Ellington** and also **Mrs Hallinman,** and cousin **Ocia Blair** and that night **Mr** and **Mrs Julian Woodard** came to see me, **Mrs Woodard** is **Dr J.F. Bullas** daughter, and is very sweet to me, and calls me Grandmother which I appreciate very much.

Tuesday Nov the 6th 1928

Clear and cool this morning. I am still feeling weak, but so thankful that I can sit up part of the day. This is the day to elect our President. and I now only lack four months of being eighty four years of age and went and Registered for the first time in my life the very day before I was taken sick, I had hoped to get able to attend the Election in person to cast my first vote. But as I am not able to go **H.S. Ragan** and one of the County Commissioners came with his wife to see me, and fixed my absentee vote so that it will be lawfully cast for **Herbert Hoover**. The Parents in this home will go to the Election and cast their votes for **Hoover**. If **Herbert Hoover** is the proper one to govern our Nation, God grant that he may be elected to that position is my prayer. "Except the Lord built the house, they labor in vain that built it."

Wednesday Nov the 7th 1928

Cloudy and cool this morning. I had more rest in sleep last night, than any night in more than three weeks. And my nose bled so freely this morning which I hope will so relieve the pain in my head that I can be up most of this day. The rest of the family are well, for which I thank our mericiful Heavenly Father for his watchful care over us all.

Thursday Nov the 8th 1928

Cloudy this morning. I had a good rest in sllep last night, for which I feel very grateful, and trust that I shall be able to be up the most of the day. The rest of the family are well. and the Parents gone over to Trinity to see **Rev** and **Mrs Reed Haris** as this is their day for leaveing their work here and going to their new field of labor in the Lords Vinyard. They will be located at Reedsville, N.C. they have been with us the last four years, and we all regret to give them up. I pray that they may be blessed with good health and have great success in their new field in bringing many souls to Christ. "His work is honorable and glorisous; and his righteousness endureth for ever." Psalm 111-3

November 1928

Friday Nov the 9th 1928

Clear and cold this morning. I am thankful to of had a good rest in sleep in the after part of the night which has given me strength sufficient to arise from my bed and sit in my chair. This is **J.W. Peaces** fifty third Birthday. They are going to bring his Mother over to take dinner with him if she is able to come. Later in the day. **Grandma Peace** came and spent the day with us, so she was here to take dinner with her son. so was **Mrs. Edd White** here to dine with her Father on his Birthday. And in the evening cousin **Sandy White** came over to see me I have been favored with the company of many kind relatives and friends since I have been sick. For which I praise the Lord for his tender care over me.

Saturday Nov the 10th 1928

Cloudy and cool this morning. I rested better than usual last night altho I did not get to sleep until late, but am so thankful to be so I can get out of bed and sit by the fire this morning and hope I shall be able to be up the most, if not all day, as I have not been able to hold up all day since I was taken sick, which will be four week tomorrow. I praise the Lord that it is as well with me as it is and that the rest of the family are in good health.

Sunday Nov the 11th 1928

Clear and cold this morning. I am feeling some better, as I had more rest in sleep last night, and my nose took another spell of bleeding this morning which relieved my head some, so that I can be up and sit by the fire. I had hoped to get able to go to Sunday School to day, as it is just four weeks to day since I attended but as I have not been able to be outside of my room door since that day, (as that was the day I was taken sick) so it is out of the question to even think of going to Mt Vernon to day, but if the dear Lord sees fit to strengthen me I so hope I shall be able by another Sabbath. Blessed be the name of the Lord for all His benefits.

Monday Nov the 12th 1928

Clear and much colder, Ice this morning. The family all in usual health. and I am thankful to the great Giver of all good that I also can arise from my bed and sit by the fire, for altho I do not get strong I am so glad that I am not confined to the bed all day as in the past, for I can now be up thru the day, by lying down only once for rest. for which I praise the Lord with my whole heart.

Tuesday Nov the 13th 1928

Clear and cold again this morning. I had more rest in sleep last night, than for several nights past for which I feel very grateful to my merciful heavenly Father for it has given me strength sufficient to get up, and to once more use my pen to write another word of thanks for the health of the family and other blessings from the Lord. Yesterday afternoon I was favored with the company of our Springfield Pastor dear **Clara I. Cox** which did me much good, always so glad of her visits, and last night until bed time. I had the pleasent surprise of a visit from **Mrs Furr** of High Point, she was **Miss Lula Davis** before marriage and is cousin of mine. I enjoyed her visit very much. I praise the Lord for putting it into the hearts and minds of my friends to come to visit me, in my loneliness.

Wednesday Nov the 14th 1928

Still clear and cold. I slept better last night than usual. and I am so thankful to be improved sufficient to go out to my breakfast for the first time in a month, instead of it having to be brought into my room. And yesterday was the very first time I had been to the dineing room to take dinner since I was taken sick. Which is now four and one half weeks ago last Sunday. I feel that I have much to praise the Lord for, that He has watched over me all along the journey of life, and since I have been left a widow, He has provided a kind and loving daughter to care for me.

Thursday Nov the 15th 1928

Clear but not quite so cold this morning. I did not rest but about half of the night, and my head is so swimming this morning that it is with difficulty that I can walk about the room, but thankful to be able to get out of bed. The rest in usual health. Praise the name of the Lord.

Friday Nov the 16th 1928

Cloudy this morning. All able to be up and at work. I am feeling quite feeble, but trying to do what little I can to help in that which is necessary to be done for the comfort of those perishable bodies. Praise the Lord.

Saturday Nov the 17th 1928

Cloudy this morning. I had a good rest in sleep last night for which I feel very thankful, but I am suffering with my head again this morning. Today is quarterly meeting at Mt Vernon, and I had hoped to get well enough to go with the rest of the family that are going, but as I am not, I will have to give it up, my desire is to be willing at all times to submit to the will of Him who knoweth all things, and we are told in His Word, "That all things work togeather for good to them that love the Lord." and I am so glad that He knows that I love Him. Blessed be His holy name now and forever. saith my soul.

Sunday Nov the 18th 1928

Clear and much warmer this morning I am still feeling feeble, but thankful to be so I can arise from my bed. The rest of the family are well as usual, **Mr** and **Mrs Gideon Bowman** and sweet babe **jr** have come in this morning. and last night **Mr** and **Mrs Grady Peace** and their fine babe **Joseph** came to visit us until bedtime. This is Preaching day at Mt Vernon and their new Preacher **Rev -Kelly** is to be there, but I shall not be able to go, but I praise the Lord that it is as well with me as it is.

Monday Nov the 19th 1928

Cloudy and warm this morning. The family are well as usual. I am still feeling weak and nervous, but I had more rest in sleep last night than usual so it has enabled me to be up this morning and use my pen to note the goodness and mercy of the Lord to us all.

Tuesday Nov the 20th 1928

Clear and cooler to day. I am still feeling weak but thankful be so I can be up, the rest of the family well as usual. Praise the Lord for all His benefits. We had the pleasure of the company of **Mr** and **Mrs Lee White** Monday evening a little while.

Wednesday Nov the 21st 1928

Much colder this morning plenty of Ice. I was favored to have a good nights rest in sleep, and can be out of bed this morning, and the rest of the family all well, for which I praise the Lord for his goodness and mercy to us all, for we are dependent upon Him for all things both spiritual and temporal. **J.W. Peace** and **Gurney Peace** went to Reedsville to day.

Thursday Nov the 22nd 1928

Clear and cold. All able to be up, I am feeling some stronger this morning, as I had a good rest in sleep last night. Nothing of importance to note only the continued goodness and mercy of the Lord to us unworthy cretures. Praise His holy name.

Friday Nov the 23rd 1928

Clear and cold. The family all up and going about daily avocations. I am feeling better altho I have not yet gained my strength as I should like, but I risked going to High Point yesterday to see **Dr Tesh** to get my glasses changed. I hope I shall be able to see more clearly, and not suffer so much with my head and eyes as I have for a month past. Praise the Lord for all His benefits.

Saturday Nov the 24th 1928

Clear and cold plenty of Ice. All able to be busy with the duties of the day for which I feel very thankful, and praise the Lord for His watchful care over us all His dependent cretures.

Sunday Nov the 25th 1928

Still clear and cold this morning. All able to arise from our beds. The family will go to Sunday School, but I do not feel like going out to day in the cold as I do not yet feel very well since my siege of suffering, but thankful to be able to be up and sit by the fire. Praise the Lord for all His benefits.

Monday Nov the 26th 1928

Clear and cold. All able to be up and going. **Clemons Peace** gone to work at the Giant Furniture company at High Point. **Mary Lee Stilwell** to High School at Trinity. **J.W. Peace** to help kill hogs at **Mr Wm Frys,** and his wife **May** and little son **J.A.** are gone with him to visit with **Mrs Fry.** This leaves **Minnie Peace** and myself in the home she is busy embroidering, and I am scribbling a few lines for my Diary. I was favored last evening with the company of my granddaughter **Sadie Blair Fouts** and her husband **Hobert Lee Fouts** of Thomasville. They were Married the 23rd of June 1928. May God bless them and may they live a long and happy life togeather on earth and afterward be reunited in the better land is the desire of my heart for them. They told us of their attendance at the funeral of **Mr Frank Lambeth** of Thomasville a few days before they were here, they said there was a very large attendance and as many as two hundred designs of fine flowers and one of this was a Chair made of flowers in honor of his being the founder of the Chair Factory in Thomasville. He was also a very influential man in many ways.

Being a great Church worker etc. It is right to give every one their due but how often do we see those who are wealthy and have great influence, highly honored, while many true Christians who are meek and lowly and do not have much of this worlds goods, get but a little recognition but we are told in Gods Word that He is "no respector of persons." So all who do His will are alike precious in His sight. Bless be His holy name now and ever.

Tuesday Nov the 27th 1928

Clear and cold. All able to be up and go about daily duties **J.W. Peace** is killing to two fine hogs today, so will be favored with fresh meat But the Dr. tells me I must not eat hog meat.

Wednesday Nov the 28th 1928

Cloudy and not quite so cold this morning. All able to be up and busy. The women folk rendering lard, makeing sausages etc. There is always plenty for the housewives to do, tending to the affairs of the home, and the most important of all is training the children to be obedient to parents, honest and truthful in all things, and above every thing else to honor God and obey His commandments one of those says, "Honor thy Father and thy Mother that thy days may be long upon the earth which the Lord thy God giveth thee." what a precious promice if we obey His holy will, but oh the fearful doom that awaits us if we are disobedient to His divine commands, for unless we sincerely repent of our sins we shall go into everlasting punishment. oh Father help us to do thy will upon earth that we may praise thee forever in heaven for Christs sake.

Thursday Nov the 29th 1928

Clear and a beautiful day for Thanksgiving. And I am very thankful that I can be up and have the use of my hands and thinking faculities to pen down the continued goodness of the dear Lord to me his unworthy child. For He puts it in the hearts and minds of his coworkers who I am thankful to state are my kindred and friends, to remember me most kindly for Thanksgiving. Last night a Car of young people came, and **Miss Nina Millikan** who is a second cousin of mine was the bearer of a lovely Tray of Fruit from The Christian endeavor Society at Springfield, Oringes, Apples, Bananas, Grapes, Pear fruit Cake etc. I can not thank them enough for this kind favor in my lonelyness and above all I thank the Great Giver of all good for it is from Him that all our blessing upon all who have remembered me so kindly. and give Him all the praise far from him cometh all our help.

Friday Nov the 30th 1928

Cloudy this morning. All able to be up and busy except the little grandson **J.A. Peace** is not very well. I had a better rest in sleep last night for which I am very thankful, and this being the last day of the month reminds me of the flight of time and that it wont be long at the longest until we will sleep our last sleep, and oh how necessary to be ready to fall asleep in Jesus to praise His name forever more.

Saturday December the 1st 1928

Cloudy and sprinkling rain this morning. All able to be up, but as always I suffer more with acheing in damp weather. This being the first day of Dec calls to mind that another year will soon have passed away and that we too shall soon pass away and have to give an account of the deeds done in the body. Dear Lord help us to so live that we may have a good account to give.

Sunday Dec the 2nd 1928

Cloudy the morning. All able to arise from our beds for which I am thankful. I hope I shall be able to attend Sunday School and Preaching to day as I have not been able to go to Church for over a month, and I am "always glad when it is said let us go up to the house of the Lord." or words to that effect. And they now have a new Preacher that I have not heard. A **Mr Kelly**. I trust he is a true servant of the Lord and will gain souls for his hire.

Monday Dec the 3rd 1928

Clear and some cooler this morning. All well as usual except the little grandson **J.A.P.** he is not feeling well. I was disappointed in not getting to S.S. and Preaching as I had hoped to do but accepted the disappointment as one of the "all things that work togeather for good to them that love the Lord." We were favored last night until bed time with the company of **Mr Fred Peace** and wife **Janett,** we are always so glad to have them. I praise the Lord this morning for His goodness to us all.

Tuesday Dec the 4th 1928

A beautiful Dec morning. The little grandson is better I am thankful to state, and the rest of the family in usual health, and are busy with daily avocations. Praise the Lord for His goodness and mercy to us His unworthy children.

Wednesday Dec the 5th 1928

Cloudy this morning. All able to be up to day, I am thankful to say. I am very grateful for a quiet nights rest in sleep, which brings to mind the words of Scripture "He giveth His beloved sleep." oh to be beloved of the Lord is worth more than the friendship of the whole world. Praise His holy name.

Thursday Dec the 6th 1928

Clear and much colder this morning. All in usual health, for which I feel thankful to the Giver of all good. "Bless the Lord O my soul and all that is within me, bless his holy name. Bless the Lord O my soul, and forget not all his benefits."

Friday Dec the 7th 1928

Cloudy and cold today. All able to be up, but some of us are not feeling very well. Today some of the Members of Mt Vernon Church are holding A Bazar for the benefit of the Church. May the name of the Lord be exalted above every other name is the fervent desire of my heart. for Christs sake.

Saturday Dec the 8th 1928

Cold this morning. All able to be up I am thankful to state **J.W. Peace** brother **Jacob,** two little girls have come to visit here a while to day.

Sunday Dec the 9th 1928

Clear and cold this morning. All in usual health and I trust will get out to Sunday School. except myself I hardly feel strong enough for the journey. May the Lord help us to make A Sabbath days journey toward heaven is the desire of my heart, for Christs sake.

Monday Dec the 10th 1928

Clear and much colder this morning. I had a good nights rest in sleep so am feeling some stronger, and the rest of the family all in usual health, for which I feel very grateful to our kind and merciful heavenly Father who watches over us, and preserves us from all harm.

Tuesday Dec the 11th 1928

Still clear and cold this morning. All in usual health and busy doing something. I had a better nights rest than usual so feel some stronger and am trying to write some letters to loved ones. **J.W. Peace** as gone to help **Lee Davis** and is brother**Will** kill hogs to day. I praise the Lord that it is as well with us all as it is. and hope we will serve Him better every day.

Wednesday Dec the 12th 1928

Clear and cold. All able to be up and busy. This is my little grandson **J.A. Peace's** fifth Birthday and he and his Mamma are gone to bring **Grandma Peace** to spend the day with him. The prayer of my heart is, that as he grows in years that he may grow in favor with God and man and that his Parents and care takers may lead, guide and direct his steps in the way of truth and righteousness for Jesus sake.

Thursday Dec the 13th 1928

Cloudy this moring. All able to be up I am thankful to state, I had a good nights rest in sleep last night, for which I praise the Lord for His goodness to me.

Friday Dec the 14th 1928

Very rainey this morning. All able to be up and busy prepareing for the Hollidays. oh that we might be as faithful day by day to prepare for the comeing of our dear Lord, who was sent into the World to redeem us from sin, and save us in Heaven to live with Him and praise him forever. As we are to get ready for the Christmas Hollidays doing those things which make for pleasure for our selves and our friends for He is a friend above all others and we should give Him all the honor and praise due to his holy name. Not only at Christmas time should we celebrate His birth appropriatly, but at all times we should glorify Him forever in Heaven. Our Father who art in Heaven, I thank thee for the gift of thy dear Son who thou didst send into the world to redeem us from everylasting punishment. Merciful Heavenly Father keep me from sining against Thee for Jesus sake.

Saturday Dec the 15th 1928

Cloudy this morning. All in usual health. The Parents in this home are going to High Point to day Shopping. We are expecting my son **Fred** and his son **Fred Blair jr** to day from Charlotte, they are

December 1928

comeing to take me home with them to spend the winter, so if my life is spared I shall be with them until after my 84th Birthday which will be March the 13th 1929.

Sunday Dec the 16th 1928

A beautiful morning. All in usual health I am thankful to state. My son and nephew came last night so I am preparing to go home with them. May the dear Lord go with us, and also be with those I leave in this home and help us all to obey His holy will.

Monday Dec the 17th 1928

Cloudy this morning. We arrived in Charlotte last evening at five oclock, found those in the home all well and ready to receive us kindly and gladly. I was of course tired after a ride of one hundred miles but so thankful that we did not meet with any accident. Praise the Lord for His goodness to us all.

Tuesday Dec the 18th 1928

Cloudy again this morning. All well as usual in this home except the ten year old daughter **May** is not well enough to go to school this morning. I had a quiet nights rest in sleep last night for which I feel like giving thanks to my kind and merciful Heavenly Father.

Wednesday Dec the 19th 1928

A beautiful morning. All in usual health to day here at my sons. I am thankful to be able to use my pen and thinking faculties, to praise the Lord for his mercy to me his unworthy child, for altho I am unworthy of all his blessings He pitties and watches over me with tender care day by day. Blessed be His holy name.

Thursday Dec the 20th 1928

Rainey this morning. All are feeling better I am thankful to note, and are on the move prepareing for the comeing of Christmas and the holidays oh that we may be an anxious to be ready for the comeing of our blessed Lord when he calls us from works to rewards, Where we can join our loved ones in praiseing Him who died to redeem us from sin. Blessed be His name forever.

Friday Dec the 21st 1928

Fair and cold this morning. All in usual health. I am thankful to state, and I prayer that we may all live in love and unity, for our Blessed Saviour hath said in His Word, "Behold how good and how pleasant It is for brethren to dwell togeather in unity."

Saturday Dec the 22nd 1928

Clear and cold this morning. All able to be up and busy I am so thankful for a good nights rest, for I often have lain awake for hours during the night so I feel like saying this morning, from my heart Bless the Lord oh my soul and forget not His benefits. My Daughterinlaw **Esther Blair** has gone up Town shopping for Christmas so I feel quite lonely.

Sunday Dec the 23rd 1928

A pretty morning, but quite cold. My son and his family are gone to Church this morning and the Lady **Mrs Willie Clary** and her little son that are boarding here are with me for the time. Praise the dear Lord for His goodness to me.

Monday Dec the 24th 1928

Anothe nice cold morning. I am so thankful that we are as well as we are for health is one of our greatest blessings. Yesterday afternoon we were favored with the company of **Mrs Charles Orsborn** who formerly lived in High Point but has been here in Charlotte with her daughter and grand children for some time. We are glad to meet with those we have known in former years. Praise the Lord for His goodness to me and my dear ones.

December 1928

Tuesday Dec the 25th 1928

A lovely Christmas morning. All able to arise from our beds and rush to the Xmas Tree to see the nice things which we all received from kindred and friends, and I feel so thankful for all the nice and good things I received and above all I am so grateful to our merciful heavenly Father for the Gift of His dear Son Jesus Christ our Lord oh that we may adore Him and prise Him above every other givt is the prayer of my heart for His dear names sake.

Wednesday Dec the 26th 1928

Clear and cold this morning. I had quiet nights rest and am so thankful that we are all as well as we are to day after indulging so freely in the many good things that were prepared for us for Christmas. Praise the Lord for His goodness to us all.

Thursday Dec the 27th 1928

Cloudy and very damp this morning which causes me more aches and pains in my aged limbs but Thankful that all are able to be up and go about daily avocations. My son **F.C. Blair** to his work in the J.H. Wearn Lumber Company, here in Charlotte, my oldest granddaughter in this Home **Emily Hayden Blair** to her work as an opperator in the Western Union Telegraph office, my daughterinlaw **Esther Hayden Blair** to her many duties in her house work. and my little ten year old granddaughter **Mary Ann Blair** washing dishes, etc. My grandson **Fred C. Blair jr** helping in the general work in the home, during the Hollidays until the School takes in again, he is takeing a buisness Course in the High School, his little sister **Mary** goes to the Common School which also closed for the Hollidays. The Lady that boards in this home has also gone to her work as a Telegraph opperator in the Wes Union Office and her little son **Billy Clary** is playing with the many Toys etc that he received for Christmas. (His mothers name is **Mrs Willie Clary**) and I am scribling a few lines in memmory of this occasion. and my heart is filled with gratitude to the Giver of all good, for His benefits to us His unworthy children.

Friday Dec the 28th 1928

A nice morning. We that constitus this family are all in reasonable good health, for which I am very grateful to our kind and merciful heavenly Father, and for putting into the hearts and minds of my many friends to remember me so nicely this Christmas by sending Cards of greeting from many places in my own native State N.C. from High Point, Thomasville, Archdale, Mt Vernon, Fairview, and other places and from Kansas City, Mo, and from Kansas City Kansas, and from Ohmaha Nebraska, by Cards and presents. Praise the Lord oh my soul and forget not all His benefits.

Saturday Dec the 29th 1928

Very damp this morning. None of us are feeling very well. My son is not able to go to his work this morning he has such a deep cold and suffered so severely with his head last night but is able to sit by the fire to day for which I am so glad. I have deep cold also and my throat is sore, but so thankful to be so I can be up and use my pen to note the continued goodness and mercy to us all in watching over and takeing care of us all day and night. Blessed be His holy name.

Sunday Dec the 30th 1928

A lovely Sabbath morning. All able to arise from our beds, and my son and his wife and their oldest daughters and their only son are gone to Church and as I am not going, I will endeavor to read my Bible and worship our blessed Lord while in the home for if it is so that we can not go to the Lords house we can worship Him in our own homes and hearts. May we all be thus engaged in worshiping Him is my prayer for Jesus sake. "Praise God from whom all blessings flow. Praise Him all cretures her below." so saith my soul this beautiful Sabbath day.

December 1928

Monday Dec the 31ˢᵗ 1928

Cloudy this morning, but not very cold, we are all able to be up and go about daily avocations after a quiet nights rest, and this being not only the last day of the month but also the last day of the year of 1928. it brings serious reflections to mind for the time is fast passing away and we shall soon be called upon to give account of the deeds done in the body, and I fervently desire to so live that I will have a good account to give, and when I reflect upon the evil deeds that are being done in many places thruout the land my heart almost bleeds at the thought of the doom that awaits those who are transgressing Gods law by perpetrateing such enormous evil deeds even to cold blooded murder, oh the horor of it, Yesterday afternoon nearly all of this family went out to the scene of that terable tragedy that was enacted last Thursday night or rather Friday morning about two oclock about one mile west of the Town of Gastonia in Gaston County, N.C. That of **J.W. Vanderburg** and his wife and two daughters and a son the oldest daughter **Miss Pauline Vanderburg** was about eighteen years of age and was a student of North Carolina College for Women Greensboro North Carolina. the other a daughter about sixteen, and the other a son about twelve years of age. The only one left in the family is **Jacob** about seventeen years of age who is being held for the murder of the whole family of five victims. What the outcome will be I can not tell now as the case has not been decided on whether the son did it or not but being held on circumstantial evidence. and he is being kept in prison. This is the most horrable murder case ever known in this State, and I can not see how anything could be worse in any State, five victims slain, and their bodies thrown in a pile and then the house set on fire and burned all their bodies beyond recognition, the chared trunks of their bodies, without their heads, arms or legs was all that could be secured to put in Caskets for burial, the chared stubs of the parents bodies were put in one Casket togeather and those of their three children were put in another, every other part of their bodies were cremated in the ruins of the building. On Sunday after this terable deed was done Friday night about two oclock, my son and family took me with them and went to the scene of that awful tragedy how dreadful to stand at the edge of the ruins and see those lone chimneys standing as mute sentinels of this horable affair and see the burned bed springs broken dishes etc and etc and small pieces of human bones and sculls my daughterinlaw is a Trained Nurse and she picked up a small piece that she knew to be a human bone, and it crumbled into sinders every particl of their bodies were perfectly cremated excep the main trunk of the body, which was so blackened and chared that there was no telling which they belonged to only by the larger and smaller bulk of the Torso. I made the mistake of stateing that all three of the children were put in one casket, the two sisters trunks of their bodies were put togather in one casket and that of the young son was put in with the parents. This is the sadest circumstance that I have ever noted, in all the more than fifty years of takeing notes.

1929

Tuesday January the 1st 1929

Real cloudy and damp for the begining of the New Year, and all of us have very deep colds and feel quite dull this morning. but I for one realise that we are entering another year of probation, and we know not what the future will bring forth, but I am praying that with the passing of the old year, we may forsake all our evil inclinations, and take on new courage to press on for the right. Leaveing the things that are behind and press forward to that which is before.

Wednesday Jan the 2nd 1929

Clear this morning, we are all suffering more or less with our colds which seem to be a mild form of Influenza, but thankful that it is as well with us all as it is. for while we can keep from being bedfast we have so much to praise God for. and I feel like saying. "I will lift up mine eyes unto the hills, from whence cometh my help cometh from the Lord which made heaven on earth.

Thursday Jan the 3rd 1929

Partly cloudy to day, we are all still suffering with cold, I had an entirely sleepless night, as my cough troubles me so badly and have difculty of breathing, but thankful to be so I can arise from my bed, and that none of us are bedfast, for there is quite an eppidemic of Flu thruout this section.

Friday Jan the 4th 1929

A beautiful sunshiney morning, but there is a cold chilly wind which makes you shiver when you are exposed to it, I am so thankful for a good nights rest in sleep, as I had none the night before. Bless the Lord oh my soul, and all that is within me bless His holy name. Bless the Lord oh my soul and forget not all His benefits.

Saturday Jan the 5th 1929

Cloudy and very damp this morning. None of us feeling well, as we are all still suffering from deep cold, and what seems to be a light attack of the Flue, but I am so thankful that it is as well with us all as it is, and feel like ascribing praise to Him from whom all blessings flow.

Sunday Jan the 6th 1929

Cloudy, cold and windy. The family here are feeling better than for several days past and I am so glad that none of us are bedfast, and altho I am not strong I am thankful to be up and pen a line in honor to my blessed Saviour who suffered so much for me that I might inherit eternal life for it was for all that He shed His precious blood therefore for me. Blessed be His holy name now and forever.

Monday Jan the 7th 1929

This is one of the coldest mornings we have had this winter, but the sun is shineing brightly, which is makeing every thing look more cheerful, and we are some better of our colds for which I am very thankful, to the Great Giver of all good for He watches over and cares for us day and night.

Tueday Jan the 8th 1929

A beautiful day but quite cold, all are some better of our deep cold but not clear of them. My daughterinlaw just started up Town Shoping which leaves little **Billy Clary** and myself alone for the time. May we look to our Heavenly Father at all times for protection and trust Him fully, for He has promiced to be a Father to the Fatherless and a husband to the widow and I am standing on his promices, Bless His holy name.

Wednesday Jan the 9th 1929

Clear and cold this morning, we are all some better of our colds, for which I feel very thankful, for there are so many that have taken on Pneumonia and we are reminded daily of the uncertainty of life and the certainty of death, for there are so many being called from works to rewards. oh that we may all be ready for the summons, when the Master calls.

Thursday Jan the 10th 1929

Some cloud, and much warmer this morning. I did not get able to arise from my bed until twelve oclock to day, as I had a dreadful attack of headache last nigh, which caused me to feel weak and nerous, but thankful to get up at last.

Friday Jan the 11th 1929

Cloudy and real damp this morning. Altho I am not over the effects of the Influenza and am still full of cold. But am so glad that I can be up this morning, and take up my pen to note down the continued goodness and mercy of our blessed Saviour toward us all, for while so many are being bereaved of some member of their family, we have been spared thru this present Epidemic. Blessed by His holy name.

Saturday Jan the 12th 1929

A nice bright morning, but quite cold. All are able to arise from our beds, I am thankful to state and my desire is that we may all be obedient to the will of Him in whom we live and move for we know that He has power to clip the brittle thread of life at any time. so our Father in Heaven I pray that we may be helped to glorify Thee on earth that we may glorify thee forever in Heaven.

Sunday Jan the 13th 1929

A lovely Sabbath morning. All nearly in usual health, for which I am thankful, Blessed be the name of the Lord who watches over us by day and by night.

Monday Jan the 14th 1929

Clear and cold. All able to be up and go about daily avocations, some to work in the home some to work in the Shop and some to work in the School room, let us all do our best whatever the ocupation and thank our Great Benefactor for sufficient health and strength to perform whatever our hands find to do and that we may do all to the glory of God.

Tuesday Jan the 15, 1929

All able to be up this morning, except the daughter Emily who is not at all well and is keeping her bed to day, but thankful that it is as well as it is with us all, Priase the Lord oh my soul.

Wednesday Jan the 16th 1929

Cloudy this morning, All better to day and are going about daily ovocations. We all had quiet nights rest for which I feel very grateful to our merciful Heavenly Father who takes care of us at all times "I will lift up mine eyes unto the hills, for whence cometh my help, My help cometh from the Lord which made heaven and earth, He will not suffer thy foot to be moved: he that keepeth thee will not slumber."

Thursday Jan the 17th 1929

Real cloudy this morning. All able to be up and busy, doing the things that are necessary to be done for the comfort and sustanance of our mortal bodies, oh that we may be concerned for the salvation of our immortal souls and obey the commandments of the Lord while on earth that we may be permited to live with Him in heaven there to praise Him with our loved ones gone before thruout the endless ages of eternity.

Friday Jan the 18th 1929

Cloudy this morning, none of us feeling very well but thankful to able to be out of bed and go about daily avocations for there has been so many years in the past that I have been entirely confined to the bed. so I say with David "Be merciful unto me O God, be merciful unto me for my soul trusteth in thee: yea in the shadow of thy wings will I make my refuge until these calamities be overpast. I will cry unto God most high: unto God that performeth all things for me." "My heart is fixed. O God my heart is fixed: I will ring and give praise."

Saturday Jan the 19th 1929

A beautiful sunshiney morning, I feel grateful to be up to enjoy it, and for having spent a quiet nights rest in sleep, and for the use of my right hand and thinking faculties to note down the contined goodness and mercy of the Lord to us His dependent children. Praise His holy name.

Sunday Jan the 20th 1929

A lovely Sabbah morning, and all except myself are gone to Church, Sunday School etc and as it is not my lot to go to day I will try to make the best use of the time possible in the home for it is our privilige to worship God in our own homes and hearts when we can not go to the house dedicated to Gods service, so I pray that I may be faithful to draw nigh to God that he may draw nigh to me, and find comfort in confideing in Him, and in doing His holy will "As the hart panteth after the water brooks so panteth my soul after thee O God." Why art thou cast down O my soul? and why art thou disquieted in me?" "hope thou in God: for I shall yet praise him for the help of his countenance." And my God."

Monday Jan the 21st 1929

Cloudy this morning. All able to arise from our beds and go about our daily duties. I was favored yesterday in the afternoon to take a drive with the family thru part of the City and the ride out in the fresh air seemed to do me good so I had a quiet nights rest in sleep for which I feel very thankful to my heavenly Father.

Tuesday Jan the 22nd 1929

Another cloudy damp day. None of feeling very well, but thankful to be able to be up and do that which is most necessary to be done for the comfort and sustanance of our perishable bodies, and I pray that we may be still more concerned for the salvation of our immortal souls. and that we may glorify God on earth, that we may glorify Him forever in heaven.

Wednesday Jan the 23rd 1929

Still some cloudy. We are all able to arise from our beds this morning for which I am very thankful and praise the Lord for all His benefits to us his dependent children. "Bless the Lord oh my soul and all that is within me. Bless His holy name."

Thursday Jan the 24th 1929

Still cloudy and very damp. All able to be up and attend to daily affairs, for which I am very thankful. and "I will lift up mine eyes unto the hills, from whence cometh my help. My help cometh from the Lord which made heaven and earth. Blessed be His holy name.

Friday Jan the 25th 1929

Cloud this morning. All of this family are able to be up to day, after listening to the Radio for several hours last night, This instrument is one of the wonders of the word brought into use in this fast age of the word. It is something to reflect upon when we consider how poor mortal man can by his God given faculties bring about such wonderful things as are now going on thruout all lands. And when we think of the infinite goodness and mercy of the Great Giver of all things which we have to enjoy. how our hearts should be filled with praise and thanksgiving to Him who has spared our lives and given us a degree of health to enjoy the many this we are permitted to hear and see.

Blessed be His name.

Saturday Jan the 26th 1929

Clear and cold this morning. All able to be up and attend the affairs of the day for which I thank Him in whom we live and move and have our being. Praise His holy name.

Sunday Jan the 27th 1929

Rainey and real cold this morning. All in our usual state of health, able to be up but not feeling stron,g but most of the family are gone to Church, but as the weather is too inclement for me to go out, I have had the privilege and the pleasure of listening to a spledid sermon over the Radio which my son has had installed in his home. The sermon was by **Dr Webb of** Columbia South Carolina who exchanged Pulpits with **Dr Little** of the first Baptist Church here in Charlotte. **Dr Webbs** sermon was founded on the second chapter of Philippians and also on a portion of the second chapter of first Corinthians, I enjoyed the sermon very much and praise the Lord for the privilege of hearing it.

January 1929

Monday Jan the 28th 1929

Still cloudy and cold, All able to be up again to day for which I give thanks, and for having rest in sleep the past night. I must note than I had the pleasure yesterday in the afternoon as well as in the forenoon of listening to a good sermon over the Radio and listening to the singing of good Hymns and the reading of Scripture all of which I greatly enjoyed for it was such a great substitute for not getting out to Church. I feel that this is a great blessings to the shutins and those who are in any way deprived of presenting themselves at the house of God, and I praise Him for all His benefits and ask Him to help us all to be faithful to do His holy will wherever we are.

Tuesday Jan the 29th 1929

A nice bright morning after several dull cloudy days, which makes us rejoice at the warm sunlight, oh that we may rejoice and sing praise to the Son of God who gave His precious life a ransom for the sins of the whole world therefore for us poor unworthy cretures as we feel ourselves to be.

Wednesday Jan the 30th 1929

Some cloudy this morning. All able to be up and attend to the affairs of the day and I call to mind that this is my granddaughter Emily Hayden Blair's nineteenth Birthday it hardly seems possible as I seem to see her as a little girl of nine or ten years of age but time flies so fast, she is now a grown young lady and is a full fleged Oporator in The Western Union Telegraph Office in Charlotte N.C. which is the home of the Parents at the time, They moved here from High Point some years ago and after Emily had finished her time in School with an aded Buiseness Course she has been industriously working ever since she was fifteen years of age, and is now an expert in the Position she now fills and is highly respected and well thought of by all who have made her acquaintance and she has numerous friends moreover is a good Christian girl which does the heart of her aged grandmother good for this is the foundation of all good.

Thursday Jan the 31ˢᵗ 1929

Cold and damp this morning, which causes more aches and pains in my aged limbs, but I am thankful to be able to be up and use my pen in noteing down the goodness and mercy of the Lord in watching over us day and night, and I am again reminded of the flight of time as this is the last day of the month of January, and we know that as the time passes we are each day that much nearer our journeys end on earth and we want to be prepared to enter the kingdom of heaven when done with the things of earth. So my prayer is this morning. Dear Lord help us to glorify thee on earth that we may glorify thee in Heaven.

Friday February the 1ˢᵗ 1929

Clear and cold this morning, All able to be up and attend to daily occupations, and as this is the first day of the month it reminds me again how fast time is passing away, and we know not what day or even an hour may bring forth, for in reflecting upon how suddenly some of the people who lived right here in Charlotte were called from works to rewards last month, when an Officer Detective **Mr Carroll** was instantly killed by a bullet shot from the hand of a negro who he was trying to arrest for robbery, and also another sad case of sudden death when a Street Car Conductor a **Mr King** was almost instantly killed by the breaking and falling of the Electric wire on the Trolley line which he came in contact in some way which Electricuted him, so we see that both those men were sent to their death without any warning, which shows us that we should always be ready for the call, let it come when or in whatever way it may, These are both very sad cases as they both left wives and several small children who were dependent upon them for their keep.

Saturday Feb the 2nd 1929

Clear and very cold this morning. All able to be up and go about daily affairs excep my daughterinlaw who is not well to day But I feel that all have much to thank our merciful Heavenly Father for that it is as well with us as it is, for we have food and rainment and fuel to keep us warm and there are many poor creatures that do not have.

Sunday February the 3rd 1929

Clear and cold this morning. All able to arise from our beds this lovely Sabbath morning, for which I am very thankful to our kind and merciful heavenly Father for His goodness to us all in careing for us by night and by day. And just at this moment there comes over the Radio the voice of the singing of a sweet Hymn in the first Baptist Church here in Charlotte and then the announcement of the reading of the twenty eight chapter of Genesis and a good sermon founded on the same. It is so nice to hear a good sermon while sitting at home when we do not have the privilige of getting to Church and to hear the good Hymns sung in praise to God.

Monday February the 4th 1929

Cloudy this morning. All able to be up and go to daily aocations as usual, but after my son had gone to work in **J. W. Wearns** Shop where he has worked and run a Saw for several years, he accidently got one of his hands cut pretty badly, and they brought him home as his hand was in too bad fix for him to work. I am very sorry he is hurt, but so thankful he did not lose his hand.

Tuesday Feb the 5th 1929

Cloudy this morning and we have about three inches of snow on a level which is our first snow in our new year of 1929 everything looks pretty this morning the trees and houses covered in the pretty white snow which makes me cry out in mind and heart "Wash me and I shall be whiter than snow." I am very thankful that we are all able to be up and look out upon this beautiful scenery. and that my son who got his left hand severely cut yesterday while runing the saw in **Mr Wearns** shop is not now suffering much with it to day and I hope it will soon heal for he is so industrious it hurts him about as bad to not be so he can work as the wound itself. so I praise the Lord that it is as well with him and all the rest of us as it is.

Wednesday Feb the 6th 1929

Real cloudy and still snow on the ground this morning and looks as tho there was plenty more in the clouds. I have had to dictate these few lines while on my bed to day as I have had a dreadful headache last night and today.

Thursday Feb the 7th 1929

The sun is shining this morning and what snow there is on the ground is melting away fast, and instead of more snow falling it looks like we are going to have a pretty day. I am still feeling weak and dizzy headed to day but thankful to be so I can be up instead of having to keep my bed as I did yesterday, and so glad that it is as well with the family here as it. my son is getting along nicely with his hand that he got Cut in the shop and I hope will soon be able to work for it is is very much against him to loose time for he is no shirker, and he also need his wages.

Friday Feb the 8th 1929

Clear and much warmer this morning. The snow has now all melted away. We are all feeling better this morning for which I am very thankful, but I am still troubled with Virtigo which causes such dizziness, that I have to be very careful not to get a fall. I had a letter yesterday from my daughter **Mrs J.W. Peace,** and she has been quite sick with the Flue. But was better, she also told me of the death of **Mrs Josephine Albertson** which was very sudden from heart Dropsy.

February 1929

Saturday Feb the 9th 1929

Rainey this morning. None of us feeling very well this damp weather, and my son has a bad headache to day. he had his laserated hand dressed yesterday and the Dr said it was doing fine, for which I am very thankful and glad that we are all able to be out of bed, for I know what it means to be confined to the bed for many years in the past and I feel it to be a great blessing when I can be up and make out to wait on myself and as my life has been spared I want to be a blessing to others, and we are daily reminded of the uncertainty of life, as there is scarely a day passes but what we learn of the death of some one or ones being killed in some way or other. Yesterday there was a Charlotte lady killed out on the Concord road by an Auto turning over on her and crushing her to death. oh how necessary that we should be ready for the final change for we know not what a day nor an hour may bring forth.

Sunday Feb the 10th 1929

A pretty sunshiny morning. All able to be up and most of the family have already gone to Church, and as I did not feel like going. I am now listening to the singing comeing over the Radio from the first Baptist Church at Charlotte N.C. and also there comes words of prayer and Scripture reading and a good sermon by **Dr Luther Little** which was very much enjoyed by those of us who were permited to be his listeners.

Monday Feb the 11th 1929

Cloudy this morning, and the Air feels like we were going to have snow again. we are all in our usual state of health, and my sons hand that was lacerated in the Shop is healing fine I am thankful to state, and he think he will be able soon to go back to work again. Praise the Lord for His goodness.

Tuesday Feb the 12th 1929

Clear and cold this morning. All up and going about their daily avocations excep my son can not yet go to his work in the Shop as his hand is not sufficiently healed but doing nicely I am very thankful to state.

Wednesday Feb the 13th 1929

Clear and much colder to day, for which I feel very grateful to our heavenly Father for all of his benefits to us his dependent children. For like "As a Father pittieth his children so the Lord pittieth them that fear Him for he knoweth our frame; he remembereth that we are dust."

Thursday Feb the 14th 1929
St Valentines Day

Clear and cold this morning. All able to arise from our beds this morning, for which I am very grateful, and my sons hand that was cut is healing fine. To day is little **Billy Martin Clarys** fourth Birthday, and his Mother is going to give him a Birthday Party here at my sons, as they are boarding here, and my daughterinlaw is busy makeing preparations for the event. May we all be truly thankful to the Great Giver of all good for all our blessings is my hearts desire.

Friday Feb the 15th 1929

Raining this morning, and looks like we would have a very rainey day. but thankful that all are able to arise from our beds. Praise the Lord.

Saturday Feb the 16th 1929

Still rainy this morning, and the dampness is very much against me, but I am very thankful that I can arise from my bed and wait on myself, and that the rest of the family are in usual health, and that my son's hand is healing fine, Last Thursday the fourteenth was not only St Valentines Day, but also little **Billy Martin Clarys** fourth

February 1929

Birthday and his Mother **Mrs Clary** gave him a Birthday Party, he invited more than a dozen little boys and they came, and little girls came also and three ladies of their acquaintance one of them was his Auntie. so we had a very nice Party. The Table was beautifully deckorated with red streamers from the corners to the electric light hanging above and small red heart shaped Boxes of Candy at each artificial plate which was supplied with a generous slice of fine Cake from the large Whie Cake that graced the midle of the Table and a block of Ice Cream there were four candles on the big Cake which little **Billy** blew out. and before serveing the meal. little **Billy** and myself gave thanks he repeating after my daughterinlaw who he calls "Mama Blair" Almighty God we give thee thanks who rulest and reignest word world without end, Amen. Then I followed by saying what was in my heart Heavenly Father thou hast said. Suffer little children to come unto Me and forbid them not for of such is the kingdom of heaven We thank Thee for all our blessings, for food for the sustanance of our mortal bodies and above all we ask that thou wilt feed us with the bread of heaven and give us the water of life to drink which alone can nourish up our souls unto life eternal through Jesus Christ our Lord. Amen.

Sunday Feb the 17th 1929

Clear and colder this morning. All able to be up and all are gone to Church exept little **Billy Clary** and myself. I wish to be faithful to worship Him who is a spirit and they that worship Him must worship Him in spirit and in truth, so if we do not have a chance to attend Church at all times we can worship Him in our homes and in our hearts.

Monday Feb the 18th 1929

Clear and cold this morning All well as usual except little **Billy Clary** who has a spell of vomiting but we are thankful that it is nothing worse. Praise the Lord for His goodness to us all.

Tuesday Feb the 19th 1929

Clear and bright this morning. All are better I am thankful to state May the sunshine of Gods love so fill our that we may be obedient to his divine will in all things to His honor and praise is my hearts desire for Christs sake.

Wednesday Feb the 20th 1929

Cloudy and very damp this morning which causes my aged limbs to ache more than when the weather is bright and clear, but I am very thankful to be so I can be up and wait on mysel, for I know what it means to be helpless for years in the past, and as I have listened to the announcements over the Radio of the many helpless and other ways afflicted shut ins, it fills my heart with sympathy for all of them and pray that the dear Lord will bless them with His presence and help them to bear all ther afflictions patiently for Jesus sake.

Thursday Feb the 21st 1929

Cloudy and real cold. and the ground covered with sleet, we are all able to arise from our beds, and I am so thankful that we have food and clothing and fuel to keep us warm, for no doubt there are those thruout the land that are not sufficiently supplied with these necessities. Oh that we may always remember the injunction in Gods holy word that "The poor you have with you always and whensoever you will you may do them good." It is the desire of my heart to observe the Golden Rule as far as it is possible to do so, God being my helper for it is my fervent to be faithful to Him in all things to His honor and praise."

Friday Feb the 22nd 1929

The sun is comeing out this morning, and it looks as tho we would have a fair day, and as this is the Aniversary of the Birth of **George Washington** to day, and stands first in the hearts of his countrymen

February 1929

as Father of our country by his achievements it is only just that we should pay tribue to his memory and while doing homage to his memory which is due, it is still more necessary that we give the praise to the King of Kings who is the Father of all Nations kindred tounge and people He in whom all people live and have our being, He who gave **George Washington** the wisdom strength and courage to do such noble deeds for our country, and for the welfare of many Nations To Him be all praise now and forever. The first great figure in the history of the United States **George Washington** was born February 22nd 1732 just 197 years ago and to him thru kind Presidents we owe our glorious independence to day.

Saturday Feb the 23rd 1929

A nice morning. All in usual health I am glad to state, for altho I am not strong I am so thankful to be so I can be up and wait on myself and pen a line in praise of my blessed Redeemer who watches over me day and night, and I have faith to believe that He hears my poor unworthy prayers for He hath said if you ask in faith you may ask what ye will and it shall be done unto you, and I am standing on His promices.

Sunday Feb the 24th 1929

Clar and cold this morning. We are all able to arise from our beds this bright morning and my three grandchildren are gone to Church and the rest of us will listen to the good things comeing over the Radio. and I trust we will also remember that all our blessings come from the source of all good, even from God our heavenly Father who gave His dear Son to die for us all.

Monday Feb the 25th 1929

Clear and much warmer this morning, all in usual health except myself. I have suffering with my head, and bleeding at the nose so I had to lie down again, but will now try to stay up and pen down a few lines, yesterday in the afternoon after I had listened to a good sermon comeing over the Radio, I went with part of the family for a drive, and calling at the Mail Box recieved a letter from my daughter **Mrs J.W. Peace** in which I got the sad news of the death of one of my cousins **Eugene Marsh** of Archdale who died of Paralysis about two weeks ago, I am so sorry for his wife for I lost my dear husband nine years ago, of Paralysis and know what the loss of companion means.

Tuesday Feb the 26th 1929

Cloudy this morning. we are all able to arise from our beds for which I am very thankful altho I feel too feeble to do much to day but I praise the Lord for giving me sweet rest in sleep the past night, for many wakeful nights have I spent during my afflictions, and I feel like saying with the Psalmist. "Unless thy law had been my delights, I should then of perished in mine afflictions." Praise the Lord oh my soul.

Wednesday Feb the 27th 1929

Cloudy and have had quite a big rain during the night. I am still feeling feeble but thankful to be so I can be up, and that the rest are all well and going about daily afocations, some to work and some to school. Praise the Lord.

Thursday Feb the 28th 1929

Still cloudy and damp this morning. I am not yet feeling as well as usual, but thankful to be up and wait on myself, and as this is the last day of Feb and also the last day of the winter season I am reminded of the flight of time, as I came here to spend three months with my son and family I now only have one month until I expect to return to my daughter in Randolph.

Friday March the 1st 1928

Clear this morning, it seems good to see the sun shining, as we have had so much cloudy and rainey weather during the past winter. We are able to be up and busy with the things that pertain to our welfare while we are permited to remain here on this earth Gods footstool. And I am anxious to do the things that He has designed that we should do to make ready for our eternal reward when done with time here below, that we may have an entrance into that home which He has prepared for those who do his holy will on earth, that they may dwell forever with Him in Heaven.

Saturday March the second 1929

Cloudy this morning but the sun is now coming out, we are all able to be up and busy to day, I am thankful to state, and hope we shall be close on our watch that we obey the divine command to love God supremely, and our neighbor as ourselves, and observe the Golden Rule to do unto others as we would have them do unto us. "I will lift up mine eyes unto the hills from whence cometh my help, my help cometh from the Lord."

Sunday March the 3rd 1929

Clear and beautiful sunshine. We are all able to be up this morning, for which I feel very grateful. The family here who belong the Catholic Church have already been to the eight oclock Mass. I have now been listening in the Radio here in my sons home to the services of the first Baptist Church at eleven oclock and heard a good sermon by **Dr Luther Little** his discourse was on he 14th chapter of St John which I could hear distinctly and the singing of good Hymns and fervent prayers etc, all of which I enjoyed very much, for altho I do not belong to any of the denominations here, I am no sectarian and love the hear the Gospel preached by any true Christian demonimation, My membership is in the Friends Church at Springfield Guilford County, N.C. and as there is no opportunity to attend my own Church while spending the winter here in Charlotte I of course miss my own Church and home associates but thankful that we have the same God, our merciful Heavenly Father wherever we may be, and desire that we may all be faithful to serve Him in spirit and in truth.

Monday March the 4th 1929

Very rainey this morning. We are able to be up and listen to the program of the Inogeration of the President of the United States **Hurbert Hoover** and the many speeches made by his Cabinet and others, and the music of the many different Bands, etc and the yelling of and claping of the thousands of people who are assembled to take part in the celebrating this eventful day, and it hardly seems believeable but nevertheless true that we could hear the rattle of the horses hoofs so plain on the pavements as a portion of many different regiments would pass the reviewing stand, and the Announcer telling how they were dressed in their respective uniforms, and how cordially the President and vice President etc greeted all concerned in the participation of this gaily day. and this has certainly been a busy day not only in Washington but thruout the many States and I am sure there will be many tired people to night, for so many have been kept busy Broadcasting the events of the day over the Radio amongst the many other transactions of the day. and it seems so wonderful to sit in the home and hear the great part of it all, as plain as tho it were in the next room. And I have thought that the Radio might well be called the eigth wonder of the World. and when will wonders ceace! and how often I have thought to day of the great pomp and granduer of this days sisplay for while our Chief Magistrates is worthy of great recognition and it is I fiting that the day should be observed properly, but oh how sadly different was our Blessed Lord generally treated when here on earth, He who made it possible for us to have a government and a good man to rule our nation, to Him belongeth the praise and honor of all nations. And in whom we live and move and have our being. Blessed be His holy name now and foreevermore.

March 1929

Tuesday March the 5th 1929

Some cloudy by appearance of clearing, we are all able to arise from our beds as usual except my daughterinlaw who has a very deep cold and headache so as to keep her bed to day, but hope she may be much better by another day, and I praise the Lord that it is as well with us all as it is, for there are many suffering ones thruout the land.

Wednesday March the 6th 1929

Clear and bright sunshine this morning which seems good after so much rain and cloudy weather most of the family are able to be up and attend to the duties of the day, **Esther** is better I am glad to state, I am suffering from deep cold and sore throast myself to day, but thankful to be so Ican wait on myself and praise the Lord for his goodness and mercy to his unworthy children.

Thursday March the 7th 1929

A pretty clear morning. all able to be up, but some of us have deep colds, the weather has been so rainey and damp for several weeks that it is hard to keep from takeing cold. but I am glad to be able to pen a few lines each day in honor of Him who watches over us all and knows our every thought. "O Lord, thou has searched me, and know me, thou knowest my down sitting and mine uprising, thou understandest my thoughts afar off. Thou compasssest my path and my lying down, and art acquainted with all my ways for there is not a word in my tongue, but lo O Lord thou knowest it altogather." I realise that these words of the 139th Psalm apply to me daily.

Friday March the 8th 1929

Clear and colder this morning all feeling some better and are busy attending to daily duties, we have so much to thank our merciful heavenly Father for as he is careing for us at all times. Blessed be His holy name.

Saturday March the 9th 1929

Cloudy this morning. All able to be up and busy I am thankful to state, but I am still suffering with cold and acheing in my chest, but so glad that I am not confined to my bed. Praise the Lord for His goodness and mercy to us all. After noon of same day, Our hearts have been saddened by hearing of the death of **Mr Bickett** who passed away about one oclock, lived but a little way from here, rite in site on the opposite side of the street. I have never met him but have some acquaintance with his wife for a few years as I have met her from time to time when I have been here in Charlotte and think a great deal of her, and she certainly has my deepest sympathy, for I know what it means to have to give up a dear life companion. And the dear Lord be with her and his dear children and comfort them.

Sunday March the 10th 1929

A bright sunshiney morning but quite cold. We are all able to arise from our bed and the family are now all gone to church services at nine thirty oclock. I hope to be able to go the funeral of **Mr. Bickett** this afternoon Sunday evening, well I must now add that I was favored to attend the funeral of **Mr. Fred Bickett** and it was one of the the largest funderals I even attendin my life. and the provusion of flowers was a show to behold. And after we returned home from the funeral. We were visited by **Mr** and **Mrs Orion Bradly** of this City which was a treat as we had not seen them in quite awhile.

Monday March the 11th 1929

Clear and cold to day, all able to be up and are some better of our colds for which I am very thankful, for many have taken on Pneumonia and passed away, while the dear has seen fit to spare our lives unworthy as we are. We were indeed glad to have **Mr. and Mrs Bradly** with us last evening for a while.

March 1929

Tuesday March the 12th 1929

Cloudy this morning, all well as usual excep **Fred** and **Emily** they are not either one able to go to work this morning but thinking they can go this afternoon as the are not seriously sick.

Wednesday March the 13th 1929

Rainey this morning. All able to arise from our beds for which I am very thankful and as this is my eighty fourth Birthday it brings up many things both of joy and of sorrow as I reflect up the past, I wish all my friends could see the beautiful Table that my daughterinlaw **Esther Blair** has dressed up for my birthday dinner with lavender streamers of fine tisue paper from the four corners of the table up to the Electric light just over the middle of the table and lovely lavender flowered napkins and pretty set of new dishes silver knives and forks and spoons and lovely drinking glasses, and in the center of the Table a large and most beautiful white cake trimmed in lavender and on it was Grandmother 84 years writen in lovely script. Praise the Lord for His goodness to me and mine.

Thursday March the 14th 1929

Cloudy this morning, we are all able to be up and busy righting up things after the delightlful time we have with our friends yesterday at my Birthday dinner. We just had a few of my special friends which I enjoyed so much as they were member of my Bibles Class when I staid here in Charlotte four years ago, **Mrs Holingworth, Mrs Ed Smith, Mrs Rogers, Mrs Kyou** and children, **Mrs Bickett** did not get to come as she had company. We had a most delightful time socially and then before parting, at my request **Mrs Holingsworth** read the 14th chapter of St John and gave a nice talk and then offered a most beautiful prayer she is such a lovely woman and lives so near to God, that she is always a welcome guest.

Friday March the 15th 1929

Rainey this morning. We are still bothered with bad colds but all better except **Mrs Clary** the lady that boards here she is not able to go to her work at the Western Union to day. But we have so much to be thankful for that that we have not been visited with Floods as in some other States.

Saturday March the 16th 1929

A beautiful morning it seems so good to see the sun shineing after so much rain oh that we may all let the Son of righteousness shine on our hearts and dispel all gloom of discouragement, and praise His holy name.

Sunday March the 17th 1929

A lovely Sabbath morning, all able to greet the beautiful sunshine, the family have all been to Church, and I was expecting to hear a sermon over the Radio at eleven oclock but owing to some mechanical defect at the Baptist Church the sermon could not be broadcast, but I hope to hear one this afternoon, but if we are sometimes deprived of listening to the sound of the Gospel preached, we can if we are faithful listeners hear That small voice speaks as yet never man spake. And I am so thankful that He puts it into the hearts of my loved one to remember me with kind letters and beautiful Birthday Cards which I have still be receiving which did not reach me on the my 84th birthday the 13th of this month. Yesterday I rec two lovely cards from my Grandaughters in Kansas City Mo.

Monday March the 18th 1929

Another bright morning, but much colder. We are all able to be up and go about daily avocations, for which I feel very thankful to the Great Giver of all good. Yesterday afternoon we had quite an interesting visit from some people who came over here from England, and as my daughterinlaw is a native of England and only lived about twenty five miles from them they were glad to meet her in America.

Tuesday March the 19th 1929

Somewhat cloudly this morning. All about as usual as to health, and are busy in the general rotine of work, and I feel like saying with the Psalmist, "I will lift mine eyes unto the hills, from whence cometh my help. My help cometh from the Lord which made heaven and earth.

Wednesday March the 20th 1929

Clear this morning. All able to go about daily duties and I am anxious that we may all do our duty not only in our household affairs but the duty we owe to our maker for His love and mercy to us, and we should love Him and each other.

Thursday March the 21st 1929

A bright sunshiney day which gives me fresh courage to put out flowers and try to beautify the yard and surondings, for we have had so much rain there has been no chance to plant flowers and vegetables, but we should be very thankful that we are spared from floods and wind storms etc which many people have had to suffer loss of property and some the loss of loved ones, so we should praise the Lord with all hearts for His goodness and mercy to us his poor unworthy dependent cretures.

Friday March the 22nd 1929

A nice clear morning after rain last night and the weather is much warmer to day and the calendar tells us that Spring begins to day and I do hope we shall realise more spring like weather than we have had thus far, for the farmers and gardeners are so far behind in planting their crops, but we are promiced in the Book of Books seed time and harvest and we should stand on the promices, both temporally and spiritually and be ready for the ingathering of our souls, when the master calls for us to lay down our earthly armor, and calls for our account.

Saturday March 23rd 1929

Cloudy this morning, it seems that we do not have but about one clear day at a time lately but we should be very thankful to our kind and merciful Heavenly Father that he has thus far spared us from the terable storms and floods that have visited many places recently with great loss of property and loss of many lives.

Sunday March the 24th 1929

This is a bright Sabbath morning and quite warm my son has been to Church this morning for early Mass, and the rest of the family are now going to the eleven oclock service and it is not my lot to attend I wish to be faithful to worship the Father in my own heart let me be where I may, Keep me as in the hallow of Thy hand.

Monday March the 25th 1929

A nice clear morning, all able to be up and busy yesterday at eleven oclock I listened to a splendid sermon by **Dr Luther Little** of the first Baptist Church his discourse was founded on the 24th Psalm and he handled it in an interesting maner and one of the Hymns they sang was, "Come thou fount of every blessing sun in the old tune which sounded like home and did my heart good and again at 7:30 oclock **Dr Little** preached from the 1st chap of Daniel, and he sure did give good advice, for people to take Daniel as a pattern to purpose in their hearts to obstain from all things harmful both to the body and soul. such as strong drink etc. and in the afternoon we went out to Belmont, N.C. to attend a Religious Drama, Presented by the Pupils of Sacred Heart Academy. For the benefit of Charity. It was such a complete discription of our blessed Lords suffering and denial, that to see Him there nailed to the Cross and the jeers of the mob and the weeping of Mary and others of His followers caused

March 1929

the tears to roll down my cheeks, my heart was so touched at the thought of our Redeemer haveing to suffer all this agony for us poor unworthy dependent cretures. and we have so much to be thankful for that our lives have been spared, whilst many others have been killed by accident one way or another. Yesterday as we were returning home and passing the aviation field we saw hundreds of people gathered there and a fog of smoke so we stoped to ascertain the cause of the excitement that seemed to prevail among the people, and found that an airplane had just a short while before we reached the place had crashed to the ground and killed the Pilot and two pasengers, a man and a woman, and the Plane had caught fire and burned all their bodies beyond recognition, while hundreds of people stood by powerless to help them, most of the acupants of our Car went to see the burning Plane which was well nigh consumed but the ambulance had taken the bodies away a few minutes before we arived at the scene. And last night at 7-30, oclock a nineteen year old girl **Miss Lula Louise Coyle** by name was instantly killed right in front of the Drug Store over at Hoskins by the Seaboard pasenger train No 22. while attempting to cross the track at Hoskins St. These things hapening so close to us makes us feel very sad, and there has been many more accidents of a similar nature taken place here in Charlotte since I came here in Dec 1928. to say nothing of those that we read about that have taken place all over our land. It is very sad indeed.

Tuesday March the 26th 1929

A nice clear and warm morning, All able to be up and busy at work for which I feel very thankful and so much to thank our merciful Heavenly Father for that we have so far been spared from any violent storms of wind and rain and from any serious accident, whilst there has been so many killed or cripled in various ways, I feel that we can not thank God enough for His goodness to us his dependent cretures, who are so liable to err.

Wednesday March the 27th 1929

A real damp morning, which causes more aches and pains in my aged limbs, but I am grateful to the Giver of all good that I am so I can be up and wait on myself and that the rest of the family here are in usual health. God be praised for all His blessings. Not unto us O Lord, not unto us, but unto thy name give glory, for thy mercy, and for thy truth's sake. Psalm 115-1

Thursday March the 28th 1929

All in our usual health at this time, which is to say that some of are not very strong, but I am thankful all are able to be up and going about daily duties, my son has gone to his work in the Shop, my littl granddaughter to school and the rest of the family have gone to church as there is special service just before the coming Easter Sunday and I am trying to take care of the household affairs whilst the others are away. I praise the Lord for His goodness to us all.

Friday March the 29th 1929

Clear and much cooler this morning, all able to be up and attend to daily affairs for which I am truly thankful. And as this is good Friday the day our blessed Lord was crucified it seems strange in a sense to call it good Friday when he had to suffer such agony on the Cross, but He gave his precious life for the good of mankind therefore it is indeed a good Friday to those of us that try to obey Him. and desire to do His will in all things.

Saturday March the 30th 1929

Real cloudy this morning, rain all thru the night, all able to arise from our bed and go about daily avocations, for which I am thankf to our merciful Heavenly Father. Later in the day I had a glad surprise as my daughter **Mrs J.W. Peace** came in very unexpected at the time for altho we had been hope she might come, we had given out getting to see her as we had not had any respone to our letter requesting her to come to day if possible to spend Easter with us.

Sunday March the 31ˢᵗ 1929

Nice morning. All well as usual except **Esther** my daughterinlaw who has a bad headache, which deprives her from going to Church this lovely Easter Sabbath, the rest of her family went to their Church which is the Catholic Church, while my daughter **Mrs Peace** and myself went to the Methodist Church at Belmot where she once had her right of membership when she resided in Charlotte there she met with many of her old acquaintances and relatives of her first husband **Arthur Lee Stilwell** and very much enjoyed seeing so many of them. Then after we returned home and had eaten a bountiful Easter dinner, which was shared with some of our friends who accompanied us, we sat down and listened to a fine program comeing over the Radio from the first Baptist Chruch, A good sermon by **Dr Luther Little** and a splendid service by **Dr Poling** and **Dr Cadman** which was very instructive and highly entertaining. Then at eight thirty my daughter and I went with my son **F.C. Blair** to the Catholic Church and heard a fine sermon by the Priest, and the beautifully lighted Church, which was a charming right at night.

Monday April the 1ˢᵗ 1929

A nice clear morning. All feeling better this morning and my daughter and I are invited out to day at **Mr Hoyle Stilwells** to spend the day so I will wait until I return to write another line.

Later we were favored to get over to **Mr Stilwells** and spent the time most enjoyably fareing sumptuously in every way, which I feel so thankful for. The praise belongs to the Giver of all our blessings.

Tuesday April the 2ⁿᵈ 1929

A nice clear morning and some cooler. We are all in usual health excepting grandaughter **Emily Blair** who was not able to go to her work this morning, but glad it is nothing serious I mentioned last evening after we returned here (to my sons) about our nice time at **Mr Hoyle Stilwells** and want to state that his wife's brother **Mr Walter Culp** lives with them, and he is sure an object for sympathy he is drawn almost double with spinal troubl cant raise himself up to look you in the face, but can walk about the rooms and even climb stairs in that drawn condition it looks like an imposibility, but he has learned by his long affliction how to manage to do this and he is so cheerful and so inteligent makes him an interesting person to converse with and having in the past been a shut in I can fully sympathise with him in is afflictions. for altho I was not drawn down as he is but I could not walk at all for many years. To day my daughter has gone out to visit some more of her friends, so we will miss her until she returns to us tomorow.

Wednesday April the 3rd 1929

Another nice morning. All able to be about daily avocations, and this being my sons forty eighth birthday, as he was born April the 3rd 1881. It brings to mind the flight of time, for it hardly seems possibl that he has arrived to that age. for it seems almost as yesterday so to speak, that my little boy babe came into the world, and I am so thankful that he has lived a Christian life thus far and trust that he will continue faithful unto the end, for as he came into the world inocent, so will he then depart out of it inocent, and ready to enter into eternal glory. My prayer is that we all may be so obedient to obey our heavenly Fathers will here on earth that we may gain an entrance into that blessed abode which He has prepard for all who love and serve Him on earth, there to praise Him with the Son of his love whoes precious blood was shed for the sins of the whole world therefore for our sins. To Father, Son and Holy Spirit, belongeth all praise now and forever. Father help us to obey Thee.

April 1929

Thursday April the 4th 1929

All able to arise from our beds this beautiful April morning I am thankful to state Afternoon of same day. I was favored to have strength to go across the street this forenoon to callon **Mrs Kjou** a lady that is very much afflicted and knowing as I do, what it means to be afflicted for many years, she certainly has my sincere sympathy, and this afternoon I call on some more neighbors that live near that I had never visited in their homes since coming to Charlotte altho I had met them as member of my Bible Class and loved them dearly. This Class was organised in my name here at my sons, some five years ago and I caried it on regular for two years, and it was with much reluctance that I had to give it up when I went back to Randolph to stay with my daughter.

Friday April the 5th 1929

A nice sunshiney warm morning all in usual health I am thankful to state, and I am prepareing to return to Randolph tomorrow after spending the winter here in Charlotte with my son and family. Praise the Lord for His goodness.

Saturday April the 6th 1929

A lovely morning. All as well as usual here at my sons, and I have now bid him goodly to return to my daughters in Randolph. Saturday after the 6th. We arrived home about one oclock having come the one hundred miles from Charlotte since eight oclock and stoped on our way to eat our lunch, and to converse with our friends, at different places, we found all well at home, and we are thankful that we came thru without any accident as the road is so conjested with Cars especially on saturdays.

Sunday April the 7th 1929

Nice clear morning, all able to arise from our beds, for which I feel very thankful, for it was a long ride from Charlotte yesterday for one of my age. My heart goes up in gratitude to our merciful heavenly Father for His goodness to us His dependent children. Praise His holy name.

Later the same day, at this time about one oclock, my daughterinlaw **Mrs Fred C Blair,** her son 16 years of age, and her ten year old daughter who brought us home from Charlottle yesterday have now started back to their home in Charlotte. Then my soninlaw **J.W. Peace** and family and myself all went to Sunday School and Preaching at Mt Vernon, we had an interesting lesson then heard a splendid sermon by their Pastor **Rev – Kelly** and I was thankful to meet again with my many friends that I had not see since December 1928. Praise God from whom all blessings flow.

Monday April the 8th 1929

Another nice clear and warm morning all able to go about daily duties for which I feel very grateful, for I see the need of many things to be done after I have been away all winter.

Tuesday April the 9th 1929

Still another nice clear morning which seems so nice after having so much rain all winter, all able to be up and busy at work, some of the women folk at the wash tub, the men in the field prepareing their crops, one son at work in Shop at High Point and one daughter in High School at Trinity, now prepareing for Anual Commencement, and as she is a Seniour this year will receie her Diploma for Graduation. God be praised for His goodness and mercy to us all.

Wednesday April the 10th 1929

Cloudy and misting rain this morning, and I am feeling the effects of the dampness, but thankful to be so I can be up and wait on myself. The rest of them here are all well. The parents are gone to Asheboro to day. **Clemons** to his work in High Point. **Minnie** is Ironing, **Mary Lee** gone to school, and little **J.A.** is playing around as usual, and I am writing a few lines in honor and praise to our merciful Heavenly Father who gives us strength of body and mind to go about our daily avocations.

Thursday April the 11th 1929

Cloudy and cold this morning, all able to be up and trying to accomplish what our hands find to do, there is such a contrast in the weather from the past few days, that it seems pleasant to have a fire to warm by this morning, insted of trying to find a cool place to rest. But the dear Lord is so mericaiful to us His unworthy and dependent children, for we have clotheing and fuel to keep us warm. whilst there are may up and down in our land who not doubt are shivering for want of these things and perhaps not a sufficency of food.

Friday April the 12th 1929

Still cloudy this morning, but not quite so cold. All in usual health I am thankful to state.

Saturday April the 13th 1929

A nice clear morning. All able to be up and go about daily avocations. The family here have now nearly all gone to High Point shoping, and my little grandson **J.A. Peace** is playing around and looking at his half brother **Clemons Peace** build a wire pen for their pet Rabits, I am thankful to still be so I can wait hon myself. And I feel like praiseing God for His goodness to us all.

Sunday April the 14th 1929

Cloudly this morning. All able to arise from our beds and I trust we shall be favored to get out to Sunday School this afternoon. I am thankful to state this evening that we were blessed to all get out to Sunday School had an interesting lesson. And I also got to meet many of my friends that I had not seen since last year before I went to my sons in Charlotte.

Monday April the 15th 1929

Raining this morning, which is very welcome to the farmers especially as they say the ground is geting too dry for plowing. Praise the dear Lord for all His benefits to His unworthy dependent cretures.

Tuesday April the 16th 1929

Rainey this morning, the ground is now well moistened We are all able to arise from our beds and go about daily work for which I am very grateful to the Giver of all our blessings. Oh that we may all be more obedient to Him.

Wednesday April the 17th 1929

Clear and much colder this morning. All in usual health. **Mary Lee** has gone to school. and **Minnie** has gone with her to Trinity to visit one of her friends, the rest of us are busy doing what our hands find to do. Praise the Lord for the strength He gives us for all our help comes from Him who shed his blood for us.

Thursday April the 18th 1929

Clear and cold this morning, considerable frost last night. All able to go about daily work. This is **Mary Lee Stilwells** seventeenth Birthday, she is now a Seniour in Trinity High School and will graduate this session, it hardly seems possible she is that age, for its so short time since she was a babe, but time flies fast, and we should all be prepared for eternity, for we know not how soon young or old may be called to give account of the deeds done in the body, oh heavenly Father help us to have a good account to give, to Thy names honor and prais is the prayer of my heart for Jesus sake. Amen.

Friday April the 19th 1929

Clear this morning and not quite so cold. All are able to be up and go about daily avocations, for which I feel very thankful, for I know

April 1929

what it means to be confined to the bed for many years in the past. and I am so thankful to my merciful heavenly Father that He puts it in the heart and mind of my dear daughter **May** with whom I now reside, to be kind and helpful to her lonely widowed Mother, and may the dear Lord bless her and family in every way according to their needs, is my ferent desire. Bless the Lord O my soul.

Saturday April the 20th 1929

A nice clear morning. All in usual health and busy. I hope that we may all be close on our watch this day and not disobey the Divine commands, for we are responsible beings, and will have to give account for every idle word spoken, and for all our deeed done in the body. Just as this time A dear aged colored woman who we call Aunt **Margaret Hoover** came in to see me. I so much enjoy her visits, because she is always ready to talk with me about what concerns our souls welfare when done with the perishiabl things of this world. and I love to give her what information I am capable of in regard to obeying Gods holy will, and His written word.

Sunday April the 21st 1929

Cloudly this morning, been raining thru the night. All able to be up this morning, and the young people are gone to the Baptiseing by Emersion at Glenola. I am now past eighty four years of age, I have seen many Christened, but have never witnessed Baptism by Emersion. We of the Friends Church believe in being Baptised with the Holy Ghost, but do not think Baptism by water is essential to the salvation of the soul. As it is simply an ordinance of the Church, I do not object to any one complying with it that feel it their duty. But while pure water is necessary for the clensing of the body, we do not believe it can clense the soul, as this must come from having our sins washed away in the blood of the Lamb, shed on Calvery. I hope we shall be able to get to Sunday School and Preaching this afternoon. Later in the day, we were favored to all get out to Sunday School and Preaching and many of the members at Mt Vernon observed the Sacrament of the Lord Supper.

Monday April the 22nd 1929

Clear and warmer this morning, All able to be up for which I am very thankful, may we all be in earnest to obey the will of the Master in all things to His honor and praise is my prayer for Jesus sake.

Tuesday April the 23rd 1929

Clear and cooler this morning. All able to be up and go about daily avocations. The family here are gone to High Point shoping to day, and as I am lonely I desided to try my strength walking out to the little house of **Aunt Margaret Hoover** the colored woman that I mentioned coming to see me the other day, this is only a few hundred yards from where I stay but is as far as I have been able to walk at one time for many years, I have enjoyed conversing with this woman for she has a knowledge of spiritual things and is trying to live so as to meet her loved ones in that happy land where there will be no differences in race or color, but will be as the angels in heaven there to join with the redeemed in singing praise to Him who gave His precious life for us all.

Wednesday April the 24th 1929

Clear and cool this morning. All about in usual health I am thankful to state, for it is such a blessing to be able to be up and attend to daily affairs, and we know of those at this time that are sick in bed and not able to do anything for themselves and family, while we are so we can be up and doing. Praise God from whom all blessings flow.

Thursday April the 25th 1929

Cloudy this morning, and been raining thru the night. All able to be up and attend to home affairs. oh that we may all be as diligent to prepare for our never ending home where we shall be forever happy if we have been faithful to do the will of the blessed Master while on earth, as we are to have everything needful for the comfort and enjoyment of these poor mortal bodies that must return to dust.

Friday April the 26th 1929

A pretty spring morning. All able to arise from our beds and go about daily duties, for which I feel very thankful, for I am so glad to still be so I can wait on myself, for I do not want to become a burden to others.

Saturday April the 27th 1929

A nice clear morning, all in usual health. To day is quarterly meeting at Hopewell and the Parents here are going, and I have the chance to go, and as I have not been there for many years if I keep able to think I will try to go. The Lord willing. Later. I was favored to attend quarterly meeting at Hopewell with the rest of the family from here and enjoyed it very much.

Sunday April the 28th 1929

A very rainey day. All in usual health I am thankful to note. my mind dwells largely to day on the many good things I heard yesterday at quarterly meeting at Hopewell. The singing of the good old sacred Hymns, and the reading of a portion of the fifth chapter of St John by **Rev James Craven** the Presiding Elder and then offered an appropriate prayer. After which **Rev – Harbinson** from High Point took his Text from the thirteenth verse of the same chapter. "And he that was healed wist not who it was for Jesus had conveyed himself away a multitude being in that place." It was a wonderful sermon, bringing to our minds how prone we are to be carried away with the mutiltude and let Jesus slip away from us. how often we let worldy pleasures lure us away from Church or from attending to the things which pertain to our souls salvation. Oh how I desire that we may all do as **Bro Harbinson** plead with us to do, to take these things home with us and profit by them, for we shall all have to give account of how we spent our time here on earth. oh heavenly Father help us to take thee at they word, and be closer on our watch to do Thy will here on earth that we may merit an entrance info thy home above.

Monday April the 29th 1929

A nice clear day, all able to go about daily affairs. I missed getting out to Sunday School yesterday, as it was so very rainey. This was the first time I have missed since I came home from Charlotte. and I always regret having to miss Sunday School or Preaching. but am trying to be in entire submision to whatever comes to my lot.

Tuesday April the 30th 1929

Some cloudy this morning. All in usual health I am thankful to state, and as this is the last day of the month it again reminds me of the flight of time, for it seems such a short time since this new year ushered in. that it causes me to see so plainly how fast we are being conveyed on the wings of time, to a never ending eternity. oh heavenly Father help us all to be prepared for an entrance into thy kingdom where we can praise thee forever and ever, is the prayer of my heart for Jesus sake.

Wednesday May the 1st 1929

Cloudy again this morning. All able to be up and busy at daily avocations for which I feel very grateful to the Giver of all our blessings. and I greatly desire to be more faithful each day to do His holy will to His names honor and praise.

Thursday May the 2nd 1929

Cloudy this morning, heavy rain and thunder during the night. all able to be up and busy, some at work some at school some visiting etc, all these activities comes from the goodness and mercy of the Lord who gives us strength of body and of mind to do that which our hands find to do. Praise His holy name.

Friday May the 3rd 1929

A clear but windy morning. All able to be up and go about daily duties as usual, and I now call to mind that this is my daughter **Mary Eliza Blair Stilwell Peace's** forty fourth Birthday. it hardly seems possible, for it seems such a short while since she was a little chubby babe sitting on the pallet on the floor in our dear old home. and to think she has passed through young womanhood and then married **Arthur Lee Stilwell** of Charlotte N.C. and lived there for fifteen years. Then after his death, in proscess of time, she married again, this time to **Jerome W. Peace** of Randolph Co. they now have one little son five years of age named **Jerome Addison Peace**, for his Father and for his Grandfather **Addison Blair**. May the dear Lord keep them all safe as in the hallow of His divine hand through the remainder of lifes journey, and then be a united band in that home above, where parting is unknown is my prayer for Jesus sake and for their never dying souls sake. Since writing the above **Mr Peaces** daughter **Mrs Gideon Bowman** came to spend the day with us, we have enjoyed having her and her sweet little **jr** with us he is such a fine promising child. **Minnie Peace** has been suffering with a bad headache. today so she could not have the enjoyment with her sister that she otherwise would, but I am thankful she is some better this evening. Praise the dear Lord for His tender care over his dependent children.

Saturday May the 4th 1929

A nice clear morning. All in usual health except the daughter who is not yet over her bad spell of headache but is better. The Parents and **Mary Lee Stilwell** are gone to High Point shopping, hope they will have a safe return, for there is so much traffic now that it is scarely safe to travel. May the dear Lord help us all to abide so close to Him and obey his holy will thruought our journey here below, that we may dwell with Him above, there to render the praise due to His name throughout eternity.

Until We Sleep Our Last Sleep

Sunday May the 5th 1929

Cloudy and windy to day. All in usual health. I was favored to get to my own Church at dear old Springfield where I have my right of membership and where I went to Sunday School and meeting from my childhood when **Uncle Allen Tomlinson** was Superintendent but since my marriage, and since becoming so much afflicted for many years, I have not been able to get there often, but it is the most sacred spot on earth to me now since the precious dust of so many of my loved ones lie there. I visited the grave of my dear husband to day and left flowers theron. My daughter and I were invited to go into **Ada Blairs** Class and it was very interesting indeed then we heard a good sermon by a gentleman from Raleigh good Hymns etc, and met many old acquaintances. Then we returned home ate our lunch, and then we and the rest of the family in the home went to Mt Vernon to Sunday School and Preaching heard another good sermon by their new Pastor **Mr Kelly,** and enjoyed their good Hymns. I feel that we have much to be thankful for, for the blessings we have enjoyed this day.

Monday May the 6th 1929

A nice clear morning. All able to be up and busy for which I want to thank the good Lord for all our blessings. Last evening we enjoyed the company of **Mr Fred Peace** and wife **Janett,** also his brother **Grady Peace** and wife **Clara** and their little son **Joseph.** and **Mr Gideon Bowman** and wife **Ollie Peace Bowman** and their little son **Gideon jr.** also had little babe **Edward Lee White,** and the childs Grandmother **Mrs Nance** from High Point. The evening seemed to slip away very quickly, chatting with friends.

Tuesday May the 7th 1929

A nice warm morning, having had rain during the night makes things look green and growing which we are glad to see. All up and able to attend to daily affairs for which I feel very thankful, and from my heart I can exclaim Blessed be the name the Lord.

May 1929

Wednesday May the 8th 1929

Clear and cooler this morning. All in usual health for which I am thankful, for to be able to be up and go about our daily affairs is one of our great blessings. "I will lift up mine eyes unto the hills, from whence cometh my help my help cometh from the Lord which made heaven and earth."

Thursday May the 9th 1929

A dark cloudy morning, had rain thru the night. All able to go about daily avocations, for which I give thanks to the Giver of all good. oh how much we have to thank God for, and we should seek to know Him better and love him more. And in the 2nd Chapter of the first Epistle to John, we are told that to Rightly know God is to keep his commandments to love our brethren and not love the world. These admonitions are for us all and he regards us here as mere children and says "my little children these things write I unto you that ye sin not, and if any man sin, we have an advocate with Father, Jesus Christ the righteous and he is the propitiation for our sins; and not for ours only, but also for the sins of the whole world. And hereby we do know that we know him, if we keep his commandments." oh dear one or ones whoever may chance to read these lines, consider well the impart of them, for thruout this chapter is given us enough of insight into the things which we should do, and those things which we should not do, to save us all from eternal damnation if needed to in time. This applies to all ages and conditions in life, let us take warning before it is forever too late, is my prayer.

Friday May the 10th 1929

Clear and much cooler this morning. All in usual health. Nothing special to note at this time, just the usual rotine of daily affairs, and the continued goodness and mercy of the dear Lord to us all.

Saturday May the 11th 1929

A nice clear morning. All able to be up and attend to what our hands find to do, which is indeed a great blessing. and I am so glad that my mind runs in a chanel that makes me want to do the things that are necessary to be done, both temporally and spiritually. for it is a great thing for us to want, to do the things that is our duty and privilige to do, and our blessed Saviour has given us the privilige to do, and our blessed Saviour has given us the privilige of takeing our choice to either serve Him and reap eternal happiness, or reject Him and go to eternal punishment. so my greatest desire is that we may all choose the way that leads to Heaven by being obedient to the Divine commands, walking in the ways of truth and righteousness in all things to His honor and praise, which will give us the blessed assurance of a home in that land where the inhabitants never say "I am sick." and where we shall have joy and peace around the Throne, singing praises to Him who has brought us with His own precious blood.

Sunday May the 12th 1929

A beautiful morning. All in usual health this beautiful Sabbath, which is set apart as Mothers Day. May we all who are Mothers be Mothers in the true sense of the word honest, upright, loveing and obedient to the Divine commands, that we may be good examples to the riseing generation. The Sunday School at Mt Vernon was held this morning at 9-30 oclock instead of at 2 oclock as usual in order that all that wished might attend the Anual Commencement Sermon at Trinity at 11 oclock. We were favored to attend Sunday School, then went to Trinity and heard the Baccalareate Sermon by **Dr Allen P. Brantley** of Winston Salem N.C. this was very interesting and instructive. At the beginning of the service they sang the Hymn "All Hail The Power." and at closeing they sang the Hymn "Take My Life And Let it Be." Then after returning home and partakeing of a good lunch some of their kindred came, and we had a very pleasant evening.

Monday May the 13th 1929

Clear and warm this morning, and I am thankful that we are all again permited to have strength to go about our daily duties, and I desire above all things that we may remember the duty we owe to our Great Creator and be obedient to perform it, to His honor and praise.

Tuesday May the 14th 1929

Cloudy this morning. All in usual health, I am glad to state, for it is one of our greatest blessings among Myriads of others, and just now we have the company of **Mr Peace's** daughter **Mrs Ed White** and children, her little two months old babe **Billy Ray** is growing fine he now weighs fifteen lbs. The Lord be praised for his goodness and mercy to us all his dependent cretures, for we are so unworthy of His tender care.

Wednesday May the 15th 1929

Still cloudy this morning. All able to go about daily affairs, some to the field, some to the wash tub, one to school, and I am thankful to still be so I can wait on myself and pen a line in praise to my Maker who is a friend above all others, for He will never forsake us, if we obey His will.

Thursday May the 16th 1929

Clear and warm this morning. All in usual health. The Parents are going to Town shopping this morning hope they will not have any accident, for there are so many takeing place keep me anxious about them. We learned yesterday the sad news of the wife of **Samuel Hodgein** killed in an Auto wreck, and he was badly hurt, we never know when there is but a step between us and death. oh let us always be ready.

Friday May the 17th 1929

Cloudy and cooler. All able to be up and busy. After attending the Commencement Exercises at Trinity High School last night everything come off splendid. The Seniours did fine. They are sure worthy of Commendation. The dear Lord be praised for the strength of body and of mind which He has given them to achieve this. May they go out into world noble and well beloved men and women is my desire for each and every one ot them.

Saturday May the 18th 1929

Still cloudy but warmer this morning. All in usual health. The young people attended the closing exercises of the Commencement at Trinity last night which was A Play. which they enjoyed very much. and they are both glad, and sory as is the usual case when school closes. Yesterday at eleven oclock we older ones also attended the exercises, listened to the Annual Literary Address by **Prof W.H. Livers**. N.C.C.W. Greensboro N.C. which was very fine, and witnessed the awarding of Diplomas, Certificates, and Prizes. They sang The Old North State at the opening at of the exercises and at the closeing sang America The Beautiful. The Graduates twenty four in number made a pretty show the girls all dressed in white and boys in dark. I enjoyed the good prayers the songs the Benediction, and all the exercises.

Sunday May the 19th 1929

Cloudy and warm this morning. All able to be up I am thankful to state, and trust we shall be able to all get out to Sunday School this afternoon. Evening of same day. We were favored to all get out to Sunday School and preaching, heard a splendid sermon by the Pastor **Rev Kelly,** who centered his remarks on a portion of the 6th chapter of St Mark concerning Christ's feeding the five thousand by aMericle his Text being the 40th verse. "And they sat down in ranks, by hundreds, and by fifties." Showing us what wonderful things Christ can and will do far all who will follow Him and be faithful to obey to His holy will.

May 1929

Monday May the 20th 1929

Rainey this morning All in usual health I am glad to note, but it is so rainy the men folk can not go to their work in the fields, but it is the same rotine of work for the housewife regardless the weather, and we should remember our duty to our Maker at all times and in all conditions in life.

Tuesday May the 21st 1929

Clear and cooler this morning. All able to arise from our beds and go about daily affairs, **Minnie Peace** is visiting for a few days at her sisters **Mrs Gideon Bowmans, Mary Lee Stilwell** attended a house party last night at **Mr Silvester Boldens** given by **Miss Mulis,** Teacher of the Seniour Class in Trinity High School, to all the members of her class. It is reported a very enjoyable occasion to all concerned.

Wednesday May the 22nd 1929

Clear and still quite cool this morning all able to attend to the affairs of the day, **Mary Lee Stilwell** our new Graduate in this home is helping her Mother at the wash tub, which shows graduation in usefulness in the many things of this life, as well as in Book education and my desire is that she may not only make good use of the Literary knowledge which she has gained, but that she may gain that knowledge from above "which is able to make wise unto salvation," thru faith and obedience to Gods holy commandments, both spiritually and temporally. Last evening while I was busy writing a letter to my daughter **Maggie Moffitt** who at this time is sojourneying with her son and family at Davenport Iowa, I looked up and there was our Pastor of Springfield Friends Church **Miss Clara I. Cox** comeing in to see me. I certainly did enjoy her visit both spiritually and socially. her prayers are so earnest.

Thursday May the 23th 1929

Clear and a very pleasent morning, all in usual health I am thankful to state. and in reading the ninety first Psalm this morning I find so many precious promices I feel that I must note a few of them down for future reference, in the three last verses it is stated, "Because he hath set his love upon me, therefore will I deliver him; I will set him on high, because he hath known my name. He shall call upon me, and I will answer him; I will be with him in trouble; I will deliver him, and show him my salvation." oh that we may all live so close to the Father of all our sure mercies obeying His holy will in all things according to his divine commandments that we may be counted worthy of those promices, and when done with the things of this life have an entrance into that home which is prepared for all those who love and serve Him on earth, there to honor and praise Him thruout eternity. is my prayer for Christs sake. This evening **Minnie Peace** returned home from her visit and her sister she and little son came with her we spent a very pleasant evening, her sister **Mrs Bowman** lives at Glenola.

Friday May the 24th 1929

A nice clear morning. All able to go about daily avocations, which strengthens my faith in prayer, for as we go to him daily in prayer for help to perform the duties of the day, He gives us strength for the same. And in Colossians fourth Chapter and second verse, Paul exorts us to "continue in prayer and watch in the same with thanksgiving." and we should take heed to this exortation, and be close on our watch that we do not deviate from the right path and be thankful for all our blessings at all times.

Saturday May the 25th 1929

Another pretty morning. All in usual health I am glad to note for it is one of the greatest among our many blessings. "Praise God from whom all blessings flow, praise Him all cretures here below, praise Him all ye Heavenly host, praise Father, Son and Holy Ghost." The words of this Hymm came so forceably to my mind after takeing up my pen to write a few lins, that I felt like inserting them here in my Diary, and hope that they may be a reminder of the many blessings we daily receive and that we may give Him the praise due to His holy name, and that of all His dear Son who died to save us from our sins.

Sunday May the 26th 1929

A nice warm Sabbath morning. All well as usual, **J.W. Peace** went over and brought cousin **Tom English** to dine with us to day we have enjoyed having him with us very much, he is getting quite feeble. We shall now all prepare to go to Sunday School at Mt Vernon at three oclock this p.m. Evening of same day we were favored to all get out to Sunday School had a very interesting lesson, and after returning home some of our friends came in, which was very satisfactory.

Monday May the 27th 1929

Cloudy this morning and quite warm. All able to arise from our beds, and are endeavoring to do what is most necessary to be done, for the comfort and sustanance of our mortal bodies, oh that we may be even more concerned for the salvation of our immortal souls for Christ the Redeemers sake, who died to save us all.

Tuesday May the 28th 1929

A nice warm morning. All in usual health I am thankful to state. and I feel that we are being watched over by a kind loveing Father. "I know not where his islands lift. Their fronded palms in air: I only know I cannot drift. Beyond his love and care." oh how good to know that we have such a kind loveing Father careing for us.

Wednesday May the 29th 1929

Cloudy this morning, the ground is thoroughly soaked since the latter rain. All are able to be up and go about the affairs of the day. oh that we may all be led this day in the strait and narrow way that leads to life and peace, looking unto Him who is able to keep us from falling. "Father I strech my hands to thee no other help I know," Thou has led me safe thus far lead me safely on. Help me to glorify Thee on earth that I may glorify thee in heaven.

Thursday May the 30th 1929

Cloudy and warm. All in usual health I am glad to note. **J.W. Peace** and **May** and myself went to High Point to day to have my glasses changed, but as they had to be sent to head quarters to be changed I will have to do without them until another day or so.

Friday May the 31st 1929

Clear and warm to day. All able to be up and attend to the affairs of the day. and to my surprise and great pleasure my glasses came to me in this mornings mail. **Dr Tesh** of High Point has been so very kind to me. I feel that I can not thank him enough for being so prompt in sending them to me, for without them I cannot read my Bible lesson, or see how to do any work.

Saturday June the 1st 1929

Another nice clear warm day. All in usual health, I am glad to note. and I am again reminded of the flight of time as this is the begining of another month, and we know that we are another month nearer our journeys end on earth, for every day and every month brings us nearer to our final sojourn here below. Father help us all to be ready.

Sunday June the 2nd 1929

A lovely Sabbath morning. All able to arise from our beds, I am thankful to state, and I hope we shall be favored to attend Sunday School and Preaching this afternoon, **Grady Peace** and wife **Clara** and little son **Joseph** have made us a call this morning, we are always glad to have them visit us. And now **Mr** and **Mrs Harison Kenedy** and **wife Nellie** and their little daughter **Minnie Lee** have come to see us and will take dinner with us, then go to Preaching this afternoon we enjoyed having them with us, and after we returned from Church **Cousin Ed** and **Anna Blair** came to spend the rest of the evening with us they had not been here for some time. And **Mr** and **Mrs Savage** and their Son and Daughter also came to spend the evening. So the evening was spent very pleasantly.

Monday June the 3rd 1929

Cloudy and some cooler, rain fell nearly thruout the night. I am feeling the effects of the dampness but thankful to be up and so I can wait on myself the rest of the family in usual health glad to state.

Tuesday June the 4th 1929

Clear and a nice pleasent morning. All able to be up and go about daily affairs, and I trust we shall be on our guard, least we enter into temptation.

Wednesday June the 5th 1929

Clear and cooler this morning. All so as to be up, but some of us do not feel at all well this morning, but I trust it is nothing serious, we are expecting company to day, if we should be disappointed I will later so state. and as we are told that all things work togeather for good to them that love the Lord we are leaving it all in His hands for he knows that we love him altho we often show our weakness by disobedience. Well we were favored with the company of **Mary Davis** wife of **Jesse Davis** to spend the day with us, I was glad indeed to have her with us, also **Grandma Peace** spent the day with us, we had a good time togeather we who are among the oldest in this neighborhood feel that our sojourn here on earth, will not be much longer at the longest.

Thursday June the 6th 1929

Clear and still quite cool, so it seem pleasant to sit by a little fire, we are all nearly as usual this morning I am thankful to note, I am so glad to be so I can still wait on myself, for many that are more than four score years like my self cannot do this, and for many years in the past I did not expect to ever walk a step again, or do any work. so I feel that I have much to thank my merciful Heavenly Father for, that it is as well with me as it is, altho I am not strong.

Friday June the 7th 1929

A nice pleasant morning. All able to go about daily avocations I am thankful to state. I think more and more each day as the time passes, how important it is to make our calling and election sure that we may be counted worthy to pass into the Holy City of God when done with time here, there to praise Him forever.

Saturday June the 8th 1929

Another nice morning. All in usual health and busy with the duties of the day. Later in the day I went with my daughter **Mrs Peace** and her little son for a drive in the fresh air, as they were going to the Store. It does me so much good to ride and in the fresh air.

Sunday June the 9th 1929

Rainey this morning, but all the family here except **J.W. Peace** went to Mt. Vernon to Sunday School which was held at nine oclock instead of in the afternoon as usual on account of the Sunday School Convention which is held at Prospect to day, in order that all who can may have the chance to attend, we as a family had intended to go but it became too rainey to go in open Car, so we gave it up and returned home, **Miss Dara Peace** came home with us. she is a sweet lively girl and we are always glad to have her company. I feel like I can not thank the dear Lord enough for His care over us all this day. Then this afternoon **Mr** and **Mrs Gideon Bowman** and little son came to see us, and also **Fred Peace** and wife came, so we had an interesting little group.

Monday June the 10th 1929

Cloudy and cool this morning. All up and attending to daily avocations. **Mary Lee Stilwell** now has a place of work in a sewing room in High Point and has gone to her work this morning. I hope she will get on fine. The rest are doing what comes to hand in the home. oh Father help us all to be obedient to Thy Divine Commands.

Tuesday June the 11th 1929

Clear and still cool this morning. All able to be up altho I for one am feeling quite feeble, but thankful I can still wait on myself, for I have a great dread of being a burden to other people. my prayer is that I may fulfil the place and purpose for which my life has been spared, bearing all the trials and provictions that more or less come into my daily life, with true Christian fortitude, "not careing what man can say or do unto me, for if the Lord be for us, who can be against us." and we are told in Gods word that "perfect love casts out fear" so my greatest desire is that my heart may be filled so full of love of God that there may be no room for anything that is impure and not well pleasing in His sight. Father be my helper, for thou knowest the "spirit is willing but the flesh is weak."

Wednesday June the 12th 1929

A nice clear morning just cool enough to be pleasant. All able to arise from our beds, and go about daily duties. I realise more and more each day as it passes that we are that much nearer our journeys end, and that we shall soon be called to give account of the deeds done in the body. Dear Lord help me to be ready.

Thursday June the 13th 1929

Clear and warmer this morning. All able to be up and doing. the Parents are gone to High Point shopping **Mary Lee** to her work in the sewing room up there and **Minnie** is cooking dinner and playing the Organ at intervals, and I am trying to do whatever my hands find to do, with what strength I have, but am not strong and feel more feble this morning than usual.

Friday June the 14th 1929

A nice bright morning. All in usual health I am thankful to note, for health is one of our greatest blessings. **J.W. Peace's** brother **Jacob** is in very poor health and has come down from High Point to day to his Mothers to see if the Country Air will make him stronger, he has such dificulty breathing.

Saturday June the 15th 1929

Another nice morning, but none of us are feeling well this morning, but hope it is nothing serious. People are very apt to feel languid at times when the weather becomes warm.

Sunday June the 16th 1929

Clear and cooler this morning. My little grandson **J.A. Peace** has been sick yesterday and to day. but is now takeing medicine so I hope he will soon be all right again. his **Uncle Jake Peace** spent last night with us and is still with us to day, The fresh air seems to be very beneficial to him, so I hope he will soon be much stronger. I am not feeling well myself to day, so I think I shall give up going to Sunday School to day. altho I regret very much to miss a day.

Monday June the 17th 1929

Cloudy this morning. My little grandson is better so he is up this morning, his uncle **Jake** as he is familliarly known is still with us and expects to stay a while to see if the change will do him good, he rested better last night, I am still feeling weak but thankful for sufficient strength to be up and wait on myself. the rest of the family able to go to their daily avocations. I praise the Lord for His goodness to us all, and trust that we shall live closer to Him every day and obey his holy will in all things to His honor and praise.

Tuesday June the 18th 1929

A nice bright morning. We as a family here are all able to be up and attend to what our hands find to do that is most necessary to be done **Jacob Peace** rested better last night and seems some stronger.

Wednesday June the 19th 1929

A nice clear moring, after a hard rain last evening. I am feeling more feeble than usual this morning but thankful to be able to arise from my bed and wait on myself. **Jacob Peace** is still with us, and feeling some stronger to day. the rest of the family here are in usual health.

Thursday June the 20th 1929

Clear and warm this morning. The family here are all in usual health, I am still feeling weak but thankful to be so I can be up and do some things to help my daughter in her daily rotine of work. **Jacob Peace** is not quite so well this morning, he seems to feel worse every other day.

Friday June the 21st 1929

Another nice warm morning, "**Uncle Jake**" did not rest well last night, think he ate more than was best for him, as it is necessary for him be careful in that matter, I am not feeling at all well to day but thankful to be up and so I can wait on myself. The family are just about in their usual health. I praise the Lord for his goodness and mercy to us his unworthy cretures.

Saturday June the 22nd 1929

A clear warm morning, the condition of the family here is much the same as for the past week, I am still feeling feeble, but so I can wait on myself, for which I thank the Giver of all our sure mercies, and there is much to thank Him for. "**Uncle Jake**" is still weak and ailing in many ways but seems to be improving some, glad to state.

Sunday June the 23rd 1929

Clear and quite warm this morning. All able to arise from our beds, altho some of us are feeling rather feeble, especially "**Uncle Jake**" but is much better than he was a week ago. The news now comes to us of the death of **Sidney J. Blair** which occured yesterday evening in High Point at his son **Rolands,** we have not yet learned the particulars of the Funeral. but we are reminded of the uncertainty of life and the certainty of death, for it is a debt we all have to pay sooner or later. oh that we may all be prepared to enter the better land. "I will lift up mine eyes unto the hills, from whence cometh my help. My help cometh from the Lord which made heaven and earth."

Monday June the 24th 1929

Cloudy this morning. All able to be up, but I do not feel strong, but hope I can have strength to attend the funeral of **Sidney J. Blair** this evening at four oclock as some of the family here want to go if the rain holds up, "**Uncle Jake**"has to lay by on account of his heart troubl can not be up only part of the time. Later in the day, **J.W.** and **May** and myself were favored to attend the funeral of **Sidney J. Blair** at Springfield at four oclock this p.m. which was conducted by **Clara I. Cox. Dougan Cox. Ruben Payne. Rev Tom Sikes. Gurney Frazier** also spoke some very appropriate words on the life and character of the Deceased. The funeral was well attended, and the profusion of flowers showed the appreciation of kindred and friend.

Tuesday June the 25th 1929

Cloudy again this morning, had rain, thunder and wind during the night. I was feeling nervous after the experience of the evening, so did not rest well, but got a sufficiency of sleep in the after part of the night to enable me to arise from my bed this morning for which I feel very thankful, the rest of the family are in usual health. **Jacob Peace** is feeling some better this morning but is far from being relieved of his afflictions.

Wednesday June the 26th 1929

Cloudy again this morning and some cooler. "**Uncle Jake**" is not feeling quite so well to day, the rest of us are about in our usual state of health. I always suffer more with aches and pains in damp weather, but thankful to be so I can be up and wait on myself. Praise the Lord for His goodness to us all.

Thursday June the 27th 1929

Raining this morning. "**Uncle Jake**" restet some better last night. All have sufficient strength to arise from our beds for which I feel thankful, for altho I am not strong, I am so glad to be so I can wait on myself and do something for others. and as the time passes I feel more and more anxious to be ready for the call that will come to us sooner or later, and there has so many of my relatives and friends near my age passed away in the past two years, that I feel that the journey will not be much longer at the longest untill I shall be called to give account of the deeds done in the body, and I want to be ready. "A good account to give." Up to this time the last funeral I attended of a relative was that of **Sidney J. Blair** at Springfield on June the 24th. he passed away on the evening of June the 22nd 1929. Seeming to be concious to the very last, he had become entirely blind for some weeks before his demise, but his spiritual sight seemed to gain strength all the while, and was perfectly resigned and ready to go. and just twenty five minutes before his breath left him, he said to his son **Roland,** I wont be here but a little while longer, let me wind my Watch one more time before I go, and he did so, and in twenty five minutes his spirit took its flight to eternity. And later his mortal remains were laid beneath the sod while his spirit had gone home to God to live forever.

Friday June the 28th 1929

Glad to see the Sun comeing out after so much rain. All able to arise from our beds this morning "**Uncle Jake**" is feeling some better but can only be up part of the time, but I am thankful that it is as well with us all as it is, for altho we have had so much rain, we have been spared from having floods and wind storms like there as been in many places. The dear Lord has been good to us, and I hope we shall all endeavor to obey His commands more diligently than we have in the past, "The Lord is good to all and his tender mercies are over all his works." "Unto thee O God do we give thanks, unto thee do we give thanks, for thy name is near, thy wonderous works declare." Psalm 75-1

Saturday June the 29th 1929

A nice clear morning. "**Uncle Jake**" is not so well to day. the rest of us so we can be up and go about daily avocations. I am thankful to state.

Sunday June the 30th 1929

Another nice morning. All just about the same as to health except "**Uncle Jake**" who seems some better to day. Later in the day. We all went to Sunday School at Mt Vernon as usual, except **J.W.** who staid with his brother and after we returned from several of his kindred and friends came in to visit and cheer up the Patient. Praise the Lord for His love and care.

Monday July the 1st 1929

Cloudy to day. and is this is the first day July it reminds us how fast the months and years are passing by for it seems such a short while since we wrote the date of Jan the 1st 1929. and my desire is that we may all keep pace with the days as they pass in prepareing for the change that will take place sooner or later when we shall enter eternity. oh Father help us to be ready.

June–July 1929

Tuesday July the 2nd 1929

Clear this morning. I am feeling quite feeble this morning but am trying to be up and wait on myself, some of the others in the family are not well to day and "**Uncle Jake**" does not seem to improve very much his daughter **Bernice Peace** is with us for a few days. Afternoon of same day, **Ollie Bowman** and little **jr** came to see us, and **Mrs Bessie Ridge** of Asheboro came to see her **Uncle Jacob Peace**, and **Mrs Harison Kenedy** of High Point also came. "**Uncle Jake**" has been highly favored with company since he has been here with us, we are all feeling some better this evening. I am thankful to note.

Wednesday July the 3rd 1929

Cloudy and some cooler this morning. "**Uncle Jake**" rested better last night and seems some stronger this morning I am thankful to be some better than for the past few days the rest of the family group here are going about their daily avocations altho feeling the burden of care and so many things that are necessary to be done. Praise the Lord for His goodness and mercy to us all.

Thursday July the 4th 1929

A nice clear morning. The most of us are feeling some better, I am thankful to note "**Uncle Jake**" just about the same as yesterday, we are rather expecting my son and family from Charlotte to day, hope we will not be disappointed Thursday evening. Well we had to submit to disappointment for our company did not come. I am sorry to state.

Friday July the 5th 1929

A very pretty day, all feeling some better I am glad to note. and altho we meet with disappointment as we had our hearts and minds set on seeing my son **Fred C. Blair** and family yesterday from Charlotte, and they did not come, yet we should feel that we have much to be thankful for, that most of us are in reasonable good health, and that it is as well with us every way as it is, for there are many that do not have the necessities of life that we have and many are confined either to their beds or to their rooms, and deprived of many privaliges that we now have and as I have been helpless for many years in the past. I feel that I cannot thank my merciful heavenly Father enough that I now in my more than four score years have the use of myself sufficient to be up and wait on myself. for I so greatly desire not to be a burden to others. and having gone thru so much suffering and privation in the past I know how to sympathise with those that suffer. and I pray that God will be with them and comfort them. as He has been with me all those years. "I waited patiently for the Lord; and he inclined unto me, and heard my cry" Psalm 40-1

Saturday July the 6th 1929

A nice clear morning. after a hard rain last night. "**Uncle Jake**" had a restless night, sick at the stomach. so is feeling weak to day. The rest of us all able to be up and trying to fulfil the duties of the day concerning our bodly needs. oh that we may all realise that we are under greater obligations to our heavenly Father to obey His holy will in all things, that we may be permited an inheritance with Him when done with the things of earth. Blessed by His holy name.

Sunday July the 7th 1929

Another nice morning, had rain again last night. All are feeling some better I am glad to note, and **Uncle Jakes** wife and little daughter spent the night with him and will remain with him until tomorrow. his Mother came over to see him this morning. Many friends of the family came to see him daily.

Monday July the 8th 1929

Some cloudy this morning, I am thankful to be so I can be up to day, but still have such giddiness in my head that I can't hardly govern my steps the rest of the family well as usual, "**Uncle Jake**"spent a restless night but seems some better to day. his wife and little daughter returned home to day.

Tuesday July the 9th 1929

Still cloudy and warm, all able to be up, except the Patient who is still feeling quite weak and restless. I am thankful to have the use of my faculties and my right hand, that I may note the goodness and mercy of the dear Lord to us all his dependent cretures. "Unto thee O God do we give thanks, unto thee do we give thanks; for that thy name is near thy wonderous works declare." Psalm 75-1. "Behold how good and how pleasant it is for brethren to dwell together in unity. It is like the precious ointment upon the head than ran down upon the beard, even Aron's beard; that went down to the skirts of his garments;" Psalm 133-1-2. Wheat thrashing is going on in this home at this time which fills my heart and mind with the thoughts of the past, for in my childhood and until I was grown up my Father **Samuel C. Millikan** owned a thrashing machine and he and some others of our good neighbors used it for many years in thrashing out the crops, and since he passed away it always fills my heart with sadness when thrashing out the grain is going on, but I trust he has been gathered, into the Heavenly garner.

Wednesday July the 10th 1929

Clear and quite warm this morning. All except the sick man in this home are up and going about daily avocations, he improves very slow. I am weak and trembly but thankful that I can still be up and wait on myself and help do some things for my daughter who is kept very busy with household affairs and careing for the sick. I pray the dear Lord to give her strength to hold up to do that which is necessary for the comfort of the sick and other members of the household from day to day and I know that she fully trusts Him all the while.

Thursday July the 11th 1929

Clear and warm again this morning. All just about the same as to health as for several days. I have nothing of importance to note only the continued goodness and loveing kindness of the blessed Lord who watches over us from day to day last night **Jacob Peace**'s wife and some of his children and some of his friends came again to see him. It seems the One that rules all things puts it into the hearts and minds of his family and many friends to visit him often as possible.

Friday July the 12th 1929

Cloudy to day. the health of this family is very much as has been noted for a week past the patient some days better and other days worse, the rest of us make out to keep up and attend to the affairs of the home. and my greatest desire is that we many all be faithful to attend to that which pertains to our never dying souls, for we shall be called to give account at the day of judgement. oh Father keep us close to thee, that we sin not.

Saturday July the 13th 1929

Cloudy again to day. nothing unusual to note at present the sick man is so he can sit up some again to day as he did yesterday, **Dr Bulla** came to see him last evening, and says his suffering now is caused by a stomach trouble, and he will have to be dieted for some time before he will get relief, the rest of us are all so we can be up and attend to daily affairs which is much to be thankful for.

Sunday July the 14th 1929

A pretty bright Sabbath morning. much to be thankful for, that we of this household are all feeling some better this morning. having had a quiet nights rest especially in the latter part of the night. Praise the Lord.

Monday July the 15th 1929

Cloudy and some cooler to day. **Jacob Peace** is some better to day than yesterday, his wife returned home this morning. the rest of the family here about as usual, not feeling very well but able to be up and attending to household affairs the two girls **Minnie** and **Mary Lee** are gone to their work in the sewing room in High Point.

Tuesday July the 16th 1929

A nice pleasent morning all feeling some better I am thankful to state. and think the sick man is improveing some, altho it seems a very slow process "In thee O Lord do I put my trust; let me never be put to confusion." "Let all those that seek thee rejoice and be glad in thee; and let such as thy salvation say continually Let God be magnified."

Wednesday July the 17th 1929

Clear this morning. I am feeling quite feeble to day. but thankful I can still arise from my bed and wait on myself. I think the sick man is still improving some, the rest of the family here are in usual health and attending the daily avocations. "Bless the Lord O my soul and all that is within me bless His holy name."

Thursday July the 18th 1929

A nice clear morning. I am feeling quite feble indeed so much so as to scarcely use my pen. but I am not one to give up as long as I can hold up my hands. and trust the dear Lord to take care of me. The sick man rested some last night the rest of the family are at their daily duties. Praise the Lord for His goodness to us all.

Friday July the 19th 1929

A very rainey morning. I am feeling some better to day for which I feel very thankful, for I suffered so much yesterday that was afraid I should be entirely confined to my bed by this time, but had strength to arise from my bed and straiten up my room as I do every morning. the sick man is resting some better at present. the family here are all up and doing as usual. I feel that we have much to thank our merciful heavenly Father for. As He cares for us daily.

Saturday July the 20th 1929

Cloudy and cool this morning. I got a fall yesterday and hurt my hand so badly that it is dificult to use my pen, but thankful it is no worse, The rest here about the same for several days.

Sunday July the 21st 1929

Still cloudy and quite cool for the time of year. The condition of the sick man in this home seems to be very much the same as for the past week some days better and other days worse, the family heare are about in their usual state of health. I am thankful to be able to be up and wait on my self altho I am still suffering with my right hand that I had bruised badly when I got a fall a few days ago, the pain goes clear up into my shoulder, so that it is with dificulty that I can use my hand and arm to write. We learn that **Thomas Finch** passed away last Friday night about two oclock, and his funeral will be preached this afternoon at the home and he will be laid to rest in his vault at Hopewell with others of his family that have gone before. Later in the day, we of this household most of us went to Sunday School and Preaching this afternoon, had a splendid lesson, then listened to a most excelent sermon by **Rev -Walton** a young man that has been conducting Vacation Bible School in this community, and it was his first sermon at Mt Vernon, and was greatly enjoyed by all.

Monday July the 22nd 1929

Cloudy yet and still cool, The Father in this home **J.W. Peace** was quite sick last night and spent a restless night, but is so he can be up to day his sick brother **Jacob Peace** seems better to day the rest of us altho not feeling well are all up. Yesterday evening after attending S.S. and Preaching at Mt Vernon. **J.W. Peace** and wife **May** who is my daughter, and myself went over to Hopewell, but as the funeral of **Thomas Finch** was held in his home we did not get to hear it but we were in time at the Church to see the funeral procession and the

Truck loads that were brought of Flowers that was beyond discription for beauty and profusion, I had seen many flowers at funerals but nothing to compare with this and the largest attendance I have ever witnessed at any place. The rich and the poor, the White and the Colored were there in great numbers to pay their last respect not merely because he was a wealthy man in this worlds goods, but because he was well beloved and was one that was ever ready to help those in need. out of his full garners.

Tuesday July the 23rd 1929

Clear this morning and not quite so cool. The sick man in this home, seems some better to day. The rest of us altho not feeling strong, are so we can all be us and attend to the daily rotine of work that is necessary to be done for the comfort of our mortal bodies, and my greatest desire is that we may not neglect to do our whole duty to God that we may be prepared for an entrance into that home which He has prepared for all those who love and serve Him on earth, there to praise Him in the name of Jesus forevermore.

Wednesday July the 24th 1929

Clear and warm this morning. I do not feel at all well, and my hand pains me so from the effects of my fall that it is with dificulty that I can write a line, but I am so thankful that I was not badly cripled that I bear the pain with patience, The sick man seems to be just about the same as for several days past, the rest in this home all up and busy. We have much to be thankful for that it is as well with us all as it is. and I want to be more closely on my watch to obey the Lord more fully every day. "I will bless the Lord at all times; his praise shall continually be in my mouth." Father help me to fulfill this Text for Jesus sake.

Thursday July the 25th 1929

Clear and much warmer to day. I had a restless night so feel weak and nervous to day, but thankful to be so I can be up and wait on myself.

the rest in this home very much the same as for several days past, the sick man so he could be moved out of his room and lie on a Cot in the fresh air, which I hope will be a great help toward restoration. Praise the Lord.

Friday July the 26th 1929

Cloudy and warm this morning. I am so thankful that we all had a reasonable good nights rest, altho the sick man as usual woke up quite often. The members of the family are all busy as usual. I am still suffering with the sprained hand but make out to scrible a few lines each day, to keep me in touch with the passing of time, and that we are accountable beings for the way we spend our time here on earth, for we shall be called to give account of the deeds done in body. and by taking a note of the date each day it keeps me closer on my watch, as I see the flight of time. "I love the Lord, because he hath heard my voice and my supplication. Because he hath inclined his ear into me, therefore will I call upon him as long as I live."

Saturday July the 27th 1929

Still some cloudy and quite warm to day. The sick man in this home does not improve as much as we had hoped in the six weeks that he has now been with us, other members of this family are not at all well to day, and I am feeling feble myself but thankful to be able to be up and wait on my self, and scrible a line praise to the Father of all our sure mercies.

Sunday July the 28th 1929

A nice clear morning. The sick man had a restless nigh and is feeling badly to day. The family in usual health, I am feeling weak to day but hope I shall have strength to attend Sunday School this afternoon as usual if the dear Lord so wills. "O Give thanks unto the Lord for he is good for his mercy endureth forever." Praise His name.

Monday July 29th 1929

A bright morning. All up except the sick man in this home, he is just about as for several days. All are very busy with daily affairs, the girls are gone to their work in High Point, and I am doing what my hands find to do as far as I able.

Tuesday July the 30th 1929

Cloudy and very warm this morning. Those of us in this home, are very much the same as to health as for the past week, the sick man does not improve much. I fear he is not going to get well, but if he is prepared for a better world, he would be relieved of suffering.

Wednesday July the 31st 1929

Still cloudy and warm, the sick man passed another restless, night, but is sleeping some to day. The rest of us very much the same as for a week past we are so we can be up and attend to daily duties, oh that we may all remember the duty we owe to our Father in heaven from whom all our blessings flow, and an another month has passed I realise that we are all that much nearer our journeys end here and earth, and that we may make our calling and election sure.

Thursday August the 1st 1929

Cloudy again to day. the sick man does not seem to improve, his wife came to see him last night and says she is going to make arrangements to have him taken to the Hospital, to see if that will help him. The rest of us in this home just about as usual. Praise the Lord.

Friday August the 2nd 1929

Clear and warm to day. The sick man **Jacob Peace** who has been in this home for over six weeks was taken to his home in High Point last evening, where he can be nearer the Drs and perhaps may have to go to the Hospital. The family here are busy to day caning the Peaches which was brought from Peach Orchard yesterday, the sand hill peaches do not seem to be as good as usual this year. There has been so much rain may be the cause of this. I am still suffering with my lame Arm and do not have much strength but thankful that it is as well with me as it is, for I am hoping to attend yearly meeting at Guilford College next week if it is the will of my merciful Heavenly Father.

Saturday August the 3rd 1929

Some cloudy this morning, All able to be up and busy we learn that **J.P.** the sick man stood his trip home last evening much better than we had expected I had a pleasant visit last evening from our Springfield Pastor **Clara I. Cox** she came to offer me a conveyance with her over to yearly meeting next week. Praise the Lord for His care over me.

Sunday August the 4th 1929

Clear and warm this morning. I am thankful to be so I can be up this morning, and that the rest of the family here are in usual health. **J.W.** and **May** are going to Town this morning to see how "**Uncle Jake**" is getting along by this time. I often feel sad and lonely, yet I can say with David, Why art thou cast down O my soul? and why art thou disquieted within me? hope thou in God; for I shall yet praise Him who is the health of my countenance and my God.

Monday August the 5th 1929

Clear and cooler to day. I am thankful to state that we are all able to be up and attend to daily affairs May God help us to do His holy will in all things, is my prayer for the sake of Him who died for us.

Tuesday Aug the 6th 1929

Fair weather and I am thankful that all the family here are able to arise from our beds I am now about ready to start to Guilford College to attend our yearly meeting I am praying that our blessed Saviour will go with me, and be with all who may attend, to His honor and praise.

August 1929

Tuesday evening August the 6th I stated this morning before leaving home that I was about ready to start to Guilford College to attend yearly meeting, I am now in the same little room that I have occupied for the past six years in succession during yearly meeting week. Cousin **Elva Blair** brought me over here this morning and I attended the forenoon session of the meeting, and being tired she advised me to go to my room and rest instead of going out to Church this p.m. and I appreciate this advice and am abideing by it, for I realy did not know how tired I was until I tried to rest. I hope I shall feel able to attend the services to night.

Wednesday Aug the 7th 1929

Nice weather this morning, I am glad to state that I got out to the services last night, heard a good sermon by a lady by the name of **Mary Cox** from the State of Ohio, other good advice from those who are attending yearly meeting from a distance, good singing etc.

Thursday Aug the 8th 1929

Cloudly this morning, had heavy rain last night which prevented many that were here in Foundrs hall from getting out to the Cherch so a group went into the Assembly room, had a good meeting heard a fine Address from A Friend by the name of **Murray S. Kenworthy** I went out to the meeting in the forenoon yesterday but did not get out in the afternoon as yet since I came Thursday night. I can now state that I got out to Church this forenoon heard a fine Address by **Elden H. Mills.** and many other interesting things and also got out this afternoon and heard a splendid sermon by **Rev Tom A Sikes** of High Point, and heard several Memorials read among others one of **Mary C. Woody** a woman that I have met here at yearly meeting in the past and a woman that was greatly beloved by her numerous acquaintance, I did not go out to Church to night as I was tired and the weather very unfavorable.

Friday Aug the 9th 1929

A lovely morning. I was favored to get out to the morning sesion, staid for the eleven oclock meeting and was invited out to the home of **Mrs Oliver Knight** to dine with them, had a splendid visit in their lovely home, his wife being one of my farmer neighbors in Randolp, before she married and moved to Guilford. At this session heard **Lewis W. McFarland,** also a fine Address by **Elden H. Mills.**

Saturday Aug the 10th 1929

A clear bright morning. Our friend **Dr Francis Anachum** of Winston Salem Friends Meeting took myself and some other Friends in his Car out to the eight oclock meeting and we staid for the eleven oclock service heard a most interesting sermon by **Dr Elbert Russell.** The morning session being presided over by **Linley M. Wells.** Both sessions were greatly enjoyed by all. Later, I did not go out to the afternoon session nor to the session at night, as I was very tired and needed my strength to recuperate ready to leave this dear old place tomorrow.

Sunday Aug the 11th 1929

A favorabl looking morning tho somewhat cloudy but I think the Sun will soon shine out I had a good nights rest and am expecting to atten the forenoon services at Church then return here for lunch as usual then leave for High Point where I am invited to visit some friends before returning to Randolp etc. I praise the Lord this morning that He has watched over me day and night and has given me rest and so many kind friends here.

Monday Morning the 12th Aug 1929

A beautiful morning. All able to be up in this home which is that of **Allen J. Blair** Route #5. High Point N.C.

According to my expectation I was favored to attend the forenoon sessions at yearly meeting yesterday. The Sunday School hour was very interesting, then the eleven oclock service was presided over **Edgar T. Hole** and **William Reagan** of New York Yearly meeting who gave us splendid advise indeed and many others gave us words of encouragement, Then returned to Founders Hall where I had my room all week, rested awhile and took lunch and conversed with my friends, then prepard to leave this dear old place. My dear friend **Clara I. Cox** our Pastor of Friends Church at Springfield brought me over here to **Allen J. Blairs** where I spent at the night, and am enjoying the day most pleasently. with him and his wife **Mary Mendenhall Blair** and their two nice children, **Elwood,** and **Evelyn.** I have known Allen from his childhood and am so glad to be in his home, May the blessing of Heaven rest upon this home. and Gods holy spirit abide with them forever is my prayer.

Tuesday Aug the 13th 1929

Clear and warm this morning, I am still in the home of my friend and relative **Allen J. Blair,** I had a quiet nights rest, so feel some stronger, and the family here are in good health for which I feel very thankful. I know that I have been watched over and cared for all along lifes journey and God will keep me to the end. "I love the Lord because he hath heard my voice and my supplication. Because he hath inclined his ear unto me, therefore will I call upon him as long as I live."

Wednesday Aug the 14th 1929

Clear and very warm this morning, I am thankful to be able to arise from my bed, as I did not get any rest in sleep last night until after one oclock just nervous and restless for no special reason that I could assign it to except being tired out as the weather is very warm and I am not strong. but I am spending the day very pleasenly, as the family are very kind to me, and provide many comforts for me, I have easy Chairs also a nice Cot on their nice Porch where I can lie down whenever I wish among the many beautiful flowers. Praise God from whom all blessing flow.

Until We Sleep Our Last Sleep

Thursday Aug 15th 1929

Some cloudy this morning, and some more fresh air stirring which makes it more comfortable, I am still in the family of **Allen Blair** as I am spending the week with them until Saturday when I expect if able to attend the Memorial services at Springfield then return to my daughter **Mrs J.W. Peace** where I make my home. The family here are in good health I am thankful to state, and I feel very grateful to our merciful heavenly Father that he has given me strength to be up and wait on myself.

Friday Aug the 16th 1929

Clear this morning very much cooler. All in this home are able to arise from our beds for which I feel very grateful to the Giver of all good. Last night the family here took me over to their brotherinlaws **Reed Mendenhalls** there we enjoyed his company and that of his nice little wife and two sweet little children a son and daughter, also the mother **Josie Mendenhall** and her other son **John** came over there and we had an Ice cream feast and a general good time.

Saturday Aug the 17th 1929

A rainey morning, and looks as if we were going to have a very unfavorable day for the services at Springfield, but all at this home are able to be up and we hope to get over to the Memorial services some time to day. I have spent the week here at **Allen J. Blairs** very pleasently, and now I am expecting to return to the home of my daughter **Mrs J.W. Peace** after I attend the Memorial at Springfield. Evening of same day, we were favord to get to the Memorial service which was very satesfactory and instructive indeed, and also met may old acquaintance and friends that I do not get to see more than once a year. It brought many things of the past so fresh to mind that it was hard to keep from being overcome by emotion. The picture of my **Uncle John Carter** was held up before this audience, and it seemed that the image of my dear Mother was revealed in his face I never saw before, until they are both gone that their faces resembled each other so much. I praise the Lord for His tender mercy and care over me this day, and for blessing me with so many kind friends.

Sunday Aug the 18th 1929

A lovely Sabbath morning. All able to be up and attend the Sunday School at Mt Vernon which was held at nine oclock, instead of two oclock as usual on account of a singing at Trinity held by **Clark Wilborn** to day which many wished to attend. We are commanded to keep the Sabbath day holy and hope that those who may attend will sing praises to Him in whom we live and have our being. "O Lord thou hast searched me, and known me. Thou knowest my downsitting and mine uprising, thou understandest my thought afar off. Thou compassest my path and my lying down and art acquainted with all my ways. For there is not a word in my tongue but lo O Lord thou knowest it altogether." Therefore I want to be kept close on my watch least I transgress thy law in anyway. "In thee Lord. do I put my trust: let me never be put to confusion. let my mouth be filled with thy praise and with thy honour all the day. Cast me not off in the time of old age: forsake me not when my strength faileth." These words of Scripture is the prayer of my heart at this time. for Jesus sak.

Monday Aug the 19th 1929

A nice morning. All able to be up and go about daily avocations I am thankful to state. We learn that **Jacob Peace** is still living this morning but no hope expressed for his recovery. I hope he has made his calling and election sure and will be admitted into the home of eternal rest and peace.

Tuesday Aug the 20th 1929

Clear and cooler this morning. All in usual health in this home, and the girls **Minnie** and **Mary Lee** are at home for the day, from their sewing room in High Point, and are helping their Mother do the washing, and will return to their work tomorrow. We learn this morning that **Mrs Balance** of Trinity passed away last night. she was eighty seven years of age. It seems that the aged will soon all have passed away and a new generation taken their places oh that all may be prepared for the change, for the old must die and the young do die, so it behooves us all to be close on our watch that we do not disobey the Divine Commands and thus forfeit a home, that is prepared for those who love and serve God while on Earth.

Wednesday Aug the 21ˢᵗ 1929

A clear and nice cool morning. All able to be up the girls are gone back to their sewing room in High Point **May** and **Clemons** went with them to see how their **Uncle Jake Peace** is getting along by this time, he was very sick yesterday. I hope that we may all be concerned for the salvation of our immortal souls more than for anything else, that we may be prepared to all meet in the better land, there to praise God togeather in eternity.

Thursday Aug the 22ⁿᵈ 1929

A clear pleasant morning. All in usual health. **Cousin F.S. Blair** who had been attending yearly meeting since been visiting his kindred and friends, surprised us last night by coming in after some of the family had gone to bed, as he could not get here any earlier. It always seems good to see him as he and I have been close friends from childhood. he went with **Jerome** and **May** and myself to High Point this forenoon, we lelf him at his brother **Winston Blairs** and we went on to see **Jeromes** sick brother **Jacob Peace** he is very sick indeed, and this afternoon we received the news of the death of **Jerome's** first wifes Father **Watson Ingram** who will be buried at Mt Vernon tomorrow afternoon.

August 1929

Friday Aug the 23rd 1929

Cloudy and some rain this morning. An Electric storm last night but I have not heard of any damage from it. We learn that "**Uncle Jake**" is much worse again and **Jerome** and **May** are gone to see him this morning. We are all in about our usual state of health to day. Later in the day, **J.W. Peace** and wife **May** and myself attended the funeral of **J.W.P's** fatherinlaw **Watson Ingram** which was held in the New Methodist Church at Archdale conducted by **Rev-Jones** the Pastor, there was large attendance and quite a profusion of beautiful flowers the Remains were taken to Mt Vernon and placed in the Cemetary there to await the Reserection.

Saturday Aug the 24th 1929

Clear this morning, we had some more rain last night and some heavy thunder, but after it passed off I had a quiet rest in sleep. and feel thankful that we are all able to arise from our beds and go about daily duties; to day is Friends quarterly meeting at Marlboro I should so much love to be there, but have no conveyance so will have to let the will suffice for the deed. May the dear Lord be very near to all those who may attend and keep us all for Jesus sake.

Sunday Aug the 25th 1929

Cloudy this morning. All in usual health in this home I am glad to state, for health is one of our greatest blessings. "Bless the Lord O my soul" and all that is within me, bless his holy name. Bless the Lord O my soul, and forget not all his benefits." Sunday evening, we were favored to attend Sunday School at Mt Vernon at two oclock as usual and after we returned home, we had a pleasant surprise from our friends **Mr** and **Mrs Fesperman** and little **Rachel**, from Salisbury giving us a call, also **Mr** and **Mrs Suggs** from High Point and their two children. We were very happy to have them with us, but the time was all too short, for they are good company.

Until We Sleep Our Last Sleep

Monday Aug the 26th 1929

Cloudy again this morning, All in usual health the girls gone back to their sewing room work and **Clemons** also went to work in High Point at the Upholstering Factory, so it leaves just **J.W.** and **May** and **little J.A.** and myself in the **Peace** home this morning. and I trust we shall always abide in Peace on Earth not only in name but in deed and in truth, and when done with time, dwell togeather in the home where all is Joy and Peace and Love.

Tuesday Aug the 27th 1929

Clear and cooler this morning. All up and busy. The girls **Minnie Peace** and **Mary Lee Stilwell** are gone to their work in a sewing room in High Point. **Clemons** has also gone to his work of upholstering in an establishment in High Point, the rest of us are doing what our hands find to do in the home. Later in the day, **Jerome** and **May** went to High Point to see how "**Uncle Jake**" is getting along they found hin resting better for the time, no real hope of recovery seems to be held out for him, but time will show, and he is in the hands of a righteous Judge.

Wednesday Aug the 28th 1929

A nice clear morning. All have sufficient strength to arise from our beds, for which I feel thankful. "I will lift up mine eyes unto the hills, from whence cometh my help. My help cometh from the Lord which made heaven and earth. The Lord shall preserve thy going out and thy coming in from this time forth, and even for evermore." What glorious promises are these that are laid down in Gods holy written Word for our comfort and help. oh that we may have perfect confidence, and obey Him fully in all things to His honor and praise. Is my prayer.

Thursday Aug the 29th 1929

Cloudly and damp to day. All up and busy as usual for which I feel very grateful, for we are such dependent cretures, but are so wonderfully favored. Yesterday we had a pleasent Call from our friends **Mr** and **Mrs Springer** of New York we have know them for several years and think of a great deal of them. **Mrs. Springer** is sister to **Mrs Edd Blair** of Progress N.C.

Friday Aug the 30th 1929

Clear and much cooler to day. All able to be up. Yesterday **Lena White, Jerome Peaces's** daughter and her children spent the day with us, and **Jerome** and **May** went to High Point to see his brother **Jacob Peace** who is still sick found him resting more comfortably for the time, but not much improvement.

Saturday Aug the 31st 1929

Still clear and cool this morning. All in usual health I am thankful to note, and hope we shall all show our appreciation by being obedient to Divine commands. for we shall all have to give account of the deeds done in the body. Dear Lord help us to have a good account to give. We learn to day that "**Uncle Jake Peace**" seems to be failing very fast.

Sunday September the 1st 1929

A nice clear morning and still quite cool. All in usual health in this home, I am glad to state. We had a very pleasent surprise yesterday by a call from one of my nieces **Ruth Laughlin,** who is my youngest sisters **Almina Davis's** daughter she is maried to **John Laughlin** and they moved to the State of Kansas several years ago. she left her oldest daughter **Almina** in the home with her Father to keep house for him while the rest were makeing their visit to N.C. they drove thru in a nice closed Car. The oldest son **Kermit** was their driver, the other three children were a fifteen year old daughter (I have forgotten her given name) and **John Laughlin jr** eleven, and **Paul** the youngest child six years of age. They have been visiting kindred and friends for the past six weeks, and have had a grand time sight seeing etc viewing the mountain scenery in The Land of the Sky which is the Switzerland of America and also visited Wilmington and saw the grand Ocean for themselves. This will be a trip those children will remember while life lasts. They aim to start for their home tomorrow the 2nd of September 1929. May God take care of them is my prayer.

Evening of Sept the 1st. We were favored to all get out to Sunday School and Preaching this p.m. heard a splendid sermon by Pastor **Rev-Kelly**, to day is the beginning of the Protracted meeting at Mt Vernon. I hope much good will be done.

Monday Sep the 2nd 1929

Another clear cool morning. All up and busy. I hope we shall be favored to attend the meeting at Mt Vernon this afternoon. Later we attended the services as we had hoped to do, had a good meeting.

Tuesday Sept the 3rd 1929

A nice clear cool morning. Yesterday as my daughter and I were returning from the three oclock meeting at Mt Vernon I desided to stop on my way home, at cousin **John Hills** and stay with them over night, as I had not visited them this year, as I was away in Charlotte the past winter at my son **Fred C. Blairs,** and did not return to Randolph until about the first of April this year, so had not visited them as I usually do once a year, and oftener when I have the opportunity, as cousin **Roxie** has to sit there in her Wheel Chair from day to day and week after week. she is quite feeble but can sit on the Porch and see the many passers by and also can roll out to her meals, and cousin **John** is so attentive to her. which is such a great blessing.

Wednesday Sept the 4th 1929

Misting rain this morning. I feel the effects of the dampness, but thankful to be able to be up and wait on myself. the rest of the family in usual health and busy with the affairs of the day. May the dear

Lord help us to be faithful to do His holy will is my great desire for Christs sake. Evening of the same day. So rainey we did not get out to Church but endeavored to be much in prayer for the welfare of all.

Thursday Sept the 5th 1929

Still cloudy, but looks as tho the Sun might come out. We of this household are all able to be up and busy I am thankful to state. Evening of the same day. **May** and myself were favored to attend the three oclock service which was very well attended for a week day and heard a splendid sermon.

Friday Sept the 6th 1929

Clear and warm this morning. All in usual health and busy attending to the affairs of the day. We learn that "**Uncle Jake**"is not better.

Saturday Sept the 7th 1929

Still clear and warm. All able to be up this morning. Praise the Lord for His goodness to us all.

Sunday Sep the 8th 1929

Cloudy this morning. All in usual health in this home I am glad to state. The evening of the same day. We were favored to go to Sunday School and Preaching this afternoon. **Rev – Kelly** the Pastor had to attend a funeral at Greensboro so **Rev – Harbison** of High Point filled his place, and gave us a splendid sermon. Also a **Mr Bacon** from High Point who accompanied **Rev Kelly**. gave us a good message and offered a most excellent prayer. I think all who had come to the years of understanding enjoyed the services very much. Praise the Lord for sending His mesengers to us. for they gave us much encouragement.

Monday Sept the 9th 1929

Cloudy and warm this morning. All in usual health in this home I am glad to state. but we learn that **Jeromes** brother **Jacob Peace** passes away last night. he had been in a severe state of suffering for the past three months. and we trust that he is now forever free from suffering and where he can sing Gods praise thruout eternity.

Tuesday Sept the 10th 1929

A nice clear pleasent morning. All in this home able to be up and prepare to attend the funeral of **Jeromes** brother **Jacob Peace**. Later. We were favored to all attend the funeral of **Jacob Peace** there was a short service held in his home at High Point conducted by **Rev W.R. Kelly** and another minister by the name of **Conrad.** Then the Remains were taken to Mt Vernon where the regular funeral was held conducted by the Pastor **Rev. W.R. Kelly** and the same **Rev Mr. Conrad.** There was a large attendance and quite a profusion of lovely flowers.

Wednesday Sept the 11th 1929

Cloudy and cool this morning. All in usual health, I am thankful to state. I feel that we have so much to thank our merciful heavenly Father for, so I can say with the Psalmist, "I will lift up mine eyes unto the hills, from whence cometh my help. My help cometh from the Lord which made heaven and earth. He will not suffer thy foot to be moved; he that keepeth thee will not slumber." Psalm 121-1-2-3

Thursday September the 12th 1929

Cloudy this morning. All in usual health and busy. **Jerome Peace's** Aunt A **Mrs Malissa Cain** is to be burried to day at Pleasent Grove, and we hope to go the the funeral. Later in the day. **Jerome** and **May** and myself were favored to go to the funeral, which wa largely attended conducted by the Pastor of Pleasent Grove Church and a **Rev Mr. Conrad.** There was quite a profusion of flowers of recognition. **Mrs Cain's** maiden name was **Miss Malissa Peace** a sister to **Jerome's** Father **Calvin Peace.** She had outlived four husbands, her first husband was a **Mr Wilborn,** the next two were **Englishes** and the fourth a **Mr Cain.** she was seventy years of age. has two daughters living and several grandchildren.

Friday Sept the 13th 1929

Still some cloudy this morning and warmer. All able to be up and go about daily avocations. It seems that attending funerals has occupied much of our time recently. which should keep us mindful that we too shall soon all pass away. oh that we may be prepared for the better land.

Saturday Sept the 14th 1929

Rainey this morning. All able to be up and some of the family had hoped to go to quarterly meeting to day at Giliad, but it looks very unfavorable. Later in the day, the clouds broke away and we **J.W. Peace, May** and myself were favored to attended the quarterly meeting at Mt Gilead there was not a large attendance, but had a good meeting.

Sunday Sep the 15th 1929

Clear and cooler this morning. I am thankful to be able to be up to day. after my drive yesterday. For I was feeling so badly yesterday morning that I thought I could not go to Church. but I took it to the dear Lord and was made to feel that it was right and best that I should go. So I went and felt much better for my effort, so it has given me fresh courage to press on to do whatever the Lord would have me do, no matter how badly and care for those who do His holy will. oh that I may be faithful to obey Him in all things to His honor and praise is my prayer for Christs sake. "O Lord God of my salvation, I have cried day and night before thee. Let my prayer come before thee; incline thine ear unto my cry."

Monday Sept the 16th 1929

Cloudy this morning. All in usual health and my little grandson **J.A. Peace** starts to school for his first term he is highly elated about it. May the Lord watch over him, and "preserve his going out and his comin in for this time forth... and forevermore."

Tuesday Sept the 17th 1929

Still cloudy this moring. All able to be up and go about daily avocations, I am thankful to state. Let thy mercy, O Lord be upon us, according as we hope thee in.

Wednesday Sept the 18th 1929

Cloudy and cool to day. I am feeling rather feeble but thankful to be so I can wait on myself and use my pen to testify to the goodness and mercy of the Lord to us his dependent cretures, who are not worthy of His blessings that we receive from day to day. The rest of the family are in usual health and my little grandson **J.A. Peace** is going to school to day.

Thursday Sept the 19th 1929

Clear and much cooler this morning. All able to be up and attend to the affairs of the day. "O give thanks unto the Lord for he is good; because his mercy endureth for ever." The Lord is my strength."

Friday Sept the 20th 1929

Clear and cold this morning. All in usual health. **May** and myself are aiming to go to spend the day with **Mrs Ed White, Jerome Peace's** daughter, Evening of the same day we were favored to spend the day very pleasently with **Lena White** as we had hoped to be able to do. Praise God from whom all blessings flow.

Saturday Sept the 21st 1929

Clear and windy to day. All up and busy with the affairs of the day. Nothing special to note only the continued goodness and mercy of the Lord to us poor unworthy cretures who are so prone to wonder away from he strait and narow way which is cast up for those who obey His commandments here on earth, and thereby merit a home of eternal rest in heaven above. oh that we may all be closer on our watch that we go not astray from the path of rectitude.

September 1929

Sunday Sept the 22nd 1929

Still windy and cold this morning. All in usual health. I am thankful to state, for health is one of God's greatest blessings, we were invited to **John Lee Kenedy** birthday dinner to day but the weather is too unfavorable to go.

Monday Sept the 23rd 1929

Raining some this morning. All able to go to their various occupations, for which I feel very thankful "O give thanks unto the Lord, for he is good: for his mercy endureth for ever."

Tuesday Sept the 24th 1929

Cloudy and misting rain at intervals. All in usual health. The girls and **Clemons** are gone to their work in High Point, the rest are busy with home affairs. **Lena White** and baby **Billie Ray,** are with us to day. May the Lord help us all to do His holy will, is my desire for Christs sake. "I love the Lord because he hath heard my voice and my supplication." Praise his holy name.

Wednesday Sept the 25th 1929

Still cloudy this morning. All able to arise from our beds and go about daily avocation.

Thursday Sept the 26th 1929

Cloudy again this morning. All in usual health.

Friday Sept the 27th 1929

A nice clear morning. All up and busy. There is nothing special to note at this time, only the continued goodness and mercy of our blessed Saviour.

Saturday September the 28th 1929

A bright sunshiney morning and some cooler. All in usual health, and busy with daily duties. Heavenly Father help us all to be close on our watch that we do not transgress thy commandments. "I will say of the Lord, He is my refuge and my fortress; my God; in him will I trust." Psalm 91-2

Sunday Sept the 29th 1929

Clear warm this morning. All in usual health. **Mr** and **Mrs Gideon Bowman** and little **jr** spent last night with us. I am invited to attend a family Reunion to day at the former home of **Sidney J. Blairs** hope to be able to go.

Monday Sept the 30th 1929

Cloudy the morning. All in usual health and attending to the affairs of the day. Well my hopes were realised yesterday in regard to attending the family Reunion at the home of the late **Sidney J. Blairs.** All the children and grandchildren of the Decesed were present, and a few invited Guests **Mrs Anna Cranford** and myself were especially Honored Guest. there were twenty five or thirty people in all. This was especially for family Reunion, and not for a big Celebration and we certainly had a very interesting time togeather in every way, They had a long Table out in the shade, well loaded with good things to eat, and Coffee for those that use it, and plenty of Ice Tea for all, and different kinds of good meats, various kinds of Pies, Pickles, and Cakes galore, and fruits, Apples, Bananas, Grapes, etc. Then after Lunch took Pictures, and conversed togeather which all seemed to enjoy. Then wound up by gathering in a room reading the 14th chapter of St. John and prayer and parted for our various destinations.

Tuesday October the 1st 1929

A very rainey morning. All able to be up and busy, but I am suffering from a very bad cold, but very thankful to not be down in bed for I have known what that means, for many years in the past. and as this is the first day of another month it reminds me how fast time flies and that it wont be long at the longest until we shall be called to give account of the deeds done in the body. Lord help us to have a good account to give that we may abide with the forever.

Wednesday Oct the 2nd 1929

Another very rainey morning. All well as usual except myself. I have deep cold which makes me feel badly, but thankful to still be able to be out of bed.

Thursday October the 3rd 1929

Clear and cool this morning. All up and busy. I feel like saying with the Psalmist. "I will lift up mine eyes unto the hills, from whence cometh my help, my help cometh from the Lord which made heaven and earth. The Lord shall preserve thy going out and thy comeing in from this time forth, and even for evermore." What a glourious promice in this Scripture Text. Psalm 121-1-2-8

Friday Oct the 4th 1929

A nice clear morning and quite cool. I am still suffering from cold in my chest but thankful to be up, the rest of the family are well as usual excep little **J.A.** he is not able to go to School this week, but hope he will soon be all right. Praise the Lord for his goodness and mercy to us all.

Saturday Oct the 5th 1929

Raining this morning. All able to be up, and today we are favored with the company of Preacher **Reed Haris** and family and some others, as they are having a Barbicue here this evening, which constitutes a family reunion and other friends, I hope we will give God all the praise for our blessing for from Him all blessings flow.

Sunday October the 6th 1929

Rainey this morning. All in usual health, with the exception of colds. This is Preaching day at Mt Vernon I trust we shall all be favored to attend. I mentioned yesterday about the Barbicue that was to be here last evening. I can now state that it was well attended by kindred and friends, who seemed to enjoy it to the full. and having had **Rev W.R. Haris** and family with us thru most of the day, and later **Rev W.R. Kelly,** wife and little **jr** came to add joy to the occasion. I trust we shall not forget from whence all our blessings flow, and give due reverence to the Source of all our joys and blessings. and now this evening I can state that we were all favored to attend Sunday School and Preaching at Mt Vernon this afternoon, heard a splendid sermon by the Pastor **Rev W. R. Kelly** his theme being centered on a portion of the 11th chap of St. Mark.

Monday Oct the 7th 1929

A nice clear day. All in usual health I am glad to state. **Ollie Peace Bowman** and her little son are with us to day we are always glad to have them visit. "Blessed is every one that fear the Lord; that walketh in his ways." oh Father help me to walk in Thy ways.

Tuesday October the 8th 1929

Clear this morning and cooler. All able to be up and attend to the affairs of the day. I am thankful to note. and hope we shall all remember that we are under obligations to our Divine Master and endeavor to do His holy will in all things, for he is so merciful to us his dependent cretures.

Wednesday Oct the 9th 1929

Nice clear morning. All in usual health and busy doing the things that are necessary for the sustanance and comfort of our mortal bodies. oh that we may be as eager to do these things which are needful for the salvation of our immortal souls.

Thursday Oct the 10th 1929

Clear and windy this morning. All able to be up and attend to daily affairs I am thankful to state Later, **Mrs Ed White** and babe spent the day with us.

October 1929

Friday Oct the 11th 1929

Clear and much cooler to day. All in usual health and busy. I must not fail to note what a pleasent surprise I was given last evening by the presence of two of the **Blair Sisters Emma and Elva** who brought a Friend Minister with them to see me. his name was **Linley Wells** of California I am always so glad of such visits, for they help me to take fresh courage to press on thru the remainder of lifes journey, and his appropriate prayer and words of comfort were refreshing to my soul. and the **Blair Sisters** brought me beautiful flowers which I appreciated so much, for it was a mark of kindness and sympathy. May the Lord bless them all, is my prayer for Jesus sake.

Saturday Oct the 12th 1929

Still clear and cool. All able to go about daily avocations I am thankful to state, Altho I am feeling feeble and nervous and have not the strength that I feel like I need to press on in the work I find to do, but am looking to Jesus who watches over me from day to day, and in whom I put my trust to help me to bear the cross and burdens of the day, for only as I lean on His strong arm am I able to bear the trials and provications of this life.

Sunday Oct the 13th 1929

A beautiful Sabbath morning. All able to arise from our beds and enjoy the bright sunshine and as we have the company of my dear son and family from Charlotte who came in late last night and gave us a pleasent surprise we are happy to have them with us at this time and trust that some of them will remain a few days.

Monday Oct the 14th 1929

Clear and cool this morning. All well as usual. We were disappointed in not haveing my daughterinlaw spend a few days with us as we had hoped she could, but she thought best to return with the rest of the family to their home in Charlotte as she is not in very good health at this time, so we had to give her up to go. and I trust they had a safe return.

Tuesday Oct the 15th 1929

Another nice clear morning. All able to be up and attend to the affairs of the day, I am thankful to state. May we all be concerned to do those things that are well pleasing in the sight of Him to whom we have to give account is my greatest desire for Christs sake.

Wednesday Oct the 16th 1929

Clear and much cooler to day. All able to arise from our beds, and do that which our hands find to do May we all do that which is well pleasing to Him to whom we own homeage for his mercy to us.

Thursday Oct the 17th 1929

A nice clear day. All able to go about daily work oh heavenly Father direct my steps this day and every day on the way that I should go, that I may merit eternal life. "Thou shalt guide me with thy counsel, and afterward receive me to glory, my flesh and my heart faileth; but God is the strength of my heart, and my portion for ever."

Friday Oct the 18th 1929

A clear bright day, but I am not feeling well enough to enjoy it, I am suffering from deep cold and shortness of breath, and am so nervous from loss of sleep etc, that I am scarely able to be up, but having been helpless and had to lie in bed of affliction from many years in the past, I am almost afraid to lie in bed even one day, when it is needful for me to do so. for fear I would have to stay there. So I am thankful to have even strength to arise from my bed and sit in a chair. The family here are in usual health is one of our greatest blessings. "I waited patiently for the Lord; and he inclined unto me, and heard my cry. He brought me up also out of an horrible pit, out of the miry clay, and established my goings." Blessed be His holy name.

Saturday Oct the 19th 1929

Another nice day but quite cool. I am still suffering but thankful to not be entirely bed fast, so use what strength I have to sit up, and pen a word of thanks to the great Giver of all good. I was so glad to have dear **Grandma Peace** spend the day with me yesterday. she is always such a comfort and help to me.

Sunday Oct the 20th 1929

A lovely Sabbath morning. I am still feeling weak but thankful that it is a well with me as it is, the rest are well as usual, and my daughter and myself are aiming if able to go to dear old Springfield to day to the eleven oclock meeting, there has been a series of meetings going on there for more than a week but I have not been at all well and have not had an oppartunity to attend any of the services which have been presided over by the Pastor **Clara I. Cox** and **Linley Wells** from California. we learn they have been having good success in this meeting.

Monday Oct the 21st 1929

Raining this morning All are feeling rather dull on account of the dampness, but thankful to be able to be up and attend to the affairs of the day. I must note, that yesterday my daughter and I were favored to get to the eleven oclock meeting at Springfield and heard a most splended sermon by **Linley Wells** of California. he is going to commence a series of meetings to day at Winston Salem. May he win many souls for Christ and receive the reward of "well done good and faithful servant" is my prayer.

Tuesday Oct the 22nd 1929

Cloudy and windy to day. None of us feeling very well, but all able to be up and attend to daily affairs for which I feel grateful to the Giver of all good, oh that we may be faithful to do His holy will on earth that we may inherit a home in that beautiful land where our blessed

Savior has gone to prepare a mantion for all who love and serve him here on earth His footstool.

Wednesday Oct the 23rd 1929

Clear and cool to day, All in our usual state of health, which is to say that some of us are not very strong, but so we can be up and attend to daily duties, and **J.W. Peace** and **May** and their little son **J.A. Peace** are gone to High Point to attend the Annual Methodist Conferance which is being held at the Wesley Memorial Church High Point. I am feeling quite lonely as I am in the home all alone, the young people of this family all being at work in High Point, the girls in the sewing room and the son in the upholstering establishment. oh that we may all endeavor to do those things that are well pleasing in the sight of God. while attending to worldly affairs is my prayer.

Thursday Oct the 24th 1929

A nice bright morning, but quite cool. I am still suffering from cold, but thankful that I can be up and pen a few lines, the rest of the family are well as usual I am glad to state. oh that we may all look to the Lord for help to live in that way and manner which is well pleasing in His sight." Lord I cry unto thee; make haste unto me; give ear unto my voice, when I cry unto thee. Let my prayer be set forth before thee as incense; and the lifting up of my hands as the evening sacrifice. Set a watch O Lord before my mouth; keep the door of my lips." Psalm 141-1-2-3. The words of this Psalm is the prayer of my heart for Jesus sake.

Friday Oct the 25th 1929

Clear and windy this morning, I am having to keep my bed to day. on account of deep cold I have couched so badly that I am weak. The rest well as usual. oh that I may keep close to the Master and trust Him fully for whatever is best for me, for I am in His hands blessed be His holy name saith my soul.

Saturday Oct the 26th 1929

Clear and quite cool to day. I am still feeling feeble and have to remain in bed. only got up long enough to scrible a line in my Diary. I had to have the Dr yesterday and am under the Influence of Medicine so do not feel like even writing a line but wish to keep it up as long as I am able to raise my hands to do so. "Bless the Lord oh my soul and all that is within me bless His holy name."

Sunday Oct the 27th 1929

Clear and cold to day. All well as usual exept myself. I have still had to keep my bed to day only sit a few minutes to rest from my bed and scrible a few lines to keep in rememberance of the date, and to give vent to my feelings by droping a line in thanksgiving and praise to my blessed Redeemer for His goodness and care over me, and all the rest of the family. oh Father in Heaven help me to do thy holy will in all things to Thy names honor and praise, I ask for Jesus sake amen.

Monday Oct the 28th 1929

Clear and cold to day. the health of the family about the same as for several days. I do not seem to improve much, but trust that my condition is improveing some, as my lungs do not seem to be quite so conjested as far several days past. But I am in the hands of the dear Lord to do as He sees best.

Tuesday Oct the 29th 1929

Somewhat rainey to day. I have not felt even as well to day, as I did yesterday, my right Lung seems more conjested to day. the rest of the family in usual health glad to note. I am endeavoring to be resigned entirely to my Masters will. Father help me to be faithful to serve thee in all the ways of thy requireings is my prayer for Jesus sake.

Wednesday Oct the 30th 1929

Cloudy to day, the family all able to be up except myself. I still do not have strenght to be up but a few minutes at a time, but glad of a few minutes rest from my bed, and still note the goodness and mercy of our blessed Saviour.

Thursday Oct the 31st 1929

Cloudy and raining some to day. I am still suffering with my cough, and am very much worn down, the rest as well as usual glad to note.

Friday November the 1st 1929

Cloudy and warmer to day I am still weak and suffering but have made out to sit up a little while at a time to day the rest of the family in usual health. As this date brings to mind the beginning of another month I am impressed with the flight of time. Father help me to be redy to spend eternity with Thee.

Saturday November the 2nd 1929

Clear bright morning. I am so I can sit up a little while at a time and enter a line in my Diary, but I have suffered so much and lost so much sleep for the past two weeks, that I am so weak and nervous that it is with dificulty that I can be up or write a line, but it is my nature to not give up as long as I have even strength enough to leave my bed a little while at a time. and I am praying for patience to endure whatever the dear Lord permits me to have to bear, for I want to bear all for His sake who suffered so much for me that I might have life eternal. oh help me to obey Thee. The family here as well as usual, glad to note.

Sunday Nov the 3rd 1929

Raining to day. I am still suffering with my cough and soreness. The rest of the family well as usual. Today is Preaching Sunday at

Mt Vernon, and as they have their same Preacher **Rev W.R. Kelly** back this year I should be glad to be able to go hear him, the young people are gone to Church, but my dear daughter staid with me. Praise the Lord.

Monday November the 4th 1929

A very cloudy day. I am still suffering from cold and pain and aches. The rest are well as usual. Cousin **Ocid Blair** came to see me this evening, which did me a lot of good as she had not been here in quite a while and I am always so glad to see her. she brought me a nice Jar of what she called Pear Honey which was of her own make and it is very fine indeed and I appreciate her thoughtful kindness so much.

Tuesday Nov the 5th 1929

Clear and cold to day. I keep just about the same still cough until it keeps me weak so that I dont gain any strength as I think I otherwise would if I could get rid of coughing so much. Cousin **Allen J. Blair** came to see me this afternoon I was so glad to see him. it does me so much good to see those who were my neighbors when I lived in my dear old home. Praise the Lord for His goodness and mercy to me and to mine. He does not fail to send kind friends to cheer me on my way. Blessed by his holy name now and forever saith my soul.

Wednesday Nov the 6th 1929

Clear and cold to day. I have still had to keep my bed with the exception of sitting up a little while for rest from the bed, but keep so weak that it is an effort to be up at all but hope I am improving some altho slow. The rest of the family all keep up glad to state and my dear daughter has been so kind to wait on me and do all she can for me, in my time of need. May the Lord bless her abundantly both spiritually and temporally according to her need and all those of her household is my prayer for Christ our Redeemer sake. Amen

Thursday Nov the 7th 1929

Clear and cold. I am still feeling quite feeble but so I can sit in a chair a little while, I am still suffering in the same way I have for the past two weeks and more, but trust that if it is the dear Lords will I may soon be better. The rest of the family are in usual health. Praise the Lord for His goodness to us all.

Friday Nov the 8th 1929

Cloudy to day. I am feeling very much the same as for several days past, my cough still troubles me, and keeps me weak the rest of the family in usual health. **Archie Spencer** came in to see me to day for a few minutes, I was glad to see him and hear from his family. Praise the Lord for His goodness to us all, his poor unworthy cretures, oh that we may all be more faithful to serve Him, is my prayer.

Saturday Nov the 9th 1929

Clear and some warmer to day. I am still feeling quite weak and nervous and my cough still holds on to me, but I had more rest in sleep last night than for many nights the past week, so I hope I may gain strength to be up before many more days, as I am so tired of the bed, having had to keep it nearly all the time for over two weeks, but I am just leaving myself in the hands of Him in whom we live and move and have our being to do with me as is His holy will for He knows what is best and I am in submission to His will. Blessed be his holy name now and forever. "Hear my prayer, O Lord and let me cry come unto thee, Hide not thy face from me in the day when I am in trouble; incline thine ear unto me; in the day when I call answer me speedily."

Sunday Nov the 10th 1929

Cloudy a good part of to day. I am still weak and have to keep my bed most of the time. The rest of the family well as usual. **J.W.** and **May** went to the Funeral this forenoon that of **Mrs June Royls** of Trinity, she was taken to Hope Well for burial. There was also another Funeral at Trinity to day, that of **Mrs Martha English** widow of **Sam English** she was laid in the Cemetary at Trinity, she was ninety one years of age. I had a pleasent visit this evening from cousin **Ed** and **Anna Blair.** Also from **Mrs Nora Ledwell** and daughters. **Mrs Ledwell** is the Teacher of what we call the Old folks Class in Sunday School at Mt Vernon. We were very glad to have them all visit us. Then later I had a very pleasent visit from **Kerney Peace** and **Mabel** and their children I was glad indeed to have them, for I get so lonely since being confined to the bed and to the room altogeather for now nearly three weeks, I am so glad of good company. Praise the Lord for His goodness in sending kind friends to comfort me. "I love the Lord because he hath heard my voice and my supplication Because he hath incline his ear unto me, therefore will I call upon him as long as I live."

Monday Nov the 11th 1929

Cloudy and damp to day. I am still feeling weak and nervous, but trust I am gaining some strength, the rest of the family in usual health. I was favored with the company of cousin **Anna Cranford** and her daughter **Estelle Carter** this afternoon I was glad indeed to see them, as it was the first time they had been to see me since I have been sick. And later this evening dear **Clara I. Cox** our Pastor at Springfield came in to see me. I was fairly rejoiced to see her, for I knew It was in answer to my poor simple prayer, for I had asked my heavenly Father to send her to me this very day if it was in accordance with His holy will, for I felt the need of encouragement which I knew I was sure to get from His faithful mesenger. Praise His holy name.

Tuesday Nov the 12th 1929

Rainey to day. I am still in feeble health but feel a little stronger to day. and hope I shall continue to gain strength so that I wont have to keep to my bed as much as I do now. The rest of the family in usual health glad to note. Praise the Lord.

Until We Sleep Our Last Sleep

Wednesday Nov the 13th 1929

Cloudy most of the day. I had some rest in sleep the past night, so can sit up a while this morning to rest from my bed. The rest of the family all well as usual. We learn that the little boy of **James White** that got run over by a Car, is dead and buried. There seems to be but a step between us and death. oh that we may all be prepared for the change for a better land. Blessed be the name of the Lord for his goodness and mercy to us all his dependent cretures.

Thursday Nov the 14th 1929

Cloudy to day. I am feeling some stronger to day, as I was favored to get more sleep last night than for several nights, but I still keep too weak to be up long at a time my cough is not so constant now but still strangles me by spells so that I am loose my breath. But I praise the Lord that it is as well with me as it is, for I have a dear daughter to care for me and provide for my bodily needs and I believe she prays for me, which I greatly appreciate, for I feel the need of prayer.

Friday Nov the 15th 1929

Cloudy this morning. I am thankful to have strength sufficient to sit up a while this morning and pen a line in recognition of my gracious Heavenly Fathers mercy to me and to mine. Blessed by His holy name.

Saturday Nov the 16th 1929

Cloudy and some cooler to day. I have had strength to sit up some more to day, than I have been able to do, hope I can soon be strong enough to be up the most if not all the time, for I am so tired of the bed. The rest well as usual I was favored this evening with the company of two of the **Blair Sisters Martha and Elva Blair.** they also brought with them **Miss Alice Baker** of Route 3 High Point. I was greatly pleased with their visit for I get very lonely sometimes. I was also so pleased to have Dear **Grandma Peace** with me part of the day.

I praise the Lord for his goodness in sending kind friends to see me and help to cheer me on my way. "God be merciful unto us, and bless us; and cause his face to shine upon us; That thy way may be know upon the earth, thy saving health among all nations." Psalm 67-1-2.

Sunday Nov the 17th 1929

Cloudy this morning I am still feeling feeble, but thankful that I can be up in a chair long enough to rest from the bed, the rest of the family in usual health. I am thankful to state, and the dear Lord has blessed me with a dear daughter to care for me, may she be wonderfully blessed for what she does for me, for I am not able to do for myself at this time.

Monday Nov the 18th 1929

Clear this morning after a heavy rain last night I am feeling some stronger this morning I am thankful to state, and the rest well as usual. Praise the Lord for His goodness and mercy to us all.

Tuesday Nov the 19th 1929

Clear and cooler, I am so I can sit up part of my time now for which I am thankful for I get so tired to have to keep my bed all the time, my cough is much better now but I keep weak and nervous. The rest here are in usual health. I feel that we all have much to be thankful for, that it is as well with us as it is. Praise the Lord.

Wednesday Nov the 20th 1929

Clear and cold this morning. I am feeling some stronger so I can be up more I am thankful to state, and that the rest of the family are in usual health. Praise the Lord for His care over us his unworthy dependent cretures.

Thursday Nov the 21st 1929

Clear and still colder to day the air feels very much like it was going to snow, I am thankful for a better nights rest than I have had for some time, and for strength to sit up more to day, do hope I shall soon be able to dress and stay out of bed during the day but want to be patient and thankful that I can now be up part of the time to rest from the bed. the rest of the family in usual health I am glad to state. Praise the Lord. My daughterinlaw who is now **Mrs Emma Conrad** having married the second time and who is now a widow again, she and my grandaughter **Corene Blair Tomlinson** came to see me last evening. I was more than glad to see them, as it had been some time since they had visited us but hearing I was sick they came at once which I greatly appreciate.

Friday Nov the 22nd 1929

Cloudy and cold this morning looks like we might have snow. I am thankful to be so I can sit up some longer now than I have since I have been sick, but still can not hold out a half a day at a time. The rest of the family all well as usual. Praise the Lord for His goodness.

Saturday Nov the 23rd 1929

Cold and plenty of sleet to day. I am very much the same as for several days past. I can sit up some and thought I was gaining strength, but I was seised with a terable pain in my right side last evening which has caused great suffering, and causes me to be weak to day, as I only got half a nights sleep, and my side still aches and is sore. The rest of the family well as usual I am glad to note. Praise the Lord for His tender care over us.

Sunday Nov the 24th 1929

Still cloudy and plenty of sleet on the trees. I had some more sleep last night so feel some stronger, but not so I can stay up long enough to dress. I have not had a dress on now in four weeks, and I am tired of bed.

November 1929

Monday Nov the 25th 1929

Still cloudy and cold. I had some more sleep the past night than usual so am able to sit up some this morning the rest as well as usual and are very busy preparing for Hog killing tomorrow. The young people are gone to Town to their work in the sewing room etc. Praise the Lord for His protecting care over all.

Tuesday Nov the 26th 1929

Cloudy yet this morning, I am feeling quite weak and nervous as I did not get any sleep at all the past night, but am trying to sit up some to day, the rest of the family all in usual health I am glad to note. Praise God from whom all blessings flow.

Wednesday Nov the 27th 1929

Clear and some colder to day. I feel so thankful for having had a good nights rest in sleep I think I had a longer nap than in any night for a month past for in this time I scarcely ever slept half of a night. I am feeling some stronger and hope I can sit up more to day. The rest of the well and busy at work. "Teach me O Lord the way of thy statues; and I shall keep it unto the end. Give me understanding, and I shall keep thy law; yea I shall observe it with my whole heart."

Thursday Nov the 28th 1929

Clear and cold, for Thanksgiving Every day should be Thanksgiving day but as this day is Nationally set apart for special Thanksgiving should be observed with true thankful hearts by all the nation, for our many blessings as a nation and as a people. I am thankful to day that I can sit up enough to note down a few lines in recognition of the many mercies of our kind and loving heavenly Father for he does not forget his dependent ones for unworthy as I feel myself to be, I have been so kindly remembered by dear friends. To day The Christian Endeavor Society of Springfield Church kindly sent out two of their number a sweet young woman a **Miss Davis** One of the Teachers in the **Allen Jay** School, and a fine young man by the name of **Hendrix**, with a lovely Basket of fruit etc to me for Thanksgiving and the young Lady sang a beautiful song for which I enjoyed very much, I think the Title of the song was The Beautiful Garden of Prayer I had not heard it before and she sang it so sweet it was inspireing indeed. and I praise the Lord for sending those dear young people to cheer me on my way.

Friday Nov the 29th 1929

Cloudy and looks as tho it was going to snow. I am feeling some stronger and have put a dress on for the first time in five weeks but will not be strong enough to stay up more than half the day the rest well as usual. **Lena White** spent the night with us and is still with us to day. I am thankful that I can say in truth that "I love the Lord because he hath heard my voice and my supplication. Because he hath inclined his ear unto me, therefore will I call upon him as long as I live."

Saturday Nov the 30th 1929

Clear and very severe cold, I am thankful to be able to sit up some more to day than I had been strong enough to do, but this cold weather makes me nervous and I have not yet been able to hold up all day, the rest all well. I am still striveing to do the will of the Master and will say with the Psalmist. "Thou shalt guide me with thy counsel and afterword receive me to glory, Whom have I in heaven but thee? and there is none upon earth that I desire beside thee, my flesh and my heart faileth, but God is the strength of my heart and my portion for ever."

Sunday Dec the 1st 1929

Clear and severe cold I am just about as I have been for the past week able to be up part of the time but am not at all strong but thankful that it is as well with me as it is and that the family here are all in good health. The begining of another month which will end the year of nineteen twenty nine brings to mind the flight of time for it hardly seems possible that another year has flown, but I have passed my four score and four and I know there will not be many more years at most allotted to me, so I am anxious to improve the moments as they pass in a way that will be well pleasing in the sight of Him in whom we live and move and have our being. Him being my helper I hope to glorify him on earth that I may glorify him in heaven. Praise His name.

Monday Dec the 2nd 1929

Very rainey and some sleet to day. The health of all here just about the same as for several days past. Praise the Lord.

Tuesday Dec the 3rd 1929

Clear and very cold. I am sure I never experienced colder weather for the beginning of winter. I am so thankful that I can now be up enough to sit by the fire instead of having to lie in bed all the times as I have for most part during the past month, the family here are all in good health I am thankful to note. My heart is lifted up in praise to the Great Giver of all our blessings for his goodness and mercy to us.

Wednesday Dec the 4th 1929

Clear and still severe cold. We of this household are now able to be up the most of the time I am thankful to state. altho I for one still have to lie down part of the time as I have not yet gained my strength, but truly thankful that it is as well with me as it is. Praise the Lord.

Thursday Dec the 5th 1929

Clear and the cold continues, This weather is the hardest on me of any I ever experiences in my life for I am so little able to bear it if I was stronger I could brave over it so much better but I am thankful that with all my suffering that I have food and shelter and a dear daughter to care for me. Praise the Lord for His tender care.

Friday Dec the 6th 1929

Clear but not quite so severe cold we are all able to arise from our beds this morning for which I feel thankful for altho I am not yet strong, I am so glad to be up I praise the Lord for His goodness to us each day. I am so thankful to now be so I can get out of my room I went to the kitchen yesterday for the first time in six weeks. And went to the kitchen again to day in the warmest part of the day, it is a treat to get out of my room that much. and I hope I shall be able to go to the dineing room each day now for I am so glad when I can wait on myself and not be a burden to another. Praise the Lord.

Saturday Dec the 7th 1929

Clear and cold but not so cold as for the past week. I am so thankful to now be so I can be up instead of being confined to the bed this cold weather, the family all in usual health. I am striveing to be in entire subjection to the will of the Lord who sees us at all times and knows all things. "O Lord thou hast searched me, and known me. Thou knowest my downsitting and mine uprising, thou understandest my thoughts afar off. How precious also are thy thoughts unto unto me, O God; how great is the sum of them."

Sunday December the 8th 1929

Cloudy this morning, I am thankful to be up and write a line in recognition of our heavenly Fathers care over us all, unworthy as we are of his watchful care over us. The family here are in good health, and **J.W. Peace** and **May** his wife are going to High Point to Preaching this forenoon to hear one of **Mays** former Pastors while she lived in Charlotte **Rev – Aycock.** she likes to hear him so well. I miss not getting to Preaching and Sunday School as that is something I always enjoy, but am trying to be like Paul when he said, "I have learned in whatsoever situation I am placed in therewith to be content."

December 1929

Monday Dec the 9th 1929

Clear and cold to day. I am truly grateful to my heavenly Father that I have strength sufficient to arise from my bed, and use my pen to note the gratitude I feel for my many blessings for altho I am not confined to the bed to bed waited on. for I do not want to be a burden to others. "Behold how good and how pleasant it is for brethren to dwell together in unity." Lord help us to do this is my prayer.

Tuesday Dec the 10th 1929

Clear but not quite so cold to day. I am thankful to have strength to be up to day. the rest of the family in usual health and busy Praise the Lord for His goodness and mercy to us all.

Wednesday Dec the 11th 1929

Clear and temperature about the same as yesterday I am thankful to be so I can be up and wait on myself for the most part, the rest are all well. **Ollie Bowman** and little **jr** are with us to day also **Lena White** and her little **Billy Ray,** we are always glad to have them visit us. May we all give thanks to the Giver of all our blessings for His tender care over us His unworthy cretures.

Thursday Dec the 12th 1929

Cloudy and damp this morning. I am not yet feeling strong but thankful to be able to be up and go to the dineing room for my meals now instead of having them carried to my room, the rest of the family in usual health, we have dear **Grandma Peace** with us to day. As it is **J.A. Peace's** sixth birthday. and as I am staying with them now, he has both of his Grandmas with him to day.

Friday Dec the 13th 1929

Still cloudy and very damp to day All able to be up and go about daily avocations which is much indeed to be thankful for.

Until We Sleep Our Last Sleep

Saturday Dec the 14th 1929

A nice clear morning. All much the same as for several days past. Praise the Lord for His goodness and mercy to us dependent ones.

Sunday Dec the 15th 1929

A pleasent Sabbath morning and all sufficiently able to arise from our beds, but I am not yet strong enough to attend Sunday School which I regret very much for I like to attend faithfully.

Monday Dec the 16th 1929

Cloudy to day. The health of the family here much the same as for the past week. We were favored yesterday afternoon with some of my relatives from Thomasville, my daughterinlaw **Emma Cloafelter Blair Conrad** as she married the second time to **Luther Conrad** and is now a widow again, my two granddaughters and their husbands also came. They are **Charance Tomlinson** and wife **Corene Blair Tomlinson** and **Hobert Lee Fouts** and wife **Sadie Blair Fouts.** I was more than glad to have them visit us. And later we also had **Ollie Peace Bowman** and her husband and little **jr** and **Grady Peace** and wife **Clara** and little **Joseph,** and **June Peace** and wife **Bessie,** and daughter **Dara Peace.** and young people had some other company. So the evening was spent very pleasently by all. The family here all except myself had attended S. School and Preaching and so had our company, before coming here so I trust the day was spent profitably as well as pleasently by all concerned. and as I have not been able to get out for a few months I thought it very kind of them to thus try too cheer me up and I feel that I can not praise the dear Lord enough that He puts it in the hearts and minds of kind friends to visit me in my lonelyness and debilitated state. and my grandchildren brought me a generous share of nice fruit Apples, Oranges, Bananas etc which I appreciate so much for fruit is medicine for me as well as a luxury. Praise the Lord saith my soul.

Tuesday Dec the 17th 1929

Real cloudy and damp this morning which causes more aches and pains to my aged limbs, but thankful to be so I can get out of bed and wait on myself, for my daughter is not at all well to day and she is my entire dependence when I cant wait on myself. the rest of the family well as usual.

Wednesday Dec the 18th 1929

Raining this morning. All able to be out of our beds for which I feel very grateful to our merciful heavenly Father for He watches over and takes care of us night and day.

Thursday Dec the 19th 1929

Still some cloudy and much cooler. All able to go about daily avocations, altho I am still feeling feeble, I am thankful to be so I can wait on myself. I am glad to state, and praise the good Lord for this.

Friday Dec the 20th 1929

Clear and very cold this morning. All up and busy but shivering with the cold as the sudden changes make it go harder with us.

Saturday Dec the 21st 1929

Clear still very cold. All able to arise from our beds and attend to the necessary affairs of the day for which she should be very thankful.

Sunday Dec the 22nd 1929

Snowing this morning for the first of the season worth mention. We are all able to be out of bed and look out at the beautiful snow as it falls to the earth Making a blanket on the fallens leaves. And it calls to mind that lovely Hymn "Wash me and I shall be whiter than snow." oh that we may all be washed in the blood and made whiter than snow.

Until We Sleep Our Last Sleep

Monday Dec the 23rd 1929

The ground is covered with snow and we had quite a sleet last night. I am thankful that we are all able to be up this cold weather, and have fuel to keep us warm. Praise God from whom all blessings flow.

Tuesday Dec the 24th 1929

Still quite cold and the snow stays on the ground. We are all able to up and enjoy the Christmas greetings by the many Cards and gifts as they have been coming in for a few days past and are anticipating more on the marrow. Praise the Lord for His goodness to us.

Wednesday Dec the 25th 1929

The ground still covered with snow and ice, which seems to stay with us longer than we have seen for several winters. But all this family have been able to be out of bed and enjoy the day We all had an invitation to help eat a Turkey dinner to day at the home of **Fred Peace** at Archdale and also at the home of **Grady Peace** who lives next door to his brother **Fred,** and as the young people here had other arrangements, they did not go, **but Jerome** and **May** and little **J.A. Peace** and myself went and had a nice time **J.W.** and **J.A.** helped eat Turkey and other good thing with **Grady** and **Clara** while **May** and myself helped eat Turkey and other good things too tedious to mention with **Fred** and **Jenett. Mr Wm Fry** also accompanied us and dined at **Freds** and enjoyed it. It was the first time I had been in their homes, and it was also the first time I had rode out since being sick and it looked rather risky this kind of weather but am trusting in the mercy of our Father in heaven who takes care of us all times, that it will not make me worse again. and we have been favored this evening with the company in this home of **Gideon** and **Ollie Bowman** and **little jr** also **Edd** and **Lena White** and their children and this morning **Rev Reuben Payne** Pastor at Archdale Friends Church called to see me and presented me with a nice Box of fruit etc from

December 1929

Friends at Archdale and Springfield which I appreciate more than words can tell.

Thursday Dec the 26th 1929

Cold this morning and the snow and ice on the ground still stays with us, we of this home are all up and busy and are enjoying our Christmas presents and Cards of greeting. Up to this time I have received two dozen lovely Cards of greeting for Christmas and the New Year. I am so grateful for so many kind friends. Praise God from whom all blessing flow.

Friday Dec the 27th 1929

Clear and cold. All able to be up and attending to things necessary to be done for the comfort of our perishable bodies. oh that we may be more concerned to make ready for time when we shall be called to give account of the deeds done in the body, that we may have a good account to give, for we want to live thruout eternity with our blessed Lord who was sent into the world to redeem us from our sins oh that we may not disobey Him by doing things that are against his holy will, for we have so much to thank him for, as we have food and rainment and are comfortaby housed and every thing realy needful. and so many kind friends I rec nine more lovely Cards of greeting yesterday and one letter more.

Saturday Dec the 28th 1929

Rainey this morning, which is making the snow melt, so we have plenty of mud, but I am glad to see the snow getting away for when the sun shines the mud will soon dry up. I am thankful that we of this household are all able to be up and enjoy the Hollidays **Lena White** and children spend last night with us, and are still with us today. I have now received ten more lovely Cards of greeting it does my heart good to be so kindly remembered by kindred and friends, several from distant States.

Sunday Dec the 29th 1929

Clear and colder this morning. All able to be up I am thankful to state, and most of the family will attend Sunday School. but I am not sufficiently able to attend as it is very windy and disagreable.

Monday Dec the 30th 1929

Clear and still colder to day than yesterday but not so windy, we are all able to be up and go about daily avocations, the girls went to their sewing room this morning in High Point after having a weak of leisure and pleasure at home **Clemons** also went to his work in Town so this leaves **J.W. Peace** and **May** and little **J.A.** and myself in the home to do what we can.

Tuesday Dec 31st 1929

Clear and cold. All able to be up and busy I am thankful to state and as this is the last day of the year 1929 it brings many reflections to my mind both of pleasure and of sadness. for it has been a pleasure to meet with loved ones, and on reflecting how it brings sadness to our hearts, but I trust that we may all take fresh courage and try to live in that way and maner that will assure us of a home when done with this earth where all sorrow and suffering is forever done away.

1930

Wednesday January the 1st 1930

Clear and cold this morning All able to arise from our beds this beautiful morning for the begining of the New Year. I am thankful to state and hope we shall all begin anew to do better in the future than we have done in the past looking to our merciful heavenly Father for strength and ability to serve Him in the way of his requireings. and bless his name for the gift of his dear Son whom He sent into world to redeem us all from sin.

Thursday January the 2nd 1930

Clear and cool this morning All able to be up and go about daily avocations, I am thankful to state.

Friday Jan the 3rd 1930

Cloudy and warmer this morning the weather is so changeable that it causes people to take cold and feel badly, but I am thankful that we of this household are now all able to be out of bed and do what is most necessary to be done. The young people are at work in Town and their cousin **Ruth Spencer** came home with them last night and some other youngsters called in and they had some Music and quite a lively time until bed time, **Mr** and **Mrs Bowman** and little **jr** also came and staid awhile so all togeather the time was spent very pleasently.

Saturday Jan the 4th 1930

Clear and much colder this morning. All well as usual except myself. I had a very hard attack with my heart trouble, such a shortness of breath that for about one hour I felt that I could not live and but for the prompt attention of my dear **May** who I called to give me a dose of Amonia I dont have any thought I would be writing this. Blessed be the name of Lord who daily watches over and mine saith my soul.

Sunday Jan the 5th 1930

Clear and cold this morning. I am still feeling feeble from the effects of my heart attace yesterday morning, but thankful to be so I can be up, and I had hoped to be able to go with the rest of this family to Church to day as it is the first Sabbath in the new year and I have not been able to attend Church for the past two months, but I find my strength is not sufficient to go with them to day so will try to be content with my lot, for I know that we can worship God in our own homes and hearts, or wherever our lot may be cast if we are faithful to obey the teaching of our blessed Lord and Master. Father help me to do this. for the sake of Thy dear Son who died to save us.

Monday Jan the 6th 1930

Cold and somewhat cloudy this morning All are able to arise from our beds, but I do not get to feeling strong since having such a hard attack of heart trouble but thankful to be able to wait on myself. We were favored last evening with the company of **Cousin Edward** and **Anna Blair,** also **Mary Davis** and **daughter Lara** and **Miss Brown** one other Teachers at Trinity, and others.

Tuesday Jan the 7th 1930

Cloudy and warmer this morning. All as well as usual except myself. I am not at all well but still keep so I can be out of bed and wait on myself. for which I am very thankful. Praise the Lord.

Wednesday Jan the 8th 1930

A clear nice morning. All able to be up and busy. I am still troubled with shortness of breath but keep so I can be up and wait on myself and do some things to help my daughter in the work for which I very thankful for I do not want to become a burden to any one. I am leaning on the strong arm of Him in whom we have our being for strength sufficient for each day to do what is required of me to do for of myself I can do nothing. "Bless the Lord O my soul; and all that is within me, bless his holy name."

Thursday Jan the 9th 1930

Clear and some colder this morning. All well as usual except myself, as I have had another attack of the trouble about my heart and have such difficulty of breathing makes me feel very badly indeed. but I am trusting in my blessed Saviour to do with me as He see and knows best, for I am in His hands.

Friday Jan the 10th 1930

A nice morning. The family in usual health. I am still suffering with shortness of breath which is very trying, but am trying to bear it with patience for I know I am dependent upon the Great Giver of life for every breath I draw. and altho I suffer greatly especially at times, I remember what agony our blessed Lord suffered on the Cross for us poor unworthy cretures, yesterday my daughter went to a general missionary meeting at Greensboro, and altho she left a woman with me to care for me in her absence, yet it was not like having my own daughter with me, for let others be ever so kind which the woman indeed was kind and helpful to me, yet we do not expect others to understand as our own children do, and we know that our merciful heavenly Father knows what is best for us better than we can know for ourselves. therefor we should be in entire subjection to His will.

Saturday Jan the 11th 1930

Cloudy this morning and much cooler. All able to be up. but I am still feeling feeble from the effects of the trouble about my heart which makes me weak and nervous. the rest in usual health.

Sunday Jan the 12th 1930

Cloudy and cool this morning. All able to arise from bed and prepare for Sunday Scool, except myself I do not feel strong enough yet to go to School and Church but thankful to be so I can be up and read my Bible. "O Lord thou hast searched me, and known me. Thou knowest my downsitting and mine uprising thou understandest my thoughts a far off." Psalm 139

Monday Jan the 13th 1930

Cloudy this morning. I had more rest in sleep last night than for some time for which I am very thankful for I am not so nervous when I get a good nights rest. The family all in general health.

Tuesday Jan the 14th 1930

A real cloudy dark morning, we had heavey rain during the night. I am suffering again to day with the weakness about my heart and shortness of breath, which is very trying for it causes me to be so weak and nervous the rest of the family here are well as usual.

Wednesday Jan the 15th 1930

Raining the morning. and the dampness makes my breathing more difficult, but thankful to be so I can still wait on myself for I do not want to be a burden to others. The family here are all well as usual. I am thankful to state.

Thursday Jan the 16th 1930

Clear and cooler this morning. I am suffering again with trouble about my heart and shortness of breath is very trying indeed, for the pain in my side added to my other suffering makes it still harder to endure, but I am very thankful that I could arise from my bed at all to day, altho it was twelve oclock before I got able to do this, and then it was quite an effort to do this. but I am always thankful when I can be able to get up and write a line in acknowledgement of the goodness and mercy of our blessed Lord. who has our lives in His hand and can clip the britle thread of life at any moment of time.

Friday Jan the 17th 1930

Cloudy and cold to day. I have been suffering with a very severe attack of Asthma to day, had to have the Dr Called this moring before I could get any relief, such shortness of breath that it seems like every breath would be the last. **Grandma Peace** came and spent the day in the room with me for company. I was so glad to have her with me for she is such a dear friend and knows how to sympathise with me in my suffering.

January 1930

Saturday Jan the 18th 1930

Cloudy this morning and still quite cool. I am still suffering with shortness of breath, but am better today than yesterday, but it is still very trying to bear. The rest of the family are well as usual and **J.W. Peace** has gone to Asheboro to pay our Taxes, and his wife **May** is busy with household affairs the daughters gone to their work in a sewing room in High Point. May the dear Lord help us all to do His holy will while on earth that we may merit a home in Heaven. for here we have no continuing City.

Sunday Jan the 19th 1930

Cloudy and quite cold to day, I have been confined to my bed to day, suffering so much with Asthma and pain about my heart. **May** my dear daughter has staid from Church to care for me, may the dear Lord bless her abundantly for her kindess is my prayer for her and all her loved ones the family here, are in good health I am glad to state.

Monday Jane the 20th 1930

Still cloudy and cool, I am still suffering with Asthma my daughter staid with me all night slept with me which was such a comfort as I lay awake so much nights I did not get to sleep last night until after twelve oclock but am so thankful for that much rest in sleep for I have spend many whole nights without one moment of sleep. so glad the family here are in good at this time. I was favored yesterday afternoon with the company of many kind friends which helps to cheer me up. **Rettie Blair English** from Archdale for one she has kindly visited me before this since I have been sick I appreciate it very much, and also the company of **Fred Peace** and his wife **Jenett,** and **Grady Peace** and wife **Clara** and little son **Joseph.** also **Mrs Earl Peace "Aunt Nannie"** we call her, and **Mrs Everett Peace Jewel,** I think a great deal of all those and am so glad of their kind visits, May the Lord bless them all.

Tuesday Jan the 21st 1930

Cloudy to day, I am still suffering with Asthma have such shortness of breath that it seems like every breath would be the last if I don't get relief. I am favored with kind friends to come to see me **Mrs Isom** came and staid with me several hours, and this evening **Cousin Anna Cranford** and her daughter **Estell Carter** and husband came. I appreciate their thoughtful kindness in comeing to see me, for I get very lonely at times. The family here are in usual health I am glad to none, for it is one of our greatest blessings.

Wednesday Jan the 22nd 1930

Cloudy again to day. I am still suffering with my dificulty of breathing, but had a little rest in sleep this a.m. which a rarity for me in the day time and often not much at night, I did not get any sleep last night until about one oclock, I am feeling quite feeble. The rest of the family are well.

Thursday Jan the 23rd 1930

It snowed enough for us this morning to make the ground white for a while but was soon gone. It is a very damp disagreeable day, and I am still suffering with Asthma which causes such trouble to get my breath that it is very trying indeed but I am trying to bear it with all the patience possible, remembering what my blessed Saviour suffered me when He died up the Cross for the sins of the whole world therefore for my sins, and I praise His holy name that He rose again for our justification and redemption. Yesterday **Rev- Kelly** the Pastor at Mt Vernon came to see me which I appreciated very much he read a portion of the 14th ch of St John and offered a most excellent prayer. The family here are well as usual thankful to state.

Friday Jan the 24th 1930

Cloudy to day. I am suffering greatly to day and suffered all night last night with shortness of breath and trouble about my heart. **Dr**

January 1930

Bulla came to see me to day and found my heart was not beating regular. left medicine for my heart and other troubles. **Nannie Lee Spencer** came to see me this evening. so did **Nannie Peace,** and **Mrs Stephens** and some others. **Nericus Millikan** for one came. I laid awake all last night which was very trying for I was so lonely in my suffering condition. The family here are well as usual.

Saturday Jan the 25th 1930

Cloudy part of the today. I am still suffering with Asthma and trouble about my heart. **Grandma Peace** came and staid with me this forenoon. I am always so glad of her company and **Jewel Peace** came to see me this evening I am always glad to have her come any time. The family here are all up and busy as usual.

Sunday Jan the 26th 1930

Cloudy and cool. I am still suffering with Asthma and trouble about my heart. I have been blessed with company to day, Cousin **Rob** and **Ocid Blair,** and **Mr** and **Mrs Tom Steed** and **Aunt Sue Steed, Mr** and **Mrs Lee White, Mr** and **Mrs Gideon Bowman** and others, oh how I thank the good Lord for puting it into the hearts of the peopl to come to see me in my loneliness and suffering The family here are in usual health I am glad to note.

Monday Jan the 27th 1930

A rainey day. I am still suffering with asthma and my heart trouble, **Dr Bulla** came to see me to day said I must be quiet and not try to talk as it makes me weaker. I know this is true but it is hard to keep from talking some when our friends come to see us, **Charles** and **Daisy Redding** came to day, so did **June** and **Bessie Peace,** and **Mona Davis,** I sure do appreciate their kind thoughtfulness in thus remembering me while confined to my bed and suffering as I surely have during this confinement. May the dear Lord bless them for their kindness to a poor unworthy creture as I feel myself to be. The family here are in usual health thankful to state.

Tuesday Jan the 28th 1930

Cloudy to day. I am still confined to the bed with Asthma and the trouble about my heart, but got more rest in sleep last night than for several nights, but am suffering again this morning with the same hard strougle for breath it is the most trying thing I ever experienced in all my afflictions, but am trying to bear with patience whatever the dear Lord sees fit to send upon me for I know He will not send more than He will enable us to bear. Blessed by His holy name. The family here are in usual good health. I am glad to note for health is one of our greatest blessings.

Wednesday Jan the 29th 1930

Cloudy to day. I had a very restless night last night, did not get any sleep until after four oclock this morning. The Dr came this morning but gave me very little relief or encouragement about being better soon, but I will live in hope. that I will be better when the right time comes. The family here are in usual good health.

Thursday Jan the 30th 1930

Snowing to day the most that it has snowed this winter. I am still suffering with trouble about my heart and shortness of breath, the rest here well as usual. I am still confined to my bed only just while I have my bed made or rest a little while in the chair. **Mrs Bowman, Gideons Mother** came to see yesterday. **Gideon** and his brother **Jonnie Gray Bowman** came with her. Praise the Lord for His goodness to us all. He blesses me with many kind friends.

Friday Jan the 31st 1930

The ground covered with snow. I am still feeling badly with the trouble about my heart. I can not describe what I suffer from this trouble it is beyond discription. I was favored to day with a sweet letter from **Clara I. Cox** our Pastor at dear old Springfield, she is so nice to me I love her dearly. The family here are all up I am thankful to note. Father in Heaven help us all to live close to thee, and do thy holy will in all things, is my prayer for Jesus sake.

Saturday February the 1st 1930

The ground still covered with snow. I am suffering with the trouble about my heart and shortness of breath. **Rev Reuben Payne** Pastor of Friends Church at Archdale came to see me last evening, he read Scripture and prayer for me which I appreciated very much. The family here are in usual good health glad to note. Bless the Lord oh my soul, and all that is within me bless His holy name.

Sunday Feb the 2nd 1930

Still snow on the ground, I am still suffering with shortness of breath. Today my dear son and wife **Esther** and **Fred jr** came to see me from Charlotte and are going to spend the night with us we are so glad to have them with us. The family here well as usual. Praise the Lord.

Monday Feb the 3rd 1930

There is still snow on the ground, but it is melting away some to day. I am quite feeble to day. my son **Fred C. Blair** and **wife Esther** and **Fred jr** went back home to Charlotte this morning. I miss them so much, but glad to get to see them a little while. Praise the Lord for His goodness.

Tuesday Feb the 4th 1930

Raining this morning. I am suffering more with shortness of breath on account of the dampness. **Kerney Peace** and **wife Mabel** came to see me this morning, I always enjoy their company. The family here are all in usual good health, thankful to state.

Wednesday Feb the 5th 1930

Clear this morning but clouding up during the day. I had a pleasant surprise to day, by my nephew **Lester Davis** from Jamestown comeing to see me I had not seen him in quite awhile. **Rev J.R. Kelly** the Pastor of Mt Vernon Methodist Church also called to see me this afternoon, and offered a nice prayer for me which I appreciated very much for I love the company of Gods mesengers. The family here are in usual health. My dear daughter **May** is my Nurse, May the Lord bless her abundantly for her care of her afflicted widowed Mother who feels lonely and dependent.

Thursday Feb the 6th 1930

Clear to day, but I am still suffering with the shortness of breath and trouble about my heart. I have been favored to day with the company of kind friends. This morning **Earl Peace** came to see me. and this afternoon cousin **Anna Blair** came, and **Ollie Bowman** and her Motherinlaw **Mrs Bowman** and **Bettie Marsh** and **Alice Hill.** and **Lena Davis,** also **Nannie Lee Spencer.** The neighbors from all around have been so nice to come to see me since I have been sick I appreciate it so much. The family here are in usual health glad to note. May we all be in entire subjection to the Masters will in all things is my prayer for Christ the Redeemers sake. who died that we might live.

Friday Feb the 7th 1930

Cloudy and cooler this morning. I am still suffering with shortness of breath, and have indigestion. The Dr came to see me this morning and says there is some improvement about my heart, but I still suffer so much. I do not get but very little rest day or night. The rest of the family in usual health. **Mrs Bulla** came with the **Dr** today. I am always glad to have her come, she is so sweet to me. **Miss Clara I. Cox** Pastor of Friends Church at Springfield came to see me to day also.

February 1930

Saturday Feb the 8th 1930

Clear and cooler. I am still suffering with such shortness of breath that it is so very uncomfortable. Today is the Funeral of **Florence Merideth** held at Fairview and the burial will be at Hopewell. **Mary Lee Stilwell** is takeing care of me, while her Mother attends the Funeral.

Sunday Feb the 9th 1930

Clear and colder to day. I am suffering severely to day from shortness of breath and acheing all over. the rest well as usual. **Cornelia Davis,** and her son **Stanley** and his wife **Esther** came to see me to day, so did **Lee White** and wife **Stella** and also **Gideon Bowman** and wife **Ollie Peace Bowman** I appreciate their kindness in coming to see me.

Monday Feb the 10th 1930

Clear this morning. I am feeling very feeble to day, the rest are well as usual. I feel like praiseing the good Lord that I have my dear daughter with me to care for me, for it is so much better than having a stranger to wait on me, as I suffer so much I want her near me as much as possible. Praise the Lord for His goodness.

Tuesday Feb the 11th 1930

Clear and cold to day, I have to sit up in bed so much to get breath, that I try sitting in the Chair once or twice a day for a change as I can rest better for a little while in a chair. **Lena White** is with us to day, the family here are well as usual. I am glad to note. This is my fourth week in bed, and I am weak and nervous. If it is the dear Lords will, I hope to soon be so I can be up and about the house even if I do not get strong. **Samaria Elder** and **Alice Hill** came to see me this evening which I appreciated very much. Bless the Lord oh my soul and all this is within me bless His holy name.

Wednesday Feb the 12th 1930

Clear and cool to day. I am still in the bed and suffering with shortness of breath and pain in my left side. To day Aunt **Margaret Hoover** and another colored woman came to see me both white and colored people have been so kind to come to see me since I have been sick. May the dear Lord bless them for their thoughtfulness of me, and may I praise His holy name daily, for I am trusting Him to take me home to glory where I can praise His for ever. and for ever.

Thursday Feb the 13th 1930

Clear and warm this morning. I am feeling quite feeble to day, so much so that it is with dificulty that I can hold up my hands to dictate a few words. The rest of the family well as usual.

Friday Feb the 14th 1930

Clear and cold. I have suffered the worst to day with my heart troubl that I have for several days. **Dr Bulla** came to see me to day, he says "he can patch me up a while longer" I am willing to die any time if it is the Lords will to take me for I want to be free from this awful suffering, but want to be willing to wait the dear Lords time and suffer for His sake who suffered so much for me. The family here are well as usual I am thankful to state. I love the Lord because he hath heard my voice and my supplication Psalm 116-1.

Saturday Feb the 15th 1930

Cloudy this morning. I had more rest in sleep the past night, but it was from the effects of the medicine. I am feeling very weak and feeble but not suffering so much pain all the time I am thankful to state. The rest of the family well as usual.

Sunday Feb the 16th 1930

Clear and cold to day. I am still suffering from shortness of breath. The family here are well as usual. **Mrs Ledwell** came to see me today which I appreciated so much. so did **Lee White and Stella,** and **Ollie and Gideon Bowman** also **Fred** and **Janette Peace.** I am always glad to see any and all of them and think it is so nice and kind of them to think of "Grandmother."

February 1930

Monday Feb the 17th 1930

Clear and cold to day. I am feeling a little stronger to day, The rest well as usual except **Minnie** who has a sore foot, but it is not serious I am glad to note. Father in Heaven help us all to do Thy will this day and every day is my prayer. for Jesus sake who suffered upon the Cross to redeem from everlasting punishment. Bless the Lord oh my soul and all that is within me bless His holy name.

Tuesday Feb the 18th 1930

Clear and cold again to day. I am feeling more feeble to day and suffering from shortness of breath. The rest of the family well as usual glad to note. I am praying that if it is the dear Lords will, that He will soon heal me of this trouble, that I may not suffer so much, and that I may get so I can wait on myself and not be a burden to others.

Wednesday Feb the 19th 1930

A lovely clear day, but I am sorry to note that I have suffered more to day than at any time for more than a week with the terable shortness of breath and trouble about my heart. oh if I could only be relieved of this trouble I think I would soon be out of bed again. The rest are well as usual. **Ollie Bowman** is spending to day with us, always glad to have her come.

Thursday Feb the 20th 1930

A nice clear day. I am still suffering with shortness of breath. **Dr Bulla,** brought **Dr G.S. Groome** of High Point to see me to day and he gave me a thorough examination and said for me to do just what **Dr Bulla** said for me to do and he thought I soon would be better. The rest all well **Miss Mona Davis** came to see to day. glad of her company.

Friday Feb the 21st 1930

A clear bright day. The family all well except myself. I do not want to murmer at my lot, but I am suffering so much with that horrible feeling caused by shortness of breath which the hardest thing to bear that I have ever had in all my afflicted days. oh that I might get some relief from this awful trouble, Dear Lord help me to be patient to bear whatever comes to my lot.

Saturday Feb the 22nd 1930

A nice clear day. I am still suffering but trying to bear it with all the patience possible. The family here are all well as usual, the Parents are gone to High Point on buisness this morning and left me in the care of the girls, **Mary Lee** is ministering to my needs while her Mother is away. I appreciate every little act of kindness so much, for I am so weak and so little able to wait on myself. May the dear Lord bless and reward all who are good and kind to me, with temporal needs, and a home in that new bright world when done with the things of earth is my prayer for Jesus sake and for the sake of their never dying souls.

Sunday Feb the 23rd 1930

Cloudy this morning, and I am feeling the effects of the dampness, the rest are well as usual. oh that the good Lord would see fit to relieve me of this suffering, I should be so thankful.

Monday Feb the 24th 1930

A clear morning. I am feeling a little stronger to day. **J.W.** and **May** are gone to High Point on buisness to day. and I am left in the care of the girls for the time. I am thankful to be so I can now sit in Chair for little while at a time as it rests me from the bed, altho I have to sit in a reclineing posture nearly all the time in the bed as I can't get my breath lying down flat.

Wednesday Feb the 26th 1930

Clear and warm this morning. I had more rest in sleep last night than I usually do, so feel a little stronger to day, the rest are all well and the girls and their Mother are busy at the Wash Tub, and the men folks busy doing farm work. Praise the Lord for His blessings.

Thursday Feb the 27th 1930

A nice clear morning. I am feeling some stronger so can sit in the Chair some to day. I had a letter from my daughterinlaw **Esther Blair** to day, they are aiming to come to take me home with them next Sunday, but as I have not been out of my room in six weeks it looks like it would not do for me to undertake the trip of one hundred miles. but I am leaving it in the hands of the good Lord and if it is His will that I should go He can give me strenth for the trip Blessed be His holy name.

Friday Feb the 28th 1930

Cloudy and much cooler this morning. I am feeling some stronger to day, but that is only to say that I do not feel quite so feeble, the rest of the family in usual health. **Lena White** and her baby are with us to day. Bless the Lord oh my soul and all this is within me bless His holy name.

Saturday March the 1st 1930

Cloudy and misting rain. I am gaining a little more strength each day, but it seems slow but perhaps I am too anxious to get stronger, as I am expecting my son from Charlotte to come for me to take me home with them to spend some time, still I am not anxious to go, for it seems like leaveing home to leave here, since I have been in my daughters care ever since I have been sick. The family here are in usual good health I am glad to note, for health is such a great blessing and all our blessings come from our merciful Heavenly Father.

Sunday March the 2nd 1930

Cold and windy to day. I am feeling some stronger to day, but not able to stay up quite a half day at one time. I have not yet been able to be up long enough to have a dress on in a month, and it begins to seem like a long time that I have had to keep my bed, with the exception of sitting in the chair a little while to rest from the bed, The rest are well.

Monday March the 3rd 1930

Clear cold and windy. I am so I can be up more now, and hope I shall soon be able to sit up all day, the rest of the family are well.

Tuesday March the 4th 1930

Still cold and windy. I am feeling some stronger so I put my dress on this morning for the first time in over a month and hope I shall be able to be up the most of the day the rest of the family in usual health glad to note.

Wednesday March the 5th 1930

Clear and cold this morning. I am thankful to be so I can get out of bed this morning and put a dress on. I hope I shall be able to be up the most of this day, the rest of the family are all able to be up and busy with daily duties.

Thursday March the 6th 1930

Clear and cold again this morning. I am thankful to be so I can get out of bed and dress myself this morning. As I have been confined to the bed nearly all the time for a month. The rest of the family are in usual good health I am thankful to state. Praise the Lord for His mercy.

Friday March the 7th 1930

Raining this morning. I am thankful to have sufficient strength to dress and make my bed but it takes all the strength I can bring into service to do this, as I gain strength so slowly but it is a relief to be so I can get out of bed and wait on myself better that I have been able to do in more than a month. The rest of the family well and busy at work. We have so much to be thankful for, as we have food and clotheing and shelter and many other blessings that many others do not have.

Saturday March the 8th 1930

Cloudy and cool this morning. I do not feel strong but thankful to be so I can arise from my bed, the rest well as usual The Parents are gone to High Point shopping. oh that we all may be careful to obey the commandments that we may have the assurance of a home where all toil and trouble are done away when done with the things of this world.

Sunday March the 9th 1930

Clear and cool this morning. I am so thankful to be able to be up, but really do not feel like I had strength for the trip to Charlotte to day. if some of my sons family come for me as they are expecting to do, but I am leaveing myself in the hands of "Him in whom I live and move and have my being." if it is right for me to go I will be given strength for the trip.

Monday March the 10th 1930

A beautiful sunshiney morning. Well sure enough according to their arrangement my daughterinlaw **Esther Blair** and my grandaughter and name sake **Emily Blair** and young man **Mr Porter Williams** came for me yesterday. and the day was so fine and we had an easy going closed care so I stood the trip much better than I had thought it possible, so we arrived at my son **Fred C. Blair** about seven oclock found **Fred** and his little daughter **May** eagerly looking for us, and had nice bountiful supper ready for us when we got there, **Fred jr** was also on hand to welcome us.

Tuesday March the 11th 1930

Cloudy and misting rain this morning. I am so thankful to be able to be up and enjoy the company of friends that I had met when in Charlotte before. and I am getting some soreness in my limbs worn off, for altho I stood the trip of the one hundred miles much better than I expected yet after sitting somewhat cramped in one position for so long my limbs were sore and stiff, but are feeling much more pliable than they were yesterday.

Wednesday March the 12th 1930

A lovely morning. and I am just back from a nice ride with my Grandaughter and name sake **Emily Blair** I enjoyed it fine as I am trying gain my strength after being quite sick for more than a month. **Emily** is having two weeks vacation from her work in the Western Union so I am having the pleasure of her company more than I would otherwise have the chance to do I am expecting to spend some time with them here if I keep able to keep up and wait on myself but should I get sick I shall perhaps return to Randolph for I do not want to be any burden to my sons family.

Thursday March the 13th 1930

A nice bright day. This is my eighty fifth Birthday. my daughterinlaw made a real nice dinner for me which I appreciated very much, but an occasion like this brings the loss of my dear companion so fresh to my mind that it almost overcomes me, but I try to be as cheerful as possible for the sake of those who are so kind as to do me many favors May the Lord bless and recompense them is my prayer.

Friday March the 14th 1930

Cloudy and damp this morning. Altho I was favored to get about half a nights sleep which is more than I often get, yet I feel feeble this morning and so nervous I can't hardly write, but am truly grateful that I can be out of my bed and so I can wait on myself for the most part. and trust He in whom I live and move and have my being, will give me strength for each day, and I pray that the dear Lord will help me to obey His holy will. in all things to His honor and praise.

Saturday March the 15th 1930

The sun in coming out after being hazy this morning and now bids fair to be a fine day. I am feeling rather feeble but am going to put forth every effort to keep up and do whatever I find to do that is in my power to do, the Lord being my helper "For in thee O Lord do I put my trust; let me never be put to confusion. Deliver me in thy righteousness and cause me to escape: incline thine ear unto me, and save me. For thou art my hope O Lord God thou art my trust from my youth." Psalm 71 -1-2-5

Sunday March the 16th 1930

A lovely Sabbath morning and altho I feel quite feeble, I am so thankful that I am so I can arise from my bed and wait on myself for I do so much crave to not become a burden to my children or any one. The dear Lord has spared me for a purpose and I desire to fulfil that purpose to His honor and glory. for having been a helpless Invalid for so many years that it looked like an impossibility for me to do anything toward building up the Kingdom in any material way. but it is my greatest desire to be instrumental in the Lords hands of helping others to prepare for an entrance into that bright world that God has prepared for those who serve Him on earth.

Monday March the 17th 1930

Some cloudy this morning. I am feeling quite feeble this morning, but thankful to be able to be up and take down a note of thanksgiving to our blessed Lord and Saviour who gave His precious life upon the Cross that we poor unworthy cretures might have life eternal in that beautiful home above which our dear Heavenly Father has prepared for all who love and serve Him here on this earth.

Tuesday March the 18th 1930

Cloudy and damp this morning. I am suffering from shortness of breath which is very trying but I am so thankful that I can be out of bed and wait on myself, for I do not want to be a burden to any one. My sons family are in usual health. My son **Fred C. Blair** is daily working in the Shop of J.W. Wearn and Company, his wife **Esther** busy with home duties, my grandson **Fred jr** is working in The Western Union, his sister **Emily H. Blair** is working in the same Company and has been for more than three years, she is taking a two weeks vacation at this time so we have the pleasure of her company in the home more than we had when she was home only at night for she is such a sweet girl we all love her so much, her only sister **May** who is eleven years old is in school and doing fine. We are a happy family enjoying the company of each other. May the Lord help us to live in His fear and do His holy will in all things. "Behold how good and how pleasent it is for brethren to dwell togeather in unity."

Wednesday March the 19th 1930

Cloudy again this morning. I still feel feeble and nervous but am so thankful to be able to be out of bed and wait on myself the family here are all in usual health at this time I am glad to state. I have been listening to the Programs that come to us over the Radio some of which are very interesting and instructive.

Thursday March the 20th 1930

A very nice morning. I am very grateful to my Heavenly Father that I am so I can be out of bed this morning and wait on myself, but I am feeling quite feeble at my best, and some of the family here are bent on taking me to see a Dr to day to try to asertain what is the cause of my keeping so weak and having such shortness of breath. so I have given up to make this trial in the hope of being benefited.

Friday March the 21st 1930

Another bright morning and some cooler. We did not get to go to see the Dr yesterday as was planed on account of some Car trouble, and as I am still suffering we think of making the trip up Town this morning to see if I can get some relief. The rest of the family here are well.

Saturday March the 22ⁿᵈ 1930

Cloudy and misting rain this morning. I am feeling quite feeble this morning so the Dr has been called to come to see me some time to day to see if he can asertain why I suffer so much we abandoned going to Town yesterday to see the Dr as I was not really able and desided it would be better to have him come out to the home.

Sunday March the 23ʳᵈ 1930

A beautiful sunshiney morning but much colder I am thankful to be so I can be out of bed. but still feel quite feeble and nervous. The most of the family are gone to Church this morning **Dr Mathews** came out to see me yesterday and prescribed quite a portion of Medicine for me he pronounced my trouble at present to be mainly Accute Gastretis I hope I shall soon get relief from this trouble for it is the most trying that I have had to bear with in years. The family here are in usual health I am glad to note. "Unto thee O God do we give thanks, unto thee do we give thanks: for that thy name is near thy wonderous works declare." Praise the Lord.

Monday March the 24ᵗʰ 1930

Cloudy this morning and very damp and cool. I am very thankful to be able to be up to day but I am far from feeling strong. but I trust that when my Medicine has time to take effect I shall feel better. The family here are in usual health. "I love the Lord because he hath heard my voice and my supplication. Because he hath inclined his ear unto me therefore will I call upon him as long as I live." Psalm 116-1-2

Tuesday March the 25ᵗʰ 1930

A very dark foggy morning. I had a quiet nights rest in sleep, and am very thankful to be so I can arise from my bed, but am still suffering from shortness of breath. I stop just here to listen to a beautiful prayer coming over the Radio, the morning service is very interesting, and as I do not get out to Church it comes in so nice to get to hear these services over the Radio each morning I love to listen not only to the beautiful prayers etc but also to the lovely Hymns. "Sing aloud unto God our strength: make a joyful noise unto the God of Jacob." Praise the God from whom all blessings flow.

Wednesday March the 26th 1930

A pretty morning, quite a contrast to yesterday which was cloudy and damp. I am suffering quite a great deal to day with my difficulty breathing, but so glad that can arise from my bed to day altho it be at a late hour. For I have been confined to the bed so much in years past that it seems such a blessing to be so I can arise and wait on myself. The family here are in usual health I am glad to note.

Thursday March the 27th 1930

Another nice morning. I am so I can be out of bed but am in a very suffering condition and my Medicine does not seem to do for me what I hoped it would, but perhaps has not had all the time necessary to bring about a change. The family are in usual health and busy.

Friday March the 28th 1930

Cloudy and damp this morning. I had a very restless night, but am thankful to so I can be up and wait on myself The family here are all in usual health. "O Lord my God in thee do I put my trust save me from all them that persecute me, and deliver me."

Saturday March the 29th 1930

A bright morning. I had more rest in sleep the past night than usual, so feel some stronger to day. but still have shortness of breath the family here are all able to be up and busy. "Not unto us, O Lord not unto us, but unto thy name give glory, for thy mercy and for they truths sake."

Sunday March 30th 1930

A lovely morning. I am in very suffering condition, and **Dr. Mathews** is having me taken to the Mercy Hospital for treatment. **Fred** and **Esther** and **Fred jr** and little **May** all came with me.

Monday March 31st 1930

Another pretty day. **Esther and Fred** came to see me this morning. and brought me some lovely flowers which I appreciate so much, I spent a very suffering night my stomach and mouth being in such a bad condition. **Dr Mathews** called to see me this morning.

Tuesday April the 1st 1930

A very pretty day. My daughter **Mrs Peace** came from home to see me and spent the afternoon and until bed time then went back to her bro **Fred** and spent the night, she left all well at her home in Randolph and will spend a few days here in Charlotte with me while I am in the Hospital.

Wednesday April the 2nd 1930

A pretty morning but cloudy and has rained some to day my dear **May** came back out here again to do and is spending to day with me. I am so glad to have her with me. I hope she can stay several days. **Dr Mathews** came to see me to day.

Thursday April the 3rd 1930

Cloudy and raining some. This is **Fred Sr** 49th Birthday he came to see me at the Mercy Hospital. His wife, son and daughter **May** came with him. His sister **May Peace** came with him.

Friday April the 4th 1930

This is a lovely day. **May** and **Esther** is with me to day, I have been taking a good rest in sleep this afternoon. **Dr Mathews** came to see me to day.

Saturday April the 5th 1930

Cloudy part of the day. **May** came to see me to day. **Hoyle and Mamie Stilwell** came to see me to day, also **Ada Bradley,** and **Mrs Bickell** and she brought me the lovely White Easter Lillys and **Mrs Ed Smith** also came in the afternoon to see me. **Esther** and **Fred jr** and **little May** and this evening **Emily** came to see me.

Sunday April the 6th 1930

This is a rainy day and I do not feel so well. **Jim Stilwell, R.O. Bradley** and wife, **Ada Swarigen** and **Luceal** and a **Miss Ball** came to see me also **Fred** and **Esther, May** and **little May** and **Emily** and **Porter** brought me some carnations.

Monday Apr 7th 1930

This is a beautiful morning and I had a good night last night and **May** came up real early and I am resting fine she said she must go to H.P. this p.m.

This is Tuesday morning April the 8th

May went back to High Point last evening as she had planed to do. I had I had a good nights rest the past night and am able to sit in Chair to eat dinner to day. My daughter (inlaw) **Mrs Fred** came to see me to day and my grandson **Fred jr.** I am glad to have them. **Dr Mathews** came in to see me to day said I was doing fine I hope I shall be able to go back to Freds next Saturday.

Wednesday April the 9th 1930

A nice clear day. **Esther** came to see me to day and staid the forenoon then back to her home. The Nurse that is waiting on me to day is **Hannah Hammond.** I love her very much she is so nice to me and seem to have so much sympathy for me and takes care of my flowers that other friends have brought me.

April 1930

Thursday April the 10th

A beautiful day the sun is shineing nice and warm. I am able to sit up a little while at a time, **Mrs Oren Bradley** came to see me to day always glad to see her. My daughterinlaw **Esther Blair** came to see me to day her family are all well. **Esther** brought me apples and Oranges. **Mrs Bradley** brought me a box of chocklate candy for which I am very thankful.

Friday April the 11th 1930

A beautiful day, I am feeling weak and nervous to day I have such shortness of breath it causes such very uncomfortable feelings and my appetite is very poor. I am anxious to go to my Sons tomorrow if they are willing for me to leave the Hospital, for altho there can not a nicer place be found than here, yet there is no place like Home.

One of the Nurses a **Miss Hammond** waits on me mostly she is a girl that is mature in her ways and seems to have so much sympathy for you in all things which pertain to your comfort in this life and in the world to come. she took me out in the Hall and roald me in a Wheel Chair this p.m. which did me so much good. Then I took a good little nap of sleep and later partook of a nice nourishing supper, but it did not take much to do me as my appetite is still very poor.

Saturday April the 12th 1930

A beautiful day. I have been suffering ever since I awoke this morning with the same shortness of breath that I have mentioned all along that I have suffered with so much. I do not seem to get rid of it and if I do not it will seem that all my deep expense has been in vain. Well just at this time my daughterinlaw **Esther Blair** and her little daughter **May** and her Son **Fred jr** came to see me. I was so glad to have them spend a little while with me, and shall expect them to come to stay a little while with me tonight for I get so lonely in the room alone as I am anxious to go home.

Well they came back and staid a while with me. which was a comfort to me in my loneliness. Then soon after they left my daughterinlaw who is now **Mrs Conrad** as she has married again came to see me, and my two grandaughters **Sadie Blair Fouts** and her husband **Hobert Lee Fouts,** and her sister **Corene Blair Tomlinson** wife of **Clarence Tomlinson** came. **Clarence** could not leave the Store to come. they all came very unexpectedly which was a glad surprise. Then soon after they left my Son **Blair** and his daughter **Emily** who is my name sake, and her little eleven year old sister **May**, and her brother **Fred jr.** came to see me and staid until bed time which was enjoyed.

Sunday April the 13th 1930

Some cloudy this morning I am so I can sit in my chair to rest a while from the bed for which I am very thankful. The Nurse that is waiting on me at this time is from Bathune S.C. her name is **Hannah Hammond** she is a real sweet girl I love her very much she is kind to me. I feel to depend so much on her help and judgement, Just now my son and wife and their son and daughter came in to see me, it is so much company to have them come in to see me this morning while they can not stay long this evening, as my grandson wants some pastime with the young people.

Monday April the 14th 1930

A beautiful day but quite warm. My daughterinlaw **Esther Blair,** and my grandson **Fred jr** came again A little while this morning to see me always glad to see any of them. This afternoon **Miss Hannah Hammond** put me in the Wheel Chair and rolled me back and forth in the Hall. it is so nice to be able to be out of the bed part of the time and take some exercise on the Chair. I shall expect some of my people in again to night. as some of my people come in almost every night which helps to while away the time.

Tuesday April the 15th 1930

The weather is some more pleasent this morning. I passed a very restless night the passed night but am thankful to be so I can sit in my Chair and take a few notes while in the Chair ready to Transcribe in my Dairy if I ever feel able to do so I hope to be able to get back to my sons home when this week is out. as I will then have been in the Hospital here for the past three weeks.

Wednesday April the 16th 1930

A very nice day. I am still hoping to get able to go back to my sons next Sunday, altho I was very sick for awhile to day my daughterin-law came over to see me awhile this forenoon, and took me out in the Hall for a ride on the Wheel Chair. I then returned to my room, and my dinner was brought in. A lovely Tray of nice things to eat, and just as I drew my Chair up to the Table to eat my dinner, I turned very sick, all at once and set in to vomiting and unloaded my stomach of more than it looked like I had eaten for several days. and did not care to take on any more ha ha, oh I was sure enough sick, so could not eat any of dinner for that time, but put it off until the next day ha ha. If I keep this up **Dr Mathews** will not let me go home next Sunday. Help me dear Lord to get able to go to my sons next Sunday.

Thursday April the 17th 1930

Some cloudy to day. I am feeling the effects of the dampness. and am still suffering which shortness of breath, but so thankful that I can be up enough to take down notes for my Diary for I am getting forgetful, and I wish to remember something that transpired each day while here and to day a young lady brought me a nice Box of flowers that came through the mail from High Point, which turned out to be from my own daughter and family who live in the Country about seven miles east of High Point, whose proper Address at this time is Trinity N.C. They were from **Mrs May Peace** and family.

Friday April the 18th 1930

Cloudy this morning. I am not feeling at all well to day. I still have such shortness of breath, but am thankful to be so I can be up and take down a few notes for my Diary. My friend **Oren Bradley** called in to see me to day he has a wife and three nice little children, he is the Son of **Preacher Bradley** that had a Pastorate at Bell Mont Church for four years but is now stationed at Greensboro as he is called here, came to see me a few minutes. He is the head one of the Catholic Church here. he seems to be very Fatherly to all with whom he meets. soon after the dear old Father left the hospital. **Mrs Hoyle Stilwell** and her daughter **Eloise** who is just recently married to a **Mr Rogers** came in to see me. I was so glad to see them, her Father **Hoyle W. Stilwell**, is brother to my soninlaw **Arthur Lee Stilwell** who is not living, and my daughter is now married again and is now **Mrs J.W. Peace.** they have one little son his name is **Jerome Addison Peace.** I am expecting to go to my Sons home next Sunday if I get able to leave the Hospital as I will then have been in here three weeks and if I am not better by then I think I shall not stay longer.

Saturday April the 19th 1930

Cloudy this morning and I am feeling quite feeble and blind to day and I still think I shall be taken to my sons Sunday if able and the weather will do for me to leave the Hospital everything is so very nice and comfortable here, but there is no place like home.

Sunday April the 20th 1930

A very nice warm day. **Mrs Holingsworth** that I think so much of came to see me to day. her little Son sent me a nice little handkerchief she was one of my Teachers when I carried on the Bible class five years ago, when I staid at my sons home which is now called Glenwood Drive which is in a new part of Charlotte.

Monday April the 21st 1930

Nice weather and I have been so rejoyced over getting to see **Mrs Holingsworth** who was one of my Bible Class Teachers here five years ago nothing would satisfy my pupils but that this class should be called the Emily A. Blair Bible Class consequently it was caried on in that name for two years until I went back to Randolph Co to my sons, and **Mrs Holingsworth** moved to another part of Charlotte.

Tuesday April the 22nd 1930

Butiful day, my son and his wife came to see me again to night his wife came and spent the day then went back home and came back and spent the evening with me.

Wednesday April the 23rd 1930

A lovely day **Freds** family came to see me to day some of them come every day.

Thursday April the 24th 1930

Esther spent this forenoon with me then went back to see after things at home like she did yesterday. then aims to come back again tonight and stay until bedtime tonight.

April 24th, 1930 was her last entry.

Until We Sleep Our Last Sleep

Emily Ann Millikan Blair passed on May 5, 1930.

Family Records

Benjamin Millikan Family Records
Transcribed by Emily A Blair 3rd mo 12th 1903

The family record of my grandfather and grandmother Millikan [whose maiden name was Bales] copied especially for the benefit of my own children and grandchildren and for all others who may be interested as well.

Benjamin Millikan was born the 21st day of 2nd month 1783
Margaret [Bales] Millikan his wife was born the 25th of 5th mo 1783

Their children are as follows

John Millikan was born 28th day of 1st mo 1807
Hannah Millikan was born the 26th of the 2nd mo 1808
Elizabeth Millikan was born the 15th of 2nd mo 1809
Sarah Millikan was born the 26th of 5th mo 1810
Susanna Millikan was born the 27th of 8th mo 1811
Ann Millikan was born the 10th of the 4th mo 1813
Samuel Millikan was born the 25th of 8th mo 1815
(Emily Millikan Blair's father)

Jesse Millikan was born 1st of 6th mo 1817
Margaret Millikan was born the 7th of 5th mo 1818 **twins**
Benjamin Millikan was born the 7th of 5th mo 1818 **twins**
Jane Millikan was born the 29th of 8th mo 1820
William Millikan was born the 25th of 3rd mo 1823
Eleazar B. Millikan was born the 14th of 10th mo 1824
Mary Millikan was born the 24th of 11th mo 1827

Until We Sleep Our Last Sleep

Samuel Millikan Family Records

Transcribed by their daughter Emily A Blair 4th mo 20th 1914
The family record of my father and mother Samuel C. Millikan and Mary [Carter] Millikan copied from the old family Bible which was a gift to my Mother from her father Samuel Carter in the 8th of 12th month 1836. Believing this will be appreciated by my own children, grandchildren, greatgrandchildren, and other kindred and friends I have done this for their sake.

Samuel C. Millikan was born the 25th of 8th mo 1815
Deceased the 18th of 1st mo 1864

Mary (Carter) Millikan his wife was born the 25th of 8th mo 1813
Deceased the 6th of the 4th mo 1902

Their children are as follows
Alpheus Lundy Millikan was born the 27th of 8th mo 1834
Deceased the 16th of 9th mo 1859

John Millikan was born the 12th of 4th month 1836
Deceased the 20th of 9th mo 1859

Emma Jane Millikan was born the 18th of 2nd mo 1838
Deceased the 31st of 5th mo 1839

Ruth Millikan was born the 19th of the 4th mo 1840

Nicholas Carter Millikan was born the 12th of 11th mo 1842
Deceased the 10th of 8th mo 1851

Emily Ann Millikan was born the 13th of 3rd mo 1845

Family Records

Margaret Ellen Millikan was born the 3rd of the 10th mo 1847 Deceased the 29th of the 6th mo 1851

Eleazer Bales Millikan was born the 15th of 11th mo 1848 (added later) Deceased the 28th of 12th mo 1927

Mary Elizabeth Millikan was born the 9th of the 4th mo 1851 Deceased the 14th of 3rd mo 1854

Martha (Mattie) Cordelia Millikan was born the 14th of 3rd mo 1854

Rachel Almina Millikan was born the 22nd of 9th mo 1856 Wife of Jesse Davis Deceased the 7th of 4th mo 1902

Thomas Coriolanus Millikan was born the 16th of 10th mo 1859 Deceased the 23rd of the 12th mo 1895

Until We Sleep Our Last Sleep

John Smith Blair Family Records

Transcribed by daughterinlaw Emily A Blair on 4th mo 21st 1914

The family record of John Smith and Eliza Blair as written in their family Bible.

John S Blair and Eliza Johnson were married the 14th of August 1839

John S. Blair was born the 26th of July 1816
Deceased the 15th of 3rd mo 1864
47 years 7 mo and 19 days

Eliza (Johnson) Blair his wife was born the 8th of April 1817
Deceased the 18th of 3rd mo 1875
57 years 11 mo 21 days

Their children ages

Jesse Clinton Blair was born the 18th of July 1840
Deceased the 17th of 1st mo 1866
25 years 5 mo 29 days

John Addison Blair was born the 14th of August mo 1843
(added later) Deceased 21st of 3rd month 1920

Family Records

John Addison Blair Family Records

John Addison Blair was born the 14th of 8th mo 1843
Emily Ann Millikan born the 13th of 3rd mo 1845
Buried at Springfield Friends Cemetary, High Point, NC

Married the 14th day of 12th mo 1864

These were the waiters (at their wedding)
<u>First</u>, Allen J. Tomlinson and Rachel E Anderson.
<u>Second</u> Joseph S. Worth and Flora M. Carter.
<u>Third</u> Franklin S. Blair and Margaret D. Hill.

A.U. Tomlinson. Chas H. Mendenhall. Thomas English. Joseph Hoggatt. M.M. Johnson. Cynthia Mendenhall. Emily A Hiatt, Rebecca Mendenhall. Bridget B. Anderson. Eliza Blair. Mary Millikan. E.P. Hoggatt. G. Frazier. Mary E. Blair. Ruth Johnson. J.A. Johnson. Wm Hill. Eli Haworth. Harrison Frazier. Joel G. Anderson. Joash Reynolds.

Until We Sleep Our Last Sleep

John Addison and Emily Millikan Blair's children

Margaret (Maggie) Ellen Blair was born the 26th of 11th mo 1865
Married Dougan Clark Moffitt the 10th of 4th mo 1890

Jesse Carter Blair was born the 18th of 9th mo 1868
Married Emma D Clodfelter the 8th of 1st mo 1896
Jesse deceased the 22nd of 9th mo 1901

Freddie Clinton Blair was born the 3rd of 4th mo 1881
Married Esther J Hayden the 11th of 5th mo 1909

Mary (May) Eliza Blair was born 3rd of 5th mo 1885
Married Arthur Lee Stilwell the 3rd of 5th mo 1905
(Later Married Jerome W. Peace)

Martha Ethel Blair was born 1st of 9th mo 1890
Deceased the 26th of 10th month 1890

Family Records

The family record of my father and mother Samuel C. and Mary Millikan copied from the old family Bible which was a gift to my mother from her father Samuel Carter in the 8th mo 12th 1834. Believing this will be appreciated by my own children, grandchildren, greatgrandchildren, and other kindred and friends I have done this for their sake.

Transcribed by their daughter Emily A. wife of John Addison Blair. 4th mo 20th 1914.

Samuel C. Millikan was born the 25th of the 8th mo 1815.

Mary Millikan his wife was born the 25th of the 8th mo 1813.

Their children are as follows.

Alpheus Lundy Millikan was born the 27th of the 9th mo 1834.

John Millikan was born the 12th of the 4th mo 1836.

Emma Jane Millikan was born the 18th of the 2nd mo 1838.

Ruth Millikan was born the 19th of the 4th mo 1840.

Nicholas Carter Millikan was born the 12th of the 11th mo 1842.

Emily Ann Millikan was born the 13th of 3rd mo 1845.

Margaret Ellen Millikan was born the 3rd of the 10th mo 1847.

Eleazer Bales Millikan was born the 15th of the 11th mo 1848.

Mary Elizabeth Millikan was born the 9th of the 4th mo 1851.

Martha Cordelia Millikan was born the 14th of the 3rd mo 1854.

Rachel Almina Millikan was born the 22nd of 9th mo 1856.

Thomas Coriolanus Millikan was born the 16th of 10th mo 1859.

Sample of the handwritten diary.

Mattie C. Millikan

Ruth Millikan Johnson

J. Alvin Johnson

Alta (left) and Erma Johnson
daughters of Alvin and Ruth Johnson

May Blair Stilwell & first husband Arthur Lee Stilwell, & Daughter Mary Lee Stilwell

John Addison Blair & Emily Millikan Blair
At their 50th Golden Wedding Anniversary

Eleazer Bales Millikan

John Addison Blair

Emily Ann Millikan Blair

Family Records

Rachel Blair Anderson   B. Franklin Blair   Frank S. Blair, a cousin of Addison Blair

Standing L to R: Ocia Redding Blair, John J. Blair, Ed & Annie Blair, Martha & Ada Blair, Walter Blair
Seated: Robert L.M. Blair, Elva Blair, Rachel A. Blair, Emma Blair
Rachel & B. F. Blair's home on Flint Hill Rd.

Cleanliness, Purity and Richness
Buy Your Milk and Cream
...of...
→Blair Dairy←
Special attention given to care of milk for babies and invalids.
H. S. Charter, Manager.

Blair Dairy Images
Courtesy High Point Historical Society, High Point, NC.

Allen Unthank Tomlinson

Rachel English Tomlinson

Faculty Guilford College 1889
L to R Top: Prof. J. Franklin Davis, Mary H. Petty, Edwood C Perisho, Julia S. White.
L to R Bottom: Mary E. Mendenhall Davis, Gertrude Mendenhall, Dr. LD Hobbs, Priscilla B. Hackney, John W. Woody

Family Records

Clara Ione Cox (1879-1940) was for many years pastor of Archdale and Springfield Quaker Meetings and a prominent community activist in High Point, NC. She was very active in a number organizations of the 1920s, 30s, and 40s which attempted to combat racism, including the Committee on Inter-racial Cooperation and the Association of Southern Women for the Prevention of Lynching (ASWPL).

The daughter of Jonathan Elwood Cox (1856-1932) and Bertha Snow Cox (1859- ?), Ms. Cox was born in Guilford College, NC, and raised in High Point. In 1902, she graduated from Guilford College; she later attended White Bible Institute and Columbia University.

Ms. Cox's interests also included the development of public welfare agencies in High Point and she helped establish that town's first public library.

Her papers are part of the Friends Historical Collection. For more information, contact archives@guilford.edu or 316-2264.

Fannie Johnson

Arrilla Johnson

Until We Sleep Our Last Sleep

L to R: Jerome, May Peace, Esther & Fred C. Blair

Mary Ann Blair

Mary Blair Stilwell Peace

Jerome A. Peace & Louise Millikan

Family Records

Esther Hayden Blair

Fred C. Blair

Esther Blair & daughter Emily
Hayden Blair

Fred C. Blair, Jr.

Emily Hayden Blair
(middle swimsuit)

Porter Williams and Emily H. Blair
Williams

Glenwood Drive Home
in Charlotte, N.C.

Amedia Louis Scarnechia and
Mary Ann Blair Scarnechia

Mary Ann Blair
and Ruble

Left: Gwendolyn Gosney Erickson Quaker Librarian & College Archivist at Guilford College

Left: Brenda Haworth, Historian of Springfield Memorial Association in Springfield Museum. My cousin on the Millikan side.

Bottom: Grainy photocopy I found at Guilford College.
Top: The original I found at Springfield Museum.

Until We Sleep Our Last Sleep

Peace Testimony
of the Society of Friends

WE UTTERLY DENY all outward wars and strife, and fightings with outward weapons, for any end, or under any pretence whatever; this is our testimony to the whole world. The Spirit of Christ by which we are guided is not changeable, so as once to command us from a thing as evil, and again to move unto it; and we certainly know, and testify to the world, that the Spirit of Christ, which leads us into all truth, will never move us to fight and war against any man with outward weapons, neither for the kingdom of Christ, nor for the kingdoms of this world.

From *A Declaration from the Harmless and Innocent People of God, called Quakers*, presented to Charles II. 1660

Emily W. Skinner

Emily Williams Skinner lives in Tampa Bay, Florida with her husband, Tom. In addition to writing, she also enjoys selling advertising, and working with their daughters, Marquel Skinner and Blair Skinner, on their film and acting projects.

Emily W Skinner sitting with her Great, Great Grandparents

Books by Emily W. Skinner

Novels by Emily W. Skinner
Marquel
Marquel's Dilemma
Marquel's Redemption

Booktrailer:
Marquel book trailer on YouTube—
featuring actor Eric Roberts & Marquel Skinner
www.youtube.com/watch?v=6e6O7iYqeVQ

Young Adult Novels by E.W. Skinner
St. Blair: Children of the Night
St. Blair: Sybille's Reign
St Blair: The Diary of St. Blair

Memoir:
Master of the Roman Noir

Sign up for email updates at:
www.emilyskinnerbooks.com

Follow Emily on:
www.facebook.com/emilyskinnerbooks
www.twitter.com/emilyauthor
www.instagram.com/emilyauthor
www.thefilmmom.blogspot.com/
www.goodreads.com/author/show/6982753.Emily_W_Skinner
Emily W. Skinner
PO Box 8590
Seminole, FL 33775-8590

Index of Names

First	Middle	Maiden	Last Name (or Last Name by First Marriage)	Relationship	Diary Entry
A - Maiden or Last Name					
Anna		Ader		Daughter of Rev Ader & Ruth Blair Ader.	2/27/1928
Rev. Olin	P		Ader	Son-in-law of Rachel Blair	6/6/1926
Ruth		Blair	Ader	Wife of Rev Ader.	2/27/1928
Ruth Jr.		Ader		Daughter of Rev Ader & Ruth Blair Ader	2/27/1928
Mrs. Josephine			Albertson		2/8/1929
Miss		Aldred		Zebidee Crokers Granddaughter	10/26/1925
Dr Francis			Anachum	Friend	8/10/1929
Allen	J.		Anderson		Also See Family Records.
Bridget	B.		Anderson		Also See Family Records.
Joel	G.		Anderson		Also See Family Records.
Joshua			Anderson	Cousin of EMB	6/5/1926
Lydia	C		Anderson		9/9/1923

Until We Sleep Our Last Sleep

First	Middle	Maiden	Last Name (or Last Name by First Marriage)	Relationship	Diary Entry
Nancy aka Nannie	Almina	Hill	Anderson / Andersen	1st Cousin of Emily Millikan Blair	9/9/1923; 7/25/1926; 7/27/1926; 7/29/1926
Rachel			Anderson	Aunt To EMB	A Reminiscence; Also See Family Records.
Thomas	E		Anderson	Husband of Nancy Anderson & he is also 1st Cousin of EMB	10/13/1889; 7/25/1926; 7/28/1926; 8/11/1927
Will / Wm			Anderson	His mother is Nannie Anderson. Nannie is a First Cousin of EMB.	9/9/1923; 8/9/1926; 8/10/1926
Thomas			Andrews	Father of Pearl Andrews Millikan	8/10/1928
Anna		Ragan	Armfiield	Daughter of Amos Ragan	8/16/1928
Rev			Aycock	Pastor in Charlotte	12/8/1929
B - Maiden or Last Name					
Mr			Bacon		9/8/1929
Rachel			Baily		9/2/1889
Miss Alice		Baker			11/16/1929
Jewel (Miss)		Baker			7/5/1926
Mrs			Balance		8/20/1929
Miss		Ball			4/6/1930
Cyrus			Balenger		8/8/1926
Dora		Balenger			8/8/1926
Julia		Balenger			8/8/1926
Arilla			Balinger		9/9/1923
Arta / Artie		Anderson	Barker	Wife of June Barker. Daughter of Tommie and Nannie Anderson.	9/9/1923; 8/11/1927; 8/12/1927;

Index of Names

First	Middle	Maiden	Last Name (or Last Name by First Marriage)	Relationship	Diary Entry
Emma		Moffitt	Barker		9/9/1923; 8/12/1927
Eliza			Barker		9/9/1923;
Fridella / Fridela			Barker	Cousin of EMB. Husband of Mattie Barker.	9/9/1923; 8/9/1926; 8/10/1926
Jerome	A.		Barker		8/12/1927; 2/14/1928
June / Junius			Barker	Husband is Arta Barker	9/9/1923; 8/11/1927; 8/12/1927
Mrs Martine		Rice	Barker	Daughter of Mrs. Lee Rice	9/23/1926
Mrs. Mary			Barker	Widow of Nericus Barker	9/9/1923; 10/26/1925; 8/12/1927 8/13/1927
Mattie		Millikan	Barker	Wife of Fridella Barker	9/9/1923; 8/10/1926
Nericus/ Nerius/ Nerias			Barker	Minister in Friends Church	9/9/1923; 10/26/1925; 8/12/1927
Tuelma		Barker		See Tuelma Barker More	8/10/1926
Mrs. (Clara)		Blair	Barnes	Granddaughter of Sidney and Della Blair; Daughter of Roland Blair	6/28/1927; 11/4/1928; 11/5/1928
Mr.			Bayles		7/2/1928
Mrs.			Bayles		7/2/1928
B.	Willis		Beede		8/10/1928
Sarah (Miss)		Benbow			9/9/1923;
Dr			Berisho		8/6/1926
Mr			Bickett/ Bickell	Neighbor in Charlotte	3/9/1929; 3/10/1929; 3/14/1929; 4/5/1930

681

Until We Sleep Our Last Sleep

First	Middle	Maiden	Last Name (or Last Name by First Marriage)	Relationship	Diary Entry
Crystal		Bird		Speaker at Guilford College	8/8/1928
Ada		Blair		Sister of Emma Blair	9/9/1923; 10/26/1925; 8/4/1926; 5/5/1929
Allen	J.		Blair	Husband of Mary Mendenhall Blair	11/5/1928; 8/12/1929; 8/13/1929; 8/15/1929; 8/17/1929; 11/5/1929
Albert	Welsh		Blair	Son of John B. and Carrie Blair	8/10/1927
Anna	Lee	Blair		Daughter of Della and Sidney Blair	4/21/1928
Anna			Blair	Wife of E.C. Blair	11/4/1925; 4/20/1926; 8/8/1926; 11/8/1926; 11/9/1926; 7/16/1928; 6/2/1929; 8/29/1929; 11/10/1929; 1/6/1930; 2/4/1930; 2/6/1930
Augustine			Blair	Son B. Franklin Blair	9/9/1923;
Aunt Rachel			Blair	See Rachel Blair	
Benjamin	Franklin		Blair	Husband of Rachel Blair. Father of Augustine Blair and Walter Blair.	9/16/1889; 9/9/1923; 5/16/1929; 5/23/1928
Carrie	Louise	Welch	Blair	Wife of John B Blair	8/10/1927
Charles	Edward		Blair	Brother of Stanley Blair	9/3/1928

Index of Names

First	Middle	Maiden	Last Name (or Last Name by First Marriage)	Relationship	Diary Entry
Della			Blair	Wife of Sidney Blair	9/13/1926; 6/28/1927; 4/21/1928; 5/16/1928; 7/29/1928
Donnel	Jesse		Blair	Son of John B. and Carrie Blair	8/10/1927
E. (Edd) Edward	C./ Charles		Blair	Husband of Anna Blair. Son of Ocia and Robert Blair	5/7/1926; 11/8/1926; 8/8/1927; 2/27/1928; 7/16/1928; 6/2/1929; 8/29/1929; 11/10/1929; 1/6/1930
Ed (Ewd)			Blair	Cousin of EMB. His Mother is Cousin Rachel Blair	11/4/1925; 8/8/1926; 11/8/1927; 11/9/1927; 2/27/1928; 4/16/1928; 4/22/1928
Elva			Blair	Sister of Emma Blair	9/9/1923; 1924; 10/26/1925; 11/1/1925; 11/2/1925; 11/3/1925; 11/4/1925; 4/20/1926; 8/13/1927; 10/26/1927; 8/13/1928; 11/5/1928; 10/11/1929; 11/16/1929
Eliza			Blair		Also See Family Records.

First	Middle	Maiden	Last Name (or Last Name by First Marriage)	Relationship	Diary Entry
Elwood			Blair	Son of Allen J & Mary Mendenhall Blair	8/12/1929
Emily	Hayden	Blair		Granddaughter of EMB	12/20/1927; 6/10/1928; 9/3/1928; 12/27/1928; 3/12/1929; 4/2/1929; 3/10/1930; 3/12/1930; 3/18/1930; 4/5/1930; 4/6/1930; 4/12/1930
Emily	Ann	Millikan	Blair	Diarist	All entries are written by Emily Millikan Blair
Emily	Corene	Blair		Daughter of Jesse C. Blair and Emma Clodfelter Blair	Notes 1895 to 1911; See Family Records
Emma		Blair		Cousin of EMB	9/9/1923; 11/4/1928; 10/11/1929
Enos	A		Blair	Uncle of John Addison Blair	4/10/1890
Enos	Cyrus		Blair	Son of John B. and Carrie Blair	8/10/1927
Enos	T		Blair	Father of John B Blair	8/10/1927
Enos			Blair	Husband of Hannah Millikan Blair, Great Grandfather of John Addision Blair.	Foreword; 10/10/1908

Index of Names

First	Middle	Maiden	Last Name (or Last Name by First Marriage)	Relationship	Diary Entry
Esther (Mrs Fred C.)	J	Hayden	Blair	Daughter in law of EMB	9/9/1923; 6/25/1926; 7/7/1928; 9/3/1928; 12/22/1928; 12/27/1928; 3/6/1929; 3/31/1929; 2/2/1930; 2/3/1930; 2/27/1930; 3/10/1930; 3/18/1930; 3/30/1930; 3/31/1930; 4/3/1930; 4/4/1930; 4/5/1930; 4/6/1930; 0; 4/8/1930; 4/9/1930; 4/10/1930; 4/12/1930; 4/14/1930; 4/24/1930
Evelyn		Blair		Daughter of Allen J and Mary Mendenhall Blair	8/12/1929
Franklin / F.	S.	Blair		Cousin of EMB, Brother of Winston Blair	9/9/1923; 8/22/1929; Also See Family Records.

Until We Sleep Our Last Sleep

First	Middle	Maiden	Last Name (or Last Name by First Marriage)	Relationship	Diary Entry
Fred Jr				Son of Fred C. and Esther Hayden Blair	6/10/1928; 7/7/1928; 9/3/1928; 12/15/1928; 12/27/1928; 3/12/1929; 2/2/1930; 2/3/1930; 3/10/1930; 3/18/1930; 3/30/1930; 4/5/1930; 4/8/1930; 4/12/1930; 4/14/1930
Freddie / Fred	Clinton		Blair	Son of EMB & John Addison Blair	7/14/1889; 10/14/1889; 4/3/1890; 9/1909; 5/1/1918; 9/9/1923; 3/23/1926; 4/3/1927; 12/3/927; 12/11/1927; 12/14/1927; 1/2/1928; 6/9/1928; 9/3/1928; 9/4/1928; 10/7/1928; 12/15/1928; 12/27/1928; 3/31/1929; 7/5/1929; 9/3/1929; 2/2/1930; 2/3/1930; 3/10/1930; 3/18/1930; 3/30/1930; 3/31/1930; 4/1/1930; 4/3/1930; 4/5/1930; 4/6/1930; 4/8/1930; 4/12/1930; 4/23/1930

Index of Names

First	Middle	Maiden	Last Name (or Last Name by First Marriage)	Relationship	Diary Entry
Garland	Augustine		Blair	Son of John B. and Carrie Blair	8/10/1927; 8/11/1927
Gladys		Edmons	Blair	Wife of Garland A Blair	8/10/1927
Hannah		Millkan	Blair	Great Aunt of EMB	Foreword; 10/10/1908
J	Winston		Blair		9/9/1923;
Jesse	Carter		Blair	Son of EMB & John Addison Blair	5/7/1891; 9/17/1926; See Notes 1895 to 1911; Also See Family Records
Jesse	Lelen/ Leolen		Blair	Son of Jesse C. Blair and Emma Clodfelter Blair. Killed by a Train at 7 years old	Notes 1895 to 1911
John			Blair	Son of Hannah Millikan Blair and Enos Balir	10/10/1908
John	Addison		Blair	Husband of EMB	10/10/1908; 5/9/1920; 3/23/1926; 5/23/1928
John	Branson		Blair	Son of Enos T. & Prisila Branson Blair. John and Prisila had 7 sons.	8/9/1927; 8/10/1927; 8/11/1927
John	J		Blair		9/9/1923;
John	Robert		Blair	Son of John B. and Carrie Blair	8/10/1927
Prof John			Blair		8/13/1928
John	Smith		Blair	Father of John Addison Blair	Also See Family Records.
Joseph	Branson		Blair	Son of John B. and Carrie Blair	8/10/1927

First	Middle	Maiden	Last Name (or Last Name by First Marriage)	Relationship	Diary Entry
Martha			Blair	Sister of Elva and Ada Blair	9/9/1923; 8/4/1926; 10/26/1927; 11/16/1929
Mary			Blair	Wife of Walter Blair	2/27/1928; Also See Family Records.
Mary	E.		Blair	Wife of Jesse Blair, Sister in law of JAB	A Reminiscence
Mary		Mendenhall	Blair	Wife of Allen Blair	11/5/1928; 8/12/1929
Mary (May)	Ann	Blair		Granddaughter of EMB	6/22/1926; 6/10/1928; 7/7/1928; 9/3/1928; 10/25/1928; 12/18/1928; 12/27/1928; 3/10/1930; 3/18/1930; 3/30/1930; 4/3/1930; 4/5/1930; 4/6/1930; 4/12/1930
Mrs. Jesse			Blair	Daughter in law of EMB	See Emma Blair Conrad
Muriel		Cook	Blair	Wife of Enos Cyrus Blair	8/10/1927
Ocid (Ocia)		Redding	Blair	Wife of Robert Blair, Cousin of EMB	11/9/1926; 5/18/1927; 11/9/1927; 2/27/1928; 7/9/1928; 9/2/1928; 11/5/1928; 11/4/1929; 1/26/1930
Pansy		Meadows	Blair	Wife of Donnel J Blair	8/10/1927

Index of Names

First	Middle	Maiden	Last Name (or Last Name by First Marriage)	Relationship	Diary Entry
Prisila		Branson	Blair	Mother of John B Blair	8/10/1927
Rachel		Anderson	Blair	Sister of Joshua Anderson; Wife of BF Blair, Mother of RLM Blair; Mother of Walter Blair & Ed Blair	9/16/1889; 11/1/1925; 3/13/1926; 6/5/1926; 6/6/1926; 10/26/1927; 11/8/1927; 2/26/1928; 2/27/1928; 2/28/1928; 4/16/1928; 4/17/1928; 4/22/1928; 5/16/1928; 5/23/1928; 5/24/1928; 7/9/1928
Robert / R	L	M	Blair	Husband of Ocid Blair, Cousin of EMB	11/9/1926; 11/10/1926; 11/11/1926; 11/12/1926; 5/18/1927; 11/8/1927; 2/27/1928; 4/16/1928; 4/17/1928; 4/18/1928; 7/9/1928; 9/2/1928; 9/3/1928; 1/26/1930
Robert Jr			Blair	Son of Ocia/Ocid and Robert Blair	11/8/1927; 11/9/1927; 2/27/1928; 4/16/1928; 4/18/1928; 9/2/1928

First	Middle	Maiden	Last Name (or Last Name by First Marriage)	Relationship	Diary Entry
Roland			Blair	Son of Della & Sidney Blai	4/21/1928; 8/1/1928; 8/2/1928; 11/4/1928; 11/5/1928; 6/23/1929; 6/27/1929
Sadie	Clodfelter	Blair	(also see Sadie Blair Fouts)	Daughter of Jesse Blair, Granddaughter of EMB	9/17/1926; 9/20/1926; 9/23/1926; 9/26/1926; 3/27/1927; 11/26/1928; 12/16/1929
Sidney			Blair		9/13/1926; 6/28/1927; 5/16/1928; 7/29/1928; 11/4/1928; 6/23/1929; 6/24/1929; 6/27/1929; 9/29/1929; 9/30/1929
Stanley			Blair		9/3/1928
Walter	E		Blair	Son of B. Franklin Blair	9/9/1923; 11/1/1925; 2/27/1928

Index of Names

First	Middle	Maiden	Last Name (or Last Name by First Marriage)	Relationship	Diary Entry
Wiliam	Ivey		Blair	Son of John B. and Carrie Blair	8/10/1927
William	A		Blair		5/2/1927
Winston			Blair	Brother of F.S. Blair	10/26/1925; 8/4/1926; 8/8/1927; 8/22/1929
Prof			Bivens	Professor at Trinity College	4/18/1926
Emily	Anita	Moffitt	Bodenheimer	Daughter of Dougan Moffitt	Notes 1895 to 1911
Mr Silvester			Boldens		5/21/1929
Gideon			Bowman	Son in law of May and JW Peace	8/15/1926; 11/21/1926; 6/17/1927; 7/11/1928; 8/26/1928; 10/18/1928; 11/18/1928; 5/6/1929; 6/9/1929; 9/29/1929; 12/25/1929; 1/26/1930; 1/30/1930; 2/9/1930; 2/16/1930
Gideon Jr			Bowman	Son of Gideon and Ollie Bowman	2/10/1928; 6/27/1928; 7/11/1928; 8/26/1928; 10/18/1928; 11/18/1928; 5/6/1929; 9/29/1929; 10/7/1929; 12/11/1929; 12/16/1929; 12/25/1929

Until We Sleep Our Last Sleep

First	Middle	Maiden	Last Name (or Last Name by First Marriage)	Relationship	Diary Entry
Ollie (Mrs. Gideon)	Bulah	Peace	Bowman	Daughter of May and JW Peace	8/15/1926; 8/16/1926; 11/21/1926; 6/17/1927; 2/10/1928; 4/24/1928; 6/27/1928; 7/11/1928; 8/26/1928; 10/18/1928; 11/18/1928; 5/3/1929; 5/6/1929; 5/21/1929; 5/23/1929; 6/9/1929; 7/2/1929; 9/29/1929; 10/7/1929; 12/11/1929; 12/16/1929; 12/25/1929; 1/26/1930; 2/6/1930; 2/9/1930; 2/16/1930; 2/19/1930
Johnnie	Gray		Bowman	Gideon's Brother	1/30/1930
Mr			Bowman	Father in Law of Ollie Peace	8/21/1926
Mrs			Bowman	Mother in Law of Ollie Peace	1/30/1930; 2/6/1930
Mrs. Samila			Branson	Widow of William Branson. John B. Blair's Step Grandmother.	8/10/1927
William			Branson	Husband of Samila Branson.	8/10/1927
Mrs.			Brewer		8/29/1926

692

Index of Names

First	Middle	Maiden	Last Name (or Last Name by First Marriage)	Relationship	Diary Entry
Mr. Orion/ Oren/ R.O.			Bradly/ Bradley		3/10/1929; 3/11/1929; 4/6/1930; 4/18/1930
Mrs. (Ada) Orion/Oren			Bradly/ Bradley		3/10/1929; 3/11/1929; 4/5/1930; 4/10/1930
Preacher			Bradley	Father of Oren Bradley	4/18/1930
Dr. Allen	P.		Brantley		5/12/1929
Rev			Byram		9/30/1926
Dr. Charles	E		Brever	President of Meredith College	5/10/1928
Miss		Brown		Teacher at Trinity College	1/6/1930
Clara		Worth	Bryan	Daughter of Joe and Minnie Worth	8/13/1926
Dr J.	F.		Bulla	EMB's Doctor	9/23/1927; 9/24/1927; 10/23/1928; 11/5/1928; 7/13/1929; 1/24/1930; 1/27/1930; 2/14/1930; 2/20/1930
Mrs			Bulla	Wife of Dr Bulla	2/7/1930
Mary (Miss)		Burge			4/9/1928
Rev			Burr		8/29/1926
Lois			Burr	Daughter of Mr.&Mrs. Walter Burr	4/25/1928
Mr. Walter			Burr	Husband of Mrs. Walter Burr	4/25/1928
Mrs. Walter			Burr	Sister to Ollie Bowman	4/24/1928; 4/25/1928

Until We Sleep Our Last Sleep

First	Middle	Maiden	Last Name (or Last Name by First Marriage)	Relationship	Diary Entry
Dr			Burrus		9//1909
Charles			Burton		10/3/1926
C - Maiden or Last Name					
Dr			Cadman	Radio show preacher	3/31/1929
Mr			Cain	4th Husband of Malissa Peace English English Cain	9/12/1929
Malissa		Peace	Wilborn; English (2nd marriage); English (3rd marriage) Cain (4th marriage)	Jerome Peace's Aunt, Sister of Clavin Peace, Jerome's Dad.	9/12/1929
Marie			Carrell		8/10/1928
Mr			Carroll	Police Detective in Charlotte	2/1/1929
Estelle / Estell		Cranford	Carter	Daughter of Anna Cranford	11/11/1929; 1/21/1930
Flora	M	Carter			Also See Family Records.
Uncle John			Carter	Uncle To EMB	8/17/1929
Grandma			Church	Grandmother of Wiliam Church	11/2/1925
William			Church		11/2/1925
Aseneth			Clark	Aunt To EMB	A Reminiscence
Ivey			Clark	California minister and missionary	8/11/1928; 9/23/1928
Billy	Martin		Clary	Son of Mrs Willie Clary	12/27/1928; 1/8/1929; 2/14/1929, 2/16/1929; 2/17/1929; 2/18/1929

Index of Names

First	Middle	Maiden	Last Name *(or Last Name by First Marriage)*	Relationship	Diary Entry
Mrs. Willie			Clary	Boarder at Fred Blair's	12/23/1928; 12/27/1928; 2/16/1929; 3/15/1929
Emma	D.	Clodfelter	Blair *Conrad (2nd marriage)*	Married to Jessie Blair, EMB Daughter-in-law, Mother of Corene Blair Tomlinson	11/21/1929; 12/16/1929; 4/12/1930; A Reminiscence
Luther			Conrad	Stepfather of Sadie Blair, EMB's Granddaughter. Second Husband of Emma Clodfelter Blair.	9/17/1926; 12/16/1929
Mr (Rev)			Conrad	Pastor of Plesent Grove Church	9/10/1929; 9/12/1929
Annie	M.		Couch		9/9/1923;
Laura (Mrs.)		Nixon	Coval	Of Indianpolis aka Mrs. Coval	11/1/1925; 11/3/1925
Clara	I	Cox		Pastor of Springfield Friends	8/5/1924; 8/4 to 9/1924; 11/3/1925; 6/1/1926; 11/11/1926; 12/30/1926; 2/2/1927; 3/22/1927; 8/2/1927; 8/8/1927; 8/13/1927; 8/14/1927; 2/7/1928; 2/14/1928; 3/24/1928; 4/2/1928; 4/3/1928; 4/17/1928; 5/21/1928; (continued next page)

First	Middle	Maiden	Last Name (or Last Name by First Marriage)	Relationship	Diary Entry
(continued) Clara	I		Cox	Pastor of Springfield Friends	(continued) 5/22/1928; 7/25/1928; 7/29/1928; 8/7/1928; 10/7/1928; 11/14/1928; 5/22/1929; 6/24/1929; 8/3/1929; 8/12/1929; 10/20/1929; 11/11/1929; 1/31/1930; 2/7/1930
Dougan	C.		Cox		7/29/1928; 10/28/1928; 6/24/1929
Mary			Cox	Speaker at Guilford College	8/7/1929
Mrs. Milener	Angel		Cox		8/6/1927
Lula (Miss)	Louise		Coyle	Mentioned in local news	3/25/1929
Anna		L	Cranford	Cousin of EMB	10/26/1925; 10/1/1926; 4/22/1928; 10/2/1928; 10/3/1928; 10/4/1928; 10/5/1928; 9/30/1929; 11/11/1929; 1/21/1930
Carrie (Miss)			Cranford	Daughter of Anna Cranford	11/7/1926; 11/7/1927; 6/25/1928; 10/5/1928
Mr Callier			Cranford		6/5/1927; 6/7/1927

Index of Names

First	Middle	Maiden	Last Name (or Last Name by First Marriage)	Relationship	Diary Entry
Mrs Merriman		Hill	Cranford	Daughter of John Hill	10/27/1928
Dr. Braxton			Craven	President of Trinity College	5/3/1928; 8/13/1928
(Rev) J. / James	D.		Craven		4/18/1926; 5/5/1928; 5/6/1928; 4/28/1929
Charle			Croker	Brother of Fannie Croker	9/30/1926; 4/22/1928
Fannie			Croker	Sister of Charlie Croker	4/22/21928; 4/27/1928; 10/18/1928
Zebidee			Croker	Grandfather to Miss Aldred and Mrs Davis	10/26/1925
Walter			Culp	Brother-in-law of Hoyle Stilwell	4/2/1929
D - Maiden or Last Name					
Almina			Davis	Sister of EMB	9/1/1929
Banner			Davis		2/14/1928
Cornelia			Davis	Mother of Stanley Davis	2/9/1930
David	Gurney		Davis		10/6/1926
Esther			Davis	Wife of Stanley Davis	2/9/1930
Jesse			Davis	Brother-in-law of EMB	1/28/1927
Jesse			Davis	Husband of Mary Coltrane Davis	8/13/1928; 6/5/1929
Laura / Lara		Davis		Daughter of Jesse and Mary Coltrane Davis	8/13/1928; 1/6/1930
Lee			Davis	Brother of Will Davis	12/11/1928
Lena			Davis		2/6/1930
Lester			Davis	Nephew of EMB	2/5/1930
Lula (Miss)		Davis		See Lula Davis Furr	

Until We Sleep Our Last Sleep

First	Middle	Maiden	Last Name (or Last Name by First Marriage)	Relationship	Diary Entry
Mary		Coltrane	Davis	Wife of Jesse Davis	8/13/1928; 6/5/1929; 1/6/1930
Mary		White	Davis	Wife of Wm Davis	2/17/1927; 2/18/1927
Miss			Davis		11/28/1929
Mrs.			Davis	Sister of Miss Aldred. Granddaughter of Zebidee Croker.	10/26/1925
Mona (Miss)		Davis			1/27/1930; 2/20/1930
Mrs. Gurney			Davis		3/2/1928;
Pattie		Spencer	Davis	Daughter of Addie Spencer	9/9/1923;
Rachel	Almina	Millikan	Davis	Youngest Sister of EMB	1/28/1927; 9/1/1929
Rev. William (Will)	Baxter		Davis	Of High Point	9/18/1927; 9/19/1927; 9/20/1927; 9/21/1927; 9/23/1927; 3/3/1928; 12/11/1928
Ruben	C.		Davis		2/14/1928
S.	L.		Davis	Of High Point	7/25/1926
Sidney			Davis	Brother of Jesse Davis	1/28/1927
Stanley			Davis	Son of Cornelia Davis	2/9/1930
Wm			Davis	Husband of Mary Davis	2/17/1927
Rev.			Drauhn		3/24/1928
Dr			Duncan	Assisted in EMB Surgery	9/9/1909
Alice		Welch	Dunman	Daughter of W.C. Welch	9/9/1923;

Index of Names

First	Middle	Maiden	Last Name (or Last Name by First Marriage)	Relationship	Diary Entry
			E - Maiden or Last Name		
Haley			Elder	Husband of Martha Elder	7/4/1926
Martha			Elder	Wife of Haley Elder	7/4/1926
Samaria			Elder		2/11/1930
Esq. Neice (Nease)			Elder	Brother of Haley Elder	7/4/1926; 7/15/1928
Mr Scales			Eldrige		7/18/1927; 7/19/1927
Mrs			Ellington		11/5/1928
David			Ensley	Husband of Hannah Ensley	9/1/1927; 8/12/1928
Hannah	Delphina	Thomas	Ensley	Sister of Eli Thomas. Wife of David Ensley	9/1/1927; 8/12/1928
Fannie			English	Cousin of EMB	11/4/1925; 10/2/1927; 8/15/1928; 8/16/19
Ginnie / Jinnie	May		English	Wife of Nerious English	11/4/1925; 8/13/1928; 8/15/1928
Prof Nerious			English		8/13/1928; 8/14/1928
Martha			English	Wife of Sam English	11/10/1929
Mildred		English		Daughter of Merley and Rettie English	10/12/1928
Murly/ Murley/ Merley			English	Son of Fannie English	11/4/1925; 8/15/1928; 8/16/1928; 8/17/1928; 8/18/1929; 10/12/1928; 11/4/1928

Until We Sleep Our Last Sleep

First	Middle	Maiden	Last Name (or Last Name by First Marriage)	Relationship	Diary Entry
Rettie		Blair	English	Merley English's Wife	9/9/1923; 11/4/1925; 8/16/1928; 10/12/1928; 1/20/1930
Sam			English	Husband of Martha	11/10/1929
Thomas			English		11/10/1889; Also See Family Records.
Tom			English	Son of Ginnie May English	11/4/1925; 8/15/1928; 5/26/1929
Venie			English	Sister of Ginnie/ Jinnie English	11/4/1925; 8/13/1928; 8/14/1928; 8/15/1928
David			Ensley	Husband of Hannah Ensley	9/1/1927
Hannah	Delphina	Thomas	Ensley	Wife of David Ensley	9/1/1927; 8/12/1928
F - Maiden or Last Name					
Edna Farlow (Mrs)			Farlow	Wife of Walter Farlow	4/18/1926
Edna	Clarice		Farlow	Daughter of Walter and Edna Farlow	4/18/1926;
L.	L.		Farlow		2/14/1928
Mamie (Miss)		Farlow			2/14/1928
Mrs. W.	M.		Farlow		2/14/1928
Muriel		Lowe	(Farlow)	Fiance and eventual Wife of Walter Farlow	7/14/1927
Walter			Farlow	Fiance of Muriel Lowe. Father of Edna Clarice Farlow.	4/18/1926; 7/14/1927
William			Farlow		2/14/1928

Index of Names

First	Middle	Maiden	Last Name (or Last Name by First Marriage)	Relationship	Diary Entry
Mrs	H	Lee	Fearns		8/17/1927
Homer			Fesperman	Husband of Cathleen Stilwell Fesperman	8/28/1926; 5/27/1927; 5/28/1927; 11/25/1927; 12/2/1927; 6/11/1928; 9/10/1928; 8/25/1929
Mrs Homer (Katheleen) (Cathleen)		Stilwell		Daughter of George Stilwell	8/28/1926; 5/27/1927; 5/28/1927; 6/3/1927; 6/9/1927; 6/15/1927; 6/17/1927; 6/18/1927, 12/9/1927; 1/2/1928; 6/11/1928; 9/10/1928; 8/25/1929
Rachel		Fesperman		Granddaughter of George Stilwell	5/27/1927; 6/15/1927; 6/11/1928; 8/25/1929
Norman			Fidler		5/2/1927;
Thomas			Finch	Well respected in His community	7/21/1929; 7/22/1929
Hobert	Lee		Fouts	Husband of Sadie Blair Fouts, Granddaughter of EMB	9/20/1926; 11/26/1928; 12/16/1929; 4/12/1930
Sadie (Mrs. Hobert Lee)		Clodfelter Blair	Fouts	(Also see Sadie Blair) Granddaughter of EMB, Daughter of Jesse Blair	See Notes 1895 to 1911; 11/26/1928; 12/16/1929; 4/12/1930
Cyrus	P		Frazier	Son of Gracett Frazier	8/13/1927; 8/19/1928

Until We Sleep Our Last Sleep

First	Middle	Maiden	Last Name (or Last Name by First Marriage)	Relationship	Diary Entry
George			Frazier		4/13/1927
Gracett			Frazier	Mother of Cyrus Frazier	8/19/1928
Gurney			Frazier	Husband of Lou Fraizer	9/9/1923; 6/24/1929; Also See Family Records.
Harison / Harrison			Frazier		8/19/1928; Also See Family Records.
J	Winston	Frazier		Uncle of Cyrus P Frazier	8/13/1927
Lou			Frazier	Wife of Gurney Fraizer	9/9/1923;
Louise		Frazier		Daughter of Gurney and Lou Frazier	9/9/1923;
Ociania			Frazier	7-year old Daughter of George Fraizer	4/13/1927
Robert			Fraizer	Grandson of Harison Fraizer	8/19/1928
Ruffin			Frazier	Son of Gurney and Lou Fraizer	9/9/1923;
Jessie		Fry		Daughter of Mrs. Fry	2/28/1928
Mrs. Wm.			Fry	Mother of Jessie Fry	2/28/1928; 4/17/1928; 4/19/1928; 9/2/1928; 11/26/1928
Paul			Fry	Son of Wm Fry	4/19/1928; 9/2/1928
Mr. Wm			Fry	Wife of Wm Fry	2/26/1928; 2/28/1928; 4/18/1928; 11/26/1928; 12/25/1929

Index of Names

First	Middle	Maiden	Last Name (or Last Name by First Marriage)	Relationship	Diary Entry
Mr. Charlie			Fulp	Husband of Mrs C Fulp	4/24/1928
Mrs. Charlie			Fulp	Wife of Charlie Fulp	4/24/1928
Mrs. Lula		Davis	Furr	Cousin of EMB	11/13/1928
G - Maiden or Last Name					
Maud (Miss)		Gainey		Secretary at Guilford College	9/9/1923; 8/12/1928
Dr. Alfred	C.		Garrett	Speaker at Guilford College	8/9/1928; 8/10/1928
Jinnie			Garver		6/1/1927
Ellen			Gray	Wife of Oscar Gray	5/16/1928; 5/27/1928;
Oscar			Gray	Husband of Ellen Gray	5/16/1928; 5/27/1928;
Abner			Grey	Husband of Hannah Blair Grey	8/12/1926
Cousin Bettie		Grey		Daughter of Abner and Hannah Blair Grey	8/12/1926
Elizabeth		Grey		Daughter of Bettie Grey	8/13/1926
Emma		Grey		Daughter of Abner and Hannah Blair Grey	8/12/1926
Hannah		Blair	Grey	Wife of Abner Grey	8/12/1926
Samuel			Grey	Son of Bettie Grey	8/12/1926
Dr. G.	S.		Groome	Physician	2/20/1930
H - Maiden or Last Name					
Laura		Petty	Hadgin		9/9/1923;
Mrs			Hallimann		11/5/1928
Congressman W.	C.		Hammer	Congressman	5/7/1927

Until We Sleep Our Last Sleep

First	Middle	Maiden	Last Name (or Last Name by First Marriage)	Relationship	Diary Entry
Hannah			Hammond		4/9/1930; 4/11/1930; 4/13/1930; 4/14/1930
Rev E./ Earnest			Harberson		10/4/1928; 10/5/1928; 4/28/1929; 9/8/1929
Margaret	B.		Hackney		9/9/1923;
Priscila		Benbow	Hackney		9/9/1923;
Rettie	S.		Harding		9/9/1923;
Warren (President)	G		Harding	President of the United States	9/9/1923;
G	C	Samuel	Haris		9/9/1923;
Mrs. (Reed)			Haris		11/8/1928
Rev. Reed (W.R.)			Haris	Pastor Mt Vernon	4/17/1926; 5/2/1926; 6/6/1926; 7/4/1926; 8/1/1926; 8/15/1926; 8/29/1926; 9/5/1926; 10/1/1926; 11/21/1926; 1/3/1927; 2/18/1927; 3/6/1927; 3/10/1927; 9/18/1927; 9/23/1927; 1/16/1928; 2/19/1928; 8/17/1927; 3/4/1928; 4/1/1928; 7/1/1928; 8/5/1928; 9/7/1928; 9/16/1928; 9/20/1928; 10/1/1928; 10/2/1928; 10/4/1928; 10/5/1928

Index of Names

First	Middle	Maiden	Last Name (or Last Name by First Marriage)	Relationship	Diary Entry
Rodema (Miss)		Harney		Nurse	8/16/1928
Byron	A		Haworth		5/2/1927
Chester			Haworth		8/4/1926
Chester	C		Haworth		5/2/1927
Eli			Haworth		Also See Family Records.
Sameul			Haworth		5/2/1927
Rev. J.	H		Haynes		8/17/1927
Elizabeth		Taylor	Hendrix	Widow of Millard Hendrix. Daughter of Martin Taylor.	5/12/1927
Millard			Hendrix	Husband of Elizabeth Hendrix	5/12/1927
Emily	A.	Hiatt			See Family Record
Stella (Mrs.)			Hiatt	Niece of Arta Barker	8/12/1927
Rev			Hiker		9/5/1926; 9/8/1926
Alice			Hill		2/6/1930; 2/11/1930
Artilica			Hill		9/9/1923;
Benjamin			Hill	Grandson of Sidney T. Hill, 1st Cousin of E.M. B	6/9/1926
Edith		Hill		Daughter of Artilica Hill	9/9/1923;

Until We Sleep Our Last Sleep

First	Middle	Maiden	Last Name (or Last Name by First Marriage)	Relationship	Diary Entry
John			Hill	1st Cousin of EMB, Brother of Sidney Hill & Nancy Anderson, His mother was a Sister of Samuel C Millikan, EMB's father.	3/13/1926; 3/31/1926; 6/8/1926; 7/29/1926; 5/18/1927; 6/26/1927; 6/27/1927; 11/9/1927; 4/18/1928; 10/27/1928; 10/28/1928; 9/3/1929
Margaret	D.	Hill			Also See Family Records.
Roxie			Hill		3/13/1926; 3/31/1926; 6/8/1926; 5/17/1927; 5/18/1927; 6/26/1927; 11/9/1927; 2/28/1928; 4/17/1928; 4/18/1928; 9/3/1929
Sidney	T		Hill	1st Cousin of EMB, Brother of John Hill & Nancy Anderson, His mother was a Sister of Samuel C Millikan, EMB's father.	6/9/1926; 7/29/1926; 4/20/1928
Terelias			Hill	Cousin, Brother of Nannie Anderson	7/29/1926
Thomas			Hill	Son of Sidney Hill	4/20/1928
William			Hill		Also See Family Records.

Index of Names

First	Middle	Maiden	Last Name (or Last Name by First Marriage)	Relationship	Diary Entry
Rev Milo			Hincle	Of Friends Greensboro	7/25/1926; 8/4/1926; 8/14/1926
Lewis	Linden		Hobbs		9/9/1923;
Evangelist Rev			Hobson		9/25/1927; 10/26/1927
Nereus	M		Hodgin	Minister	9/9/1923;
Luzena			Hockette	Aunt to EMB	A Reminiscence
Mahlon			Hockette	Uncle To EMB	A Reminiscence
Melissa	F		Hodgin	Wife of Nereus Hodgin	9/9/1923;
Mrs Samuel			Hodgein	Wife of Samuel Hodgein	5/16/1929
E.	P.		Hoggatt		Also See Family Records.
Joseph			Hoggatt		Also See Family Records.
Edgar	T		Hole	Missionary	8/4/1926; 8/12/1929
Mrs. A	C		Hollingsworth/ Holingsworth	Teacher of Charlotte home bible study	12/27/1927; 3/14/1929; 4/20/1930; 4/21/1930
Mrs			Holman		4/20/1926
Herbert			Hoover	Presidential candidate	11/6/1928
Aunt Margaret			Hoover	Neighbor	4/20/1929; 4/23/1929; 2/12/1930
Miss		Huff		Of Indana	8/6/1927
Elizabeth			Hunt	Aunt to EMB	A Reminiscence

Until We Sleep Our Last Sleep

First	Middle	Maiden	Last Name (or Last Name by First Marriage)	Relationship	Diary Entry
Sameul			Hunt	Uncle To EMB	A Reminiscence
I - Maiden or Last Name					
Watson			Ingram	Father of JW Peace's 1st Wife, Sally Ingram	8/22/1929; 8/23/1929
James			Isom	Neighbor to JW Peace	10/16/1927
Mrs			Isom		1/21/1930
J - Maiden or Last Name					
Allen			Jay		11/28/1929
Eugene	H.		Jarrett		2/14/1928
Ellen (Miss)		Jerald			10/26/1925
Mrs Everett		Peace	Jewel		1/20/1930
Lorena		Worth	John	Sister of Joe Worth	8/13/1926; 8/14/1926
Alta		Johnson		Daughter of Ruth Johnson	10/12/1889
Ermie		Johnson		Daughter of Ruth Johnson	10/12/1889
J.	Alvin		Johnson	Brother to Mattie Johnson Wilborn, Husband of Ruth Blair.	1895-1914; 9/9/1923; 2/28/1927; Also See Family Records.
Lou (Miss)		Johnson		Daughter of J Alvin and Ruth Millikan Johnson	1895-1914
M.	M		Johnson		Also See Family Records.
Prof Lemuel			Johnson	Father of Rona Johnson	7/6/1890
Rhoda	J.	Millikan	Johnson	First Cousin of EMB	3/9/1927

Index of Names

First	Middle	Maiden	Last Name (or Last Name by First Marriage)	Relationship	Diary Entry
Rona			Johnson	Daughter of Prof Lemuel Johnson	7/6/1890
Ruth		Millikan	Johnson	Sister of EMB	10/12/1889; 1895-1914; 9/9/1923; 2/28/1927; Also See Family Records.
Walter			Johnson		3/9/1927
Willie			Johnson	Jesse Millikan's Nephew	9/9/1923;
Eli			Jones	Missionary to China	11/28/1889; 8/6/1926
Mrs Nannie		Lowe	Jones	Wife of Thomas Jones	2/20/1927
Rev James	R		Jones	Friend	10/15/1889; 12/5/1889; 12/6/1889; 8/5/1926; 6/25/1928; 9/4/1928; 9/7/1928; 8/23/1929
Sibyl			Jones	Missionary to China	11/28/1889; 8/6/1926;
Thomas			Jones	Husband of Nannie Lowe Jones	2/20/1927
Wm			Jones	Father of Mrs. Wm Plummer	7/12/1890
Wright			Jones		8/11/1926
Rev H	H		Jorden/ Jordan		11/28/1927; 1/4/1928
Carrie			Judd	Writer from Buffalo NY	11/11/1889
Dr			Julian	Dr in Thomasviille	Notes from 1895 to 1911

Until We Sleep Our Last Sleep

First	Middle	Maiden	Last Name (or Last Name by First Marriage)	Relationship	Diary Entry
Mr			Julian	Husband of Mrs Julian	11/5/1928
Mrs			Julian	Wife of Mr Julian	11/5/1928
K- Maiden or Last Name					
Rev (Mr) (Pastor) W. (J.)	R.		Kelly		11/18/1928; 12/2/1928; 4/7/1929; 5/5/1929; 5/19/1929; 9/1/1929; 9/8/1929; 9/10/1929; 10/6/1929; 11/3/1929; 1/23/1930; 2/5/1930
Cameron			Kennedy	Burned at 5 year's old in accident	3/5/1927; 3/6/1927
Mrs Carina			Kenedy		10/5/1928
Harison			Kenedy		6/2/1929; 7/2/1929
Irey			Kennedy	Parent of Cameron Kennedy	3/5/1927
John	Lee		Kenedy		9/22/1929
Minnie	Lee	Kenedy		Daughter of Harison and Nellie Kenedy	6/2/1929
Nellie			Kenedy	Wife of Harison Kennedy	6/2/1929
Murray	S		Kenworthy		8/7/1929
Carras			Kerns		8/7/1889
Mrs Amos			Kersey	Daughter of Fannie English is Amos Kersey's widow	11/4/1925; 10/2/1927; 8/15/1928
Annabelle		King		Sister of Annabelle King	11/3/1925
Emma (Miss)		King		Sister of Emma King	11/3/1925

Index of Names

First	Middle	Maiden	Last Name (or Last Name by First Marriage)	Relationship	Diary Entry
Mr			King	Trolley Car Conductor	2/1/1929
Rufus	P		King		8/15/1889
Rev			Kirk		5/15/1926
Mrs. Oliver			Knight		8/9/1929
Mrs			Kyou (Kjou)	Neighbor of Charlotte Blairs	3/14/1929; 4/4/1928
L- Maiden or Last Name					
Almina		Laughlin		Daughter of Ruth Laughlin	9/1/1929
Mrs Fred			Lauglin/ Laughlin		5/25/1927; 6/8/1927
John			Laughlin	Husband of Ruth Laughlin	9/1/1929
John	Jr		Laughlin	Son of Ruth and John Laughlin	9/1/1929
Kermit			Laughlin	Son of Ruth and John Laughlin	9/1/1929
Paul			Laughlin	Son of Ruth and John Laughlin	9/1/1929
Ruth		Davis	Laughlin	Wife of John Laughlin, Daughter of Almina Davis	9/1/1929
Mr. (Frank)			Lamberth (Lambeth)	Founder of the Chair Factory in Thomasville	10/5/1928; 11/26/1928
Miss	Daisy	Leach			9/24/1926; 9/25/1926
Allen			Lay		8/18/1889
Thomas			Lay		8/15/1889
Mrs. Nora			Ledwell	Bible Teacher	12/26/1926; 6/17/1928; 11/10/1929; 2/16/1930
Mrs. Wm			Ledwell		10/24/1926

Until We Sleep Our Last Sleep

First	Middle	Maiden	Last Name (or Last Name by First Marriage)	Relationship	Diary Entry
Mrs Charlie			Lee	Daughter of Sidney and Della Blair	6/28/1927; 11/4/1928
Mary			Lee	Might be Mrs Charle Lee?	7/9/1927
Elizabeth		Levering		Server at Founders Hall, Guilford College	9/9/1923; 8/12/1928
Mrs.			Levering	Mother of Elizabeth Levering	8/12/1928
Dr. (Luther)			Little	Radio show preacher from First Baptist Church in Charlotte	1/27/1929; 2/10/1929; 3/3/1929; 3/25/1929; 3/31/1929
Prof. W.		H.	Livers		5/18/1929
Mrs. Mary	Elizabeth	Penington	Loflin		1/4/1928
Mattie		Marsh	Lowe	Childhood friend of EMB	2/20/1927
M- Maiden or Last Name					
Daisy (Miss)		Magee			8/17/1927
Bettie			Marsh		2/6/1930
Eugene			Marsh	Cousin to EMB	2/25/1929
Mr Isaac			Marsh		7/19/1927
Lenerd			Marsh	Father of Pearl Marsh Wilborn	9/9/1923;
Martha	E		Marshall		9/9/1923;
Dr			Mathews	Dr in Charlotte	3/23/1930; 3/30/1930; 3/31/1930; 4/2/1930; 4/4/1930; 4/8/1930; 4/16/1930
Lee	Charles		McCauley	Son of Mary McCauley	3/29/1927
Mrs	Mary		McCauley		3/29/1927

Index of Names

First	Middle	Maiden	Last Name (or Last Name by First Marriage)	Relationship	Diary Entry
Rev Louis (Lewis)	W.		McFarland		9/9/1923; 8/6/1926; 8/14/1926; 7/29/1928; 8/10/1928; 8/9/1929
Pearl			McFarland	Wife of Lewis McFarland	9/9/1923;
Crissie (Miss)	June	McGee			8/5/1928
Mrs. Robert			McGee	Sister to Walter Johnson	3/9/1927; 3/10/1927
Anna (Miss)		Mendenhall			2/14/1928
Chas	H		Mendenhall		Also See Family Records.
Cynthia		Mendenhall			Also See Family Records.
Elihu			Mendenhall	Dairy Farmer with Samuel Mendenhall	8/10/1927
Gertrude			Mendenhall		8/5/1926
John			Mendenhall	Son of Josie Mendenhall	8/16/1929
Josie			Mendenhall		8/16/1929
Miriam		Moffitt	Mendenhall	Sister to Dougan Moffitt	9/9/1923;
Rebecca		Mendenhall			Also See Family Records.
Reed			Mendenhall	Allen J. Blair's Brother-in-law	8/16/1929
Samuel			Mendenhall	Dairy Farmer with Elihu Mendenhall	8/10/1927
Clarance			Meredith		9/30/1926
Effie			Meredith	Wife of Clarance	10/4/1928

Until We Sleep Our Last Sleep

First	Middle	Maiden	Last Name (or Last Name by First Marriage)	Relationship	Diary Entry
Clarence / Clarance			Meredith	Son of Walter Meredith, Husband of Effie	9/13/1926; 9/24/1926; 9/30/1926; 4/22/1928; 10/4/1928; 10/5/1928
Mrs. Walter (Florence / Florance)			Meredith	Wife of Walter Meredith	10/26/1925; 9/13/1926; 10/2/1926; 10/3/1926; 4/22/1928; 10/4/1928; 10/5/1928; 2/8/1930
Julius			Meredith		9/13/1926
Mabel (Miss)		Meredith		Daughter of Florence Meredith	10/26/1925; 10/6/1928; 10/7/1928
W.W.			Meredith		9/13/1926
Walter			Meredith	Husband of Florence	10/2/1926; 10/3/1926; 4/21/1928; 10/3/1928; 10/4/1928; 10/5/1928
Aunt Polly			Millikan	Mother of EMB, see Mary Carter Millikan	4/21/1928
Benjamin			Millikan	Son of Benjamin Millikan the Sheriff. Cousin to EMB	8/11/1928
Benjamin			Millikan	Grandfather of EMB	10/10/1908; See Famly Records
Benjamin / Benjamen			Millikan	Sheriff	9/9/1923; 8/11/1928
E./Elezar	B. / Bales		Millikan	Brother of EMB	12/23/1927; 1/5/1928; 10/18/1928; See Family Records

Index of Names

First	Middle	Maiden	Last Name (or Last Name by First Marriage)	Relationship	Diary Entry
Emma	Jane	Millikan		Sister of EMB	See Family Records
J	H.		Millikan	Husband of Maggie Millikan	2/7/1928
Jesse			Millikan	Cousin to EMB	9/9/1923;
Leon			Millikan		2/14/1928
Leora			Millikan	Daughter of Maggie Millkan	8/11/1926
Maggie			Millikan	Cousin to EMB. Mother of Leora and Roger Millikan	9/9/1923; 8/11/1926; 2/7/1928; 2/14/1928
Mahlon			Millikan	Husband of Nancy Millikan	3/29/1927
Margaret		Bales	Millikan	Grandmother of EMB	See Family Records
Martha		Millikan		Twin Sister for Mary Millikan. Daughter of Mahlon and Nancy Millikan.	3/29/1927
Mary		Millikan		Twin Sister for Martha Millikan. Daughter of Mahlon and Nancy Millikan.	3/29/1927; Also See Family Records.
Mary	"Polly"	Carter	Millikan	Mother of EMB	A Reminiscence; 8/14/1926; 4/21/1928; Also See Family Records
Mattie/ Martha	Cordelia	Millikan		Sister of EMB	1/5/1928. See Family Records.
Mrs. (E.B) Sadie			Millikan	Wife of E.B. Millikan	10/13/1928

Until We Sleep Our Last Sleep

First	Middle	Maiden	Last Name (or Last Name by First Marriage)	Relationship	Diary Entry
Mrs. (E.B) Sadie			Millikan	Wife of E.B. Millikan, Sister in law of EMB	10/18/1928
Nancy			Millikan	Wife of Mahlon Millikan	3/29/1927
Nericus			Millikan		1/24/1930
Nina (Miss)		Millkan		2nd Cousin of EMB	11/29/1928
Pearl		Andrews	Millikan	Wife of Benjamin Millikan the minister, Daughter-in-law of Benjamin Milliken the sheriff. Daugther of Thomas Andrews	8/10/1928; 8/11/1928
Rachel	Almina	Millikan		Youngest Sister of EMB	1/28/1927
Roger			Millikan	Cousin to EMB. His mother is Maggie Millikan.	9/9/1923; 10/26/1925; 8/8/1926; 8/9/1926
Sameul	C		Millikan	Father of EMB	7/29/1926; 3/29/1927; 7/9/1929
Thomas	Coriolanus		Millikan	Brother of EMB	5/1/1891; See Notes 1895 to 1911; and Famly Records
Violet			Millikan		5/2/1927
Elden	H		Mills	Speaker at Guilford College	8/7/1929; 8/9/1929
Hobert			Mills	Mr & Mrs	10/1/1926
Allen			Moffitt	Friends of EMB and John Addison Blair	10/26/1889

Index of Names

First	Middle	Maiden	Last Name (or Last Name by First Marriage)	Relationship	Diary Entry
(Maggie) Margaret	Ellen	Blair	Moffitt	Daughter of EMB / Wife of Dougan Moffitt	7/14/1889; 4/10/1890; 5/18/1890; 8/12/1890; 9/9/1923; 3/13/1926; 3/23/1926; 11/26/1926; 8/12/1927; 5/22/1929
Dougan	Clark		Moffitt	Husband of Maggie Blair, son-in-law of EMB	4/10/1890; 5/7/1891; 1909; (Notes from 1895 to 1911) 9/9/1923; 3/30/1926; 8/12/1927
David	Blair		Moffitt	Son of Dougan Moffitt	Notes 1895 to 1911
Emily	Anita	Moffitt		Daughter of Dougan Moffitt	Notes 1895 to 1911. Also see Emily Anita Moffitt Bodenheimer
Ethel	Tomlinson	Moffitt		Daughter of Dougan Moffitt	Notes 1895 to 1911
Lula	Maie	Moffitt		Daughter of Dougan Moffitt	Notes 1895 to 1911
Marguerite	Elizabeth	Moffitt		Daughter of Dougan Moffitt	Notes 1895 to 1911
Wilma	Almina	Moffitt		Daughter of Dougan Moffitt	Notes 1895 to 1911
Mr Jeter			Montgomery		11/7/1926
Rev. John	W.		Moore / More	Pastor of Wesley Memorial High Point;	5/9/1926; 2/7/1928; 2/14/1928
John	S.		More	Husband of Tuelma Barker More	8/10/1926

Until We Sleep Our Last Sleep

First	Middle	Maiden	Last Name (or Last Name by First Marriage)	Relationship	Diary Entry
Tuelman		Barker	More	Wife of John S. Moore	8/10/1926
Miss		Mulis		Teacher at Trinity High School	5/21/1929
Mr.			Murphy		9/22/1926
Bernice (Miss)		Myres			10/5/1928
Mrs.			Murphy		9/22/1926
Dr John			Myres		5/1/1918
Mr Kinsey			Myres		1/4/1927; 10/5/1928
Mrs. Kinsey			Myres	Daughter of Mrs. Wall	9/25/1926;

N- Maiden or Last Name

First	Middle	Maiden	Last Name	Relationship	Diary Entry
Mrs			Nance	Grandmother of Baby Edward Lee White	5/6/1929
Mrs	Clyde		Neely	Neighbor in Charlotte	3/26/1926; 12/27/1927
Myrtle (Mrs)		W.	Nelson		9/9/1923;
Louella			Night		9/9/1923;
Alta		Winslow	Night		9/9/1923;

O- Maiden or Last Name

First	Middle	Maiden	Last Name	Relationship	Diary Entry
Arrilla		Balinger	Osborne		9/9/1923;
Mrs Charles			Orsborn		12/24/1928

P- Maiden or Last Name

First	Middle	Maiden	Last Name	Relationship	Diary Entry
Catherin			Paff		9/9/1923;
Mrs. Ralph			Parker		2/14/1928
Dr.			Pateats	Speaker at Guilford College	8/9/1928
Dr.			Paynes		3/23/1905

Index of Names

First	Middle	Maiden	Last Name (or Last Name by First Marriage)	Relationship	Diary Entry
Rev Rueben			Payne	Pastor of Friends Church Archdale	5/2/1927; 8/15/1927; 8/17/1927; 11/7/1927; 2/27/1928; 6/25/1928; 8/19/1928; 6/24/1929; 12/25/1929; 2/1/1930
Bernice			Peace	Daughter of Jacob Peace	7/2/1929
Cisero			Peace		10/1/1926
Clara (Mrs. Grady)		Ward	Peace	Wife of Grady Peace	12/28/1926; 10/15/1928; 11/18/1928; 5/6/1929; 6/2/1929; 12/16/1929; 12/25/1929; 1/20/1930
Clemons			Peace	Son of J.W. Peace	8/26/1926; 11/26/1928; 4/10/1929; 4/11/1929; 8/21/1929; 8/26/1929; 8/27/1929; 9/24/1929; 12/30/1929
Dora/Dara			Peace	Daughter of June and Bessie Peace	6/27/1928; 6/9/1929; 12/10/1929
Earl			Peace	Husband of Nannie Peace	8/22/1926; 2/6/1930
Emery			Peace	Fred Peace's Cousin	9/10/1926; 12/28/1926
Everette			Peace	Emery Peace's Brother	12/28/1926

Until We Sleep Our Last Sleep

First	Middle	Maiden	Last Name (or Last Name by First Marriage)	Relationship	Diary Entry
Fred			Peace	Son of JW Peace	12/28/1926; 10/25/1928; 12/3/1928; 5/6/1929; 6/9/1929; 12/25/1929; 1/20/1930; 2/16/1930
Grady			Peace	Son of JW Peace	12/28/1926; 4/1/1928; 7/17/1928; 10/15/1928; 11/18/1928; 5/6/1929; 6/2/1929; 12/16/1929; 12/25/1929; 1/20/1930
Grandma Levina			Peace	JW Peace's Mother	3/13/1926; 10/3/1926; 10/4/1926; 11/28/1926; 12/1/1926; 2/15/1927; 2/24/1927; 6/23/1927; 6/24/1927; 9/22/1927; 11/2/1927; 4/1/1928; 5/16/1928; 9/23/1928; 10/2/1928; 10/24/1928; 11/8/1928; 12/12/1928; 6/5/1929; 10/19/1929; 11/16/1929; 12/12/1929; 1/17/1930; 1/25/1930

Index of Names

First	Middle	Maiden	Last Name (or Last Name by First Marriage)	Relationship	Diary Entry
Jacob / Uncle Jake			Peace	Brother of JW Peace	12/8/1928; 12/31/1928; 6/11/1929; 6/14/1929; 6/15/1929; 6/16/1929; 6/18/1929; 6/19/1929; 6/20/1929; 6/21/1929; 6/22/1929; 6/23/1929; 6/24/1929; 6/25/1929; 6/26/1929; 6/27/1929; 6/28/1929; 6/29/1929; 6/30/1929; 7/2/1929; 7/3/1929; 7/4/1929; 7/6/1929; 7/7/1929; 7/8/1929; 7/11/1929; 7/15/1929; 7/22/1929; 8/2/1929; 8/3/1929; 8/4/1929; 8/19/1929; 8/21/1929; 8/22/1929; 8/23/1929; 8/27/1929; 8/30/1929; 8/31/1929; 9/6/1929; 9/9/1929; 9/10/1929; 3/26/1930

Until We Sleep Our Last Sleep

First	Middle	Maiden	Last Name (or Last Name by First Marriage)	Relationship	Diary Entry
Jenette/ Janett (Mrs. Fred)		Kerns	Peace	Wife of Fred Peace	12/28/1926; 10/25/1928; 12/3/1928; 5/6/1929; 12/25/1929; 1/20/1930; 2/16/1930
Jerome	W		Peace	Husband of Maggie Blair, Daughter of EMB	9/9/1923; 11/4/1925; 4/18/1926; 7/27/1926; 9/13/1926; 10/6/1926; 12/28/1926; 5/3/1927; 6/17/1927; 9/15/1927; 11/9/1927; 11/11/1927; 11/21/1927; 1/5/1928; 2/10/1928; 2/23/1928; 2/25/1928; 5/14/1929 3/16/1928; 4/1/1928; 4/4/1928; 4/24/1928; 5/3/1928; 5/5/1928; 6/27/1928; 5/16/1928; 7/17/1928; 8/7/1928; 8/19/1928; 8/26/1928; 8/27/1928; 8/29/1928; 9/15/1928; 9/20/1928; (continued next page)

Index of Names

First	Middle	Maiden	Last Name (or Last Name by First Marriage)	Relationship	Diary Entry
(continued) Jerome	W		Peace	Husband of Maggie Blair, Daughter of EMB	(continued) 10/14/1928; 10/15/1928; 11/9/1928; 11/21/1928; 11/26/1928; 11/27/1928; 12/8/1928; 12/11/1928; 4/7/1929; 5/3/1929; 5/26/1929; 5/30/1929; 6/9/1929; 6/24/1929; 6/30/1929; 7/22/1929; 8/4/1929; 8/22/1929; 8/23/1929; 8/26/1929; 8/27/1929; 8/30/1929; 9/9/1929; 9/10/1929; 9/12/1929; 9/14/1929; 10/23/1929; 11/10/1929; 12/8/1929; 12/25/1929; 12/25/1929; 12/30/1929; 1/18/1930; 2/25/1930; 4/18/1930

Until We Sleep Our Last Sleep

First	Middle	Maiden	Last Name (or Last Name by First Marriage)	Relationship	Diary Entry
Jerome aka J.A.	Addison		Peace	Grandson of EMB	11/12/1926; 4/4/1928; 4/24/1928; 5/23/1928; 10/14/1928; 11/30/1928; 12/3/1928; 12/12/1928; 4/10/1929; 5/3/1929; 6/16/1929; 8/26/1929; 9/16/1929; 9/18/1929; 10/4/1929; 10/23/1929; 12/12/1929; 12/25/1929; 12/30/1929; 4/18/1930
Jewel		Baker	Peace	Wife of Everette Peace	12/28/1926; 10/24/1928; 1/25/1930
Joseph			Peace	Son of Grady and Clara Peace	10/14/1928; 11/18/1928; 5/6/1929; 6/2/1929; 12/16/1929; 1/20/1930
Mr. Ferney (M. Kerney) (Gurney)			Peace	Brother of JW Peace	4/1/1928; 7/11/1928; 9/16/1928; 11/21/1928; 11/10/1929; 2/4/1930
Mr. June			Peace	Husband of Bessie Peace	6/27/1928; 12/16/1929; 1/27/1930

Index of Names

First	Middle	Maiden	Last Name (or Last Name by First Marriage)	Relationship	Diary Entry
Mrs (JW) Mary/May	Eliza	Blair	Stilwell *Peace (2nd marriage)*	Daughter of Emily Millikan Blair	10/14/1889; 5/3/1890; 9/9/1923; 8//1924; 3/13/1926; 3/23/1926; 3/31/1926; 4/18/1926; 6/8/1926; 8/4/1926; 8/15/1926; 9/26/1926; 9/27/1926; 9/30/1926; 10/4/1926; 10/6/1926; 5/3/1927; 5/22/1927; 6/7/1927; 6/24/1927; 8/2/1927; 8/13/1927; 9/12/1927; 11/11/1927; 2/25/1928; 4/4/1928; 4/22/1928; 4/24/1928; 5/3/1928; 8/7/1928; 8/18/1928; 8/19/1928; 8/27/1928; 9/2/1928; 9/3/1928; 9/10/1928; 9/16/1928; 9/23/1928; 10/1/1928; 2/8/1929; 2/25/1929; 3/30/1929; 3/31/1929; (continued next page)

Until We Sleep Our Last Sleep

First	Middle	Maiden	Last Name *(or Last Name by First Marriage)*	Relationship	Diary Entry
(continued) Mrs (JW) Mary/May	Eliza	Blair	Stilwell	Daughter of Emily Millikan Blair	(continued) 4/19/1929; 5/3/1929; 5/30/1929; 6/8/1929; 6/24/1929; 7/22/1929; 8/4/1929; 8/15/1929; 8/17/1929; 8/21/1929; 8/22/1929; 8/23/1929; 8/26/1929; 8/27/1929; 8/30/1929; 9/5/1929; 9/12/1929; 9/14/1929; 9/20/1929; 10/23/1929; 11/10/1929; 12/8/1929; 12/25/1929; 12/30/1929; 1/18/1930; 1/19/1930; 2/5/1930; 2/25/1930; 4/1/1930; 4/2/1930; 4/3/1930; 4/4/1930; 4/5/1930; 4/7/1930; 4/8/1930; 4/17/1930; 4/18/1930
Mrs June (Bessie)			Peace	Wife of June Peace	12/16/1929; 1/27/1930
Mrs. Ferney/ Kerney (Mabel)			Peace	Sister-in-law of JW Peace	4/1/1928; 7/11/1928; 11/10/1929; 2/4/1930

Index of Names

First	Middle	Maiden	Last Name (or Last Name by First Marriage)	Relationship	Diary Entry
Malissa		Peace		Jerome Peace's Aunt, Sister of Clavin Peace, Jerome's Dad.	9/12/1929. See Malissa Cain.
Minnie (Miss)	J	Peace		Step Granddaughter of EMB	5/6/1927; 11/7/1927; 11/8/1927; 11/11/1927; 11/12/1927; 11/13/1927; 11/15/1927; 11/17/1927; 11/19/1927; 3/16/1928; 3/26/1928; 4/4/1928; 5/5/1928; 10/2/1928; 11/26/1928; 4/10/1929; 4/17/1929; 5/3/1929; 5/21/1929; 5/23/1929; 6/13/1929; 7/15/1929; 8/20/1929; 8/27/1929; 2/17/1930
Mrs. Earl / Nannie (Aunt Nannie)		Crotts	Peace	Wife of Earl Peace	8/22/1926; 10/2/1928; 10/18/1928; 10/24/1928; 10/25/1928; 12/28/1926; 1/20/1930; 1/24/1930
Sally		Ingram	Peace	First Wife of J.W. Peace	3/16/1928
Erma		Mendenhall	Peele	Daughter of Miriam Moffitt Mendenhall	9/9/1923;
Rev Joseph			Peele	Husband of Erma Peele	9/9/1923; 8/5/1926
Prof (Dr) William	Howard		Pegram (Pegras)		5/3/1928

Until We Sleep Our Last Sleep

First	Middle	Maiden	Last Name (or Last Name by First Marriage)	Relationship	Diary Entry
Mrs		Craven	Pegram	Daughter of Braxton Craven	5/3/1928
Rev S.	M		Penn		8/17/1927
Mrs			Periman		9/25/1926
Dr Elwood			Perisho	Guilford College	9/9/1923; 5/6/1927; 5/7/1927; 5/8/1927; 8/7/1927; 8/11/1928
Inez		Beele	Perisho	Wife of Elwood Persiho	9/9/1923;
Mary	M		Petty		9/9/1923;
M	Victoria		Petty		9/9/1923;
Infant			Plummer	Child of Mr. & Mrs. Wm Plummer	7/12/1890
Mrs (Wm)		Jones	Plummer	Daughter of Wm Jones	7/12/1890
Wm			Plummer	Husband of Mrs Plummer	7/12/1890
Dr			Poling	Radio show preacher	3/31/1929
Rev. J	E		Pritchard		8/17/1927
R- Maiden or Last Name					
Amos			Ragan	Father of Anna Ragan Armfied	8/16/1928
H.	S.		Ragan		11/6/1928
Stokes	S		Rawlins	Speaker at Guilford College, President of North Carolina Christian Endeavor Union	8/11/1928
Alma (Miss)		Rayl			9/9/1923; 8/12/1928
William			Reagan		8/12/1929
Jinnie (Miss)		Redding			8/31/1926; 9/2/1928

Index of Names

First	Middle	Maiden	Last Name (or Last Name by First Marriage)	Relationship	Diary Entry
Charles			Redding		1/27/1930
Mrs Daisy			Redding		8/31/1926; 1/27/1930
Dr			Reitzel		9//1909
Jennie		Barker	Reynolds	Daughter of Eliza Barker	9/9/1923;
Joash			Reynolds		Also See Family Records.
Paron			Reynolds	Father of Paul Reynolds	8/12/1928
Paul			Reynolds	Son of Paron Reynolds	8/12/1928
Mrs.	Lee		Rice	Mother of Mrs. Martine Rice Barker	9/23/1926
Mrs. Bessie			Ridge		7/2/1929
Dara / Dora			Richardson/ Richerdson		9/9/1923; 1924; 11/3/1925
Wm			Richardson		10/13/1889
Allen			Robins		9/22/1927
Mrs Allen			Robins		10/24/1928
George			Robins		11/8/1926; 11/9/1926; 4/19/1928; 4/20/1928; 4/21/1928
Mrs George			Robins		11/7/1926; 11/8/1926; 4/19/1928; 4/20/1928
Mrs Nathan			Robins		4/16/1926; 4/17/1926
Mrs Nellie			Robins		7/16/1927
Mrs			Rogers		12/22/1927; 3/14/1929

Until We Sleep Our Last Sleep

First	Middle	Maiden	Last Name (or Last Name by First Marriage)	Relationship	Diary Entry
Mrs W.	D.		Rogers		3/23/1926
Mr. Lee			Roils	Husband of Mrs Lee Roils	8/14/1927
Mrs. Lee			Roils	Wife of Lee Roils	8/14/1927
Rev W	A		Rollins		1/4/1928
Dr. Howard	E		Rondthaler		5/6/1928; 5/7/1928
Mrs June			Royls		11/10/1929
Dr. Elbert			Russell	Duke University speaker	5/2/1927; 8/11/1928; 8/10/1929
Rev C	U		Ryne		1/4/1928
S - Maiden or Last Name					
Mrs.			Sayers		7/7/1928
Mr.			Savage		6/2/1929
Mrs.			Savage		6/2/1929
Mrs BD (Jessie)		Stilwell	Shoe (Shue)	Daughter of George Stilwell	5/25/1927; 5/26/1927; 5/27/1927; 6/3/1927; 6/9/1927; 10/17/1927; 11/21/1927; 11/22/1927; 11/23/1927; 11/24/1927; 11/25/1927; 11/27/1927; 12/9/1927; 1/2/1928; 1/3/1928; 1/5/1928; 9/10/1928

Index of Names

First	Middle	Maiden	Last Name (or Last Name by First Marriage)	Relationship	Diary Entry
B	D		Shoe (Shue)		5/27/1927; 6/3/1927; 10/17/1927; 11/21/1927; 11/22/1927; 11/23/1927; 11/24/1927; 11/25/1927; 1/2/1928; 1/4/1928; 9/10/1928
Mrs. H.E.			Shore		9/9/1923;
Rev Tom	Alderman		Sikes (Sykes)		10/6/1926; 7/27/1926; 5/2/1927; 2/7/1928; 2/14/1928; 6/24/1929; 8/6/1929; 8/8/1929
Mrs. Joseph			Sikes		4/18/1926
Mrs. Tom			Sykes		2/14/1928
Mr D	W		Sims		8/17/1927
Annie		Pegram	Simpson		9/9/1923;
Addie		Frazier	Smith	Daughter of Gurney and Lou Frazier	9/9/1923;
Emily	R	Newlin	Smith		9/9/1923;
Elvira		Lowe	Smith		9/9/1923;
Mrs Ed			Smith		3/14/1929; 4/5/1930
Mrs. M	L		Smith		12/15/1927
Rev Ramond			Smith		8/17/1927
Roe		Petty	Smith		9/9/1923;
Virgie			Smith		6/1/1927
Addie			Spencer		9/9/1923;

Until We Sleep Our Last Sleep

First	Middle	Maiden	Last Name (or Last Name by First Marriage)	Relationship	Diary Entry
Archie			Spencer	Son-in-law for Jesse Davis	8/13/1928; 11/8/1929
Mrs. Archie			Spencer		11/21/1926
Monroe		Spencer			3/11/1927
Nannie	Lee		Spencer		1/24/1930; 2/6/1930
Ruth			Spencer	Cousin	1/3/1930
Mr			Springer		8/29/1929
Mrs			Springer	Sister to Mrs Edd Blair	8/29/1929
Ada			Stanley		9/9/1923;
Lee			Stanley		9/9/1923;
Elizabeth			Starbuck	Sister-in-law to EMB	8/15/1889; 11/7/1889
Aunt			Steed		1/26/1930
Mr Tom			Steed		1/26/1930
Mrs Tom			Steed		1/26/1930
Mrs. George			Stephens		1/1/25; 11/1/1925; 1/24/1930
Rev George			Stephen		10/26/1925
Arthur	Lee		Stilwell	Husband of May Blair/ Daughter of EMB	5/1/1918; 5/9/1920; 9/9/1923; 8/28/1926; 10/23/1926; 5/3/1927; 10/23/1927; 5/3/1928; 9/10/1928; 10/23/1928; 3/31/1929; 5/3/1929; 4/18/1930
Eloise		Stilwell	Rogers	Daughter of Hoyle Stilwell	4/18/1930
Eva		Stilwell		Niece of Arthur Lee Stilwell	8/27/1926

Index of Names

First	Middle	Maiden	Last Name (or Last Name by First Marriage)	Relationship	Diary Entry
Everette			Stilwell		11/29/1927; 12/11/1927
George			Stilwell	Brother of Arthur Lee Stilwell	8/28/1926; 4/6/1927; 5/22/1927; 5/26/927; 6/3/1927; 6/4/1927; 6/5/1927; 6/6/1927; 6/7/1927; 6/8/1927; 6/10/1927; 6/12/1927; 6/15/1927; 11/25/1927; 11/27/1927; 11/28/1927; 11/29/1927; 11/30/1927; 12/2/1927; 12/7/1927; 12/8/1927; 12/9/1927; 12/11/1927; 12/12/1927; 6/11/1928; 9/10/1928
Harley			Stilwell		11/25/1927; 11/29/1927
Mrs Hoyle / Maime			Stilwell	Wife of Hoyle Stilwell	4/5/1930; 4/18/1930
Hoyle			Stilwell	Brother of Arthur Lee Stilwell	4/1/1929; 4/2/1929; 4/5/1930; 4/18/1930
Jim			Stilwell		4/6/1930
Margaret		Stilwell		Daughter of George Stilwell	5/25/1927; 6/8/1927; 6/28/1927; 11/29/1927

First	Middle	Maiden	Last Name (or Last Name by First Marriage)	Relationship	Diary Entry
Mary	Lee		Stilwell	Daughter of Arthur Lee Stilwell. StepDaughter of J.W. Peace	5/29/1927; 6/14/1927; 7/10/1927; 9/25/1927; 12/11/1927; 5/28/1928; 9/18/1928; 9/20/1928; 11/26/1928; 4/10/1929; 4/17/1929; 4/18/1929; 5/4/1929; 5/21/1929; 5/22/1929; 6/10/1929; 6/13/1929; 7/15/1929; 8/20/1929;
Mrs Carrie (Mrs. G.F.)			Stilwell	Wife of George Stilwell	5/25/1927; 6/8/1927; 6/10/1927; 11/28/1927; 11/29/1927; 12/12/1927; 1/5/1928; 6/11/1928; 9/10/1928
Murry			Stilwell		11/29/1927
Ottis			Stilwell		11/29/1927; 12/11/1927
Rev			Stamey	Elder of Methodist Church	7/5/1890
R			Strickland		8/12/1926; 8/13/1926
Mr			Suggs		8/25/1929
Mrs			Suggs		8/25/1929
Ada			Swarigen		4/6/1930

Index of Names

First	Middle	Maiden	Last Name (or Last Name by First Marriage)	Relationship	Diary Entry
T - Maiden or Last Name					
Martin			Taylor	Father of Elizabeth Hendrix	5/12/1927
Mr			Taylor	Sunday School Teacher	5/22/1927
Mrs			Tedwell	Sunday School Teacher	4/8/1928
Dr. J.	Fred		Tesh	Eye Doctor	4/6/1928; 11/23/1928; 5/31/1929
Eli			Thomas	Brother of Hannah Delphina Thomas Ensley	8/12/1928
Hannah	Delphina	Thomas		Wife of David Ensley	See Hannah Ensley
John	C		Thomas		5/2/1927
Nellie			Thompson		9/9/1923;
Allen	J.		Tomlinson	Uncle to EMB	5/12/1890; 5/5/1929, Also See Family Records.
Allen	U./Unthank		Tomlinson	Uncle to EMB	Also A Reminiscence; See Family Records.
Clarance (Charance)			Tomlinson	Husband of Corene Tomlison	9/23/1926; 12/16/1929; 4/12/1930
Corene		Blair	Tomlinson	Daughter of Jesse Blair and Emma C. Blair Conrad	9/23/1926; 11/21/1929; 12/16/19; 4/12/1930
Hattie	R.		Tomlinson		9/9/1923;
Prof. Julius			Tomlinson	Son of Allen Tomlinson	5/12/1890

Until We Sleep Our Last Sleep

First	Middle	Maiden	Last Name (or Last Name by First Marriage)	Relationship	Diary Entry
Rachel		English	Tomlinson	Aunt to EMB	Also A Reminiscence; See Family Records.
Sidney			Tomlinson	Son of Allen Tomlinson	5/12/1890
Amy			Trublood		9/2/1889
Rev R	G		Tuttle		5/22/1927; 5/25/1927; 6/5/1927; 1/4/1928
V - Maiden or Last Name					
Jacob			Vanderburg	Possible killer of His family	12/31/1928
J.	W.		Vanderburg	Father in Vandenburg family and victim of murder	12/31/1928
Pauline (Miss)		Vanderburg		Daughter of J.W. Vandenburg and victim of murder	12/31/1928
W - Maiden or Last Name					
Mr. J.	R.		Wall		11/22/1926
Mrs.			Wall	Widow of Henry Wall	1/4/1927
Henry			Wall		1/4/1927
Rev			Walton		7/21/1929
Yardley			Warner		8/14/1926
George			Washington	First President of the U.S.	2/22/1927; 2/22/1928; 3/4/1929
J.	W.		Wearns	Employer of Fred C Blair	2/4/1929; 2/5/1929
Dr			Webb	Radio show preacher from Columbia, S.C.	1/27/1929
Mr			Webb		6/6/1927
Mrs			Webb		6/6/1927

Index of Names

First	Middle	Maiden	Last Name (or Last Name by First Marriage)	Relationship	Diary Entry
W.	C.		Welch	Father of Alice Dunman	9/9/1923
Linley	M.		Wells		8/10/1929; 10/11/1929; 10/20/1929; 10/21/1929
Alice	Paige		White		9/9/1923;
Anna		Perisho	White		9/9/1923;
Aunt Jemima			White		8/12/1928
Billy (Billie)	Ray		White	Grandson of JW Peace, Son of Ed White / Lena White	5/14/1929; 9/24/1929; 12/11/1929
Charles			White		12/9/1926
David			White		2/2/1927
Earl			White	Husband of Mamie Steed White	11/2/1926
Edd			White	Husband of Lena White	12/25/1929
Edward		Lee	White	Grandchild of Mrs Nance	5/6/1929
Fernando	Cartland		White		9/9/1923;
H.A, (Mrs)			White		9/9/1923;
James			White		11/13/1929
Lena Mrs. (Edd)		Peace	White	J.W. Peace's Daughter	2/15/1927; 11/11/1927; 11/9/1928; 5/14/1929; 8/30/1929; 9/20/1929; 9/24/1929; 10/10/1929; 11/29/1929; 12/11/1929; 12/25/1929; 12/28/1929; 1/26/30; 2/9/1930; 2/11/1930; 2/28/1930

Until We Sleep Our Last Sleep

First	Middle	Maiden	Last Name (or Last Name by First Marriage)	Relationship	Diary Entry
Mamie		Steed	White	Wife of Earl White	11/2/1926; 11/3/1926
Emma (Miss)		White		Daughter of Thomas and Susana Wall White	1/23/1927
Mr. Lee			White	Husband of Stella White	9/9/1923; 9/10/1926; 11/20/1928; 1/26/1930; 2/9/1930; 2/16/1930
Mrs. (Ben)			White		9/26/1926
Mrs. (Lee) Stella			White	Wife of Lee White	9/9/1923; 11/20/1928; 1/26/1930; 2/9/1930; 2/16/1930
Sandy			White	Cousin of EMB	11/9/1928
Susana		Wall	White	Wife of Thomas White	1/23/1927
Thomas			White	Husband of Susan Wall White	1/23/1927
Leanna			Wibborn		9/9/1923;
Clark			Wilborn	Singer	8/18/1929
Mr. J.	Welsey		Wilborn		2/27/1927; 2/28/1927
Nerius (Dock)			Wilborn	Husband of Pearl Marsh Wilborn	9/9/1923;
Mattie		Johnson	Wilborn	Sister-in-law to Ruth Millikan Johnson, Sister of J. Alvin Johnson	2/28/1927
Pearl		Marsh	Wilborn	Wife of Nerius Wilborn	9/9/1923;
Porter			Williams	Emily Hayden Blair's date	3/10/1930; 4/6/1930
Wm			Wilson	Relative of EMB	9/9/1889

738

Index of Names

First	Middle	Maiden	Last Name (or Last Name by First Marriage)	Relationship	Diary Entry
Henry			Winslow	Father of Robert Winslow	9/9/1923; 8/10/1926; 8/11/1926; 8/12/1926; 8/8/1927
Robert			Winslow	Son of Henry Winslow	9/9/1923; 8/11/1926
Sara	E	Wilson	Winslow		8/5/1926
Laura		Balinger	Winston	Schoolmate of EMB	9/9/1923
Mr Floyd			Wolf		12/12/1927
Mr Julian			Woodard		11/5/1928
Mrs. (Julian)		Bulla	Woodard	Daughter of Dr. Bulla	11/5/1928
Mary	C.		Woody		8/8/1929
Rev J.	E.		Woosley	Pastor	4/17/1926; 7/4/1926; 7/18/1926; 1/22/1927; 1/23/1927
Mr.			Woosley	son of Pastor Woosley	7/18/1926
Joseph			Worth	Husband of Minnie Worth	8/13/1926
Joseph			Worth, jr	Cousin of EMB	8/11/1926; 8/12/1926; 8/14/1926, Also See Family Records.
Laura (Miss)		Worth		Nurse at Founders Hall	8/12/1928
Minnie			Worth	Wife of Joseph	8/12/1926; 8/13/1926
Pheobe		Worth		Daughter of Joe and Minnie Worth	8/13/1926; 8/14/1926
Wm			Worth		9/9/1923;

Until We Sleep Our Last Sleep

First	Middle	Maiden	Last Name (or Last Name by First Marriage)	Relationship	Diary Entry
Y - Maiden or Last Name					
Mary			Yates		8/8/1926
Random First Name Only					
Luceal					4/6/1930
Hendrix					11/28/1929
Unice					A Reminiscence
Lois					A Reminiscence
Timothy					A Reminiscence

www.ingramcontent.com/pod-product-compliance
Lightning Source LLC
Chambersburg PA
CBHW020415010526
44118CB00010B/255